Leiths

TECHNIQUES BIBLE

Leiths

TECHNIQUES BIBLE

SUSAN SPAULL with
LUCINDA BRUCE-GARDYNE

Foreword by Caroline Waldegrave

BLOOMSBURY

LONDON · OXFORD · NEW YORK · NEW DELHI · SYDNEY

Bloomsbury Publishing
An imprint of Bloomsbury Publishing Plc

50 Bedford Square
London
WC1B 3DP
UK

1385 Broadway
New York
NY 10018
USA

www.bloomsbury.com

BLOOMSBURY and the Diana logo are trademarks of Bloomsbury Publishing Plc

First published in Great Britain 2003

This edition published 2015

British Library Cataloguing-in-Publication Data
A catalogue record for this book is available from the British Library.

Library of Congress Cataloguing-in-Publication data has been applied for.

ISBN: HB: 978-1-4088-6933-8

2 4 6 8 10 9 7 5 3

Food styling by Susan Spaull
Line drawings by Kate Simunek
Design by Here+There

Printed and bound in China by C&C Offset Printing Co., Ltd

All papers used by Bloomsbury Publishing are natural, recyclable products made from wood grown in well-managed forests. The manufacturing processes conform to the environmental regulations of the country of origin.

To find out more about our authors and books visit www.bloomsbury.com. Here you will find extracts, author interviews, details of forthcoming events and the option to sign up for our newsletters.

Contents

Acknowledgements

We would like to thank the teachers, past and present, of Leiths School of Food and Wine whose knowledge and enthusiasm about food have made this book possible. In particular we would like to thank Jenny Stringer, Claire MacDonald and Sara Blount for reading the first draft of the manuscript and making many helpful suggestions. We would also like to thank Caroline Waldegrave for her continued support and encouragement during the writing of the book and for her many tips, tales and recipes that are found throughout the text.

On the production side we would like to thank Caz Hildebrand, Lisa Bird-wood, Kate Simunek for her brilliant drawings, Chiki Sarkar at Bloomsbury for co-ordinating this huge project, Victoria Millar for her help and patience during the proof stage and Helen Campbell for her meticulous editing, as well as insightful recommendations.

Sue Spaull would also like to thank Gowri Preece, Brooke Spatz, Rebecca Spaull, Robert Spaull and Rob Wombell for their contributions to the book. Lucinda Bruce-Gardyne would like to thank Sara Diaz, Mary and Emily Farrow and Melanie Peeke for their help.

We are also very grateful to our respective husbands and families for their understanding of late nights and imminent deadlines, and for their ability to cook a great Sunday lunch.

Susan Spaull and Lucinda Bruce-Gardyne

Foreword

Leiths School of Food and Wine began in 1975. This book details the cooking techniques we have taught our students since the school started. When we teach students how to do something we also explain *why* it should be done in that way. Sometimes the answer is a matter of science: for example, a piece of meat on the bone roasts more quickly than a piece off the bone because bone is a better conductor of heat than flesh. Sometimes the answer is one of practicality: time management is essential in any kitchen and we teach people to be efficient. We have always wanted our students to understand the reasons for doing things the right way.

The book goes right back to basic principles. You will find out how to separate an egg, boil a potato and discover what is meant by a pinch of salt. However, we then go beyond the basics into a fair degree of technicality. For example, we explain the action of yeast and we tell you why you temper chocolate. We think that, like our students, enthusiastic amateurs as well as experienced cooks will benefit from and enjoy gaining some understanding of the reasoning which lies behind our advice.

While writing *Leiths Techniques Bible* Sue and Lucinda kept having to remind themselves of the title. It is a book specifically about techniques. For example, although the cheese section defines the different types of cheese in order to illustrate the cooking methods suitable for each type given its particular taste and structure, the section is not intended to be a general guide to the cheeses of the world.

I have very much enjoyed working with Sue and Lucinda to try to distil for you more than a quarter of a century of accumulated experience in the Leiths kitchens. I hope that you enjoy the book and find that it becomes an essential Bible in your kitchen.

Caroline Waldegrave, OBE

Introduction

Leiths Techniques Bible is the essential companion for everyone who ventures into a kitchen. From choosing ingredients to the simple tasks of scrambling an egg or boiling a carrot, to the precise skills required to fillet a fish or make a cake, *Leiths Techniques Bible* has information for everyone, from the novice cook to the experienced chef.

Here you will find all the information contained in a year-long Diploma course at the renowned Leiths School of Food and Wine in London. Each technique is explained in detail, using simple but scientific descriptions, so that the cook can learn what happens during the cooking process and understand why it is important to follow certain procedures. At the end of each key recipe there is a section entitled ***What has gone wrong when*** . . . to help you diagnose any disasters.

The book is divided into three parts. The first contains the background information required for functioning in the kitchen, how to choose and use each type of knife and how to plan a menu and avoid food poisoning, for example, as well as more specialized information needed by the professional cook.

The second part is like the main course of a meal, the meat and potatoes of the book. Within this part, the sections are arranged alphabetically, so it is easy to dip in and out of the book to find quickly an answer to a question or an instruction for a certain procedure. Each section contains comprehensive information about ingredients as well as the techniques of cookery.

The recipes included throughout the book are those used at Leiths School. They have been chosen to illustrate specific skills, such as browning meat for a casserole, making pastry for a quiche or whisking egg whites for a meringue. Every recipe contains the information you need to make it work, so preparing them should be like being a student at Leiths with a teacher at your side. As a result the recipes may take a little longer to read than those in many other cookbooks, but the additional information should reassure the cook and enhance the results. Once these skills have been mastered, you should be able to tackle any recipe with confidence.

The third part of the book contains all the terms and tables a cook needs to refer to from time to time and a list of books which will enable the reader to explore specific areas of interest in greater depth than is possible to cover here.

Part one
Kitchen Basics

How to Use Recipes

When you first start to cook, using a recipe can be rather confusing. There are so many terms that are specific to cookery that reading a recipe can sometimes require half an hour spent with the dictionary. The **Cookery Terms** section of this book (page 751) should help to answer your questions and the detailed information in the sections will help you master cookery techniques.

Most cookery books, including this one, will recommend that you read through the recipe before you start to cook. It is also best to weigh and measure the ingredients before starting to cook. Although this might seem tedious it will make the actual preparation much quicker because you won't need to keep stopping and starting during cooking. Also, you will then know that you have all the ingredients required to hand.

Using Recipes: Points to Remember

- Do not mix metric weights and measures with imperial within a recipe. Use one system or the other because converting from one system to another can lead to inaccuracies.
- Teaspoon and tablespoon measures should be level unless otherwise specified.
- Ingredients should be weighed and measured accurately, particularly when baking. Baking recipes are carefully calibrated scientific ratios to produce specific results. A small change can make a big difference.
- Don't leave ingredients out.
- Use the exact size of tin specified in the recipe, particularly when baking.
- Use an oven thermometer if you are in doubt about the accuracy of your oven temperature.
- Test for doneness according to the recipe directions. If the recipe you are about to cook doesn't specify how to tell when it is done, check another similar recipe. Do not rely on the timing given in the recipe to be accurate. There are too many variables in cooking for the directions to cover all the permutations.

Menu Planning

Designing a menu that is nutritious and exciting to eat is often a daunting task. There are certain criteria any menu must satisfy in order to make a successful meal. To help decide what to cook, ask yourself the following questions:

- **What is the occasion?** Special occasions will require more expensive, elaborate food than, say, a simple family lunch. The style of the food should complement the style of the occasion.
- **Who is the menu designed to feed?** The food should be suitable for the diners' needs. How hungry are they likely to be? A ladies' lunch will require an entirely different menu from a supper for a rugger XV, for example. The age group and nationality of the diners will also influence your menu choice.
- **Are there any special diets to be catered for?** It is advisable to ask in advance to avoid any last-minute menu changes.
- **What is the season?** Seasonal produce will usually taste better and be less expensive than food that is out of season. People naturally prefer lighter food in hot weather and warming food when it is cold outside.
- **How many people are you cooking for?** For larger numbers the logistics are critical. Do you have the oven, hob and refrigerator space to prepare the food? Do you have the required pots and pans?

It is often easiest to choose a main course first, as this is the focal point or the foundation of the meal. Once you have decided on a main course, try to imagine what you would like to have for the first course. It should complement the main course as well as whet the appetite. It is important that the first course should not be more strongly flavoured than the main course.

The dessert can be decided upon once the first course and the main course have been chosen. Imagine eating the meal. What would you choose for dessert? Keep the points above in mind when choosing both the first course and the dessert.

When you have decided upon your menu, review it against the following criteria:

- Is there any repetition of ingredients? For example, do cheese, fruit or pastry appear more than once? This would be undesirable. The one exception to this rule is that it is acceptable to include fish in both the first and main courses.
- Is the menu too rich or too light? Does it contain too much cream or fat? Serving a salad is recommended with any rich meal.

- Does the menu have a variety of textures? Often texture can be added with a garnish, for example serving a crisp biscuit with a mousse or ice cream.
- Does the menu have a variety of colour? Food can often be too brown or too pale. Colour is visually exciting and will make the food seem more attractive. Add colour with garnishes and vegetables.
- Does the menu skip from one continent to another? It is usually best to keep within the same cultural realm to avoid culinary culture clashes. Try not to include too many exotic tastes in the same menu.
- Does the menu stay in style throughout? Does it feature sophisticated, restaurant-style food or is it based on simple home cooking?
- Is the menu nutritionally balanced? (see **Healthy Eating and Basic Nutrition**, page 13).
- Is it possible to cook and serve the menu easily, taking into account any limitations imposed by the kitchen, equipment, dining room, cook and/or any time constraints?
- How are you going to present and garnish the food (see **Food Presentation**, page 11)? Remember to include garnishes in your menu-planning and when writing your shopping list.

At Leiths there is always much discussion about the order of a meal. In the UK we conventionally serve dessert followed by cheese. In France, it is more usual to serve cheese before the dessert so that the dinner wine may accompany the cheese, and a dessert wine is then served with the dessert. In America cheese is often served as an appetizer with pre-dinner drinks and the salad is often part of the first course. If cooking commercially, check the order of the courses with the host/hostess.

Once the menu has been decided, make a time plan detailing when each component of the menu will be made. If you are cooking for a large number of people a time plan is vital as the preparation time will often span several days. Be sure to include time for shopping and putting away the food (see **Catering Organization**, page 77).

Catering Quantities

Few people accurately weigh or measure quantities as a control-conscious chef must do, but when catering for large numbers it is useful to know how much food to allow per person.

As a general rule, the more people you are catering for the less food per head you need to provide, e.g. 225 g|8 oz stewing beef per head is essential for 4 people, 170 g|6 oz per head would feed 60 people. These quantities are fairly generous.

Soup
Allow 290 ml|½ pint soup per head, depending on the size of the bowl.

Poultry
Chicken – 340 g|12 oz per person weighed when plucked and drawn. An average chicken serves 4 people on the bone and 6 people off the bone in a sauce.

Duck – A 2.7 kg|6 lb bird will feed 3–4 people; a 1.8 kg|4 lb bird will feed 2 people. 1 duck makes enough pâté for 6 people.

Goose – Allow 3.6 kg|8 lb for 4 people; 6.9 kg|15 lb for 8 people.

Turkey – Allow 450 g|1 lb on the bone per person – i.e. a 15 lb bird will feed 15 people.

Game
Pheasant – Allow 1 bird (roast) for 2 people; 1 bird (casseroled) for 3 people.

Pigeon – Allow 1 bird per person.

Grouse – Allow 1 young grouse (roast) per person; 1 bird (casseroled) for 2–3 people.

Quail – Allow 2 small birds per person or 1 large boned stuffed bird per person served on a crouton.

Partridge – Allow 1 bird per person.

Venison – Allow 170 g|6 oz lean meat per person; 1.8 kg|4 lb haunch weighed on the bone for 8–9 people.

Steaks – Allow 170 g–225|6–8 oz per person.

Lamb or Mutton

Casseroled – 225 g | 8 oz per person (boneless, with fat trimmed away).

Roast leg – 1.35 kg | 3 lb for 3–4 people; 1.8 kg | 4 lb for 4–5 people; 2.7 kg | 6 lb for 7–8 people.

Roast shoulder – 1.8 kg | 4 lb shoulder for 5–6 people; 2.7 kg | 6 lb shoulder for 7–8 people.

Grilled best end cutlets – 3–4 per person.

Grilled loin chops – 2–3 per person.

Beef

Stewed – 225 g | 8 oz boneless trimmed meat per person.

Roast (off the bone) – If serving men only, 225 g | 8 oz per person; if serving men and women, 200 g | 7 oz per person.

Roast (on the bone) – 340 g | 12 oz per person.

Roast whole fillet – 1.8 kg | 4 lb piece for 10 people.

Grilled steaks – 170 g–225 g | 6–7 oz per person.

Pork

Casseroled – 170 g | 6 oz per person.

Roast leg or loin (off the bone) – 200 g | 7 oz per person.

Roast leg or loin (on the bone) – 340 g | 12 oz per person.

2 average fillets – will feed 4–6 people.

Grilled – 1 × 170 g | 6 oz chop or cutlet per person.

Veal

Stews or pies – 225 g | 8 oz pie veal per person.

Fried – 1 × 170 g | 6 oz escalope per person.

Minced Meat

170 g | 6 oz per person for shepherd's pie, hamburger, etc.
110 g | 4 oz per person for steak tartare.
85 g | 3 oz per person for lasagne, cannelloni, etc.
110 g | 4 oz per person for moussaka.
110 g | 4 oz per person for spaghetti.

Fish

Whole large fish – (e.g. sea bass, salmon, whole haddock) weighed uncleaned, with head on: 340–450 g | 12 oz–1 lb per person.

Cutlets and steaks – 170 g | 6 oz per person.

Fillets – (e.g. sole, lemon sole, plaice) 3 fillets per person.

Whole small fish – (e.g. trout, slip soles, small plaice, small mackerel, herring) 225–340 g | 8–12 oz weighed with heads for main course; 170 g | 6 oz for first course.

Fish off the bone – (in fish pie, with sauce, etc.) 170 g | 6 oz per person.

Shellfish

Prawns – 55–85 g | 2–3 oz per person as a first course; 140 g | 5 oz per person as a main course.

Mixed shellfish – 55–85 g | 2–3 oz per person as a first course; 140 g | 5 oz per person as a main course.

Vegetables

Weighed before preparation and cooking, and assuming 3 vegetables, including potatoes, served with a main course: 110 g | 4 oz per person, except (per person):

French beans – 55 g | 2 oz.

Peas – 55 g | 2 oz.

Spinach – 340 g | 12 oz.

Potatoes – 3 small (roast); 170 g | 6 oz (mashed); 1 large or 2 small (baked); 110 g | 4 oz (new).

Rice

Plain, boiled or fried – 55 g | 2 oz (weighed before cooking).

In risotto or pilaf – 30 g | 1 oz per person (weighed before cooking) for first course; 55 g | 2 oz per person for main course.

Salads

Obviously, the more salads served, the less guests will eat of any one salad. Allow 1–1½ helpings of salad, in total, per head – e.g. if only one salad is served make sure there is enough for 1 generous helping each. If 100 guests are to choose from 5 different salads, allow a total of 150 portions – i.e. 30 portions of each salad.

Tomato salad – 450 g | 1 lb tomatoes (average 6 tomatoes), sliced, serves 4 people.

Coleslaw – 1 small cabbage, finely shredded, serves 10–12 people.

Grated carrot salad – 450 g | 1 lb carrots, grated, serves 6 people.

Potato salad – 450 g | 1 lb potatoes (weighed before cooking) serves 5 people.

Green salad – Allow a loose handful of leaves for each person.

Sandwiches

2 slices of bread makes 1 round of sandwiches.

Cucumber – 1 cucumber makes 15 rounds.

Egg – 1 hardboiled egg makes 1 round.

Ham – Allow 20 g | ¾ oz for each round.

Mustard and cress – For egg and cress sandwiches, 1 punnet makes 20 rounds.

Tomato – 450 g | 1 lb makes 9 rounds.

Smoked salmon – Allow 20 g | ¾ oz for each round.

Miscellaneous

Brown bread and butter – 1½ slices (3 triangular pieces) per person.

French bread – 1 large loaf for 8 people; 1 small loaf for 4 people.

Cheese – After a meal, if serving one blue-veined, one hard and one soft cheese: 85 g | 3 oz per person for up to 8 people; 55 g | 2 oz per person for over 20 people. Inevitably, if catering for small numbers, there will be cheese left over but this is unavoidable if the host is not to look mean.

Biscuits – 3 each for up to 10 people; 2 each for up to 30 people; 1 each for over 30 people.

Butter – 15 g | ½ oz per person if bread is served with the meal; 30 g | 1 oz per person if cheese is served as well.

Cream – 1 tablespoon per person for coffee, 3 tablespoons per person for pudding or dessert.

Milk – 570 ml | 1 pint for 18–20 cups of tea.

Sliced bread – A large loaf, thinly sliced, generally makes 16–18 slices.

Butter – 30 g | 1 oz soft butter will cover 8 large bread slices.

Sausages – 450 g | 1 lb is the equivalent of 32 cocktail sausages; 16 chipolata sausages; 8 pork sausages.

Chicken livers – 450 g | 1 lb chicken livers will be enough for 60 bacon and chicken liver rolls.

Dates – 50 fresh dates weigh about 450 g | 1 lb.

Prunes – A prune (with stone) weighs about 10 g | ⅓ oz.

Mushrooms – A button mushroom weighs about 7 g | ¼ oz.

Bacon – A good sized rasher weighs about 30 g | 1 oz.

Button onions – A button onion weighs about 15 g | ½ oz.

Choux pastry – 6-egg choux paste makes 150 baby éclairs. They will need 570 ml | 1 pint cream for filling and 225 g | 8 oz chocolate for coating.

Short pastry – 900 g | 2 lb pastry will line 150 tartlets.

Food Presentation

If food looks delicious, people are predisposed to find it delicious. Whilst fashions in style, garnishes and colours change almost from season to season, there are certain guidelines that can be applied to nearly every occasion, be it a formal seated dinner or a family buffet.

Restaurant food is often no different from the food you might make at home. It looks different because extra care has been taken in choosing the garnishes and in arranging the food on the plate.

By following the guidelines set out below it is possible to make all food look more appetizing and professionally prepared. These guidelines apply whether the food is plated individually or put into serving dishes.

- **Keep it simple:** Over-decorated food looks as if it has been handled excessively. The more cluttered the plate, the messier and less attractive it looks.
- **Keep it fresh:** Any garnishes should be fresh. Do not allow food to stand for longer than necessary or it becomes tired and unappetizing.
- **Keep it relevant:** Garnishes should complement the food in both taste and colour and should tell the diner something about the food if possible. The garnishes should be edible. For example, if making a couscous salad with diced peppers and cucumbers, hold back some of the diced vegetables to sprinkle over the top of the salad before serving.
- **Use centre height:** Although centre height is often taken to extremes by restaurants in the building of precariously balanced towers of food, a mound of food will always look better than food that has been flattened on to a plate or serving dish. Don't attempt to smooth the surface of the food unless you can make it perfectly smooth.
- **Use contrasting rows:** If serving 2 different types of biscuits, for example, ensure they are of different colours. Arrange them in rows of alternating colour.
- **Use diagonal lines:** Diagonal lines are easier to achieve than symmetrical straight lines. The eye is more conscious of unevenness in verticals, horizontals and rectangles.
- **Don't use too many colours:** Using a lot of colours on a plate can look garish. Using only two colours or different shades of the same colour will look sophisticated, for example a garnish of toasted hazelnuts on a coffee-coloured iced cake.
- **Contrast the simple with the elaborate** when choosing serving dishes. For example, strawberries will look pleasing piled up in a decorated bowl, whilst white dinner plates are more suited to a main course which contains many different colours and shapes.

- **Use uneven numbers:** Uneven numbers of lamb chops on a plate or rosettes of cream on a cake will look more appealing because the eye will not be looking for a symmetrical effect.
- **Be generous with your food and decorations:** Tiny rosettes of cream on a cake look mean and amateurish. Fill serving dishes generously.
- **Avoid clumsiness:** On the other hand, never cram food into a dish. Place the food on the plates or serving dishes carefully, leaving a space between the inside rim of the plate and the food. Follow the curve of the rim with the food. Think of the rim of the plate as a picture frame. Do not put any food on the rim; keep it clean.
- **Overlap slices:** Chops, steaks, sliced meats and slices of fruit look best if they are placed on the dish in overlapping slices. This way, more can be fitted on to the dish and the food will not be lying flat on the dish.
- **Use concentric circles:** For example, if placing slices of tomatoes in a serving dish, the first circle of overlapping slices should go in one direction and the next circle should go in the opposite direction.

Food Garnishes

Bouquets of Watercress

Making a bouquet of watercress

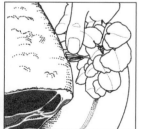

Twisting off stems

Bouquets of watercress are used to garnish dishes served without a sauce such as a roasted joint of meat or grilled meat or fish.

1 Gather a small bouquet of the watercress leaves and hold the stems tightly in one hard.
2 Twist off the stems with your other hand.
3 Immediately tuck the shortened stems underneath the food to be garnished.

Chopped Parsley

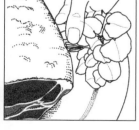

Using a bouquet of watercress to garnish

Very finely chopped parsley (see **Knife Skills**, page 65) is used to garnish dishes that are coated in a sauce, such as a meat casserole or fish in a sauce. It is also used to garnish vegetables such as boiled carrots or potatoes when the colour contrast will make the dish look more appealing.

Lemon or Lime Wedges

Preparing lemon wedges

Wedges of lemon or lime are used to garnish fish dishes.

1 Cut the top and bottom of the fruit to remove the pointed ends but do not cut into the fruit.
2 Cut the fruit in half, then cut each half into 3–4 sections, depending on the size of the fruit.
3 Cut down the length of each wedge to remove the membrane from the centre of the fruit.
4 Remove any pips.

Healthy Eating and Basic Nutrition

Food is necessary to provide the nutrients required for health as well as enough energy to live. Today, so much information about nutrition is available that it is easy to become confused and forget the basics of a healthy diet, which is needed to optimize our well-being as well as to avoid health problems that can be caused by dietary deficiencies or imbalances.

To eat a healthy diet, it is important to understand the basics of nutrition. As a cook you will be responsible for planning menus for other people. These menus need to be balanced across the different food groups (see below) as well as providing variety and satisfying the points detailed in *Menu Planning* (see page 5).

The first points to consider are variety, moderation and balance.

Variety

A varied diet should include as many different foods as possible from the major food groups (see below). Try to eat different foods within the groups each day. Every food provides different vitamins and minerals necessary for cell growth and repair. The greater the variety of food you eat within each group, the better chance you have of getting the necessary nutrition.

Moderation

Moderation means eating reasonable amounts of different foods rather than an excessive amount of any one food or of foods from one group. It does not follow that if a certain food is good for you much more of that food will be even better. An excess of one food will mean that not enough other foods are eaten.

For example, 1 or 2 oranges a day are good for you because they provide Vitamin C and fibre. If you eat 5 or 6 oranges a day, however, the acid in the fruit can start to eat into the enamel in your teeth. In addition, the Vitamin C in excess of the amount required each day (approximately the amount in 1 orange) is excreted by the body and is therefore of no use.

Balance

A diet is balanced when the principles of variety and moderation are followed and the amount of calories consumed balances with the amount expended.

The Food Groups

Each of the food groups makes an important contribution to our diet. The number of servings from each group varies according to the amount needed for a balanced diet and every individual has somewhat different requirements depending on age, gender, amount of physical activity and genetic make-up.

Variety within each group is also important. When planning a diet, do not exclude any food group unless recommended to do so by a health professional, because essential nutrients are provided from each group.

Bread, Cereal, Rice, Grains, Pasta, Potatoes: 4–6 servings daily

This group, known as *complex carbohydrates*, provides sustained energy for the muscles as well as providing B vitamins, minerals, starch and dietary fibre.

Nutritionists recommend that a minimum of 4–6 servings of foods from this group are eaten each day. For people who are very active or growing, the number of servings should be increased to 10–11 servings a day.

Examples of a serving from this group consist of *one* of the following:

- 1 slice of bread
- 1 small bun or ½ bagel
- 30 g | 1 oz cereal
- 30 g | 1 oz uncooked rice/pasta
- 1 small baked potato
- 140 g | 5 oz sweetcorn or peas

Complex carbohydrates should be the main source of energy in the diet. Energy is measured in units called calories. 1 g of carbohydrates releases approximately 4 calories of energy.

Calories from this group should provide a little more than half of the daily calorie intake, without taking into account the calories from added sauces, butter or jam.

Vegetables: 3–5 servings daily

Vegetables are sometimes classified together with fruit as a food group but for menu planning purposes it is easier to consider them separately. It is recommended that 3–5 servings of vegetables be eaten every day. Starchy vegetables, such as potatoes, peas and sweetcorn, count as complex carbohydrates and are classified in the group above.

Vegetables are the chief source of Vitamin A, which is sometimes called beta carotene. In many instances beta carotene is easily recognizable as a bright orange colour, as in carrots, squashes and sweet potatoes, but other vegetables such as broccoli, bok choy, dark green lettuce and spinach also supply beta carotene. At least one of these vegetables should be eaten every day.

Examples of a serving of vegetables consist of *one* of the following:

- 85 g|3 oz raw or cooked vegetables
- 55 g|2 oz raw leafy vegetables
- 170 g|6 fl oz vegetable juice

Several servings of cruciferous vegetables or brassicas should be eaten every week. These are cabbage, cauliflower, broccoli, Brussels sprouts and bok choy.

Fruit: 2–4 servings daily

Fruit is the dietary provider of Vitamin C as well as dietary fibre and other vitamins and minerals. Vitamin C helps to bind cells together and aids healing. A serving of citrus fruit or juice should be consumed every day.

1 serving of fruits such as apricots, mango, papaya and cantaloupe melon, which, like certain vegetables (see above), are high in Vitamin A, should also be eaten every day.

Examples of a serving of fruit consist of *one* of the following:

- 85 g|3 oz raw cooked or canned fruit
- 1 medium apple, banana, orange or pear
- ½ grapefruit
- ¼ melon
- 55 g|2 oz dried fruit
- 170 ml|6 fl oz fruit juice

Dairy Products: Milk, Yoghurt, Cheese: 2 servings daily

This food group is the main supplier of calcium to the diet. It is recommended that adults eat at least 2 servings from this group every day. Growing children and pregnant or lactating mothers should eat at least 3 servings. This group is also a good source of protein, particularly for vegetarians.

Examples of a serving from this group consist of *one* of the following:

- 290 ml|½ pint milk
- 150 g|5 oz yoghurt
- 150 g|5 oz cottage cheese
- 45–55 g|1½ – 2 oz cheese
- 2 scoops of ice cream

Many dairy products are high in fat, so the amount and type of dairy products in the diet need to be monitored if a calorie-controlled diet is being followed. Adults should eat low-fat versions of the above products, such as semi-skimmed or skimmed milk, low-fat yoghurt and cottage cheese. Children under the age of 5 should not be given low-fat products as the calories are needed for growth.

Some people are deficient in the enzyme lactase, which is necessary to digest the milk sugar lactose. As people grow older there is a tendency to become lactose-intolerant, though small amounts of cheese or yoghurt can sometimes be tolerated by lactose-intolerant people as much of the lactose has been consumed in the making of these products. Soy milk, rice milk or low-lactose milk can be substituted for milk.

Meat, Poultry, Fish, Eggs, Dry Beans, Pulses, Nuts and Seeds: 2–3 servings daily

This food group is known as the protein group because it supplies most of the protein in our diet. It is important to eat foods from this group in moderation if they are high in fat. However, they are also important sources of vitamins, in particular vitamin B_{12}, and minerals, such as iron. Iron is needed for the body to produce haemoglobin, the red substance in blood that carries oxygen to the cells.

For adults, 2–3 servings of protein every day are recommended. Examples of a serving consist of any *one* of the following:

- 55 g–85 g | 2–3 oz lean meat, poultry or fish
- 1 whole egg
- 85 g | 3 oz cooked dried peas, beans or lentils

Protein is needed for cell-building and repair on a daily basis, though often not in the quantities consumed in Western diets. Protein is made up of amino acids. Many of the amino acids are manufactured by the body, but some must be obtained from food. These are called the essential amino acids. In order for the body to be able to use the proteins in food, they must contain all the essential amino acids. These proteins are called *complete proteins*.

Examples of foods that contain complete proteins are meat, fish and eggs. Other foods, such as nuts and legumes, contain some of the amino acids but not all of them and so in nutritional terms are called *incomplete proteins*. In order for the protein from these foods to be used by the body they must be eaten in combination with another food so that all of the essential amino acids are supplied. Vegetarians need to be aware of this fact and know how to combine foods in order to avoid malnutrition.

Examples of vegetarian foods combined to make a complete protein:

- Baked beans + bread
- Lentils + rice

Protein in excess of immediate requirements cannot be used by the body and will be converted to provide future energy. 1 gram of protein supplies 4 calories.

Oils, Fats, Sugars and Salt: As little as possible

This group contains the fats, simple sugars and salt that are eaten to make food more palatable. These foods should be eaten in moderation.

Sugars and fats can add an enormous number of calories to the diet without supplying any nutritional benefit. That is why they are called 'empty calories'. It is important not to let these foods satisfy your hunger and deprive you of food that is good for you.

Examples of oils, fats and sugars:

- butter, margarine
- salad dressing
- sweetened fizzy drinks
- sweets
- crisps and other snack food

Fat is not all bad, however. It provides energy, and some fat is needed for healthy hair and skin and for a number of metabolic processes. Most of the required fat, however, is 'hidden' in other foods, such as meat, some types of fish, cheese and other dairy products.

Nutritionists recommend that the level of fat in our diet is kept to 30 per cent of our calorie intake: 1 g of fat supplies 9 calories.

There are two categories of fat: saturated and unsaturated. The fat from animals is saturated fat. Most types of saturated fat, such as lard and butter, hold their shape at room temperature, although coconut oil and palm oil are saturated fats that are liquid at room temperature. Margarine is usually a polyunsaturated fat (see below) that is stabilized through the addition of gelatine. Saturated fats clog the arteries, increasing the risk of cardiovascular disease.

Unsaturated fats come from seeds and plants. There are two types of unsaturated fat: polyunsaturated and monounsaturated. Polyunsaturated fats make the blood less sticky whilst monounsaturated fat has no effect on the blood. Polyunsaturated fat, from plants such as the sunflower, should be used in preference to saturated or monounsaturated fat. Monounsaturated fat is found in olive oil.

Oily fish contains mainly both mono- and polyunsaturated fat. The omega-3 oils, which are thought to be beneficial in lowering cholesterol, are found in the tissues of fish.

Some vegetable oils are hydrogenated, a process that changes their molecular structure and makes them solid at room temperature. Unfortunately this change in structure turns these oils to saturated fat.

Sugar, known as sucrose, is one of the simple carbohydrates, that provides energy quickly. Other simple carbohydrates are glucose and fructose from fruits and vegetables and lactose from milk. Fruits, vegetables and milk provide nutrients in addition to energy but the foods providing sucrose do not. Whilst it is recommended that everyone should eat fruit and vegetables daily, the consumption of sweets and sugary drinks is not advised. Consuming large quantities of these is likely to result in weight gain and tooth decay.

Salt is naturally present in many foods and is added in quantity to most processed foods. Excess salt in the diet can cause hypertension and is to be avoided.

Water

Water is an essential part of the daily diet. It is the main constituent of the body fluids, such as blood and urine, and acts as a solvent for minerals and vitamins. The adult body consists of about 60–65 per cent water. Daily fluid intake should be at least 1.5 litres│2½ pints and can be in the form of water, juices and sauces. Anyone who exercises strenuously or suffers fluid loss through illness should increase their liquid intake to avoid dehydration.

Vitamins

Vitamins are a group of organic compounds that are essential to the body in small quantities. They perform specific roles in the metabolic processes: energy metabolism, blood-clotting and the absorption of nutrients.

Vitamins are found in a wide range of food sources, so a varied diet which includes plenty of fresh fruit and vegetables should meet vitamin requirements sufficiently. Supplemental vitamins should only be necessary in exceptional cases.

Vitamins are divided into 2 groups: fat-soluble and water-soluble. The water-soluble vitamins will leach into any water they come in contact with. For that reason, vegetables should not be soaked in water or cooked in large quantities of water. Water-soluble vitamins are also destroyed by heat.

Certain vitamins called the anti-oxidants, Vitamins A, C and E, have been recognized as particularly important in maintaining health by their abilities to neutralize free radicals, the by-products of the body's normal processes. Free radicals are believed to play a role in cardiovascular disease, ageing and cancer.

Fat-soluble Vitamins

Vitamin*	Functions*	Sources in food*
A	Essential for healthy skin and tissues, light perception and resistance to disease. Anti-oxidant	Fish-liver oils, eggs, carrots, green and yellow vegetables, fortified margarine
D	Controls and maintains the absorption of calcium essential for healthy bones and teeth	Oily fish, eggs, fortified margarine, butter, cereals
E	Protects cell membranes. Anti-oxidant	Wheat germ and green vegetables
K	Blood-clotting	Green vegetables, egg yolk, liver

Water-soluble Vitamins

Vitamin*	Functions*	Sources in food*
C	Maintains connective tissue, e.g. skin and gums. Important role in wound healing. Anti-oxidant	Potatoes, green vegetables, fruits, particularly citrus fruits
B_1 (Thiamin)	Release of energy from carbohydrate	Milk, wholegrain bread, fortified bread and cereals, meat, especially offal
B_2 (Riboflavin)	Utilization of energy from food	Milk, dairy produce, meat, especially liver, yeast extracts
B_3 (Niacin)	Utilization of energy from food	Meat, especially liver, fish and wholegrain cereals
B_6	Metabolism of amino acids and formation of haemoglobin	Occurs widely in food, especially meat and fish, eggs, wholegrain cereals
B_{12}	Growth and metabolism, red blood cells	Occurs only in animal products: offal, fish, eggs, milk and dairy foods
Folic acid	Many functions in the body. Important for the reduction of risk of neural tube defects	Offal, leafy green vegetables, fortified bread and cereals

Minerals

Minerals are inorganic substances that are essential in almost every body process, from the regulating of the heartbeat to the function of enzyme systems. The macro minerals, which are needed in the largest amounts, are calcium, magnesium and phosphorus. Trace minerals are needed in smaller quantities.

Mineral*	Functions*	Sources in food*
Iron	Formation of haemoglobin, which transports oxygen around the body. Deficiency can lead to anaemia	Meat, especially offal, cereal products, egg yolk and green leafy vegetables. Absorption improved in combination with Vitamin C
Calcium	Gives strength to bones and teeth, in combination with phosphorus. Required for muscle contraction, nerve activity and normal blood-clotting	Milk and dairy products, leafy green vegetables, fish with edible bones, flour, bread
Sodium	Essential for muscle and nerve activity. High intake related to increased blood pressure	Table salt, bread, cereals, meat products such as bacon and ham, processed foods
Potassium	Complements sodium in function of cells and fluid balance	Fruit, fruit juices, vegetables, meat and milk
Magnesium	Enzyme function and energy utilization	Wide range of foods, especially those of vegetable origin
Zinc	Wound healing, component of many enzymes	Meat, dairy products, eggs and oysters

*Dietary Reference Values for Food Energy and Nutrients for the United Kingdom, Department of Health, 1991

Food Safety

Knowledge of how to prepare food safely and hygienically is essential in the kitchen as many foods may contain harmful organisms that can cause illness if consumed. It is also important to know the sources of potential food contamination. Remember that contaminated food will not necessarily look or smell 'off', hence the need to be vigilant.

Food poisoning is contracted by consuming food that has been contaminated by bacteria, viruses or poisons. Bacteria will grow to toxic levels if given the chance. In order to grow they need time, warmth, moisture and food. A tiny colony of bacteria is capable of multiplying rapidly to an extent that anyone eating the food could become very ill and require hospitalization. If the victim is a baby with an immune system that is not yet fully developed or an elderly person or an invalid, death could result. See below (page 25) for the different types of food poisoning.

Some foods are considered to be high-risk. These foods are usually moist and high in protein. They include cooked poultry and meats, shellfish, dairy produce, soups, sauces and stock, cooked rice and raw eggs.

In the UK, people preparing food commercially are required to have the Basic Food Handler's Certificate, which can be achieved by taking a short course and passing an examination. Contact your local Environmental Health Office for details of a course nearby. Commercial food sites are advised to prepare a Hazard Analysis and Critical Control Point (HACCP) assessment to show that the risks involved in preparing food for public consumption have been identified and assessed and are being properly monitored. Help in preparing an HAACP can be obtained from the Chartered Institute of Environmental Health Officers.

Safe Food Preparation

Fortunately some simple precautions can be taken to prevent food poisoning. You can kill organisms with heat, i.e. thorough cooking; some organisms can be washed from the food before preparation; bacterial growth can be slowed by refrigeration, and you can prevent cross-contamination by washing your hands, chopping boards and knives between tasks.

Washing
Wash all food if it is to be eaten raw. It is good practice to wash all fruits and vegetables even if they are going to be peeled because bacteria can be spread to the food in the process of peeling and cutting. Wash eggs just before using as the shells

are porous and salmonella is more likely to be present on the shell than inside the egg.

Refrigeration

Refrigeration is useful for keeping food for a longer time than would be possible otherwise. Refrigeration slows down the growth of bacteria and the enzyme activity that causes food to spoil. Commercial food premises are legally required to keep their refrigerators at or below 8°C│47°F, although it is recommended that the temperature is kept between 1–4°C│34–40°F. It is a good idea to keep a thermometer in the refrigerator to monitor the temperature. If the refrigerator is warmer than this, food will not keep for as long as it might otherwise. Restaurants and food shops are required by law to monitor and record the temperature of their refrigerators at frequent, regular intervals every day.

Refrigerate all meat, fish, poultry, dairy products and eggs until you need to use them. Until the discovery of salmonella in eggs, refrigeration of eggs was not thought to be necessary. Although the danger remains slight, it is still present, and eggs will keep fresh for a longer period of time if refrigerated. Opened jars of jam, jelly, mustard and ketchup should be refrigerated.

Bacteria grow most prolifically at temperatures between 5° and 63°C│40° and 145°F. This temperature range is known in the food trade as the 'danger zone'. Beneath the lower temperature the growth of bacteria slows dramatically, and above the higher temperature they start to die. Room temperature is usually about 20°C│68°F, and this is a perfect temperature for bacteria to multiply rapidly. Never leave cold, cooked food sitting at room temperature for more than an hour.

Do not put hot food into a refrigerator because the heat will cause the temperature to rise and put all the food in the refrigerator at risk of bacterial growth.

As far as possible, always keep raw and cooked foods separate from each other. Bacteria can enter the kitchen on raw food and can be transferred to cooked food where they might be able to multiply easily.

When storing food in the refrigerator, place cooked food on a higher shelf than raw food to avoid the chance of the raw food dripping or falling on to the cooked food and thereby contaminating it.

Cover food whenever possible, but not if it is hot (see *Cooling*, below). Air contains bacteria that can settle on uncovered food.

Buy from reputable suppliers

Purchase your food from a reputable supplier with a high turnover. Ensure that the food is transported and stored in a clean environment at the correct temperature.

Check 'use by' dates

Discard any food that has passed its 'use by' date. Ensure that food is stored in accordance with the directions recommended on the packaging.

Cooking

Food must be cooked thoroughly in order to destroy any bacteria present. In particular, chicken, chopped meats, rolled joints and burgers must be cooked completely through in order to destroy any bacteria present inside the meat. Test either with a thermometer or by cutting into the meat near to the bone at the thickest point. The juices should not be pink or bloody and the fibres of the meat should be set, not soft. Bacteria will die if the temperature is held at 60°C | 140°F for at least 10 minutes or 72°C | 165°F for 2 minutes. When cooking for the very old, young, pregnant or infirm, ensure that egg yolks are cooked through completely.

Consumption of raw meat and fish carries a risk of food poisoning. Fish and meat that are traditionally served raw, such as oysters, sushi and steak tartare, must be of the freshest and best quality and should be prepared and eaten immediately. Some traditional dishes such as smoked salmon, gravadlax or Parma ham can be kept for a few days under refrigeration because they have been cured with either salt or smoke which helps to preserve the food (see **Preserving**, page 549).

Cooling

Cooked food should be cooled as quickly as possible to avoid bacterial growth. If cooling large quantities of food, divide it into several shallow containers to create the maximum surface area. Large saucepans can be placed in a sink full of cold water. Keep the cold tap running and allow the water to drain from the sink at the same time to keep the water bath cool. Stir the food to help it cool quickly.

Do not leave hot food covered with a lid – uncovered food cools more quickly. If you need to keep food from drying out or to prevent a skin from forming, place a piece of wet greaseproof paper (thin enough not to prevent cooling) directly on to the surface of the food.

Wrapping

Do not wrap hot food in clingfilm. Any air pockets can provide the perfect environment for bacteria to grow. Clingfilm may also contain chemicals that can leach into food, particularly food high in fat, when it is hot. Choose non-PVC clingfilm to prevent this.

Reheating

When reheating food, make sure that it is served piping hot, which means that the food should be near boiling, right through to the centre. The interior of the food can be tested with an instant-read thermometer, or a skewer can be inserted to the centre of the food. Leave the skewer for 10 seconds, then test it on the back of your wrist. If it is hot enough to make you jump, this means it has been warmed through thoroughly. This is what the instruction to make food 'piping-hot' means. If possible, the food should be stirred during reheating to ensure it is heated through evenly. The food should be held at the very hot temperature above for at least 10 minutes.

Do not pour hot sauces on to cold food unless you are going to reheat the whole dish through immediately. Do not add warm food to cold. Always reheat any mixture immediately if combining two foods of different temperatures or that have been prepared at different times. Remember that the cool food might contain bacteria and the hot food will provide enough warmth to start the bacteria growing but not enough heat to kill them.

Reboil stocks daily if the weather is hot. In the winter, reboil them every 3 days.

Keeping food warm

If food must be kept warm, make sure it has been heated through to a sufficiently high temperature to kill all bacteria, as instructed above under *Cooking*. Then keep it really hot, i.e. above 63°C | 145°F.

Freezing

Do not refreeze completely thawed food without cooking it first. Freezing does not kill bacteria, it merely prevents it from growing. Follow the guidelines on freezing times given throughout this book. (See *Freezing*, page 31, for methods and temperatures.)

Cooking from frozen

Never cook large, thick, whole items such as a chicken from frozen. When the bird looks cooked on the outside, the inside, where the salmonella bacteria thrive, will still be uncooked. It is unwise to stuff large birds because the stuffing usually does not become hot enough to kill the salmonella bacteria.

Defrosting

The defrosting process can be started at room temperature but once the food begins to thaw it should be put on to a low shelf in the refrigerator. It should not be placed on a higher shelf than cooked food because the juices might leak on to the cooked food and contaminate it. Food can also be placed in a leak-proof bag under cold water.

Do not try to defrost food quickly by placing it in a warm oven or under hot water. The outer layer will stay at the incubating temperature for bacteria for too long.

Defrosting in a microwave is safe because the process is quick enough to prevent any bacteria from growing in sufficient numbers to be dangerous. The food should be cooked as soon as it is defrosted, however, because many microwave ovens warm food unevenly.

Utensils

Do not use the same knife or chopping board for raw and cooked food without washing it in between tasks. If you have jointed a chicken, then sliced cooked beef with the same knife, you have transferred bacteria from the chicken to the beef. The bacteria will be killed when the chicken is cooked but they will grow unimpeded in the beef.

Potential allergens can also be passed by cross-contamination. A knife used to cut a nut loaf, then a lemon tart, will pass the nut allergens to the tart which can be fatal to anyone with a severe nut allergy.

Professional caterers have separate chopping boards for cooked and raw foods and large catering establishments have separate refrigerators as well as different boards for each type of food. The home cook need not go to these lengths but should practise good food hygiene and take sensible precautions.

Cleaning

Keep the kitchen area clean. This means washing tools frequently in near-boiling water with detergent. Clean as you go. Tools and dishes should be rinsed with clean hot water and left to drip-dry or wiped dry with a clean tea towel. Boards and work surfaces should be scrubbed, rinsed, disinfected and dried.

Tea towels and cloths should be changed as soon as they are dirty or damp. A damp cloth left over a warm cooker provides the perfect incubating conditions for germs. Cracked wooden spoons, dishes or knives should be discarded for the same reason.

Keep pets away from food preparation areas.

Personal hygiene

Hair should be tied back if possible or covered with a hair net and if you are preparing food commercially it must be covered with a hat. Never comb your hair where food is being prepared or stored.

Hands must be washed before preparing food and in between tasks. Always wash your hands after visiting the lavatory, handling rubbish, and touching your nose or hair. Nails should be short and clean without polish. Use liquid soap and a nail brush when washing your hands, then dry them on a paper towel. Do not wear rings, earrings or a watch.

Clothing should be clean and covered with a clean apron. Do not wear outdoor clothing in the kitchen. Shoes should be clean and flat and sturdy with closed toes to protect your feet from a dropped knife or heavy items of kitchen equipment.

If preparing food commercially, it is illegal to smoke in food preparation areas.

Types of Food Poisoning

In the majority of cases there will be no indication that a food is contaminated: it will not taste, smell or look any different from uncontaminated food. The following bacteria and spores are the usual culprits in cases of food poisoning.

Salmonella is one of the most common causes of food poisoning and is brought into the kitchen on poultry, meat, fish, shellfish, unpasteurized milk and eggs, particularly if the shells are cracked. The bacteria can cause symptoms any time from 6 hours to 3 days after consuming the contaminated food and these may last from 2 to 4 days. The symptoms are flu-like, including nausea, vomiting, diarrhoea, headache, fever and chills.

Salmonella is caused by improper cooking or food storage and/or poor hygiene. The bacteria thrive at temperatures between 7° and 47°C | 47° and 115°F. They will die if heated to 60°C | 140°F for at least 10 minutes or to 72°C | 165°F for at least 2 minutes.

Other foods can be contaminated if they come into contact with bacteria that have been spread to chopping boards or knives. This is called cross-contamination. For example, cross-contamination can occur when uncooked poultry is prepared on a chopping board and the same chopping board is then used to prepare salad or to carve cooked meat without being adequately cleaned in between tasks. The cook must be careful to avoid cross-contamination by cleaning knives, chopping boards and work surfaces between tasks. Hands must be washed before cooking and between tasks.

Salmonella can also be contracted from undercooked poultry and eggs. Mousses, cold soufflés, Hollandaise Sauce, mayonnaise and dishes containing mayonnaise are all potential sources of salmonella infection and should not be served to anyone with a potentially deficient immune system, such as the very young, the very old or infirm or pregnant women.

It is important that poultry be cooked thoroughly before it is eaten. Test the meat in the thickest part next to the bones. The fibres should be firm. If the flesh is pressed, the juices must run clear, not pink. The internal temperature of the meat must have reached a temperature of 75°C | 170°F.

Campylobacter enteritis is a common food-borne disease that usually enters the kitchen on raw poultry and can be contracted by consuming undercooked poultry or unpasteurized milk, or through cross-contamination. The symptoms of abdominal cramps, diarrhoea and fever may not appear for up to 10 days.

Clostridium perfingens is often present on raw meat and unwashed vegetables. The bacteria is present in the intestinal tracts of mammals and is therefore carried in the soil. Thus it is important to wash all soil from fruit and vegetables. The bacteria grow in reduced-oxygen (anaerobic) conditions. If allowed to grow, these toxic bacteria produce heat-resistant spores. The symptoms of windy pain, diarrhoea and sometimes vomiting occur between 8 and 24 hours of consuming the bacteria.

Staphylococcus aureus is usually spread by a food handler who has the infection. The bacteria are present in the nose and mouth as well as in open wounds of both people and animals. It can cause nausea and vomiting within 2 to 4 hours which will last from 1 to 2 days. All broken skin must be covered by waterproof plasters and food handler's gloves. Infected staff must not be allowed to prepare food. In commercial kitchens, blue plasters are used so they can be located if they become separated from the wearer.

Staphylococcus bacteria can be contracted from infected meat, poultry, cheese and egg products. Coleslaw and starchy salads that have been improperly stored are also potential sources of infection. The bacteria are killed by heating to 60°C|140°F for at least 10 minutes. However, if they are allowed to multiply due to improper food storage, enterotoxins are produced that are resistant to heat, freezing and chemicals.

Listeria is commonly found in many foods but listeriosis is very rare as most people's immune systems cope well with listeria. Listeria can be removed from raw vegetables by careful washing. Listeria can multiply at temperatures just above 0°C|32°F.

The special dietary advice regarding listeriosis applies to vulnerable groups of people who are most at risk. These are pregnant women and people with illnesses that result in impaired resistance to infection. These groups are advised to avoid pâtés and soft-ripened cheeses of the Brie, Camembert and blue-veined types and to reheat ready-cooked meals until piping-hot.

Clostridium botulinum produces the sometimes fatal form of food poisoning known as botulism. It is most often contracted through the consumption of contaminated canned foods. The spores are widespread in the environment but are inactive in the presence of oxygen. The toxin affects the central nervous system resulting in a general weakness, headache and double vision. Immediate medical treatment is necessary.

Do not eat food from cans that bulge, leak or spurt liquid upon opening. Home-canned foods that have not been properly heat-processed should also be avoided.

E. coli 0157 is found in the excreta of mammals and is both soil- and water-borne. It can be fatal. The bacteria produce toxins that cause bloody diarrhoea and attack the kidneys and the brain. Symptoms appear within 3 to 4 days. Cases have been contracted through the consumption of infected minced beef that has not been thoroughly cooked as well as through contaminated water supplies. The bacteria are killed when the food is heated to at least 72°C|165°F for 2 minutes. Washing hands after using the lavatory and washing soil from fruits and vegetables are vital precautionary measures.

Bacillus cereus can be present in starchy salads, particularly rice salad. Diarrhoea and vomiting will occur within 30 minutes of consumption and last up to 6 hours. It is important to keep cooked rice in the refrigerator for no longer than 24 hours.

Trichinosis, now rare in developed countries, is a still a common infection on a world-wide basis. The worms are contracted from consuming infected raw or undercooked pork or pork products. Fever will be present within 1 to 2 days, followed by pain and respiratory problems. Pork should be cooked to an internal temperature of 75°C|170°F, ensuring that it is no longer pink.

Paralytic shellfish poisoning results from a marine micro-organism that is contracted by consuming infected shellfish. The toxin, which survives cooking, is present in coastal areas that have a 'red tide'. The symptoms of facial numbness, difficulty in breathing and muscle weakness occur within 30 minutes.

'Off' Foods

Never serve food that smells or looks at all peculiar. Although salmonella is completely tasteless and has no discernible odour, unpleasant odours or appearance are an indication of age and poor condition, and food-poisoning organisms are likely to be present along with the ones causing obvious deterioration. If in doubt, throw the food out.

Poisonous Foods

Some foods are naturally poisonous and must be treated with care or avoided altogether. For example, rehydrated red kidney beans must be boiled for 10 minutes to destroy a potentially fatal enzyme. Cooking the beans until soft at a very low temperature is not sufficient to do this, so if using a slow cooker, give the beans a fast boil before putting them into the pot.

Green potatoes (see *Potatoes*, page 541), rhubarb leaves and many wild mushrooms are mildly poisonous and can cause gastric upsets. Some wild mushrooms are lethal, so do not cook mushrooms picked in the wild unless you have the knowledge to distinguish between the safe and poisonous varieties.

Food Storage

Storage conditions and the length of time food can be stored vary tremendously depending on the type of food. Food must be stored safely at the correct temperature to avoid waste and contamination. Food storage instructions are given throughout this book, but a few general principles of food storage apply to all types of food items. These are discussed below.

Today many foods are stamped with a 'use by' date that should be adhered to. However, the food must be stored in the correct conditions prior to use. A food that is still within its 'use by' date can be 'off' if it has not been stored correctly. If a food tastes or smells 'off' or unusual, throw it out.

Stocks of food should be rotated. This means that you should use the supplies you already have on hand before using the newly purchased items.

Dry Food Storage

Dry foods such as rice, flour, sugar, pasta and dried herbs and spices should be kept in airtight containers in a dry, well-ventilated room or cupboard. Food should never be stored on the floor. The storage area should be kept clean and tidy.

Any cans that are rusty, dented, bulging or past their 'best before' date should be thrown away. Never open a bulging can as the pressure that has built up inside could cause the contents to spray, along with harmful bacteria.

Once cans are opened, the contents should be removed and stored, covered, in a glass, ceramic or stainless-steel container. Food should not be kept in opened cans because it can react with the metal of the can.

Fruit and Vegetables

For maximum nutritional benefit fruits and vegetables should be used as soon as possible. They should be kept in a cool room and stored off the floor. If there is a possibility of insect contamination, they should be covered. Any vegetable with soil still attached to it should be stored away from other food to prevent cross-contamination from contact with the soil. Fruit and vegetables rot quickly so they should be checked daily. Any that are beginning to rot should be discarded.

See *Fruit* (page 275) and *Vegetables* (page 715) for storage instructions for each type of fruit and vegetable.

Perishable Foods

Perishable foods such as meat, fish, dairy products and ready-made dishes spoil quickly so must be refrigerated. They naturally contain bacteria which multiply when the food is not chilled sufficiently. The bacteria can cause the food to spoil and cause food poisoning (see **Food Safety**, page 21) if consumed.

See individual food types throughout the book for storage instructions.

Refrigerators

Refrigerator temperatures should be held at 1–4°C | 34–40°F. If the temperature is above this range the food will not keep for as long as it might according to its 'use by' date and should be used as soon as possible. Inexpensive thermometers can be purchased to check the temperature of your refrigerator on a daily basis.

There are a number of rules to follow when using a refrigerator. These are:

- Always place food that needs to be chilled in the refrigerator as soon as possible. If the weather is warm, transport food using a cool-box.
- Always cover food and wrap it well to prevent cross-contamination.
- Store cooked food above raw and uncooked food.
- Clean refrigerators on a weekly basis.
- Dairy products are easily contaminated and should be kept away from other foods.
- Raw meat should be covered and placed in a container, then stored in the bottom of the refrigerator.
- Check perishable food every day for spoilage and use in order of purchase.
- Never put hot food into a refrigerator as it raises the temperature and can cause condensation that might result in contamination.
- Don't overload the refrigerator. Air needs to circulate freely for maximum cooling efficiency.

Freezers

Freezing food keeps it in good condition because bacteria are dormant at very low temperatures. In addition, the moisture in the food is frozen and therefore not available for bacterial growth (see also **Kitchen Equipment**, page 37).

The freezer temperature should be held at −18°C | 10°F which gives it a ★★★ 3-star rating. This rating is often marked on freezers and on frozen food packages and relates to the length of time a food can be stored. If the freezer is a compartment within the refrigerator, it will have a ★ 1-star rating.

Freezer rating	Length of food storage
*1-star	1 week
**2-star	1 month
***3-star	3 months
* ***3-star plus	3 months plus, capable of freezing fresh food

Freezers operate more efficiently when they are full but should never be filled above the 'load line' for a chest freezer or so full that the door does not shut easily.

Freezers need to be cleaned and defrosted regularly. Try to defrost the freezer when stocks are low and the weather is cool. Keep the frozen food in another freezer or in cool-boxes while defrosting.

Freezing Food

Food that has been purchased already frozen can be placed in the freezer in its packaging. Any frozen food that is soft on the surface should be defrosted and used as soon as possible. Never refreeze frozen food once it has been thawed as during thawing any dormant bacteria have had a chance to multiply. A cycle of freezing, thawing and refreezing food could result in the bacteria multiplying to dangerous levels.

Fresh food that is to be frozen should be closely wrapped in clingfilm, then wrapped again in a plastic freezer bag or foil. It should be labelled with the contents and the date of freezing. Food that is not wrapped closely is likely to develop 'freezer burn' which appears as a white patch. This means that the food has dried out. The white patch can be cut out and discarded.

The quicker the freezing process, the smaller the ice crystals in the food will be. Large ice crystals can damage the cell walls of the food. When the food is defrosted, liquid will escape from the cells, resulting in loss of nutrients and possible dryness. Only small amounts of food should be frozen at a time. Large quantities of unfrozen food raises the temperature of the freezer and the freezing process would be too slow.

Liquids, such as soups, can be poured into a large plastic box lined with a plastic freezer bag. Once the contents are frozen, remove the bag from the box. This means that you will need fewer boxes and space in the freezer can be maximized. Liquids in plastic containers should be frozen with a space of about 2.5 cm|1 in between the surface and the lid to allow for expansion on freezing.

Food such as casseroles and stews should be frozen in blocks of not more than 10 cm|4 in thick or defrosting will take too long. The meat must be covered with sauce or it will dry out during freezing.

Frozen food should be used in the date order of freezing: first in, first out.

Open-freezing

Vegetables and fruits are sometimes 'open-frozen' before packaging in plastic freezer bags or boxes. This method is sometimes referred to as 'dry pack' freezing. To open-freeze, blanch the vegetable according to the recipe directions and then dry them. See *Vegetables* (page 715) for detailed instructions on blanching and freezing vegetables, and storage times. Fruit such as raspberries can be washed, dried and frozen without blanching. Place them in a single layer on a tray in the freezer. Once they are frozen, place them in a freezer bag or container. This allows you to use only as much of the food as you need at any one time. Small cuts of meat such as chicken portions or chops should be wrapped individually in clingfilm then placed in a larger plastic bag or container.

Defrosting Food

In most cases food should be thawed as slowly as possible so that its quality is maintained. If time is short, casseroles and soups can be double-wrapped in plastic bags, then immersed in cold water to speed up the thawing time.

Some frozen items, such as vegetables or ready-prepared frozen foods, can be cooked from frozen. Baguettes can be wrapped in foil and reheated from frozen. Sliced bread can be toasted from frozen. However, large joints of meat need to be thoroughly defrosted before cooking or else the outside of the joint will be cooked while the inside is still raw.

Joints of meat should be placed on a tray or plate to catch any juices that escape from the packaging during defrosting. They should be defrosted in the bottom of the refrigerator. Small pieces of meat and fish should thaw within 6 hours. Larger joints will take up to 1–2 days. Once meat has thawed it should be cooked within 24 hours. Never refreeze meat or fish that has thawed.

Foods That Cannot Be Frozen Successfully

Although most food will be prevented from spoiling if kept at freezing point, some foods cannot be frozen successfully as their texture is ruined by freezing. This is particularly true of foods with a high water content such as bananas, cucumbers, lettuce and watercress. However, some of these may be frozen if wanted for soups or purées, in which case they should be frozen in purée form.

Emulsions such as mayonnaise or Hollandaise Sauce do not freeze successfully as they separate when thawed.

Yoghurt, milk and cream can be frozen but will not be totally smooth when thawed. Double cream freezes better if whipped first. Storage time: 4 months.

Eggs cannot be frozen in the shell, but both whites and yolks freeze well, either lightly beaten together or separated. Boiled eggs become rubbery when frozen. Storage time: 9 months.

Jelly, both savoury and sweet, loses its texture if frozen, and would have to be melted and allowed to set again after thawing if required jellied.

Mousses and soufflés set with gelatine tend to go rubbery, but can be frozen up to 1 week.

Strawberries keep their colour and flavour well, but become soft on thawing.

Melon is too watery to remain crisp when thawed. It is best frozen in balls in syrup, but even this is not totally satisfactory.

Tomatoes emerge mushy when thawed, but are good for soups and sauces. One bonus of freezing tomatoes whole is that they can be easily peeled if placed, still frozen, under running hot water. They can, of course, be frozen as purée or juice.

Fats, or foods with a high fat content, freeze less successfully as a rule than less fatty foods. They have a tendency to develop a slightly rancid flavour if stored for more than 3 months.

The Larder

This somewhat old-fashioned term evokes a picture of ordered rows of jars of bottled fruits and vegetables in a small room with marble shelves and mesh over the window. Few homes have such rooms today, relying instead upon refrigerators and freezers.

Although for many people obtaining food is relatively easy, certain items are worth keeping on hand either as supplies that are used frequently in cooking or for those times when you need to put together a quick meal and don't have time to shop.

The list below includes dry ingredients and foods that are useful to have on hand in the kitchen. These lists will, of course, vary from home to home, depending on personal taste.

- Caster sugar
- Plain flour
- Strong flour
- Cornflour
- Bicarbonate of soda
- Baking powder
- Fast-action yeast
- Salt
- Chocolate
- Cocoa powder
- Vanilla essence
- Canned tomatoes
- Sundried tomatoes
- Dried mushrooms
- Olives
- Canned tuna
- Canned sweetcorn
- Canned baked beans
- Canned or dried lentils
- Canned or dried chickpeas
- Canned or dried kidney beans
- Dried fruit, such as apricots, raisins
- Nuts, such as almonds, hazelnuts, pine nuts

- Canned peaches
- Soy sauce
- Olive oil
- Vegetable oil
- White wine vinegar
- Balsamic vinegar
- Bouillon powder
- Tomato purée
- English mustard powder
- Dijon or wholegrain mustard
- A good curry powder or paste
- Pasta
- Basmati, risotto, and long-grain rice
- Couscous
- Dry Madeira
- Vermouth
- White wine
- Amaretti biscuits
- Stem ginger in syrup

The following frozen foods are useful to keep stored in the freezer:

- Peas
- Chips
- Sliced bread
- Breadcrumbs
- Sausages
- Mince
- Chicken portions
- Prawns
- Salmon steaks
- Pastry
- Butter
- Ice cream/sorbet

Kept in the refrigerator, the items listed below will serve as basics for many recipes:

- Onions
- Garlic
- Lemons
- Milk
- Crème fraiche
- Butter
- Eggs
- Parmesan cheese
- Cheddar cheese

Recommended Basic Kitchen Equipment

- 1 cook's knife with a 20 cm|8 in or 25 cm|10 in blade
- 1 cook's knife with a 10 cm|4 in blade
- 1 flexible filleting knife with a 15 cm|6 in blade
- 1 serrated fruit knife
- 1 serrated bread knife
- 1 palette knife
- 1 stockpot
- 1 large saucepan, 20 cm|8 in diameter, with lid
- 1 small saucepan, 15 cm|6 in diameter, with lid
- 1 frying pan with 25 cm|10 in diameter base
- 1 colander
- 2 wooden spoons
- 1 fish slice
- 1 rubber spatula
- 1 sieve
- 1 vegetable peeler
- 1 set of scales
- 1 rolling pin
- 1 pastry brush
- 1 set of measuring spoons
- 1 whisk
- 1 measuring jug with 1 litre|2 pint capacity
- 1 pair of kitchen scissors
- 2 × 570 ml|1 pint ceramic basin
- 2 large stainless-steel bowls
- 1 cheese grater/fruit zester
- 2 plastic or wooden chopping boards
- 2 roasting tins; 1 small, 1 large
- 1 wire rack
- 2 baking sheets
- 20 cm|8 in flan ring
- 20 cm|8 in cake tin
- 1 lb loaf tin

Kitchen Equipment

Although a wide selection of cooking equipment is available in the shops, many of the items are not needed by the home cook to produce good food. The basic set of kitchen equipment listed opposite should prepare the cook for most tasks. It is important to buy the best quality you can afford, however. Good-quality equipment should last a lifetime, if not longer, and will make all the difference when preparing food.

Sharp knives slice cleanly and effortlessly through food; heavy-based pans cook their contents evenly; and well-designed, robust utensils make specific cooking processes easy. Conversely, poor-quality or unsuitable tools are likely to make food preparation frustrating and are more likely to produce dishes that could taste and look much better.

Many of the tools listed here are extremely useful for general and specific cooking processes, but many more can be collected over time.

Cutting Implements

Knives

When buying a knife, choose one that feels well balanced and substantial in the hand. Pivot the handle/blade junction on the edge of your open hand and the handle should fall back gently into your palm. The weight, balance, shape and metal from which a knife is made are important factors. The handle-end of the blade, known as a tang, fits into the handle and is encircled with a bolster or hand-grip. The tang should run the whole length of the handle to give the knife balance and should be riveted into place so that it cannot work loose from the handle. The heads of the rivets should be flush with the surface of the handle to make cleaning easy.

Knives must be looked after carefully to maintain the sharp cutting edge of the blade. Always clean and dry them immediately after use and sharpen them regularly with a steel. Use a wooden knife block to protect and neatly store knives or store them in a drawer separate from other kitchen tools as blades can be damaged and are dangerous in a cluttered drawer.

See also *Knife Skills* (page 65) for further information on knives and how to use them.

Types of Blade

Carbon-steel blades
Carbon steel is a good material for knife blades as the carbon hardens the steel so that the blade retains its sharpness and is easy to resharpen. Carbon-steel knives do, however, require a high level of maintenance as carbon steel rusts and discolours when used to cut onions and acidic food and the blades must be wiped, cleaned and dried immediately after use. When carbon-steel knives become stained, clean them with half a lemon sprinkled with salt. If that does not work, occasionally use a scouring pad. To remove rust, rub the blade with a burnt cork.

Stainless-steel blades
A stainless-steel blade can be used to prepare every type of ingredient as the metal is strong and does not rust or react with foods. Blades made of stainless steel are relatively soft and dull easily so require very regular sharpening.

High-carbon stainless-steel blades
Although high-carbon stainless-steel knives are expensive, they have all the advantages and none of the disadvantages of carbon-steel and stainless-steel knives. It is easier to maintain a sharp edge to the blade as the metal is harder than normal stainless steel and does not react with foods.

Knife Sharpeners

It is important not to allow a blade to become blunt. The knife then becomes harder to use as more pressure is required to slice through an ingredient. As a result, blunt knives can be more dangerous than sharp ones as they are liable to slip. It is worth taking your knives to a butcher or to a professional knife sharpener every month or so to maintain the blade. In between, a knife steel will be sufficient to maintain a sharp edge provided you know how to use it (see **Knife Skills**, page 65).

Whetstone (sharpening stone)
Grinding stones, often referred to as oil stones, are made of silicon carbide. Its very fine grain gives a good edge to a knife, making it extremely sharp. All good knives should be ground periodically to maintain their original sharpness.

Knife steel
A cylindrical, finely grooved rod, made from high-carbon steel, used for sharpening knife blades. A steel only gives a temporary edge.

Diamond steel
The surface of this stainless-steel rod is encrusted with ground industrial diamonds for extra grinding power. A diamond steel must only be used by someone who knows how to sharpen knives properly as this steel is highly abrasive and will blunt a blade very quickly if used incorrectly.

Ceramic steel

A lighter-weight knife sharpener made of roughened ceramic material. It is very effective at sharpening but easy to break if knocked or dropped.

Other Cutting Implements

Apple corer

Choose one with a sharp, rigid stainless-steel blade to withstand the force of twisting when coring.

Canelle knife

A blunt stainless-steel blade with a sharpened notch for cutting decorative grooves in the surface of vegetables and fruit.

Carving knife and fork

A knife with a rigid blade gently tapering from a wide heel to a pointed tip, measuring at least 20 cm | 8 in in length, for carving joints of meat with long clean slices (see *Knife Skills*, page 65). A carving fork has a long handle, a hinged hand guard and two long curved or straight prongs. The fork is used to hold the meat in place during carving.

Cherry stoner

Choose a sturdy stainless-steel stoner to stone cherries and olives.

Citrus zester

A square stainless-steel blade with a row of holes with sharpened edges, used to remove the zest of citrus fruits in thin strips known as julienne or needleshreds. Various sizes are available.

Clam knife

This is similar to an oyster knife (see below), with a longer, round-tipped blade.

Double-handed herb chopper or mezzaluna

A wide, curved blade with a handle at each end, used for chopping herbs. Available with up to 4 parallel blades, for chopping herbs in bulk.

Grapefruit knife

A stainless-steel fully serrated blade curved to fit the shape of the fruit. The knife is used with a sawing action to separate the segments of fruit from the pith and membranes.

Ham knife

The blade should be at least 25 cm | 10 in long, narrow and slightly flexible. The blade often has indentations along its cutting edge to reduce friction and keep thin slices intact.

Kitchen scissors

Choose sturdy scissors with stainless-steel blades that are strong enough to cut through the soft cartilage and fine bones of small birds.

Mandolin

Mandolin

A manually operated slicer, made of stainless steel with adjustable slicing blades. It is used to thinly slice, julienne and waffle-cut firm fruit and vegetables. Its narrow, rectangular body sits on the work surface at a 45° angle. Foods are sliced uniformly by moving it back and forth across the blade. The blades are extremely sharp. Use a hand guard if possible or protect your hand with a rubber glove.

Meat cleaver or Chinese cleaver

A knife with a large, heavy, rectangular blade, 15–20 cm | 6–8 in long. Used for cutting through and chopping bones. Choose a heavy one for extra cutting power. The blade usually has a hole punched in it for hanging it up out of the way.

Melon baller

A small stainless-steel metal scoop at each end of a central handle. One scoop is for cutting melon balls, the other is usually smaller and used for making small potato balls to sauté for Pommes Parisienne.

Mincers

Designed for mincing meat. The meat is placed in a funnel and is drawn towards the blades by a large screw operated by turning a handle. The blades can often be changed to determine the coarseness of the mince. Choose a mincer with a clamp rather than a suction base. Sharpen or replace the blades regularly and ensure they come apart easily for cleaning.

Oyster knife

A thick-handled knife with a short, rigid, flat blade, used to prise open oyster shells. Choose one with a handle that has a good grip and a guard between the blade and handle in case the knife slips (see **Shellfish**, *Oysters*, page 633).

Poultry shears

Large stainless-steel scissors about 25 cm | 10 in long, used to cut the bones of small and medium-sized birds. The notch cracks bone, the spring keeps the blade open between cuts, and one blade is usually serrated for cutting cartilage. Poultry shears should be made of stainless steel to prevent them from rusting as they often need to be immersed in water.

Smoked salmon knife

(See *Ham knife* above.)

Peelers are used to peel the thin skins from firm fruit and vegetables. There are 2 types of peeler, fixed and swivel. The swivel type has a blade that pivots freely to adapt to the shape of the ingredient being peeled. The blade is held either at the end of a cylindrical handle, with a pointed end for removing the eyes from potatoes, or horizontally between 2 arms. Both types have a double-cutting edge so that you can peel in an up or down motion.

Measuring and Weighing Equipment

It is essential to have accurate weighing and measuring equipment for successful cooking, especially when ingredients need to be measured precisely, as in recipes for baked goods.

Measurements are based on weight for dry ingredients and on volume for liquids. Therefore it is important to have several measuring devices, including scales and measuring jugs as well as liquid and dry measuring cups for American recipes.

Useful measuring charts can be found on pages 768–70.

Weight Measures

Scales

The 2 main types are spring-mechanism scales and balance scales. Spring-mechanism scales have a flat tray used as a platform for the measuring bowl. As the ingredients are weighed, a spring-mechanism moves the rotating dial marked with imperial and metric measurements. Spring-mechanism scales are also available in electronic models that display the weight on a digital screen. Choose scales that weigh in small units, e.g. 2 g, and switch easily from metric to imperial, and 'zero' easily, so that you can weigh different ingredients one after the other in the same bowl.

Balance scales are more traditional and use a 2-tray and free-weights counter-balance system, where weights are placed on one tray and ingredients are placed on the other until the 2 trays balance, as displayed by a marker. Although they can be very accurate, they are more difficult to use than spring-mechanism scales.

Volume Measures

American cup measures

American recipes measure dry and liquid ingredients by fractions of a 225 ml|8 fl oz cup. It is usual to buy a set of American cups measuring 1 cup down to $\frac{1}{4}$ cup or 55 ml|2 fl oz.

Measuring jug

Used to measure liquids. Buy a large jug that will hold at least 1 litre|2 pints of fluid, so that both large and small quantities of liquid can be measured. It is important that the jug features both metric and imperial measurements. 30 ml | 1 fl oz demarcations are useful for measuring accurately.

Measuring spoons

Sold in sets which usually include $\frac{1}{4}$ teaspoon, $\frac{1}{2}$ teaspoon, 1 teaspoon, and 1 tablespoon. 1 tablespoon = 3 teaspoons. They can be used for measuring small volumes of dry and liquid ingredients.

Saucepans

Saucepans are smaller and shallower than pots. They have straight or sloped sides, 1 or 2 handles and a lid. They are available in a range of sizes and are used for general cooking, to heat or reduce liquids, to cook food in liquids and to sweat aromatic vegetables as well as to sauté or fry small quantities of food.

Saucepans are made of many materials: aluminium with or without non-stick finishes, stainless steel, cast iron, enamelled steel, copper-plated and ovenproof porcelain. Saucepans should be substantial in weight, with a heavy base and a long handle riveted to the side of the pan. Choose a pan edged with an outwardly curved pouring lip so that a liquid can be poured at any point around the pan. It is also important that the base is curved along the inside edge to make cleaning easier and to prevent food from catching and burning. Pans often come in sets of 5 different sizes; however, it is better to have 2 or more of certain sizes for general use. (See list of *Recommended Basic Kitchen Equipment*, page 36.)

Materials Used to Make Saucepans and Other Cookware

Saucepans and other cookware for use on the hob and in the oven must be selected for their size, shape, construction, the material from which they are made and their efficiency for conducting and evenly distributing heat. Saucepans and other cooking equipment that do not distribute heat evenly may cause hot spots and burn foods. Different metals conduct heat at different rates and thicker layers of metal conduct heat more evenly than thinner ones. No one material suits all cookware and some materials are better suited than others to a specific process. It is therefore important to select durable equipment made of the most appropriate material for the job.

Aluminium

Aluminium is used commonly in the manufacture of pans as it is the second most effective heat conductor after copper and is light in weight. Aluminium is a soft metal so the pans need to be treated with care to prevent dents. A major disadvantage is that aluminium reacts with and discolours acidic, sulphurous and light-coloured foods, particularly when these are stirred with a metal spoon. As a result, the interiors of aluminium pans are often coated with a non-stick surface or are anodized to produce a hard, dark corrosion-resistant surface to prevent food from sticking or discolouring. Aluminium is frequently sandwiched between stainless steel in the base of stainless-steel pans to improve their heat conductivity.

Cast iron

Cast iron distributes heat evenly and holds high temperatures well. It is often used to make griddles and large skillets, both of which are used over a high flame. Although relatively inexpensive, cast-iron pans are heavy and difficult to lift. They must also be kept oiled and dry to prevent rusting and must be proved when new. Rub a new pan with sunflower oil and place in a 200°C|400°F|gas mark 6 oven for 20 minutes. Allow to cool. Repeat whenever the pan rusts.

Ceramics

Earthenware, porcelain and stoneware are used primarily for baking dishes, casseroles and baking stones as they conduct heat uniformly and retain temperatures well. Ceramics are non-reactive, inexpensive and generally suitable for the microwave oven, although most stoneware is too high in iron to use in the microwave. Ceramics chip or crack easily and most types are not suitable for use over direct heat.

Copper

Copper is an excellent heat conductor as it heats and cools rapidly and evenly. Although copper pans are wonderful to cook with, there are disadvantages: copper reacts with certain foods, producing a toxic substance. As a result, copper pans are always lined with tin. They are also heavy, expensive and require a high level of maintenance. They must be relined with tin periodically and cleaned frequently to remove the unsightly copper oxide that forms on the pan's outer surface during cooking. Copper is frequently used to improve the heat conductivity of pans made of other materials by sandwiching the metal between layers of stainless steel or aluminium in the base.

Enamel

Heavy pans, usually made of cast iron coated in enamel, are non-reactive and conduct heat efficiently and evenly. Enamel pans can be used both on the hob and in the oven, and are ideal for cooking casseroles and braising meat. Although good enamelled pans are relatively hard-wearing, the enamel can chip or crack, providing places for bacteria to grow, and the chemicals used to bond the enamel to the cookware can cause food poisoning if ingested. Only wooden spoons should be used in enamel pans as the enamel is easily scratched by metal. Enamel pans are rarely used professionally.

Glass

Tempered heat-proof glass conducts heat poorly but is sometimes used to make domestic pots and pans for use on the hob, in the oven and for microwave cooking. Glass is non-reactive, looks attractive and is ideal for watching the contents of a pan but shatters easily.

Non-stick coatings

Without affecting a metal's ability to conduct heat, a polymer plastic called polytetrafluoroethylene (PTFE), marketed under the trade name Teflon, is often applied to many types of cookware. It provides a non-reactive finish that prevents food from sticking, so less fat is required for cooking. Non-stick coatings on pans can be scratched or chipped by metal spoons so it is best to use wooden spoons only. Do not scour or scratch the non-stick surfaces when washing up.

Stainless steel

Although stainless steel conducts and retains heat poorly, it is a hard, durable metal, particularly useful for keeping food warm, and for low-temperature cooking. Stainless-steel pots and pans are available with aluminium or copper bonded to the base or with an aluminium-layered core to combine the rapid, even heat conductivity of copper or aluminium with the strength, durability and non-reactivity of stainless steel. Stainless-steel pans are very popular in the professional kitchen.

Types of Pan

Crêpe pan

A thick-based round pan with a shallow rim, designed so that a palette knife can be slid easily under a crêpe, to turn it over during cooking. The ideal size for *Crêpes* (see **Batters**, page 111) has a 15 cm|6 in diameter base. If possible, reserve your pan for cooking only crêpes, so that you do not need to wash it: just scour with salt and rinse. Over time a non-stick surface will build up in the pan.

Deep-fat frying pan

A deep-frying pan is thicker and deeper than an ordinary saucepan so it can hold sufficient oil or melted fat for immersing items of food. Deep-frying pans are fitted with a fine mesh basket to make it easy to remove the food and to keep the fat free of food particles. Choose a pan large enough to fry a portion of fish.

Double saucepan or double boiler

A metal pan that fits snugly into a second pan that holds a small quantity of boiling water below the base of the upper pan. Steam is produced by the boiling water and gently heats the top pan for making delicate sauces and melting chocolate where direct heat from the hob would be too intense.

Fish kettle

A long, deep, metal pan with a handle at each end, a removable platform and a lid. Fish kettles are most commonly made of aluminium or stainless steel and are used to poach or steam whole fish such as salmon or sea bass in court bouillon, either in the oven or on top of the hob. The fish rests on a removable platform that fits snugly into the base of the kettle, so that once the fish is cooked, it can be lifted out and transferred to a serving dish with minimum disturbance. Make sure that the platform has handles long enough to stand proud of the poaching liquor for easy lifting. The fish kettle should be large enough to hold a fish measuring at least 50 cm|20 in long.

Frying pan or skillet

A round, shallow pan with a long handle and shallow sloped or vertical sides, used for frying or sautéing food. The classic frying pan is made of cast iron for even heat distribution over a high flame. To prevent it from rusting it must be dried thoroughly after cleaning and then wiped with an oiled cloth. Lighter pans are often more popular as they are easier to lift. Stainless-steel pans are bad conductors of heat so must have copper or aluminium incorporated in the base. Aluminium frying pans with a non-stick coating are good conductors of heat and are easy to clean, but are easily scratched. The base of a non-stick frying pan must be strengthened and of reasonable thickness so it does not buckle over a high heat or develop hot spots.

Girdle pan

Thick cast-iron pan used for frying drop scones and crumpets.

Griddle pan

Ridged cast-iron pan used for char-grilling meat, fish and vegetables. Choose a heavy model.

A griddle pan can also be a heavy aluminium, iron or steel plate used to make griddle scones and crumpets. The base should be flat and thick to distribute the heat evenly. The handle usually folds down for easy storage.

Omelette pan

A small, round pan, 15–20 cm|6–8 in in diameter, made from carbon steel or other metal, with a thick base to ensure the eggs cook evenly. The sides are sloped to make folding and serving the omelette easier (see **Eggs,** Omelettes, page 222). To maintain the non-stick surface, it is best only to wipe clean, using a little salt as an abrasive, never scour. Omelette pans can also be used for making crêpes.

Roasting tin

Stainless-steel or aluminium rectangular tins used to bake or roast foods in the oven at high temperatures. Heavy-duty roasting tins can also be placed over direct heat for making gravy.

Roasting rack

The roasting rack fits inside the roasting tin to hold roasting meat off the base of the pan and enable air to circulate underneath for even cooking.

Sauté pan

Similar to a frying pan, a sauté pan is a round, shallow pan with straight or gently flared sides and a handle. Made of stainless steel, aluminium or tin-plated copper. Used to fry meat, fish and vegetables that are often cut up into pieces. The sides are slightly higher than those of a frying pan so that ingredients can be easily stirred to coat them with fat to brown them evenly on all sides.

Wok

A wok is used to prepare Asian foods quickly over high heat. Woks have round bottoms and curved sides that help to diffuse the heat and make it easy to toss or stir the contents. Their domed lids trap steam for steaming vegetables. Woks are useful for quickly sautéing strips of meat, simmering a whole fish or deep-frying appetizers. They range in diameter from 30 cm | 12 in to 50 cm | 30 in and are available with a long wooden handle or a metal handle on each side. Choose a heavy wok, preferably made from stainless steel. Cast iron woks periodically need to be rubbed with oil then heated to prevent rusting.

Pots

Pots are tall, large, round vessels with straight sides and 2 loop handles. Available in a range of sizes, they are used on the hob for making stocks or soups or for boiling or simmering foods, particularly when rapid evaporation is not desired. Flat or fitted lids are available.

Casserole dish

A casserole dish is a wide, lidded pan or container with handles, made of heavy-duty metal, earthenware or enamelled cast iron, available in various sizes. Used for long, slow cooking on the hob or in the oven. Oval casserole dishes are suited to pot-roasting or braising joints of meat and round casserole dishes are used for cooking stews and ragouts.

Stockpot

A large, deep pan with a capacity of several litres, a stockpot is designed to hold a substantial quantity of stock ingredients and water. They are made from heavy-duty stainless steel, tinned copper or aluminium. Commercial stockpots, due to their size, often have a tap near the base for draining the stock into a clean pan, and a handle on each side to facilitate lifting.

Steamers

You can buy steamers in the form of a saucepan with a second perforated pan that fits on top. This is more expensive than the readily available perforated steamer top, with a lid and a gradated base that fits on to any saucepan.

Folding steaming platform

This perforated platform stands on legs with adjustable folding side panels and is particularly useful for steaming small quantities of vegetables in any size of saucepan.

Steaming basket for wok

A small bamboo basket that fits neatly into the wok, leaving a gap of about 5 cm|2 in between the interior platform and the wok's base.

Utensils

Hand utensils are designed to aid in shaping, moving or combining foods. It is important to select tools that are sturdy, durable and easy to clean.

Basting spoon

For spooning melted fat or the cooking juices over meat during roasting or braising. The spoon should be large with a deep bowl and a long handle for safely spooning hot fat or liquid. Also used for folding in ingredients in cake-making. As a basting spoon is large, it is useful to buy one with a hooked or pierced handle for hanging up.

Bulb baster

A long, tapering tube marked in millilitres and fluid ounces with a rubber bulb fitted at its top. Used to transfer a liquid from one container to another, for example when extracting fat-free stock from beneath a layer of liquid fat. A clear plastic tube on the baster is the most useful.

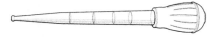

Chinois

Cone-shaped sieve made of very fine metal mesh. Used for straining stocks and sauces of impurities.

Corkscrew

Choose one with a very thin, sharp coil that disturbs the wine as little as possible but grips the cork efficiently. Pulling the cork out of the bottle can be made easier by choosing a corkscrew with arms or with the screw-pull system.

Fish slice

Used to lift cooked fish from a pan or to turn it over without damaging the delicate flesh. A fish slice should be broad and long for larger pieces of fish or other delicate foods.

Garlic press

A gadget with two metal handles, hinged in the centre. A foot located at the end of one handle closely fits a perforated garlic container at the end of the other. The container is filled with a skinned whole garlic clove and the foot is pressed into it by squeezing the handles together, until the garlic appears through the perforated surface as a purée. Look for a press with a built-in cleaner as presses are difficult to clean. Cherry or olive stoners are also often integrated in the handle. Garlic presses are invaluable in the kitchen as the smell of garlic is difficult to remove from wooden boards or a pestle and mortar.

Graters

Hand-held graters come in a variety of shapes and sizes. Choose a grater with a variety of faces ranging from fine 'nail' holes for grating nutmeg and zesting citrus fruit to large 'half-moon' holes for grating vegetables, fruit and cheese. Microplane and Accutec graters are particularly sharp and easy to use.

Small hand-held mouli graters are ideal for grating nuts and cheese.

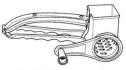

Hand-held mouli grater

Ice-cream scoop

A deep, spherical spoon used to mould ice cream into balls. The spoon is made of metal so that it can be heated in hot water before use to make scooping easier and to produce smooth balls of ice cream. A spring-action lever running inside the bowl of the spoon is also useful for turning the ice cream out cleanly.

Ladle

A bowl-shaped spoon with a long vertical handle usually made of stainless steel. Ladles are used for transferring liquids between pans for serving soups and stews at the table and for skimming fat from liquids. Smaller ladles often have lips to assist pouring and are used for spooning sauces on to plates or for transferring drinks, such as mulled wine or punch, into glasses.

Larding needle

A hollow stainless-steel skewer, with teeth at one end and a wooden or metal handle at the other. Used to thread lengths of lard or strips of bacon fat through lean meat, game and poultry to improve their flavour and moisten the flesh during cooking (see **Meat,** Veal, Veal Fricandeau, page 377).

Lobster crackers

For cracking the claws of lobsters to extract the sweet flesh. They resemble pliers (see **Shellfish,** *Lobster*, page 625).

Lobster pick

A long steel prong used to remove the flesh from the legs and claws of lobsters.

Meat-tenderizing mallet

A heavy wooden mallet with a spiked head, used to flatten or beat meat to break down the muscle fibres. Often used to prepare meat for pan-frying and other fast modes of cooking.

Mouli or moulinette

Used to strain and purée food by forcing it through a perforated metal plate with a rotating paddle. Choose a model that can be taken apart for cleaning.

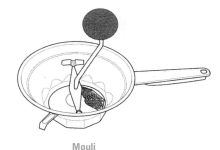

Mouli

Pasta wheel

A metal wheel with a sharpened edge, attached to a handle, for slicing through rolled-out pasta dough.

Pastry brush

A pastry brush has soft 2.5 cm | 1 in bristles, usually made of nylon, set in a short wooden handle. Used to brush off excess flour, to apply glazes or to wet the surface of rolled pastry so that smaller pieces of pastry can be stuck on for decoration. Make sure that the bristles are securely bound as they can work loose and stick to the food. Have one pastry brush for using with oil and another for using with flour.

Potato masher

A long-handled implement with a flat, perforated metal plate, held by 2 arms. It is used to crush drained root vegetables, especially potatoes. A smoother purée should be made using a mouli or bowl sieve.

Scraper

A flat, rectangular blade with a rounded handle along one side. Made of stainless steel or plastic and used for scraping pastry boards clean or drawing chopped ingredients together (see **Cake Icings and Decoration**, page 115).

Sieve

A bowl-shaped utensil made of wire or plastic mesh, with a long handle and a hanging loop for sitting over a bowl or pan, used for puréeing, straining liquids and sifting dry ingredients. Stainless-steel sieves are recommended as carbon steel discolours acidic purées. Although nylon sieves are not very sturdy, they are good for passing sauces that might be tainted by metal, such as *Raspberry Coulis* (see **Sauces, Sweet**, page 617).

Skewer

A long, thin, stainless-steel rod pointed at one end and looped at the other. Used to hold stuffed, boned or rolled meat in place during cooking. Metal kebab skewers are used for char-grilling pieces of marinated meat, fish, shellfish and vegetables. Choose skewers made of flat metal if possible as they are less likely to roll. Wooden skewers are also available. If using on the barbecue or under the grill, soak them in water for 1 hour before skewering the food and cooking, to prevent them from burning.

Spatula

A paddle-shaped implement with a long handle made of rubber, plastic or wood. A rubber spatula is more effective for scraping food from the surface and corners of containers. The rubber or plastic should be thin and flexible but strong enough to hold a quantity of food on its tip. Wooden spatulas are wide and flat and are used for moving food in a non-stick pan.

Spider

A long-handled tool with a wire-mesh flat spoon, used to remove food quickly from a liquid.

Tongs

Made of stainless steel and used for lifting and turning over pieces of food on barbecues, char-grills and in frying pans. Make sure the tongs are long, that the ends meet and that there is a spring mechanism for opening and closing.

Trussing needle

A thin rod of stainless steel, pointed at one end with an eye at the other. Used to pass string through the body, legs and wings of poultry or game birds to retain their shape during cooking (see **Meat, Poultry, Trussing**, page 418). Also used to sew up stuffed meats and birds to produce a regular shape and prevent the stuffing from escaping during cooking.

Whisks

Utensils made of stainless-steel wire bent into loops and held together in a handle. Whisks are used for different tasks and their design differs accordingly.

Balloon whisks: designed specifically to whisk air into egg whites or cream. The flexible wire loops are arranged in a short, rounded balloon shape that is held together by a wooden or metal handle. They are used for whipping cream and whisking egg whites.

Sauce whisk: A small metal whisk with tight loops of wire set in a spoon shape. It is used to beat and emulsify sauces and to beat lumps out of roux-thickened sauces (see *Sauces, Savoury*, page 579).

Sauce whisk

Wooden spoons

Wooden spoons are used to stir and mix foods while they cook, as they withstand heat well but do not conduct it. They have a shallow bowl and come in a variety of sizes to stir varying quantities of food. Choose long-handled heavy spoons as they are more practical to use over high heat and will be more hard-wearing. Some wooden spoons have a square corner to reach into the corners of a pan to prevent a mixture from catching and burning.

Other Kitchen Equipment

Bread board

A wooden board, often with an integrated serrated knife for slicing bread. A board with a removable slatted tray is useful for catching crumbs.

Chopping board

A board made of hard wood or toughened plastic in a variety of coded colours. Used as a surface for slicing and chopping foods (see *Knife Skills*, page 65).

Colander

A deep, perforated metal bowl with one or two handles, used for draining food. Choose a colander with a stand sufficiently tall to hold the contents clear of the draining liquid. The stand also facilitates pouring hot foods safely from a pan into the colander while using both hands.

Funnel

Conical in shape with a long narrow stem. Used for pouring liquid safely into bottles. Make sure it is made of heat-resistant plastic or stainless steel and has a wide, flared top and a tube that fits narrow bottles.

Flour dredger or sifter

A metal container with a close-fitting lid perforated with large holes. It is filled with flour, turned upside-down and shaken rhythmically to flour a work surface or the surface of food evenly to prevent sticking.

Jelly bag

A fine mesh bag held open with a wooden hoop for straining solids from unset jelly (see **Jams, Jellies and Other Preserves**, page 321).

Lemon squeezer

A ribbed, domed lid, perforated with small holes around the edge, fits on to a bowl with a pouring spout. Lemon squeezers are usually made of plastic, stainless steel or glass and are used to squeeze, strain and collect the juice from citrus fruit.

Marble slab

A tile of marble measuring at least 60 × 45 cm | 24 × 18 in for preparing foods that need to be kept cool during preparation, such as tempered chocolate, pastry and biscuit dough.

Mixing bowls

Wide-rimmed bowls with a heavy base and curved or sloping sides used for mixing, beating and folding ingredients together. It is useful to buy mixing bowls in a range of sizes. Large bowls are used to beat or fold mixtures or to mix large quantities of ingredients together. Smaller bowls are useful for blending or emulsifying smaller quantities. Stainless-steel bowls are durable and have a curved lip for easy pouring. Mixing bowls are also available in plastic and toughened glass but are not so hardwearing.

Oven gloves

A pair of gloves, or 2 gloves attached by a length of material, used to protect the hands from hot cooking utensils. They are made of non-heat-conducting material such as layered, woven cotton, or foil-lined foam in a cotton cover. Choose good-quality, thick gloves as cheaper varieties are often not very effective and quickly fall apart.

Pan rest

A heavy wooden, ceramic or cast-iron stand on which hot pans are placed to protect the work surface.

Pestle and mortar

A heavy bowl, called a mortar, and a short, round-ended stick, called a pestle. They are made from heavy materials such as stone, glass, ceramic or wood and used to crush or pound food to a paste or powder. Stone and ceramic mortars are most effective for breaking down herbs and spices due to their naturally fine, abrasive grain. They are also heavy and sturdy to use and do not absorb aromas and flavours like wood. The pestle and mortar must be made of the same material otherwise one will grind the other away. The pestle and mortar is often replaced with a food processor these days but is ideal for processing small quantities.

Pie dishes
Round, oval or rectangular glazed ceramic or porcelain dishes, with a lip available in a variety of sizes and depths (usually 5–7 cm | 2–3 in) for baking pastry-topped foods.

Piping bag and nozzles
A cone-shaped nylon or disposable plastic bag for use with metal or plastic plain, starred, fluted or slit-shaped nozzles. Piping bags are used for decorating cakes (see page 155), pâtisserie (see page 531) and confectionery with icing, chocolate or cream. They are also used for shaping pastries, such as eclairs, and for piping puréed potato, pastes and meringue. Plain $\frac{1}{2}$ cm | $\frac{1}{4}$ in and 1 cm | $\frac{1}{2}$ in nozzles are the most generally useful.

Preserving jar
A wide-necked glass container, also known as a Kilner™ jar. It is hermetically sealed with either a metal screw top or with a glass lid fitted with a rubber seal and a metal clip.

Pressure cooker
A hermetically sealed saucepan that cooks food under pressure at a higher temperature to reduce the cooking time. The pressure cooker is suited to cooking steamed, braised and stewed dishes (see **Pressure Cooking**, page 555).

Pudding basins
Heavy ceramic bowls with curved sides, a heavy base and edged with a thick lip for securing string. Pudding basins are available in a variety of sizes and are used for moulding and cooking steamed puddings (see **Steaming**, page 673) as well as for all-purpose mixing bowls (see above).

Salad spinner
Used to dry washed salad leaves. A perforated bowl for holding salad leaves sits in a larger bowl fitted with a lid and spinning handle. Projections attached to the handle inside the lid grip the perforated bowl so that when the handle is turned the bowl spins, forcing the water into the bowl below.

Salt and pepper mills
Choose a wooden mill with a screw top rather than a turning handle. It is well worth investing in a good make as the grinding mechanism in cheaper models can often be unreliable and give an uneven result. Choose mills with metal grinding mechanisms for pepper and plastic for salt as the salt corrodes the metal.

Smoker

A metal box divided by a perforated shelf. Wood chips are burnt in the bottom whilst the food to be smoked is placed on the perforated shelf above. The box is then sealed to contain the smoke during the smoking process.

Storage containers

Storage containers are necessary for keeping leftovers and opened packages of food safe for consumption. Proper storage can also reduce the costs incurred by waste or spoilage. The most useful storage containers are those made from hard-wearing, high-density plastic. They are available in clear or white plastic to protect light-sensitive foods. It is important that the containers have well-fitting lids and are available in a range of sizes. Flat, snap-on lids ensure an air-tight seal and stack easily for space-efficient storage.

Tammy or drum sieve

A fine, double-wire mesh sieve, held firm and flat in a circular wooden or metal frame. Forcemeat, fruit and cooked vegetables are pushed through the fine mesh to produce smooth pastes and purées (see **Mousselines**, page 487).

Tea towels

Buy linen or 100 per cent cotton towels as they absorb more water than mixed-fibre varieties and can also be boil-washed. Run new tea towels through a wash before use to make them more absorbent.

Timer

Used to remind the cook to check food that is cooking. Buy one with increments of 30 seconds. A timer that you can pin to your shirt is useful in case you are out of the kitchen.

Baking Tins

Baking tools are often specialized and make specific tasks easier but can be quite expensive. As always, when purchasing baking equipment, look for quality and durability.

Baking tins are made of tinned steel, stainless steel or aluminium, so that heat is evenly conducted. It is important to select heavy-duty tins that will distribute heat evenly and will not warp in the oven. Choose dull, light-coloured tins, not shiny or dark ones, as these cause over-browning.

Angel cake tin

A 20 cm | 8 in deep cake tin with gently sloping sides and a tube in the centre to allow for even baking. Used for angel cakes, American whisked-sponge cakes made with egg whites.

Barquette tins

Boat-shaped tins made in various sizes from 3.5 cm | 1 ½ in to 12.5 cm | 5 in and used to mould sweet and savoury pastries for canapés (see page 167), petits fours and pâtisserie (see page 531).

Brioche tin

A fluted, tinned–metal mould for baking brioche dough. They come in a variety of sizes to make large and individual brioches (see **Bread, Yeast**, page 134).

Croquembouche tin

Conical-shaped stainless-steel tin for moulding the French wedding cake, Croquembouche.

Deep cake tin

Metal tins with sides 10–12.5 cm | 4–5 in deep, with fixed or loose bases. These tins are usually round or square, but are also available in novelty shapes.

Flan ring

Metal rings of different diameters and depths, with either a plain or a fluted edge. Placed on a baking sheet to mould rolled-out pastry into a flan base suitable for filling.

Loaf tin

A deep, rectangular tin used to mould and bake a loaf of bread, traditionally weighing 450 g | 1 lb or 900 g | 2 lb.

Moule à manqué

A classic French cake tin, traditionally 20–22.5 cm | 8–9 in in diameter, made from aluminium or tinned steel. The sides are about 5 cm | 2 in deep and slope gently outwards from the base to give the turned-out cake an attractive tapered shape when it is served upside down (see **Cakes**, page 137).

Patty tin

Metal baking tray containing 6, 9 or 12 round indentations with rounded or sloping sides, used to mould and bake small cakes and pastries.

Raised pie tin

Oblong or oval tin with decorative indentations and hinged or loose sides that unclip once the pie is baked. Used to mould meat pies encased in hot water pastry (see **Forcemeat**, page 271, and **Terrines, Pâtés and Raised Pies**, page 703).

Sandwich tin

Shallow tin, 5 cm | 2 in in depth, made from tinned steel or aluminium, sometimes with a non-stick coating. They are available in round, square, oblong and novelty shapes (see *Cakes*, page 137).

Spring-form tin
A deep aluminium or tinned-steel tin with sides that unclip to remove the sides from the base. Often useful for deep, moist cakes where turning out is likely to be difficult, and for cheesecakes. Also available with a tube insert.

Swiss roll tin
A shallow, oblong tin, $25 \times 35\,\text{cm} \mid 10 \times 14\,\text{in}$ and $2\,\text{cm} \mid \frac{3}{4}$ in deep, for baking whisked sponge for roulades and Swiss roll (see *Cakes*, page 137).

Tartlet tins
Individual tinned-steel fluted tins in various shapes and sizes for moulding petits fours and pâtisserie.

Other Baking Equipment

Baking sheet
A flat metal sheet used to bake foods such as pastries and biscuits that do not require moulding. Choose heavy steel sheets with a lip on one side to make it easy to slide the baked food on to a plate or wire rack. Do not buy thin, flexible baking sheets as they warp in the heat of the oven, which is likely to damage the baking food. Pale, dull sheets are best as dark or shiny sheets can cause the food to over-brown.

Blind-baking beans
Usually dried pulses which are used specifically for the purpose. Also available are ceramic beads the size of small beans (see *Pastry, Baking a Pastry Case Blind*, page 509). Uncooked rice is also suitable.

Palette knife
A long, flexible blade with a rounded end and no cutting edge for easing under breads, cakes, biscuits and pâtisserie. Also used for spreading icing on to cakes.

Pastry cutters
Thin-tinned steel or aluminium strips, moulded into round, fluted and novelty shapes, used to cut pastry and biscuit dough into shapes. The top edge is rolled to safeguard the fingers and to keep the cutter shape rigid, while the lower edge is sharp for cutting cleanly through the dough.

Rolling pin
Wooden rolling pins are the best. Choose one without handles; it is easiest to use. Pasta rolling pins have slightly tapering ends.

Wire cooling rack

Wire mesh platforms, used to cool baked foods. Steam can escape evenly from all surfaces of the food, preventing the underside of the food from becoming soggy. Make sure that the racks have good stands, which hold the food at least 1 cm $\vert$ $\frac{1}{2}$ in away from the work surface for optimum air circulation.

Moulds

A mould is a receptacle that holds food in a certain shape while it sets or bakes so that it retains its moulded shape when it is turned out. Moulds can be tall, shallow, plain or patterned with indentations. Poor heat-conducting ceramic or glass moulds are used where heat or cold retention is an important factor, but most moulds are made of metal because of its quick reaction to heat change.

Charlotte mould

Made from aluminium or tinned steel, copper or ovenproof glass. The shape is deep and round, with slightly sloping sides, and the mould has two small handles. The sloping sides make it easier to line the sides with fingers of bread or sponge.

Chocolate mould

Moulds made of clear plastic are available in many shapes such as animals, eggs or figures, and can be used for making filled chocolates and festive hollow chocolate novelty shapes (see **Chocolate**, page 189).

Cream horn mould

A tinned steel conical mould for shaping individual pastry and biscuits into cones for filling with cream or thick custard and fruit (see **Pastry,** *Flaky Pastry*, page 520).

Dariole mould

Made from tinned steel or aluminium. It is a small flowerpot-shaped mould, with gently rounded sides, used to make individual steamed puddings, small cakes, and savoury or sweet mousses.

Fish mousse mould

Decorative mould for setting fish mousse. The mould is shaped like a fish, to indicate the main ingredient, and decorated with patterned indentations to depict scales and other details. Traditionally made of copper, lined with tin, but most frequently available in aluminium, glass or porcelain.

Ice-cream mould

Made of tinned steel or copper with a lid, for making iced bombes and layered iced desserts. Ice-cream moulds are conical, square or spherical. The best moulds have a vacuum-release top, otherwise the bombe is very difficult to turn out. Do not use old metal moulds because the metal can taint the ice cream.

Jelly mould

Traditionally made of copper lined with tin, aluminium, glass or porcelain to set clear fruit jellies. The moulds can be tall or shallow and extravagantly patterned with decorative indentations depicting fruit, or shaped like a castle so that light enhances the clarity and finished appearance of the jelly.

Ring mould

Made from aluminium or tinned steel. They can be deep, shallow, plain or decorated for baking cakes or setting sweet or savoury mousses and jellied desserts.

Shortbread mould

A wooden mould, usually engraved with a thistle pattern, in which the shortbread dough is rolled to shape it before being turned out on to a baking sheet for cooking.

Soufflé dishes/Ramekins

Round ceramic or porcelain bowls with fine, straight, ribbed sides used specifically for baking soufflés in a hot oven.

Terrine mould

A round, oval or rectangular lidded earthenware or enamelled cast-iron container used for shaping and baking layered and minced meat or fish mixtures.

Timbale

Small conical moulds made from tinned steel or aluminium for shaping individual portions of mousse, custard, ice cream, fruit or vegetables. Their slightly flared sides allow the contents to release cleanly when inverted. The term is often used interchangeably with dariole mould (see above).

Electrical Equipment

Deep-fryer

An insulated metal bowl, fitted with a wire mesh basket, heating element and thermostat used to cook food quickly by immersing it in hot fat. Depending on the food to be deep-fried, the thermostat is set to retain the heated fat at a pre-set temperature so that it does not overheat. Choose one that is easy to drain.

Food mixer

Consists of a motor that powers a rotating head at a selection of speeds, controlled by a dial or lever, above a large metal bowl. A whisk, paddle or dough hook is fitted on to the rotating head to whisk cream and eggs, cream or beat cake mixtures and knead bread dough. Good for mixing cakes and meringues, whipping cream and kneading bread.

Food processor
Consists of a motor that powers a revolving S-shaped blade in the base of a deep bowl fitted with a lid and funnel for dropping in ingredients. The food processor will only work if the lid is correctly fitted for safety and to prevent spillage. The motor is powered by a selection of buttons so that the blade can chop ingredients both roughly and finely, as well as purée foods, emulsify sauces, liquidize soups and make pastry. Discs can be used instead of the blade to slice, shred or julienne foods. Select a processor with a powerful motor and a large bowl. Food processors with the bowl sited directly over the motor are the most durable.

Hand-held whisk
An electric motor, fitted with plastic or steel beating and whisking attachments. Electric whisks remove the physical effort and time involved when whisking by hand. Buy one with a heavy-duty motor for whisking larger quantities. Used for making cakes and meringues, whipping cream and emulsifying mayonnaise.

Ice-cream machine
Used to churn ice cream and sorbets (see *Ice Creams*, page 311).

Juicer for citrus fruits
An electric alternative to the traditional lemon squeezer used to extract the juice of citrus fruits. A motor powers a revolving dome-shaped squeezer set above a perforated tray that strains the juice into a bowl below. The motor is activated when the halved fruit is pressed down on to the squeezer. Useful for squeezing large quantities of fruit.

Liquidizer
A motor-driven 4-pronged blade sits in the base of a tall, cylindrical container of clear glass or reinforced plastic. The lid, which has a plugged hole for adding ingredients, fits securely on to the container. Liquidizes foods such as soups and sauces to a smooth consistency but it is also used to blend batters, prepare smooth drinks and emulsify sauces and dressings. Choose a machine with a large container and a lid that fits securely to prevent the food escaping whilst liquidizing is in progress.

Multi-practic
A hand-held, stick-shaped liquidizer, consisting of a handle with a power button that drives a small revolving blade located at the end of a detachable, washable arm. Used for liquidizing soups and sauces or puréeing fruit and vegetables, either in the pan in which they were cooked, or in a long, cylindrical container, often sold with it. Immerse the blade completely before turning on the motor.

Pasta machine

A hand-operated or electric stainless-steel machine for kneading, rolling and cutting pasta dough (see *Pasta*, page 499).

Freezers

Either in chest or cupboard form, used to preserve food for up to twelve months at a temperature of at least −18°C|0°F. The upright model is easier to access and occupies a minimum of floor space. The chest freezer offers greater usable volume for the same capacity as an upright. It is useful to have a temperature gauge so that it is obvious if the temperature inside is rising abnormally. Clear drawers are also useful so that it is easy to see what is stored. Some modern models of freezer have a 'super-freeze' facility where food is frozen at a faster rate. Freezers can also be kept free of frost by a 'no frost' feature where dry air is circulated by a fan located on the interior back wall (see *Food Storage*, page 30).

Refrigerators

Proper refrigeration space is essential in a kitchen as many foods must be stored at low temperatures (below 5°C|40°F) to maintain quality and safety. It is therefore sensible to choose the largest refrigerator possible for your kitchen. It is important that the refrigerator has well-fitting, sturdy shelves that can be adjusted to make way for large containers. Reinforced glass shelves and a cooling element hidden behind the back wall of the refrigerator make the interior surfaces easier to clean. Salad drawers, found in the bottom of the refrigerator, provide a humid atmosphere to increase the length of time vegetables and salad ingredients can be stored. Refrigerators often feature a built-in thermometer and display the temperature digitally above the door for peace of mind during warm weather (see *Food Storage*, page 30).

Thermometers

Freezer thermometer

Used to check that the freezer is running at the required temperature (see *Food Storage*, page 30).

Instant-read thermometer

A thin metal thermometer with a sharp point to insert into food. An accurate reading is obtained within a few seconds.

Meat thermometer

Insert into meat during cooking to obtain internal temperature readings from the deepest part of a joint of meat. The thermometer has markings for rare, medium and well-done meat. The reading is displayed on a dial denoted by an arrow. It is important to ensure the thermometer does not touch the bone in a joint of roasting meat. Bone conducts heat readily and will be hotter than the surrounding meat, which may lead to an inaccurate reading.

Oven thermometer
Placed in the centre of the oven to measure the oven temperature, displayed on a dial, accurately.

Sugar or deep-fat thermometer
Measures temperatures up to 200°C|400°F, using mercury in a glass column. It gauges when fat is ready for deep-frying and indicates the temperature, termed the degree of 'crack', of boiling sugar (see **Sugar, Sweetners and Sugar Syrups**, page 695). As sugar thermometers are normally made of glass, do not insert them into hot food. They should be placed into cold or cool food and warmed gently.

Other Cooking Equipment

Barbecue
In its most basic form a barbecue consists of a rack suspended over a fire. More sophisticated barbecues feature adjustable racks to move the food closer or further away from the burning coals. As the burning charcoal throws off so much heat, specialized barbecue accessories are useful, such as long-handled tongs for turning the food over and bellows for encouraging the charcoals to burn more intensely. More sophisticated still are barbecues containing lava stones heated by electricity or butane gas, often fitted with a spit for roasting joints of meat, kid or suckling pig. They do not heat as intensely as charcoal-burning barbecues and do not give food the characteristic smoky, blackened taste of burning charcoal (see **Meat,** *Barbecuing*, page 350).

Fondue pot
A ceramic or enamelled cast-iron pot placed on a stand fitted with a spirit lamp. The flame heats the contents of the pot before food spiked on to a 2-pronged, long-handled fork is dipped into it.

Grills

Cooking apparatus, located in the top of an oven or as a separate entity, where food is quickly cooked, toasted, caramelized or browned, from above, by an electric element or powerful gas flame. Gas grills are preferred by professional cooks as they heat up more quickly than electric models and are easier to regulate.

Salamander
An overhead gas grill used to finish or brown the surface of foods, mostly used in a professional kitchen.

Char-grill

A cast-iron grill suspended above burning wood or charcoal. Char-grills are heated intensely before use, so that the surface of the food placed on the grill chars and takes on the characteristic blackened appearance and flavour of the wood or charcoal beneath. Used to cook meat, fish, shellfish and vegetables.

Rôtisserie

Similar to an overhead grill except that the food is placed on a revolving spit in front of the heat source. Some domestic ovens offer this facility. Mostly suited to poultry or joints of meat.

Gas and Electric Hobs

Hobs are usually fitted with 4 gas burners or electric rings on which pans are heated. Gas hobs are the type used professionally as the flame supplies a direct heat that is easy to control. Electric plates are relatively slow to heat and cool. A pan may have to be removed altogether whilst the ring cools, to prevent burning.

Ceramic hob

A ceramic hob has a completely smooth surface and is made of a special glass panel, which is highly shock-resistant and can withstand large variations in temperature. Heat is transmitted by radiation to the base of pans placed on to marked areas on the hob's surface. It is therefore important to use heavy-based pans to use the heat most efficiently. Ceramic surfaces must be cleaned using a specific non-abrasive cleaning fluid.

Induction hob

This method of heating is known as the cold-heat hob as it has an active element in the form of a coil that creates a powerful magnetic field when an alternating current is passed through it to produce a powerful, even heat. The inductors are located beneath marked heating areas on the hob's surface, which is perfectly flat and made of a non-conducting material such as ceramic glass. The efficiency of an induction hob far exceeds gas or electric hobs, but induction hobs are far more expensive. Ceramic hobs often include one or two induction burners for their quicker response time.

Ovens

Convection/fan oven

Convection ovens use internal fans to circulate the air heated by either gas or electricity. This tends to cook foods more quickly and evenly. Convection ovens cook foods more quickly so temperatures may need to be reduced by $10°C|25°F$ from those recommended for conventional ovens. Convection ovens can be tricky to bake with because the food tends to brown more quickly than it would in a conventional oven. For baking, it is best to choose an oven that has the option of turning the fan off, or cover the food when it becomes brown.

Microwave oven

An electrically powered oven using high-frequency short waves, called micro-waves, as a source of cooking energy. The microwaves are directed into the oven cavity and bounce off the metal walls and floor in all directions to cook food. Even cooking is assisted by a rotating glass tray located in the base of the microwave oven on which the food is placed in microwave-proof plastic, ceramic or glass containers. Dishes made of or trimmed with metal will reflect the microwaves and are therefore not suitable.

Microwaves have a number of power settings: low settings for defrosting food and more powerful settings to cook or reheat pre-cooked food. Choose one with time settings in increments of 10 seconds. Microwave ovens do not radiate heat and will therefore not brown foods unless fitted with special browning elements, such as a grill. Although they are not suitable for roasting meat, when used properly, microwaves are useful for cooking fish, fruit and vegetables, heating sauces and soups and cooking steamed sponge puddings in a fraction of the time taken using the traditional cooking method (see *Microwave Cookery*, page 483).

Aga

A heavy iron oven traditionally heated by solid fuel, but also by electricity, oil or gas. The Aga has a hot and cool oven, a warming oven and two covered hot plates. Solid-fuel ovens are the cheapest to run. As the Aga loses heat rapidly when the hot plates are uncovered, it is mainly used for long slow cooking and simmering inside the oven.

Slow cooker

Sometimes called a 'crockpot', a slow cooker is a large electric pot used to cook soups and stews with slow, moist heat. It is useful to cook food during the day when you are away from home. Most cookers have a 'fast' setting that takes 4–6 hours or a 'slow setting' that takes 8–12 hours. If food needs to be browned this should be done in a frying pan before adding to the cooker. Beans that require fast boiling (see *Pulses*, page 559) should be boiled on a conventional hob before being added to the slow cooker.

Using Knives: Points to Remember

- **Buy the best knives that you can afford**

- **Choose an appropriate work surface**
  Use a large chopping board that sits firmly on the work surface. Place a damp J-cloth underneath the board to prevent it from slipping. Choose plastic or wooden chopping boards, both of which are kind to blades and provide a comfortable surface to chop on. Avoid surfaces such as metal, marble or glass as they are likely to damage the knife blade or even cause the knife to slip, which could be dangerous.

- **Keep the work surface clear**
  A crowded board makes it difficult to chop accurately and could be dangerous. To help you keep your work surface clear, transfer cut ingredients directly into pots placed within easy reach as you work.

- **Choose the correct knife for the job**
  Before cutting an ingredient, decide which type of knife is most suitable for the purpose.

- **Make sure the knife blade is sharpened**
  A blunt knife is more dangerous than a sharp one because it is more likely to slip.

- **Hold the knife correctly**
  The handgrip is determined by the type of knife, the size and firmness of the ingredient and the style of cut.

- **Always cut away from yourself to avoid injury**

- **Make the ingredient safe to cut**
  For safety and ease of chopping, trim rounded ingredients on one side to create a flat surface so that they will sit firmly on the chopping board while you cut them.

- **Hold the ingredients correctly and safely**
  Hold the ingredients on the work surface with a claw-like grip, the large finger joints pointing upwards, the fingertips curled under, and the thumb tucked under the palm. The blade of a cook's knife is deep and specifically designed to be held against the finger joints which act as a guide, helping to cut the ingredients evenly.

- **Do not force the knife**
  Always allow the blade's cutting edge to do the cutting. Never force the blade through the ingredient. Use smooth, even strokes.

- **Washing knives**
  Always wash knives by hand immediately after use. Never place a knife in the sink as it will not be visible in washing-up water and could be dangerous. Dishwashers are also to be avoided as the heat and washing chemicals can damage the knife blade and riveted handle.

Knife Skills

The first lesson in a cook's training is to learn to select, handle and maintain knives. Each knife has a specific purpose for which it is best suited. Learning to use each knife confidently and accurately takes a great deal of practice.

Knives Most Frequently Used in the Kitchen

A set of 6 knives is sufficient for the preparation of most ingredients.

- The 20–30 cm|8–12 in **cook's knife** has a deep blade and is used for general cutting and chopping, slicing and dicing.
- The 10 cm|4 in **paring or office knife** is used to slice or dice smaller ingredients finely.
- The **boning knife** is sturdy and is used like a dagger to remove bones from joints of meat and poultry as well as trimming fat from filleted meat.
- The **filleting knife** is thin and pliable and is used mainly for filleting and skinning fish and removing membranes from meat.
- The serrated **fruit knife** is used to prepare fruits and soft vegetables.
- The **bread knife** is used to slice bread, cakes and sweet and savoury pastries.

Other Knives That Have Their Place in a Well-equipped Kitchen

- The **turning knife** is used to shape vegetables and fruit garnishes.
- The **carving knife** is used to slice large joints of meat thinly.

See *Kitchen Equipment* (page 37) for information about other types of knife.

Knife Sharpening

A knife can only be used correctly and safely if it is well sharpened. The knives listed above are almost useless without investing in a good knife sharpener such as a steel or whetstone to keep the blades sharp.

In order to cut ingredients effortlessly, evenly, thinly and/or finely it is extremely important to maintain the edge of the blade. Restaurant chefs sharpen their knives with a steel a number of times each day and send them to be ground on a whetstone once a week to keep the blade razor-sharp. Although it is not

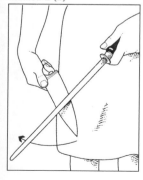

necessary to sharpen knives in the domestic kitchen quite so regularly, it is important to maintain them, particularly if you have invested in good-quality knives. While the knife steel helps to maintain a blade's edge, the knife must be ground periodically to keep its original sharpness.

Knife Steel

The knife steel is a thin, rounded, slightly tapered length of steel with a handle and a hand guard. It is used to smooth out any rough spots on the edges of the blade and realign the metal. Ceramic knives have a specific type of steel, so ensure the type of steel is the correct type for your knives.

Sharpening a Knife with a Knife Steel
Method 1

The safest method is as follows:

1 Place the point of the steel firmly on a work surface, holding the handle with one hand. With the other hand, hold the knife blade at a 30° angle to the steel.
2 With a smooth, sweeping action, slide the knife down the steel, slowly pulling the knife towards you so that only the point is in contact with the steel as it reaches the work surface. Ensure that the blade remains angled at 30° throughout the action to sharpen the first edge evenly.
3 Repeat the action, holding the other side of the blade at the same angle against the opposite side of the steel. Repeat the action several times on each side of the blade until it is sharpened sufficiently.
4 The knife should not be pressed hard against the steel but passed lightly and smoothly over it. A knife held at too great an angle or dragged heavily down the steel will be blunted further.

Method 2

Once you are well practised at sharpening:

1 Hold the steel at waist-height with the tip pointing away from you to allow freer movement and faster sharpening. Hold the knife firmly in a horizontal position, with the thumb and forefinger gripping the heel of the blade for added control.
2 Rotate the knife so that the blade is held at a 20° angle against the steel.
3 Start with the heel of the blade at the hand-guard end of the steel and sweep the knife blade down the steel with a downward curving action until the tip of the blade reaches the tip of the steel. Repeat the action several times on each side of the blade.

Sharpening a Dull Knife Blade with a Whetstone (Sharpening Stone)

1 Place the heel of the knife blade against the whetstone at a 20° angle. Maintaining this angle, press down on the blade while pushing it away from

you in one long arc, as if to slice off a thin piece of the stone. The entire length of the blade should come into contact with the stone during each sweep.

2 Repeat the action an equal number of times on each side of the blade until it is sufficiently sharp.

How to Tell if a Knife Is Sharpened Sufficiently

If the sharpened blade slices through the skin of a tomato or red pepper with minimal downward pressure, it requires no further sharpening.

The Cook's Knife

The cook's knife is without doubt the most versatile cutting tool used in the kitchen. It is used for precise cutting, rough or fine chopping and thick or thin slicing.

Many home cooks are put off by the size of the cook's knife as initially it feels heavy and far too large to control. Once you know how to use the long, curved blade correctly and safely, you will be able to prepare food more precisely and efficiently.

The cook's knife should be 20–30 cm | 8–12 in long. It should have a long, deep blade with a curved cutting edge and a recessed, well-balanced handle. The heel of the blade is deep and heavy and gradually tapers to a sharp point. The heel, middle and point of the blade are used for different cutting purposes. The point is used for delicate slicing, while the heel is more suited to heavier jobs such as slicing through hard root vegetables or chicken carcasses. The middle of the blade is used for everything in between. Knives that are made from one piece of metal or that have rivets through the handle holding the tang in place are likely to last longer than knives with handles that have been attached by adhesive.

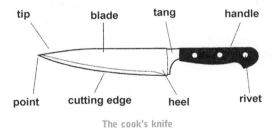

The cook's knife

Using the Cook's Knife

Roll-slicing
This technique is used to slice small onions and other vegetables and herbs.

1 With the tips of your fingers and thumb tucked under towards the palm of your hand, hold the ingredient to be cut in a claw-like grip. (a)

Roll-slicing – the claw grip (a)

2 Hold the knife in your other hand. Rest the side of the knife blade against the flat area between the knuckles at the tip and middle of the fingers. Lift the heel of the knife, keeping the tip on the cutting board. Push the knife down and away from you, sliding the middle part of the blade through the food. (b)

3 Use the second joint of your index finger as a rest. Adjust the position of the guiding finger back on the food after each slice to produce slices of equal width. After every few slices, slide your fingertips and thumb down the length of the ingredient and continue slicing, keeping the tip of the knife on the board. (c)

4 The action of slicing becomes easier if you develop a rhythm, guiding and rocking the blade over the ingredient at a comfortable, even speed.

Chiffonade

The roll-slicing action is used to cut soft and delicate foods, such as lettuce, spring greens and herbs, into ribbons. Stack several leaves on top of one another, then roll them into a cigar shape and slice as described above, holding the rolled leaves firmly.

Diagonals

Long round vegetables such as carrots and cucumber look more attractive when sliced on the diagonal to produce oval slices. Use the roll-slicing action for smaller vegetables such as carrots or celery and the action described below for slicing larger vegetables such as cucumber.

Slicing large ingredients

To cut or slice large or hard ingredients such as large onions, squashes, potatoes and parsnips, move your hand well back on to the knife handle and grip firmly. Even if the knife blade is extremely sharp, it will not cut as efficiently if used in a simple downward motion instead of a sliding motion. To slice through large, hard ingredients, position the tip of the blade on the front edge of the ingredient and slice forward and down through it so that when the blade reaches the board, most of the downward pressure is on the heel of the knife.

Thin slicing

If a high degree of control is required over the knife blade for tasks such as thinly slicing onions, grip the handle as close to the blade as possible, with your thumb on one side of the blade and your forefinger on the other. The pointed tip slices the ingredient with a fast, curving downward motion: draw the blade forwards and then backwards with every slice so that the tip of the blade always leads the way.

Horizontal slicing

Horizontal slicing is often used to thinly slice food that is flat in shape or too soft to slice vertically. Using this technique, pockets are cut into thin, flat portions of meat, poultry or fish, to stuff with flavoured butters and soft forcemeats. (See **Meat,** *Poultry, Stuffing a Chicken Breast*, page 434.)

Portions of meat are often 'butterflied', a term used to describe a boneless portion of meat sliced almost through horizontally and opened out for frying or grilling (see *Meat,* **Lamb**, page 380).

To slice horizontally, place your hand flat on top of the food, with your fingertips curved upwards. Holding the knife parallel to the board, slice a pocket towards the centre of the portion of food, or cut through completely, as required.

Slicing large ingredients

Slicing uncooked joints of meat

Place one hand flat against the end of the meat to support it. Pull the knife towards you through the meat, with the handle higher than the tip. Pull the sliced section of meat away, then repeat the long slicing stroke.

Thin slicing

Chopping

Chopping involves cutting an ingredient into small pieces of roughly the same size. Chopping is used to prepare many aromatic and strongly flavoured ingredients such as onions, herbs and garlic as they lend more flavour to a dish when cut very small. It is a technique called for in many recipes and can be done effortlessly and effectively with a food processor.

Horizontal slicing

Cross-chopping

This action is used primarily to chop herbs. In most instances the hard stems are removed and only the leaves are chopped. Wash the herbs before chopping. Parsley is chopped as finely as dust; other herbs are chopped into $1-2$ mm $| \frac{1}{24} - \frac{1}{12}$ in pieces (see *Herbs*, page 305). Because parsley is chopped so finely, excess moisture should be removed by squeezing it dry in kitchen paper. This will enable it to be sprinkled easily.

1 Hold the knife handle firmly and place your other hand flat along the top of the blade, making sure that your fingertips are well away from the sharp edge. Position the herbs under the middle part of the knife.
2 Move the blade of the knife up and down while holding the tip of the knife firmly on the chopping board. At the same time, sweep the knife forward and back again to chop over the entire pile of herbs. As the herbs spread out over the board, use the blade to gather the pieces together and chop again to the required size.

Cross-chopping

Cross-chopping using 2 knives

If a large amount of ingredients need to be chopped, or if the ingredients are very firm, such as meat, use 2 knives of equal sizes to chop. The action is the same as for chopping parsley, above.

Cross-chopping using 2 knives

Rough chopping

Rough chopping does not mean carelessly cutting food into random pieces. Instead, the curved blade of the cook's knife is rocked backwards and forwards

Bruising garlic

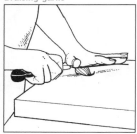

Reducing garlic to a purée

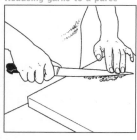

Chopping an onion (a)

Chopping an onion (b)

Chopping an onion (c)

over the ingredient until it is reduced to pieces measuring roughly 1 cm | ½ in on all sides. This technique is used to prepare ingredients for soups and rustic dishes.

Bruising/peeling garlic

1 Place an unpeeled garlic clove on the chopping board. Place the broad end of the knife blade flat over the clove.
2 Holding the knife handle firmly with one hand, place your other hand flat on to the blade, above the clove, and press down quickly, exerting just enough pressure to crack and loosen the skin around the garlic. Too much pressure will crush the clove, making it difficult to peel and slice afterwards.
3 Peel the garlic, then chop it using the *roll-slice* action, above.

Reducing chopped garlic to a purée

4 Once the garlic is finely chopped, scrape any garlic sticking to the knife blade back on to the chopping board and gather the garlic together. Sprinkle the chopped garlic with a pinch of salt: this acts as an abrasive and assists in breaking the garlic down to a purée.
5 Using the knife as a paddle, with the blade held at a shallow angle, crush and smear the garlic against the board with the sharp edge of the blade. Hold the blade near its tip to guide it and exert pressure on the garlic underneath it.

Chopping an onion

1 Trim the pointed top off the onion to make a flat surface.
2 Rest the onion on its cut top and cut it in half lengthways through the root.
3 Peel the papery outer leaves back towards the root and pull them away from the root at the base. Do not slice off the root as it holds the onion together while it is being chopped.
4 Place the halved onion on the chopping board, cut side down. Cut equidistant parallel slices of the desired thickness vertically through the onion, just short of the root. **(a)**
5 Make a single cut on a small onion, or 2 cuts on a large onion, horizontally through its width, being careful to keep the root intact. **(b)**
6 Slice the onion vertically across its width, perpendicular to the second series of cuts. Make sure that the distance between each cut is equal so that the onion is evenly and precisely chopped. **(c)**
7 Repeat with the other half of the onion.

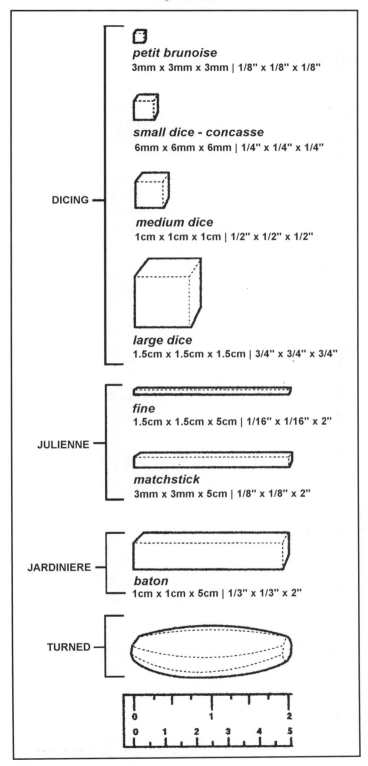

DICING

petit brunoise
3mm x 3mm x 3mm | 1/8" x 1/8" x 1/8"

small dice - concasse
6mm x 6mm x 6mm | 1/4" x 1/4" x 1/4"

medium dice
1cm x 1cm x 1cm | 1/2" x 1/2" x 1/2"

large dice
1.5cm x 1.5cm x 1.5cm | 3/4" x 3/4" x 3/4"

JULIENNE

fine
1.5cm x 1.5cm x 5cm | 1/16" x 1/16" x 2"

matchstick
3mm x 3mm x 5cm | 1/8" x 1/8" x 2"

JARDINIERE

baton
1cm x 1cm x 5cm | 1/3" x 1/3" x 2"

TURNED

Cutting Batons, Dice and Julienne

Ingredients are cut into batons, dice and julienne with specific, uniform dimensions so that they cook evenly and enhance the appearance of a dish (see following definitions). Batons and julienne are cut into matchstick shapes as follows. To cut dice, see step 6.

Blocking off a carrot (a)

1 Peel the vegetable if required, and square off the sides, losing as little of the vegetable as possible. **(a)**

2 Place the tips of 4 fingers close together against the long side of the vegetable to measure the cut length of each baton or julienne. A 4-finger tip length is roughly equal to 5 cm|2 in. **(b)**

3 Cut one 4-fingertip length and use this as a template to cut the rest of the vegetable into equal lengths. Use the vegetable trimmings and ends for soup or stock.

4 Cut each length of vegetable into even slices of the desired thickness, being careful to keep the slices together. **(c)**

5 Stack the slices neatly and cut into matchstick-sized lengths. **(d)**

6 To cut dice, stack the batons or julienne and cut across the stack, using the *roll-slice* action, above. **(e)**

Cutting four fingertip lengths (b)

Vegetable Cuts

Baton

A term used to describe vegetables and other foods cut into thin sticks measuring $\frac{3}{4} \times \frac{3}{4} \times 5$ cm $| \frac{1}{3} \times \frac{1}{3} \times 2$ in.

Cutting batons (c)

Brunoise

Cubed vegetables used raw, cold or sautéed in butter to garnish soups, sauces and stuffing.

Petit brunoise

Very small cubes of 3 mm $| \frac{1}{8}$ in used to garnish soups, sauces and stuffing.

Small dice

Vegetables cut into dice measuring 6 mm $| \frac{1}{4}$ in. *Concassé* is the term used to describe peeled and deseeded diced tomato.

Cutting dice (d)

Medium dice

Cubes measuring 1 cm $| \frac{1}{2}$ in. Croûtons used to garnish soups and salads are often cut into dice this size (see *Soups*, **Soup Garnishes**, page 667).

Large dice

A cube-shaped cut, measuring 1.5 cm $| \frac{3}{4}$ in, used especially to garnish meat, poultry, fish, game and for vegetables in casseroles and other rustic dishes.

Julienne

Ingredients, especially vegetables, cut into fine sticks measuring approximately $1.5 \times 1.5\,\text{mm} \times 5\,\text{cm} \mid \frac{1}{16} \times \frac{1}{16} \times 2\,\text{in}$ or matchstick lengths measuring $3 \times 3\,\text{mm} \times 5\,\text{cm} \mid \frac{1}{8} \times \frac{1}{8} \times 2\,\text{in}$. Potatoes cut into matchsticks are known as *allumette* and a mixture of carrots, turnips and French beans, cut into sticks of even length, is known as *jardinière*. These are served as a garnish for roast or sautéed meat. Vegetable julienne are softened in butter and used to garnish soups and consommés or are served raw in hors d'oeuvres. Other foods often cut into julienne include citrus fruit peel, peppers, truffles, ham and tongue. Cut thin strips, then layer the strips in stacks. Use the *roll-slice* action, above, to cut to the desired thickness.

Paysanne

A mixture of vegetables such as potatoes, carrots and turnips cut into flat, square shapes measuring $6\,\text{mm} \mid \frac{1}{2}$ in. Used to make soups or to garnish braised meat and fish dishes.

Cutting brunoise, small, medium and large dice

1 Follow the technique used to cut batons or julienne, above, to produce the size of dice required.
2 Turn the batons or julienne 90° and slice again to the same thickness to obtain perfect dice.

The Paring or Office Knife

The paring or office knife has a short blade with a gently curved cutting edge and pointed tip. It is used for peeling, trimming, coring, thinly slicing and finely dicing small vegetables and fruit and is also used in preference to a cook's knife or boning knife for boning small birds.

Using the Paring or Office Knife

The hand should be positioned well up on to the heel of the blade for maximum control. To cut small ingredients into thin slices or brunoise, place the tip of the blade where the cut should start and draw the heel back and down towards the chopping board.

Paring the peel from an apple

Paring

This action is used to remove thin peel from fruit and vegetables. Hold the knife firmly in your palm with your fingers wrapped around the blade. The first finger should be crooked around the blade where it meets the handle: make a cut into the peel by pressing with your crooked first finger towards your thumb.

Thinly slicing or chopping shallots

Use the same technique described for *Chopping an onion*, above, making the pieces as small as possible with very close parallel cuts.

The Boning Knife

The boning knife is used to bone joints of meat, poultry and larger game birds. It has a long, thin rigid blade with a pointed tip to reach deep into a joint of meat to separate the flesh from the bone.

Using the Boning Knife

See also **Meat,** *Boning Meat* (page 387) and **Meat,** *Boning Poultry* (page 440).

The underhand grip

The underhand grip

For larger cuts of meat such as lamb, beef and venison, which have large bones situated deeply in the meat, the underhand grip is most suitable. The knife is gripped in a fist with the four fingers around the handle and the thumb on the end. The knife is held at a 45° angle so that the pointed tip of the blade cuts the meat away from the bone with an up-and-down sawing action.

The Fish Filleting Knife

The fish filleting knife has a slim, flexible blade that tapers to a pointed tip.

Using the Fish Filleting Knife

The fish filleting knife is used to cut the delicate flesh of fish cleanly away from the bone as it follows the contours of the rib bones and to trim thin membranes from fish such as monkfish, and meat such as pork fillet. See also **Fish** (page 237).

Trimming fat and membrane

Removing membranes from meat

Hold the knife horizontally and with the pointed tip cut just through the membrane, at the edge or end of the cut of meat, being careful not to cut the meat beneath. Use small horizontal strokes to cut a flap of membrane away from the meat, large enough to hold firmly with your free hand. Holding the flap of membrane away from the meat, carefully trim the membrane away from the meat in long strips, along its length (rather like peeling a banana), using long, smooth, horizontal strokes. Be careful not to cut into the meat below.

The Serrated Fruit Knife

This knife, with its long, thin, slightly flexible serrated blade, is used in a sawing action to prepare soft fruits and vegetables. It is used to peel and segment citrus fruit and slice tomatoes as well as to prepare mangoes and papayas (see **Fruit,** page 275).

The Bread Knife

The bread knife has a long serrated blade and is used to cut cleanly through bread and cakes with a long, smooth, sawing stroke.

The Turning Knife

The turning knife has a short, curved blade with a sharp tip and is used to cut short lengths of vegetables into barrel and boat shapes or to decorate small vegetables with a spiral design. Vegetables shaped or decorated in this way are known as turned vegetables and are used to garnish meat and fish dishes (see also *Vegetables, Carrots*, page 727).

Turned vegetables are either served individually or *à la bouquetière*, when turned potatoes, carrots and turnips are served together with roast meat. Turned vegetables can also be added to braised dishes and casseroles to enhance and formalize their appearance.

Turning vegetables so that each piece is precisely the same shape and size requires a high degree of skill and takes considerable practice but is well worth the effort for special occasions.

The turning knife

Turning root vegetables into barrel shapes

Root vegetables are traditionally turned to a barrel shape, 4 – 5 cm | $1\frac{1}{2}$ – 2 in length, with 7 equal sides and 2 blunt ends.

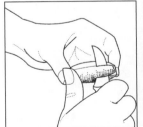

Using the turning knife to turn carrots, etc.

1 Cut the vegetable into 5 cm | 2 in lengths, using the 4 fingertips of your free hand as a measure. Each length should be at least 2 cm | $\frac{3}{4}$ in thick to obtain sufficiently curved edges. If a carrot is large, it can be cut into quarters lengthways, to minimize waste. Spherical root vegetables such as potatoes and turnips are cut lengthways into 4, 6 or 8 pieces, depending upon their size, before turning.
2 Make sure each 5 cm | 2 in length has flat ends, which are held with the thumb and forefinger while the turning knife cuts the 7 curved sides.
3 Shape each curved side by cutting the vegetable in a single stroke from top to bottom.
4 Turn the vegetable a few degrees to cut the second of the 7 sides and repeat 5 more times.

Turning cucumber, courgettes and apples into boat shapes

1 Cut cucumber or courgettes into 5 cm | 2 in lengths, using the 4 fingertips of your free hand as a measure.

2 Place each length on its flat cut end and cut the vegetable into 4–6 pieces, depending upon its width.

3 To obtain the boat shape, hold the vegetable away from you at 45°, with your thumb and forefinger at each flat end. Retaining the skin on one side, trim the straight sides of the cucumber or courgette into 3 curves, as in the diagram above.

● To turn apples, slice the apple into 4–6 pieces, depending upon its size. Core each wedge and retaining the skin on one side, cut into boat shapes using the technique described above.

The trimmings of turned vegetables can be used to make soups and purées.

Cooking turned vegetables
To ensure that the turned vegetables are cooked perfectly without damaging their appearance, cook a piece of the vegetable, cut roughly to the same size, in the pan with the others and use this for testing.

The Carving Knife

The carving knife has a long thin blade and is used to slice meat and poultry thinly and cleanly with long, smooth strokes. The tip of the blade has a very sharp point for reaching between bones and joints. The carving knife is used with a carving fork to hold the meat firmly in place while it is being sliced.

See also **Meat** (page 359), **Meat**, *Poultry* (page 421) and **Meat**, *Game* (page 469) for carving instructions.

Catering Organization

Any meal, no matter how simple, will benefit from forward planning.

Time Plans

Small dinner parties and lunches are relatively simple and take little more than half an hour to organize once you have decided upon your menu (see **Menu Planning**, page 5). Make a time plan to cover both cooking and serving. This is simply a list of the order in which your tasks must be completed in order to have the meal on the table at the specified time.

Large events are not very different, except that your time plan will span several days or even weeks. Make sure to include space in your time plan for shopping and putting away all the food. It is necessary to make lists of required equipment to ensure you have enough (see *Hiring Equipment*, page 79).

Try to intersperse tasks when drawing up your time plan so that you make the most efficient use of your time. That means that you should be doing more than one thing at a time, for example, preparing vegetables while the casserole is cooking. Some preparation can be done in advance. In restaurants the chefs often prepare much of their food and garnishes during the day so that when the customers arrive it can be assembled and served quickly. The tasks that are done ahead of service time are called *mise en place*. Use this technique when possible to save time.

Let's assume you are going to cook the following menu for a family Sunday lunch. You have 8 people to cook for, including yourself.

- Write out the menu, including garnishes.
- Think about which items can be prepared in advance.
- Decide on the time when you are going to serve. Calculate the cooking time for the meat, remembering that it should come out of the oven at least 30 minutes before serving so that it can rest and you can make the gravy.
- Deduct the cooking time from the service time to determine what time the meat must go into the oven.

Sample menu

Smoked Salmon Terrine   Watercress and lemon garnish
Melba Toast

Roast Beef
Yorkshire Pudding
Red Wine Gravy
Horseradish Sauce
Broccoli
Glazed carrots   Chopped parsley garnish

Apple and Blackberry Crumble
Vanilla Ice Cream

The terrine, Melba toast, ice cream and crumble topping can all be made a day in advance. The Yorkshire Pudding ingredients can be weighed out in advance.

Your time plan will look something like this:

Saturday

a.m.	Shop.
p.m.	Make ice-cream base, chill.
	CLEAR UP.
	Make Melba Toast.
	Churn ice cream.
	Make terrine.
	CLEAR UP.
	Weigh ingredients for Yorkshire Pudding.
	Lay table.

Sunday

10.15 a.m.	Preheat oven to 200°C|400°F|gas mark 6 and prepare beef for oven.
10.30	Put beef into oven.
	Make Yorkshire Pudding batter. Chill.
	CLEAR UP.
	Prepare potatoes, place in water with salt.
11.00	Parboil potatoes.
	Prepare broccoli and carrots.
	Wash watercress, cut lemon wedges.
	CLEAR UP.
	Place roasting tin with oil in oven for potatoes.

11.30	Roast potatoes.
	Prepare Horseradish Sauce.
	CLEAR UP.
	Baste beef.
12.00	Prepare fruit for crumble.
	CLEAR UP.
	Turn potatoes.
	Heat oil in oven for Yorkshire Pudding.
12.30	Remove beef from oven.
	Turn potatoes.
	Put Yorkshire Puddings into oven.
	Place crumble in oven below Yorkshire Puddings.
	Transfer beef to serving dish and tent with foil to keep warm. Use dripping to prepare gravy.
12.45	Boil carrots with butter and sugar.
	Remove terrine from refrigerator, put on to plates with garnish.
	Sieve gravy into small saucepan to hold.
	Turn carrots into serving dish to hold. Cover.
	Place saucepan of water on to boil for broccoli.
1.00	Serve terrine.
	Remove potatoes and Yorkshire Puddings from oven, keep warm.
	Check crumble, turn oven down if necessary.
1.20	Clear table, cook broccoli.
	Take crumble out of oven.
	Put ice cream into refrigerator to soften.
1.30	Serve main course.
1.45	Clear main course.
	Serve crumble with ice cream.
2.15	CLEAR UP.

Although this time plan is simply an order of work, details about each recipe can be added. For example the step for making ice cream could read: make custard base, sieve and cool, or scald milk, combine yolks and sugar, pour milk on to yolks slowly, cook until thick, sieve and cool. A time plan should include all the information you need in order to prepare the meal and serve it on time. Remember to include 'clear ups' after each preparation step.

Hiring Equipment

For large functions caterers are often asked to arrange the hire for tables, chairs, marquees, china and cutlery, etc. A fee can be charged for this or it is perfectly acceptable for you to organize a discount from the supplier and charge the customer the retail price.

When dealing with hire companies for large functions, it is important that you make your booking with the company as early as possible because certain times of the year, such as June for weddings, are especially popular.

Chairs

If there is to be dancing check that the chairs are stackable and arrange for staff to be on hand to help move the chairs after the meal has been served.

Tables

If you are using long tables, allow a 45–60 cm | 18–24 in length per person. A 1.8 m | 6 ft trestle table will seat 3 people along each side and one person at either end, i.e. 8 people in total. Trestle tables are usually very narrow, so there will not be enough room to place serving dishes down the centre of the table.

With round tables, the simple rule is to double the diameter in imperial measures, e.g. a 1.2 m | 4 ft table will seat 8 people and a 1.5 m | 5 ft table will seat 10 people.

If you need to advise on spacing for a sit-down dinner, allow 3–3.7 m | 10–12 sq ft per person: for example, a 184.7-sq m | 600-sq ft room will seat 50–60 people. For a reception where people will be standing, allow 1.8 sqm | 6 sq ft per person. Remember to allow for any pillars, doorways and passageways when making your calculations.

When arranging tables you will need to allow space between them. Allow a 45 cm | 18 in space the chairs plus 30–45 cm | 12–18 in space for passage between the tables.

Tableware

China: Calculate the number of plates that you need, then allow for an additional 10 sets per 200 people. Order extra plates for crumbing down (clearing crumbs from the tables) if required.

Serving dishes: Always order a few extra serving dishes.

Butter dishes, salt and pepper sets and mustard pots: Allow 2 per table of 10. Remember to take salt, pepper and mustard to fill the containers.

Cutlery: Order an extra 10 sets per 200 people. Remember to include butter knives and service cutlery.

Glasses: For a reception allow 1–2 glasses per person. For a dinner allow 2 wine glasses plus 1 water glass per person. Order 10 extra glasses per 100 people.

Ashtrays: Allow 3 per table of 10 to allow for regular emptying, plus extras for the bar.

Bread baskets: Allow 2 per table of 10.

Tablecloths: Allow 1 per table plus an extra 1 per 10 tables. Order extras if required for the bar, cake stand, tombola, etc.

Napkins: Allow 1 per person plus an extra 10 per 100 people and 1 per 10 people for crumbing down.

Service cloths: Allow 2 per waitress.

Service trays: Allow 1 per waitress.

Drinks trays: Allow 1 per 30 guests.

Additional Equipment to Remember

Ice bins and ice (make sure the hire equipment arrives before the ice)
Corkscrews and bottle openers
Coat rails and hangers
Easel and board menu holders
Cake stand and knife
Coffee urns, coffee pots, milk jugs and sugar bowls, teaspoons
Extension leads
Tablemats
Jugs for water or juice
Tea towels (lots)
Dish cloths
Bin liners
Clingfilm
Washing-up liquid
Plate rings for stacking plates
First-aid kit
Sound system
Extension leads
Staff food and drink

Staffing

Silver service: 1 waitress per 6–10 guests
Butler service: 1 waitress per 25 guests
Canapé party: 1 waitress per 25 guests and 1 person in the kitchen per 25 guests
Full bar: 1 butler per 25 guests
Simple bar: 1 butler per 50 guests
Supervisor: 1 per 80 guests
Porter: 1 per 80 guests
Master of ceremonies

Wine

Generally allow 1 bottle of wine per head, ordered on a sale-or-return basis. Most wine merchants will not accept return of wine with damaged labels so take care not to leave bottles soaking in a wine cooler, as the labels will fall off. Order champagne and other white wine ready chilled, if possible.

Other Drinks

Orange juice and water are the most usual soft drinks to have on hand. Allow 1 bottle of water per head if the weather is warm or $\frac{1}{2}$ bottle if the weather is cold. Generally neither water nor orange juice can be acquired on a sale-or-return basis.

Ice

A 10 kg | 25 lb bag of ice will chill 2 cases of champagne or 3 cases of white wine (champagne is usually served cooler than other white wine). Remember to arrange to have your hire order arrive before the ice. Wine and champagne will take approximately $1\frac{1}{2}$ hours to chill properly.

Other Items

You might be asked to recommend or organize a marquee, photographer, balloons, flowers and/or a band. It is a good idea to have the names of several sources and to be able to discuss the options available.

Serving Style

How much formal convention is followed at the family table or at a simple supper with friends depends, of course, on the character and personal style of the person hosting the meal. But it is useful to know how things ought to be done when giving a formal party or when cooking for someone else.

Laying the Table

As a rule, cutlery is laid so that the diner works from the outside in – his first-course knife will be the furthest from the plate on the right because he is to pick up the knife with his right hand. His first-course fork will be on the left, the furthest from the plate.

Similarly, if the first course is soup, the soup spoon will be on the right, at the extreme outside of the cutlery collection. If a course requiring a knife and fork is followed by soup, the soup spoon will be in second place, and so on, working towards the dessert spoon and/or cheese knife on the inside. Dessert cutlery is sometimes, though primarily at home rather than in restaurants, laid across the top of the place setting, with the spoon above the fork and the handles pointing towards the hand that will pick them up. This style of place setting is also used on more formal occasions when space is limited.

Logic prevails in the same way with glasses, which are set out in a diagonal row just beyond the knife tips. The first glass, for the wine that will go with the first course, is set nearest the plate, and so on. If space is limited, the glasses can be placed in a triangle above the knife tips.

Place setting

The bread plate is placed on the diner's left, to the left of the cutlery. The napkin is placed either on this plate or in the middle of the place setting if the first course is not yet on the table. Individual ashtrays, fingerbowls, and salt cellars are placed within comfortable reach of the diners.

It is important to leave enough space between the banks of cutlery for a dinner plate. It is a good idea to use a plate as a guide when laying the table. Any table decorations such as flowers and/or candles should be low enough for the diners to see and converse with each other across the table.

The Etiquette of Serving

At a family supper, people may help themselves and pass around the serving dishes as individual tastes dictate, but at a formal occasion convention is followed. The women should be served before the men. The female guest of honour seated to the right of the host is served first, then the woman seated to the left of the host. The hostess is served last, then the men are served. The most important male guest, usually to the right of the hostess, is served first, then the male guest to the left of the hostess, with the host being served last. Once everyone has been served the hostess, or host in the absence of a hostess, begins to eat, which is the signal for everyone else to start.

Types of Service

- **Family service:** Serving dishes are filled and are passed from one diner to the next with each person helping himself or herself.

- **Butler service:** Serving dishes are offered to each diner in the order detailed under *The Etiquette of Serving*, above. The platter is offered to the diner from his right. The platter is held low enough so that each guest can help himself or herself.

- **Silver service:** The food is placed on each guest's plate by the waitress or butler in the order specified above. The waitress or waiter usually uses two spoons or a spoon and a fork held together in one hand to lift the food. The food is served from the left of the guest.

- **Restaurant service:** The food is arranged on individual plates that are placed in front of each diner.

- **Gueridon service:** The food is placed in serving dishes on a trolley that is wheeled into the dining room. The food is placed on the plates by the waitress or waiter.

- **Buffet service:** see *Buffet Parties*, below.

- **Serving drinks:** Wine and water are poured from the right of the diner. Do not reach across the diner unless it is impossible to avoid. When serving try not to interrupt conversations.

How Much to Serve

A daunting plateful tends to take away the appetite, so do not over-help the guests to food. Take trouble to arrange things neatly and attractively on the plate. Place the first spoonful to the side, not in the middle, then arrange the food around the plate, keeping the piles separate. Drips and spills look messy, so have a clean cloth to hand to wipe the plates.

Clearing the Table

This should be done as unobtrusively as possible. Nothing should be touched until everyone has finished their food and indicated this by putting their knives and forks together. The plates are then removed from the right of the diner. The plates should not be stacked on top of each other or scraped in view of the diners.

When the plates are cleared, everything else on the table pertaining to that course, such as salt cellars, gravy boats, etc. should be removed from the table.

Nothing connected with the dessert should go on to the table before everything has been cleared. The same goes for coffee – it should not be served until the dessert plates and any accompanying sauce jugs have been removed.

Buffet Parties

At a buffet, the food is served from a long table. The plates are stacked at one end of the table and each guest takes a plate, then either help themselves to food or are helped by someone standing on the other side of the table. If the guests will be eating at tables the cutlery can be laid on the tables as described above, or if they are to eat whilst standing up, the cutlery can be wrapped in napkins and placed at the opposite end of the buffet table from the plates so the guests do not have to hold their cutlery while taking their food.

As a general rule it is not a good idea to serve more than 25–30 people from one buffet table or the queue waiting will be very long. For example, for 40 guests and if space allows, it would be preferable to have two identical tables and direct guests to one table or the other. Service is also much quicker if the food is served to the guests. One person serving can manage two or three different dishes adequately. If a large number of dishes are to be served, it is helpful to have several people serving.

If the guests help themselves they will inevitably take more than if served by a waitress or waiter. The eyes are so often greedier than the stomach! You will need to cater for more generous quantities if the guests are helping themselves. Don't serve all the food at once. Have several serving dishes of the same recipe so that when one dish becomes depleted it can be taken away and another put in its place.

If the food is to be consumed while standing it must be possible to eat it with a fork. At a buffet, guests tend to take a little bit of everything, so it is important that the flavours and textures of the dishes are compatible (see ***Menu Planning***, page 5).

Part two
Leiths Kitchen Techniques

Aspic

Aspic is a clear jelly made from meat, fish or vegetable stock or sugar syrup that has been clarified and set with gelatine. Aspic was popular during the eighteenth century, particularly in France where moulded dishes made using aspic jelly, 'aspics', were served at buffets. During Victorian times aspics and other dishes made using gelatine were thought to be highly nutritious, but it is now known that the protein in gelatine is incomplete (see *Healthy Eating and Basic Nutrition*, page 13) and is therefore not as valuable a nutritional source as was previously thought.

Using Aspic

Clear aspic is used as a lining for moulded dishes or as a glaze for cold fish, meat, poultry or eggs. Aspic is combined with a Béchamel Sauce for a chaudfroid (see below). It also can be set with garnishes on to a plate for a mirrored effect or cubed to use as a garnish.

Adding aspic to a pie

Aspic is funnelled into cooked pâtés en croûte and cold meat pies to fill the gaps created when the meat filling shrinks during cooking. The aspic helps to preserve the meat filling, keeps it from drying out and holds the pie together when it is sliced. Place a large piping nozzle in the steam hole in the crust and drip the nearly setting aspic into the pie. The pie should be cool, but not cold, or the aspic will set upon contact with the meat and will not drip down to the bottom.

Ready-made powdered aspic can be purchased in dried form, then reconstituted with water and a little sherry or herb vinegar for flavouring. When using ready-made aspic, follow the package directions.

The gelatine content of aspic can be varied depending on its use. For buffet display work where it is unlikely that the aspic will be eaten, the aspic jelly can be made very firm. In contrast, aspic jelly used to garnish plated food, to bind mousses or to fill meat pies should be firm when cold, wobble easily at room temperature and be sufficiently tender to melt in the mouth when eaten.

Lining a Terrine Mould

Chill a metal mould in an ice-bath and pour in the liquid aspic. Quickly swirl the aspic around the mould so that it will set evenly over the base and sides. Pour out any excess. Repeat as necessary to achieve the desired thickness. 3–4 mm | $\frac{1}{8}$ in is appropriate for an individual serving mould and up to 6 mm | $\frac{1}{4}$ in for a large loaf tin.

Glazing

Place the pieces of food to be glazed on a sterilized wire rack set over a sterilized tray. The tray should have a lip to contain any excess aspic. Allow the aspic to cool until it becomes syrupy, then *napper* the aspic over the food, using a large basting spoon. If additional coats of aspic are required, chill the food until the aspic becomes tacky to the touch, then napper with another layer of aspic.

A whole poached salmon can be covered with thin slices of cucumber dipped in aspic to resemble scales. Slice the cucumber as thinly as possible. The pieces should be pliable. Make a 570 ml | 1 pint quantity of aspic and allow to stand until syrupy. Dip each cucumber slice into the aspic and layer over the fish, starting from the tail end. Refrigerate to set the aspic.

As a Garnish

For a traditional presentation, mirror a plate by tipping a small amount of syrupy aspic on to the sterilized plate. Tip the plate to coat it evenly. Tap it on the work surface to remove any air bubbles. Any remaining bubbles can be burst with a clean cocktail stick. Chill until set.

Garnishes can be set into the aspic. Soft herbs, thin slices of mushroom or carrot, tomato peel or red pepper peel are suitable. The vegetables should be blanched briefly first to soften them. Pat the garnish dry, then dip the garnish into the syrupy aspic, using sterilized tweezers. Place on a layer of set aspic. Allow the aspic on the garnish to set, then coat with an additional layer of aspic. The garnish should be completely encased in aspic.

Aspic can be set in a 3 mm | ⅛ in layer on a sterilized tray, then cut into dice or diamonds with a sharp, thin knife. The aspic can also be set more thickly and roughly chopped.

Clearing

Stock for aspic is often cleared before use to make it brilliantly clear and therefore more attractive. A gelatinous stock that has been made using bones such as calf's or pig's trotters, chicken feet or veal knuckles will help the aspic set, but powdered gelatine is added to the stock to ensure a good set.

Clearing: Points to Remember

- The flavour of the stock can be enhanced with wine, brandy, sherry or herbs.
- All equipment must be clean and grease-free. Aspic is an ideal environment for the growth of bacteria (see *Food Safety*, page 21), so scrupulous hygiene is vital.
- All equipment used for clearing must be sterilized by boiling before using. The following items are required for clearing:

  a large saucepan, a whisk, a metal sieve, a bowl, a ladle, muslin or kitchen paper to line the sieve, 3 egg shells per litre | 1¾ pints stock

Clearing Aspic

860 ml | 1½ pints fat-free stock   55 g | 2 oz powdered gelatine
  (see **Stocks**, page 683),   2 egg shells, sterilized
  well seasoned   2 egg whites

1 Sterilize all equipment to be used (see list above).

2 Remove any traces of fat from the stock. Place the cold stock in a large saucepan. The stock should not fill the saucepan more than halfway.

3 Sprinkle the gelatine over the surface of the stock and allow it to stand for a few minutes. Shake the pan so the gelatine is absorbed.

4 Crush the egg shells lightly and whisk the egg whites to a froth, then add to the cold stock.

5 Place the saucepan over medium heat and beat the stock with a sterilized wire whisk, using a violent downward-thrusting motion. Continue to beat in this way until the mixture starts to steam. The egg whites should have formed a thick white crust.

Method for clearing stock

6 At this point the stock will be bubbling underneath the crust. As the crust cooks the impurities will be trapped. Meanwhile, rotate the pan so that the edge of the crust separates from the sides of the pan.

7 Place the pan centrally over the heat and allow the mixture to boil so that the crust rises up in the pan. If the mixture starts to boil through the crust, remove the pan from the heat. When the crust rises to the top of the pan, remove the pan from the heat and allow the crust to sink.

8 Place the pan over the heat one or two more times to allow the crust to rise. Remove from the heat and allow the pan to stand for 2 minutes.

9 Place a sterilized sieve over a sterilized bowl. Line the sieve with sterilized muslin or a 2 ply piece of white kitchen paper.

10 Take a large spoonful of the crust and place it in the sieve. Discard the remaining crust. Ladle the clear stock through the crust in the sieve, taking care that the sieve is not resting in the stock in the bowl. Allow the stock to strain through the muslin without squeezing. The aspic should be clear. If not, the process can be repeated, omitting the addition of gelatine. Use as required, flavouring the aspic with wine, sherry or tarragon vinegar, if wished.

Cooling the aspic

The bowl of aspic can be placed in a cold bain-marie and given one or two strokes with a spatula every few minutes to ensure that it cools evenly. Do not stir the aspic vigorously or air bubbles will be introduced into it, destroying its clarity.

Jelly

Clear Lemon Jelly with Strawberries

SERVES 6

whites and crushed shells of 3 eggs
860 ml|1½ pints water
200 g|7 oz granulated sugar
thinly pared zest of 4 unwaxed lemons

290 ml|½ pint lemon juice
2.5 cm|1 in cinnamon stick
55 g|2 oz powdered gelatine
6 perfect strawberries, hulled

1 Sterilize the equipment and egg shells as instructed above.
2 Heat the water, sugar, lemon zest and juice and cinnamon stick in a deep saucepan over low heat to dissolve the sugar. Stir to help the sugar dissolve.
3 Allow the mixture to cool. Remove the zest and cinnamon stick.
4 Sprinkle the gelatine over the mixture. Shake the pan to help the gelatine become absorbed.
5 Froth the whites with a fork then add to the pan along with the egg shells.
6 Place the pan over medium high heat and whisk with a downwards-shooting motion to form an egg white crust. Stop as soon as the mixture begins to steam.
7 Continue heating the mixture until the crust comes away from the sides of the pan. Rotate the pan over the heat to heat the mixture evenly, if necessary.
8 Allow the mixture to boil so that the egg white crust rises up in the pan but do not allow it to boil so vigorously that it bubbles through the crust. Remove the pan from the heat and allow the crust to subside. The egg white will trap the sediment in the liquid and clear the jelly.
9 Boil the mixture once more then let it cool for 2 minutes.
10 Fix a double layer of muslin or kitchen paper over a sterilized sieve placed over a sterilized bowl. Place one large spoonful of the egg-white mixture in the sieve, then carefully ladle the liquid into the sieve. Do not try to hurry the process by squeezing the cloth, or murky jelly will be the result. If the jelly begins to set before is completely strained, warm it enough to melt it.
11 Place 6 sterilized, dampened timbale moulds into a cold bain-marie.
12 Add 1 cm|½ in of jelly and allow to just set. Suspend a strawberry, pointed end down, over each timbale using 3 or 4 cocktail sticks.
13 Add another layer of jelly to come half-way up the strawberries. Allow to just set.
14 Remove the cocktail sticks then add enough jelly to come within ½ cm|¼ in of the top of the timbale moulds.
15 Refrigerate to set completely, about 4 hours.
16 To turn out the jellies, loosen the top edges of the jellies around the edges with your finger. Immerse each timbale in hand-hot water for about 10 seconds. Invert on to individual dampened dessert plates. Holding each plate and timbale securely, give each in turn a sharp shake to release the jelly. Remove the moulds.

Aspic and Jelly: What has gone wrong when...

The aspic is cloudy.
- The stock contained fat that was dispersed in the stock when the stock was boiled.
- Whisking continued after the stock began to steam and the crust was beaten into the stock.
- The bowl and/or other equipment was not sterilized properly.

The aspic has a lot of bubbles in it.
- The aspic was stirred vigorously during cooling.
- Bubbles were not removed with a cocktail stick before the aspic set.

The aspic splits into layers after it has set.
- The first layer of aspic was set too firmly before the second layer was added.

Chaudfroid

Literally translated from the French *chaud* (hot) and *froid* (cold), this term is used to describe cooked food served cold, coated thinly with set white or brown sauce (see **Sauces, Savoury**, page 579) and decorated, then glazed with aspic. Chaudfroid dishes featured in the grand buffets in of nineteenth-century France. Today chaudfroid might appear on the buffet tables of grand hotels or perhaps as a cold first course for a formal dinner.

Chaudfroid of Sole

SERVES 2

1 sole, about 675 g | 1½ lb, filleted and skinned

For the farce
85 g | 3 oz salmon
½ egg white
salt and freshly ground white pepper
cayenne pepper
2 tablespoons double cream

For the aspic
860 ml | 1½ pints fish stock (see **Stocks**, page 683), flavoured with white wine
55 g | 2 oz powdered gelatine
2 egg whites and 2 egg shells

For the Béchamel Sauce
290 ml | ½ pint milk
6 peppercorns
1 blade of mace

1 slice of onion
30 g | 1 oz butter
20 g | ¾ oz plain flour
1 tablespoon double cream

To finish the chaudfroid sauce
1 tablespoon double cream
2 tablespoons water
1 level teaspoon powdered gelatine
75 ml | ⅛ pint aspic

For the garnishes
fresh chervil
tomato peel
carrot
mushroom

1 Lightly bat the thick end of the sole fillets to obtain an even thickness. Trim each fillet, reserving the trimmings, so that when it is folded in half it will form a neat V-shaped parcel. Refrigerate.

2 Make the farce (see **Mousselines**, page 487). Pureé the salmon and sole trimmings with the egg white in a food processor. Take care not to let the mixture become warm. Season with salt and pepper and cayenne. Pass the mixture through a fine-mesh drum sieve into a cold bowl.

3 Place the bowl over ice and beat in the cream, $\frac{1}{2}$ a tablespoon at a time, using a wooden spoon. Taste the mixture for seasoning.

4 Place the sole fillets skinned side uppermost on a work surface. The skinned side will have a noticeable V-pattern on it. Season with salt and pepper. Spread a layer of salmon farce over half of the sole fillet so that the thickness of the salmon mixture is equal to the thickness of the sole. Fold over the sole. Refrigerate.

5 Poach the fish (see **Fish**, page 237), then drain and chill.

6 Infuse the milk for the Béchamel Sauce with the peppercorns, mace and onion.

7 Clear the stock as described above under *Clearing Stock for Aspic*. Allow the aspic to stand until syrupy.

8 Place the water in a small bowl and sprinkle over the gelatine for the chaudfroid.

9 Make the Béchamel Sauce (see **Sauces, Savoury**, page 579). Add the cream.

10 Scrape the sponged gelatine into the hot Béchamel Sauce and stir to dissolve.

11 Place the sauce in a muslin-lined sieve and gently squeeze it to *tammy* the sauce. Place over an ice bath and leave until thickened to the consistency of double cream, stirring frequently.

12 Meanwhile, prepare the garnishes, blanching them if necessary.

13 Place the poached fish on a wire rack over a tray with a lip. Napper with the chaudfroid sauce. Refrigerate until just set. If the fish is still showing through the sauce, napper again with the chaudfroid. Any excess chaudfroid sauce or aspic can be used again by scraping the excess from the tray and gently reheating it.

14 When the aspic has become syrupy, napper the fish with it. Refrigerate until just set.

15 Dip the garnishes in the aspic and arrange over the fish. Refrigerate again.

16 Napper with the aspic one or two more times to encase the garnish completely. Refrigerate until ready to serve. Trim away any excess sauce or aspic, using a hot sharp knife, before serving.

VARIATION

Chicken Chaudfroid is a classic buffet preparation and can be prepared with a whole chicken or with supremes. The chicken should be poached and cooled overnight (see **Meat**, **Poultry**, page 414). The poaching stock can be used for the aspic, cleared as described above.

Prepare as for Chaudfroid of Sole from step 6. Very thinly sliced truffle can be used to garnish Chicken Chaudfroid.

Notes

Baking: Points to Remember

Certain cooking practices are recommended for success in all types of baking, as follows:

- Weigh all the ingredients carefully and accurately before starting to cook.
- Ensure the ingredients are at the correct temperature. Many recipes require soft butter and eggs at room temperature.
- Use good-quality, heavy metal tins and baking sheets that are light in colour. These heat evenly, will not warp in the oven or over-brown the food.
- Use the recommended tin size and type. Prepare the tin as required before starting to cook.
- Arrange the shelves in the oven at the required level.
- Heat the oven to the specified temperature. Use an oven thermometer if in doubt about the accuracy of your oven.
- If using a fan-assisted oven, consult the manufacturer's directions to adjust the oven temperature.
- When batch-baking, take care to make all items the same size and shape so that they cook evenly.
- When baking biscuits and bread, rotate the items in the oven half-way through the baking time to ensure even browning.

Baking

Baking is the cooking in the oven of various flour-based foods, such as cakes, breads, biscuits and pastries. When baking many of the same types of item, the term 'batch-baking' is used. Perfect uniformity is the goal when batch-baking.

See also the following sections:

- **Bread, Yeast** (page 117)
- **Cakes** (page 137)
- **Pastry** (page 507)
- **Pâtisserie** (page 531)

Biscuits

Originally biscuits were the hard, thin wafers found in ships' galleys called hard tack. It was not until the 1800s that the flavoursome biscuits we eat today began to evolve. The commercial production of biscuits became prevalent from the mid-1800s with the availability of inexpensive flour and sugar and the invention of chemical raising agents, such as bicarbonate of soda and baking powder.

Every country seems to have its own specialities, with the recipes often being passed from one generation to the next. In Britain and France the word 'biscuit' is used to describe a small, crisp pastry, either sweet or savoury. *Biscuit* is a French word meaning 'twice-cooked'; Italian *biscotti* has the same meaning.

In America the word 'cookie' is used to describe these same crisp biscuits, as well as soft and/or chewy small cakes. It is derived from the Dutch *koekje*, the diminutive word for cake. Biscuits are served as a snack, often at tea-time, or as a crisp accompaniment for desserts such as a mousse, fruit salad or ice cream, or with cheese.

Biscuits can be divided into the following types:

Drop: These biscuits, often called jumbles, especially in the USA, are roughly formed, slightly domed small mounds that are somewhat bumpy in appearance. They can be crisp or soft and are made by either the rubbing-in method (see **Pastry**, page 507) or the creaming method (see **Cakes**, page 137). *Chocolate Chip Biscuits* (see below) are an example.

Bar: These are rather like cakes and are baked in a shallow roasting tin to a depth of about 2.5 cm|1 in, then cut into small rectangles after baking. They are usually made by either the melting or the creaming method (see **Cakes**, page 137). *Brownies* (see below) are an example.

Shaped or moulded: These biscuits are usually crisp and tender. The dough is shaped by hand, working quickly and lightly to avoid making the biscuits tough and greasy. They are made by the rubbing-in method (see **Pastry**, page 507) or creaming method (see **Cakes**, page 137); *Shortbread* (see below) is an example.

Biscuits such as *Tuiles* (see below), *Florentines* (see below) and *Brandy Snaps* (see **Sugar, Sweetness and Sugar Syrups**, page 695) are technically shaped biscuits but they are made by the melting method (see **Cakes**, page 137).

Rolled or refrigerator: These crisp biscuits have a high butter content and are made by the creaming method (see **Cakes**, page 137) or rubbing-in method (see **Pastry**, page 507). The dough requires chilling before being rolled thinly and cut with shaped cutters. *Gingerbread Biscuits* (see below) are an example.

Piped: biscuits are crisp and tender when baked. They are made from a very soft, short dough by the creaming method (see **Cakes**, page 137). *Langues de chat* (see below) are an example.

Meringue: These biscuits are made with egg whites and sugar (see **Meringues**, page 475). Ground nuts are often added to the mixture. Macaroons are traditionally baked on sheets of edible rice paper. The biscuit mixture sticks to the paper when it is baked then after baking the excess paper is carefully torn away.

Biscotti: These Italian biscuits are baked then slowly dried out in the oven to make them very crisp. They are traditionally dipped into a liqueur or sweet wine when eaten. *Almond and Pine Nut Biscotti* (see below) are an example.

Storing Biscuits

Crisp biscuits should always be stored in an airtight container separately from soft biscuits and cakes. Keep in a cool, dry cupboard. If it is likely that the biscuits will stick together, interleave them in layers with greaseproof paper. Most biscuits will keep for up to 5 days, but some crisp biscuits, such as shortbread, will keep for up to 1 month. Biscuits that are high in fat and/or dried fruit or that have a low moisture content, such as biscotti, usually keep the best.

Biscuits can be frozen if closely wrapped for up to 1 month. Unbaked dough can be kept in the refrigerator for up to 3 days or frozen for up to 1 month.

Most biscuits can be refreshed by placing them in a single layer on a baking sheet in a preheated 150°C|300°F|gas mark 2 oven for 5 minutes. This treatment will also improve store-bought biscuits.

Biscuits: Points to Remember

- Use very little extra flour when rolling biscuits. Too much will make them dry.
- Do not re-roll the dough more than once.
- Arrange the biscuits in staggered rows on the baking sheet to aid even cooking.
- Use flat, dull, heavy metal baking sheets with no or very low edges in preference to dark-coloured trays with lips.
- When making a batch of biscuits it is worthwhile baking an individual biscuit as a test before baking a whole tray.
- Remove the biscuits from the baking sheet as soon as they are set, usually within 1 minute of removal from the oven.
- Cool the biscuits on wire racks.
- Cool completely before storing in an airtight container
- See also **Baking: Points to Remember** (page 96).

Chocolate Chip Biscuits

MAKES 30

110 g | 4 oz butter, softened	125 g | 4½ g plain flour
55 g | 2 oz caster sugar	¼ teaspoon bicarbonate of soda
85 g | 3 oz soft light brown sugar	a pinch of salt
1 teaspoon vanilla essence	100 g | 3½ oz walnuts, roughly chopped
1 medium egg, beaten	170 g | 6 oz chocolate chips

1 Preheat the oven to 180°C | 350°F | gas mark 4.
2 Cream the butter and the sugars until light. Stir in the vanilla.
3 Gradually add the egg, beating between each addition.
4 Sift together the flour, bicarbonate of soda and salt. Stir into the creamed mixture.
5 Stir in the walnuts and chocolate chips.
6 Drop tablespoons of dough on to ungreased baking sheets, leaving the space of one mound between each biscuit to allow for spreading.
7 Bake in the middle of the oven for about 10 minutes until pale golden and set in the centre. Rotate the tray from back to front half-way through the cooking time.
8 Cool on the baking sheet for 1 minute, then remove the biscuits with a fish slice and place on a wire rack to cool completely.

Brownies

MAKES 36 VERY SMALL OR 16 LARGE BROWNIES

110 g│4 oz butter

140 g│5 oz good-quality plain chocolate, chopped

170 g│6 oz caster sugar

2 medium eggs, beaten

½ teaspoon vanilla essence

55 g│2 oz plain flour

30 g│1 oz cocoa powder

100 g│3½ oz pecans or walnuts, roughly chopped

1 Preheat the oven to 180°C│350°F│gas mark 4. Line a 18 cm│7 in square tin with baking parchment (see *Cakes, Lining a Tin*, page 140).

2 Melt the butter and chocolate over a very low heat, stirring occasionally.

3 Stir in the sugar, then remove from the heat and allow to cool to room temperature.

4 Stir in the eggs and vanilla.

5 Sift together the flour and cocoa and fold into the chocolate mixture.

6 Stir in the nuts.

7 Spread the mixture out evenly in the tin and bake for 30 minutes or until just set in the centre. A skewer inserted into the centre will have a small amount of crumbs, but not wet mixture, stuck to it.

8 Allow to cool for 20 minutes, then cut into squares.

9 When completely cool, wrap in foil and store in the refrigerator for up to 3 days.

Shortbread

The ground rice makes this recipe particularly short. If you don't have any in stock, plain flour can be used instead of rice flour.

MAKES 6–8 PIECES

110 g│4 oz butter, softened

55 g│2 oz caster sugar

55 g│2 oz ground rice

110 g│4 oz plain flour

2 teaspoons caster sugar

1 Preheat the oven to 160°C│325°F│gas mark 3.

2 Stir together the butter and sugar. Do not beat the mixture as too much air will cause the shortbread to puff up when baking and lose its shape.

3 Stir in the ground rice and then the plain flour. If the mixture is rather dry, draw it together with your fingers to make a dough.

4 Smooth the shortbread into a circle about 1 cm│½ in thick on a baking sheet.

5 Crimp the edges (see *Pastry, Pâte Frollée*, page 517.). Prick all over with a fork, all the way through to the baking sheet. Mark the top into 6–8 segments with a knife.

6 Refrigerate until firm.

7 Bake for about 30 minutes or until pale golden.

8 Remove from the oven, dredge with caster sugar, then run a palette knife under the shortbread to prevent it from sticking to the baking sheet when cold. Cut through the marked segments to make individual pieces. When set, place on a wire rack to cool.

9 Store as described above (see *Storing Biscuits*, page 98).

VARIATIONS

Hazelnut Shortbread: Add 30 g | 1 oz browned and skinned roughly chopped hazelnuts with the flour.

Ginger Shortbread: Add 1 teaspoon ground ginger and 55 g | 2 oz chopped crystallized stem ginger with the flour.

Orange Shortbread: Add the finely grated zest of 1 large orange to the butter.

Tuiles

The French word *tuile* means a tile and these shaped biscuits, made by the melting method, look very similar to roof tiles. To shape them quickly and evenly, make a template. Cut a 7.5 cm | 3 in circle out of the lid of a plastic box, such as an ice-cream container. Use a palette knife to spread the mixture over the circle in a thin, even layer. Remove the template.

MAKES 20

55 g	2 oz butter	110 g	4 oz caster sugar
2 egg whites	55 g	2 oz plain flour

1 Preheat the oven to 190°C | 375°F | gas mark 5.

2 Line 2 baking sheets with baking parchment, cut into 4 equal squares a little larger than the template.

3 Melt the butter and allow it to cool to room temperature.

4 Beat the egg whites lightly with a fork to break them up, then stir in the sugar.

5 Stir in the melted butter, then the flour.

6 Spread the mixture into very thin rounds on to the paper squares.

7 Bake for 5–7 minutes or until lightly browned. Lift the biscuits, using the paper to protect your hand, and drape over a rolling pin. Alternatively, the biscuits can be wrapped around the handle of a wooden spoon. Allow to cool.

8 Store as described above (see *Storing Biscuits*, page 98).

VARIATIONS

Almond Tuiles: Sprinkle a few flaked almonds on to the biscuits before they are baked.

Orange Tuiles: Add the grated zest of 1 orange to the uncooked mixture.

Tuile Baskets: Drape the pliable, cooked biscuit over a brioche mould or ramekin to make a cup shape. For baskets, use a 15 cm | 6 in circle template.

Florentines

MAKES 20

55 g | 2 oz butter	45 g | 1½ oz chopped mixed peel
55 g | 2 oz caster sugar	45 g | 1½ oz glacé cherries, finely chopped
2 level teaspoons clear honey	45 g | 1½ oz blanched almonds, finely chopped
55 g | 2 oz plain flour	110 g | 4 oz plain chocolate, melted

1 Preheat the oven to 180°C | 350°F | gas mark 4. Line 2 baking sheets with baking parchment.
2 Melt the butter, sugar and honey in a saucepan. Allow to cool to room temperature.
3 Stir in the flour, then the peel, cherries and almonds.
4 Drop teaspoonfuls of the mixture on to the baking sheets, leaving plenty of space in between to allow for spreading.
5 Bake for 8–10 minutes, until pale brown. Leave on the sheets for 2 minutes to set, then transfer to a wire rack to cool completely.
6 Ideally, the chocolate should be tempered (see *Chocolate* page 189). Spread the bottom of the biscuits with a thin layer of chocolate. Refrigerate until set. Spread a second slightly thicker layer of chocolate on to the first layer, then scrape a fork across the chocolate in an 's' to make the characteristic wavy pattern. Allow to completely set. Do not refrigerate or the chocolate will lose its sheen.
7 Store as described above (see *Storing Biscuits*, page 98).

NOTE: These biscuits are notoriously difficult to make. If the mixture seems too cakey, add a little more honey. If they have too many holes when baked, add a little more flour next time.

Gingerbread Biscuits

These biscuits can be decorated and hung on the Christmas tree if a small hole is made in each biscuit with a skewer before baking.

MAKES ABOUT 48

225 g | 8 oz butter, softened	1 teaspoon bicarbonate of soda
170 g | 6 oz light muscavado sugar	2 teaspoons ground cinnamon
1 level tablespoon treacle	1 teaspoon ground ginger
1 egg, beaten	½ teaspoon ground cloves
340 g | 12 oz plain flour	a pinch of salt

1 Beat the butter, sugar and treacle in a bowl until fluffy. Gradually beat in the egg.
2 Sift together the remaining ingredients and stir into the butter mixture.
3 Roll the dough between 2 sheets of greaseproof paper to a thickness of 3 mm | ⅛ in for crisp biscuits, thicker for softer biscuits. Refrigerate until firm.

4 Preheat the oven to 190°C│375°F│gas mark 5.

5 Cut the dough into shapes, using a biscuit cutter. Dip the cutter into flour if it sticks to the dough.

6 Bake the biscuits for 8–10 minutes or until the edges are very lightly browned. Do not overbake or the biscuits will taste bitter. Transfer to a wire rack to cool.

7 Store in an airtight container for up to 2 weeks.

Langues de Chat

Langues de Chat, or cats' tongues, are thin, crisp biscuits that are ideal for serving with a dessert mousse.

MAKES 30–40

100 g│3½ oz butter, softened
100 g│3½ oz caster sugar
a few drops of vanilla essence

3 egg whites
100 g│3½ oz plain flour

1 Preheat the oven to 200°C│400°F│gas mark 6. Line a baking sheet with baking parchment.

2 Beat together the butter and sugar until pale and fluffy. Stir in the vanilla.

3 Whisk the egg whites lightly with a fork to break them up, then gradually beat into the creamed mixture.

4 Sift the flour over the top of the mixture and fold in.

5 Place the mixture in a piping bag fitted with a 6 mm│¼ in plain nozzle. Pipe fingers 5 cm│2 in long on to the baking parchment, leaving 5 cm│2 in between the biscuits to allow for spreading.

6 Tap the baking sheet on the work surface to release any air bubbles.

7 Bake for 5–7 minutes or until pale biscuit-coloured in the centres and golden at the edges.

8 Cool slightly, then lift off the baking sheet with a palette knife and transfer to a wire rack to cool completely. Store as described above (see *Storing Biscuits*, page 98).

Almond and Pine Nut Biscotti

MAKES 36

100 g│3½ oz blanched almonds
100 g│3½ oz pine nuts
225 g│8 oz plain flour
pinch of salt
½ teaspoon baking powder

85 g│3 oz caster sugar
2 eggs, lightly beaten
55 g│2 oz butter, melted and cooled
1 egg white, to glaze

1 Preheat the oven to 190°C│375°F│gas mark 5. Grease a baking sheet.

2 Place the almonds and pine nuts on the baking sheet and bake for 6–8 minutes or until golden brown. Remove from the oven and cool. Chop roughly.

3 Sift the flour, salt and baking powder into a large bowl. Mix in the nuts and sugar.

4 Make a well in the centre and add the eggs and butter. Mix to a firm dough.

5 Divide the dough into 2 equal pieces and roll into long sausage shapes, about 5 cm|2 in wide and 25 cm|10 in long.

6 Place the rolls at least 5 cm|2 in apart on the baking sheet.

7 Lightly whisk the egg white and brush over the rolls.

8 Bake in the oven for 20 minutes.

9 Remove the rolls and turn the oven down to 80°C|175°F|gas mark $\frac{1}{4}$. Using a serrated knife, cut the rolls at a 45° angle into 1 cm|$\frac{1}{2}$ in slices. Place on the baking sheet cut side up.

10 Bake for a further hour, turning over halfway through the baking.

11 Cool on a wire rack then store in an airtight container.

Biscuits: What has gone wrong when...

The biscuits are tough and dry.
- The biscuits have been overbaked.
- The dough was overworked when the flour was added.
- There is too much flour in the recipe or too much flour was used when rolling out.

The biscuits lose their definition and spread while baking.
- The butter was overbeaten, incorporating too much air.
- The dough was not chilled long enough before baking.
- The biscuits contain too much butter or sugar. Add a little more flour.

The biscuits are not evenly browned.
- The baking trays were not rotated during baking.
- The oven temperature was too high.

The biscuits are greasy.
- The biscuits were not chilled for long enough before baking.
- The dough was overworked.
- The dough was underbaked.

The biscuits are hard.
- The biscuits were overbaked.
- The eggs were too large.

The biscuits are too thick and cakey.
- The biscuits contain too much flour.
- The oven temperature was too high.
- The biscuits were poorly shaped.

Quick Breads

Quick breads are made without yeast from batters that require no kneading and do not have to rise before they are baked. Instead of yeast, chemical raising agents such as bicarbonate of soda, cream of tartar and/or baking powder are used in these breads. Quick breads have a close, cake-like texture and tend to stale more quickly than yeast-raised breads so they are best eaten on the day they are made.

Brown or *Irish Soda Bread* (see below) is the most common example of this type of bread. Other types of quick breads can be found in American cookery books – *Banana Bread* (see below) is one of the most popular. Muffins are a quick bread baked in individual serving-sized muffin tins.

For a well-risen quick bread, it is very important to get the mixture into the oven as soon as it is mixed in order to capture the gas given off by the chemical raising agents. The oven must be preheated and the tins prepared before mixing begins. A wooden skewer is needed to test whether the bread is done.

The chemical raising agents used are sodium bicarbonate (an alkali) and cream of tartar (an acid). Cream of tartar is a fine white powder found in deposits on the inside of wine barrels. Occasionally soured milk or buttermilk is used as the acid in place of cream of tartar. When the alkali and acid combine with each other and liquid is added, carbonic gas is formed. This gas, along with the conversion of the liquid in the dough to steam and the expansion of the eggs, serves to raise the bread. Baking powder, the mixture of an acid, cream of tartar, with an alkali, sodium bicarbonate, was developed in England around 1835. Commercial baking powder became available commercially from about 1850.

Some types of baking powder are also heat-activated so that a second chemical reaction occurs in the oven. It is very important to sift the raising agents with the flour several times to ensure they are well combined. Badly mixed raising agents will show in a bread as yellow deposits in the crumb.

As a raising agent for quick breads, baking powder can be substituted for sodium bicarbonate and cream of tartar in a recipe. Use 4 level teaspoons baking powder per 250 g/9 oz of flour.

Irish Soda Bread

Many soda bread recipes call for buttermilk, which in times past was the liquid left after butter had been churned. Today, buttermilk is made by the addition of bacteria and flavourings to low-fat milk to give the characteristic acid tang. Using buttermilk to make soda bread will help the chemical reaction and therefore the rise and will give a more complex flavour to the finished loaf. However, regular milk will work in this recipe or, if you wish, a tablespoon of lemon juice can be added to the milk before using.

It is important to sift the flours with the raising agents and salt 3 times before using to incorporate the raising agents fully. Soda bread is best eaten on the day it is baked. It is particularly delicious with cheese.

MAKES 1 LOAF

oil, for greasing	1 tablespoon sugar
225 g⎪8 oz wholemeal flour	2 teaspoons bicarbonate of soda
225 g⎪8 oz strong white flour	55 g⎪2 oz butter
1 teaspoon salt	290–425 ml⎪½ –¾ pint buttermilk

1 Preheat the oven to 190°C⎪375°F⎪gas mark 5. Oil a baking sheet.
2 Sift the dry ingredients together 3 times. Reserve any bran in the sieve.
3 Rub the butter into the flour.
4 Pour in 290 ml⎪½ pint buttermilk and mix to a soft dough. Add more buttermilk if the mixture seems dry. Knead lightly to bring together.
5 Place the dough on to the baking sheet and shape into a round loaf.
6 Sprinkle with the reserved bran.
7 Flour a wooden spoon handle, then holding it horizontally press it into the dough twice to make a cross in the top of the bread. The cross should be deep, coming to within 1 cm⎪½ in of the baking sheet.
8 Immediately place in the oven and bake for 35–40 minutes. The cross in the surface of the bread should appear dry when the loaf is cooked.
9 Cool on a wire rack.

NOTE: If buttermilk is unobtainable, use regular milk and add 2 teaspoons cream of tartar to the dry ingredients at step 2.

Banana Bread

Banana bread, with its soft crumb and moist texture, is more like a cake than a bread. It is risen using bicarbonate of soda and baking powder. The bananas take the place of some of the fat in the recipe, making the loaf lower in fat than a cake. For the best flavour use bananas that have ripened to a deep brownish-black colour. Banana bread is even better the day after it is made.

MAKES 1 LOAF

55 g⎪2 oz butter, melted and cooled, or vegetable oil	2 medium eggs, beaten
	225 g⎪8 oz plain flour
225 g⎪8 oz peeled weight ripe bananas, about 3 medium	3 teaspoons baking powder
	½ teaspoon bicarbonate of soda
110 g⎪4 oz caster sugar	100 g⎪3½ oz walnuts, roughly chopped

1 Line the base and sides of a 900 g⎪2 lb loaf tin with baking parchment. Preheat the oven to 190°C⎪375°F⎪gas mark 5.
2 Place the melted butter or oil in a large bowl. Slice the bananas into the bowl and add the sugar. Mash with a potato masher or fork until nearly smooth.
3 Stir in the eggs.
4 Sift together the flour, baking powder and bicarbonate of soda.

5 Quickly fold into the banana mixture, using no more than 10 strokes.

6 Fold in the walnuts.

7 Turn the mixture into the tin. Bake for 45 minutes to 1 hour or until well risen, browned and a wooden skewer inserted into the centre comes out clean.

8 Cool for 5 minutes, then remove from the tin and transfer to a wire rack. Leave to cool completely.

9 Store wrapped in foil for up to 3 days.

Quick Breads: What has gone wrong when . . .

The bread is heavy and wet in the centre.
- The bread was underbaked.
- The oven temperature was too low.

The top of the bread has cracked.
- Nothing is wrong, a crack is characteristic of quick breads.

The crumb of the bread is flecked with yellow and the bread has a sour taste.
- There was too much raising agent in the recipe or the balance of alkali with acid was not right.
- The dry ingredients were not sifted thoroughly enough.

Muffins

Muffins are small cakes made from a batter of eggs, flour, milk and sugar. They are risen by bicarbonate of soda, baking powder and an acid, such as buttermilk or brown sugar, which contains acid. Muffins are best eaten on the day they are made.

Muffins: Points to Remember

- Mix quickly. Overmixing produces tough muffins riddled with tunnels. The best tool to use for mixing muffins is a large wire whisk. It will mix the batter quickly and help to lighten it.
- Only mix the wet and the dry ingredients sufficiently to moisten the flour.
- To keep any fruit or nuts in the batter from sinking to the bottom, dredge them lightly in flour before folding them in, or fold them in with softly beaten egg white.
- Fill muffin tins quickly by using a spring-release ice-cream scoop.
- To tell when muffins are done, stick a wooden skewer into the centre: it should come out clean. The muffins should also spring back if pressed gently in the centre. Cool the muffins for a minute or two in the tin before transferring them to a wire rack to cool completely.

Lemon Poppy-seed Muffins

MAKES 12

250 g | 9 oz plain flour

2 teaspoons baking powder

½ teaspoon bicarbonate of soda

a pinch of salt

110 g | 4 oz butter, melted and cooled

110 g | 4 oz soft light brown sugar

2 eggs, beaten

85 ml | 3 fl oz milk

grated zest and juice (55 ml | 2 fl oz) of 2 small lemons

2 tablespoons poppy seeds

1 Preheat the oven to 190°C | 375°F | gas mark 5. Line 12 muffin tins with paper liners or greaseproof paper discs.

2 Sift the flour, baking powder, bicarbonate of soda and salt together and set aside.

3 In a large bowl, mix together the butter, sugar, eggs, milk, lemon zest and juice.

4 Fold the flour into the wet mixture in the bowl using no more than 10 strokes.

5 Stir in the poppy seeds. Do not overmix.

6 Quickly fill the muffin tins, using an ice-cream scoop or small cup. They will be full to the top. Do not level.

7 Bake in the middle of the oven for 20–25 minutes until the muffins are well-risen and golden-brown and a wooden skewer inserted into the centre comes out clean. Cool on a wire rack.

VARIATIONS

Chocolate Chip Muffins: Omit the lemon zest and juice. Use a total of 150 ml | ¼ pint milk. Add ½ teaspoon vanilla essence to the milk. Omit the poppy seeds and stir in 110 g | 4 oz chocolate chips.

Chocolate Walnut Muffins: Use 200 g | 7 oz plain flour and 55 g | 2 oz cocoa powder in place of 250 g | 9 oz flour. Omit the lemon zest and juice. Use a total of 150 ml | ¼ pint milk. Omit the poppy seeds and stir in 110 g | 4 oz chopped walnuts.

Scones

Scones are made by the rubbing-in method (see **Pastry**, page 507), which gives a crumbly, moist texture. The raising agent is either bicarbonate of soda, added to plain flour, or self-raising flour. Scones are the most similar of all baked goods to pastry and together with rock cakes are classic examples of the rubbing-in method.

Adding the liquid

Add three-quarters of the liquid all at once, stirring with a table knife. This should be done quickly as the raising agent will begin to work immediately. Add the remaining liquid to any remaining dry ingredients in the bowl.

Scones

MAKES 6–8

225 g | 8 oz self-raising flour
½ teaspoon salt
55 g | 2 oz butter

30 g | 1 oz caster sugar (optional)
150 ml | ¼ pint milk
1 egg, beaten, to glaze

1 Preheat the oven to 220°C | 425°F | gas mark 7.
2 Sift the flour with the salt into a large bowl.
3 Cut the butter into small cubes. Toss it in to the flour, then use your fingertips to rub in the butter until the mixture resembles coarse breadcrumbs.
4 Stir in the sugar, if using.
5 Make a well in the centre of the flour, then pour in the milk. Quickly bring the mixture together by stirring with a table knife. The mixture should be sticky.
6 On a floured surface knead the dough two or three times until smooth. Roll or pat it into a flat block about 2.5 cm | 1 in thick.
7 Cut into rounds with a floured cutter, taking care not to twist the cutter or the scones will be lopsided.
8 Brush the tops of the scones with the beaten egg for a glossy crust or dust with flour if a soft crust is preferred.
9 Bake the scones in the top of the oven for 15–20 minutes or until well-risen and golden-brown. The cracks on the sides should be starting to dry out.
10 Transfer to a wire rack covered with a clean tea towel. Leave to cool.

VARIATIONS

Fruit Scones: Add 55 g | 2 oz raisins or sultanas with the flour.
Parmesan Chive Scones: Omit the sugar. Add 30 g | 1 oz grated Parmesan cheese and 1 tablespoon finely chopped chives to the flour.

Scones: What has gone wrong when...

The scones are heavy and badly risen.
- Not enough liquid was added.
- Not enough raising agent was used.
- The scones were not put into the oven quickly enough.

The scones are tough.
- The mixture was overworked when the liquid was added.

The scones have risen unevenly.
- The oven heat was uneven.
- The scones were shaped unevenly.
- The cutter was twisted when the scones were cut out.

Batters

A batter is a mixture of flour, eggs, milk or water and sometimes fat. It is used to make *Scotch Pancakes (Drop Scones), Crêpes* and *Yorkshire Puddings* (see below). Batter is also used to coat food before deep-frying (see **Deep–frying**, page 207).

It is important that batter is free from lumps when making pancakes, crêpes and Yorkshire puddings. Batter can be made by hand or more quickly in a food processor or liquidizer.

Making a Batter

Making Batter by Hand

1 Sift the flour with the salt and sugar, if using, into a large bowl. Make a well in the centre.
2 Place the beaten eggs and 2 tablespoons of the liquid used into the well.
3 To make a smooth, lump-free batter, use a wooden spoon to stir the eggs to make a whirlpool to gradually draw in the flour. Do not stir in the flour but allow the liquid to incorporate the flour very gradually.
4 When the mixture in the centre is the thickness of double cream, add 2 more tablespoons of liquid and continue stirring as before. Repeat this procedure until all the liquid has been added and all the flour has been incorporated.
5 Stir in any oil or melted, cooled butter.
6 If lumps form in the batter at any time, the flour has been incorporated too quickly. Do not add any more liquid. Beat the batter hard until the lumps disappear.
7 The batter should be allowed to stand for at least 30 minutes before using so that the starch grains in the flour have a chance to swell. This will result in a lighter cooked product because the softened starch grains burst upon contact with heat. The batter will usually thicken upon standing. If necessary, add a little more liquid. Place in the refrigerator as batter is an ideal medium for bacterial growth.

Making Batter in a Food Processor or Liquidizer

1 Place all the ingredients in the machine.
2 Process until the mixture is smooth, scraping down the sides of the bowl once or twice.
3 Refrigerate for 30 minutes.

Storing Batter

Once made, the batter must be stored in the refrigerator because it is an excellent medium for the breeding of bacteria such as salmonella (see **Food Safety**, page 21). Keep it in the refrigerator for up to 24 hours. However, a batter made with self-raising flour is best cooked as soon as it is mixed.

Crêpes (French Pancakes)

These crêpes can be served with melted butter, lemon juice and sugar or be used for making Crêpes Suzette. They can also be used for savoury dishes, filled with cooked meat, vegetables or fish.

MAKES ABOUT 12

110 g	4 oz plain flour	1 egg yolk
a pinch of salt	290 ml	½ pint milk or milk and water mixed
1 medium egg	15 ml	1 tablespoon oil

1 Make the batter according to the directions given above.
2 Prove a crêpe pan (see **Eggs,** *Omelettes*, page 222 for directions).
3 Wipe the pan with a little oil and heat over a medium heat. To test if the pan is hot enough to cook the batter, sprinkle a little cold water into the pan. If it splutters and hisses, the pan is ready to use.
4 Swirl about 2 tablespoons batter over the base of the pan, pouring out any excess into a bowl.
5 Cook for 1–2 minutes until the edges of the crêpe look dry. Prise up the crêpe, using a palette knife. The underside should be golden-brown.
6 Turn the crêpe over and cook on the other side for 1–2 minutes until brown speckles appear. The side cooked first is the presentation side.
7 Serve immediately, or layer the crêpes between greaseproof paper to keep them from sticking together.

Storing crêpes

When cool, the crêpes can be layered between greaseproof paper and placed in a plastic bag. Store in the refrigerator or freeze for up to 1 month.

Crêpes: What has gone wrong when...

The crêpes have stuck to the pan.

- The pan has not been proved correctly. Prove the pan again. Wipe the pan with a little oil or butter after cooking each crêpe.

The crêpes are pale.

- The pan is not hot enough.

The crêpes are rubbery.

- The batter was beaten too hard.
- The egg was too large.
- The batter was not allowed to stand for long enough.

The crêpes are too thick.

- The batter was made with too much flour or too little liquid. Add a little more milk or water.
- Too much batter was put in the pan.

Scotch Pancakes (Drop Scones)

MAKES ABOUT 12

110 g|4 oz plain flour

2 teaspoons baking powder

a pinch of salt

1 medium egg, separated

150 ml|¼ pint milk

1 tablespoon melted butter

additional butter, for frying

1 Sift the flour with the baking powder and salt into a large bowl. Make a well in the centre.

2 Place the egg yolk and a little of the milk into the well and proceed as for *Making a Batter*, above.

3 Whisk the egg whites to the medium-peak stage (see **Eggs,** *Whites*, page 232) and fold into the batter.

4 Heat a frying pan over a medium heat until a drop of water sizzles in the pan.

5 Add enough butter just to coat the bottom of the frying pan.

6 Pour in batter to make pancakes of the desired size.

7 Cook for 2–3 minutes or until the pancakes are golden-brown on the underside, bubbles start to break through the batter and the top surface of the pancakes begins to look dry.

8 Turn the pancakes over with a palette knife and cook on the other side until brown.

9 Remove the pancakes from the pan and place in a folded tea towel to keep warm.

10 Serve warm with butter and syrup or jam.

VARIATIONS

Sweet Scotch Pancakes: Add 1 tablespoon caster sugar to the flour in step 1.

Herb Scotch Pancakes: Add 2 tablespoons finely chopped fresh herbs to the batter.

Sultana Scotch Pancakes: Add 55 g|2 oz sultanas to the batter.

Scotch Pancakes: What has gone wrong when...

See also *Crêpes: what has gone wrong when . . .*

The edges of the pancakes are fried and hard.
- Too much butter was used in the pan.

The pancakes are flat and tough.
- The batter was not used quickly enough.
- The raising agents have exceeded their shelf life.

Yorkshire Pudding

Yorkshire Pudding is a traditional accompaniment to roast beef. It can be made in a roasting tin or in individual Yorkshire Pudding tins or muffin tins. Beef dripping gives the best flavour but if none is available use vegetable oil instead.

SERVES 4

110 g | 4 oz plain flour
a large pinch of salt
2 medium eggs, beaten

290 ml | ½ pint milk or milk and water mixed
55 g | 2 oz beef dripping or vegetable oil

1 Preheat the oven to 200°C | 400°F | gas mark 6. Make the batter according to the directions above for *Making a Batter* and refrigerate for about 30 minutes. While the batter is standing, heat the dripping or oil in a roasting tin or individual Yorkshire Pudding tins in the oven. The fat should reach a depth of 3 mm | ⅛ in.

2 Remove the roasting tin or Yorkshire Pudding tins from the oven and place over the hob set to medium-low to keep the fat hot.

3 Carefully pour the batter into the hot fat. It should sizzle and bubble. The batter should reach a depth of about 1 cm | ½ in.

4 Return the tin or tins to the top third of the oven and bake until risen and golden-brown. Individual puddings will take 20–30 minutes and a larger pudding about 35–40 minutes. Do not open the oven door until 5 minutes before the puddings are done.

Storing Yorkshire Puddings

Yorkshire Puddings can be kept warm in a low oven, 100°C | 200°F | gas mark ½, for about 30 minutes, placed in a single layer and not covered. They can also be frozen for up to 1 month in a rigid freezer container. Reheat from frozen on a baking sheet in the oven preheated to 200°C | 400°F | gas mark 6 for about 20 minutes or until crisp.

Yorkshire Puddings: What has gone wrong when...

The puddings have not risen.
- The dripping or oil was not hot when the batter was added.
- The batter was not cold when it was added to the hot fat.
- The oven door was opened before the puddings were set.
- The batter was too dry.
- The oven temperature was too low.

The puddings are greasy.
- The oil was not hot enough when the batter was added.
- The puddings were not cooked for long enough.
- Too much dripping or oil was used.
- The oven temperature was not hot enough.

The puddings are soggy.
- The puddings were undercooked.
- The oven was not hot enough.
- The puddings have been stored in a covered dish. To correct, place on a baking sheet in a single layer and reheat in the oven preheated to 200°C|400°F|gas mark 6 until crisp.

Stages of Bread-making

The following stages apply to making most types of yeast bread. It is important to understand the various stages and to know when it is time to move from one stage to the next.

- **Mixing** is the combining of the yeast, flour, salt and liquid. Fat and sugar are also sometimes added at this stage.

- **Kneading** is the manipulation of the dough in order to develop the gluten and distribute the yeast. A yeast bread dough is kneaded until it is smooth and elastic. Test the dough by shaping it into a tight ball and pressing it. It should feel springy.

- **Rising** is when the dough is left to rest for a period of time so that the yeast can reproduce and thereby stretch the gluten. A dough is risen when it has doubled in size and the indentation will remain when the dough is prodded.

- **Knocking back/Shaping** means kneading the dough for a short time, then forming it into the shape required for the finished bread. Knocking back is done to even out the texture of the bread and to redistribute the yeast. If nuts, herbs or fruit are to flavour the bread, they are added at this stage.

- **Proving** is the last rising before the dough is baked. It allows the shaped dough to rise again to nearly its final size. When the dough is proved it will feel soft and pillowy and when prodded the indentation will spring back only about half-way.

- **Baking** is the cooking of the dough to make it edible. Bread is baked in a hot oven to kill the yeast and set the dough. It is done when the dough is well-browned and feels light and in most cases sounds hollow when tapped on the underside.

Bread, Yeast

Wheat has been a staple part of the diet of the Western world for centuries. For a very long time wheat grain was coarsely ground, mixed with a little water, then baked or dried on a hearth. It was not until a method for rising the dough was discovered, probably by accidentally leaving a dough to stand for longer than usual before baking, that the slightly raised 'flat' breads, such as Middle Eastern pitta breads, were made.

Natural yeasts are present in the environment, so a dough left to stand for a length of time would capture these wild yeasts. The yeast would grow in the dough, making the loaf lighter and nicer to eat than the usual hard, unleavened bread. Perhaps the dough had been mixed with wine, fruit juice or ale. It is recorded that thousands of years ago the Egyptians used the froth on the top of beer, the barm, which is full of yeast, to leaven their bread.

In the 1800s, naturally leavened bread became popularly known as sourdough (see *Sourdough Bread*, page 129). Although loaves made this way were a staple of many European countries such as Poland and France, the sourdough method of bread-making became associated with the gold miners in the western states of the USA and with ranchers in the Australian outback. It is a way of leavening bread when baker's yeast is not available and is a method that is still used today. A piece of dough is set aside from a loaf before it is baked, then used as a 'starter' to leaven the next loaf. This piece of dough was often stored in the saddlebag and gave the name 'sourdoughs' to the gold miners.

By the mid-1800s a method for growing yeast commercially was developed, allowing bakers to produce a dough that would rise reliably to make an acceptable loaf. With the advent of factory-made bread, bread-making almost became a lost art for a while among home cooks. It has been rediscovered in recent years, prompted by the fashion for exotic, flavoured breads. Frequently, making a successful loaf ignites a passion for bread-making and it becomes part of the pattern of a cook's life, if only to recapture the unequalled smell and intense pleasure of eating a freshly-baked loaf.

Bread-making is as much a science as a craft and the product can be improved by understanding the process and the ingredients. The basic ingredients for making a loaf of bread are flour, yeast, salt and liquid. These can be varied to produce bread of different flavours and textures. Each of these ingredients and their effects on the finished loaf are discussed in detail below.

Bread Flour

(*See also **Flour**, page 267.*)

Wheat flour, used either alone or in combination with other types of flour, is the main ingredient in bread. Wheat flour has a higher protein content than flours made from other grains, so it is the most suitable flour to use for yeast-risen (leavened) bread.

The strong flour used for making bread is produced from the hard winter wheat grown principally in northern regions of the USA and in Canada. Commercial flours are usually blended to give a uniform product. Today white flour is often enriched with vitamins and minerals in order to replace those extracted during milling and sifting. For example Vitamin C is added because it has been found to help strengthen gluten. Some flours contain certain enzymes that have an effect on gluten development and yeast activity.

Wholemeal flour is once again very popular due to its higher nutritional value, having been very much the 'poor relation' to white flour for centuries. Wholemeal flour has a slightly lower gluten content than white flour due to the presence of the bran and the wheatgerm in the flour. The fat and the abrasive qualities of the bran and wheatgerm have a softening effect on gluten development, so a loaf made with wholemeal flour will require a slightly longer kneading time. A loaf made entirely of wholemeal flour will be very dense and heavy so equal quantities of wholemeal and strong flour can be mixed to produce a more palatable loaf.

Gluten

Two proteins in the flour called glutenin and gliadin bond with the liquid in the recipe to form a substance called gluten. When the dough is kneaded the gluten is developed and forms elastic strands. The dough becomes firmer and has a smooth, almost satiny appearance when the gluten is fully developed. When the yeast reproduces and gives off carbon dioxide gas, the gas stretches the strands of gluten, rather like a bubble blown in chewing gum. Baking the dough sets the open network of bubbles in place and air replaces the carbon dioxide. It is the gluten which is chiefly responsible for giving bread its open, chewy texture. Kneading strengthens gluten. Although it is unlikely that a dough would ever become overkneaded by hand, it is possible to overknead a dough when using a machine. When this happens, the gluten strands are stretched so much that they break and the dough disintegrates into a soft, runny mass.

Yeast

Yeast is a single-celled micro-organism of the fungus family, which is used in bread-making to rise the dough (leaven) and give the finished loaf a lighter, more open texture. In order to raise the dough the yeast needs to grow or reproduce. Yeast requires warmth, moisture and food to reproduce. Too much heat will kill it, so care must be taken to ensure that the liquid added to the yeast is not too hot. When the yeast reproduces it gives off carbon dioxide and alcohol and stretches the strands of gluten in the dough.

The yeast uses the starch available in the flour for food as well as any sugar or sweetening ingredient in the recipe. Too high concentrations of sugar, salt, alcohol or fat will inhibit the reproduction of the yeast, slowing down the rising. If the dough is high in any of these ingredients it is advisable to use a greater amount of yeast and/or expect a longer rising time.

Either fresh baker's yeast or dried yeast can be used to make bread. Fresh yeast comes in a block and is a creamy, pale beige colour. It has a pleasant, slightly yeasty smell. The texture should be smooth and it should break with a clean snap. On no account should it smell 'beery' or feel slimy. When it is old it discolours and eventually dries out. Old yeast is not reliable for rising bread and will produce a loaf with an unpleasant yeasty flavour.

Storing Yeast

Fresh yeast can be stored in the refrigerator for up to 1 week if wrapped tightly in clingfilm or it can be frozen for up to 1 month. To freeze yeast, divide it into 30 g | 1 oz pieces, wrap individually, then overwrap. The yeast will liquefy upon defrosting so it should be used immediately.

Using Yeast

In most bread recipes the yeast is first mixed with some of the liquid and a little sweetener in order to make a smooth cream. For fresh yeast, the liquid is usually warmed to blood heat, 37°C | 100°F, which feels slightly warm to the touch. If you do not have a thermometer and are uncertain about the liquid temperature, one-third boiling water mixed with two-thirds cool tap water will produce a temperature of about 37°C | 100°F.

Dried yeast is sold in granular form in foil packages that will normally have a 'use by' date. It should be kept in a cool, dry place. It will usually keep for about 6 months but it should be discarded if the 'use by' date has passed.

If a recipe calls for fresh yeast and you wish to substitute dried, use half the amount in weight of dried yeast.

Dried yeast requires a slightly higher temperature than fresh yeast – about 39°C | 110°F – in order to be reconstituted successfully. It is very important, though, that the temperature of the liquid is not too hot as too high a heat will kill the yeast and the dough will not rise.

'Fast-action' or 'easy-blend' yeast is dried yeast that has been designed to be mixed in its dry form directly with flour, making it somewhat easier to use than the other types of yeast. This dried yeast has been very finely milled so that it disperses well when the flour is mixed with the liquid. The method of making bread using fast-action yeast is abbreviated because the yeast is so reliable and so active. A dough made with this yeast only needs to be kneaded once after mixing and is then placed directly into the prepared tin to rise. As soon as the dough has doubled in size it can be baked immediately. It does not need to be knocked back and risen again before baking. The texture is only very slightly coarser than that of a loaf that has had the usual rising and proving.

Fast-action yeast can be used in recipes that require the yeast to be reconstituted with liquid before it is added to the flour. It will dissolve in liquid of a cooler temperature than standard dried yeast, slightly lower than blood temperature, although the warmer temperature of 37°C | 100°F will help it rise more quickly. As with all yeast, too high a heat will kill it.

The quantity of yeast recommended to raise 340 g | 12 oz flour in a standard bread recipe is as follows:

3.5 g | ⅛ oz fast-action yeast = 1½ teaspoons fast action-yeast or
7 g | ¼ oz dried active yeast = 3 teaspoons dried active yeast or
15 g | ½ oz fresh yeast = 1 cake of fresh yeast (USA)

Salt

Salt is an essential ingredient to make bread palatable. Without salt, bread would taste stale and dull and the texture would be coarse. Either ordinary table salt or sea salt can be used. The presence of salt in the flour also helps gluten development.

Sea salt is popular with chefs as it has a more complex flavour than table salt – it contains flavourful minerals in addition to sodium chloride. Coarse salt should be ground finely or dissolved in liquid before it is added to the flour.

A high concentration of salt in a dough will inhibit the growth of the yeast so it is important to measure the salt accurately. The standard amount required for a savoury loaf is 1 teaspoon per 225 g | 8 oz flour. Use a level 5 ml teaspoon.

Liquid

Water or other liquid, such as milk, cream or juice, is an essential ingredient in bread-making. Water makes a loaf with an open texture and a hard crust. Milk will produce a loaf with a finer crumb than water due to the fat in the milk. Bread made with milk will keep better than a loaf made with water.

It is thought that the serum proteins in milk interact with the proteins in the flour, inhibiting the development of gluten and producing a weak, slack dough. For this reason it is recommended to scald the milk before using it to make bread.

Beer makes a flavourful bread but it must be boiled to drive away the alcohol before use as the alcohol would interfere with yeast activity. When adding liquid to flour, most of the liquid should be added all at once. It is better to have a slightly wet dough than a dry one. Softer doughs are easier to knead and produce lighter loaves. If the dough is too sticky, add flour as necessary.

Fat

Fat is not an essential ingredient in bread-making but it is used in many recipes for flavour, to help the browning of the crust and to produce a finer texture. The most usual types of fat for making bread are butter, olive oil, eggs and milk. Wholemeal flour has a higher fat content than white flour. Fat slows the action of the yeast and softens the gluten in the flour.

Butter gives a good flavour and a well-browned crust as well as improving the keeping qualities of the loaf. Oil makes the dough easy to knead and produces a slightly chewy loaf.

Too much oil in a dough – more than 30 g | 1 oz fat per 225 g | 8 oz flour – can result in bread with a slightly oily crumb.

Sugar

Sugar is not absolutely necessary in a dough but a small amount, 1–2 teaspoons per 225 g | 8 oz flour, is often included as a source of food for the yeast. The presence of sugar in a dough will help the bread to brown in the oven.

White, demerara and brown sugar can be used in bread doughs, as can honey, molasses, treacle and golden syrup.

A high concentration of sugar will inhibit the growth of the yeast, so for sweet breads the quantity of yeast is often increased. The sugar in a sweet bread makes it more moist and extends the keeping time.

Sugar also has a softening effect on gluten, so doughs with a high sugar content often require two risings to give the yeast longer to stretch the gluten, which will result in bread with a better texture.

Gluten Development and Yeast Activity, in Summary

To summarize, gluten is formed by the addition of liquid to flour and is strengthened by kneading as well as by the presence of salt and/or Vitamin C in the dough. Gluten is softened by fat and/or sugar and enzymes in the dough.

Yeast needs moisture, warmth and food in order to grow. High concentrations of sugar and/or fat and/or salt inhibit yeast growth. Only too high a heat kills yeast.

The Stages of Bread-making

Almost all cooks would agree that yeast cookery is a particularly satisfying craft. Whether it evokes the homely folk memory of a floury-handed grandma or the noble notion that one is producing the staff of life, the smell of baking bread unquestionably produces one of the most appealing kitchen environments. But for all its inherent romance, bread-making is a scientific process. By understanding how this works it is possible to create reliable results time after time, even when conditions change. Bread-making can be broken down into the 6 stages described below. To help our students remember these stages, we remind them to think of the sentence *Mary knits red knickers pretty badly*, where the initials stand for *mixing, kneading, rising, knocking back and shaping, proving* and *baking*.

Mixing

This is the process of combining the basic ingredients. Many recipes call for 'creaming the yeast'. This means mixing the yeast with some of the liquid specified in the recipe and, perhaps, a little of the sugar or other sweetener, to the consistency of thin cream. Creaming the yeast makes it easier to distribute evenly in the flour. If the yeast is active, it should start to go frothy within about 10–15 minutes of creaming. If it does not, it is likely that the yeast has died, so it is advisable to start again with some fresh yeast.

Some recipes specify mixing a little of the flour with the yeast liquid to make a sponge or starter, then leaving the sponge to stand for at least 20 minutes or up to several days. This process is discussed under *Sourdough Bread*, page 129.

The dough can be mixed in a large bowl with a wooden spoon or in an electric mixer fitted with a dough hook.

There are two basic methods for mixing the dough. One is to sift the flour into a large bowl with the salt and make a well in the centre. The yeast mixture is poured into the well along with enough liquid to make a soft dough. At least three-quarters of the liquid should be added immediately and stirred in quickly, then the remaining liquid is added as required. The amount of liquid required will vary depending on the flour used and the humidity of the weather.

The other method, called the fountain method, is to place the liquid and the yeast in the bowl, then stir in enough flour to make a soft, but not sticky, dough.

Kneading

Kneading is the process of manipulating the dough in order to distribute the yeast and develop the gluten. When the liquid is added to the flour, the water molecules combine with the protein in the flour to form gluten. When the dough is kneaded these protein strands are stretched and toughened.

To knead bread by hand, place the heel of your hand on the top of the dough and push away from you, moving from one side of your body to the other. **(a)** With your fingertips, flip the ball of dough over, pulling the dough back towards you. **(b)** Give the dough a quarter turn. Repeat the process with your other hand. Continue to knead, alternating hands. **(c)**

The majority of doughs will require kneading for 10 to 15 minutes by hand or for 5 to 10 minutes in a mixer with a dough hook. To tell if a dough has been kneaded enough, roll it into a tight ball and prod it with your finger. **(d)** It should spring back readily and will also be smooth and satiny in appearance.

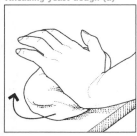

Kneading yeast dough (a)

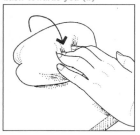

Kneading yeast dough
Flip the dough over and bring it back towards you (b)

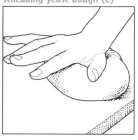

Kneading yeast dough (c)

Circular kneading

Rising

This is the stage at which the dough is allowed to stand in order for the yeasts to reproduce. As this happens, the yeasts emit carbon dioxide gas which stretches the gluten in the dough causing it to expand. This process will give the final loaf its texture.

Usually the dough is allowed to rise until it has doubled its original size. Place it in a lightly oiled bowl or a large oiled plastic bag. Turn the dough to coat the surface with the oil. This keeps the dough from developing a dry outer layer, which might inhibit rising. If using a bowl, cover the bowl with lightly oiled clingfilm and place in a warm, but not hot, place.

At a room temperature of $22°C|75°F$ – an ideal temperature for raising dough – the dough should double in size in approximately 1 hour. The dough can be raised at a cooler temperature than this, but obviously it will take longer. Some recipes call for a long cool rise, often in the refrigerator, for 8 hours or more. This procedure will produce bread with a more complex flavour due to enzyme activity and bacterial growth in the dough.

Bread that is raised at too high a temperature or for too long can have an unpleasant beery taste and smell. The dough might collapse if left for too long. If this happens, knead the dough for a few minutes, then shape it as required.

To tell if the dough has risen sufficiently, prod it with your finger. It should feel soft and pillowy and the indentation made by your fingertip should remain. This indicates that the gluten in the dough has been stretched to its full capacity.

Knocking Back and Shaping

Once the dough has risen until it has doubled in size, it will need to be knocked back. Knocking back redistributes the yeast in the dough and evens out the texture of the bread by kneading out the air bubbles that have formed during rising. It is done by the same procedure as *kneading* (see the description above).

Generally, knocking back needs to be done for only one to two minutes. In certain speciality breads an uneven texture with large holes is desirable, so the dough does not require knocking back. The recipe will indicate if this is the case. Do not cut into the dough to check the texture because this breaks the strands of gluten and will interfere with the final texture of the bread.

Some bread recipes will call for a second rising. The dough needs to be knocked back after the first rise, then left to rise again in the manner described above. Two risings are often called for with *enriched breads* (see page 132). Dough that has been allowed to rise twice will have a finer texture.

For recipes which have additional ingredients such as fruit or nuts, add these ingredients after the dough has been knocked back and before the final shaping.

Shaping is the process by which the dough is given its final shape, whether it is a traditional loaf baked in a tin, a free-form bloomer or dinner rolls. As knocking

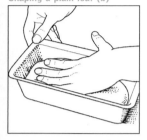

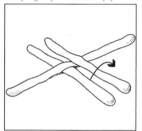

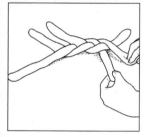

back can cause the gluten in the bread to tighten, it may be necessary to let the dough stand for up to 10 minutes to allow the gluten to relax before shaping.

Once the bread is shaped it should be put in the oiled tins or on an oiled baking sheet immediately and allowed to prove (see below). Bread is best baked in a dull metal loaf tin that has been lightly oiled. Rolls should be baked on lightly oiled or floured dull metal trays. Shiny trays will make the rolls brown too much.

Pizza stones are good for baking pizza or free-form loaves as they slow down the crusting process and produce a thicker, chewier crust. The dough must first be proved on a baking sheet, then transferred on to the hot pizza stone which has been preheated in the oven. To make transferring the risen loaf easier, dredge the baking sheet with polenta, flour or ground rice before placing the shaped dough on it.

Examples of bread shapes are as follows.

Plain loaf: Cup both hands around the edges of the dough and roll the dough on the work surface, using a circular movement, for about 30 seconds. This movement aligns the gluten, giving the finished bread a more even texture.

Using both hands, pull the dough towards you over the work surface. **(a)** This should smooth the surface of the dough. Gently roll the ends of the dough with both hands to form a slightly elongated shape. Place in the prepared tin. Flatten into the corners, using your fingers. **(b)**

Plaited loaf: Divide the dough into 3 equal pieces and shape each piece into a sausage about 40 cm | 16 in long. Place 2 of the pieces parallel to each other, about 2.5 cm | 1 in apart. Put the third piece perpendicularly across the middle, over one piece and under the other, to form an 'H'. **(a)** Starting from the middle, take the left-hand piece and place it in the centre of the 2 other pieces and proceed to plait the dough. **(b)** At the end, press the ends together to secure, then turn the whole plait over. **(c)** Proceed from the middle with the unplaited pieces as before. Turn the ends underneath to secure and place on a lightly oiled baking sheet. To bake in a tin, fold the long plait into thirds, rather like a business letter, and place in the prepared tin.

Bloomers are large oval loaves. Shape as for a plain loaf, then roll the dough at the ends to taper. Slash the loaf 3 times with a serrated knife or single-edged razor blade before proving.

Cottage loaf: Divide the dough into 2 pieces, one 3 times larger than the other. Shape both pieces into balls as for *dinner rolls* (see below). Make a small indentation in the centre of the top of the large ball and place the smaller ball on it, on the prepared baking sheet. Using a floured finger or wooden spoon handle, press a hole through both rolls right down to the baking sheet below, thus fixing the top to the bottom.

Dinner rolls are made using approximately 35–45 g | 1¼–1½ oz dough for each roll. Place the dough on a smooth work surface and working around the circumference of the dough, bring the edges up to meet in the centre. **(a)** Cup your hand over the dough ball and roll gently on the work surface. **(b)** Turn the ball over so that the smooth side is uppermost.

Baps are made using 55 g | 2 oz dough for each bap and are shaped in the same manner as for *dinner rolls* (above). They should be flattened with the palm of the hand once placed on the baking sheet.

Knots are made by rolling 45 g | 1½ oz of dough for each knot into a 10 cm | 4 in sausage shape which is then tied into a knot with the ends tucked underneath.

Proving

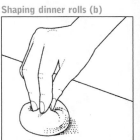

Proving is the last rising before the dough is baked. During this last rising the dough assumes its final shape and most of its final size. Proving can be done in a slightly warmer environment than rising to speed up the process – 25°C | 80°F is the recommended temperature. Usually proving will take approximately half the time of rising because the previous rising will have stretched the gluten strands, making the dough more elastic.

The shaped dough needs to be covered loosely with lightly oiled clingfilm to keep the surface from drying out.

The dough is ready to be baked when it has risen to 75–100 per cent of its original size. If the dough is prodded gently, the indentation made will spring back about half-way. The dough will feel soft and pillowy.

Dough that has been underproved will result in bread that has a close, heavy texture and a thick crust. *Oven-spring*, a crack in the bread where the crust has separated from the body of the loaf, may result. If the dough proves for too long, i.e. overproves, the bread will have large bubbles under the surface of the crust and may collapse in the oven.

Slashing

Loaves are sometimes slashed before baking to give a rustic appearance and to help prevent oven-spring. Slashing also avoids the formation of bubbles under the crust which can form when the steam in a baking loaf is trapped under the crust. Slashing is best done with a sharp, serrated knife or a single-edged razor about 10 minutes before the bread is due to go into the oven.

Glazing

Before the dough is baked it is often glazed to improve the appearance of the crust. Beaten egg will give the crust a shine and help it brown. Milk will also help the crust brown but will produce a softer crust with a matt appearance. It is important to apply the glaze thinly, using a pastry brush. The glaze should not be allowed to drip into the crack between the dough and the tin or it may act as glue once cooked and the finished loaf will be difficult to remove from the tin. Dough can also be dusted with flour before baking to give the bread a dusty, rustic appearance with a soft crust.

Baking

Baking cooks the dough in its final shape. During baking the dough continues to rise for a short while due to the formation of steam and continued action from the yeast. It will stop rising when the dough hardens and the yeast dies – when the internal temperature of the dough reaches 60°C|140°F. This usually happens within the first 10 minutes of baking. The moisture in the dough and the alcohol from the yeast reproduction evaporate and are replaced by air, leaving a network of fine bubbles in the dough that gives the bread its open texture.

It is important to preheat the oven before baking. Most bread is baked at 200°C|400°F|gas mark 6 near the top of the oven, the hottest part. Some recipes may call for preheating the oven to 225°C|425°F|gas mark 7, then turning the oven temperature down to 200°|400°F|gas mark 6 when the dough is put into the oven as a falling oven temperature is well suited to bread baking. Other recipes, particularly those for *enriched breads* (see p. 132) may call for a baking temperature of 190°C|375°F|gas mark 5.

A loaf of bread is baked until it is golden-brown all over and sounds hollow when tapped on the underside. If the top crust has browned well but the sides are still pale, the bread can be turned on its side and returned to the oven to continue baking for about 5 minutes until brown all over.

When the bread is done, remove it from the tin immediately and cool on a wire rack. The bread is still cooking during the cooling process, so it is important to leave it to cool completely before consuming. This can take up to 2 hours.

Storing Bread

Wrap the cooled loaf in greaseproof paper. Placing bread in a plastic bag will cause it to sweat, making the crust soft. Bread is best stored at room temperature because it stales more quickly if stored in the refrigerator. However, if the weather is very warm and there is a risk that the bread will go mouldy, it can be refrigerated.

White Bread

MAKES 1 LOAF OR 12 DINNER ROLLS

225 g|8 oz strong white flour

5 ml spoon|1 teaspoon salt

170 ml|6 fl oz water

10 g|⅓ oz fresh yeast or 1 teaspoon fast-action
    yeast or 2 teaspoons dried yeast

1 teaspoon caster sugar

30 g|1 oz butter, melted and cooled

extra flour, for kneading

oil, for greasing

1 egg, beaten with a pinch of salt, to glaze

1 Sift the flour with the salt into a large bowl and make a well in the centre.
2 Warm the water to 37°C|100°F (blood temperature) if using fresh yeast, or to 40°C|110°F if using fast-action or dried yeast.
3 If using fast-action yeast, mix the yeast and sugar with the flour and continue with step 5. Otherwise, place the fresh or dried yeast in a small bowl and add the sugar. Stir in enough water to dissolve the yeast and make a smooth cream.
4 Tip the yeast mixture into the well. Rinse the yeast bowl with a little of the water, then tip all of the water and the butter into the well.

5 Stir the mixture in the bowl with a wooden spoon to make a soft dough, adding more water or flour as necessary.

6 Turn the dough out on to a work surface. Knead for 10–15 minutes by hand or for 5–7 minutes in an electric mixer, adding extra flour if the dough is too sticky, until the dough is smooth and elastic.

7 Place the dough in an oiled bowl, turning it over to coat the surface with the oil. Cover the bowl with oiled clingfilm and leave to rise in a warm place, about 22°C|75°F. A good place to put a dough for rising is on a wire rack near a warm cooker. Airing cupboards are usually too warm.

8 When the dough has doubled in size, punch your fist into the centre of the dough to deflate it. Turn it on to the work surface and knead for 1 minute to knock it back. Let the dough rest for 5 minutes before shaping as required. For a plain loaf, lightly oil a 450 g|1 lb loaf tin.

9 Preheat the oven to 200°C|400°F|gas mark 6.

10 Cover the dough loosely with oiled clingfilm and leave to prove (rise again) until nearly doubled in size.

11 Glaze the dough with the beaten egg, taking care not to let the glaze drip into the tin. This would seal the bread into the tin, making it difficult to remove after baking.

12 Place the dough in the top third of the oven (the hottest part). Bake for 30 minutes or until the loaf is golden-brown and sounds hollow when tapped on the underside. Cool on a wire rack before slicing.

VARIATIONS

Wholemeal bread: To make a wholemeal loaf or rolls, replace 110 g|4 oz of the white flour with wholemeal flour. Increase the quantity of water by 2 tablespoons.

Bread-making: What has gone wrong when...

The bread has risen only a little.
- The dough was too dry.
- The shaped dough was proved for too short a time.
- Too much salt or sugar was added to the dough.
- The yeast was stale and not sufficiently active.
- The dough was overproved and collapsed in the oven.
- The liquid was too warm and some of the yeast was killed.

The bread has a cake-like texture.
- The kneading was insufficient for the gluten to develop properly.
- The dough was proved for too short a time.
- The dough contained too much salt.
- Plain flour was used instead of strong flour.
- The recipe contains a lot of fat.

The bread has a coarse texture.
- Too little salt was added to the dough.
- Too much liquid was added to the dough.
- The dough was risen for too short a time.
- The dough was overproved.

The bread has an uneven texture and/or holes.
- The dough was not knocked back sufficiently.
- The dough was overproved.

The bread has a sour and/or yeasty flavour.
- The dough was risen/proved at too high a temperature.
- The dough was risen for too long a time.
- The yeast was stale.
- Too much yeast was used.

The bread has a cracked crust (oven-spring).
- The oven was too hot.
- The dough was proved for too short a time.
- The dough formed a leathery crust when it was proving because it was not covered properly. Slashing the loaf during proving, before the loaf is baked, will help prevent oven-spring.

The bread has a wrinkled crust.
- The bread was cooled too quickly. Cover it with a tea towel while cooling.
- The dough was overproved.

The bread has holes underneath the crust.
- The dough was overproved.
- The oven was too hot so the crust formed too quickly. Slash the proved loaf before baking.

Olive Oil Bread

This Italian-style bread has a chewy, slightly coarse texture. It is very easy to make, requiring only one rising. It will not have as open a texture as ciabatta, however.

MAKES 1 SMALL LOAF

225 g|8 oz strong flour
5 ml spoon|1 teaspoon salt
15 g|½ oz fresh yeast or 1½ teaspoons fast-action yeast or 3 teaspoons dried yeast
a pinch of caster sugar

170 ml|6 fl oz warm water
2 tablespoons olive oil, plus extra for greasing
a 10 cm|4 in sprig of fresh rosemary
coarse sea salt (optional)

1 Sift the flour with the salt into a large bowl and make a well in the centre.
2 Mix the fresh yeast, if using, and the sugar with 3 tablespoons of the warm water to make a thin cream. Pour the mixture into the well, then rinse any remaining yeast from the container with a little additional water.

3 Pour 1 tablespoonful of the oil into the well.

4 Pour the remaining water into the well, then stir quickly with a wooden spoon to make a soft dough. As the dough comes together, add more water or flour as needed to make a soft, slightly sticky dough.

5 Knead the dough for 8–10 minutes by hand or for 5–6 minutes in an electric mixer until it is smooth and elastic. Allow to rest, covered for 5 minutes.

6 Oil a baking sheet, then roll the dough with a rolling pin into an oval about 2 cm│¾ in thick. Cover with oiled clingfilm and leave in a warm place to rise.

7 Preheat the oven to 200°C│400°F│gas mark 6.

8 When the dough has doubled in size and feels soft and pillowy, use your finger to make about 8 dimples in the dough. Drizzle the remaining oil into the dimples, then insert a little sprig of rosemary into each dimple.

9 Sprinkle with the sea salt, if using.

10 Place the dough in the top third of the oven (the hottest part).

11 Bake the bread for about 25 minutes or until well-risen and golden-brown. Then remove the bread from the baking sheet and place directly on the oven shelf for 5–10 minutes so that the underside can brown.

12 The bread is done when it feels light and sounds hollow when tapped on the underside. Cool on a wire rack.

NOTE: To use fast-action yeast, mix the yeast with the flour in step 1 and continue with the recipe, omitting the fresh yeast addition in step 2.

Olive Oil Bread: What has gone wrong when...

In addition to the points mentioned under *Bread-making*, above:

The bread has a greasy crumb.
- Too much oil was used in the dough.

Sourdough Bread

The sourdough method of making bread produces a dense, chewy loaf with a thick crust and a sour tang. The loaves are frequently made either partially or wholly from wholemeal flour, sometimes with the addition of rye flour, and are shaped into a free-form loaf that is slashed several times. The bread keeps well and is particularly good served with a strong cheese.

The original sourdough breads were made using the wild yeast present in the environment to leaven the flour, following a process that was used for centuries to produce a raised loaf, long before baker's yeast became available commercially. It is thought that the first raised loaf was made by accidentally capturing these yeasts, probably on the inside of a vessel used for wine.

Sourdough bread was widely made in the American West and in the Australian outback, where it is still popular today. San Francisco is renowned for its sourdough bread which owes its particular taste to a strain of bacterium, *Lactobacillus sanfrancisco*, which is unique to that city. Sourdough bread is also very popular in Central Europe and in France where it is known as *La Poilane*, after a famous family bakery in Paris.

Sourdough bread is leavened with a 'starter'. Originally a piece of bread dough was kept back from the loaf being baked. This piece of dough was stored in the flour sack and then mixed with fresh water and flour to make the next loaf. This type of starter is known as a dry or firm starter. Today it is a useful way to add flavour to bread.

A second type of starter, called a wet starter, is made by mixing organic flour and water to the consistency of a batter or thick cream, then allowing it to stand uncovered for about 3 days to capture the wild yeast present in the air. The starter should become foamy and sweetly yeasty. If it smells 'off', it is best to discard it and start again. Organic yoghurt, honey, grapes, and even beer can be used to help feed the starter. A starter can be made more successfully in a rural environment, rather than in a city where the air is polluted. It is important to use organic ingredients when making sourdough bread. Bleached flour and chlorinated water contain chemicals that inhibit yeast growth.

The wet starter is also referred to by other names, such as *biga* (Italian), *Poolish* (Central European) or *levain* (French).

A loaf raised entirely by a natural yeast starter can take up to 24 hours to make (not including the time required to make the starter) from the time the loaf is mixed to the time it is baked, because of the relatively small amount of yeast in the dough. For this reason many bakers today add a small amount of commercial baker's yeast, usually half the usual quantity, to the flour along with the starter. This produces a loaf with the flavour of a sourdough bread in a much shorter time.

Adapting a Bread Recipe to the Starter Method

Most bread recipes can be adapted to the starter method by mixing the liquid with half of the yeast, any sugar or sweetening called for in the recipe and enough flour to make a batter. The batter is then left to stand for at least 20 minutes and as long as 3 days in a cool kitchen or larder. The longer the starter is left to stand, the more intense the tangy flavour will be. This starter is also called a pre-ferment.

To make the dough, add the starter to the remaining flour along with the salt and any fat called for in the recipe. Cream the remaining half of the yeast with a little warm liquid of the type specified in the recipe and add to the flour. Mix to form a soft dough. Knead, rise and prove in the usual way.

The finished bread should have a more complex flavour and a more open, chewy texture. The crust should be thicker and chewier.

This method of mixing the dough is particularly suitable for olive oil breads (see recipe above), where an open texture and a thicker crust are particularly desirable.

Sourdough Bread

The starter needs about 6 days to become sufficiently active to raise a loaf. Once it starts bubbling, it can be stored in the refrigerator and fed every 3 days. A loaf can be produced from the starter in approximately 24 hours.

For the starter

225 g | 8 oz organic wheat grains, ground
225 ml | 8 fl oz warm natural mineral water
225 g | 8 oz organic plain flour
1 teaspoon organic honey
150 ml | ¼ pint warm natural mineral water

For the loaf

170 g | 6 oz starter
55 ml | 2 fl oz warm natural mineral water
1 tablespoon honey or barley malt syrup
170 g | 6 oz strong plain organic flour
55 g | 2 oz organic rye flour or wholemeal flour
1 slightly rounded teaspoon sea salt

For the starter

1 Place the ground wheat grain in a bowl and stir in the water. Leave to stand uncovered for 3 days at room temperature or in the garden. A few whole unwashed organic grapes can be added to the mixture.

2 On the third day stir in the flour, the honey and the water. Let stand for a further 3 days. The mixture should begin to bubble. If not or if it smells off, start again. Remove 170 g | 6 oz of starter to make the bread. Feed the remaining starter with 100 g | 3½ oz organic flour, and 100 ml | ½ fl oz organic mineral water, then place in the refrigerator.

For the bread

3 Place 170 g | 6 oz of the starter in a large bowl and stir in the water and honey. Sift together the flours then add enough flour to make a soft but not sticky dough.

4 Knead for 10 minutes by hand or 5 minutes by machine until the dough is smooth. Place in an oiled bowl, cover with oiled clingfilm and let stand at room temperature to rise until doubled in bulk. This will take 12–24 hours.

5 Knock back the dough and knead for one minute. Return to the oiled bowl, cover with oiled clingfilm and let rise again until doubled in bulk, about 3–8 hours.

6 Sprinkle the salt over the dough then knead the dough to knock back for 1 minute. Cover the dough with clingfilm and let the dough rest for 10 minutes. Line a 20 cm | 8 in diameter basket with a heavily floured linen tea towel.

7 Shape the dough into a smooth round (boule) and place in the basket. Cover with oiled clingfilm and let rise in a warm place until nearly doubled, about 3 hours.

8 Meanwhile, preheat the oven to 225°C | 425°F | gas mark 7. Place a pizza stone in the middle of the oven.

9 When the dough has proved, remove the stone from the oven and sprinkle the stone liberally with flour. Carefully turn the dough onto the stone then slash it with a razor or serrated knife in a noughts and crosses pattern.

10 Place the dough in the hottest part of the oven then pour a cup of cold water onto the floor of the oven to create steam. Bake for 35–40 minutes or until the loaf is well browned and sounds hollow when tapped on the underside. Let cool for 1 hour before slicing.

11 To serve: slice thinly and serve with butter or cheese.
12 To store: the bread keeps well for up to 1 week if kept closely wrapped and stored in an airtight container. Freeze for up to 1 month. Defrost at room temperature for approximately 3 hours then refresh in a 180°C│350°F│gas mark 4 oven for 10 minutes.

Enriched Breads

Enriched breads are yeast-raised breads in which the dough has been made richer by the addition of significant quantities of fat and/or sugar. The fat is usually butter or oil, but lard is sometimes used. Milk, cream, eggs and the bran and wheatgerm in wholemeal flour also contain fat.

Bread made from an enriched dough has a softer, finer texture because the fat weakens the gluten in the flour. For this reason enriched doughs often require a longer kneading time and are frequently allowed to rise twice before knocking back and shaping.

Enough sugar or honey is often added to enriched doughs to give them a sweet taste. A large amount of sweetening ingredients in a dough inhibits yeast growth, so these breads are often made with a greater quantity of yeast to compensate. Examples of enriched breads are hot cross buns, brioche, Chelsea buns and panettone.

Enriched Dough

200 ml│7 fl oz milk	5 ml spoon│1 teaspoon salt
40 g│1½ oz fresh yeast or 4 teaspoons fast-action yeast* or 8 teaspoons dried yeast	85 g│3 oz butter
	55 g│2 oz caster sugar
450 g│1 lb strong plain flour	2 eggs, beaten

1 Scald the milk and allow it to cool to blood temperature.
2 Cream the yeast with 1 teaspoon of the sugar and 3 tablespoons of the milk.
3 Sift the flour with the salt into a bowl. Rub in the butter.
4 Stir in the caster sugar, then make a well in the centre of the flour.
5 Tip the yeast mixture and the eggs into the well then add enough of the remaining milk to make a soft dough.
6 Knead for about 12–15 minutes by hand or for 6–9 minutes in an electric mixer until the dough is smooth and elastic.
7 Place the dough in an oiled bowl and turn it so that it is covered with a thin film of oil. Cover with oiled clingfilm and leave in a warm place to rise until doubled in size, about 2 hours.
8 If two risings are desired, knock the dough back by kneading for 1 minute, then return the dough to the bowl, cover, and leave to rise a second time until doubled in size.
9 Knock back the dough by kneading lightly for 1 minute. Add any dried fruit or nuts to the dough at this stage (see below).

10 Preheat the oven to 190°C|375°F|gas mark 5.

11 Shape the dough as required. Cover with oiled clingfilm.

12 Place in a warm place to prove until soft and pillowy.

13 Bake for 15–20 minutes for rolls, 25–30 minutes for a loaf. Allow to cool on a wire rack.

*NOTE: To use fast-action or dried yeast, omit step 2 and mix the yeast with the flour in step 3. Add all the sugar in step 4.

VARIATIONS

Hot Cross Buns

1 Sift 4 teaspoons ground mixed spice with the flour.

2 After knocking back, add 110 g|4 oz currants and 30 g|1 oz candied peel into the dough. Shape into 24 buns for small buns or 16 for large buns. Prove.

3 Just before the buns are to go into the oven, combine 110 g|4 oz plain flour with 1 tablespoon oil and enough water to make a thin paste. Using a serrated knife, mark a cross on the tops of the buns.

4 Pipe the paste over the marked crosses and bake for 15–20 minutes. Five minutes before the buns are due to come out of the oven, brush the tops with a little sweetened milk. Return to the oven to finish baking.

Rolling Chelsea bun dough (a)

Chelsea Buns

1 After knocking back the dough roll it into a 20 cm × 40 cm|8 × 16 in rectangle.

2 Mix together 55 g|2 oz softened butter, 55 g|2 oz caster sugar and 1 teaspoon ground mixed spice.

3 Spread over the dough, leaving a 1 cm|½ in margin round the edges. Sprinkle with 55 g|2 oz sultanas and 55 g|2 oz currants. Roll up from one long edge. Pinch the join to seal. Slice into 16 rounds.

4 Place the rounds in 2 lightly oiled 20 cm|8 in sponge tins or on 2 oiled baking trays with the joins in the rolls facing inwards. Cover with oiled clingfilm and prove. Sprinkle with a little caster sugar and bake for 20–25 minutes.

5 Brush with apricot glaze (see **Pâtisserie**, *Apricot Glaze*, page 533). Cool on a wire rack.

Chelsea buns (b)

Enriched Doughs: What has gone wrong when...

The dough takes a very long time to rise.

● The additional fat and sugar in the recipe inhibit yeast action. More yeast could be used next time, or plan for longer risings.

Chelsea buns (c)

Brioche

Brioche is the ultimate enriched bread. It contains a large amount of butter and eggs which give it a fine, cake-like texture and buttery flavour. It is thought that the name brioche is a derivative of the French verb *broyer*, or the German verb *brechen*, both of which mean break, in reference to the effect of the butter on the gluten during the making of brioche.

Originating in Normandy, for centuries renowned for its butter production, brioche was being consumed in Paris, usually for breakfast, by the 1700s. It is traditionally baked in a deep fluted tin with sharply sloping sides, although it can be baked in a loaf tin for slicing and toasting. The tins can be small for individual brioches or large enough to serve 10–12 people.

Recipes call for 450–675 g | 1–1 ½ lb butter per 1 kg | 2.2 lb flour, although a less rich version can be made for wrapping pâtés and sausages.

Brioche can be sweetened or not, depending on how the finished product is to be used. Plain flour produces a brioche with a fine, cake-like texture, whilst strong flour produces a brioche with a more open, bread-like texture.

Brioche

MAKES 12 INDIVIDUAL OR 1 LARGE BRIOCHE

85 ml | 3 fl oz milk

15 g | ½ oz fresh yeast

30 g | 1 oz caster sugar

500 g | 1 lb 2 oz flour (see above for type)

1 ½ teaspoons salt

6 medium eggs, beaten

340 g | 12 oz unsalted butter, softened

melted butter and flour, for the tins

1 egg yolk, beaten with 1 tablespoon milk, to glaze

Kneading brioche

1 Scald the milk, then allow to cool to blood temperature.
2 Cream the yeast with the milk and a pinch of the sugar.
3 Sift the flour with the salt into a large bowl and make a well in the centre.
4 Place the milk/yeast mixture and the eggs in the well, then stir to make a soft, very sticky dough.
5 Beat the dough in an electric mixer or by hand. If kneading by hand, take a lump of the dough and pull it up vertically, then push it back down and away from you. Continue this process until the dough becomes smooth and elastic and forms a cohesive ball.
6 Cover the dough with lightly oiled clingfilm and place in a warm place to rise until doubled in bulk.
7 Beat the butter and the rest of the sugar together to dissolve the sugar and bring the mixture to the same texture as the dough.
8 To add the butter to the dough using a mixer, beat a tablespoon of the butter at a time into the dough, only adding more butter when the previous addition has been incorporated. To add the butter by hand, turn the dough on to a work surface. Bury the butter a tablespoon at a time in

the centre of the dough, then knead the dough as above until it becomes a smooth, silky mass. Continue adding butter in this fashion until it has all been added.

9 Place the dough in a bowl and cover with oiled clingfilm. Allow to rise until doubled in bulk. It should not be risen in a very warm place, i.e. no more than 21°C|70°F, or the butter could become too soft which would result in a greasy brioche.

10 When the dough has risen, gently knock it back by folding the edges of the dough over the centre and patting it down lightly.

11 Cover the dough with oiled clingfilm and refrigerate for at least 8 hours or overnight.

12 Generously grease the brioche tins with 2 coatings of butter and dust with flour, tapping any excess flour on to the work surface.

13 Half fill the prepared tins with the cold brioche dough. For brioche *à tête*, make a hole in the centre of the dough all the way to the bottom. Place an elongated 'head' of dough into the hole and secure it by pressing through the centre of the 'head' with the floured handle of a wooden spoon.

14 Preheat the oven to 190°C|375°F|gas mark 5. Cover the brioche tins with oiled clingfilm and leave to rise until the dough is mounding slightly over the top of the tins.

15 Brush the dough with the egg yolk glaze, taking care not to let any of the glaze drip between the edge of the dough and the tin or the glaze could 'glue' the dough to the tin, making the brioche difficult to remove.

16 Bake in the top third of the oven (the hottest part) for 8–10 minutes for individual brioches or 30–40 minutes for a large mould. Larger brioches will need to be covered with greaseproof paper after about 15 minutes baking to prevent then from overbrowning. The brioche is done when it is deep brown on the top and pale golden brown and firm where it was covered by the tin. It should feel light for its size.

17 Allow to cool on a wire rack. Eat within 1 day or freeze for up to 1 month.

Shaping brioche *à tête* (a)

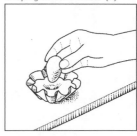

Shaping brioche (b)

Brioche: What has gone wrong when...

The brioche is heavy.
- The brioche was underproved.

The brioche is greasy.
- The dough was raised/proved at too high a temperature.
- The dough became too warm when the butter was added.

The brioche is very crisp on the outside.
- The brioche was overbaked.
- The brioche was baked at too high a temperature.

Methods of Cake-making

Rubbing-in Method
- The fat is rubbed into the flour with the fingertips or in a food processor, then the liquid ingredients are added. These cakes, raised by chemical raising agents, are dense and heavy. Example: *Scones* (see **Baking**, page 108).

Melting Method
- The butter is melted with the sugar and allowed to cool. The eggs are mixed in, then the flour. These cakes, raised by chemical raising agents, are moist and heavy. Example: *Gingerbread* (see page 141).

Creaming Method
- The softened butter and sugar are beaten together until light to incorporate air. The eggs are beaten in gradually, then the flour is folded in. These cakes are raised by chemical raising agents, by the air beaten into the cake and the expansive properties of the eggs. These cakes are moist with a soft crumb. Example: *Victoria Sandwich* (see page 144).

Whisking Method
- Several types of cake are made by the whisking method. The simplest is a plain *Whisked Sponge* or *Swiss Roll* (see pages 149 and 150). The eggs are whisked with the sugar and the flour is folded in to make a light, somewhat dry cake (see page 147).

  With Génoise cakes, melted butter is folded into the mixture before the flour is added. This gives the cake a tender texture and a moist crumb (see page 150).

Cakes

Although historically the differences between cakes, bread and biscuits are blurred – often a round shape was the only factor which qualified certain types of baked goods to be described as cakes – the definition is now more involved. Today we expect a cake to be a raised, sweet, baked mixture of flour, sugar or other sweetening, fat and eggs. It will have been raised by the air beaten into the mixture, by the expansive properties of the eggs and possibly by chemical raising agents. The texture is significant in determining whether baked goods are cakes, biscuits or bread. A cake should be tender and moist, without the chewiness associated with bread or the crispness of a biscuit. The crumb of a cake should be very small.

A cake mixture is basically a batter with a high proportion of fat, sugar and eggs in relation to the flour. These enriching ingredients inhibit the formation of gluten in the flour (see **Flour**, page 267), giving the resulting cake a tender texture. By varying the order and the method of combining these ingredients, different types of cakes can be produced.

Fat

Fat keeps a cake tender and gives richness and flavour. The fat coats the flour molecules, helping to protect the protein in the flour from the liquid in the batter that would cause gluten to form.

Butter will produce a cake with the best flavour, but some recipes call for other types of fat. Vegetable shortening will give a finer texture but will not give any flavour. Margarine, particularly the soft tub variety, is good for both flavour and speed of mixing as it is already soft. Most recipes will specify soft butter, the texture of soft tub margarine.

Lard is sometimes called for in old-fashioned recipes. It gives a characteristic flavour and a somewhat greasy crumb so it is not used very often in cake-making.

Vegetable oils are often specified in recipes using carrots or bananas. Oil cannot be beaten to incorporate air so a cake made with oil will have a close, dense texture with a moist crumb.

Sugar

Sugar sweetens a cake and helps it to brown. Sugar also interferes with gluten development in the flour, helping to keep the cake tender.

Caster sugar is the most suitable for cake-making because it can be creamed with the fat to incorporate air. Coarser granulated sugar can give a speckled appearance to a finished cake unless it is first ground finely in a food processor or liquidizer. Icing sugar is not suitable for cake-making because the smooth surface of the individual grains cannot hold tiny air bubbles. Golden caster sugar, an unrefined, raw cane sugar (see *Sugar, Sweeteners and Sugar Syrups*, page 695) will give a richer, slightly caramelized flavour to a cake, but the darker brown sugars, whilst suitable for gingerbread and fruit cakes, would give a sponge cake a drab appearance and too strong a caramel flavour.

Other sweetening ingredients such as golden syrup, honey, treacle and molasses are used in cakes made by the melting method. The crumb tends to be moister and heavier in these cakes because it is not possible to incorporate much air with the melting method. These cakes are cooked at a lower temperature than sponge cakes, as the sweetening agents tend to caramelize and burn at higher temperatures.

Flour
(See also *Flour*, page 267)

The best flour to use for making a cake is plain white flour or self-raising flour, as specified in the recipe. Cake flour, a low-gluten flour, is available in some countries and is ideal for both cakes and pastries. The high proportion of low-gluten wheat in European flour makes it particularly suitable for cake-making. Too high a gluten content in the flour would produce a tough, chewy cake.

Flour should be folded into a cake mixture very gently so as not to develop the gluten in the flour. Vigorous stirring of the mixture once the flour has been added and overfolding of the flour will produce a tough texture in a cake.

Self-raising flour has raising agents added to it so should only be used if specified in the recipe. All flour, even if labelled 'ready-sifted', should be sifted before use to eliminate any lumps and to incorporate air.

Eggs
(See also *Eggs*, page 213)

Eggs give a cake flavour and colour and are responsible for much of the volume. They constitute part of the liquid in cake-making. Unless otherwise specified, it is assumed that medium eggs weighing 55 g|2 oz should be used.

It is best to use the eggs at room temperature. Cold eggs are difficult to incorporate into the butter and sugar mixture without curdling. Curdling results in a cake that is badly risen and coarse in texture. Eggs can be warmed by placing them in their shells in a bowl of warm water for a few minutes before using.

Raising Agents

Air is incorporated into cake mixtures by agitating the ingredients, by sifting the flour, beating the butter and creaming it with the sugar and by whisking the eggs. The liquid in the wet batter turns to steam during the baking process and the steam also raises the cake mixture to a small extent.

Bicarbonate of Soda

Chemical raising agents such as bicarbonate of soda or baking powder are also used to raise cakes. Bicarbonate of soda is a white powder which when mixed with an acid ingredient such as molasses, buttermilk, yoghurt, soured cream or cream of tartar produces carbon dioxide. This gas is trapped in the batter and expands as it heats. The heat then sets the structure of the batter and the carbon dioxide is replaced by air.

When using bicarbonate of soda, it is important to put the cake into the oven as quickly as possible to capture this chemical reaction in the cake and make it rise. A large amount of bicarbonate of soda can leave an unpleasant flavour in a cake and give the crumb a yellowish taint, so it is usually used in strongly flavoured cakes such as gingerbread.

Baking Powder

Baking powder in its commercial form is a white powder that is a mixture of sodium phosphate, an acid (usually cream of tartar) and a filler such as cornflour to keep the mixture dry. The chemical reaction created by baking powder is activated when it is mixed with a liquid so cakes made with baking powder also need to be mixed quickly and put in to the oven immediately. In the USA a 'double-action' baking powder which has a second, heat-activated reaction, is available.

Too much baking powder in a recipe will produce a cake with an 'off' taste. The amount used should not exceed 2 teaspoons per 110 g|4 oz flour. Baking powder is perishable, so if in doubt about its efficacy, mix 1 teaspoon in 55 ml|2 fl oz hot water. It should bubble vigorously.

To make your own self-raising flour, add 4 level teaspoons baking powder per 250 g|9 oz plain flour.

Yeast

Yeast can also be used to raise flour mixtures through the growth of the yeast cells. However, these cakes, such as Lardy Cake and Tea Cakes, are classified as sweetened *enriched breads* (see **Bread, Yeast**, page 132).

Methods of Cake-making

There are 4 basic methods of cake-making, the rubbing-in method, the melting method, the creaming method and the whisking method. These are described in detail below. In each of the methods a batter is produced in which tiny air bubbles are held in suspension by the mixture. Technically this mixture is a foam. As the mixture bakes, the bubbles of air and carbon dioxide expand and the liquid in the batter turns to steam, stretching the batter and raising the cake. As the mixture continues to bake, the proteins in the eggs and flour coagulate and the starch gelatinizes, stabilizing the foam and setting the fine, sponge-like texture in the cake.

Successful cake-making depends on measuring ingredients precisely and following mixing and baking instructions carefully. To ensure a well-made cake follow the recommendations below:

Cakes: Points to Remember

- Set the oven to the correct temperature before starting to mix the cake.
- Place the oven shelf at the correct level, usually in the middle of the oven.
- Use the size of tin called for in the recipe and prepare it as specified.
- Weigh and measure all the ingredients.
- Ensure your ingredients are at the correct temperature.
- Sift the flour with the raising agents.

Rubbing-in Method

The rubbing-in method produces a fairly heavy cake with a crumbly, moist texture. In this method the fat is rubbed into the flour with your fingertips or in a food processor. The raising agent is either bicarbonate of soda or self-raising flour. These cakes are the most similar of all the cakes to pastry. *Scones* (see **Baking**, page 108) are classic examples of cakes made by the rubbing-in method (see also **Pastry**, page 510).

Melting Method

The melting method is the easiest and most foolproof of all the cake-making methods. In the melting method the fat and sugar are melted together, then allowed to cool to room temperature before the eggs are added. The dry ingredients are sifted together, then folded into the wet ingredients. This method produces cakes with a moist, dense crumb, such as *Gingerbread* (see below).

Preparing a tin for cakes made by the melting and creaming methods
The cake tin(s) should be prepared before starting to make the cake. Brush the tin(s) lightly with a flavourless oil, such as vegetable oil. To line the base of the tin

accurately, use the tin as a template and draw around the outside of the base of the tin on to greaseproof paper or baking parchment with a pencil. Cut just to the inside of your pencil mark. Place the paper inside the tin and brush lightly with oil if greaseproof is used. Baking parchment has been treated with silicone to be non-stick, so does not need to be brushed with oil. If there are any pencil marks on the paper, be sure to turn it over to avoid marking the cake.

Lining a cake tin (a)

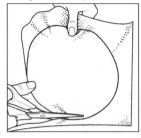

Lining a cake tin (b)

Melting-method Cakes: Points to Remember

- Let the melted sugar and fat cool to room temperature before adding the eggs or the eggs will cook in the heat.
- Sift the dry ingredients together thoroughly.
- Work quickly when folding the dry ingredients into the wet ingredients and put the cake into the oven as quickly as possible.
- The cake is done when a wooden skewer inserted into the centre comes out without any wet mixture adhering to it.

Black Sticky Gingerbread

This is a classic, dark gingerbread, aromatic with spices. It is better if made a day or two in advance as the flavours mellow upon standing. It keeps for up to 1 week if wrapped closely in clingfilm. It can be frozen for up to 3 months.

MAKES 24 PIECES

oil, for greasing
225 g | 8 oz butter
225 g | 8 oz soft dark brown sugar
225 g | 8 oz black treacle or molasses
340 g | 12 oz plain flour

2 teaspoons ground ginger
1 tablespoon ground cinnamon
2 teaspoons bicarbonate of soda
2 eggs, beaten
290 ml | ½ pint milk

1 Preheat the oven to 150°C | 300°F | gas mark 2. Prepare a 30 × 20 cm | 12 × 8 in roasting tin by brushing lightly with oil, then lining the base with greaseproof paper or baking parchment and brushing lightly with oil if greaseproof is used (see *Preparing a tin for cakes made by the creaming and melting methods*, above).

2 Melt the butter, sugar and treacle or molasses in a saucepan. Tip the mixture into a large bowl and allow to cool to room temperature.

3 Sift the flour, ginger, cinnamon and bicarbonate of soda into a large bowl and make a well in the centre.

4 Stir the eggs and milk into the butter mixture.

5 Tip the butter mixture into the well in the flour and fold in quickly with a large metal spoon or wire whisk.

6 Turn into the tin and place in the middle of the oven.

7 Bake for about 45 minutes or until the cake is well risen and will spring back when pressed lightly in the centre, and a wooden skewer inserted into the centre will come out clean.

8 Place on a wire rack to cool. Wrap in foil and store in a cool dry cupboard for up to 5 days or freeze for up to 1 month.

Melting-method Cakes: What has gone wrong when...

The cake sinks in the middle.
- The oven door was opened before the cake was set.
- The cake is underbaked.

The surface of the cake is covered with little holes.
- The cake was not placed in the oven quickly enough.
- The oven temperature was too low.
- The bicarbonate of soda was not mixed into the flour well enough.

The top of the cake is thick and crusty.
- The oven temperature was too high.
- The cake is overbaked.

The top of the cake is domed and cracked.
- The oven temperature was too high.

The cake has a sour flavour and/or a greenish tinge.
- Too much bicarbonate of soda was used.

Creaming Method

The creaming method is used to make many cakes, including the classic sponge cake, the *Victoria Sandwich* (see below).

Prepare the tins as described under *Preparing a tin for cakes made by the creaming and melting methods*, above.

Creaming the butter and sugar

In the creaming method the butter is beaten until soft, then the caster sugar is added gradually while beating continues. This can be done by hand with a wooden spoon or with an electric mixer. The creaming of the butter and sugar incorporates a great deal of air into the mixture that will help the cake to rise in the oven. As the mixture is beaten it will become fluffy and mousse-like and nearly white in colour due to the large amount of air that is beaten in. The butter should not be allowed to melt or become oily or the cake will not rise well and will have a greasy crumb.

The mixture is stabilized by the presence of some of the sugar that does not dissolve but is held in suspension in the butter. Caster sugar is the best type to use because the grains are very small, unlike granular sugar that would produce a speckled effect when the cake is baked. Icing sugar is too fine and the crystals would not give the required stabilizing effect in the beaten butter.

Adding the eggs

After the butter and sugar have been well creamed the eggs are beaten, then added a teaspoonful at a time to the creamed mixture. It is important that the mixture is beaten well after each addition of egg. Eggs at room temperature should be used as cold eggs can cause the butter to cool down so that it sits in separate lumps with a coating of egg. This means that the mixture is curdling. A tablespoon of the flour can be added to help stabilize the mixture if it the butter starts to separate from the egg. However, if a mixture appears to be curdling badly and rescue attempts fail, it is best to continue with the recipe and add the flour as quickly as possible. The butter–sugar–egg mixture is an unstable emulsion that will split if left to stand for any length of time.

It is the air that is beaten in that makes the cake light and tender. The amount of air incorporated into the mixture is dependent on the expansive properties of the eggs. As the mixture is beaten, the proteins in the eggs stretch, holding the tiny air bubbles in place (see **Eggs**, *Uses in Cooking*, page 224). It is important to take time to incorporate the eggs into the butter mixture so that the mixture does not curdle. Cakes made from curdled mixtures have a less delicate, more open and coarse texture than those made from a mixture that has not curdled.

Folding in the flour

Once the eggs have been incorporated, the flour is folded in gently. A large metal spoon is ideal for folding because the sharp edge will cut through the mixture with ease. To fold, start at the middle of the bowl and cut vertically through the centre of the mixture, then across the bottom of the bowl and up the other side. Gently continue this motion, giving the bowl a quarter turn after each stroke so that a 'figure-eight' shape is being made with your spoon. It is important not to overfold the mixture or air will be knocked out and the gluten in the flour will be developed, making the cake tough.

1–2 tablespoons of warm water or milk can be added at the end to help lighten the mixture. The uncooked mixture should be of a dropping consistency, i.e. a table-spoonful of the mixture should drop easily from a spoon when given a sharp shake.

Baking

During baking the air trapped in the mixture expands and the raising agent produces carbon dioxide bubbles causing the cake to rise. As the mixture heats, the proteins in the eggs and flour set to hold the fine network of bubbles in place. Any disturbance before the cake has set will cause it to fall, resulting in a flat, dense cake. Do not open the oven door to check if the cake is done until it has had a chance to set, i.e. only open the door approximately 5 minutes before the end of the specified cooking time.

To test if the cake is done, stretch your arm inside the oven and gently press the cake in the centre. If it is done it will feel firm and will spring back. If the indentation from your finger remains, continue baking the cake for a further 2–3 minutes before checking it again. The cake should be well-risen and golden-brown. The cake will also pull away slightly from the edges of the tin when it is done.

Allow the cake to cool in the tin on a wire rack for 5 minutes before inverting it on to the rack to remove it from the tin. Peel the paper from the base of the cake, then carefully turn the cake over so the wire rack does not make grooves on the top of the cake. Allow to cool completely before icing and/or serving.

Victoria Sandwich

The recipe for a Victoria Sandwich contains equal weights of eggs, butter, sugar and self-raising flour. A medium egg weighs 55 g | 2 oz, so a 2-egg Victoria sandwich cake will require 110 g | 4 oz each of butter, caster sugar and self-raising flour. A 3-egg Victoria Sandwich will require 170 g | 6 oz butter, sugar and flour, etc. By keeping these proportions any size of cake can be made and eggs of different sizes can be used.

oil, for greasing
110 g | 4 oz butter, softened
110 g | 4 oz caster sugar
2 medium eggs

110 g | 4 oz self-raising flour, sifted
warm water
2 tablespoons raspberry jam
caster sugar, for dusting

1 Preheat the oven to 180°C | 350°F | gas mark 4.
2 Prepare 2 × 15 cm | 6 in sandwich tins by lining the base of each with a disc of greaseproof paper or baking parchment and brushing lightly with oil if greaseproof is used (see *Preparing a tin for cakes made by the creaming and melting methods*, above).
3 Cream the butter in a bowl, then gradually beat in the sugar. Continue beating until light and fluffy.
4 Mix the eggs together in a separate bowl, then beat them into the creamed mixture a teaspoonful at a time. If the mixture begins to curdle, beat in a tablespoon of the flour.
5 Fold in the flour, adding enough water to bring the mixture to a *dropping consistency*.
6 Divide the mixture between the tins and smooth the tops.
7 Bake in the middle of the oven for about 20 minutes or until the cakes are well-risen, golden-brown and spring back when pressed lightly with a fingertip.
8 Allow to cool in the tins on a wire rack for 5 minutes. To remove from the tins, insert a table knife between the edge of the cake and the tin. While pressing against the tin with the knife, use your other hand to rotate the tin 360°, thereby cutting with the knife between the cake and the tin.
9 Turn the cakes on to the wire rack and invert them so they are sitting top side up to avoid the wire rack marking the tops. Carefully remove the lining paper and allow to cool completely.

10 To serve, place the less attractive layer top side down on a serving plate. Beat the jam with a fork or pass it through a sieve to make it easier to spread. Spread the cake with the jam, then top with the second layer. Sprinkle with caster sugar.

Creaming-method Cakes: What has gone wrong when...

The cake has risen a little but has a dense, heavy texture.
- The eggs were added too quickly and the mixture has curdled.
- The mixture was overfolded when the flour was added.

The cake is flat and dense.
- No raising agent was included in the mixture.

The cake has tiny holes on the surface.
- The cake was not put into the oven quickly enough.
- The oven temperature was too low.

The base and sides of the cake are damp and soggy.
- The cake was left in the tin to cool.

The cake is domed and/or cracked in the centre.
- The oven temperature was too high.
- The tin size was too small.
- Too much raising agent was used.

The cake has sunk in the middle.
- The cake was underbaked.
- The oven door was opened before the cake was set.

The edges of the cakes are thick and crunchy.
- Too much oil was used to coat the tin.

Fruit Cake

Preparing a tin for fruit cake

Fruit cakes with a high proportion of dried fruit are baked very slowly because the fruit would scorch at higher temperatures and become unpleasantly bitter. To help protect these cakes from the heat of the oven, the high-sided fruit cake tins need to be lined on the base and sides with a double thickness of greaseproof paper lightly brushed with vegetable oil.

Several thicknesses of newspaper are then wrapped around the outside of the tin and secured with string. The tin is placed in the oven on several thicknesses of newspaper making sure to keep it well clear of the gas flame, if there is one.

Lining a fruit cake tin (a)

Lining a fruit cake tin (b)

Although fruit cakes are often so densely packed with fruit that it is difficult to determine whether or not the texture of the surrounding cake is light, the following version of the creaming method is suitable for fruit cakes.

Softened butter and sugar are creamed in a mixing bowl to incorporate air, then the eggs are beaten in a little at a time. The flour is added alternately with the last few additions of the egg to avoid curdling. The dry fruit is then folded in well to distribute it throughout the cake. The mixture should have a soft, dropping consistency. The cake mixture is turned into the prepared tin (see above), then a large well going all the way to the base of the tin is formed. Scrape the cake mixture from the centre and mound it on the sides. As the cake starts to cook the mixture will level out. The well will prevent the cake from peaking in the centre during cooking.

To tell if a fruit cake is cooked, insert a skewer into the centre of the cake all the way to the base. There should be no uncooked mixture adhering to the skewer when it is removed.

Fruit Cake

This recipe is for the traditional Christmas cake. It will improve on keeping for a couple of months if well wrapped in kitchen foil and stored in an airtight container.

MAKES A 22.5 CM | 9 IN CAKE

110 g | 4 oz glacé cherries, halved

55 g | 2 oz mixed peel

450 g | 1 lb raisins

285 g | 10 oz sultanas

110 g | 4 oz currants

200 ml | 7 fl oz ale or sweet sherry

225 g | 8 oz butter, softened

225 g | 8 oz soft dark brown sugar

2 tablespoons treacle

grated zest of ½ lemon

5 medium eggs, beaten

285 g | 10 oz plain flour

2 teaspoons ground mixed spice

110 g | 4 oz ground almonds

55 ml | 2 fl oz brandy or sherry

1 Wash the fruit and dry it on kitchen paper. The day before baking, combine the fruit with the ale or sweet sherry in a large bowl or plastic bag. Refrigerate overnight.

2 Prepare the tin as described above.

3 Preheat the oven to 170°C | 325°F | gas mark 3.

4 Cream the butter with the sugar, treacle and lemon zest in a bowl until fluffy.

5 Beat in the eggs gradually. If the mixture starts to curdle, stir in a little of the flour.

6 Sift together the flour and mixed spice. Mix in the ground almonds.

7 Drain the fruit in a sieve over the bowl of creamed mixture to catch any remaining ale or sherry and stir in. Fold in the flour, then the fruit.

8 Turn the mixture into the cake tin and make a well in the centre right to the bottom of the tin. This will ensure that the cake is level when it is baked. Use a dampened spoon to smooth over the surface and to push any fruit into the batter. Fruit left on the surface tends to burn.

9 Bake in the lower third of the oven for $2\frac{1}{2} - 3$ hours or until a skewer inserted into the centre of the cake comes out clean.

10 Cool in the tin for 10 minutes before turning out on to a wire rack. Leave to cool completely. Wrap the cake in kitchen foil when cold. After 1 day and at least 2 days before decorating, skewer the cake all over and drip 55 ml|2 fl oz brandy or sherry into the holes. Wrap again in foil and store in a cool place but not the refrigerator.

Fruit Cakes: What has gone wrong when...

The top of the cake is domed.
- The well in the centre of the cake mixture was not large enough.
- The tin was too small.
- The oven was too hot.

The fruit has sunk to the bottom of the cake.
- The cake mixture was too thin.
- The fruit was not mixed in well enough.

The cake has a hard, dark crust around the outside.
- The oven was too hot.
- The cake was overbaked.
- The cake tin was not wrapped in newspaper.

Whisking Method

In the whisking method the only raising agent is the air that has been trapped in the cake mixture during mixing. The texture of the cake is entirely dependent on the expansive properties of the eggs and the skill of the cook. Beating eggs causes the proteins in the eggs to unwind and stretch. This results in an expansion in volume of the egg as the unwound proteins trap tiny air bubbles. When the cake is baked, the air expands in the heat of the oven and the cake rises. *Whisked Sponge* (see below), *Swiss Roll* (see below) and *Génoise* (see below) are examples of cakes made by this method. The American cake called Angel Cake because of its white colour is made with the egg whites only and does not contain any fat.

Preparing a tin for cakes made by the whisking method
The cake tin needs to be brushed with a thin film of flavourless oil, then lined on the base with greaseproof paper or baking parchment, as for cakes made by the *melting method* (above). The paper is brushed again with oil, then the tin is given a

dusting of caster sugar and flour. To dust a tin, place a tablespoon of sugar in the tin and tip it to coat the tin with the sugar. Invert the tin over the sink and rap the tin lightly on the tap to knock out any excess sugar. Repeat the process with the flour.

A Swiss Roll is made in a special shallow baking tin approximately 25 × 35 cm | 10 × 14 in. A roasting tin of the same size can also be used. If using a Swiss Roll tin, line as for whisked sponge, above. To make a paper case, cut a doubled piece of baking parchment 10 cm | 4 in longer and wider than a sheet of A4 paper. Fold the parchment over the A4 paper to form the sides. Remove the A4 paper. Fold the corners as shown in the diagram and secure with a paper clip. Place on a baking sheet.

Making a Swiss Roll tin

A Génoise is traditionally baked in a moule à manqué tin, which is a tin with sloping sides approximately 20 cm | 8 in in diameter at the base and 22.5 cm | 9 in at the rim (see **Kitchen Equipment**, page 55). The base of the Génoise becomes the top of the cake once it is baked. A Génoise is usually split in half, then filled with a rich buttercream.

Beating the eggs and sugar to the ribbon

The classic Whisked Sponge is made by whisking the eggs with the sugar over a pan of steaming water until they are thick enough to leave a ribbon trail over the top of the mixture when the beaters are lifted. The bowl should not touch the water or it is likely that the eggs will become too hot and cook, losing their elasticity. The gentle heat of the steam speeds up the dissolving of the sugar and slightly thickens the eggs, encouraging the mixture to hold the maximum number of air bubbles. The mixture should change colour from yellow to nearly white and increase to 4 times its initial volume. When the mixture leaves a ribbon trail, the bowl is removed from the heat source and whisking continues until the mixture has cooled to room temperature.

A more complicated technique for making a Whisked Sponge requires separating the eggs then whisking the yolks with the sugar over heat as described above. The whites are whisked separately, then folded in alternately with the flour. Some recipes will call for a portion of the sugar to be whisked into the whites to make a meringue. This makes the whites more stable and less likely to lose volume when folded into the yolk and sugar mixture. See recipe for *Biscuit Fin au Beurre*, below.

Folding-in technique

Folding in the flour

The flour is sifted over the surface of the egg and sugar mixture and is folded in with a large metal spoon as quickly as possible, taking care to preserve the volume. The mixture is tipped into the prepared tin and gently eased to the edges. A whisked mixture tends to be self-levelling, so perfection is not required here.

Baking a Whisked Sponge

Whisked Sponges are baked at 180°C | 350°F | gas mark 4 in the middle of the oven. The cake needs to be placed in the oven as soon as it is mixed as the mixture is very unstable. The door of the oven must remain closed for 25 minutes. Only then can the door be opened a crack to check the cake, as Whisked Sponges are very prone to collapse. The cake is done when it is well-risen and golden-brown and will look slightly wrinkled around the edges. It will spring back when touched lightly in the centre with a fingertip. If you listen carefully you will be able to hear a faint creaky, popping sound when you press the cake. Immediately after removing the cake from the oven, place it upside down on a wire rack to cool. Leave the tin sitting over the cake for about 10 minutes. This keeps the cake stretched and gives a more open texture.

When the tin is cool enough to touch, remove it from the cake and carefully peel off the lining paper to allow the steam to escape. Cakes cooked in a moule à manqué tin are served upside down, i.e. the side with the smallest diameter is at the top, so the cake does not need to be turned over once it has been unmoulded from the tin.

Whisked Sponge

oil, for greasing
extra sugar and flour, for dusting
85 g | 3 oz plain flour, sifted
a pinch of salt
3 medium eggs

85 g | 3 oz caster sugar
1½ tablespoons warm water
2–3 drops vanilla essence
3 tablespoons warmed jam

1 Preheat the oven to 180°C | 350°F | gas mark 4.
2 Prepare a moule à manqué tin by brushing the bottom and sides with a little oil. Line the base with greaseproof paper or baking parchment, then brush with a little oil if greaseproof is used. Dust the tin with sugar then flour.
3 Sift the flour with the salt.
4 Put the eggs and sugar into a heatproof bowl set over a saucepan of steaming water. Whisk the mixture, preferably with an electric hand-held whisk, until pale and thick. The mixture should leave a ribbon trail when the beaters are lifted.
5 Remove the bowl from the water and continue to whisk for 2–3 minutes or until the mixture is no longer warm to the touch.
6 Using a large metal spoon, fold the water and vanilla into the mixture.
7 Sift the flour over the surface of the mixture, then fold in.
8 Pour the mixture into the tin.
9 Bake in the oven for 25–30 minutes or until no impression remains when the sponge is lightly pressed with a fingertip and the edges look very slightly shrunken. When pressed the cake will sound 'creaky'.
10 Allow the cake to cool in the tin for 5 minutes, then turn out on to a wire rack and leave to cool completely before removing the lining paper.
11 When the cake is cool, split it in half and fill with the jam. Replace the top and dredge with caster sugar.

Ribbon trail

Swiss Roll

The mixture for a Whisked Sponge can be used to make a Swiss Roll.

1 Prepare a 25 × 35 cm | 10 × 14 in tin as for Whisked Sponge (above). Bake for 12–15 minutes. Allow to cool for 15 minutes.
2 Place a piece of greaseproof paper on a work surface and sprinkle it evenly with caster sugar. Loosen the edge of the baked sponge with a knife, then invert the sponge on to the sugared paper. Peel away the lining paper. Trim the edges of the cake.
3 Sieve 3 tablespoons raspberry or strawberry jam. While the cake is still warm, spread it with the jam.
4 Using the paper underneath the cake to help you, roll up the cake firmly from one of the shorter sides.
5 Turn on to a serving dish and dredge with caster sugar.

NOTE: If the cake is to be filled with cream, it must cool completely before filling. To help rolling and prevent cracking, roll the unfilled cake while still warm. Wrap the rolled cake in greaseproof paper and until leave cold. Unroll carefully, spread with 200 ml | 7 fl oz lightly whipped double cream and roll up again.

Génoise

A Génoise is a Whisked Sponge to which melted butter has been added, producing a light cake with a soft crumb. It is named after the Italian city of Genoa where bakers have made this cake since the seventeenth century. It is a particularly tricky cake to make because the texture depends on the correct amount of whisking and gentle folding. The addition of butter often causes the foam to deflate, particularly in *Génoise Fine* which contains twice as much butter as *Génoise Commune* and so is more difficult to make.

Decorating a Génoise

Génoise is used most frequently for a filled layer cake. (For instructions on how to cut a cake into layers and for recipes for fillings, see **Cake Icings and Decoration**, page 155.) A Génoise is best made the day before filling so that it is easier to cut into layers. A filled cake can be kept for 3 days in the refrigerator. An unfilled cake can be frozen for up to 1 month.

Génoise Commune

oil, for greasing tin
extra sugar and flour, for dusting
4 medium eggs
125 g|4½ oz plain flour

a pinch of salt
125 g|4½ oz caster sugar
55 g|2 oz unsalted butter, melted and cooled

1 Preheat the oven to 180°C|350°F|gas mark 4. Place the shelf in the middle of the oven. The eggs should be placed in warm water for 1–2 minutes. Sift the flour with the salt.

2 Prepare a 20 cm|8 in moule à manqué or deep cake tin as described above under *Preparing a tin for cakes made by the whisking method.*

3 Break the eggs into a large heatproof bowl and add the sugar.

4 Whisk the eggs and sugar with an electric hand-held whisk to combine them, then place the bowl over a pan of steaming water. Whisk until the mixture is pale and thick and feels warm to the touch. It should leave a ribbon trail that holds its shape for just 5 seconds on the surface of the mixture when the beaters are lifted. The mixture will feel slightly warm.

5 Remove the bowl from the pan of water and continue beating until the mixture is no longer warm to the touch, about 1–2 minutes.

6 Pour the butter around the edge of the bowl and give it 2–3 folds, with a large metal spoon.

7 Sift half the flour over the surface of the mixture and give 2–3 folds to partially fold it in. Sift over the remaining flour and fold in.

8 Pour the mixture into the tin. Bake in the oven for 30–35 minutes. The cake is done when it springs back when pressed lightly with a fingertip and has pulled away from the top edge of the tin.

9 Turn the cake upside down, still in the tin, on to a wire rack and allow to cool for 10 minutes before removing the tin. Cool completely before removing the lining paper.

VARIATION

Chocolate Génoise: Substitute 30 g|1 oz cocoa powder for 30 g|1 oz flour. Sift the flour with the cocoa powder 3 times before folding in, to combine and aerate.

Génoise Fine

This version of Génoise has nearly twice as much butter as *Génoise Commune* and less flour, giving it a more tender texture and a richer flavour. It is also more difficult to make.

oil, for greasing
extra sugar and flour, for dusting
4 medium eggs
100 g|3½ oz plain flour

a pinch of salt
125 g|4½ oz caster sugar
100 g|3½ oz unsalted butter, melted and cooled

Make as for *Génoise Commune*, above.

Biscuit Fin au Beurre

This recipe makes a Génoise with a slightly firmer texture. It is particularly good for cutting into small cakes to ice with *Fondant* (see **Cake Icings and Decoration**, page 159). Use the recipe for *Génoise*, above, following the directions below.

1 Preheat the oven to 180°C | 350°F | gas mark 4. Place the shelf in the middle of the oven. If the eggs are cold, place them in warm water for 1–2 minutes.

2 For a large cake prepare a 20 cm | 8 in moule à manqué tin as described under *Preparing a tin for cakes made by the whisking method*, above. For a cake to cut into smaller cakes prepare a paper case as described under *Making a paper case for a Swiss Roll*, above, and place on a baking sheet.

3 Place 1 whole egg and 3 yolks into a heatproof bowl with all but 1 tablespoon of the sugar. Place the whites in a large clean bowl and set aside.

4 Whisk the eggs and sugar with an electric hand-whisk to combine them, then place the bowl over a pan of steaming water. Whisk until the mixture is pale and thick and feels warm to the touch. It should leave a ribbon trail that holds its shape for 5 seconds on the surface of the mixture when the beaters are lifted.

5 Remove the bowl from the pan of water and continue mixing until the mixture no longer feels warm to the touch, about 1–2 minutes.

6 Pour the butter around the edge of the bowl and give it 2–3 folds with a large metal spoon. Sift half the flour over the surface and give 2–3 folds to partially fold in, then repeat with the remaining flour.

7 Whisk the egg whites until stiff peaks just form then whisk in the reserved tablespoon of sugar. Whisk again for 5 seconds.

8 Fold 1 large tablespoon of the whites into the mixture to loosen it, then carefully fold in the remaining whites.

9 Turn the mixture into the prepared tin or paper case and bake until it is golden brown and firm to the touch, about 30 minutes for a large cake or 15–20 minutes for a cake in a Swiss Roll case.

10 Cool a large cake upside down on a wire rack, removing the tin after 10 minutes. If you have made a cake in a Swiss Roll tin, place it right side up on a wire rack to cool. Cool completely before removing the lining paper.

Génoise: What has gone wrong when...

The egg and sugar mixture fails to double in volume.
- The water underneath the bowl is not hot enough.
- The mixture has not been whisked for long enough.

The egg and sugar mixture cooks around the edge of the bowl.
- The water underneath the bowl is too hot.

The cake has bubbles on the surface.
- The oven was not hot enough.

The cake is badly risen.
- The eggs were not whisked enough or they were whisked too much before the flour was added.
- The mixture was overfolded when the butter and/or flour were added.

The cake is badly risen and has a very hard crust.
- The egg and sugar mixture was too hot when the flour was folded in.

There are pockets of flour in the cake.
- The flour was not folded in well enough.
- The butter was not properly folded into the cake before the flour, so the flour formed lumps with some of the butter.

The cake has a greasy, dense layer at the bottom.
- The eggs and sugar were not whisked enough before the butter was added.
- The butter was not folded in well enough.
- The butter was too cool when folded in.

The cake sinks badly in the middle.
- The cake was not baked for long enough.
- The oven door was opened before the cake was set.

Pain de Gênes

This Genoese sponge cake was invented in the nineteenth century in France to mark the siege of the city of Genoa. Developed by the chef Fauvel who was working for the pastry cook Chiboust, it is thought that the cake was flavoured with almonds because almonds were the only food the citizens of Genoa had left to eat before they surrendered.

This is a tricky cake to make because the ground almonds make the mixture heavy. It is very moist and is firm enough to use for *Petits Fours* (see **Pâtisserie**, page 531).

melted butter, for greasing	½ teaspoon baking powder
110 g | 4 oz blanched almonds	a pinch of salt
140 g | 5 oz caster sugar	85 g | 3 oz butter, melted and cooled
3 medium eggs	1 tablespoon Amaretto or Kirsch
55 g | 2 oz potato starch or flour	icing sugar, to dust

1 Preheat the oven to 180°C | 350°F | gas mark 4.
2 Brush a moule à manqué tin or 20 cm | 8 in round deep cake tin with melted butter. Line with baking parchment and prepare as for a Whisked Sponge.

3 Grind the almonds finely with 1 tablespoon of the sugar.

4 Whisk the eggs with the remaining sugar, using an electric hand-held whisk, until thick and mousse-like and a ribbon falls from the beaters when lifted.

5 Sift the potato starch or flour with the baking powder, salt and ground almonds.

6 Fold half of the flour mixture into the egg mixture.

7 Fold in the melted butter and the Amaretto or Kirsch.

8 Fold in the remaining flour.

9 Turn the mixture into the tin and bake on the middle shelf for 35–40 minutes. The cake should be brown and spring back when pressed lightly in the centre.

10 Allow to cool in the tin for 5 minutes, then turn out on to a wire rack and leave to cool completely before peeling off the lining paper.

11 Serve dusted with icing sugar.

NOTE: This cake is very delicate and prone to falling. Do not open the oven door before 35 minutes has passed. For help in correcting problems, see *Génoise: What has gone wrong when* ... above.

Cake Icings and Decoration

The art of cake decoration is a specialist skill requiring great dexterity, artistic ability and much patience. This section is an introduction for cooks whose forays into cake decoration are reserved for Christmas, birthdays and perhaps the occasional wedding or christening cake. A list of specialist books can be found in the bibliography. (See the previous section, *Cakes*, for cake recipes.)

Cutting a Cake into Layers

To cut a cake into layers, use a large serrated bread knife to cut a horizontal groove halfway down the sides of the cake. Place two cocktail sticks one over the top of the other, one near the top of the cake and the other near the bottom; this will help you line the cake up later. Place your hand on the top of the cake, then use a sawing motion to cut the cake in half horizontally, keeping your knife level using the groove as your guide. **(a)**

Cutting a cake into layers (a)

A day-old Génoise can be cut into layers using a long piece of thin cotton thread. (A freshly baked genoise will tear instead of cut with this method.) Cut a groove around the sides of the cake as described above. Place the thread around the cake in the groove. Cross the ends over and pull gently. **(b)**

Cutting a cake into layers (b)

Traditional Decorations

Victoria Sandwich

Traditionally a Victoria sandwich is served with the centre filled with a thin layer of sieved raspberry or strawberry jam or with a layer of lemon curd (see *Eggs*, page 230). The top of the cake is sprinkled with caster sugar.

This cake can be filled and/or iced with Simple Butter Icing (see below), if desired.

Whisked Sponge

These cakes are very light and often slightly dry. They are nicest filled with a mixture of lightly whipped cream and soft fruit, then sprinkled with caster or icing sugar.

Génoise

A classic Génoise is usually split into two or three layers (see above) and then filled and iced with a buttercream (see below). These cakes can be elaborately decorated with rosettes, crushed praline (see *Caramel*, page 178), caraque (see *Chocolate*, page 195), toasted flaked or nibbed almonds or candied julienne citrus peel (see below).

Icings

Simple Butter Icing

FILLS AND COVERS A 20 CM 8 IN CAKE

225 g 8 oz unsalted butter, softened
170 g 6 oz icing sugar, sifted

1 teaspoon vanilla essence

1 Beat the butter until light and creamy.
2 Gradually beat in the icing sugar.
3 Flavour with the vanilla.

Simple Chocolate Butter Icing

FILLS AND COVERS A 20 CM 8 IN CAKE

225 g 8 oz plain chocolate, chopped
2 tablespoons water
2 teaspoons instant coffee granules

110 g 4 oz unsalted butter, softened
225 g 8 oz icing sugar, sifted

1 Place the chocolate with the water and the coffee in a heatproof bowl placed over, but not touching, simmering water and stir until melted. Remove from the heat and allow the mixture to cool until it no longer feels warm.
2 Beat the butter until light and creamy. Gradually beat in the icing sugar.
3 Beat in the melted chocolate a little at a time. If the icing is very soft, refrigerate for 15 minutes then beat again before using.

Buttercreams

The following buttercreams are cooked icings and require more skill and time than the Simple Butter Icings, above. The buttercreams, with their rich flavour and light texture, are used for filling and icing Génoise cakes (see *Cakes*, page 150).

Coffee Custard Buttercream

Toasted flaked almonds pressed on to the sides of the cake would complement the coffee flavouring in this buttercream.

Have a bowl and a sieve ready to strain the custard before beginning to cook.

FILLS AND COVERS A 20 CM|8 IN CAKE

225 ml|8 fl oz milk
170 g|6 oz caster sugar
2 tablespoons instant coffee granules

3 egg yolks
170 g|6 oz unsalted butter, softened

1 Place the milk with half of the sugar and the coffee granules in a small saucepan and heat until the mixture steams.
2 Place the egg yolks in a bowl with the remaining sugar and stir with a wooden spoon until pale and thick.
3 Slowly pour the hot milk on to the yolk and sugar mixture in a thin stream while continuing to stir.
4 Rinse the saucepan and return the mixture to the pan. Cook the custard over a medium-low heat, stirring, until thickened (do not allow to boil). It should coat the back of a wooden spoon.
5 Strain the custard to remove any eggy threads and allow to cool.
6 Beat the butter until very soft and creamy.
7 Beat the cooled custard into the butter, a tablespoonful at a time. The buttercream is ready to use as required.

NOTE: If the mixture curdles when the custard is beaten into the butter, it is likely that it has become too cold. Place the bowl over a saucepan of steaming water and beat vigorously.

Crème au Beurre Meringue

This filling has a cooked meringue base which makes it very light and fluffy. It is particularly suitable for flavouring with chocolate. For a dark, fudgy chocolate icing use ganache (see **Chocolate**, page 197).

FILLS AND COVERS A 20 CM|8 IN CAKE

3 egg whites
170 g|6 oz icing sugar
250 g|9 oz unsalted butter, softened

Suggested flavourings

200 g|7 oz plain chocolate, melted, or finely grated zest of 2–3 oranges, lemons or limes, or strong coffee essence to taste

1 Place the egg whites in a large bowl and sift the icing sugar over the top. Stir to combine.
2 Place the bowl over a saucepan of simmering water and beat, preferably with an electric hand-held whisk, until the mixture is thick and glossy.

3 Remove from the heat and continue to whisk until the mixture is thick enough to hold a teaspoon inserted into the mixture in a vertical position.

4 Beat the butter with the whisk until soft and creamy. If using chocolate, substitute the chocolate for half of the butter. Beat the cooled melted chocolate into the butter.

5 Gradually beat the butter into the meringue.

6 Citrus or coffee flavourings should be added at this point. The buttercream is ready to use as required.

Crème au Beurre Mousseline

This is a rich, creamy cake filling. It is particularly suitable for flavouring with citrus juice and zest.

FILLS AND COVERS A 20 CM | 8 IN CAKE

170 g | 6 oz granulated sugar
170 ml | 6 fl oz citrus juice or water
4 egg yolks

grated zest of 1 lemon and 1 orange
225 g | 8 oz unsalted butter, softened

1 Place the sugar and the juice or water in a small saucepan over low heat. Stir gently to help the sugar dissolve. If desired, a sugar thermometer can be placed in the pan at this point.

2 Place the yolks in a large bowl and stir in the citrus zest.

3 When the sugar has dissolved, raise the heat and boil the mixture until it reaches 120°C | 250°F, (see **Sugar, Sweeteners and Sugar Syrups,** *Stages of Sugar Syrups,* page 701).

4 Immediately pour the boiling syrup on to the yolks while whisking, taking care not to pour the syrup over the beaters. Continue whisking until the mixture is thick and cool.

5 Beat the butter with the whisk until it is soft and creamy.

6 To combine the yolk mixture with the butter, gradually whisk the thinner of the two mixtures into the other.

Buttercreams: What has gone wrong when...

The mixture splits.
- The butter was too cold.
- The flavouring liquid was added too quickly.
- The flavouring liquid was too cold.

To correct, place the bowl over a second bowl of steaming water and beat vigorously.

Decorating with Citrus Zest

Cakes flavoured with citrus can be decorated with strips of zest called needleshreds. Pare 5 cm | 2 in strips of zest from the fruit, taking care not to cut into the bitter white pith. Scrape any pith from the back of the zest with a knife. Cut the zest into 1 mm julienne strips (see **Knife Skills**, page 71). Boil the zest until just tender, about 3 minutes, in a sugar syrup (see **Sugar, Sweeteners and Sugar Syrups**, page 699) made with 150 ml | ¼ pint water and 75 g | 2½ oz granulated sugar. Drain in a sieve, then separate the shreds and roll them in granulated sugar.

Fondant Icing

Fondant icing is the soft sugary icing often used on commercial cakes. It makes a good surface for piping messages or decorations. It can also be tinted with a little food colour. Fondant icing can also be used to coat small pieces of the genoise type cake, *Biscuit Fin au Beurre*, to make Petits Fours (see **Cakes**, page 152).

Fondant is made from sugar syrup that has been taken to the soft ball stage then crystallised slowly. It can be tricky to make so a familiarity with sugar syrups (see **Sugar, Sweeteners and Sugar Syrups**, page 699) is very useful. The glucose syrup helps to prevent rapid crystallization. When making both fondant and fudge (see **Sugar, Sweeteners and Sugar Syrups**, page 699) it is important that the mixture cools slowly so that the crystals formed are small.

A 225 g | 8 oz sugar quantity of fondant icing is enough to ice the top and sides of a 20 cm | 8 in cake. Fondant can be stored for several weeks in the refrigerator if it is closely covered with clingfilm.

225 g | 8 oz granulated or loaf sugar
110 ml | 4 fl oz water

½ teaspoon liquid glucose or a pinch of cream of tartar mixed with 1 teaspoon water

1 Dissolve the sugar in the water over a low heat without boiling.
2 Mix in the glucose syrup or cream of tartar mixed with water.
3 Wash down the sides of the pan with a pastry brush dipped into water then bring to the boil.
4 Boil until the syrup reaches 116°C | 240°F on a sugar thermometer, the soft ball stage (see **Sugar, Sweeteners and Sugar Syrups**, *Stages of Sugar Syrups*, page 701). Stop the sugar from cooking any further by dipping the base of the saucepan in cold water. Let it stand for 5 minutes.
5 Dampen a marble or metal work surface and pour the syrup on to the surface.
6 Using a palette knife, work the syrup back and forth, folding the outsides of the mixture into the centre. Continue this for about 5 minutes until the mixture starts to crystallize. This happens when the mixture turns white and is no longer workable with the palette knife.
7 Immediately dampen your hands and knead the fondant until smooth, for about 2 minutes.
8 Place the ball of fondant into a dampened bowl. Place a piece of dampened kitchen paper directly on the surface of the fondant and then cover with clingfilm. Store in the refrigerator until required.

To use:

1 Place the bowl containing the fondant in a sauté pan with hot water to come up the sides of the bowl to the level of the fondant. Keep the water warm by placing it over heat, but do not allow it to boil. The fondant must not become warmer than 66°C|155°F or it might split.

2 Melt the fondant to the consistency of double cream, thinning it with a little light sugar syrup (see *Sugar, Sweeteners and Sugar Syrups*, page 699). The fondant will be at a usable consistency when it reaches 48°C|120°F.

3 Brush the surface of the cake with a thin apricot glaze (see *Pâtisserie*, page 533). Place the cake on a wire rack set over a plate. Any fondant that drips on to the plate can be scraped up and re-melted.

4 Pour the fondant over the surface of the cake or using a large metal spoon quickly *napper* the fondant over the items to be covered. The fondant will set within a minute but do not move the cakes immediately or the fondant might crack.

Fondant Icing: What has gone wrong when...

The fondant has crystallised and is hard and crumbly.
- The sugar syrup was taken to too high a temperature.
- The fondant was not kneaded as soon as the mixture turned white.
  It cannot be used.

The fondant has turned white but it is still sticky and stretchy.
- The sugar syrup was not heated to a high enough temperature. As long as it is possible to knead, the fondant can be used although it will take longer to set.

The fondant is lumpy.
- The fondant was not kneaded quickly and/or efficiently enough. Continue kneading and crush the lumps with your fingers.

Decorating Fruit Cakes

Traditionally fruit cakes are served at weddings, christenings and for Christmas. They are covered with marzipan then with either a hard white icing called *Royal Icing* (see below) or with a fondant icing (see above). The marzipan adds flavour to the confection while protecting the pristine white icing from being stained by the rich fruit cake. It will take about a week to cover a cake with marzipan and 3 layers of royal icing allowing for drying time in between coats.

Marzipan or Uncooked Almond Paste

If you are concerned about salmonella in eggs, pasteurized eggs can be used in the following recipe.

COVERS A 20–22 CM | 8–9 IN CAKE

225 g | 8 oz caster sugar
225 g | 8 oz icing sugar, plus extra for dusting
450 g | 1 lb ground almonds
2 egg yolks

2 medium eggs, beaten
2 teaspoons lemon juice
6 drops of vanilla extract

1 Sift the sugars together into a bowl and mix in the ground almonds.
2 Mix together the yolks, whole eggs, lemon juice and vanilla.
3 Stir into the sugar and almond mixture, beating briefly with a wooden spoon.
4 Lightly dust a work surface with icing sugar, then knead the paste lightly. Take care not to overwork or the oil will be drawn out of the almonds, making the paste greasy.
5 Wrap well in clingfilm and store in a cool place for up to 24 hours or use immediately.

Covering a Round Cake 20–22 cm | 8–9 in with Marzipan

110 g | 4 oz apricot jam
lemon juice
icing sugar, for dusting

a cake board 5 cm | 2 in larger in diameter than the cake

1 Heat the apricot jam until it just starts to boil, then pass it through a sieve to remove any pieces of fruit.
2 Sharpen the jam with a little lemon juice.
3 If the cake is not level, trim it with a serrated knife. Turn it upside down on to a cake board so that the smooth base becomes the top.
4 Using a piece of string, measure from the bottom edge on one side of the cake across the top and down to the bottom edge on the opposite side.
5 Brush the cake all over with the warm jam.
6 Sift a little icing sugar on to a work surface. Roll the marzipan out into a round, using the string to give you the diameter.
7 Place the cake on the marzipan, jam side down.
8 Wash your hands.
9 Carefully smooth the marzipan up on to the sides of the cake, taking care not to tear or fold the marzipan.
10 Turn the cake over and place on the cake board.
11 Trim any excess marzipan from the edges and/or fill any gaps with a little extra marzipan.

12 Let the cake stand for 24–48 hours to allow the surface of the marzipan to dry slightly so that the oil from the almonds does not stain the icing.

Covering a Square Cake with Marzipan

1 Measure the length of one side of the cake with a piece of string.
2 Take two-thirds of the marzipan. On a work surface lightly dusted with sifted icing sugar roll out 4 pieces to the length of the string and to the depth of the cake.
3 Brush one side of the cake with the warm, sieved jam.
4 Pick the cake up and press the side with the jam on to a strip of marzipan. Repeat with the remaining 3 sides.
5 Place on a cake board 5 cm│2 in larger than the diameter of the cake.
6 Roll the remaining marzipan into a square to fit the top of the cake. Place in position and roll gently with a rolling pin.
7 Use a knife to trim the edges. Allow to dry for 24–48 hours.

Icing a cake with ready-made fondant

This fondant remains soft and easy to cut. It is also relatively easy to work with. Use 450 g│1 lb ready-made fondant for a 20–22 cm│8–9 in cake covered with marzipan.

1 Roll the fondant on to a surface lightly dusted with sifted icing sugar, following the method with the string described above under *Covering a Round Cake with Marzipan*.
2 Lightly brush the marzipan with vodka or water to make the surface tacky.
3 Lift the fondant from the work surface, using the rolling pin. Guide the fondant over the cake, gently pressing it on to the marzipan.
4 Trim the edges if necessary.

Icing a Cake with Royal Icing

Royal Icing is the hard, usually white, icing used to coat traditional wedding fruit cakes. The icing is spread on to the cake in several layers to produce a perfectly smooth surface. Additional piping is then done to decorate the surface. Icing a cake with Royal Icing is an advanced skill and many specialist books have been written on the subject (see **Bibliography and Suggested Further Reading**, page 771). A fruit cake covered with Royal Icing should keep for several weeks in a dry, airtight container.

Royal Icing can be made using powdered egg whites or pasteurized egg whites, to avoid the risk of salmonella contamination.

Equipment

To ice a cake with Royal Icing you will need a cake turntable, a cake scraper and a metal ruler.

Consistency of Royal Icing

A marzipanned fruit cake needs to be covered with 2–3 coats of Royal Icing. Each coat requires icing of a slightly different consistency.

- **First coat:** The icing needs to be very thick. It should stand up in stiff peaks when the beaters are lifted.

- **Second coat:** The icing is a little thinner than the first coat. The tips of the peaks should flop over when the beaters are lifted.

- **Third coat or float:** The icing should be of thick pouring consistency.

Royal Icing

MAKES ONE COAT OF ICING FOR A 22.5 CM│9 IN CAKE

500 g│1.1 lb icing sugar   2–3 egg whites

Additions to Royal Icing

a drop of blue food colouring

1 teaspoon lemon juice per 500 g│1.1lb icing sugar

1 teaspoon glycerine per 500 g│1.1lb icing sugar

1 Sift the icing sugar to ensure the icing is lump-free.
2 Mix the egg whites with 3 tablespoons of the icing sugar and add lemon juice

and/or glycerine if required. Lemon juice will make the icing sharper and less sickly. Glycerine keeps the icing softer. Without glycerine the icing will eventually harden to the extent that it is impossible to cut. However, do not add more glycerine than specified or the icing will not hold its shape. If the cake is to be served within 24 hours of icing, glycerine is unnecessary.

3 Gradually add the remaining sugar.

4 Mix well until the icing holds its shape without sagging. Add a drop of blue colouring to counteract the tendency of icing to look yellow.

5 Cover the surface of the icing with a damp cloth, then with clingfilm. Allow to stand for several hours or overnight so that any air bubbles in the icing can work their way to the surface.

Using Royal Icing

For the first coat: Use a small spoonful of the icing to stick the cake to the cake board. The top of the cake is iced first, then allowed to dry overnight before the sides are iced. If the cake is square, it is iced in 3 stages, with the first pair of opposing sides being allowed to dry before the second pair of sides is iced.

Icing the top

1 Spoon half the icing on top of the cake with a palette knife, then, using a paddling action to remove any air bubbles, spread the icing to the edges.

2 Pull a straight metal ruler across the icing to give a smooth surface. Dampening the ruler slightly under the hot tap makes it easier to use.

3 Use the palette knife to remove any excess icing that has fallen down the sides of the cake.

4 Allow to dry for 24 hours.

Icing the sides

Smoothing the royal icing on a turntable

1 Place the cake on its board on an icing turntable or upturned bowl.

2 Spread the icing on to the sides, using the palette knife.

3 Use a cake scraper to smooth the icing around the edges of the cake, holding the straight edge against the cake and perpendicular to the board. Try to do this in one smooth motion.

4 Allow the sides to dry for 24 hours.

For the second coat: Apply the second coat in the same manner as the first coat, using a slightly thinner icing. Allow to dry for 24 hours between coats.

For the third coat or float: A three-tier wedding cake or a cake that has not been perfectly iced may need a third coat. This coat is often called the float because it is very thin.

Pipe a thin line around the outer edge of the cake, using the icing from the second coat. Add a little egg white to the remaining icing to make it the consistency of double cream. Place it in a piping bag, wrap in clingfilm and allow to stand for at least 30 minutes. This will allow any air bubbles to work their way out of the icing. Use the piping bag to guide the icing on to the top of the cake, avoiding the piped line. Use the handle of a teaspoon to move the runny icing to meet the piped line. The piped line will prevent the icing from running off.

Decorating with Royal Icing

Have a clear idea of your design before beginning. Patterns can be drawn on to tracing paper then transferred to the cake by pricking the iced surface with a pin. Fill the piping bags only half full.

Shells: Use a star nozzle. Hold the bag at an angle of 45°. Pipe a shell, then release the pressure on the bag and begin a new shell one-eighth of the way up the first one so that each new shell overlaps its predecessor.

Star piping: Fit the bag with a star nozzle. Hold the nozzle upright, immediately above and almost touching the top of the cake. Squeeze gently from the top of the bag. Stop pressing and lift the bag away.

Dot or pearl piping: Use a plain nozzle and pipe as for stars (above). If the dots are too small, use a larger nozzle.

Straight lines: Use a plain nozzle. Hold the point of the nozzle about 4 cm | 1½ in above the surface of the cake and, pressing gently as you go, guide rather than drag the icing into place. The icing can be directed into place more easily if is allowed to hang from the tube.

Run-in work: Use a writing nozzle to pipe the outline of a design on to baking parchment. Float runny icing into the centre and allow to set for at least 24 hours. Lift off and stick on to the cake with wet icing.

Piping with Royal Icing: What has gone wrong when...

The lines are broken.
- The icing was too stiff.
- The icing was pulled along rather than being allowed to flow from the nozzle.
- The icing contained air bubbles.

The lines are wobbly.
- The icing was squeezed out of the bag too quickly.
- The icing was too liquid.

The lines are flattened.
- The icing was too liquid.
- The nozzle was held too near to the surface of the cake.

Canapés

Canapé is a French word meaning couch, which has come to be used for small pieces of food usually served on small pieces of toast or dried bread. *Amuse-gueule* is another French term (literally, 'amusement of the mouth') for these small savouries served at the table before a meal.

The canapé party as we now know it first became popular in the 1920s when canapés were served with the then newly fashionable cocktails. Canapés are often served at drinks parties where they are useful for lining the stomach and whetting the appetite, in addition to being delicious in their own right. As canapés are consumed with the fingers, usually by someone who is holding a drink in the other hand, they must be easy to eat and small enough to be consumed in one or two bites.

A drinks party is an efficient and relatively easy way to entertain a large number of people. In England, people are invited for drinks at a stated time: it is generally expected that the party will last about 2 hours after which guests will make their way on to lunch or dinner. If the party is expected to last longer, the quantities recommended below should be increased accordingly. Generally the canapés are not meant to take the place of a meal unless served in copious quantities.

If you are catering as a business and have been asked to prepare canapés, discuss the purpose and the length of the proposed party with the host before preparing the menu and giving a quotation.

Food for a 'finger buffet' is made larger than canapés. It should be large enough to eat in about 4 bites. At finger buffets the food is served from a buffet table on to small tea plates, then picked up with the fingers to eat. Food served in this manner takes the place of a meal, often lunch, so frequently includes sandwiches.

What to Serve

The type of ingredients that can be used for canapés is only limited by your imagination. Many of the Asian street foods, such as satay (marinated chicken, pork or beef with a peanut sauce) and kofta (spiced minced meat skewers) work particularly well for drinks parties. Many recipes can be prepared in miniature sizes, such as choux-buns, pastry cases and bouchées (see *Pastry*, page 525), Yorkshire Puddings and tiny Drop Scones (see *Batters*, pages 114 and 113).

The considerations given in the *Menu Planning* section (see page 5) should be reviewed when planning the food for a drinks party. The food served should be attractive to look at and full of flavour. Have a mixture of hot and cold food, some fish canapés, some meat and some vegetarian. Dips (see below) are always popular and can be served with raw vegetables, small pieces of French bread, or with any of the many varieties of crisps and savoury biscuits now available in supermarkets. Include popular, familiar food, such as smoked salmon, prawns and/or cocktail sausages, as well as a few more exotic canapés.

Plan the menu so that approximately half the canapés are served cold and the others hot, bearing in mind that the hot canapés will need last-minute attention. If desired, have a couple of sweet offerings to finish the menu.

It is usually better to serve only one or two types of canapé on each tray so that guests do not have to stop their conversation to study the food. Serving the canapés in this way also means that the trays don't become picked over as everyone vies for the favourite prawn. Arrange the food carefully on the trays, leaving enough space to make it easy to pick up the items with the fingers.

Be inventive with your choice of trays, bowls and garnishes. Lacquered slates can look stunning, decorated with a few leaves or a single flower. Strew a simple basket with a bunch of flat-leaf parsley. Savoy cabbages and other fruits and vegetables can be hollowed out to serve as containers for dips. See **Food Presentation** (page 11) for additional considerations.

Wait until the first guests have had their drinks in hand for about 15 minutes, then start by offering one or two cold canapés. Begin with the milder-flavoured ones, working up to the spicier flavours. Reserve the hot food until the bulk of the guests have arrived, then alternate the cold canapés with the hot. Sweet canapés to serve near the end of the party could include mini mince pies or Christmas puddings at Christmas, or tiny chocolate brownies or mini *tartes au citron*.

How Much to Serve

Choose a variety of canapés that work together well as a menu. The following quantities are recommended.

Pre-lunch drinks: 8–10 items per head if the guests will be going on to a meal.
Pre-dinner drinks: 10–12 items per head if the guests will be going on to a meal.
Before a meal at the same venue: 2–3 items per head.
As a substitute for a first course: 5–6 items per head.
As a substitute for a meal, e.g. wedding reception, christening: 15–16 items per head.

Organizing Your Time

Preparing the food for a drinks party can be very labour-intensive because the items are small and need individual attention. For a party of 100 guests for which 10 different types of canapé are prepared, it is likely that the preparation will take about 40 hours.

When preparing a large number of the same item, work in an assembly-line fashion in order to make the most efficient use of your time. The food should be prepared entirely in advance as there is little time during the course of a drinks party to do anything other than warm food through quickly and restock trays. Hot food should be prepared to the stage where all that has to be done is to heat it through quickly.

Staff

If the party is for more than 20 guests it will be necessary to have people to help in the kitchen and serve during the party if you want to have a chance to speak with your guests.

We recommend that for each 20–25 guests you have one person serving food, one person serving drinks, and a third person in the kitchen warming the food and stocking the trays. If any of the food needs to be cooked on site, such as tempura or fish goujons, we recommend that a fourth person be dedicated entirely to this task. Have several trays so that some can be restocked while the others are circulating. Offer small napkins with messy or crumbly food.

Smoked Salmon Canapés

These canapés can be made a day in advance if stored in the refrigerator layered between clingfilm. They can also be frozen for up to 1 month. Defrost overnight in the refrigerator before serving.

MAKES 40

5 slices of brown bread
55 g | 2 oz butter, softened
freshly ground black pepper

cayenne pepper (optional)
1 lemon, cut into wedges
225 g | 8 oz smoked salmon

1 Spread the bread thinly with the butter, taking care to spread the butter to the edges of the bread to prevent it from becoming soggy or drying out.
2 Cut the crusts from the bread and discard.
3 Sprinkle the bread lightly with black pepper and cayenne, if using.
4 Place 2 layers of sliced smoked salmon over the bread, using scissors to cut the fish to line up with the edges of the bread.
5 Use a large cook's knife to cut the bread into 8 triangles.
6 Serve garnished with the lemon wedges.

Simple Sushi

Sushi makes an excellent canapé and the ingredients for making it are now readily available in the supermarkets. Sushi, traditionally, is filled with a variety of fillings such as avocado pear, peeled cucumber, smoked salmon, raw fish, cooked prawns, squid and scallops and strips of sweet omelette. This recipe simply uses smoked salmon, avocado and cucumber. A bamboo sushi mat makes rolling the sushi easy but is not necessary. Large squares of clingfilm can be used instead of Sushi mats.

MAKES 40

225 g | 8 oz sushi rice
450 ml | 16 fl oz water
1 piece kombu seaweed
5 tablespoons rice wine vinegar
1 tablespoon caster sugar
2 teaspoons salt
½ packet nori seaweed, ready roasted

½ cucumber, peeled and cut into long pencil lengths
110 g | 4 oz smoked salmon, cut into strips
1 avocado pear, peeled and cut into strips

For the dipping sauce

1 red chilli, finely chopped
3 tablespoons soy sauce
wasabi paste

1 Rinse the rice under running cold water. Put the rice into a saucepan with the water and kombu, bring up to the boil, cover and simmer for 12 minutes. Remove the kombu and add the vinegar, sugar and salt. Mix and leave to cool.

2 Lay a sushi mat or a square of clingfilm on a work surface. Cover with a piece of nori seaweed. Spoon a layer of rice over two thirds of each sheet, up to the edges.

3 Arrange a couple of cucumber and avocado strips and a piece of smoked salmon on the rice. Roll up firmly as for a Swiss Roll. Wrap in clingfilm and refrigerate for at least 15 minutes. Repeat with the remaining ingredients.

4 Trim the edges of the rolls and cut, crosswise, into 8–10 even slices.

5 Mix the soy and chilli together.

6 Stir the chilli into the soy sauce and season with a little wasabi. Serve with the sushi.

Toastie Cases

Toastie cases are one of the caterer's staples. They can be made up to a week in advance and stored in an airtight container and, best of all, once filled, they will hold without going soggy for a much longer time than pastry.

You need mini muffin tins to make these cases. If you are making them in bulk and have an electric pasta machine, you can save time and effort by running the bread through the rollers, but do not make the bread too thin or the toasties will be too hard.

1 loaf of stale thinly sliced white bread   110 g | 4 oz butter, melted

1 Preheat the oven to 180°C | 350°F | gas mark 4.
2 Cut the crusts from the bread and discard.
3 Flatten the bread by rolling with a rolling pin or by passing it through a pasta machine.
4 Cut 5 cm | 2 in circles from the flattened bread.
5 Brush both sides of the circles thinly with the melted butter, then press into mini muffin tins.
6 Bake for 10–15 minutes, or until the cases are lightly browned around the edges.
7 Turn the cases out of the muffin tins, then place them upside down on a baking sheet.
8 Return to the bottom third of the oven and bake for a further 10–15 minutes, or until an even golden-brown.
9 Cool on a wire rack, then store in an airtight container until required.
10 Fill just before serving.

Suggested cold fillings

- Taramasalata (see **Fish**, page 266)
- Crème fraîche and lumpfish caviar or keta (salmon roe)
- Cream cheese mixed with roasted garlic and herbs
- Smoked Trout Pâté (see **Fish**, page 264)

The toastie cases can be filled quickly by piping in the filling.

Suggested hot fillings

- Spinach topped with a poached quail's egg and Hollandaise Sauce (see **Eggs**, *Poaching*, page 218, and **Sauces, Savoury**, page 602)
- Wild mushrooms with tarragon and cream

Dips

Dips are simple combination sauces of thick coating consistency (see **Sauces**, **Savoury**, page 579) served with raw vegetables (*Crudités*, see below), biscuits or toast as an appetizer. Other classic cold sauces that will cling to food, such as *Tartare Sauce* for fried fish or *Aïoli* for seafood or chicken (see **Sauces, Savoury,** *Mayonnaise*, page 598) are popular for dipping foods. The dip should be thick enough to cling to the dipper (vegetable baton, crisp or toast) without dripping off but not so thick that the dipper snaps off in the dip. See **Pulses** (page 562) for a recipe for the popular Middle Eastern dip, *Hummus bi Tahini*.

Guacamole

Guacamole is a Mexican recipe for a spicy avocado dip (see **Fruit**, page 283, for information about avocados). This recipe uses many of the skills from the **Knife Skills** section (page 65). It should be made not more than 1 hour before eating as the avocado tends to discolour.

2 ripe avocados

2 Kenyan fresh green chillies, finely chopped (see **Vegetables**, page 730)

1 large clove of garlic, crushed (see **Knife Skills**, page 70)

3 tablespoons chopped fresh coriander leaves

juice of 1 lime

1 large tomato, concassé (see **Knife Skills**, page 74)

1 teaspoon mild chilli powder

½ teaspoon salt

1–2 spring onions, thinly sliced on the diagonal

crudités (see below) or tortilla chips, to serve

1 Cut the avocados in half and remove the stones.

2 Scrape the flesh from the avocados with a teaspoon, taking care to scrape as close to the skin as possible to extract the dark green flesh.

3 Mash the avocado flesh with a fork, leaving it slightly lumpy, then stir in all the remaining ingredients except the spring onions.

4 Turn into a bowl and garnish with the spring onions.

Crudités

Crudités are raw vegetables cut into batons or small pieces to be used for dipping into a thick sauce. The pieces of vegetable should be long enough so that they can be stuck in the dip without the fingers getting messy, but not long enough to encourage 'double dipping'. A length of about 5 cm | 2 in for carrots, celery and peppers is recommended (see **Knife Skills**, page 71). Try to make the size of the batons as uniform as possible for the purposes of presentation.

The following vegetables are suitable for serving as part of a crudités tray:

Carrots

Celery

Red and yellow peppers

Baby sweetcorn, raw or lightly blanched (see **Vegetables**, page 744)

Cucumber

Radishes

Cauliflower florets

Asparagus spears, raw or lightly blanched (see **Vegetables**, page 719)

Broccoli florets

The vegetables can be prepared in advance. Wrap each type in damp kitchen paper and place in a plastic bag in the crisper drawer of the refrigerator.

Alternate the different coloured vegetables when arranging the crudités on a serving platter.

Spinach and Ricotta Strudels

MAKES 20

110 g | 4 oz butter, melted
225 g | 8 oz frozen chopped spinach
110 g | 4 oz ricotta
salt and freshly ground black pepper

a pinch of freshly grated nutmeg
4 sheets of bought filo pastry
1 egg, beaten, to glaze

1 Preheat the oven to 200°C | 400°F | gas mark 6.
2 Defrost the spinach and squeeze dry.
3 Heat 30 g | 1 oz of the butter in a sauté pan over medium heat until pale brown. Stir in the spinach and cook for 1 minute. Turn into a bowl and cool. Stir in the ricotta. Season with salt, pepper and nutmeg.
4 Brush the filo sheets with the remaining butter.
5 Cut each sheet of pastry into strips 5 cm | 2 in wide.
6 Place a spoonful of the filling at the bottom of each strip and fold over into a triangle (see diagram). Continue folding until the end of the strip, then tuck the end of the pastry into the fold to secure.
7 Place the triangles on baking sheets in a single layer.
8 Brush with the egg glaze, taking care not to let it drip on to the baking sheet.
9 Bake in the oven for about 10 minutes until golden-brown. Serve warm.

Making filo parcels

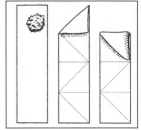

Making Caramel: Points to Remember

- Use a clean, heavy-based saucepan.

- Use granulated sugar; it is cleaner than caster as it is less finely ground and contains less sugar dust, so is less likely to crystallize. It will dissolve more quickly because it is easier for the water to move between the grains.

- Stir the sugar gently with a wooden spoon to help it dissolve.

- Do not stir the sugar syrup once it has begun to boil.

- Wash down the inside of the saucepan with a pastry brush dipped in water to remove any sugar crystals.

- Once the sugar has started to colour, watch it carefully. Sugar turns from caramel to charcoal within seconds.

- Ensure that the handle of the pan is turned away from the front of the hob.

Dry Caramel: as above, plus:

- Caster sugar is normally used for a dry caramel, but granulated sugar also gives successful results.

- Melt the sugar over a low heat, shaking the pan occasionally.

- Do not allow the flames of a gas burner to lick up the sides of the pan. This can cause uneven browning.

- Brush down the inside of the pan with a pastry brush dipped into water only if sugar crystals have appeared on the sides of the pan.

- Dip the bottom of the saucepan into a bowl of cold water to stop the cooking when the desired state of caramelization is reached or if the caramel has gone too far.

- When making caramel chips or praline, have an oiled baking tray ready to immediately pour the finished caramel on.

- Once the caramel has been removed from the saucepan, fill the saucepan with water and heat to remove the caramel that has stuck to the pan.

Caramel

Caramel is sugar that has liquefied then been cooked to a deep, rich brown. It is used in desserts as well as a flavouring for soups, stocks and sauces, both savoury and sweet.

See also:
- **Mousses,** *Caramel Mousse* (page 490)
- **Sauces, Savoury**, *Gastrique* (page 597)
- **Sauces, Sweet,** *Caramel Cream* (page 619)

It is important that the sugar is cooked to a deep amber colour, otherwise the caramel will be sickly-sweet. However, if it has cooked too long the caramel will become bitter and inedible. It is a very fine line between the two stages and much practice is usually needed to get the caramel to the correct stage.

The temperature at which sugar caramelizes is $170°C\,|\,340°F$, which is extremely hot, so great care must be taken when making caramel. If adding water or cream to the caramel, cover your hand and arm as the mixture often splashes. If some of the caramel splashes on to you immediately dip the affected part into cold water. Do not put it to your mouth.

Wet Caramel

Wet caramel is made with granulated sugar and water. It is used primarily for sauce, as in the following recipe.

Oranges in Caramel Sauce

SERVES 4

225 g | 8 oz granulated sugar
290 ml | ½ pint water

4 large oranges

1 Place the sugar in a heavy saucepan with half of the water.
2 Heat over a low heat until the sugar has dissolved, then brush down the inside of the saucepan with a pastry brush dipped in water.
3 Turn the heat to high and boil the syrup until the mixture turns a deep caramel.
4 Protecting your hand with an oven glove and averting your face, tip the remaining water into the caramel to stop the cooking.
5 Place the caramel over a low heat to dissolve it, if necessary. Allow to cool.
6 Segment the oranges as directed in *Fruit* (see page 282), reserving any juice.
7 Pour the caramel over the oranges. Refrigerate for at least 1 hour or up to 48 hours.

VARIATIONS

Liqueurs such as Armagnac or Grand Marnier can be added to the caramel. Allow 2 table-spoons liqueur for the above recipe. Liquid caramel can also be infused with citrus zest and spices such as cinnamon and star anise: add the whole spices to the hot caramel and allow it to cool. For a stronger flavour, infuse the caramel with the spices overnight in the refrigerator, then strain.

Microwave Method: Caramel can also be made in the microwave. See **Microwave Cookery**, page 483.

Storing Liquid Caramel

Caramel can be kept for up to 3 weeks in the refrigerator, covered with clingfilm or sealed in an airtight container.

Dry Caramel

Dry caramel is normally made with caster sugar and can be used to make caramel chips for decoration.

Making caramel

1 Heat caster sugar to a depth of 6 mm $|\frac{1}{4}$ in in a heavy-based saucepan over a low heat. Shake the pan gently from time to time as the sugar starts to melt.
2 When the sugar turns a dark caramel, quickly dip the base of the pan into a bowl of cold water to stop the cooking.
3 Immediately pour the caramel on to an oiled baking tray.
4 Allow to cool completely, then break into caramel chips. Do not touch the caramel while it is hot.
5 Use immediately or store overnight in an airtight container.

Crème Brûlée

SERVES 4

290 ml $|\frac{1}{2}$ pint whipping or double cream
1 vanilla pod or 1 teaspoon vanilla essence
4 egg yolks

1–2 tablespoons caster sugar, plus extra for the topping

1 Heat the cream with the vanilla pod, if using, to scalding point. This is just below boiling point, when small bubbles form around the edge of the pan. Allow to stand for 10 minutes, then scrape the tiny seeds from the inside of the pod and add to the cream. Discard the pod.
2 Preheat the oven to 170°C $|325$°F $|$ gas mark 3. Prepare a warm bain-marie.

3 Mix the egg yolks and the sugar in a small bowl to combine, then slowly stir in the cream.

4 If using vanilla essence add it now.

5 Sieve the mixture into a jug, then pour into 1 large dish or 4 small ramekins and place in a warm bain-marie.

6 Place in the oven and cook for about 20–25 minutes or until a visible skin forms on the top of the custard and the mixture only just wobbles when the dish is shaken.

7 Remove from the bain-marie and allow to cool. Refrigerate, uncovered, overnight. This ensures that the custard is very cold and a good skin has formed to support the sugar.

8 To brûlée the custard, use one of the methods below. Once the topping has been added, the custards can be refrigerated for up to $1\frac{1}{2}$ hours; however, the caramel softens in the refrigerator and will eventually liquefy if left for too long.

NOTE: Some recipes use Demerara sugar for the topping. This is acceptable but gives a different flavour.

To brûlée using a domestic grill

1 Preheat the grill to its highest setting.

2 Dredge the custard with caster sugar to a thickness of $6\,\text{mm} \big| \frac{1}{4}$ in. To do this, place the custard on a tray or sheet of greaseproof paper and sift the sugar from a height over the custard. This will give an even layer of sugar.

3 Wipe any excess sugar from the rim of the dish and place the custard on a baking sheet. Place under the grill about $5\,\text{cm} \big| 2$ in from the heat.

4 Watch the custard and turn the dish frequently to ensure the sugar caramelizes evenly.

5 When the sugar is a deep golden caramel, remove from the grill and allow to cool.

To brûlée using a blow-torch

This is the method most often used in commercial kitchens.

1 Dredge the custard with caster or icing sugar as above but only to a thickness of $2\,\text{mm} \big| \frac{1}{16}$ in.

2 Spray the sugar lightly with water using a plant mister. This helps to dissolve the sugar.

3 Use the blow-torch in a sweeping motion across the sugar from a distance of about $10\,\text{cm} \big| 4$ in to caramelize the sugar. This will take several minutes.

4 Allow to cool.

Making a dry caramel in a saucepan

This method produces an evenly coloured caramel but works best if individual ramekins as used.

1 Make a dry caramel following the directions above, using $110\,\text{g} \big| 4\,\text{oz}$ caster sugar.

2 When the colour of the caramel reaches a deep amber, pour the caramel over the individual custards.

3 Allow to cool.

Praline

French in origin, praline is a confection of almonds coated with caramelized sugar. It is used widely in desserts as an addition to cream fillings for cakes and pastries. Crushed roughly, it is used as a topping for ice cream. Finely crushed praline can also be used to coat the outside of cakes.

Almonds are the traditional nuts for praline but other nuts, such as hazelnuts or pistachios, can be used in their place.

oil, for greasing   55 g | 2 oz caster sugar
55 g | 2 oz whole blanched almonds

1 Oil a baking sheet.

2 Put the almonds and sugar into a heavy-based saucepan and place over a low heat.

3 Stir gently with a metal spoon as the sugar begins to melt and brown.

4 Use a table fork to turn the almonds over to cook both sides evenly.

5 When the almonds have started to make a cracking sound and the sugar is a deep amber colour, tip the mixture on to the prepared baking sheet.

6 Spread the almonds apart using the spoon. Allow to cool completely.

7 Fill the saucepan with water and heat to remove the caramel.

8 Pound the praline to a powder with a mortar and pestle or break into pieces and crush in a food processor.

9 Store in a dry, airtight container for up to 1 month.

Notes

Types of Cheese

Fresh Cheeses have a soft texture due to their high moisture content. These cheeses, such as fromage blanc (quark), ricotta, cottage cheese, cream cheese, mascarpone and curd cheese, are intended to be consumed quickly. They are eaten fresh and can be used in baking (see *Cheesecake*, page 183).

Whey Cheeses are made from the whey that is drained from the curds during cheese-making. Ricotta is the best-known example of this type of cheese. Ricotta means 'twice cooked' in Italian. The cheese is cooked once during the clabbering stage (see below) then, once formed, the cheese is dipped in very hot water, to soften it.

Acid-cured Cheeses, such as cottage cheese and curd cheese, are made from skimmed milk that has been soured by the introduction of lactic acid bacteria. Cream is added after the curds are drained and washed.

Vacherin Mont d'Or is a special uncooked and unpressed cheese made in the Rhône-Alps region. It is moulded into small rounds held in place by thin strips of spruce bark. The ripening process is very short so the cheese remains creamy while absorbing a woody flavour imparted by the spruce. The surface rind is washed with diluted cream and should be creamy-white, never mouldy.

Dried Fresh Cheeses, such as goat's cheese crottins, have a natural rind that forms when the cheese begins to dry. These cheeses are good for grilling.

Soft, Surface-ripened Cheeses such as Camembert, Brie and Pont L'Evêque are best for eating. They have not been cooked or pressed. These cheeses are made into flat cakes and then impregnated with penicillin mould and special bacteria and cured in a humid cellar. Other soft cheeses, known as double and triple crème, have had cream added at the clabbering stage. These cheeses, such as Explorateur, are very high in fat.

Some soft cheeses, such as Reblochon, have their crusts washed during ripening with cider, wine, brandy, beer or whey. These cheeses are very sticky and smelly, although the interior is usually mild. Other surface-ripened cheeses are dusted with ash or rolled in herbs.

Semi-soft Cheeses have a rubbery, elastic texture, making them good for grilling, but as they become stringy when heated they are not good for Cheese Sauce. An example of semi-soft cheese is St Paulin. Mozzarella is a semi-soft cheese that has been given a special process called *pasta filata*. The curd is dipped in hot whey, then kneaded and stretched to give it an elastic, stringy texture.

Hard-pressed Cheeses, such as Cheddar, Cheshire and Gruyère, are low in moisture and firm. They have been cooked, pressed and aged for a shorter time than very hard cheeses, about 6 months to 1 year. They are excellent for eating as well as grating to add to sauces (see **Sauces, Savoury**, *Mornay Sauce*, page 589).

Very Hard Cheeses, such as Parmesan and Pecorino, and cooked, pressed and aged for 2–4 years. They are excellent for grating and are added to sauces in small quantities to enhance the flavour of other cheeses.

Blue-veined Cheeses have been injected and/or sprayed with spores of *Penicillin roqueforti* or *Penicillin glaucum* to produce the veins of flavourful mould. Some of these cheeses have a crumbly texture that makes them ideal for adding into salads or soups; others are creamy and spreadable. Blue cheeses are too strong for most sauces but make a good soufflé if mixed half and half with a drier cheese such as Gruyère.

Cheese

Cheese is made from the milk of cows, goats, ewes, sheep and water buffalo. Cheese-making originally evolved as a method of preserving excess quantities of milk. Milk is rich in both calcium and protein and provides an excellent form of nutrition. Man has made and consumed cheese for thousands of years: there is evidence of cheese-making going back as far as 6000 BC and cheese from 3000 BC has been found inside an Egyptian tomb.

Although today there are more than 1,500 different types of cheese world-wide, cheese can be divided broadly into 2 categories: fresh and ripened. The ripened, or aged, cheeses divide into 6 major subdivisions relating to the method of production. How cheese is produced has a great influence on the end product and will determine the behaviour of the cheese when heated and, therefore, its cooking qualities.

The flavour of a cheese will depend not only on its origin, how it was made and the kind of milk it was made from, but on what the animal has eaten and the time of year the cheese was made. Many people feel that cheeses made with unpasteurized milk have a more complex flavour due to the presence of certain bacteria. However, many cheeses today are made from pasteurized milk in order to standardize the product and protect the consumer. Pasteurization involves heating the milk to kill any micro-organisms that might be harmful to consume. Cheese made from unpasteurized milk could carry listeria (see **Food Safety**, page 21) so pregnant women and the infirm are advised not to eat these cheeses. A well-made cheese produced from pasteurised milk can be every bit as good as a cheese made from unpasteurized milk, without the health risk.

The texture of cheese depends on its water content as well as its fat content. Soft cheese has a higher water content than hard cheese and therefore, contrary to what many people would expect, soft creamy cheeses do not always contain a higher percentage of fat than hard cheeses. For example, Camembert contains 21 per cent fat, whilst Cheddar contains 33 per cent fat. The French system of measuring fat content is different to that in the UK; in France the percentage of fat is calculated as a percentage of dry matter, whilst in the UK it is calculated as a percentage of the whole. Therefore a Brie might be labelled '48 per cent fat' but the actual fat content according to the English method of measuring will be only 24 per cent.

The Cheese-making Process

Cheese is made by warming milk then letting it ripen. During this process the milk is kept warm to help the bacteria grow. The lactic acid which produces bacteria in the milk turns the milk sour. It is the lactic acid that gives cheese its sharp flavour.

The milk is then curdled either with rennet, which is a powdered form of the coagulating enzyme from the stomach of an unweaned calf, or a vegetarian coagulant. The process is called clabbering. The milk separates into semi-solids, the curds, and a liquid called whey. The curds are then ladled into a sieve or mould to drain. Some cheeses, such as ricotta, are made from the whey, which is reheated. For fresh cheeses such as fromage blanc, cottage cheese and curd cheese, the curds are drained and the product is packaged.

For ripened cheese the curds are worked to achieve the desired texture. Salt is added for flavour and to help preserve the cheese. Before being stored and left to age the cheeses are moulded. Some cheeses, such as Camembert and Brie, are made into flat cakes that are placed in humid cellars where they are sprayed with penicillin bacteria. The bacteria ripen the cheese by softening the casein (protein) in the cheese, working from the outside in.

Other types of soft cheese have their crusts washed repeatedly with cider, wine, whey, beer or brandy. This gives the cheese a soft, sticky crust and makes the cheese rather smelly, although the inside of the cheese is usually mild in flavour.

For the hard-pressed and very hard cheeses, the curds are heated and stirred to break them down into fine particles. The heating denatures the proteins slightly and squeezes out some of the water. The curd is sometimes cut to help the whey run off. In the process called cheddaring, the cheese is stacked and weighted. This pressure removes further moisture and produces a hard cheese with a low moisture content. These cheeses are kept cool during ripening. The ripening process for these cheeses takes between 6 months and 4 years, depending on the type of cheese.

Choosing

Buy cheese from a supplier with a high turnover, preferably from a cheese shop that doesn't wrap the cheese in clingfilm or keep the cheese too cold. Buy cheese in small amounts and use within a few days. It never benefits from home refrigeration.

A soft, surface-ripened cheese such as Camembert and Brie should feel moist and slightly springy, not hard, when pressed in the centre. It should not have a strong ammonia smell as that indicates an over-ripe cheese. Hard cheese should show no sign of surface mould or sweating.

Storing

Fresh cheese should be stored in a closed container in the refrigerator and used within 5 days. Discard it if any mould appears on the surface.

Ripened cheeses should be wrapped in greaseproof or waxed paper, then placed in a plastic bag in the warmest part of the refrigerator. Semi-soft cheeses keep for up to 1 week. Hard-pressed and very hard cheeses will keep for up to 3 weeks. Any surface mould should be cut from the cheese before eating.

Leftover cheese can be frozen to use in cheese sauces, soufflés and quiches although it will never taste as good as recently purchased cheese. Grate or cut the cheese into small cubes so it can be used from frozen. Store tightly wrapped in a plastic bag and use within 3 months.

Using Cheese in Cooking

Fresh Cheeses

Fresh cheese, such as fromage blanc or its German equivalent, quark, can be served as an accompaniment to fruit or cakes. Cottage cheese is usually eaten on its own or with fruit. It can be used to prepare uncooked cheesecakes and similar foods, but it will retain its granular texture.

Cheesecake is one of the classic preparations using cream cheese or curd cheese. Cream cheese is higher in fat than curd cheese so it will give a slightly richer, creamier result. Cheesecakes are either baked, which gives the cake a firm texture, or made with cream and set with gelatine to give a soft texture rather like a mousse.

Baked Cheesecake

It is important to use good quality cream cheese for the best texture. Allow the cream cheese and eggs to come to room temperature before starting to cook.

SERVES 6–8

melted butter for greasing

For the crust

200 g | 7 oz digestive biscuits
85 g | 3 oz butter, melted

For the filling

225 g | 8 oz best-quality cream cheese
85 ml | 3 fl oz double cream

1 egg yolk
1 egg
1 teaspoon vanilla essence
3–4 tablespoons sugar

For the topping

75 ml | 2½ fl oz crème fraîche
ground cinnamon

1 Preheat the oven to 180°C | 350°F | gas mark 4. Brush 20 cm | 8 in flan ring or springform tin with butter.
2 Crush the biscuits by placing them in a plastic bag and bashing them with a rolling pin.
3 Mix together the biscuit crumbs and the butter. Use a fork to press the crumbs on to the base and 2.5 cm | 1 in up the sides of the tin.
4 Chill the crust for 10 minutes to set the butter, then bake for 10 minutes until just starting to brown. Set aside.
5 Turn the oven temperature down to 150°C | 300°F | gas mark 2.
6 Beat the cream cheese with the sugar until it is very soft, then gradually beat in the egg yolk and the whole egg.

7 Stir in the cream and vanilla.

8 Pour the mixture into the crust and bake in the lower part of the oven for about 30 minutes, until the filling has nearly set. It should still have a slight wobble in the centre.

9 Turn off the oven and allow to cool in the oven.

10 Remove the cheesecake from the oven, spread with the crème fraîche and refrigerate overnight.

11 Sprinkle with the cinnamon just before serving.

Cheesecake: What has gone wrong when...

The cheesecake is dry and hard.

- The cheesecake was overbaked.
- The cream cheese was not beaten for long enough.
- The cream cheese was not of good quality.

The cheesecake has a grainy texture.

- The cheesecake was overbaked.
- The oven temperature was too high.
- The cream cheese was not of good quality.

The cheesecake has cracked in the middle.

- The cheesecake was overbaked.
- The cheesecake was cooled too quickly.

The cheesecake is too runny.

- The cheesecake was not refrigerated overnight.
- The cheesecake was underbaked.
- The oven temperature was too low.

Hard Cheeses

Cheeses that are high in fat, such as hard cheeses, melt easily; low-fat cheeses are not good for melting. The cheese needs only just enough heat to melt it. As coagulation starts at 60°C|140°F, overheating will result in stringiness, graininess and oiliness as the protein in the cheese hardens squeezing out the fat. For example, Gruyère, grated, is used for the Swiss speciality, fondue. The fondue is kept warm over a small flame to ensure that the cheese does not become too hot otherwise it will become grainy and oily.

Average Fat Content of Selected Cheeses

Ripened Cheeses	% Fat
Roquefort	29
Stilton	40
Brie	23–35
Camembert	21–23
Cheddar	33
Edam	23
Gouda	23
Gruyère	33
Parmesan	30

Fresh Cheeses	
Cottage cheese (low-fat)	0–5
Cream cheese	33
Curd cheese	12–25
Mascarpone (Italian cream cheese)	40
Mozzarella	22
Quark/fromage blanc	0.2
Ricotta	10

Grating Cheese

For incorporation in a sauce, cheese is grated using the 'half-moon'-type hole on the grater. A dry cheese such as Cheddar is the best cheese to use for grating to add to sauces. The cheese should be strong-flavoured as its flavour will be diluted by the sauce. To make a mild cheese taste stronger, grate it and leave it uncovered at room temperature for 1 hour to let it dry slightly.

Grated cheese is also used in pastry, quiches and for a gratin topping. Cheddar and Gruyère are best for these purposes. The cheese should be finely grated, using the smallest of the 'half-moon'-type holes on the grater.

Grating cheese for a gratin topping

Parmesan is the cheese to use for risotto (see **Rice**, page 569) and for mixing with breadcrumbs to make a gratin topping for dishes such as *Cauliflower Cheese* (see below) and Macaroni Cheese. If the grated cheese is sprinkled on top of the dish without being mixed with breadcrumbs the fat will create an oily surface on the food. Parmesan should be very finely grated from a block of fresh cheese. Ready-grated Parmesan is made from poor-quality cheese and has a nasty, stale flavour.

Making cheese shavings

Parmesan is the best cheese for making shavings to use as a garnish for pasta dishes and salads. Parmesan is sold in 2 qualities: Parmagiano-Reggiano, with the best flavour and highest price, and Grana Padano which has a milder flavour and a more granular texture.

Use a large block of Parmesan and a vegetable peeler. Scrape the peeler along the length of the block. You need to press against the cheese firmly as it is very hard.

Cauliflower Cheese

SERVES 4

1 large or 2 small cauliflowers

290 ml | ½ pint milk
55 g | 2 oz strong Cheddar or Gruyère cheese, grated
salt and freshly ground black pepper

For the cheese sauce
20 g | ¾ oz butter
20 g | ¾ oz plain flour
½ teaspoon dry English mustard
a pinch of cayenne pepper

For the topping
15 g | ½ oz Parmesan cheese, freshly grated
2 tablespoons breadcrumbs

1 Preheat the oven to 190°C | 375°F | gas mark 5.
2 Break the cauliflower into florets, removing most of the stalk, and cook in boiling salted water until tender. Drain thoroughly in a colander.
3 Meanwhile, make the cheese sauce: heat the butter in a saucepan and remove from the heat. Stir in the flour and spices.
4 Return to the heat and cook, stirring, until the mixture bubbles. Remove from the heat and gradually add the milk to make a smooth sauce.
5 Return to the heat and bring to the boil, stirring. Boil for 2 minutes.
6 Remove from the heat and stir in the cheddar or Gruyère cheese. Season to taste with salt and pepper.
7 Fold in the cauliflower. Turn into an ovenproof dish. Mix together the Parmesan cheese and the breadcrumbs and sprinkle over the top.
8 Place in the oven and cook for about 20 minutes, until golden-brown and bubbling.

Cauliflower Cheese: What has gone wrong when...

See also *Flour-thickened Sauces: What has gone wrong when* . . . (page 593)
The cheese sauce is greasy and stringy.

- The sauce was overheated after the cheese was added.

There is an oil slick on the surface of the dish.

- The cheese was sprinkled on without being mixed with the breadcrumbs.

The sauce tastes floury.

- The sauce was not boiled.
- Not enough salt has been added

Deep-frying Cheese

Small deep-fried wedges of cheese are popular served as first course with a tart fruit sauce and a salad garnish. Camembert and Brie are the best cheeses to use for deep-frying. Chill the cheese well before frying.

Camembert Fritters

Brie can be used instead of Camembert.

SERVES 4

1 Camembert cheese, chilled

1 egg, beaten

dried white breadcrumbs

oil, for deep-frying (see **Deep-frying**, page 207)

To serve

Gooseberry Sauce (see **Fruit**, *Berries*, page 284)

green salad

1 Cut the chilled Camembert into 8 wedges. Dip in the beaten egg, then in the bread crumbs. Refrigerate for 30 minutes.
2 Heat the oil until a crumb browns lightly in 10 seconds.
3 Deep-fry the cheese until pale brown. Drain on kitchen paper. Sprinkle lightly with salt.
4 Serve immediately with the Gooseberry Sauce and salad.

Grilling Cheese

Certain cheeses are especially good for grilling because they melt well yet retain their shape. Mozzarella is particularly well known for its melting qualities and is used as a topping for pizza.

One of the few cheeses that melts well yet retain its shape is haloumi from the Middle East. This firm, salty cheese is often made from sheep's milk. Haloumi will hold its shape whilst melting on the inside so it can be cooked on the barbecue or skewered with vegetables and grilled.

Other cheeses melt well but become runny and sticky. Goat's cheese crottins are a favourite for melting to serve with a salad for a first course. Crumbly Greek feta also melts well.

Welsh Rarebit

SERVES 2

55 g | 2 oz Gruyère cheese, grated
55 g | 2 oz Cheddar cheese, grated
2 teaspoons Dijon mustard
salt and freshly ground black pepper
a pinch of cayenne pepper

½ egg, beaten
1 tablespoon beer
2 slices of bread, toasted
butter, for spreading

1 Preheat the grill.
2 Combine the cheeses with all the remaining ingredients except the toast and butter.
3 Spread the toast with the butter, then with the cheese mixture, taking care to spread the mixture to the edges.
4 Grill until golden-brown and serve immediately.

Grilling Cheese: What has gone wrong when...

See also *Flour thickened Sauces: What has gone wrong when . . . (page 593)*

The cheese becomes very stringy and oily.
- The cheese has been overheated.

Baking Cheese

Soft, ripened cheeses are good for baking whole. Wrap cheeses such as Camembert in puff or filo pastry or bread dough and bake until the covering pastry or dough is cooked. The cheeses Vacherin Mont d'Or and Camembert can be heated in their wooden containers until runny, then served by spooning the cheese from the container, accompanied by French bread.

Preparing a Cheese Board

A cheese board for a cheese course traditionally consists of at least 3 cheeses, the standard rule being to include 1 hard, 1 soft and 1 blue cheese. This provides variety and looks attractive on the plate, an odd number being preferable to an even number. However, one large perfect cheese is also acceptable if you know your guests' tastes. Allow 85 g | 3 oz cheese in total per person if catering for up to 8 people, 55 g | 2 oz for up to 20 people and 30 g | 1 oz per person for over 20 people.

The cheese should be cut so that each triangular wedge has some rind attached. Cheese boards are often garnished with small bunches of red and green grapes, dates or wedges of apple. Stilton is traditionally served with celery stalks. Biscuits for cheese can include water biscuits, oatcakes, and/or Bath Olivers. Many people, however, prefer bread with their cheese.

Chocolate

Chocolate, the product of the cocoa tree, *Theobroma cacao*, literally meaning the food of the Gods, has a grand reputation and a long history. Cultivated by the Mayas and the Aztecs and used by Native Americans as a form of currency, chocolate was brought to Europe by the Spanish Conquistadors in the sixteenth century.

The word chocolate is derived from an Aztec word meaning 'bitter water', and for most of its history, chocolate was consumed as a drink. 'Chocolate houses', similar to coffee houses, were popular in London in the 1800s.

The sweetened chocolate tablet is a relatively recent invention which was developed by an Englishman in the mid-nineteenth century. Until this time, due to scarcity and high taxation, chocolate was primarily consumed by royalty. To this day the Queen has her own special blend of chocolate.

The cocoa tree grows in equatorial regions of the world between latitudes 20°N and 20°S. Its fruit is the rugby ball-shaped, ridged cocoa pods which are 15–25 cm | 6–10 in long. Each contains up to 40 cocoa beans. These beans are fermented then roasted. The flavour of the chocolate is determined by the variety of tree the beans come from as well as the fermenting and roasting times and temperatures.

There are three varieties of cocoa tree, the Criollo, Forastero and a hybrid of these, the Trinitario. Within these varieties there are many other hybrids which differ from location to location.

The Criollo, native to Venezuela and Equador, has the highest-quality beans but produces only about 5 per cent of the world's supply. Beans from the Criollo trees are high in cocoa butter and low in bitterness. The Forastero trees that grow primarily in Africa and Brazil produce about 85 per cent of the world's harvest but their beans are more bitter than the Criollo. The Trinitario trees were developed in Trinidad at a time when the Criollo tree population was dwindling. These beans have characteristics of both of their parents and represent about 10 per cent of world production.

In chocolate manufacture the beans from different types of trees are often mixed to take advantage of their individual characteristics. The nibs are then removed and ground to produce chocolate liquor. This chocolate liquor is comprised of cocoa solids and cocoa butter and, in its unprocessed form, is very bitter. The cocoa solids are separated from the liquor by pressing. The resulting cakes of cocoa solids are ground finely to make cocoa powder. To manufacture a chocolate tablet, the cocoa butter is added back to the cocoa powder, then the mixture is kneaded, or 'conched', for up to 72 hours to produce a smooth, fine-textured chocolate.

To make the chocolate more palatable, the chocolate is mixed with sugar and sometimes with lecithin, an emulsifying agent. Milk solids and vanilla are added to make milk chocolate. Lesser-quality chocolate has a greater amount of sugar than the best-quality chocolate and will often have vegetable fat in place of some of the cocoa butter. The quality of chocolate varies tremendously, so it is important to know about its composition to ensure you are buying the best chocolate for your needs.

Many people find chocolate to be addictive, hence the term 'chocoholics'. The Aztecs and the Spanish considered chocolate to be a powerful aphrodisiac. Containing small amounts of caffeine and theobromine, it has a slight stimulating effect. Another chemical present in chocolate in small quantities is phenylethylamine, a substance that is purported to influence the mood centre of the brain in a manner similar to the emotion of 'falling in love'.

Types of Chocolate

Plain chocolate: This varies tremendously in the amount of sugar that has been added and the quantity of cocoa solids. When choosing a chocolate to use in cooking, look for the percentage of cocoa solids on the list of ingredients. If this is between 50 and 70 per cent the chocolate will have a full chocolate taste that most people will find acceptable. Above 70 per cent cocoa solids, the chocolate will be very dark with a more bitter taste. Generally, the higher the percentage of cocoa solids, the more expensive the chocolate will be. As the flavour and texture of each brand of chocolate vary, it is important to taste the chocolate before using it in cooking to ensure it has the flavour you require.

Semi-sweet chocolate: This term is used primarily in the USA. It is similar to plain chocolate but has slightly more sugar.

Couverture: Couverture is a plain dark chocolate with a relatively high proportion of cocoa butter. It is more free-flowing than plain chocolate when melted. This is the type of chocolate to use for confectionery because when it hardens after the process called tempering, it is shiny and breaks with a sharp snap. It is used for coating, hence its name: the word *couverture* means 'blanket' or 'covering' in French.

Milk chocolate: This chocolate has added milk solids or cream as well as sugar. Vanilla is often added. The quality of milk chocolate varies tremendously.

Unsweetened chocolate: This is widely available in the USA and is available commercially in the UK. It is also known as bitter or baking chocolate. It does not contain any sugar. During processing the cocoa solids are ground very finely and an emulsifier such as lecithin is added, then the chocolate is pressed into blocks.

White chocolate: Technically this is not chocolate at all, but a manufactured concoction of milk solids, sugar, cocoa butter and vanilla.

Cocoa powder: This consists of cocoa solids and varying amounts of sugar. Cocoa powders vary tremendously in the intensity of chocolate flavour. Many recipes require the addition of boiling water to cocoa powder to release the flavour.

Certain brands of cocoa powder are described as 'Dutch processed'. This means that the cocoa powder has been treated with an alkaline solution to make it less bitter. This process gives the powder a darker colour. This type of cocoa powder is preferable for culinary use.

Melting Chocolate

Part of the magical attraction of chocolate is that it melts in your mouth. It has a sharp melting point which means that within a narrow temperature range it changes from solid to liquid. Chocolate is sensitive to heat and it can change from melted to burnt within a matter of seconds. For this reason, chocolate is notoriously tricky to work with.

When melting chocolate, avoid dripping small amounts of water or other liquid into the chocolate. Even the smallest amount of liquid, for example, drips from the underside of the bowl, will cause the chocolate to *seize* and harden into a solid, unworkable lump. If the chocolate seizes, it can sometimes be rescued by adding 1 teaspoon of flavourless oil per 55 g | 2 oz of chocolate and then reheating the mixture. The result can still be used in cooking but cannot be tempered – only pure chocolate can be tempered (see *Tempering Chocolate*, below).

It is also very important not to overheat chocolate. As the temperature of the chocolate approaches 50°C | 120°F, the cocoa butter will start to separate from the cocoa solids. The solids will burn if the chocolate is overheated and the texture of the chocolate will be dry and crumbly. If the chocolate burns there is nothing that can be done to save it.

Melting Chocolate: Points to Remember

- Chocolate should be chopped into small pieces, no more than 1 cm | ½ in before being melted.
- It should be stirred during melting to keep the temperature even throughout the mass.
- Half fill a saucepan with water and heat until it simmers. Turn off the heat, then place a heatproof bowl containing the chopped chocolate over, but not touching, the water. Stir frequently until the chocolate has melted.
- Place in a heatproof bowl – glass is ideal – then microwave on 50 per cent power for sessions of 30 seconds. Stir the chocolate after each session. Milk and white chocolate should be heated at 30 per cent power.
- Do not overheat the chocolate.
- Do not allow any liquid or steam to come in contact with the melted chocolate.

Chocolate Mousse

Chocolate mousse can be made successfully from plain or milk chocolate, but for mousse with an intensely chocolate flavour, use a chocolate with up to 70 per cent cocoa solids. Remember, however, to follow the rules for melting and using chocolate above.

SERVES 4
110 g|4 oz good quality plain or milk chocolate
4 medium eggs at room temperature, separated

1 Chop the chocolate into 1 cm|½ in pieces and melt by one of the methods described above. Allow to cool slightly.
2 Place the egg yolks in a large bowl and stir to break them up.
3 In a separate bowl, whisk the whites to the medium peak stage (see **Eggs**, page 234).
4 Stir the melted chocolate into the egg yolks.
5 Using a large metal spoon, carefully fold the whisked whites into the chocolate mixture, taking care not to overfold. Turn into 4 small ramekins or a serving dish.
6 Refrigerate for at least 2 hours or overnight.

Chocolate Mousse: What has gone wrong when...

The chocolate and egg yolk mixture becomes very thick.
- The chocolate has cooled too much or the yolks were cold.
- The yolks were added to the chocolate rather than the chocolate to the yolks.

The egg whites won't combine easily with the chocolate.
- The chocolate has cooled too much. Work more quickly next time.

The surface of the mousse is covered with little holes.
- The egg whites weren't whisked enough.

The mousse is dense and fudgy.
- The mixture was overfolded when the egg whites were added.

Adding Liquid to Chocolate

Melted chocolate will seize with even a small addition of water as the liquid combines with the dry cocoa solids. It is necessary to add a large enough quantity of liquid to enable these solids to form a solution.

If a recipe requires the addition of a small amount of liquid, add it to the chocolate before it is melted. If adding liquid to melted chocolate, ensure that the liquid measures at least 1 tablespoon per 55 g|2 oz of melted chocolate. Warm the liquid before using.

If possible, add the melted chocolate to the liquid ingredient. Do not add melted chocolate to cold ingredients as this could result in the cocoa butter solidifying.

If the chocolate seizes, add more liquid and heat it, stirring, until it becomes smooth again.

Hot Chocolate Sauce

Chocolate sauce is served warm with profiteroles (see **Pastry**, *Choux*, page 525), hot soufflés (see **Soufflés**, page 647), ice creams (see page 311) and traditionally with desserts containing pears or raspberries. As chocolate varies tremendously in flavour, choose one to your taste. For ease of melting and to ensure the chocolate and water combine without clumping, this recipe adds the water to the chocolate before it is melted. As there is a large amount of water in the recipe, the chocolate can be placed directly in a saucepan to melt rather than in a bain-marie.

170 g|6 oz plain chocolate, chopped
4 tablespoons water
1 tablespoon golden syrup

1 teaspoon instant coffee powder, dissolved in 1 tablespoon boiling water
15 g|½ oz butter

1 Place all the ingredients in a small saucepan and heat over a low heat stirring occasionally, until the chocolate has melted and the sauce is smooth.
2 Serve warm or cold.

NOTE: Store the chocolate sauce in a bowl covered with clingfilm or in an airtight container. When required, heat it gently until smooth and glossy.

Tempering Chocolate

Tempering is a method of heating then cooling chocolate to a particular temperature so that when the chocolate cools and hardens it has a shiny surface and breaks with a sharp snap. It is necessary to temper chocolate before using it to line moulds for making filled chocolates, for coating and when making chocolate bands, curls and shapes. If chocolate is melted, then used without tempering, it will have a dull, streaky appearance when it hardens.

Tempering changes the alignment of the molecules in the chocolate and results in the desired type of cocoa butter crystals remaining unmelted in the chocolate. It is best to work in a cool, dry environment when tempering chocolate.

Couverture, dark chocolate with a high proportion of cocoa butter and cocoa solids, is the best chocolate to use for tempering. Plain chocolate with a high proportion of cocoa solids can also be tempered successfully, as can good-quality milk and white chocolate.

To temper plain chocolate, melt it by one of the methods described above under *Melting Chocolate* so that it reaches a temperature of 45°C|115°F. Milk and white chocolate should be melted to 2° lower. The cocoa butter will melt at this temperature. An accurate and sensitive thermometer such as a digital probe thermometer is necessary for tempering chocolate. Professional chocolatiers often use their upper lip for gauging the temperature of the chocolate because the upper lip is very sensitive.

The chocolate must then be cooled to 27°C|84°F, or 2° lower for milk or white chocolate. It must not become any cooler than 25°C|82°F or the chocolate will have to be reheated again to 45°C|115°F. The chocolate can be cooled in one of the following ways:

- Add an additional 20 per cent of unmelted chocolate and stir constantly. This is called 'seeding'.
- Pour half the melted chocolate on to a cool, dry work surface. Spread the chocolate back and forth with a palette knife until it thickens and becomes difficult to spread. Stir this into the remaining melted chocolate. This is called 'tabling'.
- Place the bowl in a cool water bath and stir to keep the temperature even and to speed cooling.
- Use a tempering machine to melt the chocolate, then add 20 per cent unmelted chocolate. The machine does the stirring. A tempering machine consists of a metal bowl with a heating element underneath to melt the chocolate and a motor that rotates the bowl so that the chocolate is stirred continuously. A thermostat is used to control the temperature of the chocolate so that it is maintained at the correct temperature.

The cooled chocolate must then be reheated to 31°C|88°F for plain chocolate, 27°C|81°F for milk and white chocolate. If the temperature exceeds 33°C|92°F the chocolate must be reheated to 45°C|115°F. Take care not to overheat the chocolate. Chocolate that has seized cannot be tempered.

To test if the chocolate has been tempered successfully, dip a palette knife into the chocolate and tap the knife on the edge of the bowl to remove the excess. Allow the chocolate to stand for up to 5 minutes. It should harden and have a shiny appearance. If the chocolate is not set and shiny, repeat the tempering process.

Once tempered, the chocolate must be kept at 31°C|88°F in order to stay 'in temper'. To hold the chocolate at this temperature, place the bowl of tempered chocolate in a roasting tin half-filled with lukewarm water or on an electric heating pad set to the lowest setting. Special heat lamps are often used by professionals.

Using Tempered Chocolate

Piped chocolate shapes: Tempered chocolate can be piped on to baking parchment, using a small piping bag. Place in the refrigerator to set, then layer the shapes

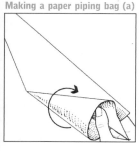
Making a paper piping bag (a)

between baking parchment or clingfilm and store in an airtight container in a cool place. The shapes should be small enough not to dominate the dessert or cake they are to decorate.

Chocolate leaves: Chocolate leaves can be made by painting several layers of tempered chocolate on to the underside of clean rose leaves. Once the chocolate has set, the leaf can be carefully peeled away from the chocolate. Store as for *Piped chocolate shapes*, above.

Caraque, or chocolate curls, can be made by using a palette knife to spread the thinnest possible layer of tempered chocolate on to a cool marble slab or work surface. Allow the chocolate to cool until nearly set, then pull the edge of a thin sharp knife through the chocolate at a 20° angle. The chocolate should roll into cigarette shapes. If the chocolate is still slightly warm, large curls can be made. The curls can be used to decorate desserts and cakes. Store as for *Piped chocolate shapes*, above.

Chocolate teardrops: To make chocolate teardrops to hold ice cream or mousse, cut a rectangular band about 20 × 5 cm|8 × 2 in from acetate. Spread a thick layer of tempered chocolate on to one side of the acetate. Press the ends together with the chocolate on the inside and secure with a paper clip. Place on a plate or tray in the refrigerator until set, then carefully peel the acetate from the chocolate.

Making Moulded Chocolates

Small items, such as teaspoons can be successfully moulded from chocolate. and used to decorate desserts or to stir cappuccino. Fill a small container to a depth of 2 cm with cocoa powder. Carefully press the item to be moulded into the cocoa powder to make an impression. Drizzle melted chocolate into the impression then flick cocoa powder over the top of the chocolate. Place in the refrigerator until set. Allow the chocolate item to harden for a few hours before using.

Chocolate can be moulded using any smooth plastic container. Specialized chocolate moulds can be purchased from catering suppliers or good cookware shops. Clear plastic is the best material for a mould. The thicker the plastic, the more durable the mould will be. Paper cupcake liners or petits fours cases can also be used for moulds.

Chocolate shrinks slightly when it hardens, so the inside, not the outside, of the mould should be coated with several layers of tempered chocolate. This can be done either by painting the chocolate on to the mould with a small brush or by pouring the chocolate into the mould, then tipping out any excess. Allow the chocolate to harden in between coats. The moulds can be placed in the refrigerator to speed the process. The hardening should not take more than 5–10 minutes.

Small moulds that are to be filled need only enough coats for no light to be seen when the mould is held up to the light. Larger chocolate moulds, such as those for Easter eggs, and those which are not going to be filled, will need a coating thickness of up to 6 mm cm|¼ in to make them strong enough to withstand unmoulding.

To fill a mould with a truffle filling, pipe the filling into the hardened chocolate shell, leaving enough space for a layer of chocolate to encase the filling. Chill the chocolate to harden the filling. Pour tempered chocolate over the filling and draw a palette knife or icing scraper over the chocolate to smooth the surface and remove any excess chocolate. Any excess chocolate along the edge of the mould should be carefully cut away with a small, sharp knife when hardened.

To put 2 sides of a mould together, heat a baking sheet in the oven. Quickly place the two halves on to the baking sheet to melt the edges, then hold the halves together until the melted edges set.

Truffles

This recipe can be used to make free-form truffles, or can be enrobed with melted chocolate. It can also be used to fill chocolate moulds (see above).

MAKES ABOUT 40

For the filling
250 g | 9 oz dark plain chocolate
110 ml | 4 fl oz double cream
55 g | 2 oz unsalted butter
1 tablespoon glucose syrup or golden syrup
2 tablespoons liqueur of choice

To coat
110 g | 4 oz cocoa powder, sifted, or toasted chopped nuts, or crushed Amaretti biscuits, or finely ground praline (see *Caramel*, page 178)

To enrobe
225 g | 8 oz tempered melted chocolate

1 Make the filling: chop the chocolate into pea-sized pieces and place in a heatproof bowl.
2 Bring the cream to the boil, then pour over the chocolate. Stir to combine. If the chocolate has not melted completely, place the bowl over a saucepan of steaming water and heat, stirring, until smooth.
3 Stir in the butter, the glucose or golden syrup and the liqueur.
4 Refrigerate until starting to thicken, about 10 minutes.
5 Using an electric hand whisk, beat the mixture until it lightens in colour. Refrigerate until firm, about 10 minutes.
6 Line a baking sheet with baking parchment. Pipe the mixture in a piping bag fitted with a plain 1 cm | ½ in nozzle or use a teaspoon to mound the mixture into rounded teaspoonfuls on the baking parchment. Don't worry if they are not perfectly rounded. Tap down any pointed tops.
7 Roll in sifted cocoa powder, toasted chopped nuts, crushed Amaretti biscuits or finely ground praline.

VARIATION

To enrobe the truffles, omit step 7. Chill the truffle centres until firm but not icy cold. Dip in melted tempered chocolate, then allow to set on baking parchment or roll whilst still wet in sifted cocoa powder, nuts or praline.

To store: If the weather or room is warm, i.e. above 20°C | 70°F, store the truffles, tightly covered, in the refrigerator.

Ganache

Ganache is used primarily as a filling for cakes or meringue discs. It is similar to a truffle mixture but is softer in texture and lighter in colour.

FILLS 2 × 20 CM | 8 IN CAKES

340 g | 12 oz plain chocolate   225 ml | 8 fl oz double cream

1 Chop the chocolate into 1 cm | ½ in pieces and place in a heatproof bowl.
2 Bring the cream to the boil, then pour over the chocolate. Stir until the chocolate is melted and the mixture is thoroughly combined.
3 Allow the mixture to cool until it starts to thicken, then beat it with an electric hand-whisk until thick but still creamy, about 2 minutes. Use as required.

Storing Chocolate

Chocolate should be wrapped in foil and stored in a cool, dry place: 17°C | 65°F is the ideal storage temperature. Avoid storing chocolate in the refrigerator unless your room is too warm. Chocolate stored in the refrigerator must be closely wrapped to avoid condensation.

Plain and unsweetened chocolate have an indefinite shelf life but can easily be spoiled if incorrectly stored, either in too warm an environment or by placing near to strong-smelling foods. The high fat content of chocolate means that it will easily pick up the flavours of other foods, so be careful what other foods are stored nearby. Milk and white chocolates have a tendency to become rancid and should be kept for no longer than 1 year.

If chocolate is stored at a temperature which is too warm it will form 'bloom', a white mottling on the surface. This is the cocoa butter rising to the surface of the chocolate. It can still be used for cooking, however.

Sugar *bloom* can form on chocolate that has been wrapped too loosely. Any moisture that condenses on the surface will dissolve the sugar in the chocolate. When the moisture evaporates, the sugar is left behind as a white crust. Chocolate that has formed a sugar bloom can still be used for cooking.

Dairy Products

Dairy products have formed a very important part of the Western diet since the domestication of cows and sheep about 3,000 years ago. Man is the only animal that continues to consume milk past infancy. Although many people now have concerns about consuming dairy products because of worries about the fat content in regard to both calories and cholesterol, dairy products remain an important ingredient in nutrition and everyday cooking.

Information about the fat content, storage and uses for each dairy product is given in this section. Recipes and methods of using dairy products are to be found in the following sections:

- *Cheese* (page 181)
- *Eggs* (page 213)
- *Sauces, Savoury* (page 579)
- *Sauces, Sweet* (page 611)

Milk

Milk is an emulsion of fat and water. It contains proteins, salts and lactose (milk sugar). The protein casein is responsible for making milk curdle. Milk is used in many recipes, primarily in sauces and milk-based desserts. It is an important source of calcium, protein and Vitamin D in the diet.

Whole milk, with a fat content of 3.5 per cent can be used for extra creaminess in recipes. It is generally recommended that children under the age of 5 should be given whole milk because the additional calories are needed for growth.

Semi-skimmed milk, with a fat content of 1.5–1.8 per cent, can be substituted for whole milk in recipes without much of a noticeable difference.

Skimmed milk has a fat content of 0.3 per cent and is useful in a calorie-controlled diet. It seems watery in comparison to semi-skimmed milk but can be substituted for whole and semi-skimmed milk in recipes.

Milk Treatments

Pasteurization: All milk in the UK is pasteurized, i.e. it has undergone heat treatment that destroys bacteria that might cause disease. Raw milk is sometimes used in cheese-making (see *Cheese*, page 181). Milk will keep for longer if it is pasteurized.

Homogenization: Homogenized milk has been forced through a fine jet under pressure on to a hard surface to break up the fat molecules and disperse them evenly throughout the milk. This gives it a creamier flavour and texture without increasing the fat content and prevents the fat from separating to the top of the milk. Homogenized, whole milk is the best type to use for frothing when preparing cappuccino.

Storing Milk

All milk should be stored in the refrigerator away from light as light destroys the vitamin content. Most milk today is sold stamped with a 'use by' date; however, if it is left at room temperature it can spoil before this date.

Using Milk

Heating milk: Milk will curdle, that is, separate into hard lumps and runny liquid, when mixed with an acid such as lemon juice or partially cooked onion. Always heat milk gently to avoid scorching the proteins.

Scalding milk: To help prevent it from curdling, milk is scalded in many recipes, which means it is heated to just below boiling point. Heat the milk slowly to avoid scorching the casein and whey proteins on the bottom of the pan. Small bubbles form around the edge of the saucepan and steam rises from the milk. This helps to stabilize it. It is also important that any acidic vegetables, such as onion, are cooked until very soft before they are combined with milk.

Avoid boiling: Boiling milk gives it an unpleasant flavour and results in a skin forming on top. This skin contains a large amount of nutrients which will be lost when it is discarded.

Cream

There are many types of cream available. Their fat content determines whether or not they can be whipped or heated and therefore their use in cooking.

Storing Cream

As for milk, take the 'use by' date into account. Cream will keep for up to 3 days in the refrigerator once the container has been opened. Whipping and double cream can be frozen for 1 month. Whip lightly, then freeze in an airtight freezer container. Rewhisk slightly upon defrosting. Cream will not whip as firmly after freezing.

Using Cream

Single cream has a fat content of 18 per cent. It is used for pouring over desserts and in coffee. It cannot be boiled without curdling and cannot be whipped.

Whipping cream has a fat content of 36 per cent. It can be used for pouring, heating or whipping, although its lower fat content means that it is not quite as stable as whipped double cream. It is the best cream to use for ice cream. It gives a lighter, less fatty texture to the ice cream and is less likely to become overworked. Double cream gives the ice cream a grainy texture when it is overworked.

Double cream has a fat content of 48 per cent. It is used for pouring and for whipping (see *Sauces, Sweet, Crème Chantilly*, page 615). Whipped double cream is also used for decoration and for lightening mousse mixtures (see *Mousses*, page 489).

Whipping cream to the soft peak stage

Whipped cream is a foam stabilized by the protein in the cream. Use a balloon whisk or an electric mixer. As soon as the cream starts to thicken, watch it carefully. When whipping cream it is important not to overwhip or the butterfat will become grainy, spoiling the texture and the appearance of the cream. If the cream reaches the stiff peak stage, a little milk should be added to help soften it. If the cream is whipped further, the butterfat will start to clump together and separate from the whey, a thin liquid.

For both decorating and folding the cream should be whipped to the soft-peak stage. Overwhipped cream is difficult to fold into other mixtures. It tends to form clumps that will not combine with the base mixture.

When whipping cream in hot weather, when the temperature is above 25°C | 80°F, it is advisable to chill the bowl and beaters as well as the cream before starting to whip, otherwise the foam may not form.

Extra thick cream has stabilizing ingredients added to make it spoonable without having to whip. It is used as a sauce for desserts.

Cultured Milk Products

Yoghurt is a fermented milk product made from cultured skimmed or whole milk. It has a fat content of 0.5–4 per cent. It is made by heating the milk to about 35°C | 110°F, then adding *Lactobacillus bulgaricus* and *Streptococcus thermophilus*. The bacteria change the lactose into lactic acid, thickening the milk and giving it a sharp flavour.

Yoghurt is usually suitable for people who have lactose intolerance because most of the lactose has been consumed by the bacteria. It has a reputation for being a healthy food as the 'live cultures' in certain types of yoghurt are thought to help colonize bacteria in the intestines and aid digestion. Some yoghurt is sweetened with sugar and flavoured with fruit.

Unsweetened, plain yoghurt can be stirred into curries to enrich them, although it should not be boiled (see *Sauces, Savoury*, page 585) or it will curdle.

Greek yoghurt is made from cow's or sheep's milk. It has a higher fat content than commercial plain yoghurt because it has been partially strained. Sheep's milk yoghurt has a tangier flavour than yoghurt made from cow's milk and is more stable in cooking.

Buttermilk traditionally is the liquid remaining after cream has been churned into butter. Today buttermilk is produced by adding bacteria to low-fat milk to thicken and slightly sour it. It has a fat content of about 2 per cent.

Buttermilk is primarily used in baking recipes which include bicarbonate of soda, such as *Irish Soda Bread* (see **Baking,** *Quick Breads*, page 105), pancakes and scones. The acidity from the buttermilk combines with the alkaline bicarbonate of soda to produce carbon dioxide, which raises the baked goods. If buttermilk is not available, milk can be substituted, but a better result will be obtained if 1 tablespoon lemon juice is added to 290 ml|½ pint milk before using.

Soured cream is made from single cream that has been soured through the addition of lactic-acid producing bacteria which thicken it and give it a tangy flavour. It has a fat content of 18 per cent.

Soured cream can be used as a topping for baked potatoes or for blinis or drop scones served with caviar. It can be used in place of yoghurt for enriching sauces. Like yoghurt, it cannot be boiled.

Clotted cream has a fat content of 55 per cent. It is a speciality of the West Country made by heating cream to concentrate it slightly, then allowing it to stand. The butterfat rises to the top, forming a thick, creamy crust that is skimmed off to use as a spread. It has a rich, creamy flavour and is traditionally served on scones with jam as part of a cream tea. Clotted cream will keep for 5 days in the refrigerator.

Crème fraîche is traditionally made from unpasteurized milk that has been allowed to age. The bacteria present in the cream thicken it and give it a slightly tangy, nutty flavour. Crème fraîche is a speciality of the Normandy region in France. Today crème fraîche made from pasteurized milk is produced by introducing the bacterial culture into the cream. It has a slightly tangy flavour so it tastes less rich than double cream even though the fat content is 48 per cent. It can be whipped or added to sauces and boiled.

Crème fraîche is often very thick when refrigerated but becomes softer at room temperature and when it is stirred. It can be served as an accompaniment to desserts or stirred into sauces to enrich them (see **Fish,** *Braised Noisettes of Salmon with Leeks and Mustard*, page 260). Crème fraîche can be boiled. Low-fat crème fraîche tends to split or separate into lumps and liquid when boiled.

Storing Cultured Milk Products

The cultured milk products listed above should be stored, covered in their containers, in the refrigerator according to their 'use by' dates or for up to 1 week.

Butter

Butter was produced in early times as a method of preserving milk. Today butter is made from cream that has been ripened through the addition of lactic acid-producing bacteria. The cream is churned, which brings the fat molecules together with some of the water in suspension. The remaining liquid, the buttermilk, is drained away, then the butter is washed and worked to improve its texture. Salt is often added for flavour and as a preservative. The type of cow producing the cream as well as its diet have a great influence on the flavour of the butter.

Butter, a water-in-oil emulsion, contains approximately 80 per cent fat, with the remaining 20 per cent consisting of milk solids and water. It is solid at room temperature and is a saturated fat (see *Healthy Eating and Basic Nutrition*, page 17) so is best consumed in limited quantity.

Storing

Butter should be kept tightly wrapped in the refrigerator, away from strong-smelling foods as it will absorb flavours. Most butter is marked with a 'use by' date. Butter should not be left at room temperature. It quickly becomes rancid due to the oxidation of the fat and develops a noticeably sour smell and taste. Butter can be frozen for 1 month.

Using

Butter is widely used in cooking as a seasoning for vegetables, for frying (see *Meat*, page 345), for cooking eggs and as an ingredient in pastry (see *Pastry*, page 507) and cakes (see *Cakes*, page 137). Unsalted butter is used for the emulsion sauces (see *Sauces, Savoury, Hollandaise Sauce*, page 602). In some countries unsalted butter is called sweet or sweetened butter. Butter is also used to make *Maître d'Hôtel Butter*, a simple seasoning for grilled meat (see below), and *Brandy Butter* (see below) to serve with *Christmas Pudding* (see *Steaming*, page 677) and mince pies.

Maître d'Hôtel Butter

55 g│2 oz butter, softened	1 teaspoon finely chopped parsley
2 teaspoons lemon juice	salt and freshly ground black pepper

1 Mix together all the ingredients and shape into a cylinder.
2 Wrap in clingfilm and refrigerate.
3 Cut into 3 mm│⅛ in discs and place on top of hot grilled meat.

Brandy Butter

SERVES 4

110 g│4 oz unsalted butter, softened	grated zest of 1 small orange
55 g│2 oz caster sugar	2 tablespoons brandy

1 Cream the butter until very soft.

2 Add the sugar and orange zest and beat until light and fluffy.

3 Gradually beat in the brandy.

4 Pile into a serving bowl and refrigerate until required.

NOTE: Icing sugar can be used in place of caster sugar, if desired.

Flavoured Butters: What has gone wrong when...

The liquid ingredients will not mix into the butter.

- The butter is too cold. Beat it for a longer time to soften it.
- Too much liquid has been added.

Creaming Butter

Many recipes for cakes and biscuits require the butter to be 'creamed', sometimes with sugar. This means that the butter is beaten either with a wooden spoon or in an electric mixer until it is very soft and almost white in colour. The change of colour occurs as air is beaten into the butter. When sugar is added, it will dissolve in the whey and lose its granular texture. If possible, letting the butter come to room temperature before creaming makes the process easier. Otherwise heat the bowl in hot water and dry it. Cut the butter into small pieces and place in the warmed bowl to beat.

Butter for Frying

When used for frying food, butter is often combined with an equal quantity of flavourless oil which allows it to be heated to a higher temperature without burning. The butter gives the fried food a good flavour and helps it to brown.

Clarified butter (sometimes called drawn butter) is butter that has had the whey and the milk solids removed. This allows the butter to be heated to a higher temperature without burning. Clarified butter is used for frying meat when a butter flavour is desired. Clarified butter is also used to seal the surface of pâtés to protect them (see **Terrines, Pâtés and Raised Pies**, page 710).

Making clarified butter

1 Heat the butter in a saucepan over a medium heat. The butter will sizzle and pop as the water evaporates. Continue to heat until the sizzling stops but not for so long that the milk solids at the bottom of the pan start to turn brown.

2 Skim the froth from the top of the melted butter (this is the whey).

3 Pour the butter through a sieve lined with a sterilized J-cloth or piece of muslin, to trap the milk solids.

4 Store tightly covered in the refrigerator for up to 3 weeks or freeze for 3 months.

Noisette Butter and Black Butter

Noisette butter (*noisette* is the French word for hazelnut) is butter that has been heated until it has turned nut-brown and gives off a nutty aroma. The cooking of the proteins in the butter produces the brown colour. It is used as a sauce for skate (see **Fish**, *Skate with Brown Butter and Capers*, page 254) and to finish cooked spinach. Black butter (Beurre Noir), which results when the proteins burn, and is also used as a sauce for skate.

Beurre Noir

Serve with eggs, fish and asparagus.

55 g|2 oz butter	1 tablespoon chopped fresh parsley
1 tablespoon lemon juice	salt and freshly ground black pepper

1 Melt the butter in a heavy-based pan and cook over a medium heat until it is nut-brown and smells lightly toasted. Be careful not to allow the butter to darken excessively or it will taste burnt.
2 Mix the lemon juice with 1 tablespoon water and stir into the hot butter to make an emulsion.
3 Stir in the parsley and pour over the food.

VARIATIONS

Add 2 teaspoons rinsed and roughly chopped capers to Beurre Noir to serve with skate. For **Beurre Noisette**, make as for Beurre Noir but heat the butter only until the milk solids turn a medium-brown colour and smell nutty. Serve with *Sole Meunière* (see **Fish**, page 256).

Ghee is clarified butter that has been heated until the milk solids brown, giving it a nutty flavour. It is widely used in Indian cookery.

Margarine, a butter substitute, is a fat made from hydrogenated vegetable oil. Hydrogenation is a chemical process that changes a fat that is liquid at room temperature to a fat that is solid (see **Healthy Eating and Basic Nutrition**, page 13). Margarine is dyed to give it a similar appearance to butter and the best-quality margarine has 80 per cent fat, as does butter. Margarine can be substituted for butter in cakes and pastries, but it is not recommended for butter sauces or for seasoning food. Most margarines are not good for frying because they separate when melted.

Deep-frying: Points to Remember

- Use a fat with a high smoke point (see below).
- Check the temperature of the oil. If the deep-fryer is not thermostatically controlled, use a thermometer to test the temperature of the fat or test by timing the browning of a cube of bread, as follows:

  60 seconds = 160°C | 325°F = low
  40 seconds = 180°C | 350°F = moderate
  20 seconds = 190°C | 375°F = very hot

- If the fat becomes any hotter than 190°C | 375°F it is dangerous. Turn off the heat source and add slices of bread to the fat to cool it down.
- If using a commercial fryer, dip the basket in the hot oil before adding the food to prevent it from sticking to the basket.
- Cook the food in small batches. Large amounts will cause the fat to cool down too much and the food will absorb fat and will not brown.
- When frying food from frozen, do not compensate for the fact that it is frozen by turning up the heat. The food needs to be fried at a moderate temperature in order to cook through completely.
- Drain the cooked food well on kitchen paper. This will absorb fat from the surface of the food.
- Sprinkle savoury food with salt to help absorb any additional fat on the surface of the food. Sprinkle sweet food with a little caster sugar.
- If keeping fried food warm, do not cover it or it will become soggy. Spread it on a hot baking sheet in a single layer. Place in a warm oven with the door ajar so there is free circulation of air.
- To re-use fat, sieve it when cool to remove any particles of cooked food.
- As soon as the fat becomes dark it should be discarded: it has started to break down.

Safety Precautions when Deep-frying

- Never leave unattended an operating deep-fryer or a saucepan heating with hot fat. The fat can burst into flames.
- Never move a hot deep-fryer or pan of hot fat.
- Turn any handles away from the front of the cooker.
- Have a fire extinguisher or blanket and a lid within easy reach of the frying area.
- If the fat bursts into flames, do not spray it with water: this could cause the flames to spread. If possible, smother the flames.
- Turn off the heat source if the oil smokes or if it bursts into flames.
- Never fill a deep-fryer or pan more than two-thirds full with fat.
- Dry food thoroughly before frying: do not put wet food into the hot fat, it will splutter and could cause the fat to splash.

Deep-frying

Deep-frying is one of the fastest methods of cooking small, tender cuts of meat and fish. It is also suitable for many vegetables, particularly potatoes, and for dough mixtures such as fritters and doughnuts.

Deep-frying is a potentially dangerous cooking method because of the very high temperatures to which the fat is heated. It is important to follow the safety precautions listed opposite.

Smoke Point of Oils

The smoke point is the temperature at which the molecular structure of the oil begins to break down and the oil begins to smoke. These smoky fumes are toxic. At this point the oil is becoming unstable and is in danger of bursting into flames. The heat source should be turned off and bread should be added to the fat to reduce the heat quickly. Oil that has reached its smoke point will give food an unpleasant, rancid flavour.

Peanut, Safflower, Soybean, Grapeseed	225°C | 450°F
Rapeseed (Canola)	210°C | 435°F
Corn, Olive, Sesame	200°C | 400°F
Sunflower	190°C | 375°F

Safflower, corn oil, or oil marketed as 'vegetable' oil are the best oils to use for deep-frying. Peanut (groundnut) oil could possibly provoke allergic reactions. Grapeseed oil is expensive, and rapeseed, olive and sesame oils are too strongly flavoured. Butter cannot be heated to the high temperatures needed for deep-frying without burning (see **Dairy Products,** *Butter,* page 202).

Coatings for Deep-frying

With the exception of potato crisps, which are only fried for a very short time, and chips, which are given 2 fryings (see *Chips,* below), most foods are given a protective coating before frying. The coating should cover the food completely. This protects delicate food from the very hot fat, helps to prevent overcooking and seals in the juices as well as keeping the fat from absorbing the flavours of the food.

The coating also gives the food a crisp outer layer which provides a delicious contrast with the soft interior.

The type of coating should be in keeping with the food being coated. A delicate fish fillet needs only a thin coating. A more robust, chunky piece of fish can hold up to a thicker batter. The coating should only enhance and flavour the food, never dominate it.

Applying a simple coating of flour, beaten egg and crumbs is known as to *paner*. It is the classic coating for *Goujons* of *Fish* (see recipe below) and is also used to coat mashed potatoes for croquettes and small pieces of cheese. Dried, sieved bread-crumbs will give a fine, crisp coating. The coarser the coating, the crisper and more fatty it will be. Fresh breadcrumbs, oatmeal or crushed cereal flakes can be used in place of dried crumbs.

Batter is often used for coating larger pieces of fish and for vegetables. Batter (see **Batters**, page 111) is made by mixing a liquid such as water, milk or beer with eggs and flour to a consistency of thick cream. The Japanese dish tempura is made by coating the fish and vegetables with a batter, as is the fish for traditional English fish and chips (see recipe for *Beer Batter*, below). A thick, cool batter will adhere to food better than a thin, warm batter. Before dipping food in batter, it should be coated first with seasoned flour to help the batter adhere.

The fat content of the coating will affect the rate of fat absorption. Batters made with egg white will be lighter and crisper, whilst batters containing egg yolk will be more tender and rich.

Tempura is a Japanese dish made by coating fish, vegetables or fruit in a light batter made with cornflour and fizzy mineral water. The packet mix produces the best results.

Food should be coated just before frying otherwise the coating absorbs some of the moisture from the food and will not become crisp when fried. The one exception to this rule is fried ice cream. The ice cream must be dipped in the batter, then refrozen before frying.

Goujons of Fish

A goujon is a piece of fish measuring about 5 × 1 cm|2 × ½ in.

110 g|4 oz white fish fillets, such a lemon sole or plaice, skinned, per person
plain flour, seasoned with salt and freshly ground black pepper
1 egg beaten with a little oil, sieved dried white breadcrumbs, sieved

To serve
Tartare Sauce (see **Sauces, Savoury**, *Mayonnaise*, page 601)
lemon wedges (see **Food Presentation**, *Garnishes*, page 12)

1 Cut the fish across the grain or on the diagonal, if possible, into finger-like strips.
2 Heat the oil to moderate temperature (see above).

3 Put the seasoned flour, beaten egg and crumbs on to 3 separate plates or roasting tins. If possible, ask one or two other people to help you with the flour-egg-crumb (*paner*) procedure. For best results do not paner in advance or the coating will soak up the juices from the fish and become soggy.

4 Dip the fish pieces into the flour, then shake gently to remove any excess.

5 Dip the pieces of fish into the egg. It is important to keep the pieces separate from each other so that they are coated evenly and completely.

6 Dip the pieces of fish into the crumbs.

7 Place each piece of fish on a plate or tray in a single layer so that they do not touch each other.

8 Fry a few pieces at a time until crisp and golden-brown.

9 Drain on kitchen paper and sprinkle with a little salt.

10 Serve with Tartare Sauce and lemon wedges.

Goujons of Fish: What has gone wrong when...

See *Deep-frying: What has gone wrong when* ... below.

Beer Batter

Before making a batter read the section on *Batters* (page 111). Food to be coated with a batter should first be dipped into seasoned flour to help the batter adhere evenly to the food. This recipe can be used to coat fillets of fish, vegetables or courgette flowers.

110 g | 4 oz plain flour

a pinch of salt

1 egg, lightly beaten

1 tablespoon vegetable oil

100 ml | 3½ fl oz beer or ale

plain flour, seasoned with salt and freshly
    ground black pepper

1 Sift the flour with the salt into a large bowl and make a well in the centre.

2 Put the egg, oil and half the beer into the well.

3 Stir the liquid gently to slowly draw in the flour to make a lump-free batter.

4 Stir in the remaining beer.

5 Cover the batter and refrigerate for 30 minutes.

6 To use, dip the food to be fried into seasoned flour, then into the batter. Fry immediately in small batches in fat heated to 180°C | 350°F until golden-brown.

7 Sprinkle with a little salt and serve immediately. To keep fried food warm, see instructions under *Deep-frying: Points to Remember*, above.

Beer Batter: What has gone wrong when...

See *Deep-frying: What has gone wrong when* ... below.

Beignets

Choux pastry can be deep-fried to produce delicious crisp morsels. See **Pastry,** *Choux* (page 525) for the basic recipe. A slightly slack mixture will produce the best beignets.

Savoury: To the basic recipe add 55 g|2 oz Cheddar cheese, cut into 3 mm|⅛ in cubes.
Sweet: After frying the beignets, fill them with a 290 ml|½ pint quantity *Crème Pâtissière* (see *Pâtisserie*, page 532). Dust with a mixture of caster sugar and ground cinnamon.

1 Heat the oil to 180°C|350°F.
2 Drop teaspoonfuls of the choux pastry into the hot oil one at a time so that they do not stick together. Dip the teaspoon in the hot fat first so that the pastry will slip off easily.
3 Tap the floating beignets lightly to help them puff. Turn them over. Fry for about 3–5 minutes or until golden-brown. They should feel light when done.
4 Remove from the oil with a slotted spoon and drain on crumpled kitchen paper.
5 Roll the beignets in sugar or sprinkle with salt.
6 The beignets can be split open and filled with *Crème Pâtissière* (see **Pâtisserie**, page 532), if desired.

Deep-frying: What has gone wrong when...

The food is pale and greasy.
- The oil was not hot enough.
- The food was not cooked for long enough.
- The food was not fried immediately after coating.

The coating is soggy.
- The food was not fried immediately after coating.
- The fried food was covered and the coating was softened by the steam of the hot food.

The coating browns too quickly before the food is cooked.
- The oil was too hot.
- The coating contains too much sugar or egg.

The coating falls off the food when fried.
- The food was not dusted with flour before coating.
- The food was not fried immediately after coating.

Chips

Home-made chips are a rare treat. Use floury potatoes such as Maris Piper or King Edward (see **Potatoes**, page 540). The potatoes need to be deep-fried twice: first at a slightly lower temperature to cook them through, then again at a higher temperature to brown them. The first frying gelatinizes the starch in the potatoes; the second frying browns the starch on the outside.

SERVES 4
675 g | 1½ lb potatoes
oil, for deep-frying
salt

1 Cut the potatoes into 5 × 1 cm | 2 × ½ in sticks. Place in a bowl of cold water to prevent discoloration.
2 Heat the oil in a large saucepan or deep-fryer to 160°C | 325°F.
3 Drain the potatoes and dry them thoroughly. If they are still wet they will cause the oil to splutter.
4 Fry the potatoes in small batches (too many will stick together) for 7–8 minutes or until soft. Place on crumpled kitchen paper to drain.
5 For the second frying, heat the oil to 190°C | 375°F.
6 Fry the chips again, in small batches, until well-browned and crisp.
7 Drain on kitchen paper and sprinkle with salt. Serve immediately.

VARIATION
Pommes Allumetes are matchstick pieces of potato (see **Knife Skills**, page 71) that are given only 1 frying.

Chips: What has gone wrong when...

The chips are soggy.
- The chips were not pre-cooked.
- The second cooking was not long enough.
- The chips were covered to keep warm.

The chips are dry in the centre.
- The chips have been overcooked.

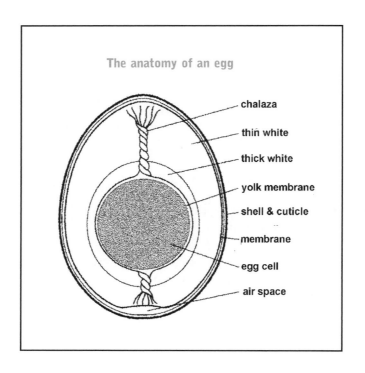

The anatomy of an egg

chalaza

thin white

thick white

yolk membrane

shell & cuticle

membrane

egg cell

air space

Eggs

Eggs are inexpensive and are probably the most versatile and nutritious of cooking ingredients. Eggs supply complete protein (see **Healthy Eating and Basic Nutrition**, page 16), fat, Vitamins A, B, D and E and iron and mineral salts. They are easily digested. Their neutral, rich flavour provides an ideal background for a vast array of flavouring and seasoning ingredients, both savoury and sweet.

Eggs can be boiled, scrambled, poached, fried, baked and served with a diverse array of garnishes. They are also used to emulsify and thicken sauces, to bind forcemeat and to make pasta, biscuits, pastry, cakes and batters as well as a glaze for baked goods.

It is best to avoid serving dishes that contain raw eggs, such as home-made mayonnaise, chocolate mousse or dishes containing partially cooked eggs such as Hollandaise Sauce to vulnerable groups, including the pregnant, old, infirm or very young.

Types of Eggs

Although hens' eggs are most frequently used in the kitchen, other types of egg can be used in a number of dishes. The following types are available fresh from farms, specialist shops and good supermarkets and should be stored in the same way as hens' eggs (see *Storing Eggs*, below).

Turkey and goose eggs, due to their high fat content, are too strongly flavoured and rich to be eaten alone but are useful for enriching and lightening baked goods. Goose eggs, which have a white shell and are 4–5 times larger than a hen's egg, make particularly good sponge cakes. Duck eggs have an off-white shell and when boiled, the white turns bluish in colour and the yolk a deep orange. They can be used for most purposes.

Quail, guinea fowl and gulls' eggs make very good first courses served with celery salt, paprika and brown bread and butter. Quail eggs are small with brown speckles and have a creamy texture and rich flavour; they are often served as a canapé, hard-boiled and peeled, with celery salt, or soft-boiled or poached in salads. Gulls' eggs are served as a delicacy as they are available only in May and June. The shell is pale blue with light or dark brown markings and they have a slightly fishy flavour, due to the birds' diet. They vary in size and are sold ready boiled. The cooked white is translucent and bluish and the yolk is pale yellow.

To use other egg varieties in the place of hens' eggs, such as goose eggs for a cake, weigh the goose egg and divide by 55 g | 2 oz, the average weight of a hen's egg, in order to calculate how many hens' eggs the goose egg is replacing.

The Anatomy of an Egg

The main constituents of an egg are the yolk, the white and shell. The average weight of a hen's egg is 55 g | 2 oz, of which the yolk weighs around 25 g | 1 scant oz and the white weighs around 30 g | 1 oz.

The Egg Shell

The hard, brittle shell contains and protects the white and yolk from physical damage, from losing moisture and from infection by bacteria. Egg shell is made of a calcium carbonate and protein mesh, densely perforated with pores and covered in a protective protein cuticle. The colour of the shell has no effect on the quality, flavour or nutrition of the egg but is determined by the breed of hen and varies from white to reddish-brown.

To crack an egg: Have a bowl ready. Tap the side of the egg on the rim of the bowl to crack the shell. Place your thumbs either side of the crack on the underside of the egg and pull apart. Allow the egg to drop into the bowl.

To separate an egg: When pulling the two halves of the shell apart, catch the yolk in one half. Allow the white to drain into the bowl. If any yolk falls into the white, use the sharp edge of the egg shell to scoop it out.

Inside the Shell

Inside the shell are 2 white membranes that separate to form an air sac at the wider end. Between these 2 membranes lies the egg white, or albumen. Forming 58 per cent of the total weight of the egg, egg white is a viscous, colourless liquid made up of 88 per cent water, with the remaining 12 per cent composed of protein, minerals and vitamins, including riboflavin. The egg white is made up of an outer thin white, an inner thick white and a third extremely thin layer which coats the chalaziferous layer surrounding the yolk membrane.

The chalaziferous layer is visible as opaque fibrous chords or white strings, called chalazae, on opposite sides of the yolk. The chalazae hold the yolk in the centre of the egg, stretching from the yolk, through the white, to the membranes located right against the inner surface of the shell. Prominent chalazae signify that an egg is fresh and may be strained out of the egg white before cooking or whisking.

The yolk constitutes 42 per cent of the egg's total weight and contains three-quarters of the its calorific value. It is made up of 19 per cent protein, 30 per cent fat and 51 per cent water. The yolk is a thick liquid containing the entire fat content of the egg, a wide range of vitamins and minerals, the emulsifying protein lecithin and an iron-based pigment called haematogen that gives the yolk its yellow colour.

Identifying a Fresh Egg

As an egg ages, the structure of the white and yolk begins to break down, affecting both its cooking properties and flavour. Cracking an egg on to a plate can show the cook just how old it is. If the white has body, does not spread widely and the chalazae are clearly visible, the egg is very fresh. As an egg ages, the thick part of the egg white deteriorates and becomes watery. The yolk of a fresh egg should be domed and stand firmly above the white. Over time, the yolk membrane becomes weaker, causing the yolk to flatten and spread. As a result, older eggs do not hold tightly together during poaching, fried eggs look flat and shapeless and in both cases the yolk is liable to break. Older eggs can be successfully scrambled, however, and the shell is easier to remove from hard-boiled older eggs as the membrane no longer clings tightly to the inside of the shell.

With the gradual breaking down of the egg white, carbon dioxide is released into the enlarging air sac and out through the shell. Air from outside passes through the pores in the shell to fill the increasing space left by the egg white. Knowing this, it is possible to test whether an egg is fresh without breaking it, by gently immersing it in a bowl of water. If the egg lies flat on the bottom, this means that the air sac is small, and the egg is very fresh. If the egg stands up and bobs on the bottom of the bowl, this means that it is older and more buoyant, due to the enlarged air sac, but is suitable for scrambling. If the egg floats to the surface, this means that it is full of gas and should be thrown away as it is most probably rotten.

Storing Eggs

Eggs are potentially hazardous as they are rich in nutrients and provide the ideal conditions for the growth of harmful bacteria such as salmonella (see *Food Safety*, page 26), which is commonly found in the intestines of chickens. Most bacterial contamination is present on the shell of a dirty or cracked egg but can also be found inside. Eggs that are dirty and/or cracked should be discarded.

Store eggs in a refrigerator: To reduce the risk of salmonella poisoning as well as to slow the rate of deterioration, store eggs at temperatures below 4°C|40°F. Eggs age faster at room temperature than if kept in the refrigerator. Shop-bought fresh eggs are stamped with a 'best before' date set at 3 weeks from laying, provided they are kept in the refrigerator. Egg shells are porous and pervious to air, water and odours. To prevent the flavour of eggs from becoming tainted it is best to store the eggs in their box away from strongly flavoured, pungent foods. They will also keep better if they are stored standing upright on their pointed end so that the air sac, at the wide end, is facing upwards.

Storing Separated Eggs

Egg whites can be refrigerated for up to 3 weeks as they contain a natural bactericide, or may be frozen for up to 3 months. Yolks can be refrigerated for 2–3 days, covered with a little cold water and clingfilm to prevent a hard crust from forming. They can also be frozen for up to 3 months.

Storing Egg Dishes

Egg dishes should be stored below 4°C|40°F or above 63°C|145°F or eaten within 1 hour of being prepared if held at room temperature.

Cooking Eggs

Eggs are rich in protein that coagulates and solidifies when heated. The exact temperature at which coagulation occurs varies depending upon how quickly the eggs are heated and if they are combined with other ingredients. If a whole beaten egg is heated slowly without any added ingredients, coagulation will begin at 70°C|160°F. By the time the temperature reaches 82°C|180°F the egg will be fully coagulated.

Raw egg white is clear and watery as the uncooked protein allows light to pass through it. As the protein unwinds, or denatures, with heat, the protein molecules pack densely together so that light is no longer able to pass through and the white becomes opaque and solidifies. If the egg continues to cook after coagulation occurs or if it is heated very rapidly, the protein continues to pack more and more densely together until the water in the egg is squeezed out and the remaining protein becomes hard, dry and rubbery. To prevent this from happening it is important to heat eggs gently even when boiling eggs (see below).

Boiled Eggs

Boiled eggs are eaten for breakfast with buttered toast, used whole, halved or grated in salads, in egg mayonnaise or as a garnish in soups and sauces. Boiled eggs should really be called 'simmered' eggs as they should not be boiled hard but simmered gently in water where bubbles are only just breaking the surface.

Timing boiled eggs

Boiling-water start (Medium size egg)

- 4½ minutes will give a runny yolk and a white that is just set.
- 6 minutes will give a well-set white and a moist but runny yolk, set on the rim and thick but wet inside.
- 8 minutes will give a hard-boiled egg that is just set to the centre of the yolk (this is known as *œuf mollet*).
- 12 minutes will give a yolk sufficiently cooked to be dry and crumbly when mashed.
- 15 minutes will give a yellowish-green rim to the dry yolk ands make the white tough and unpalatable.

Serving soft-boiled eggs

Following the cooking times above, once the eggs have simmered for the required time hold them under cold running water for a few seconds, to prevent them from cooking further.

To serve boiled eggs, place the pointed end of the egg in an egg cup. Carefully crack the shell across the broad end, 1 cm | ½ in from the tip, with a sharp knife and serve immediately. Eat the egg from the shell with a small spoon accompanied by hot buttered toast.

Hard-boiled Eggs

Hard-boiled eggs are peeled once they are cooked and this can be difficult when using very fresh eggs as the membrane inside the shell is firmly attached to the egg white. To make peeling easier, crack the shells during cooling. Choose eggs that are about 7–10 days old so that the membrane comes away cleanly from the white as the shell is peeled off.

Place the eggs in a saucepan of cold water and bring to the boil. Once the water has started boiling, turn the heat down to a simmer and cook for 10 minutes.

Cool the eggs by placing under cold running water for 5 minutes. Tap them gently to crack the shells all over and make peeling easier.

To remove the shell, roll the egg back and forth on a work surface, applying gentle downward pressure. Hold the egg under cold running water and start to peel the shell at the broad end, starting above the air sac.

To store hard-boiled eggs, refrigerate them in their shells for up to 5 days.

Hard-boiled Eggs: What has gone wrong when...

The yolks have turned green around the edge.
- The eggs have been overcooked. The iron contained in the yolk and the sulphur in the white combine with prolonged cooking at high temperatures to produce hydrogen sulphide.

The eggs are difficult to peel.
- The eggs are very fresh.
- The shells were not cracked during cooling.

The white is rubbery.
- The egg was cooked at a rolling boil. Never boil eggs at more than a gentle simmer.

The yolk is powdery.
- The egg was cooked for too long.

Poached Eggs

To poach eggs, use the freshest eggs available as the white of a fresh egg is thick and holds tightly together when the egg is lowered into simmering water. The membrane surrounding the yolk is also stronger and less likely to break. It also helps if the eggs are cold as the whites are less inclined to spread. Small quantities of salt and vinegar (2 tablespoons vinegar per litre $|$ 1¾ pints water) can be added to the water to denature and solidify the white more quickly so that the poached egg is more likely to hold its shape during cooking.

The white of a poached egg should be sufficiently set to encase the yolk completely in a neat teardrop shape but the yolk should still be runny. Poached eggs are generally served on hot buttered toast or with Hollandaise Sauce (see *Sauces, Savoury*, page 602), or on warm salads or with asparagus.

Poaching Eggs

1 Fill a saucepan with water at least 5 cm|2 in deep and bring to simmering point.
2 Crack a very fresh, cold egg into a cup.
3 Swirl the water in its pan to make a whirlpool (the current encourages the egg to set in a compact shape). As the whirlpool slows and almost disappears, tip the egg into its centre, holding the cup as near to the water as possible.
4 Raise the heat so that the water bubbles gently. The gently boiling water will set the outside of the egg white and prevent the egg from spreading.
5 Once the egg white appears to be just set, reduce the heat to a simmer to cook the egg slowly.
6 Poach each egg for 2–3 minutes or until the white next to the yolk feels firm and set. The yolk should be still runny but warm.
7 Lift out the egg with a slotted spoon, pat dry with kitchen paper and trim the white with kitchen scissors if it is ragged at the edges.
8 Serve as required.

If a number of poached eggs are required, they can be poached in advance and held for up to 1 day as follows:

1 Prepare an ice-bath.
2 Cook the eggs as above until the whites are set and the yolks are still runny.
3 Remove each egg from the pan with a slotted spoon and place gently in the ice bath to stop the cooking process and to cool them quickly.
4 Store the eggs in iced water in the refrigerator until needed.
5 Reheat the eggs by placing them in a pan of barely simmering water until just hot.

Poached Eggs: What has gone wrong when...

The egg is misshapen.
- The egg was dropped into still water that might have been too cool and as a result had too long to set. The egg has spread out in the water, rather than holding together, while it was still unset and as a result is very uneven in shape.

The egg white has broken away from the yolk.
- If an egg is dropped into a very fast whirlpool this can cause the white to break up and away from the main body of the egg.
- The egg was old.

The egg has a flat shape.
- The water was not simmering.
- The egg was old.

Fried Eggs

Pan-frying is one of the simplest ways to cook eggs. The temperature at which an egg is fried will determine its texture and the amount of fat it absorbs. An egg fried at a very high temperature becomes brown, crisp and tough and the white traps bubbles of fat, which can make the egg greasy. An egg fried gently will be tender and moist and will absorb little fat. Fried eggs are traditionally served as part of an English or American cooked breakfast.

It is important to use very fresh eggs as the yolk holds its shape better and the white spreads less. The two most popular ways to serve fried eggs is, as the Americans say, 'sunny side up' and 'over easy'. Sunny side up eggs are fried on the first side only, over a medium to low heat, long enough (about 4 minutes) to firm the whites and partially firm the yolk. The yolk can be basted with the fat from the pan for flavour and to cook it slightly.

For over easy, the egg is partially cooked on one side (about 3 minutes), then gently turned over with a spatula and cooked on the other side until the yolk is partially cooked but runny in the middle. The egg white should be firm but not browned and the yolk should never be broken. Cook for longer if a firmer egg is required. Eggs can be fried in vegetable oil or a mixture of oil and butter, or clarified butter. Butter produces a fried egg with a richer taste.

Fried eggs do have a tendency to stick to the pan, so use a well-seasoned or non-stick heavy pan that conducts heat evenly. Warm the fat in the pan before adding the eggs but make sure it does not get so hot that the eggs brown the moment they touch the pan.

Frying Eggs

1 Select a sauté pan just large enough to accommodate the number of eggs to be cooked. A 20 cm|8 in pan is suitable for 3 eggs.
2 Add a small amount of vegetable oil and butter or clarified butter and heat over a medium-low heat until the fat just begins to sizzle.
3 Carefully break the eggs into the pan.
4 Continue to cook over a medium-low heat until the whites are set. Baste the yolk or turn the eggs over as required.
5 Gently slide the cooked eggs on to a serving plate, season and serve immediately.

Fried Eggs: What has gone wrong when...

The base of the egg is brown, crisp and bubbly.
- The egg was cooked in oil that was too hot.

The egg white has spread and is uneven in shape.
- The egg was not fresh enough. For perfectly compact, evenly shaped fried eggs, use the freshest possible.

- The eggs were added to the pan while the oil was still cool.
- The pan was unseasoned and / or a poor conductor of heat.

Scrambled Eggs

Scrambled egg should consist of large flakes of softly set egg. It is very important not to overcook scrambled egg as the flakes of egg become tough and rubbery. To allow large flakes of egg to form, slowly move the eggs around the pan over a medium heat until they are almost set. By the time the pan has been removed from the heat and the scrambled eggs have been transferred to a serving dish, they will have set to a soft, creamy consistency. Scrambled eggs are served with hot buttered toast, or with smoked salmon and are often served with sautéed mushrooms and grilled tomatoes.

Scrambled eggs have a tendency to stick and catch on the base of the pan. Use a well-seasoned or non-stick heavy-based pan that conducts heat evenly and warm the butter gently in the pan before adding the eggs.

Scrambled Eggs

SERVES 1

2 eggs

1 tablespoon creamy milk or water (optional)

salt and freshly ground black pepper

15 g | ½ oz butter

1 In a bowl, whisk together the eggs, milk or water and the seasoning with a fork or balloon whisk.
2 Melt the butter in a heavy-based saucepan and warm until the butter starts to bubble gently.
3 Tip in the egg mixture and using a wooden spoon, slowly and smoothly move the egg around the base of the pan until the egg is thickened and creamy.
4 Remove from the heat and serve immediately.

Scrambled Eggs: What has gone wrong when...

The eggs are watery.
- The eggs have been overcooked.

The eggs are rubbery.
- The eggs were cooked at too high a temperature and are overcooked.

Omelettes

An omelette can be either savoury or sweet. It is made from beaten whole eggs, cooked gently in a frying pan and served plain or with the addition of flavouring and garnishing ingredients. An omelette is usually prepared as an individual serving using 2–3 eggs and served flat or folded and hot for breakfast, a light lunch, supper or even as a dessert. An omelette may also be sliced thinly to garnish salads and soups.

A number of different preparation and cooking methods are used to make omelettes.

Plain folded omelette: Cooked with finely chopped herbs and seasonings incorporated into the basic egg mixture.

Filled omelette: A filling of hot pre-cooked ingredients such as sautéed vegetables, diced ham or bacon and grated cheese is spread over the surface of the half-set omelette which is then folded.

French garnished omelette: A slit is made in the surface of the cooked, folded and plated omelette and filled with a garnishing ingredient often bound in a sauce.

Flat open-faced omelettes: Frittatas (Italian) or tortillas (Spanish) made with a large proportion of filling ingredients added to the uncooked egg mixture, then cooked on both sides on the hob or finished in the oven or under the grill. The result is a thick cake that can be served hot or cold, cut into wedges. As with all egg dishes, it is important not to overcook flat omelettes as they will become tough and dry.

Soufflé omelettes: Light-textured omelettes filled with savoury or sweet fillings. A soufflé omelette is made by whisking the egg whites and yolks separately, then folding them together before partially cooking the omelette on the hob, then transferring it to the oven where the omelette soufflés. Omelette Arnold Bennett is a classic savoury example which is flavoured with smoked haddock and cheese. Sweet soufflé omelettes are usually filled with jam or poached fruit, sprinkled with icing sugar, glazed under the grill and sometimes flamed with liqueur.

Although omelettes are very simple to make, they have a tendency to stick to the pan and can be difficult to serve without practice. They can also be tough and rubbery as a result of cooking at too high a temperature and/or for too long.

Omelettes: Points to Remember

- Omelettes have to be cooked in a well-proved pan (see below), or non-stick pan.
- A small amount of cold water added to the eggs will lighten the omelette.
- Prepare all filling ingredients before starting to cook.

Proving a Pan

Omelette pans are heavy-based wide pans with shallow sloping sides and one long pan handle. The omelette pan is designed to cook the base of the omelette evenly and to assist turning the omelette on to the plate. It is then folded in half or into three for serving.

- Place 1 tablespoon vegetable oil and 1 tablespoon salt in the pan and heat until the oil starts to smoke.
- Remove the pan from the heat and allow to cool.
- Rub the sides and base of the pan with kitchen paper, using the salt as an abrasive to remove any impurities from the surface that could cause food to stick.
- Once the pan is clean, remove any remaining oil and salt by wiping the pan out with kitchen paper.
- If the pan is reserved for cooking omelettes and crêpes, it is better not to wash it with detergent, just wipe it out thoroughly with kitchen paper after cooking.

Folded Omelette

SERVES 1

2–3 eggs at room temperature
salt and freshly ground black pepper
1 tablespoon cold water

15 g | ½ oz butter
any filling and garnishing ingredients, ready prepared

1 Cook any ingredients for the omelette filling. Warm a serving plate.
2 Break the eggs into a bowl and with a fork mix in the seasoning and water.
3 Melt the butter in a heavy 15 cm | 6 in omelette pan and swirl it around to coat the bottom and sides. When foaming, pour in the egg mixture.
4 Hold the pan handle in your left hand and move the pan gently back and forth over the heat to distribute the egg evenly over the base. At the same time, move the mixture slowly, pulling the set egg from the sides of the pan towards the centre, allowing raw liquid egg to run underneath the cooked egg. Tilt the pan to help this process. (a)
5 Once the omelette is almost set (the bottom is set but the top is still moist and creamy), shake the pan to loosen the omelette from the base, then remove from the heat. If the omelette is sticking, loosen it with a spatula. Spoon over any filling ingredients.
6 Using a palette knife, fold the edge of the omelette next to the pan handle over the centre third. (b) Tilt the pan downwards and place the edge of the pan with the omelette over the serving plate. Grasp the handle from underneath them turn the pan upside down to fold the omelette out of the pan and over on itself so that it lands folded in thirds with the seam hidden underneath on the warmed plate. (c) Alternatively, fold the omelette in two and slide it on to the plate.
7 Spoon any sauce or garnishing ingredients on top and serve immediately.

Making an omelette (a)

Making an omelette (b)

Making an omelette (c)

Omelettes: What has gone wrong when...

The omelette is tough and rubbery.
- The omelette was overcooked.
- The pan was too hot.

The omelette is heavy and flat.
- The egg was not moved about the pan enough during setting.
- Water was not added to the uncooked egg.
- The pan was too cool when the egg was added.

Use of Eggs in Cooking

Eggs contain a large quantity of protein, water and fat. These three constituents work together, separately or mixed with other ingredients, to bind, set, thicken, aerate and lighten as well as to enrich, emulsify, clarify and glaze.

Setting

Eggs thicken liquids when their protein content is partially denatured by gentle heat. The protein molecules bond to each other to form a loose network through the liquid to thicken or set it.

Both egg yolks and whole eggs are used to set baked custards (see *Custards*, below).

Binding

Eggs are used to bind the liquid, fat and protein components of meat and fish forcemeats (see ***Forcemeat***, page 271) to improve their texture. Forcemeat bound with eggs should be moist and hold together well. Forcemeat made without eggs often becomes crumbly and dry when cooked and is difficult to slice. The egg protein coats both the meat or fish fat and protein, binding them together as well as setting the liquid constituent that would otherwise drain out of the forcemeat as it cooks. It is important not to use too much egg or the forcemeat will become tough and rubbery. 1 egg will generally bind approximately 450 g | 1 lb forcemeat.

Eggs also bind dry and fat ingredients together in cakes, pastries and biscuits.

Leavening

Whole eggs, egg yolks and egg whites have the ability to trap air when whisked or beaten and are used to lighten and leaven baked products such as meringues, cakes, hot soufflés and choux pastry, and to lighten meringue-based ice creams, cold soufflés, and mousses. The leavening properties of eggs are covered below.

Thickening and Enriching

Some savoury and sweet sauces are enriched, bound and thickened to a smooth, creamy coating consistency by the high protein and fat content of egg yolks. To thicken savoury sauces, egg yolks are mixed with milk, stock or double cream to form an egg liaison which is warmed, added to the hot sauce and stirred over a medium heat until the sauce is thickened. (see **Sauces**, **Savoury**, *Allemande* and *Supreme* page 591).

Sweet sauces thickened with egg yolks are known as custards. Custard is also used as the base for ice cream (see **Ice Creams**, page 311). Eggs are also used to thicken *Lemon Curd* (see below).

Emulsifying Fats and Liquids

Egg yolks form stable emulsions with oil to make mayonnaise and with butter to make Hollandaise, the two mother sauces of the emulsified sauces. The protein lecithin in egg yolks has the unique ability to hold oil and water in suspension, to create a stable emulsion. 1 egg yolk will form a stable emulsion with up to 200 ml|7 fl oz oil or 55 g|2 oz melted butter (see **Sauces, Savoury**, *Emulsion Sauces*, page 597).

Enriching Colour, Flavour and Texture

Due to the deep yellow colour and high protein and fat content of egg yolk and the lightening quality of egg white, eggs are used to enrich the colour, flavour and texture of food in a variety of ways. They add characteristic smoothness and creaminess to sauces and custard-based dishes, colour, moisture and softness to cakes, and a firm but crumbly richness to biscuits and pastries. Egg whites used alone will produce crisp, dry products such as meringues.

Glazing Baked Goods

An egg wash, or glaze, made from whole eggs, egg whites or egg yolks broken down with a little sugar or salt is brushed on to the surface of bread and pastries before they are baked. The protein content in an egg glaze made from whole eggs or egg yolks browns to a deep golden colour in the heat of the oven to give baked goods a rich, shiny glaze. Egg white used alone will give a baked product a colourless shine.

Filtering or Clarifying Stock for Clear Consommé and Aspic

The protein content in egg white traps impurities as it coagulates in the heat of a simmering liquid, clearing it of all particles too small to be caught in a fine strainer. The clarifying properties of egg white are covered under **Aspic** (see page 91).

Preventing Ice Crystallization

Egg whites control ice crystal formation in sugar syrup- or purée-based sorbets to promote a smooth texture and slow down the rate of melting (see **Sorbets**, page 643).

Custards

There are 2 types of custard, custard sauce, also known as Crème Anglaise (see **Sauces, Sweet**, page 612), and baked custard. Custard sauce is thickened to a creamy coating consistency on the hob and is served with desserts. Baked custard is cooked gently in the oven, protected by either a bain-marie or pastry case, until it is sufficiently set to hold its shape when turned out of the baking mould or sliced. Moulded baked custards include the classic dessert *Crème Caramel* (see below). Custards set in a pastry case include fillings for quiches (see below) as well as savoury and sweet custard tarts.

Baked Custards

A baked custard is milk thickened by the binding and partial coagulation of denatured egg protein. Baked custards include simple mixtures of eggs, sugar and milk, such as *Crème Caramel* and *Crème Brulée*, as well as custard mixtures in which other ingredients are suspended, such as custard tarts and quiches. A perfectly baked custard should have a smooth texture throughout, just firm enough to slice, and should taste smooth and creamy.

Baked custard can be made with whole eggs or egg yolks, or both. The egg whites in whole eggs are powerful setting agents but used in excess may make the custard rubbery.

Egg yolks or a mixture of egg yolks and whole eggs produce a rich, softer-set custard with a tender, creamy texture. Sugar slows the setting ability of eggs, while acidic fruits and vegetables increase it. The proportion of eggs to liquid determines the thickness and richness of the set custard.

For a moulded dessert custard such as *Crème Caramel*, where the custard must hold its shape firmly yet be smooth and delicate, use 1 egg to 150 ml | ¼ pint milk.

For a quiche the custard should be rich, smooth and thick enough to support the other ingredients. The ideal ratio of eggs to liquid is 1 egg and 1 yolk to 150 ml | ¼ pint milk and cream, half and half.

Baking custards in dishes and moulds

Baked custards are baked in large or individual-sized dishes, moulds or in a pastry case.

As the egg proteins are so sensitive to heat and can easily overcook, the custard must be baked slowly at a temperature not exceeding 93°C | 200°F. To achieve the correct cooking conditions the oven is preheated to 150°C | 300°F and a bain-marie is used to protect the custard from the strong, dry heat of the oven. The underside of the custard may also be protected from the heated oven shelf by placing folded kitchen paper or a J-cloth beneath the dish.

Throughout cooking it is important to maintain the water level at half the depth of the mould to prevent the custard from being exposed to strong heat. This is done by partially pulling the oven shelf supporting the custard out of the oven from time to time, so that water can be added to the bain-marie easily, before gently sliding the shelf back into place. Do not attempt to lift the bain-marie and custard dish on to the hob as the movement and drops of water may break the surface of the setting custard, causing cracks to form and spoil its appearance. It is also important that temperature of the water is maintained at just below simmering point. If the water level is allowed to get too low the water is likely to boil which will cause the custard to overcook.

Testing if the baked custard is set

Do not press the custard with your finger, as you are liable to break the smooth skin that forms on the surface. Gently shake or flick the mould with a finger. The custard is perfectly cooked when the centre wobbles very slightly. If the custard ripples in the centre it requires more cooking.

Crème Caramel

SERVES 4–5

110 g | 4 oz granulated sugar	4 eggs
4 tablespoons water	2 tablespoons caster sugar
570 ml | 1 pint milk	vanilla essence

1 Preheat the oven to 150°C | 300°F | gas mark 2. Heat a flan dish in the oven and heat a roasting tin half-filled with water in the oven.
2 Place the sugar in a heavy-based saucepan with the water and allow it to melt over low heat. When it has dissolved, boil rapidly to a deep caramel (see **Caramel**, page 175 or **Microwave Cookery**, page 485).
3 Pour the hot caramel into the hot dish, tipping it so that the caramel coats the bottom and the sides.
4 Heat the milk until it steams.
5 Beat the eggs with the sugar to combine.
6 Slowly stir the hot milk into the eggs. Flavour with vanilla. Sieve the mixture into the caramel-lined dish.
7 Place the dish in the warm bain-marie and bake for 1 hour or until the custard wobbles only very slightly when the dish is given a shake.
8 Remove the custard from the bain-marie and allow to cool until tepid or cold.
9 To serve, place a serving plate with a lip to contain the caramel over the top of the flan dish. Gently press the edges of the custard with your finger to release it from the sides of the dish. Invert the two dishes to remove the Crème Caramel from the dish.

Crème Caramel: What has gone wrong when...

The custard is rubbery and cracked.

- Despite the bain-marie, the custard is overcooked. It has been cooked for too long or the oven temperature was too high.

Small bubbles have set in the base and sides of the custard.

- The water in the bain-marie was allowed to get too low and the custard has overheated.

The custard has not set.

- The custard was not baked for long enough.
- The temperature of the oven was too low.

Quiches and Custard Tarts

Both quiche and custard tart consist of a blind-baked pastry case (see **Pastry**, page 509) filled with set custard, often flavoured and garnished with other ingredients. Quiche is always savoury; custard tarts may be savoury or sweet. The pastry case provides some protection for the custard against the strong, dry heat of the oven but it is important to cook the quiche or tart gently at around 150°C|300°F to prevent the custard filling from overcooking.

Quiche fillings

Filling ingredients may include sautéed diced ham or bacon, fish or shellfish, vegetables such as sweated onions and mushrooms and blanched spinach, asparagus or broccoli. Strong-flavoured cheese such as Gruyère or Cheddar is also added to flavour the custard. The filling ingredients should provide contrasting texture and flavour, without overpowering the delicate egg custard.

Quiche Lorraine

SERVES 4–6

170 g|6 oz flour quantity rich shortcrust pastry (see **Pastry**, page 512)

For the filling
15 g|½ oz butter
1 onion, finely chopped
110 g|4 oz streaky bacon, diced

225 ml|8 fl oz milk
225 ml|8 fl oz single cream
3 medium eggs, beaten
3 yolks
85 g|3 oz strong Cheddar or Gruyère cheese, grated
salt and freshly ground black pepper

1 Roll out the pastry and use to line a flan ring 20 cm|8 in in diameter, 4 cm|1½ in deep. Refrigerate until firm.
2 Preheat the oven to 200°C|400°F|gas mark 6. Bake the pastry case blind (see **Pastry**, page 509).

3 Melt the butter is a small saucepan and stir into the onion. Cover with a dampened piece of greaseproof paper and a lid. Cook over low heat until soft, but not coloured.

4 Remove the lid and the paper and stir in the bacon. Cook over medium heat until cooked through but not coloured.

5 Remove the onion and the bacon from the pan with a slotted spoon to drain away excess fat and juice. Place on a plate to cool.

6 Mix together the milk, cream, beaten eggs and yolks. Pass through a sieve to remove and eggy threads.

7 Stir in the onion and bacon mixture and the cheese. Taste, adding salt and pepper as required.

8 When the pastry is cooked through, remove from the oven and turn the oven temperature to 150°C|300°F|gas mark 2.

9 Using a slotted spoon remove the solids from the filling mixture and distribute over the bottom of the pastry case. Pour enough of the cream mixture into the pastry to fill it to the top

10 Bake in the lower third of the oven for about 40 minutes. The filling will be set, that is, not wobbly, when cooked. It should not take on a brown colour.

11 If the pastry is still very pale, the flan ring can be removed and the quiche returned to the oven for a further 5 minutes.

12 Serve warm or cold.

Quiche: What has gone wrong when...

The filling is watery and rubbery.
- The quiche was overcooked.
- The quiche was cooked at too high a temperature.
- The onions were not cooked for long enough and their acidity has caused the milk to curdle.

Little bubbles have set in the custard mixture.
- The quiche was cooked at too high a temperature.

The custard has not set.
- The quiche was not cooked for long enough.
- The quiche was cooked at too low a temperature.

The quiche has souffléd (risen up).
- The quiche was cooked at too high a temperature or for too long.

Custard Tarts

A custard tart is similar to a quiche with the addition of sugar and sometimes the juice and/or zest of citrus fruits, such as the classic French lemon tart, Tarte au Citron. In England a custard tart is traditionally flavoured with vanilla, nutmeg and/or cinnamon. Often the custard is made using whole eggs, taking advantage of the setting power of the whites to ensure that the custard sets firmly enough to hold its shape when the tart is cut into slices. The custard is sometimes enriched with the addition of 1 egg yolk per 4 eggs. Rich Shortcrust pastry is used for both savoury and sweet custard tarts, while Pâte Sucrée is frequently used for classic French sweet tarts (see **Pastry**, page 516).

Using Eggs to Thicken

Eggs are also used to thicken other liquids, such as the lemon juice for *Lemon Curd* (see below). Unlike custard sauce, lemon curd can be boiled. The eggs do not curdle because of the high proportion of sugar, which inhibits the binding and thickening ability of the egg protein, and the butter coats the protein molecules, preventing them from binding to each other. By boiling the lemon curd the protein molecules are forced together, causing them to partially coagulate and thicken the lemon curd to coating consistency. As the curd cools, the proteins continue to bind, thickening the curd to spreading consistency.

Lemon Curd

MAKES 450 g | 1 lb

2 large lemons	225 g	8 oz granulated sugar
85 g	3 oz butter	3 eggs, lightly beaten

1 Grate the lemons on the finest gauge on the grater, taking care to grate the zest only, not the pith, and set aside.
2 Squeeze the juice from the lemons.
3 Put the lemon juice, butter, sugar and eggs into a heavy-based saucepan or double boiler and heat gently, stirring all the time, until the mixture is thick and a few large bubbles rise to the surface of the mixture.
4 Sieve to remove any eggy threads, then stir in the lemon zest. Spoon into warmed jam jars and cover.
5 Store in the refrigerator for up to 1 week.

Lemon Curd: What has gone wrong when...

The mixture has a granular texture.
- The eggs have curdled because the mixture got too hot or was not stirred continuously.

The cooled lemon curd is very thick and stiff.
- Too much time was taken making the curd and much of the liquid evaporated.

Leavening and Lightening Properties of Whole Eggs

Eggs are widely used in baking as a lightening and leavening agent. Whole eggs, egg whites and egg yolks have the ability to lighten the texture and increase the volume of otherwise dense foods by aerating them or allowing them to rise and set, the process known as leavening, when cooked at high temperatures. The ability of eggs to form bubbles of trapped air enables the cook to lighten and leaven a wide variety of savoury and sweet foods. For eggs to introduce air into a mixture they must be whisked and folded into the food or added to a mixture that is then beaten until it becomes light and fluffy.

Whole eggs are used as the leavening agent in choux pastry (see **Pastry**, page 525) and whisked sponge cakes such as *Whisked Sponge* and *Génoise* (see **Cakes**, pages 148 and 150). Both egg yolks and whites, whisked separately, will lighten cakes and soufflés. Yolks add creaminess and moistness and egg whites make baked food light, dry and crisp.

Whole Egg Foams

An egg foam is formed by whisking air into eggs to form a mass of air bubbles. The action of whisking causes a proportion of the egg protein to denature, which means that each molecule unwinds and straightens, exposing sites for other denatured proteins to bond to. The denatured protein molecules link up (coagulate) with other molecules to form an airtight coating around a bubble of air. As the egg is whisked the proteins continue to coagulate and form an increasingly thick, voluminous foam in which a high density of small air bubbles are supported.

Leavening Properties of Whisked Whole Eggs and Yolks

Whisked whole eggs and yolks are used to leaven cakes. Their protein content forms and sets the sponge-like structure of their cake by trapping air bubbles that expand and then set in the heat of the oven. Their fat content, meanwhile, tenderizes, moistens and improves the storage time of the baked cake.

If both egg whites and yolks are called for in a recipe they are often whisked separately as egg white retains its volume when carefully folded into yolks or other fatty mixtures. Soufflés, mousses and many cakes are leavened in this way. Whole eggs or egg yolks are often whisked over gentle heat to facilitate protein coagulation so that the egg thickens sufficiently to trap air and double or even triple in volume. Whole eggs or egg yolks are whisked 'to the ribbon' to aerate *Whisked Sponges* and the dessert Zabaglione.

Whole eggs or yolks are normally whisked with sugar in a heatproof bowl set over simmering water to encourage the yolk proteins to denature and create air bubbles. The fat contained in the yolk interferes with the bonding sites of denatured proteins, making it difficult for them to link up and dramatically reducing their ability to trap air and gain volume. By heating the egg and sugar mixture the sugar readily dissolves and egg proteins partially coagulate to thicken the mixture and trap the maximum number of air bubbles.

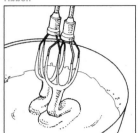

Whisking to the ribbon: As the egg and sugar mixture becomes aerated, the colour of the yolks is diluted from yellow almost to white and thickens to a dense foam. The mixture is ready when it is thick and foamy enough to leave a ribbon-like trail on the surface of the mixture for some seconds before sinking, when drizzled from the whisk. At this stage the consistency of the egg and sugar mixture is termed 'to the ribbon' (see **Cakes**, *Whisked Sponge* (page 148) and *Génoise* (page 150)). Some recipes use a large proportion of sugar to egg yolks but because the yolks contain 31 per cent fat they may not contain enough water to dissolve it. Adding a tablespoon or so of tepid water helps to dissolve the sugar and loosens the yolks for easier whisking. Although the egg and sugar mixture is traditionally whisked by hand, the same results are achieved with less effort using an electric hand-held whisk.

Leavening and Lightening Properties of Egg Whites

Egg whites have an enormous capacity for trapping air when whisked. They can increase 8 times in volume to aerate and lighten mousses and cold soufflés and leaven meringues, hot soufflés and cakes.

When soufflé, cake or meringue mixtures are placed in the oven, the air bubbles which have been incorporated heat up and expand, causing the lightened mixture to rise. As the mixture gets hotter the egg white coating surrounding each bubble coagulates, sets and dries to become stiff and inflexible, setting the mixture in its risen state.

It is important to recognize the extent to which an egg foam has set. Soufflés are removed from the oven once they are risen but should still wobble when shaken gently. At this stage the consistency of the partially set, leavened soufflé is described as *baveuse*. The egg foam is softly set and still moist and will remain risen only while the soufflé is hot. As it cools, the partially set air bubbles shrink to their original size and the soufflé collapses. Cakes, on the other hand, are baked until the egg coating the air bubbles is dry and rigid enough to support the cooked cake mixture so that when it cools the cake retains its risen volume.

Whisking Egg Whites

To obtain an elastic, moist foam with maximum volume, as much air as possible should be beaten into the egg whites without reducing the elasticity of the protein coating around each air bubble. In order to achieve an egg-white foam that will successfully leaven and lighten a mixture a number of basic rules should be followed.

Old egg whites produce the greater volume: The albumen proteins in older, thin egg whites form weaker bonds and denature more readily than protein in fresh egg whites. This means that they whisk into a foam of greater volume in less time than fresh egg whites, but are liable to collapse if used to lighten a heavy mixture as the protein bonds are weak and unstable. Older egg whites are used mainly to produce expansive foams for making meringues.

New egg whites produce a foam that is stable and elastic: The foam will leaven soufflés and cakes more successfully than that from old egg whites. Egg whites that have been frozen whisk more easily than fresh and make good foams and cakes of high quality.

Bring egg whites to room temperature before whisking: The colder the egg whites, the longer it will take to whisk them to the required volume, so it is recommended to bring eggs to room temperature before whisking them.

Use a copper, stainless-steel, ceramic or glass bowl: The bowl should be large enough to contain comfortably egg whites whisked to 8 times their original volume. Avoid plastic bowls as they are prone to harbour grease even after a thorough clean.

Copper bowls have been proven to make a more stable foam with more leavening power than egg whites beaten in stainless-steel, ceramic or glass bowls. As the egg whites are whisked a chemical reaction affects the behaviour of the albumen, causing it to denature more slowly and retain its water content, even when whisked to stiff peaks. The resulting foam is moist, soft and elastic, holds its shape and expands well when cooked. Due to the relatively high water content of an egg-white foam whisked in a copper bowl, the foam will take longer to coagulate in the heat of the oven, allowing the incorporated air bubbles to expand to maximum capacity before setting. As a result, meringues are feather-light and soufflés achieve maximum height.

Although it is considered perfectly safe to whisk eggs in a copper bowl, it is important not to leave them there for any length of time as a further chemical reaction could take place, resulting in discoloration of the egg whites.

Use a large flexible balloon whisk: A large whisk will beat air efficiently into the whites. If using an electric hand whisk, rotate it round the bowl to whisk the whites more quickly. Start whisking on a slow setting to establish a foam of big, stable bubbles. Once the foam is established, increase the whisking speed to whisk the egg whites to the required stiffness. If whisking with a standing mixer, use the wire whisk attachment.

Whisking Egg Whites: The Three Basic Stages

The extent to which egg whites are whisked depends on how they are to be used. For further tips on Whisking Egg whites see *Meringues*, page 475.

Soft peak: Egg whites whisked to a soft peak are most frequently used to lighten loose or soft mixtures of thick coating or dropping consistency, such as foaming Hollandaise Sauce or pancake batter. As egg whites reach a soft peak very quickly, it is best to beat them manually with a large balloon whisk to avoid overwhisking them. Whisk until the foam begins to hold its shape but remains soft and moist. To test the consistency of the foam, dip the tip of the whisk into it. Invert the whisk so that the peak of foam is held upright. The foam peak should bend over by 90°, just hold its shape and wobble when shaken.

Whisked egg whites: soft peak

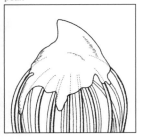
Whisked egg whites: medium peak

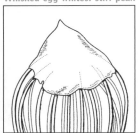
Whisked egg whites: stiff peak

Medium peak: Egg whites whisked to a medium peak are used to lighten or leaven a wide variety of mixtures such as soufflé *panades*, cake mixtures and mousses. The foam should be soft and moist but hold its shape firmly when held on the tip of the whisk. The tip of the foam peak should bend over by 40° and wobble only slightly when shaken.

Stiff peak: Egg whites whisked to a stiff peak are used for most varieties of meringue (see ***Meringues***, page 475). The egg foam should hold its shape firmly and no longer wobble on the tip of the whisk. The foam should not be too dry but still appear moist, elastic and stable so that it holds its shape and expands well when cooked. An electric whisk is very useful for whisking eggs to a stiff peak as it can be a long, arduous process by hand, but be careful not to overwhisk the foam or it will collapse.

Whisking Egg Whites with Added Ingredients

Egg whites are often whisked with acidic ingredients such as vinegar or cream of tartar (the powdered salt of tartaric acid) to improve their stability, or with sugar and salt to improve their flavour.

Cream of tartar or vinegar: The acid in these ingredients speeds up the rate at which egg proteins denature and link up around air bubbles as well as strengthening the bonds between the linked proteins. As a result the egg-white will support, leaven and lighten heavier mixtures very successfully. In order to stabilize whisked egg whites, $\frac{1}{8}$ teaspoon cream of tartar or white wine vinegar per egg white should be added to the egg whites before whisking.

Salt: Recipes will often call for the addition of salt to egg whites before whisking to add flavour and to increase the rate at which the egg whites foam. Although the flavour of the egg white may be improved, salt actually weakens the bonds between the protein molecules, forming an unstable foam which readily breaks down and loses volume. Salt can, however, help to thin very fresh egg whites for easier whisking as well as break down prominent chalazae that would otherwise be visible in the prepared food.

Adding Ingredients to Whisked Egg Whites
An egg-white foam will be destabilized when a substantial quantity of an additional ingredient, such as sugar, nuts or cocoa powder is folded into it. It is therefore important to add such ingredients only when the egg foam reaches stiff peak and is at its most stable. The added ingredients must be folded in very carefully to maintain the volume of the foam.

Sugar: Adding sugar to an egg-white foam is termed 'to meringue the foam'. The addition of sugar to egg whites decreases their ability to foam as sugar dissolves in the water contained in egg white to form a sugar syrup that coats the protein molecules. The sugar syrup coating reduces the ability of egg whites to denature or to bond to other proteins, making it difficult for them to link up around air bubbles and form a foam. Therefore the sugar is added only when the whites have reached a stiff peak.

Once the sugar is successfully incorporated, it will stabilize the foam by preventing the egg protein from coagulating further. Caster sugar dissolves quickly in egg whites, making it fast to incorporate. Although icing sugar dissolves in even less time, it contains cornflour to separate the powdered sugar crystals, causing the meringue mixture to become light but very hard when cooked (see *Meringues*, page 475).

Nuts and Cocoa Powder: These dry ingredients will cause the foam to lose volume so should be carefully folded in once all the sugar has been added.

Incorporating Whisked Egg Whites into a Heavier Mixture
Incorporating whisked egg whites into a heavier mixture requires skill and gentle handling. Air bubbles making up the foam burst each time the foam is stirred or knocked, causing the foam to lose volume. As the maximum foam volume is required to successfully lighten or leaven a mixture, the foam must be incorporated with as little disturbance as possible to its structure.

Loosening the mixture: To assist the incorporation of whisked egg whites quickly and easily, with minimum volume loss, the heavier mixture must first be lightened or 'loosened' by stirring in 1 large tablespoonful of egg white. Then the remaining foam is incorporated, using a technique known as folding.

Folding in whisked egg whites: Whisked egg whites are folded into the mixture by gently lifting the mixture from the base and sides of the bowl into the centre, cutting through the mixture in a smooth three-dimensional figure-of-eight motion, in order to break as few of the air bubbles in the foam as possible. Use a large metal spoon or a spatula with a thin edge that will cut between the bubbles and move a large proportion of the foam and mixture with each stroke, to minimize the number of times the mixture needs to be folded. Stop folding while there are patches of egg white still visible or the foam is likely to deflate to almost its original density and volume.

Folding in whisked egg whites

As the lightened mixture is poured into the mould or baking tin, any patches of egg white can be teased into the mixture with the tip of the spoon or spatula. Once the lightened mixture is ready to be set or baked, continue to treat it gently. Do not bang the side of the tin or dish with the spoon to loosen any remaining mixture as this will cause the aerated mixture to lose volume. Place the filled mould or tin carefully in the oven and do not slam the oven door.

Fish Terminology

Cartilaginous fish: Fish with cartilage instead of a bony skeleton, such as shark and skate. These fish have no swim bladder so need to keep moving in order to float. They contain a large amount of urea, which gives off an unpleasant ammonia smell and taste so they must be eaten very fresh.

Coarse: Freshwater fish, such as roach and tench, that have no value commercially because they are not particularly good to eat although they are eaten by anglers.

Demersal: Fish that feed on the bottom of the sea or river bed, such as monkfish, cod, Dover sole and catfish. Some demersal fish have a sensory feeler under their chin.

Dextral: Flat fish with the eyes on the right side of body, such as lemon sole, plaice and halibut.

Eggs: Hard roe of the female fish, which is sold smoked, salted or canned.

Fin: Used by fish for swimming, balance and steering. The dorsal fin is on the top of the back, the pectoral fins below and slightly behind the gills, and the anal fin is on the underside near the tail. The tail, which propels the fish through the water, is called the caudal fin.

Fry: Very young, small fish.

Grilse: Young salmon, approximately 1.4 kg|3lb, that has returned to spawn within the first year at sea.

Kipper (salmon): Male salmon that has developed a hooked lower jaw to attract the attention of the female salmon during its journey upstream to spawn. The hooked jaw gives the fish a rather fierce look. The kipper will have a relatively low body weight due to the exertion of the journey.

Landlocked: Fish that would normally migrate (see below) but have become trapped in fresh water, such as the Arctic char that became landlocked in the lakes in the north of England in pre-historic times.

Lateral line: A sensory line that runs down the middle of each side of a fish. It detects pressure and vibration.

Migratory fish: Fish that travel long distances to spawn or breed, such as salmon, sea trout and eels.

Milt: Soft roe from the male fish. Milt from flat fish can be used to flavour sauces or dipped in seasoned flour and fried in butter.

Oily fish: Fish with the majority of its fat dispersed in the flesh, such as salmon and mackerel, usually pelagic (see below).

Pelagic: Fish that feed on or near the surface of the water, usually oily fish such as tuna and herring.

Pinbones: Small bones that protrude perpendicularly from the backbone of the fish and run through the flesh. The pinbones are often left in the flesh after filleting and need to be removed with tweezers or pliers (see below).

Shellfish: See *Shellfish* page 621.

Shoaling: Fish that swim in large groups called a shoal.

Sinistral: Flat fish with the eyes on the left side of the body, such as brill and turbot.

Sweet fish: Freshwater fish.

Wet fish: General term for all fresh and previously frozen fish.

White fish: Fish with most of its fat content stored in the liver such as cod and haddock, usually demersal.

Fish

Fish is a valuable source of protein that historically has been readily available to people living near coastal waters, lakes and streams. Archaeological evidence of fish consumption dates back to pre-historic times. In the Middle Ages, the Church encouraged the eating of fish as it was thought to have a cooling effect on man's fiery nature. Although fish consumption has declined in the last 50 years while cost has been rising due to the depletion of stocks through over-fishing, consumption is now on the increase because fish is a healthy food.

In addition to being an excellent source of protein, fish is low in fat in comparison with meat. Even oily fish rarely have more than 20 per cent fat content. The oil in fish is polyunsaturated (see **Healthy Eating and Basic Nutrition**, page 17) and contains Vitamin D and Omega 3 fatty acids that have been found to be helpful in lowering cholesterol. Fish also supplies calcium and phosphorus, iodine, fluorine and some of the B vitamins.

Classification of Fish

Fish can be divided into several categories, the broadest being sea fish and freshwater fish. Fish differ from shellfish in that their skeleton is internal and they have fins (see also **Shellfish**, page 621). It is useful to the cook to know how to classify fish in order to identify a fish and to choose the most suitable cooking method (see below).

Freshwater Fish

Freshwater fish can be further divided into sport and coarse fish. Trout and pike are 2 types of fish caught both for sport and the table. Coarse fish, such as roach, gudgeon and tench, have a muddy flavour and poor-quality flesh, so are usually eaten only by anglers and their families. Many freshwater fish, such as bass, sea trout and salmon, spend most of their adult lives in the sea, swimming back up the rivers to spawn, but they are still classified as freshwater fish despite the fact that most of them are caught by trawl at sea.

Sea Fish

Sea fish are categorized further according to whether they are flat or round, and by the oil content of their flesh. To fillet a fish, you must first recognize whether the fish is round or flat. Freshwater fish are always round.

Flat Fish

Flat fish dwell on the ocean bed. The dark greyish brown colour of their top side serves as camouflage for the fish at the bottom of the sea. These fish have very small scales and fins that run the length of their body. Flat fish have both eyes on the top of their body, one eye having moved from one side to the other soon after birth. Some fish, such as plaice, haibut and lemon sole, have their eyes on the right-hand side of their body and are classified as dextral. Fish with their eyes on the left side of their body, such as turbot and brill, are classified as sinistral. Flat fish are always classified as white (see below).

Round Fish

Round fish, such as trout and salmon, have a central backbone and eyes and gills on either side of their bodies. Round fish can be either freshwater or sea fish. Round fish are kept upright by their swim bladder, an air sac that is situated underneath the backbone which can sometimes be seen when the fish is gutted. Round fish can be either oily or white (see below).

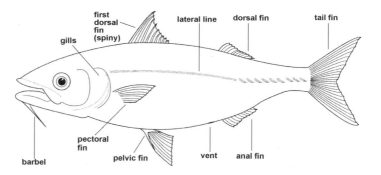

Oily or White Fish

Fish with a high oil content are described as oily whereas fish with a low oil content are described as white. Both types have a distinct texture and flavour which will influence the choice of cookery method. The classification of fish into white and oily can be found in the table below.

In fish classified as oily, the fish oil is dispersed between the flakes of the flesh. In white fish, the oil is primarily contained in the liver of the fish.

Farmed Fish

Several types of fish, notably salmon and trout and also sea bass and tilapia, are now farmed very widely, guaranteeing availability in the shops throughout the year. As wild fish stocks are becoming increasing depleted by over-fishing, fish farms have become important suppliers of this popular food.

Farmed fish can vary in quality depending upon the conditions in which they have been raised. The quality cannot be determined by the appearance of the fish and farmed fish should be chosen in the same manner as wild fish (see *Choosing Fish*, below). Their diet, which can vary from one farm to another and from the farm to the wild, will affect their flavour. Once cooked, farmed fish will often have a softer texture and a milder flavour than their wild namesakes. This difference is primarily due to lack of exercise.

The Structure of Fish

Fish is made up of approximately 70 per cent water, 20 per cent protein, 7 per cent fat and 3 per cent connective tissue. The fibres in the flesh are short and arranged in bundles called myotomes, separated into flakes by thin layers of connective tissue.

The tender texture and mild taste of the majority of fish are due to the high percentage of water in the flesh as well as the structure of the muscle fibres. The majority of fish have short muscle fibres, which are used primarily for quick, rather than long, sustained, movement. These muscle fibres are known as 'short twitch fibres': they are nearly white in colour and very delicate.

The darker flesh seen along the sides of round fish, called the swim muscle, is used for continuous movement. Fish that swim longer distances, such as mackerel, will have a greater amount of darker flesh than fish that languish at the bottom of the sea, such as cod. The swim muscle is particularly noticeable in the salmon as the grey flesh along the outside of the fillets. The pink colour of some fish such as salmon and trout is due to a pigment from the insects and crustaceans that the fish eat.

Categories of Fish

The table below gives the classification of the fish more commonly found in the UK market and groups them together by texture. In most instances, fish within these groups can be substituted one for another in recipes. Some fish appear more than once.

Fish group	Habitat	Type	Category
Salmon (farmed and wild)	Sea and freshwater	Oily	Round
Trout (farmed and wild)	Sea and freshwater	Oily	Round
Sea bass	Sea	White	Round
Cod	Sea	White	Round
Haddock	Sea	White	Round
John Dory	Sea	White	Round
Bass	Freshwater	White	Round
Mahi mahi	Sea	White	Round
Icefish	Sea	White	Round
Whiting	Sea	White	Round
Carp	Freshwater	White	Round
Hake	Sea	White	Round
Pike	Freshwater	White	Round
Tuna	Sea	Oily	Round
Monkfish	Sea	White	Round
Swordfish	Sea	Oily	Round
Mahi mahi	Sea	White	Round
Marlin	Sea	Oily	Round
Shark	Sea	Oily	Round
Eel	Sea	Oily	Round

Categories of Fish—*contd*

Fish group	Habitat	Type	Category
Turbot	Sea	White	Flat/sinistral
Brill	Sea	White	Flat/sinistral
Halibut	Sea	White	Flat/dextral
Cod	Sea	White	Round
Dover sole	Sea	White	Flat/dextral
Lemon sole	Sea	White	Flat/dextral
Plaice	Sea	White	Flat/sinistral
Sea bream	Sea	White	Round
Red snapper	Sea	White	Round
John Dory	Sea	White	Round
Parrot fish	Sea	White	Round
Sea bass	Sea	White	Round
Tilapia	Freshwater	White	Round
Mackerel	Sea	Oily	Round
Blue fish	Sea	Oily	Round
Herring	Sea	Oily	Round
Sardine	Sea	Oily	Round
Red/grey mullet	Sea	Oily	Round
Pilchard	Sea	Oily	Round
Gurnard	Sea	White	Round

Choosing Fish

Fish is at its very best straight from the water so you are fortunate if you can buy it directly from the boat. Most of us will have to rely on the fishmonger or one of the larger supermarkets where the fish is often a few days old. Avoid buying fish on a Monday as it will certainly have been frozen or will be more than 3 days old: fish markets are not usually held on Sundays or Mondays.

Choosing Fresh Fish: Points to Remember

- The fish should have a slight smell of the sea or no aroma at all. If the smell is strongly 'fishy', the fish is old. There should be no smell of ammonia.
- Fish with scales, such as salmon, sea bass, herring and snapper, should have an even covering of scales. The scales should not be coming loose in large patches. The fins should not be damaged.
- The eyes of the fish should be clear and bright, not sunken and dull.
- The gills should look bright red, not pale. Red gills indicate that oxygen is still present in the blood and that the fish is very fresh. The colour of the gills fades with time to light pink, then grey, and eventually to green or brown.
- The flesh of the fish should feel firm, not spongy.
- The fish should have a thin covering of slime. It should not look dry.
- Cuts of fish should be moist, shiny and plump.

How Much Fish to Buy

Fish is lighter to eat than meat so a typical main-course serving size would be from 110 g|4 oz if the fish is oily, such as salmon, and 225 g|8 oz if the fish is white, depending on appetite and the menu. A first-course serving should be approximately half the size of a main-course serving.

Storing Fish

Fish contain enzymes that continue to be active at very low temperatures, making fish highly perishable. Fish should be stored in the coldest part of the refrigerator at not more than 1°C|34°F. It should be cooked and eaten within 24 hours. If fish is stored at 4°C|40°F, the length of time it can be kept is halved.

Whole fish should be stored surrounded by crushed ice. The tray should be perforated so that the water can drain away or the crushed ice should be placed in plastic bags.

Ready-frozen fish has been quick-frozen, which is preferable to home-freezing. Home-freezing is best avoided because the process damages the delicate cells of the fish, causing it to lose moisture and in some cases become tough. If home-freezing is unavoidable, wrap the fish closely in clingfilm, then in a plastic freezer bag, excluding all air. Freeze for up to 3 months. All frozen fish should be stored in a freezer at −18°C|0°F or below.

Preparing Fish

Use a fish filleting knife (see **Kitchen Equipment**, page 65) for filleting fish. The flexible blade allows you to cut next to the bones and remove as much of the flesh as possible.

Flat Fish

A flat fish has 4 fillets, 2 on each side. The fillets on the darker side of the fish are thicker than the fillets on the white side. Sometimes fishmongers will remove the fillets from each side in one piece, giving 2 double fillets per fish. If ordering fish over the telephone it is helpful to clarify the size of fillet required, to avoid misunderstandings.

Filleting flat fish

Filleting flat fish (a)

1 Place the fish on a chopping board with the dark side uppermost.
2 Cut through the skin down to the bones along the lateral line from the head of the fish to the tail. (a)
3 Feel the fish near the head to determine where the fillets end. Cut just below the head in an exaggerated 'Y' shape. (b)

Filleting flat fish (b)

4 Use your knife to stroke along the cut, starting from the head and moving towards the tail and working on the left side of the fish if you are right-handed. Use long strokes and put pressure on the knife so that it bends against the fish. You should feel the knife shudder against the bones. (c)
5 While cutting with one hand, use your other hand to hold the fillet back away from the centre of the fish.
6 When you have reached the edge of the fish, cut through the skin to remove the fillet. Alternatively, grasp the fillet near the head of the fish and pull towards the tail of the fish; the fillet should come away easily.
7 Turn the fish so that the head is now closest to you and remove the second fillet on the dark-skinned side by repeating the procedure, starting from the centre of the fish.

Filleting flat fish (c)

8 Turn the fish over and repeat steps 1–7 on the white side of the fish.

Skinning a fish fillet, flat or round
The method of skinning a fish fillet is the same whether the fillet is from a round or a flat fish. Very young flat fish can be skinned by pulling the skin from the fish: see *Skinning a slip sole*, below.

When skinning a flat fish, remember which side of the fillet was next to the skin.

The side which was next to the skin should be on the inside if the fillet is rolled, or cooked second if the fillet is sautéed flat because it has an unattractive grey tinge when cooked. Once the fillet has been skinned, the skin side can be identified by a silvery herringbone pattern. The side that was next to the bone will be comparatively rough and slightly rounded.

Skinning a fish fillet

1 Place the fillet on a chopping board with the tail end close to you and the head end furthest away.
2 Grasp the tail end of the fillet with one hand and hold the knife with your other hand. If the fish is particularly slippery, pile a little salt on the tail to help your grip.
3 Make a cut through the flesh but not through the skin, about 1 cm|½ in from the end of the tail.
4 Holding the knife at an angle of 30°, saw back and forth across the fillet while pushing the knife away from you. Keep tension on the fillet by pulling the fillet towards you, using the hand holding the tail. The knife should also be in contact with the board.
5 Continue until the knife reaches the other end of the fillet.
6 If the knife cuts through the skin, pare the skin away from the fillet to release some skin to grasp onto and continue as above.

Skinning a slip sole

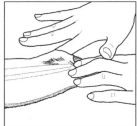

Skinning a slip sole (a)

A slip sole is a young sole, usually no bigger than your hand. Certain recipes call for removing the skin prior to grilling. Traditionally only the dark skin is removed.
1 Make a cut in the skin across the tail of the fish.
2 Push your fingers under the skin next to the fins along the edges of the fish to release it from the flesh. (a)

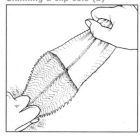

Skinning a slip sole (b)

3 Firmly grasp the loosened skin and pull it towards the head of the fish. (b)
4 If it is difficult to pull in some places, use a small knife to help ease the skin from the flesh.
5 Cut the skin from the fish at the head end if necessary.

Round Fish

Scaling round fish

Scaling round fish

A round fish usually has scales and these should be removed before the fish is filleted or gutted.

1 Place the fish in a deep sink or in a large plastic bag such as a carrier bag (the scales have a tendency to fly everywhere).
2 Grasp the tail and scrape the scales from the tail to the head of the fish, using either a fish scaler or the back of a heavy knife.
3 Rinse the fish.

Gutting round fish

Round fish are gutted before cooking if they are going to be cooked whole. If the fish are going to be filleted it is easier to do so if they have not been gutted.

1 Cut the fish from the anal vent to the fins just below the gills, using scissors or a sharp, small knife. Try to cut the skin only and not to dig into the entrails.
2 Scoop the entrails out of the abdominal cavity with your fingers. Discard.
3 Rinse the fish under the cold tap.
4 Scrape away the blood line running along the backbone, using the end of a teaspoon to break through the membrane.
5 Rinse all the blood from inside the fish. It tastes bitter when cooked.

Gutting round fish

Removing the gills from round fish

The gills of a fish are filled with blood that tastes bitter when cooked so they are removed before cooking.

1 Lift the flap of the gill and cut in a semi-circle from one end to the other with the points of scissors. Discard the gill.
2 Repeat with the gill on the other side of the fish.
3 Rinse the fish.

Slashing round fish

Slashing the sides of a round fish before baking or grilling helps it to cook evenly and more quickly but can result in loss of moisture in the fish. After gutting, cut diagonal slashes about 2.5 cm|1 in apart and halfway through to the bone in the sides of the fish.

Filleting round fish

It is easier to fillet a round fish if it is not gutted before filleting. Very large round fish can also be filleted according to the method for *Filleting flat fish*, above.

1 Place the fish on a chopping board with the back (top) of the fish facing you.
2 Cut across the fillet at the head end and the tail end.
3 Place your hand flat on the fish.
4 Use the knife to cut horizontally into the fish slightly above the middle where the backbone lies.
5 Using a stroking action with the knife against the bones, continue to cut through the flesh until the knife reaches the other side of the fillet. Either cut through the small lateral bones extending perpendicularly from the backbone or gently lift the fillet off the bones.
6 Remove the fillet from the fish.
7 Turn the fish over and repeat the procedure on the second fillet.

Filleting round fish

Pinboning a fish fillet

Pinboning round fish

Pinbones are the tiny bones sometimes found in the flesh of the fillets of round fish. They extend into the flesh from either side of the backbone and are frequently left in the fillet. The bones can be removed either before or after cooking.

1 Run your finger along the flesh side of the fillet from the head end to the tail end. The bones will be found about one-third of the way down from the top edge.
2 Pull the bones out with your fingers or use tweezers or pliers to pull them out.

Butterfly-boning small round fish

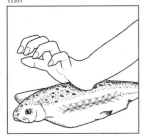

Butterfly-boning small round fish

Small round fish such as herring and sardines are often boned by the following method because their small size makes the usual method of boning difficults. The bones of these small fish are still pliable, making butterfly-boning possible.

1 Gut the fish as described under *Gutting round fish*, above.
2 Place the fish on a board and open out the abdominal cavity.
3 Press with the heel of your hand along the backbone of the fish from the head to the tail.
4 Turn the fish over and use scissors to cut the backbone at the head end and the tail end.
5 Peel out the backbone. Remove any pinbones (see *Pinboning round fish*, above).

Preparing a fish noisette

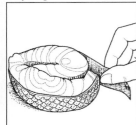

Preparing a fish noisette

A noisette, or boneless fish steak, can be prepared from steaks of round fish such as salmon and cod. The preparation enhances the presentation and makes the fish easier to eat. (see *Noisettes of Salmon*, page 260)

1 Cut out the bones on the inside of the abdominal cavity of the fish.
2 If the bones extend towards the middle of the fish, remove them by cutting on either side of the bones. Do not cut through the skin.
3 Feel for any pinbones and remove them as described above under *Pinboning round fish*.
4 Release the skin from one of the ends of the steak halfway towards the top by cutting between the fish skin and the flesh.
5 Roll the separated flesh into the middle of the abdominal cavity.
6 Wrap the other end over the rolled fish.
7 Wrap the flap of skin around the outside of the noisette. Tie with string. Do not tie too tightly or the centre of the fish will pop up during cooking.

Methods of Cooking Fish

Although the main principle behind cooking fish is similar to cooking meat, that is, the proteins are heated until they coagulate, the practice is often much trickier. The flesh of fish is made up of short muscle fibres that require quick, careful cooking. All that is needed for the proteins to coagulate is a little heat, or in some recipes, acid in the form of citrus juice or wine. This happens quickly with fish and at a lower temperature – 41°C|105°F – than with most meats. If the fish is subjected to too much heat or heated for too long, the flesh will dry out and begin to fall apart.

The method of cooking chosen will depend upon the type of fish (see *Categories of Fish* table above). Different types of fish are recommended for each method of cooking. Within the groups, which are based on texture, one type of fish can be substituted for another reasonably well. Fish tends to overcook if it is kept warm so it is better to leave cooking till the last minute.

How to Tell When Fish Is Cooked

When the fish is cooked and the proteins have denatured, the flesh will have turned from translucent to opaque. The flesh will have become firmer and it should flake and come away from the bones easily. The flakes can be felt easily on fish with large flakes, such as cod and haddock, if you run your finger over the surface of the fish.

As cooking continues, beads of white albumin will become noticeable around the edges of the fish and between the flakes. Further cooking will lead to moisture being squeezed out from the individual protein molecules and more visible albumin. Unlike the tougher cuts of meat, most fish, with the exception of the cephalopods, squid and octopus (see *Shellfish*, page 639), do not become more tender with longer cooking times. In fact, overcooking gives fish a woolly, dry and even tough texture.

When a whole fish is cooked, the eye of the fish will turn white and opaque. This is a good indication that the fish is done if its thickness is uniform along the length, as with trout. It is not, however, a reliable indicator of doneness for larger fish, such as salmon.

Another test that a whole round fish is done is to tug on the dorsal fin. If the fish is cooked it should pull out easily. When cooking large whole fish, such as a 3 kg|7 lb salmon, it is a good idea gently to apart prise the fish fillets where the dorsal fin was and look inside. The flesh at the centre of the fish should be almost opaque.

Cooking Fish: What has gone wrong when . . .

(See also information under individual cooking methods, below.)

The fish is dry.
- The fish has been overcooked.

The fish falls apart.
- The fish has been overcooked.
- The fish was handled roughly.

The fish is mushy.
- The fish is undercooked.

The fish is tough.
- The fish has been overcooked.
- The fish has been frozen.

Marinating

Fish can be 'cooked' by marinating it in citrus fruit juice. The acid in the juice denatures the proteins in the fish, causing it to turn from translucent to opaque and the texture to become firm. The recipe for *Céviche*, below, demonstrates this method.

Céviche

Céviche is a popular appetizer in Spain and Latin American countries. The fish is marinated in citrus juice, usually lime juice, along with olive oil, onions and other flavourings. Only very fresh fish should be used for Céviche. Sole, halibut, monkfish, salmon and red snapper are all recommended for this recipe.

SERVES 4

340 g | 1 lb fish (see above), cut into 6 mm | ¼ in slices

1 small onion, finely chopped

juice of 4 limes or 2 lemons

1 tablespoon olive oil

2 fresh green or red chillies, deseeded and finely chopped

2 tablespoons chopped coriander

To garnish

1 ripe avocado, peeled and diced

1 tablespoon lemon juice

2 small tomatoes, peeled and concasséd

1 yellow pepper, deseeded and diced

2 tablespoons good-quality olive oil

salt and freshly ground black pepper

1 Place the fish in a shallow non-corrosive dish and scatter over the onion.

2 Sprinkle with the citrus juice, oil, chillies and half the coriander. Cover with clingfilm and refrigerate for about 2 hours, turning the fish occasionally until it is opaque. The length of time will depend on the thickness of the fish.

3 For the garnish, combine all the ingredients with the remaining coriander. Season with salt and pepper.

4 Place the fish on individual plates and garnish with the salad.

Grilling

Fish steaks, fillets and small, whole fish are ideal for grilling, although the thickness of each should be no more than 5 cm | 2 in. If the fish is too thick, the outside will be overcooked by the time the inside is cooked. Fish thicker than 2.5 cm | 1 in should be slashed (see *Slashing round fish*, above).

Oily, meaty fish steaks, such as tuna or swordfish, are particularly good for grilling because they hold together well when cooked and the oily texture of their flesh does not dry out too much under the fierce heat of the grill. Marinate white, non-oily fish steaks in an oily marinade and take care not to overcook when grilling. Brill, cod, halibut, haddock, turbot and salmon cutlets are all suitable for grilling. Cooking time for grilled or barbecued fish varies with the type and size of the fish as well as its density and the distance from the heat source. See *How to Tell When Fish Is Cooked*, above.

1 Preheat the grill until it is really hot. It is important that the fish sizzles and browns under the grill to add flavour.
2 The fish should be brushed with melted butter or oil before cooking and seasoned with salt and pepper.
3 Place the fish about 5 cm|2 in from the heat source. When the surface has browned slightly, turn the fish over, brush the other side with oil and season. Grill the second side. If the fish seems to be cooking too quickly, move it further from the heat source. The cooking time should be approximately 5–7 minutes in total for fish steaks 2.5 cm|1 in thick.

Grilling Fish: Points to Remember

- Take the fish out of the refrigerator 30 minutes before grilling. Unless the pieces are relatively thin, the cooking time is too quick to warm the inside adequately if the fish is cooked straight from the refrigerator.
- Salt the fish just before cooking, not earlier. Salt draws the moisture out of the fish, making browning difficult.
- Turn the fish over with a fish slice. Don't pierce it or the juices will run out and the fish will break up.
- The first side grilled is the presentation side.

Grilled Dover Sole

1 × 340 g|12 oz Dover sole per person
melted butter
salt and freshly ground black pepper

To garnish
lemon wedges (see **Food Presentation**, page 12)

1 Make a cut in the belly of the fish just below the head and remove the entrails.
2 Wash the fish thoroughly in cold water.
3 Snip the fins off with scissors, then make a cut through the skin across the tail with a sharp knife.
4 Preheat the grill.
5 Push your index finger underneath the skin along the fins, on each side of the fish, from the tail to the head.
6 Loosen the skin with a small knife at the tail end, then grasp the skin and pull towards the head to remove the skin. Use a little salt on your fingers to help the grip. Repeat on the other side of the fish.
7 Brush the grill pan and the fish with melted butter.
8 Season the fish with salt and freshly ground black pepper, then place under the grill for 3–4 minutes. Turn the fish over and cook the other side for a further 2–3 minutes. Serve with the first side grilled as the presentation side.

Griddling

Griddling is very similar to *Pan-frying* (see below) because it is done on the hob. A griddle pan is made from heavy cast iron so it can be heated to a very high temperature. It is a popular method of cooking steaks of oily fish such as tuna, meaty fish such as monkfish, or pieces of shellfish such as scallops. Delicate white fish tends to break up when griddled.

1 Marinate the fish in a little olive oil. See under *Grilling Fish: Points to Remember*, above.
2 Brush the griddle pan with a thin layer of oil.
3 Place over a medium high heat until the pan just begins to smoke.
4 Season the fish with salt and freshly ground black pepper.
5 Cook the fish for 2–3 minutes per side, depending on the thickness of the fish and how you like it cooked.

Griddled Tuna with Green Chilli Pesto and Pepper Salad

This recipe also works well with swordfish steaks.

SERVES 4

4 × 170 g|6 oz tuna steaks about 2.5 cm|1 in thick

For the marinade

6 tablespoons olive oil
2 tablespoons balsamic vinegar
freshly ground black pepper

For the chilli pesto

2 green chillies, deseeded
55 g|2 oz fresh coriander
55 g|2 oz pine nuts, toasted (see **Nuts**, page 494)
2 cloves of garlic, crushed
55 g|2 oz Parmesan cheese, freshly grated
6 tablespoons olive oil
salt and freshly ground black pepper

For the peppers

3 red or yellow peppers
3 tablespoons olive oil
1 tablespoons balsamic vinegar

1 Place the tuna steaks in a flat dish or a plastic bag. Pour over the marinade ingredients and refrigerate for 2 hours.
2 To make the pesto, purée the chillies, coriander leaves and stalks, pine nuts and garlic in a food processor. Add the Parmesan cheese, then dribble in the oil while the motor is running. Thin with water if necessary, then season with salt and pepper. Cover and refrigerate until required.
3 For the peppers, preheat the grill.
4 Remove the stalks and seeds and cut the peppers into 4 flat pieces. Grill them skin side up until the skin is blackened. Place the peppers in a plastic bag until cool enough to handle. The steam will help loosen the skins.
5 Cut the peppers into 1 cm|½ in wide strips and toss with the oil and vinegar. Set aside.

6 To cook the tuna, lightly oil a griddle pan and heat until it starts to smoke. Griddle the tuna steaks on each side for about 2 minutes per side for rare and 3 minutes for medium. The colour of the fish on the sides of the steaks becomes paler as it cooks.

7 To serve, divide the pepper salad between 4 plates and top with a tuna steak. Garnish with a mound of the chilli pesto.

Grilled/Griddled Fish: What has gone wrong when...

The fish is dry.
- The fish is overcooked.
- The fish was not marinated in oil.

The fish sticks to the griddle pan.
- The griddle was not hot enough.
- The fish was moved too soon.
- The fish was not marinated in oil.

Barbecuing

Meaty, oily fish such as tuna or swordfish steaks can be barbecued very successfully. Take care not to overcook the fish and be sure to turn it with a fish slice (metal spatula), not a fork, or it will break up. Whole fish can be barbecued if slashed (see *Slashing round fish*, above) but barbecuing is most successful with smaller fish, such as sardines, because the fish stick to the rack and break up if cooked for too long a time. It is possible to buy special wire-mesh fish-shaped holders to barbecue whole fish.

Tender white fish sticks to the grill, breaks up and falls apart when barbecued. Non-oily white fish fillets are best marinated, then wrapped in a foil parcel and placed on the barbecue to bake; indeed any fish can be wrapped in foil then baked on the barbecue (see *Baked Red Snapper*, below). Special racks are available for barbecuing fish. They are made of fine mesh to support the fish. Oil the racks thoroughly before using to help keep the fish from sticking.

Poaching

Poaching is a classic method for cooking fish because it is gentle and moist. It is suited to all types of fish and is often used for cooking white fish fillets or steaks. The fish is poached in a *court bouillon* (see **Stocks**, page 693) or in the case of smoked fish, a mixture of milk and water. The milk helps to lessen some of the smokiness of the fish.

Poached fish can be served on its own or with a sauce. *Hollandaise*, *Beurre Blanc*, and fish *Velouté Sauces* (see **Sauces, Savoury**, pages 579) are all classic accompaniments to poached fish. Poached fish is also used in composite dishes such as *fish pie* and *fish mousse* (see **Mousses**, page 491). A mousseline of raw fish is poached to make *quenelles* (see **Mousselines**, page 487).

1 Scale, gut and remove the gills of the fish, as described above under *Preparing Fish*.
2 Half fill a fish kettle (see **Kitchen Equipment**, page 44) with water and add 150 ml | ¼ pint vinegar and *court bouillon* ingredients (see **Stocks**, page 693).
3 Simmer the court bouillon for 20 minutes. Strain and cool.
4 Put the fish into the kettle and bring slowly to the boil. Poach, allowing 5 minutes per 450 g | 1 lb of fish.
5 Remove from the heat and allow the fish to stand in the liquid. Check every 10 minutes to see if it is cooked by pulling on the dorsal fin. When the fin comes out easily, use a table knife to prise the fillets apart gently and check whether the fish is cooked in the centre. It will have turned from translucent to opaque when cooked. It is best to undercook the fish slightly because it continues to cook in its own heat.
6 Remove the fish from the kettle and place on a tray.
7 Carefully peel the skin away from the fish if serving warm, or allow to cool before removing the skin if serving cold.

Hot poached salmon is traditionally served with *Hollandaise Sauce* (see **Sauces, Savoury**, page 602), whilst cold poached salmon is served with *Mayonnaise* (see **Sauces, Savoury**, page 598) or Watercress Sauce.

Dressed Poached Salmon

1 cold poached salmon
290 ml | ½ pint Mayonnaise (see **Sauces, Savoury**, page 598)
1 cucumber, very thinly sliced

1 bunch of watercress
lemon wedges (see **Food Presentation, Garnishes**, page 12)

1 Carefully peel the skin from one side of the fish, then turn the fish over on to a serving platter.
2 Cut through the top fillet down to the bone next to the head and the tail. Remove the skin. Separate the top fillet from the bottom one by inserting a knife along the backbone of the fish. Lift off the top fillet so that the pinbones are left attached to the skeleton and invert onto a baking sheet.
3 Cut the backbone next to the head and tail, then peel the backbone from the bottom fillet. Remove any pinbones.
4 Spread the bottom fillet with Mayonnaise.
5 Using 2 fish slices if the salmon is large, carefully replace the top fillet on to the bottom fillet to reshape the fish.
6 Mitre the tail by cutting it into a 'V' shape.
7 Use the cucumber slices to cover the surface of the fish, resembling scales. Start from the tail end and work towards the head, overlapping the cucumber slices slightly.
8 Garnish with watercress and lemon wedges.

Fillets of fish can be poached either in the oven or in a sauté pan on the hob.

1 If using the oven method, preheat the oven to 180°C│350°│gas mark 4.

2 Pinbone the fish (see *Pinboning round fish*, above). Leave the skin on to help hold the fish together during cooking.

3 Place the fish in an ovenproof dish or a sauté pan. If poaching in the oven, place the fish skin side up. If poaching on the hob, place the fish skin side down.

4 Pour over enough *court bouillon* (see **Stocks**, page 693) or milk, if poaching smoked fish, to nearly cover it.

5 Place a piece of dampened greaseproof paper (a *cartouche*) over the surface.

6 Place in the oven or heat over a medium heat until the surface of the liquid trembles and an occasional bubble rises to the surface. Do not let the fish boil or it could become tough and/or fall apart.

7 Maintain the liquid at this temperature until the fish is done (see *How to Tell When Fish Is Cooked*, above).

8 Remove the fish from the liquid with a fish slice. Use as required.

Poached Smoked Haddock Florentine

Poaching is a good method for cooking fillets of smoked fish, such as haddock or cod. The cooking liquid helps to keep the fish moist whilst reducing some of the strong, smoky flavour.

The heat should be regulated so only the occasional bubble rises to the surface of the cooking liquid. The liquid should never be allowed to boil. Boiling can cause the fish to toughen and dry out by tightening the proteins and squeezing the water out of the tissue.

The word Florentine often denotes the use of spinach in a dish.

SERVES 4

450 g│1 lb smoked haddock fillet, divided into 4 × 110 g│4 oz portions

570 ml│1 pint milk

1 slice of onion

1 bay leaf

4 eggs, poached

2-egg yolk quantity Hollandaise Sauce (see **Sauces, Savoury**, page 602)

15 g│½ oz butter, melted

340 g│12 oz fresh spinach, cooked and chopped (see **Vegetables**, page 742)

salt and freshly ground black pepper

a pinch of freshly grated nutmeg

1 If using the oven method, preheat the oven to 180°C│350°F│gas mark 4.

2 Prepare the fish as described under *Poaching Fillets of Fish*, above.

3 Pour the milk over the fish and add the onion and bay leaf.

4 Place a piece of dampened greaseproof paper over the surface of the fish.

5 Place in the oven or over a medium heat until the surface of the liquid trembles and the occasional bubble rises to the surface.

6 Maintain the liquid at this temperature for about 20 minutes, until the fish is done (see *How to Tell When Fish Is Cooked*, above).

7 Poach the eggs (see **Eggs,** *Poached*, page 218) and keep warm.

8 Remove the fish from the cooking liquid with a fish slice. Remove the skin and pat the fish dry. Keep warm in the oven turned down to 55°C|130°F|gas mark ¼ .

9 Put 4 plates into the oven to warm.

10 Make the Hollandaise Sauce and keep warm.

11 Melt the butter in a large sauté pan until it begins to turn brown, then stir in the spinach to reheat quickly. Season with salt, pepper and nutmeg.

12 Place the spinach on the warm plates. Top each serving with a piece of haddock.

13 Pat the poached eggs dry and place one on each piece of haddock.

14 Napper with the Hollandaise Sauce and serve immediately.

Skate with Brown Butter and Capers

Skate is a cartilaginous fish which is usually sold cut into small portions, or wedge-shaped wings. It needs to be eaten very fresh as it starts to smell of ammonia quite quickly. Serving it with brown butter (*beurre noisette*) and capers is a classic preparation.

SERVES 4

900 g|2 lb skate wings	1 tablespoon lemon juice mixed with
570 ml|1 pint *court bouillon* (see **Stocks**,	1 tablespoon water
page 693)	1 tablespoon capers, rinsed and roughly
85 g|3 oz unsalted butter	chopped

Removing skate from the bone (a)

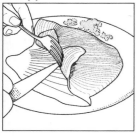

1 Wash the skate and divide it into 4 portions by cutting vertically between the bones.

2 Place the skate pieces in a single layer in the cold *court bouillon* in a sauté pan. Place a piece of dampened greaseproof paper directly on top of the fish. Heat slowly until the occasional bubble rises to the surface.

3 Cook gently for 15–20 minutes or until the skate feels firm to the touch. Insert a knife vertically into the thick part of the fish near the bone to see if the flesh has changed from translucent to opaque.

4 Remove the fish from the cooking liquid then scrape the grey membrane from the fish.

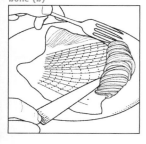
Removing skate from the bone (b)

5 To present the skate without bones, insert a fish knife underneath the flesh next to the thick bone at the point of the triangle. **(a)** Scrape against the bone to remove the fish from the bones. Roll towards the edge of the skate **(b)**.

6 Cover the fish with dampened greaseproof paper (a *cartouche*) and keep warm in a low oven while preparing the butter sauce.

7 Heat the butter in a sauté pan over a medium heat until it is golden-brown and smells nutty.

8 Using a small sauce whisk, whisk in the lemon juice and capers.

9 Pour over the fish and serve immediately.

Deep-frying

Deep-frying is a popular method of cooking fish. It is suitable for white fish, but not oily fish, as the oiliness of the fish combined with the oil in the cooking would make the fish rather indigestible. Cod, haddock, plaice and sometimes skate are deep-fried for traditional English fish and chips (see ***Deep-frying***, page 208).

The fillets of fish are coated in either egg and breadcrumbs or a batter to protect the fish from the fierce heat of the oil and to give the outside of the fish a tasty, crisp texture. Whitebait, small whole fish, are tossed in seasoned flour and are fried and eaten whole.

Pan-frying or Shallow-frying

Pan-frying, where the fish is cooked in a sauté pan with enough fat just to cover the base of the pan, is a good method for cooking most types of fish. Butter or a mixture of oil and butter which allows the pan to be heated to a higher temperature is used. Some ethnic cuisines use peanut (groundnut) oil or season the oil with a small amount of sesame oil.

Whole fish should be gutted and the gills removed (see *Preparing Fish*, above) then coated with seasoned flour. When the eye turns opaque and the dorsal fin will pull out easily, the fish is done.

Shallow-frying is a term used almost interchangeably with pan-frying but generally calls for more oil or butter, usually about 1 cm|½ in in the base of the pan. As with deep-frying, the oil used in the cooking makes this method less suitable for oily fish, although whole oily fish, such as mackerel, herrings or sardines, can be shallow-fried. The fish is usually coated in flour seasoned with salt and freshly ground black pepper, then in beaten egg, then in crumbs or oatmeal before frying to protect the fish from the heat of the pan and give it a crisp coating.

Sole Meunière

SERVES 4

3 lemon sole, filleted and skinned
seasoned plain flour
salt and freshly ground black pepper
55 g | 2 oz clarified butter (see **Dairy Products**, *Butter*, page 204)
1 tablespoon lemon juice mixed with 1 tablespoon water

1 tablespoon finely chopped fresh parsley

To garnish
4 lemon wedges (see **Food Presentation**, *Garnishes*, page 12)

1 Wash the fillets of sole and pat dry on kitchen paper.
2 Immediately before cooking, dredge the fillets in the flour, shaking them to remove any excess. Keep them all with the skin side in the same direction, i.e. either up or down. The side next to the bone is the presentation side and must be cooked first as the side next to the skin turns an unappetizing grey colour when cooked.
3 Place the fillets in a single layer on a plate.
4 Heat a quarter of the butter in a large sauté pan until it foams. As the foaming subsides, add 2 of the fillets bone-side down. Cook for 1–2 minutes until golden-brown.
5 Turn the fillets over, using a palette knife, and cook the second side until golden-brown. By now the fish should have turned from translucent to opaque.
6 Place the cooked fish on a warmed serving plate and cover with foil.
7 Wipe out the pan with kitchen paper, then cook the remaining 2 fillets from step 4.
8 When all the fillets are cooked, wipe out the pan and return it to the heat.
9 Place the remaining butter in the pan and heat over a medium heat until it turns pale brown and smells nutty.
10 Quickly whisk in the lemon juice and water mixture, then the parsley. Pour over the fish immediately and garnish with the lemon wedges.

Pan-frying a whole fish

This method of cooking is suitable for whole fish that are small enough to fit into a frying pan, such as trout, mackerel and herring.

1 Gut the fish and remove the gills (see *Preparing Fish*, above). Remove the head, if desired. Leave the dorsal fin intact.
2 Wash the fish and pat dry with kitchen paper.
3 Just before cooking, dredge the fish in seasoned flour, shaking away any excess. Place in a single layer on a plate.
4 Over a medium heat, warm enough butter in a frying pan to coat the bottom of the pan by 3 mm cm | ⅛ in.
5 When the butter has foamed and the foaming has started to subside, put the fish into the pan and cook for 2–3 minutes on each side until golden-brown.

Trout with Almonds

SERVES 4

4 medium rainbow trout	**To garnish**
seasoned plain flour	chopped fresh parsley
85 g⎮3 oz clarified butter (see **Dairy Products**,	lemon wedges (see **Food Presentation**,
Butter, page 204)	Garnishes, page 12)
55 g⎮2 oz flaked almonds	
lemon juice	

1 Preheat the oven to 170°C⎮325°F⎮gas mark 3.

2 Gut the trout and remove the gills (see *Preparing Fish*, above).

3 Wash the fish well, ensuring that the bloodline beneath the backbone is clean.

4 Dip the trout in the seasoned flour and shake to remove any excess.

5 Heat 30 g⎮1 oz of the clarified butter in a large frying pan until it sizzles. Add the trout and brown them on both sides over a medium heat, then transfer them to an ovenproof dish.

6 Bake the trout in the oven for 10–15 minutes, or until the dorsal fin pulls away easily and the eye is opaque.

7 Wipe out the frying pan, then fry the almonds in the remaining butter until golden.

8 Stir the lemon juice into the butter, then pour over the trout immediately.

9 Garnish with the parsley and lemon wedges.

Steaming

Steaming is a suitable method of cooking all types of fish. White, non-oily fish, such as cod or haddock, is often steamed for invalids because it is bland and easily digestible (see **Steaming**, page 674).

Baking or Roasting

Baking or roasting is a good method of cooking fish because the fish will cook quickly. The fish will not be in the oven long enough to benefit from the added flavour created by browning that is associated with roasting joints of meat; however, it can be browned on the hob before baking. Fish is likely to dry out during baking due to its lack of fat and connective tissue, so care must be taken not to overcook the fish.

Although a piece of fish about 2.5 cm⎮1 in thick will take about 10–12 minutes to cook at 200°C⎮400°F⎮gas mark 6, a piece of fish 5 cm⎮2 in thick will take more than double the time due to its density: a 5 cm⎮2 in piece of fish will take approximately 25–30 minutes to cook. Test the fish for doneness as instructed in *How to Tell When Fish Is Cooked*, above.

Roast Cod with Garlic

This recipe is most successful with thin fillets of cod.

SERVES 4

4 × 170 g | 6 oz cod fillets, unskinned
150 ml | ¼ pint good-quality olive oil
4 cloves of garlic, unpeeled
salt and freshly ground black pepper

seasoned flour
lemon wedges (see **Food Presentation**, *Garnishes*, page 12), to serve

1 Preheat the oven to 200°C | 400°F | gas mark 6.
2 Pinbone the cod fillets if necessary (see *Pinboning round fish*, above).
3 Place the olive oil and garlic in a roasting tin and heat in the oven for 15 minutes.
4 Season the cod fillets and dredge in the seasoned flour, shaking off any excess.
5 Remove the roasting tin from the oven and place directly over a medium heat on the hob. Place the cod fillets in the hot oil, skin side down, and place over direct heat for 2 minutes.
6 Turn the cod over, then place in the oven and cook for a further 5–10 minutes, depending on the thickness of the fish. It should be opaque and firm when done (see *How to Tell When Fish Is Cooked*, above).
7 To serve, place a cod fillet skin side up on each plate with a clove of baked garlic and a lemon wedge.

Baked Red Snapper with Herbs and Lime

This recipe for baking a whole large fish can also be used for individual small fish. For small fish to serve 1 person, plan on about 340 g | 12 oz per person; for a whole fish 250 g | 9 oz per person is sufficient because there is proportionately less waste on a large fish. Red mullet, bream or sea bass can also be used in this recipe.

SERVES 4

4 × 340 g | 12 oz or 1 × 1 kg | 2.2 lb whole large fish
vegetable oil, for brushing

For the marinade

4 tablespoons olive or vegetable oil
grated zest and juice of 2 limes
1 teaspoon ground turmeric
2 cloves of garlic, crushed
salt and freshly ground black pepper

For cooking

290 ml | ½ pint dry white wine or vermouth
4 tablespoons chopped fresh chives, parsley and tarragon

To garnish

sprigs of fresh herbs
lime wedges (see **Food Presentation**, *Garnishes*, page 12)

1 Clean and scale the fish, then slash on both sides (see *Preparing Fish, Slashing round fish* above).
2 Brush the marinade on to the fish, working the marinade into the slashes and inside the fish. Refrigerate for 1 hour or overnight.

3 Preheat the oven to 200°C|400°F|gas mark 6.

4 Boil the wine to reduce by half, then stir in the herbs.

5 Place the fish on a large piece of aluminium foil.

6 Pour the wine over the fish and fold the foil over to make a sealed parcel. Place in a roasting tin and bake in the oven for 15 minutes for small fish or 25–30 minutes for a large fish.

7 Test if the fish is done; it should have turned from translucent to opaque and feel firm. See also the instructions under *How to Tell When Fish Is Cooked*, above.

8 Serve in the foil, garnished with herb sprigs and lime wedges.

Baking en Papillote

A 'papillote' is a sealed parcel of greaseproof paper or baking parchment in which a single portion of food is cooked in its own steam, which keeps it moist. This cookery method is a combination of steaming and baking. The parcels are normally served to each diner at the table so when they are opened the aroma of the food is released.

Trout en Papillote

SERVES 2

oil, for brushing

55 g|2 oz butter

1 tablespoon very finely julienned white part of leek (see **Knife Skills**, page 71)

1 tablespoon very finely julienned carrot

55 g|2 oz button mushrooms, thinly sliced

1 teaspoon chopped fresh tarragon or dill fronds

salt and freshly ground black pepper

4 × 110 g|4 oz unskinned trout fillets, pinboned (see *Pinboning round fish*, above)

lemon juice

2 tablespoons dry white wine

1 Preheat the oven to 220°C|425°F|gas mark 7. Place a baking sheet in the oven.

2 Cut 2 heart shapes from a piece of greaseproof paper or baking parchment, about 30 × 30 cm|12 × 12 in. Brush the paper with a little oil.

3 Melt half the butter in a frying pan, add the leek and carrot and sweat for about 5 minutes until soft.

4 Add the mushrooms and cook for 2 further minutes, then stir in the herbs. Season with salt and pepper. Allow to cool.

5 Sandwich the trout fillets, skin side outside, with the vegetables, then place a sandwich on one side of each paper heart.

6 Drizzle the fish with a little lemon juice and the white wine. Dot with the remaining butter.

7 Fold the other half of the heart shape over the fish. Seal the parcel by twisting the edges of the 2 halves together, beginning from the pointed end of the heart.

8 Press the twisted edges down to hold them together as you work your way around the edge of the paper.

9 Place the parcels on the hot baking sheet so that they do not touch each other. Bake for 10–12 minutes.

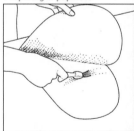

Preparing a papillote

Securing the edges of a papillote

10 It is difficult to tell if the fish is done without unwrapping the parcels. However, if you press through the paper it should feel firm.

11 Serve each diner with a puffed-up parcel. If the fish is not cooked it can be resealed and returned to the oven.

Baking Fish: What has gone wrong when...

See *Cooking Fish: What has gone wrong when...*, page 247.

Braising

Braising is a method of cooking where the food is baked in a closed container in the oven with a little liquid and sometimes aromatic vegetables at the bottom of the dish. As with *Baking en Papillote*, above, the food cooks by a mixture of baking and steaming to keep it moist. Braising is suitable for most types of fish, including whole fish.

Braised Noisettes of Salmon with Leeks and Mustard

SERVES 4

4 × 140 g|5 oz salmon steaks
110 g|4 oz white and pale green part of leeks
30 g|1 oz butter
10 g|⅓ oz fresh dill
2 tablespoons white wine
salt and freshly ground black pepper

1 tablespoon vegetable oil
100 ml|3½ fl oz full fat crème fraîche
55 ml|2 fl oz White Fish Stock (see **Stocks**, page 689)
2 teaspoons wholegrain mustard

1 Prepare the salmon (as instructed under *Preparing a Fish Noisette*, above). Set aside.

2 Preheat the oven to 200°C|400°F|gas mark 6.

3 Slice the leeks into matchstick strips, 5 cm × 2 mm|2 × ¹⁄₁₆ in (see **Knife Skills**, page 71). Wash well.

4 Melt the butter in a small saucepan and stir in the leeks. Cover with a piece of dampened greaseproof paper (a *cartouche*) and sweat for about 5 minutes until soft. Place in an ovenproof dish large enough to hold the salmon noisettes in a single layer.

5 Sprinkle with half of the dill and the wine.

6 Season the fish with salt and pepper, then heat the oil in a sauté or griddle pan over a medium heat and lightly brown the salmon on both sides. Place on top of the leeks.

7 Cover the dish with foil and bake for 20 minutes or until the salmon has nearly turned from translucent to opaque in the centre.

8 Combine the crème frâiche, stock, mustard and the remaining dill.

9 Remove the salmon from the oven and place each noisette on a plate. Remove the string.

10 Pour the leeks and the cooking juices into a small saucepan and heat, stirring, until the juices have reduced to 2 tablespoons.

11 Stir in the crème fraîche mixture and heat through until warm. Season. Divide the sauce over the noisettes and serve.

Stir-frying

Stir-frying is a quick method of cooking used primarily for Chinese food. It can be done in either a wok or a large frying pan over high heat while continuously stirring the contents of the pan. Because of the constant agitation, it is not a method of cooking that is suitable for most fish as it would break up. However, a firm fish that does not flake easily, such as monkfish, is suitable for stir-frying.

Monkfish with Mangetout and Spring Onions

SERVES 4–6

800 g | 1¾ lb monkfish tail

140 g | 5 oz mangetout

1 tablespoon vegetable oil

1 teaspoon sesame oil

2 cloves of garlic, cut into slivers

1 cm | ½ in piece of root ginger, peeled and sliced

For the marinade

2 tablespoons soy sauce

1 tablespoon dry sherry

For the sauce

55 ml | 2 fl oz rice wine vinegar

2 teaspoons caster sugar

2 tablespoons light soy sauce

2 red chillies, deseeded and finely chopped

1 clove of garlic, crushed

1 teaspoon cornflour

4 spring onions, shredded

To garnish

2 tablespoons chopped fresh coriander

1 Cut down both sides of the monkfish bone and remove the bone. Trim the membrane from the monkfish, then slice the fish into 2 × 1 cm | 1¾ × ½ in strips. It is important to remove all the membrane because it turns an unpleasant grey when cooked.

2 Toss the fish in the marinade ingredients and refrigerate for 30 minutes.

3 Blanch the mangetout in boiling salted water for 2 minutes, then refresh under cold water (see *Vegetables*, page 716). Drain and set aside.

4 Combine the ingredients for the sauce.

5 Heat the oils in a wok or large frying pan, then add the garlic and the ginger.

6 Cook until light brown, then remove with a slotted spoon and discard.

7 Stir-fry the monkfish over a high heat for about 3 minutes until firm.

8 Add the sauce ingredients to the hot pan and cook, stirring, to coat the monkfish.

9 Add the mangetout and the spring onions to the sauce and heat for 1 minute to warm through.

10 Turn into a warmed serving dish and garnish with the coriander.

Microwaving

The microwave oven can be used successfully to cook small quantities of fish (see *Microwave Cookery*, page 483), however care must be taken not to overcook it as it might explode in the oven. Choose pieces of fish of even size and thickness. Steaks or thick fillets of fish are the most successful choice.

1 To serve 2, place 2 × 170 g | 6 oz pieces of fish 2.5 cm | 1 in thick in a microwave container with a few tablespoons of white wine, or a combination of water and lemon juice.

2 Cover with clingfilm, then microwave on HIGH (650 watts) for 2 minutes. Let stand for 1 minute.

3 Turn the dish and microwave for a further 1½ minutes. Stand for 3 minutes before serving.

Preserved Fish

See *Preserving* (page 551) for a recipe for *Gravadlax*.

Canned Fish

Canned fish, such as tuna, salmon, anchovies and sardines, are useful store-cupboard ingredients.

Tuna can be used to make dips and sandwich fillings or can be added to a *Béchamel Sauce* (see *Sauces, Savoury*, page 589) and served on toast for a quick meal. Tuna canned in olive oil has the best flavour for sandwiches, dips and salads, but tuna canned in brine contains fewer calories. Choose cans labelled 'white tuna steaks' for better-quality fish. Drain the tuna in a sieve before using.

Salmon is useful for sandwich fillings and pâtés. Drain the salmon in a sieve, then remove any bones and skin.

Anchovies are brined, then packed in oil. Drain them before use, then rinse them in cold water to remove excess salt or soak briefly in milk. Anchovies are used in small quantities as a garnish and in *Caesar Salad Dressing* (see *Salad Dressing*, page 577).

Sardines are packed in oil or in a sauce. Choose sardines in olive oil for the best flavour. To eat, drain of excess oil.

Smoked Fish

For a description of hot and cold smoking, see *Preserving* (page 549).

Choosing smoked fish

Look for smoked fish that is plump and moist in appearance and firm to the touch. It should not be soft or have a strong fishy odour. The fish should smell mildly smoky.

Storing smoked fish

The smoking preserves the fish to some extent but it can still 'go off'. If the fish is vacuum-packed, be guided by the 'use by' date on the package. Once opened, wrap the fish in greaseproof paper, place in a plastic bag and store in the refrigerator for up to 3 days.

Using smoked fish

Smoked fish is a popular first course. It is often served with a small garnish of salad, lemon wedges, and brown bread and butter. It is also delicious made into a pâté and served with *Melba Toast* (see *Smoked Trout Pâté*, below).

Cold Smoked Fish

Smoked salmon, trout and **halibut** can be purchased ready-sliced. Look for thinner slices; the fish will be of better quality than thickly sliced fish.

A whole side of salmon can be purchased more cheaply than the sliced product. Wild salmon has the best flavour. To slice a side of salmon, first remove the pinbones (see *Pinboning round fish*, above). Use a very sharp, thin, straight-bladed knife such as a ham knife to cut the thinnest possible slices, slicing across the grain and working from the head to the tail.

Smoked haddock and **cod** are cooked before eating (see *Poaching*, above). Buy undyed fish in preference to dyed.

Kippers are smoked herrings. The darker the fish, the lesser the quality. Kippers are delicious grilled but many people are put off by the strong smell of the cooking fish that can linger in the house for days. Kippers can also be cooked by immersing them in boiling water to cover. Turn off the heat and allow them to stand for 10 minutes.

Bloaters are herrings that have been brined and smoked without being gutted. This gives the fish a gamy flavour and means that they should be consumed within 2 days. To use, pour boiling water over the fish and allow to stand for 2 minutes. This will loosen the skin. Bloaters are usually mashed into a paste with lemon juice and served with toast.

Hot Smoked Fish

Arbroath smokies are haddock that have been gutted and beheaded then smoked whole. Their flavour is milder than that of cold smoked haddock. They are always sold in pairs. To use, split them in half, dot with butter and grill to heat through. They also make an excellent pâté.

Smoked eel is dense and rich, with a slight sweetness. It is good as part of a smoked fish plate or mashed into a pâté.

Smoked mackerel is rich, with a creamy texture. It can be eaten cold with salad or made into a pâté. It is sometimes sold coated with crushed peppercorns.

Smoked trout is one of the most popular hot smoked fish. It has a more subtle flavour than smoked mackerel, a finer texture and an attractive pale pink colour. It is excellent on its own or made into a mousse or pâté.

Smoked Trout Pâté

Other types of smoked fish can be substituted for the smoked trout in this recipe.

SERVES 4

2 smoked trout, 250 g | 9 oz total after skinning
   and boning
170 g | 6 oz cream cheese
2–3 teaspoons creamed grated horseradish
lemon juice, to taste
salt and freshly ground black pepper

To serve
Melba Toast (see following recipe)
lemon wedges (see **Food Presentation,**
   Garnishes, page 12)

1 Skin and bone the trout.
2 Mash the fish with a fork and beat in the remaining ingredients, or mix all the ingredients together in a food processor. Season, carefully with salt and pepper.
3 Turn into a dish and refrigerate until required.

NOTE: To keep the pâté for more than 1 day and up to 3 days, seal it with clarified butter (see **Dairy Products**, *Butter*, page 204). Pack the pâté tightly into ramekins and pour cool, melted clarified butter over the surface to a depth of 3 mm cm | ⅛ in.

Melba Toast

SERVES 4

4 slices of white bread

1 Preheat the oven to 150°C|300°F|gas mark 2.
2 Toast the bread, then cut off the crusts while still warm.
3 Using a bread knife, cut the bread in half horizontally so that you have 2 very thin slices of bread, each toasted on one side. Scrape any excess uncooked bread from each slice.
4 Cut each slice of bread into 4 triangles.
5 Place the triangles on a baking sheet, untoasted side up, and bake until an even golden-brown on both sides. This can take up to 30 minutes.
6 Store in an airtight container for up to 2 days.

Salted Fish

Salt cod or baccalau is cod that has been preserved by salting and drying, an ancient method of preserving fish. It is very popular in the Mediterranean countries where it is used to prepare *Brandade*, a pâté made with salt cod, garlic, olive oil or mayonnaise and breadcrumbs or mashed potato.

In order to use salt cod it must first be soaked in several successive changes of cold water to remove the salt and rehydrate the fish. This process can take up to 48 hours. Taste a small piece of the fish in order to tell if it has been soaked for long enough.

Pickled Fish

Pickled herrings have been marinated in white wine vinegar and aromatics. Like *Céviche* (see page 248) the protein is denatured by the action of the acid. Various names are given to the herrings depending on the ingredients of the pickle. Serve pickled herring with thinly sliced rye bread and a soured cream and cucumber salad.

Fish Roe

Caviar is the best known of the fish roes. It is the roe of the sturgeon that has been salted and cured with borax. There are three types of caviar, beluga, sevruga and oscietra. Each type is named after the species of sturgeon from which the eggs are taken. Beluga is the rarest and most expensive. Sevruga is cheapest. Oscietra is golden in colour with an oily texture. All caviar is graded, with malassol being the finest. Malassol caviar is slightly salted and is from fish caught at the beginning of the season. Eggs from fish caught later in the season is stronger in flavour and is normally processed to make 'pressed caviar'.

Lumpfish roe or mock caviar is the roe of the Arctic lumpfish. The tiny eggs are dyed red or black, then packed in glass jars. It has a salty flavour. It is useful for a garnish or for canapés.

Storing caviar

Keep in the refrigerator as close to 0°C|32°F as possible. Once the jar has been opened, consume within 5 days.

Using caviar

Serve caviar in a glass bowl set on a bed of crushed ice. It becomes oily if it is too warm. Caviar spoons are made from bone – a silver spoon will react with the caviar, giving it a metallic taste. Caviar is traditionally served with blinis, small yeast-raised buckwheat pancakes, soured cream, chopped onion and chopped hard-boiled eggs.

Keta is the roe of the salmon. It is larger than sturgeon caviar and bright orange-pink in colour. It has a mild fishy taste. It is excellent for garnishing fish pâtés or for serving as a canapé with crème fraîche (see ***Canapés***, page 202).

Cod's roe has been smoked, which turns it a deep red. It is used to make the dip *Taramasalata* (see below). Taramasalata is served with bread.

Taramasalata

225 g|8 oz smoked cod's roe	juice of ½–1 lemon
1 clove of garlic, crushed	150 ml|¼ pint olive oil
55 g|2 oz fresh white breadcrumbs	boiled water, cooled

1 Cut the cod's roe in half across its width and scrape out the inside, using a spoon. Discard the skin.
2 Put the roe into a food processor with the garlic, breadcrumbs and juice of ½ lemon.
3 Process the roe until smooth. Add the oil slowly through the feed tube while the motor is running.
4 Season with additional lemon juice if wished.
5 Add water if needed to thin the dip.

Flour

Flour is the finely ground and sifted meal of various edible grains such as wheat, corn, rye or rice. Flour is also made from nuts, starchy vegetables and pulses, such as chestnuts, potatoes or chickpeas. Unless a type of flour is specifically called for, 'flour' in a recipe is assumed to be plain white wheat flour. Self-raising flour is a soft, white flour that contains chemical raising agents added at the mill (see *Cakes*, page 138). It is used primarily for cakes.

Wheat

The importance of wheat in cooking lies in its combined proteins, glutenin and gliadin, which when mixed with water form an elastic substance called gluten. It is the gluten which gives bread its body. All flours contain protein, starch, fat, water, fibre, vitamins and minerals in varying quantities. Millers mix flours from different wheat crops in order to produce a standard product.

Wheat that has a relatively high amount of protein is said to be 'hard'. Although there are over 30,000 different strains of wheat, the important distinguishing factor between them is their degree of hardness. The types of wheat can be put into 3 categories: hard, soft or durum. Flour with a protein content of 12 per cent or higher is termed 'hard' or 'strong' and is best suited to bread-making. Flour with a protein content of 7–9 per cent is termed soft and is suitable for cakes, biscuits and some pastries. Durum wheat is very hard and is used for making dried pasta.

The structure of a grain of wheat looks something like this:

The **bran** is the outer coating of the grain. It contains a high proportion of B vitamins and about 50 per cent of the mineral elements in the grain. The bran consists mainly of indigestible cellulose which is a useful source of fibre (roughage) in the diet. The bran is separated from the grain during the milling process and is removed from white flour by sifting.

The **germ** is the embryo of the grain. It is rich in fats, proteins, B vitamins, Vitamin E and iron. Most of the germ is lost during the milling process; however, wheat germ can be purchased from heath food shops. Due to its high fat content it goes rancid quickly so is best stored in the refrigerator.

The **scutellum** is a membranous tissue that separates the germ from the endosperm. It is rich in thiamin.

The **endosperm** is the floury part of the grain, consisting mainly of starch and carbohydrate. It is very low in mineral elements and contains no vitamins. The endosperm contains the proteins glutenin and gliadin which when mixed with water combine together to form gluten, as described above.

The **aleurone layer** is a single layer of cells surrounding the endosperm. It contains some proteins but is lost during the milling process.

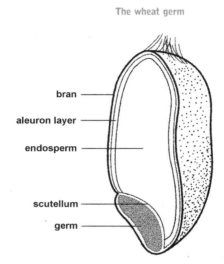

The wheat germ

- bran
- aleuron layer
- endosperm
- scutellum
- germ

Types of Wheat Flour

Wholewheat flour contains the whole of the cleaned wheat grain. 'Stoneground' refers to the old method of grinding the wheat grain between 2 slowly moving stones. This process crushes the grain without generating heat or separating the germ from the grain. Stoneground flour contains a higher quantity of the bran and the germ than does white flour. Wholemeal flour contains 80–90 per cent of the cleaned wheat grain. This percentage is termed the rate of extraction. It is the percentage of the whole grain that remains in the flour after milling.

Strong flour/Bread flour is milled from hard spring wheat which is grown in climates where the winter is very cold and the ground freezes to a depth of at least 20 cm|8 in, primarily Canada, the northern USA and Russia. This wheat has a higher protein content, usually 12–15 per cent, than the wheat grown in warmer climates. This flour is used for bread-making because of its high protein content.

Plain flour/All-purpose flour is a fine-textured flour milled from the endosperm. White flour is usually made from 70 to 72 per cent of the cleaned wheat grain. It contains neither the bran nor the germ. It is milled from winter wheat that produces a flour with a protein content of 9–11 per cent, somewhat lower than strong flour. Plain flour is higher in starch than strong flour and absorbs less liquid than strong flour. It is used for general cooking purposes, particularly to thicken sauces and make pastries, cakes and biscuits which do not require the tougher texture provided by the gluten in strong flour.

White flour in its natural state is a creamy colour but is often bleached to make it whiter. Unless a flour package is marked 'unbleached', it will have been bleached.

Self-raising flour is plain white or wholemeal flour to which raising agents have been added. It is used for cakes and other baked goods. The raising agent, usually baking powder, reacts with the liquid in the recipe to produce bubbles of carbon dioxide. Baking powder is a combination of bicarbonate of soda, an alkali, and cream of tartar, an acid. If the bubbles of carbon dioxide are captured in the flour during baking, a risen effect will be produced in the baked goods.

Plain flour can be converted to self-raising flour by the addition of 4 teaspoons baking powder per 250 g|9 oz plain flour. Too much raising agent will produce a sour, chemical taste in the baked goods.

Cake flour is a white flour milled from soft wheat. It has been ground very finely and is particularly suitable for cakes.

Other Types of Flour

Gluten-free flour is a product manufactured for people who are intolerant of gluten. It is a blend of rice flour, potato flour, buckwheat flour and maize flour. Although it cannot be used for yeast-leavened products, it can be substituted for plain flour in other recipes, such as pastry, scones, pancakes, and flour-based sauces. Gluten-free flour can be converted to self-raising flour by adding 4 teaspoons baking powder per 250 g|9 oz flour. The gluten-free flour will absorb slightly more liquid than would plain flour so the liquid quantity in a recipe may need to be increased.

Semolina flour/Pasta flour is a pale yellow, grainy flour that is ground from durum wheat. Durum wheat is a variety of hard wheat, so semolina is high in protein. It is used primarily for making pasta and gnocchi. In Italy durum wheat is ground into different degrees of fineness or 'types', *tipo* in Italian. The very fine grind of 'OO' is commonly used for making pasta.

Spelt flour is made from an ancient grain, spelt, grown in Southern Europe. It was popular with the Romans and was brought to England during the Roman occupation. Spelt has a light brown colour and a nutty flavour. It is more digestible than wheat and is therefore tolerated better by people who are sensitive to wheat. It can be purchased in health food stores. Spelt flour can be substituted for wheat flour in recipes.

Barley flour is a staple in Scotland and Northern England. It is low in gluten and has a nutty flavour. It can be added to wheat flour in small proportions.

Besan flour/Gram flour is made by grinding dried chickpeas. This fine, golden-yellow flour is used primarily in Indian cooking for making chapatis.

Buckwheat flour is extracted from the seeds of a herb native to Asia and Russia. Light brown in colour with flecks of black, it is used for the Russian pancakes called blinis and for the large crêpes made in Brittany. It contains no gluten and has a nutty flavour. In recipes, it is usually mixed with a similar quantity of wheat flour.

Chestnut flour is made from dried ground chestnuts. It has a strong, nutty flavour and is used in Europe, where it was once a staple in Corsica and the poorer areas of France and Italy. Chestnut flour can be used in cakes to give a nutty flavour.

Cornmeal/Maize flour is available in several degrees of fineness. As it does not contain gluten it needs to be combined with wheat flour for baking.

Polenta is a fine ground cornmeal used in Italian cooking (see *Grains*, page 302).

Masa Harina is a finely milled and sifted cornmeal that has been treated with lime to make it digestible. It is used to make tortillas.

Cornflour is a farinaceous thickening agent made from the starch of the corn. It is gluten-free. In addition to thickening sauces it can be used in baking, for example in combination with wheat flour for shortbread.

Potato flour is the dried starch from potatoes. It is used as a thickening agent and in cakes to impart a light, dry texture. It does not contain gluten so is a useful addition to gluten-free diets.

Rice is ground into rice flour, a very fine powder, and ground rice, a slightly gritty powder. It is mainly used for thickening puddings and for giving shortbread its characteristic sandy texture.

Oat flour is made from ground oat groats, the hulled oat grain. It does not contain gluten. The oat bran is particularly high in soluble fibre. It can be combined with wheat flour in small quantities.

Rye flour is milled from a hardy cereal grass. It is a staple of Central and Eastern Europe where the soil is too poor and the climate too harsh for growing wheat. Bread made from rye flour is a very dark brown. Although rye flour is high in protein, the type of protein it contains will not form gluten, so bread made from rye flour is dense and heavy. For bread-making rye flour is best mixed with strong white flour. The type of bread called pumpernickel is made using rye flour and black treacle (or molasses). Pumpernickel flour does not exist.

Soy flour is made from ground, dried soy beans. It contains twice the protein of wheat flour. As it has a strong flavour, it is normally used in small amounts as a 'flour improver' to increase the protein content of wheat flour.

Storing Flour

Flour should be stored in a cool, dry place, where it will keep for about 6 months. It is best stored in an airtight container. Alternatively, the bag of flour can be kept in a sealed plastic bag. Wholewheat flour will not keep as long as other flours, due to its higher fat content. In hot climates it is best stored in the refrigerator.

Forcemeat

The term forcemeat is derived from the French word *farce*, meaning stuffing. Forcemeat is made from uncooked minced meats, poultry, fish or shellfish, mixed with fat, spices, herbs and a generous quantity of seasoning. Forcemeat is used either on its own or with other ingredients to make pâtés and terrines (see **Terrines, Pâtés and Raised Pies**, page 703) and other products such as galantines (see **Meat**, *Poultry*, page 443) and sausages (see **Meat**, *Pork, Sausagemeat*, page 404).

Types of Forcemeat

The texture of forcemeat depends upon how finely the ingredients are prepared. Coarse forcemeat has a rough, chunky texture with visible pieces of meat and fat. It is used for country pâtés and terrines en croute and is often garnished with diced meats or nuts. The smoothest forcemeat has been laboriously sieved to remove any coarse bits of meat or connective tissue. It is used for pâtés and *mousselines* (see page 487). A mousseline is a delicate mixture, usually made with finely pounded shellfish or fish as the main ingredient (see **Aspic,** *Chaudfroid of Sole*, page 93).

Forcemeat Ingredients

The principal ingredient in forcemeat may be meat, poultry, fish or shellfish. When preparing the main ingredient it is important to remove all membranes, connective tissue and small bones to facilitate mincing.

Meats

Forcemeat based on meat usually contains minced pork as it adds moisture and smoothness. Without pork, forcemeats made with lean meats such as poultry and game tend to become dry and grainy when cooked. Pork usually makes up one-third of the meat content.

Pork and chicken livers are also often added to forcemeats to add flavour and help to bind the ingredients together. When a fine texture is required, the livers are minced and passed through a fine-mesh drum sieve, to remove any unwanted membranes, before adding to the forcemeat mixture.

Forcemeat: Points to Remember

- **Use fresh ingredients.** Meat and fish contain a protein called albumen that allows them to bind well with other ingredients. With age, the albumen disintegrates, losing its binding qualities, so it is important that meat or fish for forcemeat should be as fresh as possible. This is especially crucial when making smooth forcemeats as these forcemeats rely on the emulsification of albumen and fat to form a mixture that remains stable while it is cooked. A correctly made forcemeat will remain smooth and moist, whereas improperly emulsified forcemeats lose their fat, shrink and become dry and grainy after cooking.

- **The ingredients used to make the forcemeat must be kept chilled.** Forcemeats contain raw meat, liver, eggs and dairy products, all of which if incorrectly handled are potential breeding grounds for hazardous micro-organisms.

- **The equipment must be scrupulously clean and well chilled.** Forcemeats are prepared in a food processor or using a mincer with various-sized mincing discs. The equipment must be scrupulously clean, and when possible, chilled to below 4°C|40°F in the refrigerator or freezer to prevent the forcemeat warming while it is being processed.

- **Ensure the forcemeat ingredients are used in the correct proportions.** The ratio of ingredients in forcemeat is especially important with regard to the emulsification and binding of proteins and fats and to the texture of the cooked forcemeat.

- **Cut ingredients to the appropriate size for processing, no larger than 2.5 cm|1 in.** Process or mince the meat, pork, fat and any other ingredients to the required size. Mince once through the largest-sized disc and again through the next size for rough-textured pâté, or rub through a fine sieve after mincing for smooth-textured forcemeat.

- **Test the seasoning and texture of the forcemeat by cooking a teaspoonful of the mixture.** Coarse forcemeats can be fried in a little oil. Smooth forcemeats can be poached in water. Either type of forcemeat can be cooked in a microwave over for 30 seconds on MEDIUM power. A 450 g|1 lb quantity of minced meat requires approximately 5 ml|1 teaspoon salt; however, herbs and spices will compensate for salt so it is best to add the seasoning by degrees to avoid over-seasoning.

- **Adjust the texture of the forcement.** When cooked, forcemeat should not be dry and crumbly, or so soft that it fails to hold its shape. Forcemeat should be sufficiently firm to cut cleanly into slices or portions, but not set to the extent that it becomes rubbery. If the texture of the forcemeat is too dry, add a little double cream. If it is too soft, add a small quantity of egg white and test again.

Fish

Mousseline forcemeats made with shellfish bind more successfully if fine-textured white fish, such as sole, makes up 25 per cent of the total weight. Forcemeat made with lobster is enhanced in appearance and taste if the coral and eggs are used.

Fats

Pork fat, bacon fat and double cream are most commonly used in forcemeat to add a rich flavour and smooth, moist texture. Suet, butter and dripping are also used for the same purposes. Coarse, rustic forcemeats use half the weight of fat to meat and smoother mousseline forcemeats use 1 litre|1¾ pints of double cream to 1 kg|2¼ lb of meat or fish.

Binding Ingredients

Although the process of emulsifying fat and meat or fish protein is often sufficient to bind smooth forcemeats, the addition of other binding ingredients may be necessary to improve the overall texture. The binding ingredients hold the forcemeat together while it cooks and cools, to produce a smooth, moist texture and a product that holds together well when sliced. The two principal binding ingredients are *panades* and eggs.

Panade or panada: A *panade* is a term given to a thick paste made of flour and water or milk and a small quantity of butter. Often amounting to 20 per cent of the total forcemeat ingredients, it is used cold to bind meat or especially fish (as fish mousseline can be grainy) and produce a stable, smooth-textured forcemeat. The mixture is then passed through a sieve before other enriching ingredients such as butter or eggs are added.

Eggs: Eggs or egg whites are used to bind and set forcemeat if it contains a large quantity of liquid or liver. Four egg whites are required to bind and set a mousseline made with 1 kg|2¼ lb of meat or fish and 1 litre|1¾ pints of double cream. If too much egg white is used, the mousseline may have a rubbery texture when cooked, or if too little is used, the mousseline ingredients may not bind sufficiently, giving a grainy and crumbly result.

Béchamel Sauce: To bind vegetable forcemeat, a thick *Béchamel Sauce* (see **Sauces, Savoury**, page 589) replaces the heavier *panade*.

Bread: Bread soaked in hot milk or cream can be used to bind forcemeats.

Flavouring Forcemeat

Forcemeat can be bland and uninteresting unless carefully flavoured and seasoned. The flavour is enhanced with a wide variety of ingredients, including table salt, curing salt, marinades, herbs and spices. Salt not only adds flavour to forcemeat but also promotes emulsification of the meat and fat and for this reason is usually added in the early stages of preparation. Curing salt, a mixture of salt and sodium nitrite, is used in small quantities in forcemeat to inhibit bacterial growth and help retain the fresh pink colour of meat by preventing it from oxidizing. Without sodium nitrite, forcemeat made with meat turns grey and unappetizing in appearance within a matter of hours after contact with air.

Marinating

Forcemeat ingredients are often marinated for anything between 1 hour and 2 days before mincing, to tenderize the ingredients and enhance their flavours. Marinades for forcemeat may include herbs, citrus zest, spices, wine, port and brandy.

Spicing

Spices most commonly used to flavour forcemeat are those associated with winter food, such as cloves, nutmeg, juniper, ginger, paprika, and black and white pepper. Herbs include those with robust flavours such as bay leaves, thyme, sage, rosemary, parsley, tarragon and marjoram.

Garnishes

Forcemeat is often garnished with small quantities of diced or chopped meat, fat and/or vegetables or dried fruit to enhance its flavour, texture and appearance. Garnishes most commonly used are pistachio nuts, diced pork fat, truffles, diced ham and tongue. Vegetables, ham and tongue should be pricked before adding to the forcemeat or they may shrink during cooking, leaving unsightly air pockets.

Storing Uncooked Forcemeat

Once forcemeat is made, it should be covered in clingfilm, placed immediately in the refrigerator and used within 24 hours. Raw forcemeat may also be frozen for up to 3 months.

Fruit

Fruit is a delicious and important part of man's diet, providing vitamins, minerals and fibre. Nutritionists recommend that at least 2 servings of fruit are eaten every day. Try to eat fruit that is in season: it should taste better, be more nutritious and be less expensive than fruit that has been stored for a long time or that has been picked unripe several weeks before being shipped for thousands of miles.

Fruit contains fructose, a simple sugar that gives it wide-ranging appeal. Some fruit, however, contains tannins, astringent compounds that make your mouth pucker. As the fruit ripens, the tannins soften. Most fruit continues to ripen once picked. Guidelines for choosing fruit are given in this chapter.

When fruit is packed close together it produces a gas called ethylene which softens the cell structure of the fruit. Bananas produce a large amount of this gas and a ripe banana can be used to ripen other fruit by placing it in a bag with a piece of unripe fruit.

Some fruits, such as apples, pears and bananas, turn brown when their flesh is exposed to air. This is called oxidation. It is caused by the enzymes called phenolases. Brushing the exposed fruit with lemon juice or submerging it in liquid to which lemon or orange juice or ascorbic acid (Vitamin C) powder has been added can slow the discoloration. The acid retards the enzyme action.

Wash all fruit before cutting and eating, but if possible, not before storing as washing encourages the cells to soften.

The season in the UK is indicated where appropriate in the list that starts on page 278.

Methods of Cooking Fruit

Stewing (see *Apple Sauce*, page 279)

Stewing is a good method for cooking fruit that needs a lot of sugar to make it palatable and is suited to most fruit with the exception of citrus fruit. It is the method used to make a thick fruit sauce such as *Apple Sauce*. Other fruits that stew particularly well are plums, gooseberries, rhubarb and cranberries.

Fruit that has been stewed may be frozen for up to 1 year.

To stew 450 g | 1 lb fruit

Peel, de-seed or stone and cut the fruit into 2.5 cm | 1 in chunks and place in a saucepan with 2 tablespoons water, the juice of ½ lemon and sugar to sweeten as required. Place a piece of dampened greaseproof paper (a *cartouche*) directly on top of the fruit and cover with a lid. Cook over a medium-low heat, stirring frequently to prevent the fruit from catching and scorching, until the fruit is softened. Adjust the consistency as required by adding water to thin or by boiling to thicken. Season with more sugar or lemon juice as required. The fruit can be passed through a sieve to make a smooth purée or it can be used as a chunky sauce. Cool completely before freezing.

Stewed fruit can be folded together with an equal quantity of lightly whipped cream, thick yoghurt or thick custard to make a quick dessert called fool.

Poaching (see *Mulled Wine Poached Pears*, page 280)

Whole or large pieces of fruit can be cooked by poaching in a sugar syrup (see **Sugar, Sweeteners and Sugar Syrups**, page 699). This method of cooking is particularly suitable for fruit that is underripe because the poaching softens and sweetens the fruit. Most fruit, other than very soft berries which would disintegrate, is suitable for poaching – pears, apricots and peaches are the most popular. Fruit compote is made from poached fruit.

The sugar syrup can be flavoured with wine or with spices such as cinnamon sticks, vanilla pods, slices of fresh ginger or pods of star anise or cardamom.

Fruit that has been poached can be frozen in the sugar syrup for up to 1 year.

To poach 450 g | 1 lb fruit

Place 1 litre | 1¾ pints water or half wine and water and 450 g | 1 lb granulated sugar in a saucepan large enough to hold the fruit and the syrup. Add spices, if using. If the fruit is likely to discolour, add the juice of 1 lemon (see information about individual fruit below).

Heat over a low heat, stirring, until the sugar has dissolved, then turn up the heat and boil for 5 minutes.

Peel the fruit if necessary. Apples and pears are peeled before poaching but peaches, nectarines and apricots are easier to peel after poaching. The skins are left on plums.

Add the fruit to the hot syrup so that the fruit is submerged. Place a piece of greaseproof paper directly on the surface of the fruit and then place a small saucer on top of the paper to keep the fruit submerged. Regulate the heat so that occasional bubbles come to the surface of the liquid. Cook until the fruit is just tender when pierced with a skewer.

The cooking time will vary depending on the ripeness and size of the fruit. If the fruit is in danger of overcooking, remove it with a slotted spoon and leave to cool in a dish in a single layer, otherwise it can be cooled in the poaching syrup.

Baking (see *Baked Apples*, page 278)

Cooking apples are the classic fruit used for baking because their cells soften more quickly than those of eating apples. Plums, peaches, nectarines and apricots are also good baked, particularly if they are slightly underripe. The heat of the oven softens the cells of the fruit and intensifies its flavour by drying it slightly.

To bake fruit other than apples, cut the fruit, cored or stoned as necessary, into large bite-sized pieces. It the fruit is likely to discolour, toss it with lemon juice. Berries can be baked whole. Wrap individual servings of fruit loosely in foil parcels with sugar to sweeten and 2 tablespoons water, wine or fruit juice. Bake in the oven preheated to 180°C|350°F|gas mark 4 for about 20 minutes or until the fruit is softened and hot.

Baked fruit is not suitable for freezing.

Grilling

Most fruit is suitable for grilling. Preheat the grill until it is very hot. Cut the fruit, cored or stoned as necessary, 1–2.5 cm|½–1 in thick. If the fruit is likely to discolour, brush it with lemon juice. Place the fruit in a single layer on a baking sheet and sprinkle with caster sugar. Place the fruit under the grill, about 7 cm|3 in from the heat, and grill for about 5 minutes until the fruit is softened and lightly caramelized. Serve warm.

Grilled fruit is not suitable for freezing.

Deep-frying

Fruit tempura is the most usual form of deep-fried fruit. Slices of banana or apple are most often used (see **Deep-frying**, page 208).

Frying

Although fruit is not usually shallow-fried, 1 cm|½ in thick slices of apple, pear or banana are sometimes cooked in buttered caramel in a sauté pan to use as a garnish for sweet or savoury dishes.

Heat 30 g|1 oz butter with 4 tablespoons caster sugar over a medium heat until the sugar begins to brown. Add the fruit slices in a single layer and cook, turning in the caramel to coat, for about 5 minutes or until the fruit has softened.

The caramelized fruit slices are not suitable for freezing.

Jams, Jellies and Preserves

Many types of fruit can be used for making jams, jellies and chutneys. Underripe fruit contains pectin which forms a gel when heated and is necessary for setting jams and jellies (see **Jams, Jellies and Other Preserves**, page 321).

Orchard Fruit

Apples

Imported or cold-stored available all year round; UK: September–December

Choosing

Apples can be divided into cooking or eating apples. Choose apples that have no signs of bruising, have smooth skins, are heavy for their size and are not beginning to soften. Cooking apples such as the Bramley are large, slightly bulbous and a bright green colour.

Apples that have a brown spotting that runs throughout the fruit have been damaged with the disease called 'bitter pit'. The diseased part of the fruit should be discarded.

When apples are 'out of season', it means that they have been held in cold storage since harvest so will not have a lot of flavour.

Storing

Store apples in a cool place or in the fruit drawer of a refrigerator. If apples are to be stored for longer than 1 week, ensure that they are not touching each other as the fruit will soften and start to rot at the point where they touch.

Using

Apples discolour when their cut surfaces are exposed to air, so they need to be tossed with lemon juice if they not going to be used immediately.

Cooking Apples

Cooking apples are tarter than eating apples and need the addition of sugar to be palatable. When cooked, they soften and release their juices faster than eating apples because their cell walls are softer. Cooking apples and crab apples, cherry-sized reddish-orange apples, make excellent jelly (see *Jams, Jellies and Other Preserves*, page 321)

Stewed Bramley apple makes an excellent apple sauce for accompanying roast pork (see below). Bramleys are also suitable for baking and poaching (see *Baking* and *Poaching*, above) or making into pies or crumbles (see *Pastry*, page 510).

Baked Apples

1 small cooking apple per person
soft light brown sugar
sultanas

1 Preheat the oven to 180°C│350°F│gas mark 4.
2 Wash the apples and remove the cores with an apple corer. Using a sharp knife, cut a ring just through the apple skin about two-thirds of the way up each apple.

3 Put the apples into an ovenproof dish and stuff the centres with a mixture of sugar and sultanas.

4 Sprinkle 2 teaspoons sugar over each apple, then pour water over the apples to come to a depth of 1 cm | ½ in.

5 Bake in the oven for about 45 minutes, or until the apples are soft when pierced with a skewer.

Apple Sauce

Apple sauce is the traditional accompaniment to roast pork (see **Meat, Pork**, page 398). This recipe uses cooking apples, which are much more tart than eating apples. Eating apples can also be made into apple sauce but half the amount of sugar should be used and the cooking time will be longer.

450 g | 1 lb cooking apples
110 g | 4 oz sugar
4 tablespoons water

1 Peel and core the apples. Cut them into chunks. Put them into a heavy-based saucepan with the sugar and water and simmer gently until they are soft and pulpy. Beat out any lumps with a wooden spoon.

2 If the purée is too sloppy, boil it rapidly to reduce and thicken it stirring frequently, but leave the pan half-covered in case it splashes dangerously.

Eating Apples

Eating apples come in an enormous number of varieties although many are now becoming scarce. The most commonly found eating apples in the market today are Cox's Orange Pippin, Gala, Granny Smith, Red Delicious and Golden Delicious. Granny Smith apples are the tartest of the eating apples and are also suitable for using in fruit desserts (see **Nuts,** *Normandy Apple Tart*, page 496).

Pears

Imported available all year round; UK: September–November

Choosing
Pears are picked unripe. It is best to buy under-ripe pears a few days before you need them as pears that have ripened in the shop are often damaged. Avoid any pear that shows browning at the base because it is likely to be brown throughout.

Storing
Pears can be ripened in a single layer at room temperature. It is important that they do not touch each other as they have a tendency to rot at the point of contact.

Depending on the variety, the colour of a ripe pear will vary from gold to green to brown. Pears do not freeze well.

Using

Pears are wonderful eaten raw when ripe, but can also be poached whole or in pieces, or grilled. They make a delicious topping for a tart filled with *frangipane*, an almond paste (see **Nuts**, page 497).

Pears discolour when their cut surface is exposed to air and need to be brushed with lemon juice if they are not going to be used immediately.

Mulled Wine Poached Pears

These are particularly delicious made a day or two in advance. The pears will become a deep garnet colour and translucent as they stand in the syrup.

SERVES 4

150 ml | ¼ pint water	1 cinnamon stick
290 ml | ½ pint red wine	2.5 cm | 1 in piece of fresh root ginger, peeled
110 g | 4 oz granulated sugar	and sliced
thinly pared zest of 1 orange and 1 lemon	4 pears
1 teaspoon whole cloves	juice of 1 lemon

1 Place the water, wine, sugar, citrus zests and spices into a saucepan and bring to a simmer. Simmer for 5 minutes, then let stand for a further 10 minutes.
2 Peel the pears with a vegetable peeler or knife, leaving the stems intact. Place the pears in a bowl of water with the lemon juice to prevent discoloration.
3 Immerse the pears in the wine mixture and cover with a piece of greaseproof paper. Place a saucer on top of the paper to submerge the pears.
4 Keep the mixture at a poach, so that the occasional bubble rises to the surface, for 30–60 minutes. The pears should be tender when pierced through the base with a skewer.
5 Remove from the poaching wine and place in a serving dish. Boil the wine until syrupy, then sieve over the pears.

Poached Fruit: What has gone wrong when...

The fruit is still hard.
- The fruit was undercooked.

The fruit is mushy.
- The fruit was overcooked.
- The fruit was boiled.
- The fruit was bruised before cooking.

Quinces

Available October, November

Quinces are a hard, golden fruit that look rather like a misshapen apple. When ripe they have a heavenly perfume, rather like that of a very intense, tart apple.

Choosing

Quinces should be a deep golden-yellow with no brown or soft spots and with no signs of wrinkling.

Storing

As for apples (see above).

Using

Quinces can be grated or diced and added to an apple pie or crumble. They can also be poached, baked and made into jam or jelly.

Citrus Fruit

Lemons, Limes

Available all year round

Oranges, Grapefruit

Available all year round; best November–March

Blood Oranges

Available February

Seville Oranges

Available January and February

Choosing

Choose fruit that are heavy for their size and show no signs of bruising or softening. There are now many varieties of oranges, grapefruit and citrus hybrids available in the market. The flavour and degree of sweetness varies from type to type.

Storing

Citrus fruit keeps well. Store at room temperature for up to 1 week or in the refrigerator for up to 1 month. Oranges for marmalade can be frozen whole. Defrost before using.

Using

High in Vitamin C, segments of oranges and grapefruit are used in fruit salads and to accompany meat dishes, especially rich meats such as pork and duck. Occasionally the segments are warmed but they are seldom cooked as high heat dulls their fresh, sharp flavour and destroys their Vitamin C content. The ascorbic and citric acids in citrus fruit are useful for marinades for meat and fish because the acids denature (soften) proteins.

- **Seville oranges** are small bitter oranges used for making *Marmalade* (see ***Jams, Jellies and Other Preserves***, page 328).
- **Blood oranges** are tart oranges, used for both eating and cooking. Their flesh is speckled with ruby, a result of crossing the orange with a pomegranate.

The juice and zest of lemons and limes is used widely to flavour food. Wedges of the fruits are used to garnish fish dishes (see ***Food Presentation***, *Garnishes*, page 12).

Peeling citrus fruit

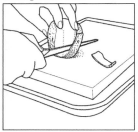

Peeling citrus fruit

1 Use a serrated fruit knife (see ***Kitchen Equipment***, page 74).
2 Create a firm base for the fruit to stand on by cutting off the peel and pith at the top and bottom, exposing the tips of the segments.
3 Following the contour of the fruit from top to bottom, cut away the peel, pith and outer membrane of the fruit in narrow strips. Use the cut edge of the peel as a guide for the blade of your knife. Rotate the fruit clockwise. Be careful not to cut into the flesh or the segments will lose their natural shape.

Segmenting citrus fruit

Segmenting citrus fruit

Citrus fruit can be segmented for use in fruit salads and other recipes (see ***Caramel***, *Oranges in Caramel Sauce* page 175).

1 Peel the citrus fruit, using the method described above.
2 Trim any remaining pith and membrane off the peeled fruit, being careful not to cut into the flesh.
3 Place the fruit on a board set over a tray to catch the juice. Cut on either side of the segments, between the fruit and membrane, using a sawing motion.
4 Once a few segments have been removed, cut down the side of the membrane, then twist the knife to cut back up the other side. Work your way around the fruit.
5 Each segment should still retain its curved outer surface, be fully intact and free of membrane and pith.

Zesting citrus fruit

The zest of oranges, lemons and limes is widely used in cookery for flavouring. It contains the essential oils of the fruit and thus much of the flavour. Usually the zest is removed using a small 'nail-hole' grater for a fine zest. For shreds of zest, use a 'half-moon' grater. Scrub the fruit well before zesting to remove pesticides, then dry it thoroughly. Only the coloured part of the peel should be removed. Do not grate into the white pith because it is bitter.

Removing zest with a peeler

Making needleshreds: The blanched julienne peel of citrus fruits is often called 'needleshreds' in reference to the fineness of the cut. It is used to decorate desserts that have been flavoured with the juice of the citrus fruit and is an important ingredient in *Cumberland Sauce* (see below).

Use a vegetable peeler to remove strips of the peel, working from the top to the bottom of the fruit. Flatten the strips of zest on the board, cut side up, and using a serrated fruit knife carefully scrape off any pith. To cut julienne strips of about 1 mm × 5 cm|$\frac{1}{25}$ × 2 in, first trim off the ragged edges and use a cook's knife to cut the zest into even julienne (see **Knife Skills**, page 71). Blanch in boiling water until tender, then immerse in cold water to stop the cooking.

Cutting needleshreds

Crystallized needleshreds: Crystallized needleshreds are good for decorating cakes and mousses. Poach the needleshreds in sugar syrup (see **Sugar, Sweeteners and Sugar Syrups**, page 699) for about 5 minutes until tender. Drain, then roll in granulated sugar. Allow to dry on baking parchment, then store in an airtight container.

Cumberland Sauce

This fruit sauce is traditionally served with country pâtés and cold meats such as gammon.

2 oranges	150 ml|$\frac{1}{2}$ pint port
1 lemon	$\frac{1}{2}$ teaspoon Dijon mustard
225 g|8 oz redcurrant jelly	a pinch of cayenne pépper
1 shallot, finely chopped	a pinch of ground ginger

1 Remove the zest from the citrus fruits, using a vegetable peeler. Cut away any white pith. Cut the zest into needleshreds.

2 Squeeze the juice from the fruit and strain into a saucepan.

3 Add the remaining ingredients along with the needleshreds. Simmer for 10 minutes, then allow to cool.

4 Store in the refrigerator, covered, for up to 2 weeks.

Soft Fruit and Exotic Fruit

Avocados

Available imported all year round

Choosing

The avocado is a pear-shaped fruit that is usually used in savoury recipes, such as salads, Mexican dishes and dips. There are 2 types of avocado: the smooth green-skinned avocado and the smaller black knobbly-skinned Haas avocado. An avocado should yield to gentle pressure at the stem end when ripe.

Keep at room temperature. Avocados that have been refrigerated often develop brown spots in the flesh. Place an unripe avocado in a paper bag with a ripe banana to help it ripen more quickly.

Using

Cut in half, from top to bottom, just before using. Twist to separate the halves, then tap the large stone with the sharp edge of a cook's knife and twist the knife to remove the stone. Brush the cut avocado with lemon or lime juice to help avoid discoloration (see **Canapés,** *Guacamole*, page 172).

Bananas

Available imported all year round

Choosing

Bananas ripen quickly at room temperature so choose bananas that are slightly less ripe than you need. As a banana ripens it turns from green to yellow to brown. Preferences regarding ripeness for eating vary tremendously but a banana that has lost its green tinge will be sweeter and have more flavour than a green banana. As brown freckles appear on the skin, the sweetness of the fruit increases and the banana flavour strengthens. For baking, a banana that is nearly entirely brown but not yet mushy to touch will give the best flavour.

Storing

Bananas are best kept at room temperature. If bananas are refrigerated or frozen, the skins will turn soft and black although the fruit will still be suitable for baking. Placing a ripe banana next to unripe fruit will cause the fruit to ripen more quickly due to the ethylene gas that is emitted by the ripe banana.

Using

Bananas turn brown when their flesh is exposed to air, so if peeled bananas are going to be left for any length of time they should be tossed in lemon juice.

Bananas can be used in cake mixtures for baking (see **Baking**, *Quick Bread, Banana Bread*, page 106) or can be baked in their skins until soft. They can also be used for fruit tempura (see **Deep-frying**, page 208) or can be peeled and grilled (see *Methods of Cooking Fruit*, above). Bananas can be split in half and shallow-fried in butter and sugar, then flambéed with brandy before serving with vanilla ice cream.

Berries

Blackberries *Available August–October; frozen available all year*

Blueberries *Available imported most of the year; UK: July, August*

Cherries *Available May–July*

Cranberries *Available October–December*

Currants, Red, Black and White *Available July, August*

Gooseberries *Available June, July*

Mulberries *Available July–September*

Physalis (Cape gooseberry) *Available imported most of the year*

Loganberries *Available July, August*

Raspberries *Available imported most of the year; UK: July, August*

Strawberries *Available imported most of the year; UK: June, July*

Tayberries *Available July, August*

Choosing berries

Choose berries that are plump and show no signs of bruising, crushing or mould.

Storing berries

Store in the refrigerator for up to 3 days. The berries can be stored in their punnets but they will keep better if they are placed on a tray in a single layer without touching each other, covered with clingfilm before being refrigerated. Do not wash or hull berries until just before using or they will become mushy.

Berries are suitable for freezing for up to 1 year but when defrosted they become soft. Open-freeze (see **Food Storage**, *Freezing*, page 32) the berries, then store in a rigid box or plastic freezer bag.

Using

Blackberries, blueberries, cherries, loganberries, raspberries, strawberries and tayberries are all suitable for eating raw. Any berries can be made into a sauce (see **Sauces, Sweet**, *Fruit Coulis*, page 617), added to a fruit parcel for baking (see *Methods of Cooking Fruit*, above) or to apples for a fruit crumble (see **Pastry**, page 510). Puréed berries can be used for ice cream and sorbets (see **Ice Cream**, page 311 and **Sorbets**, page 643).

- Tart **Morello** cherries are used for baking and making into jam.
- Green **gooseberries** and **cranberries** are too tart to eat raw and are most often stewed to make into a sauce. Stew 225 g|8 oz berries with 110 g|4 oz caster sugar and 150 ml|¼ pint water (see *Stewing*, above). When half of the berries have burst, the sauce is done.
- **Currants** are used for making sauces and for the favourite British dessert *Summer Pudding* (see below), along with raspberries and other berries.

Summer Pudding

A mixture of summer berries are lightly cooked to make this classic dessert. Summer pudding can be frozen for up to 3 months.

SERVES 4–6

150 ml | ¼ pint water
110–170 g | 4–6 oz caster sugar
900 g | 2 lb mixed berries, such as
    blackcurrants, raspberries, redcurrants and
    blackberries, destalked

2 tablespoons crème de cassis
oil, for greasing
6–9 slices of stale white bread, crusts removed
290 ml | ½ pint double cream or crème fraîche,
    to serve

1 Place the water and the sugar in a large sauté pan over a low heat. Stir to dissolve the sugar.
2 Add the berries and cook for 5–10 minutes until they have softened and their juices have started to run. Stir in the crème de cassis and turn off the heat.
3 Meanwhile, lightly oil a pudding basin or 6 timbale moulds and line with clingfilm.
4 Cut the bread into strips, dip one side in the juice, and use to line the base and sides of the basin or moulds, placing the dipped side next to the mould.
5 Place the fruit in a sieve over a bowl to catch the juices (reserve this). Spoon the warm fruit into the bread-lined basin or moulds, pressing down lightly.
6 Cover the fruit with juice-dipped bread, then cover with clingfilm. Place a disc of cardboard over the top and place a weight on top of the cardboard.
7 Refrigerate overnight.
8 Boil the juice to a light syrup consistency. Cool then refrigerate.
9 Turn out the pudding or puddings and spoon over the juice. Serve with cream or crème fraîche.

Figs

Available imported most of the year; UK: August–October

Choosing

Figs range in colour from green to purple to black. When ripe, they feel plump and moist. They should feel also slightly soft and be heavy for their size. Avoid fruit that is dry or cracked. Figs will not ripen further once picked.

Storing

Figs do not keep well and should be consumed as soon as possible. Store in the refrigerator for up to 2 days.

Using

Figs can be baked at 180°C | 350°F | gas mark 4 for about 30 minutes, or until they start to collapse, and served with crème fraîche or Greek yoghurt. They can also be baked in a tart with custard or frangipane (see *Nuts*, page 495). Figs have a special affinity with goat's cheese and can be served with the cheese as part of a salad. Cut the fruit in half from top to bottom. Peeling is not necessary.

Kiwi Fruit

Available imported all year round
The kiwi, imported from New Zealand, is a relatively new fruit in the UK, but it is now ubiquitous. The fuzzy brown oval fruit opens to reveal a bright green or golden translucent interior with a central white core and tiny black edible pips. A kiwi fruit has up to 5 times more Vitamin C than an orange.

Baby kiwi are now available. They taste like physalis crossed with a kiwi. They have bright green edible skins.

Choosing

Choose kiwi fruit that yield slightly to pressure but are not squishy.

Storing

Kiwi will ripen if left at room temperature in a single layer. Refrigerate when ripe for up to 2 weeks.

Using

Kiwi fruit are best eaten on their own or as part of a fruit salad or fresh fruit tart. Heating destroys their Vitamin C content. Kiwi fruit is a traditional part of the dessert *Pavlova* (see *Meringues*, page 478). As the fruit contains the enzyme bromelin, which interferes with the setting powers of gelatine, Kiwi fruit should not be used in jellies or other gelatine-set desserts.

To peel a kiwi fruit, cut the skin from the top and the bottom and use a serrated fruit knife or vegetable peeler to peel around the fruit to remove the skin. Do not slice too thinly or the fruit will break up. Use gloves to protect your hands if peeling several kiwi fruit.

Peeling a kiwi fruit

Lychees

Available imported November–February

Choosing

Lychees should be a dusty red colour, never brown, and firm. Avoid any that are starting to soften or dry out.

Storing

Keep at room temperature for 2 days or in the refrigerator for up to 1 week. Lychees can be poached in a sugar syrup and frozen for up to 1 year, although they are best eaten fresh.

Using

Cut through the tough skin at the stem end with a knife then peel. The skins are rough, so use gloves if peeling several. To remove the large stone, cut around the peeled fruit from top to bottom and pull the fruit from the stone.

Mangoes

Available imported most of the year, particularly May–September

Choosing

Dicing a mango (a)

Choose mangoes that are heavy for their size and 'give' slightly when pressed. Although the colour of mango skin varies according to variety, mangoes available in the UK usually have a more golden-red colour than green. Avoid any mangoes that are bruised or very soft. The riper a mango, the stronger its aroma. The Alphonse mango is the most delicious.

Storing

Keep mangoes at room temperature for up to 1 week or in the refrigerator for up to 2 weeks.

Dicing a mango (b)

Using

Mangoes can be sliced and poached in a sugar syrup (see *Methods of Cooking Fruit*, above) or made into a fruit sauce (see **Sauces, Sweet,** *Fruit Coulis*, page 617) or chutney (see **Jams, Jellies and Other Preserves**, page 330).

Preparing a mango

Dicing a mango (c)

1 Before taking a knife to the fruit, decide which way the stone lies by holding the mango narrow end up and looking down it. In cross-section, mangoes are oval in shape and the stone lies along the length of the oval.

2 Once you have discerned which way the stone lies, take a serrated fruit knife (see **Kitchen Equipment**, page 74) and, holding the mango on a board with the narrower end uppermost, cut it in half along its length, as close as possible to the stone lying in the centre of the fruit. (a)

3 Cut on the other side of the mango stone towards the board to obtain the second half of the mango.

4 Lie one half of the cut mango on the board, skin side down.

5 Make a series of diagonal cuts through the mango flesh, taking care not to pierce the skin. (b)

Dicing a mango (d)

6 Turn the mango by 90° and cut the same way across the fruit to obtain even dice.

7 To separate the dice, turn the mango inside out by pushing the skin towards its cut side. (c)

8 Hold the fruit above a bowl and with a gentle sawing action, remove the mango dice by cutting as close to the skin as possible. (d)

9 Any mango flesh still attached to the stone can be trimmed off and cut to dice of a similar size.

Melons

Imported available most of the year

Choosing
Melons come in many different varieties, many of which have a strong fragrance when ripe. Choose a fruit that is heavy for its size and without any bruising. When ripe, the fruit at the stem end should give slightly when pressed.

Storing
Ripen melons at room temperature then store in the refrigerator for up to 5 days. Wrap the melon in a plastic bag because their strong fragrance can taint other foods. Once cut the melon should be stored with the seeds intact to help prevent dehydration. Eat within 3 days.

Using
Melon is usually eaten raw, but the denser varieties such as cantaloupe and honeydew melon can be poached in sugar syrup then frozen for up to 1 year. The fruit softens upon defrosting.

Papaya (Pawpaw)

Available imported all year round

Choosing
Choose fruits that are heavy for their size and show no sign of browning. Papaya is ripe when it feels slightly soft when pressed gently and the colour has changed from green to yellow.

Storing
As for mangoes (see above).

Using
Cut the fruit in half and use a teaspoon to remove the round black seeds, which are not usually eaten. A sprinkling of lime juice complements the flavour of papaya. Papaya contains the enzyme bromelin which softens protein, so it cannot be used in dishes set with gelatine.

Passion fruit

Available imported all year round; UK: July–September

Choosing
Most varieties of these small round fruits with their leathery brown skins are ripe when the skins are heavily wrinkled. The fragrant pulp surrounding the tough

black seeds is used to perfume fruit salads, sauces and meringues. Look for South American passion fruit with their smooth firm orange shell; they have a wonderful flavour.

Storing

Passion fruit will continue to ripen at room temperature. Once ripened, store in the refrigerator for up to 1 week. To freeze, dry-pack the whole fruit in sugar (see **Food Storage,** *Freezing*, page 30) and freeze for up to 1 year.

Using

Cut in half through the middle and use a teaspoon to scrape out the pulp and the black seeds. The seeds and pulp can be used in fruit salads and sprinkled over Pavlova (see *Meringues*, page 478). Passion fruit complements the flavour of mango beautifully and can be used with mango to make a *Coulis* (see **Sauces, Sweet**, page 617). To remove the pulp from the seeds, pulse in a food processor very briefly, then sieve.

Pineapple

Available imported most of the year

Choosing

Choose fruit that is heavy for its size with a noticeable 'pineapple' aroma. Most types of pineapple will start to turn golden-brown when ripe, although a few varieties remain green. Another test for ripeness is to tug on a leaf: it should pull out easily from the fruit.

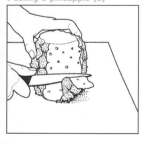
Peeling a pineapple (a)

Storing

Ripen at room temperature, then store in a tightly closed plastic bag in the refrigerator for up to 5 days. Pineapple slices or chunks can be poached in a sugar syrup, then frozen for up to 1 year.

Using

To peel a pineapple, top and tail the fruit using a serrated fruit knife (see **Kitchen Equipment**, page 74), then peel as for an orange (a). To remove the eyes, cut V-shaped groves in the flesh on either side of the eyes. (b) Like kiwi fruit and papaya (see above), pineapple contains the enzyme bromelin, which prohibits its use with gelatine.

Peeling a pineapple (b)

Rhubarb

Forced available from November, main UK season, March–June
Although rhubarb is a vegetable, it is almost always sweetened and served as a fruit.

Choose firm, not flabby stalks without any sign of dryness or wilting.

Remove any leaves before storing because they are poisonous. Place the stalks in a plastic bag, then keep in the refrigerator for up to 1 week. Rhubarb can be frozen without any preparation for up to 1 year although it may lose some of its colour. Alternatively, the fruit can be poached or stewed, then frozen for up to 1 year.

Never eat rhubarb raw. It should be stewed with sugar or poached in a sugar syrup (see *Methods of Cooking Fruit*, above). Rhubarb can also be cut into pieces and baked until tender before using in fools, pies and crumbles. It does require a lot of sugar to be palatable, however. Never cook rhubarb in an aluminium pan as it will cause a dangerous chemical reaction.

Stone Fruit

Stone fruit is round with a noticeable groove giving the fruit a lobed appearance. To cut these fruits in half, cut along the groove around the circumference of the fruit, then twist the 2 halves apart. This will allow the stone to be removed easily.

Apricots

Available imported most of the year; UK: July, August
A truly ripe apricot is a delight but often they have a woolly texture and are lacking in flavour as they have been picked unripe.

The fruit should feel heavy for its size and be slightly soft.

Apricots can be stewed or poached. As the skin is very thin, the fruit does not need to be peeled.

Keep at room temperature for up to 1 week to ripen, then store in the refrigerator for up to 5 days.

Nectarines

Available imported May–August; UK: July, August

Choosing

As for peaches (see below) except the smooth skin of nectarines should be more red than gold.

Storing

As for apricots (see above).

Using

Nectarines are slightly sweeter and juicer than peaches, with a thinner, slightly bitter, skin. Eat raw or cook as for peaches (below).

Peaches

Available imported most of the year; UK: July, August

Choosing

Peaches will ripen slightly once picked but it is best to choose fruit that is slightly soft. The lightest colour on the skin, either gold or green-gold, will be the colour of the flesh and thereby give an indication of ripeness. White-fleshed peaches, particularly delicious eaten raw, are available as well as the better-known yellow peaches.

Storing

As for apricots (see above).

Using

Ripe fruit will peel easily but slightly under-ripe fruit needs to be immersed in boiling water for 10–15 seconds, then plunged into cold water. The skin should then peel away easily. Peaches can be baked, stewed, poached or grilled.

Plums

Available imported most of year; UK: August, September
There are many different varieties of plum, from the tiny purple-blue damson to the large black Opal plum. Very tart plums such as the damson are most suited to jam-making or stewing but the other plums are good eaten raw.

Choosing

Ripe plums will be slightly soft to the touch. Under-ripe plums will ripen if left at room temperature for 2–3 days.

Storing

Place in a single layer and leave at room temperature for up to 5 days, then refrigerate for a further 5 days.

Using

In addition to eating raw, plums can be baked, grilled or poached.

Dried Fruit

Drying is an age-old method of preserving fruit (see **Preserving**, page 549). Drying removes the moisture from the fruit and concentrates the sugar, thereby preserving the fruit. Today most types of dried fruit are treated with sulphur dioxide, although untreated fruit can be purchased from health food shops and the organic section of large supermarkets. Sometimes dried fruit is irradiated to preserve it more thoroughly. All dried fruit should be washed before using (see **Cakes**, *Fruit Cake*, page 145).

Grapes are dried to make raisins, and plums are dried to make prunes. Other types of dried fruit include apricots, bananas, dates, mangoes, papaya, peaches and pears.

Glacé fruit, such as cherries and lemon and orange peel, has been simmered slowly in a sugar syrup. Wash and dry before using.

Choosing

Look for fruit that is still plump and moist, not hard and dry. Discard any that has mould on it.

Storing

Wrap in plastic, then store in an airtight container for up to 1 year, or follow the use-by date on the package.

Using

Wash and dry thoroughly before using unless the package states that this is not necessary. Sometimes dried fruit requires soaking in hot water before use. This will normally be specified in the recipe. Fruit that has become too dried-out for use can be soaked in hot water, tea or a sugar syrup to soften.

Gelatine: Points to Remember

- Measure the gelatine accurately.
- Sponge the gelatine. Powdered gelatine needs to be reconstituted or 'sponged' before using in a recipe so that it will dissolve completely (see below).
- Melt the sponged gelatine over a low heat until it is a clear liquid.
- Do not stir the gelatine as it will stick to the spoon and some of the quantity will be lost.
- Do not allow the gelatine to get too warm. Never allow the gelatine to boil or it will smell of its source (pig) and possibly lose some of its setting ability.
- The food that the gelatine is added to should be at room temperature. If it is cold the gelatine will set into strings.
- Once the gelatine has been added to the base, the mixture can be placed in a cold bain-marie to speed setting. Stir every now and then to prevent the mixture from setting on the bottom of the bowl while the centre remains liquid.
- Do not add whisked egg whites or whipped cream to the mixture until setting point has been reached (see below).
- Always add thin mixtures to thick mixtures to prevent the thick mixture forming lumps.

Gelatine

The word gelatine comes from Latin *gelare*, meaning to freeze. Gelatine is a setting agent, available in both powdered and leaf form, that is made commercially from pig skin. Having little taste or colour, it is used widely in home cooking and industrial food preparations to set jellies, mousses, cold soufflés and commercial ice cream.

Until the commercial product became available in the late 1800s, cooks had to make their own gelatine by boiling the trotters, bones, cartilage and tendons of calves and pigs. This was a laborious task, so jellied dishes were usually served only at banquets and for special occasions.

Although gelatine is a protein, it is not a complete protein (see **Healthy Eating and Basic Nutrition**, page 16) and therefore has little nutritional value of its own. When it is dissolved, then cooled, it sets to form a jelly. If it is beaten during the setting process, the protein strands are stretched and will hold tiny air bubbles in a foam, making it particularly useful commercially.

Using Powdered Gelatine

Gelatine can be tricky to use but if the guidelines below are followed it should be uncomplicated.

Sponging Gelatine

To sponge gelatine, sprinkle it over cool water or some of the liquid from the recipe. One teaspoon of gelatine requires 2 tablespoons of liquid to sponge. If any dry gelatine is left on top of the sponged gelatine, sprinkle it with a little additional liquid. Let the gelatine stand for 3–5 minutes. It will absorb the liquid, like a sponge.

The Setting Power of Gelatine

To set 570 ml|1 pint of liquid, use:

- 11 g|$^2/_5$ oz powdered gelatine, or
- 3 level teaspoons, or
- 3 sheets of leaf gelatine

Gelatine melts at 27°C | 80°F and sets at 20°C | 68°F.

Fresh pineapple, papaya and kiwi fruit contain an enzyme called bromelin that interferes with the setting power of gelatine. These fruits should not be used in dishes containing gelatine.

Setting point is when the gelatine is beginning to set and the mixture starts to thicken. You can tell when that point has been reached by running a spoon or plastic spatula along the bottom of the bowl. The mixture will stay separated: this is called the parting of the waves.

In certain circumstances a mixture will require a greater quantity of gelatine than those specified above in order to set. This is necessary if:

- the weather is hot
- the mixture is very acidic
- the mixture contains alcohol
- the mixture is to be transported

Preparing Moulds

If the mixture to be set with gelatine contains cream, the mould should first be lightly brushed with a flavourless oil, then placed upside down on a piece of kitchen paper so that any excess oil can drain out. For mixtures such as jellies that do not contain cream, the jelly moulds can be wetted. However, if the mould is an elaborate one, it is better to coat it lightly with flavourless oil as this will make unmoulding easier.

Unmoulding Jellies

Metal moulds are the easiest to unmould jellies from because they conduct heat easily. Dip the mould into a sink containing enough hot water to cover the base and sides of the mould. Hold the mould in the water for 8–10 seconds or longer if using a ceramic mould. Remove from the water, then gently push the edge of the jelly away from the edge of the mould with your finger in one spot, to release the vacuum. Dampen the serving plate before unmoulding the jelly on to it. This will allow the jelly to be moved if it is not in the centre. Place a serving plate large enough to hold the jelly over the mould, then invert the jelly on to the plate, giving the mould a sharp downward shake.

Orange Jelly

Making this simple jelly is an easy way to learn to use powdered gelatine.

SERVES 4

3 tablespoons water
4 level teaspoons powdered gelatine
570 ml | 1 pint orange juice

1 Place the water in a small saucepan and sprinkle over the gelatine. Allow to stand for 3 minutes.

2 Warm half the orange juice in another saucepan.

3 Dissolve the gelatine over a low heat, without allowing to boil, and pour into the warm orange juice.

4 Add the remaining orange juice to the warm mixture, then pour into a wetted jelly mould or pudding basin.

5 Refrigerate for 4 hours or until set.

6 Unmould as described above on to a serving plate.

Gelatine: What has gone wrong when...

The jelly has not set.
- The jelly has not been chilled for long enough.
- Not enough gelatine was used.
- The gelatine was boiled and lost its setting ability.

The jelly is rubbery.
- Too much gelatine was used.
- Too little liquid was used.

  If the jelly does not contain cream, the whole mixture can be rewarmed to dissolve the gelatine, then reset with the addition of more gelatine or more liquid as required.

The jelly contains rubbery lumps.
- The base was too cold.
- The gelatine was not warm enough when added to the base and set in lumps.

  If the jelly does not contain cream, the mixture can be rewarmed to dissolve the gelatine, then reset. If the mixture contains cream, the gelatine can be removed by sieving the mixture and some additional gelatine can be added. This is a drastic rescue, however, as sieving will remove the air from the mixture and make it heavier.

Using Leaf Gelatine

Leaf gelatine is gelatine that has been set into thin transparent sheets about $5 \times 10\,cm | 2 \times 4\,in$. Widely used on the Continent and by professional chefs, it is an easy and accurate way to use gelatine. Substitute 1 leaf of gelatine for 1 level $5\,ml | 1$ teaspoon of powdered gelatine.

To use leaf gelatine, soak it in cold water for about 5 minutes until it becomes soft and pliable. Do not let it stand in the water for too long, or it will dissolve completely. Remove the gelatine from the cold water and shake off any excess, then stir it into the warm base to dissolve.

Coffee Cream Bavarois

A Bavarois is a rich custard set with gelatine.

SERVES 4

200 ml | 7 fl oz milk
20 g | ¾ oz plain chocolate, finely chopped
1 tablespoon instant coffee powder
oil, for greasing
3 egg yolks
85 g | 3 oz caster sugar

1 leaf of gelatine or 1 level 5 ml | 1 teaspoon
   powdered gelatine
150 ml | ¼ pint double cream

To serve

double cream, lightly whipped
shavings of chocolate (see *Chocolate*, page 195)

1 Place the milk, chocolate and coffee in a small saucepan over a low heat. Stir occasionally until the mixture steams and the chocolate melts.
2 Brush a 570 ml | 1 pint cake tin or flan dish or 4 × 150 ml | ¼ pint ramekins with the oil. Invert on to kitchen paper to allow any excess oil to drain away.
3 Mix the yolks and the sugar in a bowl. Pour the chocolate milk on to the eggs in a thin stream, while stirring.
4 Rinse out the saucepan. Place the chocolate custard mixture in the pan and cook over a medium heat, stirring, until the mixture thickens and coats the back of the spoon. Do not allow the mixture to boil. Pass through a sieve to remove any eggy threads.
5 Soften the gelatine in a bowl of cold water. When pliable, remove from the water, shake off any excess water and stir the gelatine into the warm custard. Alternatively sponge the powdered gelatine in 2 tablespoons cold water. Melt as directed above.
6 Pour the custard into a bowl and place in a large bowl filled with ice and cold water.
7 Stir the custard frequently until it begins to thicken and parts to reveal the bottom of the bowl.
8 Whip the cream to soft peaks (see *Eggs, Egg Whites*, page 233), then fold into the custard using a large metal spoon or spatula.
9 Turn the mixture into the prepared tin, flan dish or ramekins. Refrigerate for 4 hours or until set.
10 Unmould (see *Unmoulding Jellies*, above) on to a serving plate to serve.

Substitutes for Gelatine

Carrageen or Irish Moss is a seaweed found on the coasts of Brittany and Ireland. It can be used as a vegetarian substitute for gelatine. To use, it must be soaked for 20 minutes then boiled for 15 minutes before stirring into the mixture to be set.

Agar-agar is also known as Kanten or Japanese gelatine. This complex carbohydrate is made from seaweed. It melts at 90°C|194°F and sets at 45°C|112°F. It is the medium used for cultures in laboratory Petri dishes. Agar-agar has a brittle texture and does not melt in the mouth like gelatine. It can be used for dishes containing pineapple, papaya or kiwi which cannot be set with gelatine.

Agar-agar's setting qualities are affected by the nature of the food to which it is added, and so required quantities will vary, but as a general rule 1 teaspoon powder or 1 tablespoon flakes will set 570 ml|1 pint, and twice the quantity should be used to set a firm jelly.

Using agar-agar

1 Soak the agar-agar in the full liquid measurement specified in the recipe, in a saucepan; leave powder for 5 minutes, flakes for 10–15 minutes.
2 Dissolve the agar-agar in the pan over a medium heat, stirring continuously. Turn up the heat and boil for 2–3 minutes, continuing to stir to prevent sticking. Use as required. (Agar-agar may be re-boiled without impairing its setting ability.)
3 If properly prepared, agar-agar sets quickly on contact with anything much cooler than itself. Therefore, the ingredients to which it is added must be warm. To test whether it is ready for use, spoon a small quantity on to a cold plate: a skin should form very quickly, and wrinkle if a finger is pulled over the surface.

Isinglass is made from the swim bladders of sturgeon. It needs to be boiled to dissolve. To use to set a liquid, use isinglass in a ratio to the liquid of 1:30. 35 g|1¼ oz isinglass sets 1 litre|1¾ pints of liquid.

Rennet is an enzyme extracted from the stomach of an unweaned calf. It can be used to set milk for junket. It is also used in cheese-making.

For other recipes using gelatine see also:

- *Aspic* (page 89)
- *Mousses* (page 489)
- *Soufflés*, *Cold Soufflés* (page 647)

Grains

Grains, the edible seeds of plants from the grass family, have been a staple food for man since pre-historic times. Many grains today have been pre-cooked so the package instructions vary depending on the quality and any pre-processing. The instructions given for each grain below are general. Follow the instructions on the package.

Barley, an oval, creamy-coloured grain with a nutty flavour, dates back to the Stone Age. When it has been husked, steamed and polished, it is known as pearl barley. Scotch barley is husked and coarsely ground.

In food use, barley is also added to soups, most famously Scotch broth and in stews, where it has a thickening effect. It can be used in place of rice in a pilaf. Ground barley is used in unleavened griddle breads called bannocks. Malted barley is used to make beer and whisky.

Bulghur (burghul) wheat is made from wheat grains that have been steamed, dried and crushed. It is a staple in the Middle East where it is the principal ingredient in Tabbouleh salad. It can also be used in place of rice in a pilaf or salad and as a binder for minced meats. Bulghur wheat can be used inter-changeably with *cracked wheat* (see below), although cracked wheat usually takes longer to soften.

To use, place in a large bowl and pour over boiling salted water or stock. Let stand for 15 minutes, then drain. Spread on a clean tea towel or kitchen paper to dry before using.

Couscous is a granular semolina (see below) which is eaten as a staple in North Africa, notably in Morocco where it is steamed over a tagine, a conical-lidded cooking pot, with a fragrant stew (also called a tagine) in the bottom. It is often served with a spicy sauce flavoured with harissa, a sauce made with chillies. This method of cooking can be approximated by the home cook by placing the couscous in a large sieve over a pot of simmering stew until tender. The couscous should be raked with the fingers to keep the grains separate.

Couscous can also be used in salads. Place the couscous in a large bowl and cover with double the quantity of cold water. Allow to stand for 20 minutes, stirring occasionally with a fork until the couscous is tender.

Cracked wheat is wheat kernels that have been cracked. It can be substituted for bulghur wheat (see **Meat, Game, Warm Pigeon Breasts and Cracked Wheat Salad**, page 463) but needs to be boiled.

Oats are the most nutritious of the cereal grasses. Before use, the oats are cleaned, toasted and hulled, then steamed and flattened with rollers to become rolled oats. Although higher in protein than wheat, oats are lacking in gluten, the special protein that gives bread its texture (see **Bread, Yeast**, page 118), so they are unsuitable for making bread unless combined with flour. Oats are used for porridge, oatcakes, flapjacks, for coating herrings before frying and in stuffings.

Different grades of oats are available as follows:

Pinhead: Used for haggis and combining with flour to make bread
Medium: Used for porridge and baking
Jumbo: Used for porridge and baking

Polenta, a staple of northern Italy, is made from ground dried corn (cornmeal). It became popular after the Venetians imported maize from America in the mid-1600s. It is thought that a similar preparation had previously been made with barley.

When warm, polenta has a soft texture, rather like mashed potato or porridge, and is served as a starchy accompaniment to meat stews or as a first course. When it becomes cold it has a firm texture, like a pressed cheese. Firm polenta is often cut into wedges and then fried before being eaten hot or cold.

Polenta

This recipe is for a firm polenta. It can be flavoured with a few tablespoons of grated Parmesan cheese if desired. Stir in the cheese to taste at the end of step 3.

SERVES 4–6

2 litres|3½ pints White Stock (see **Stocks**, page 688)
1 teaspoon salt
285 g|10 oz polenta

To serve
85 g|3 oz butter or olive oil, for frying

1 Place the stock in a large saucepan with the salt and bring to the boil.
2 Remove from the heat and sprinkle on the polenta, in a stream while stirring to prevent lumps from forming.
3 Return the pan to a medium heat, cover, and allow to simmer, stirring frequently, until thick enough to hold a spoon upright.
4 If serving immediately, stir in the butter.
5 If serving cut into wedges, spread the polenta into an oiled 30 × 18 cm|12 × 7 in shallow tin. Allow to cool.
6 When cold, cut the polenta into wedges and fry in a little oil until golden-brown, or brush the polenta wedges with oil and griddle on a hot griddle pan.

Semolina is made from durum wheat, a hard wheat that has been ground either coarsely or finely into flour. It is used to made puddings, gnocchi and bread. Coarse semolina has a gritty texture when cooked. It is often dyed a pale yellow colour.

Finely ground semolina is used for making pasta (see **Pasta**, page 499).

Gnocchi alla Romana

Gnocchi is sometimes served rolled with a fork into small cocoon shapes, which takes much manual dexterity. This semolina gnocchi can be cut with a small pastry cutter or knife. Serve as a first course before a dish of fish or grilled meat.

SERVES 4–6

1 litre ǀ 1¾ pints milk	3 egg yolks
1½ teaspoons salt	85 g ǀ 3 oz Parmesan cheese, grated
freshly grated nutmeg	85 g ǀ 3 oz butter, plus extra for greasing
225 g ǀ 8 oz coarse semolina	

1 Lightly dampen a baking tray.
2 Bring the milk, salt and plenty of nutmeg to the boil in a large saucepan.
3 Remove from the heat and sprinkle over the semolina, stirring continuously with a wooden spoon.
4 Return the pan to a medium heat and cook, uncovered, for 10–15 minutes, stirring occasionally to prevent sticking. The semolina should be gently bubbling. The mixture should be thick enough to hold a spoon upright.
5 Remove from the heat and cool slightly.
6 Beat in the egg yolks, 30 g ǀ 1 oz of the cheese and 30 g ǀ 1 oz of the butter. Taste for seasoning.
7 Pour the semolina on to the baking tray and smooth with a dampened spatula to a thickness of about 1 cm ǀ ½ in.
8 Refrigerate for about 1½ hours until firm.
9 Preheat the oven to 225°C ǀ 425°F ǀ gas mark 7. Melt the butter.
10 Cut the semolina into rounds, using a small pastry cutter.
11 Butter an ovenproof dish. Arrange the semolina rounds in overlapping circles in the dish.
12 Melt the remaining butter and pour over. Sprinkle with the remaining cheese. Bake for 15–20 minutes until crisp and golden.

Quinoa, pronounced 'keen-wa' and available from health food shops, is an ancient grain of South American origin. The tiny round grains resemble tapioca in both shape and texture. Quinoa was an important staple of the Incas, being high in usable protein and nutrients. With its mild, nutty flavour, it can be used as a substitute for rice and is cooked in the same way.

Rice: See **Rice** (page 563).

Wheat is the staple grain for most of the Western world. See **Flour** (page 267) and *bulghur* and *cracked wheat*, above.

Grains of durum wheat are also cooked as an accompaniment to other foods, particularly in France, where they are used as a substitute for rice. The grain is usually pre-cooked so will only need to be boiled for 15–20 minutes.

Herbs and Their Uses

Herb	Flavour	Uses
Basil (sweet)	Pungent, slightly peppery-beef flavour with a hint of cloves and liquorice	Used in Mediterranean cooking, particularly tomatoes, pesto sauce
Bay leaves	Musty, slightly bitter vegetal flavour	Soups, stews, milk puddings. Remove before serving. Part of a *bouquet garni*
Chervil	Mild parsley/aniseed flavour	Member of the parsley family and one of the traditional *fines herbes* (see below) used in French cooking for chicken, fish and egg dishes
Chives	Mild onion aroma and flavour	Thin, needle-like shoots used to flavour fish, potatoes, eggs and to garnish soups
Coriander/Cilantro (leaves, stems and roots)	Pungent citrus/celery scent and flavour	Widely used in Asian cooking. Similar in appearance to flat-leaf parsley
Dill	Aniseed flavour	Fine fronds used in Scandinavian and Central European cooking for fish, potato and egg dishes
Lemon balm	Lemon and soap	Used to infuse fruit salad
Lemon grass	Strongly lemon/citronella aroma and flavour	Stems are used to infuse and are used chopped in South/East Asian cuisine
Marjoram	Similar to oregano but slightly bitter and woody	Slightly furry leaves are used in Mediterranean cooking
Mint (many varieties, spearmint is most common)	Sharp menthol scent and flavour	Used to flavour new potatoes, lamb and chocolate. Doesn't mix well with other herbs
Oregano	Peppery scent and flavour	Used in Greek, Italian and Mexican cuisine, especially in meat and tomato dishes
Parsley, (curly and flat)	Green grass and slightly salty scent and flavour. Flat has a stronger flavour	Used widely in Western cuisines alone or as base for herb blends, and as a garnish
Rosemary	Very pungent aroma and flavour of pine resin	Grey-green spiky leaves used in Mediterranean cuisine, particularly with lamb
Sage	Balsam and camphor aroma and flavour	Very strong-flavoured downy grey-green leaves used in turkey stuffing, forcemeats and pork dishes
Sorrel	Lemon, becoming acidic and bitter as it ages	Cream soups, omelettes, sauces for fish
Tarragon (French)	Aniseed/dried grass scent and flavour. Avoid Russian tarragon as it lacks flavour	Slender blue-green leaves used in French cuisine traditionally in poultry and fish dishes. A principal ingredient in *Béarnaise Sauce* (see **Sauces, Savoury**, page 605)
Thyme (many varieties available)	Mild menthol and lemon scent and flavour, slightly woody	Tiny oval, grey-green leaves. Part of a *bouquet garni* (see below), used widely to flavour stews, soups and stocks

Herbs

Herbs are the fragrant leaves and sometimes stems of plants that are used to add flavour to food. In most cases herb plants do not have woody stems. Herbs are sold in both fresh and dried forms; some herbs are also sold frozen, and puréed and packaged in plastic tubes.

Fresh Herbs

Fresh herbs are far superior in flavour to dried and frozen herbs and should be used in preference to processed herbs wherever possible. Choose herbs that are bright in colour and show no sign of wilting, bruising or yellowing and avoid any that have started to flower. In most recipes, fresh herbs should be added to the dish at the end of cooking, immediately before being served. Heat deadens the flavour of the volatile oils in the soft herbs — basil, chervil, chives, coriander, dill, mint, parsley and tarragon — and changes their bright green colour to a dull khaki. The hardier herbs — bay, marjoram, oregano, rosemary, sage and thyme — are often added to soups and stews at the beginning of cooking to infuse the food with their flavour. Although their colour dulls during heating, their robust construction usually survives the cooking process.

The flavour added by herbs can be used as a salt substitute in a salt-reduced diet.

Chopping Fresh Herbs

Chop the leaves of the herbs just before using to capture the vibrancy of flavour. Herbs should always be washed just before use and dried in a salad spinner or by shaking gently in a tea towel.

· Unless directed otherwise by a recipe, only the leaves of the herbs are used. They should be removed from the stems before chopping because the stems do not chop down finely and remain as hard bits in the food. Coriander is the main exception to this rule. The stems and roots of fresh coriander are often used in Asian cooking because they have a very intense flavour.

Place the leaves in a small pile on a chopping board. Use a large cook's knife with a deep blade or a mezzaluna to cross-chop across the pile (see *Knife Skills*, page 69). Continue chopping to the required fineness, stopping to gather the herbs back into a pile every so often. If the herbs have been chopped very finely they will need to be dried again before use so that they will sprinkle without clumping. Place the chopped herbs in a double layer of kitchen paper and squeeze to extract the juice. Spread the chopped herbs in a thin layer to finish drying.

Parsley: Parsley is chopped until it is of even texture and no larger pieces are visible. For garnishing classic French dishes it should be as fine as dust. Casseroles and boiled root vegetables are traditionally garnished with finely chopped parsley. For less formal bistro dishes or for garnishing Italian food, the parsley is chopped more coarsely into individual pieces about 2 mm | $^1/_{12}$ in in size (see **Food Presentation,** *Garnishes*, page 12).

Basil: It is recommended that basil leaves be torn, rather than chopped with a knife, although this is not always practicable if a large amount is required. Basil leaves can also be rolled and sliced into a *chiffonade* (see **Knife Skills**, page 68).

Storing Fresh Herbs

Fresh herbs should be purchased as required. They are best stored by placing the stems in water with a piece of damp kitchen paper wrapped around the leaves and then covering the damp paper with a plastic bag. This treatment will keep the herbs fresh for about 3 days. Change the water daily.

Classic Herb Combinations

Fines herbs: This preparation is a mixture of finely chopped parsley, tarragon, chervil and chives, traditionally used in classic French dishes, such as *Omelette Fines Herbes* (see page 00).

Bouquet garni: This is a classic flavouring for stews and soups. It is prepared by placing a sprig of thyme, a few parsley stalks and a bay leaf in the groove of a 5 cm | 2 in piece of celery stalk and securing them by tying with a piece of string. Alternatively, the aromatics can be tied in a muslin bag. The bouquet garni is added to the food at the beginning of cooking and is removed before serving.

Dried Herbs

Dried herbs need to be used in a different manner to fresh. Substitute 1 teaspoon dried herbs for 1 tablespoon chopped fresh herbs. In order to release the flavour of dried herbs and make them palatable they need to be softened and are normally added to food at the beginning of cooking. Soups and stews utilize dried herbs successfully because the moisture in the dish will rehydrate the herbs and facilitate an exchange of flavours.

Dried herbs lose their potency rapidly and should be kept in an airtight container in a cool, dark place for no longer than 6 months after opening.

Mint Sauce

Mint Sauce is a traditional accompaniment to roast lamb (see **Meat, Lamb**, *Roast Leg of Lamb*, page 382).

15 g|1½ oz fresh mint
2 tablespoons caster sugar

2 tablespoons hot water
2 tablespoons white wine vinegar

1 Wash the mint and remove the leaves from the stalks. Discard the stalks and finely chop the leaves.
2 Place the chopped leaves in a bowl with the sugar.
3 Pour the hot water over the mint and let stand for about 5 minutes to dissolve the sugar.
4 Stir in the vinegar. Allow to stand for 1–2 hours before serving.

NOTE: Mint can be preserved by chopping it and mixing to a paste with golden syrup. Store in the refrigerator for up to 6 months. To make mint sauce, stir a spoonful of the syrup with boiling water and a little white wine vinegar.

Pesto

Pesto is an Italian sauce originating in Genoa. It is traditionally made from a combination of basil, garlic, pine nuts, cheese and olive oil, liquidized to a fine purée and served with pasta or spread on crostini as a canapé. Other ingredients are also used, such as sun-dried tomatoes for Red Pesto.

2 cloves of garlic, crushed
2 large cups of fresh basil leaves
55 g|2 oz pine nuts

55 g|2 oz Parmesan cheese, freshly grated
150 ml|¼ pint olive oil
salt and freshly ground black pepper

1 Process the garlic and basil together in a liquidizer or with a mortar and pestle to form a paste.
2 Add the pine nuts and cheese. Take care not to over-process or the mixture will become very oily.
3 With the motor still running if using a machine, add the oil gradually to make a thick paste. If the paste begins to look oily and too thick, add 1 tablespoon water.
4 Taste and add seasoning if required

NOTE: Pesto can be kept in a covered jar in the refrigerator for up to 2 days although it will lose some of its bright colour and vibrant flavour. Pesto can also be frozen, closely wrapped, for 1 month.

VARIATIONS

- **Almonds or walnuts** can be substituted for the pine nuts. Nuts can be toasted for additional flavour (see *Nuts*, page 494).
- **Garlic** can be roasted for a more gentle, mellow flavour.
- **Red Pesto** is made with sun-dried tomatoes and purple basil. Use for crostini or pasta.
- **Rocket or Coriander** can be substituted for the basil. Use for fish and chicken (see **Fish,** *Griddled Tuna with Green Chilli Pesto*, page 250).

Bases for Ice Cream

There are 4 bases for ice cream, each with different ingredients, textures and 'mouth-feel'. Each type of ice cream is made by a slightly different method.

Custard base: Traditional creamy, rich ice cream is made with a flavoured custard base and cream. The base needs to be churned. It is best for traditional flavours that combine well with cream, such as vanilla, coffee and chocolate.

Mousse base: This method produces an ice cream known as a parfait. It is made by whisking hot sugar syrup on to egg yolks, then folding the resulting mousse into lightly whipped cream. Classically it is flavoured with coffee or alcohol but is also good for making fruit-flavoured ice cream. The base does not need to be churned.

Meringue base: Hot sugar syrup is whisked on to egg whites to make a meringue. The foam is folded together with fruit flavouring and lightly whipped cream. The mixture can be frozen in a terrine and does not need to be churned. The method suits strongly flavoured fruits.

Yoghurt base/All-in-one method: This is the simplest of all the ice-cream methods. Greek yoghurt is combined with a fruit purée, then frozen. This ice cream is lower in fat than the other ice-cream types. It does not require churning but can be churned for extra smoothness.

Ice-cream Terms

Churning: Agitating the ice-cream mixture during freezing to break down the ice crystals and add air.

To 'come to': To allow an ice cream to stand at room temperature or in the refrigerator for 30 minutes to soften before serving.

Overrun: The increase in volume from the unfrozen base to the finished ice cream.

Method of Churning

Still-freezing: A time-consuming process by which the ice-cream base is placed in a shallow container in the freezer. Stir the frozen crystals that form around the edges into the unfrozen mixture, using a fork. Repeat every 2 hours until the ice cream is completely frozen.

Mechanical churn: The chilled ice-cream base is placed in the freezing compartment of an ice-cream machine which stirs the mixture to break up the ice crystals during freezing. The most effective method for churning ice cream.

Food processor: The ice-cream base is frozen, then allowed to soften slightly before being processed briefly to break up the ice crystals. The ice cream then needs to be refrozen. This method is effective but will not give as smooth a result as churning with an ice-cream machine.

Ice Creams

Ice cream is a marvellous treat, enjoyed by young and old throughout much of the world. Today we take the availability of ice cream for granted, but before refrigeration, ice cream was only enjoyed by the privileged few who had access to ice.

Although Catherine de Medici is widely credited with introducing ice cream to the French court in the sixteenth century, it is now thought that the Chinese experimented with frozen milk products several hundred years after Christ. In England, ice cream was quickly adopted by Charles II who served it to his guests at court in 1671. From the eighteenth-century ice-houses – underground shelters – became prevalent at many country estates throughout England. The ice was harvested from frozen lakes during the winter months, then stored in the ice-house for use during the summer.

Ice cream consists of tiny ice crystals composed of pure water, solid globules of fat from milk and cream, sugar and solids from flavourings. It is made into a foam by the churning process. The churning process simultaneously breaks down the ice crystals that form during freezing and beats air into the mixture.

Freezing stabilizes the foam by solidifying most of the liquids and trapping the tiny air bubbles. Even after freezing, some of the ice-cream mixture will not have frozen. It is this liquid, along with air, that prevents the formation of a solid block. Ice cream without air and a small portion of unfrozen liquid would be difficult to serve, scoop or eat.

Commercial ice creams have a great deal of air churned into them, particularly the 'soft-scoop' variety. The added volume in the product achieved by churning in air is known as 'overrun' in the industry. Some commercially produced ice creams have as much as 100 per cent overrun. That means that only 50 per cent of the volume of the container is filled with ingredients, the other 50 per cent is air. So the size of an ice-cream container can be misleading and it is important to check the weight of a container when purchasing commercial ice creams. Ice creams with a large amount of overrun will taste 'warmer' in the mouth due to the fact that they have a smaller proportion of icy crystals.

The Chemistry of Ice Cream

The proportions of the ingredients in relation to each other and to the whole are very important in making an ice cream that is smooth and creamy. Outside of certain boundaries, changes in these relationships will cause the ice cream to freeze too hard, or be too syrupy or fudgy or granular in texture.

For a well-flavoured ice cream it is necessary to over-flavour the unfrozen mixture because freezing dulls the flavour and the addition of air through churning dilutes it. The ice-cream base should taste slightly too strong and sweet.

Milk solids help break up the ice crystals by keeping them apart. It is advisable to scald and cool milk before using it in an ice cream, as this will produce a smoother result. Too much milk in an ice cream can result in a gritty, sandy texture because the lactose (milk sugar) does not dissolve as easily as sucrose. The lactose will freeze into tiny, gritty granules that remain in the mouth when the ice cream melts.

Cream contains less lactose than milk and more fat. The fat coats the ice crystals to give the ice cream a smooth 'mouth-feel' and a rich flavour. The fat also prevents large ice crystals from forming, keeping them small and separate. Whipping cream is usually the cream of choice when making ice cream, but double cream can be used instead. However, too much cream will produce an ice cream that is dense and chalky due to the high fat content. Cream is also good for holding air. The recommended ratio of milk to cream in ice-cream making is between 1:1 and 2:1.

Fat is also provided by egg yolks. 3 egg yolks per 570 ml | 1 pint ice-cream base is usually the minimum requirement for custard-based ice cream. Some recipes call for up to 8 yolks per 570 ml | 1 pint. Egg yolks contain the emulsifier lecithin, which helps make the ice cream smooth by coating the ice crystals. Gelatine instead of egg yolks is often used for this purpose in commercial ice cream.

Sugar lowers the freezing point of a mixture. Although it is desirable that some of the mixture should remain in a liquid state so that the ice cream does not freeze into a solid block, too much sugar produces a mixture that will not freeze solidly enough and an ice cream with a syrupy consistency. Approximately 30 per cent of an ice-cream mixture should be sugar. Excess sweetness can be balanced to a certain extent through the careful use of lemon juice.

Salt is required in some ice-cream recipes. Salt is a flavour enhancer and can be used in the proportion of $\frac{1}{8}$ teaspoon per 570 ml | 1 pint of ice-cream base.

Alcohol also lowers the freezing point. Too much alcohol will keep a mixture from freezing. The alcohol content should be no more than about 10 per cent of the mixture. Liqueur can be poured over the finished ice cream just before serving if a more intense flavour is desired.

Custard Base

The custard-based method is used to make ice cream from a mixture of a rich custard and cream. These ice creams have a rich, smooth flavour. The custard base contains eggs, sugar, milk and flavourings. (For detailed instructions for making custard, see **Sauces, Sweet**, *Crème Anglaise*, page 612.) Additional cream is then added to the cooled custard base before freezing and churning. Whipping cream (with a fat content of 36 per cent) is recommended, but double cream (fat content 48 per cent) can also be used. If the fat content of the ice cream is too high, however, the ice cream will be dense and crumbly rather than smooth. When churned it is the proteins in the milk that stretch and trap the air bubbles.

The custard ice-cream base ideally should be stored in the refrigerator for between 4 and 24 hours before churning to allow the flavour to mature.

It is not recommended that the very young, the elderly, pregnant women or infirm consume this type of ice cream because it is possible that the eggs may contain salmonella.

Vanilla Ice Cream (custard base)

SERVES 4–6

290 ml | ½ pint whole milk

1 vanilla pod, split lengthways

4 medium egg yolks

110 g | 4 oz caster sugar

290 ml | ½ pint whipping or double cream

1 Place the milk in a saucepan with the vanilla pod and heat over a medium heat until the milk steams and tiny bubbles form around the edge of the pan.
2 Remove from the heat and let stand for 10 minutes to infuse.
3 Remove the vanilla pod from the milk and reserve.
4 Mix the egg yolks with the sugar in a bowl.
5 Slowly stir the warm milk into the yolk and sugar mixture.
6 Rinse the milk pan to remove any coagulated milk proteins. Return the milk and egg mixture to the pan.
7 Place a sieve and a bowl next to the hob, then cook the mixture over medium-low heat, stirring continuously with a wooden spoon, until the mixture thickens enough to coat the back of the spoon. Do not overheat the mixture or it will curdle.
8 Immediately sieve the thickened mixture to remove any eggy threads.
9 Place the bowl in an ice bath, stirring occasionally, until cool. Using a sharp knife, scrape the seeds from the inside of the vanilla pod and add it to the mixture.
10 Stir in the cream. If time allows, store in the refrigerator for up to 24 hours to allow the flavour to mature before churning.
11 Freeze and churn following one of the methods given below under *Churning Ice Cream*.

NOTE: The flavour of vanilla ice cream improves if it is kept in the freezer for 24 hours before eating.

VARIATIONS

Strawberry Ice Cream: Omit the vanilla pod and add 250 g | 9 oz fresh strawberries, puréed, to the cooled custard. Flavour with 1 tablespoon balsamic vinegar.

Chocolate Ice Cream: Add 2 tablespoons good-quality cocoa powder, ½ teaspoon instant coffee powder and 85 g | 3 oz grated plain chocolate to the milk before heating.

Mousse Base

The mousse-based method produces a type of ice cream that is also known as a parfait. *Parfait* is the French word for perfect. This base is made with a hot sugar syrup whisked into egg yolks. The whisking causes the proteins in the egg yolks to stretch while the heat cooks the proteins, stabilizing them and enabling them to hold air bubbles. The cream is whisked to incorporate more air, then the two mixtures are folded carefully together. In mousse-based ice creams there is no need to churn the mixture because air has already been incorporated. This type of ice cream is therefore useful for cooks who do not have access to a churn or ice-cream machine.

Mousse-based ice creams are particularly suited to fruit flavours. They can be frozen in ramekins with a collar tied around the edge to give the appearance of a risen soufflé. As with custard-based ice creams, it is not advisable that this ice cream is eaten by the very young, the elderly, pregnant women, or the infirm due to the risk of salmonella poisoning.

Raspberry Parfait (mousse base)

SERVES 4–6

450 g | 1 lb raspberries
85 g | 3 oz icing sugar, sifted
3 egg yolks
70 g | 2½ oz granulated sugar

110 ml | 4 fl oz water
lemon juice, to taste
290 ml | ½ pint whipping cream

1 Line an oiled loaf tin with clingfilm or tie greaseproof paper collars around 4–6 ramekins.

2 Purée the raspberries and push them through a sieve to remove the seeds.

3 Stir the icing sugar into the raspberry purée. Set aside.

4 Place the egg yolks in a heatproof bowl and whisk lightly.

5 Place the sugar and the water in a saucepan and dissolve the sugar over low heat. Bring to the boil, then lower the heat and simmer to the firm ball stage, 120°C | 248°F on a sugar thermometer (see **Sugar, Sweeteners and Sugar Syrups**, *Stages of Sugar Syrup*, page 701).

6 Pour the hot sugar syrup on to the yolks in a thin stream, whisking with an electric hand whisk. Take care not to pour the syrup on to the beaters as it might stick to them.

7 Continue to whisk until the mixture is thick and mousse-like and forms a ribbon trail from the beaters when they are lifted up from the mixture. Allow the mixture and the bowl to cool to room temperature.

8 Fold in the raspberry purée. Taste for flavour balance, adding more sugar or lemon juice as required.

9 Whisk the cream until soft peaks form (see **Eggs**, *Egg Whites*, page 233), then fold into the mixture. Turn into the prepared dishes and freeze for about 24 hours, until solid.

Meringue Base

Meringue-based ice cream requires the making of an Italian meringue using sugar syrup and whisked egg whites (see **Meringues**, page 478). The flavouring is folded into this base along with the whipped cream. This type of ice cream is suitable for fruit-flavoured ice creams as the acidity of the fruit counterbalances the sweetness of the meringue nicely. As the base and the cream have already been whisked, this ice cream does not require churning, so it is particularly useful for cooks who do not have an ice-cream machine.

Blackcurrant Ice Cream (meringue base)

SERVES 6–8

For the purée

250 g | 9 oz fresh or frozen blackcurrants

100 ml | 3½ fl oz water

For the Italian meringue

225 g | 8 oz granulated sugar

150 ml | ¼ pint water

2 egg whites

1–2 tablespoons lemon juice

oil, for greasing

290 ml | 10 fl oz double or whipping cream

1 For the purée, place the blackcurrants and water in a saucepan over a low heat until the juices run and the berries soften.

2 Pass the blackcurrants through a sieve to remove the seeds. Allow the purée to cool.

3 Lightly oil a 1 litre | 2½ pint loaf tin, then line with clingfilm.

4 For the meringue, place the sugar and water in a saucepan over a low heat. Stir until the sugar is dissolved. Wash any sugar crystals from the side of the saucepan using a dampened pastry brush.

5 Turn up the heat and boil the syrup to the firm ball stage, 120°C | 248°F on a sugar thermometer (see **Sugar, Sweeteners and Sugar Syrups**, *Stages of Sugar Syrup*, page 701).

6 Meanwhile, whisk the egg whites to the stiff peak stage and whip the cream to the medium peak stage (see **Eggs**, *Egg Whites*, page 233).

7 As soon as the sugar syrup reaches the firm ball stage, whisk the boiling syrup into the whisked egg whites. Whisk until the mixture no longer feels warm.

8 Fold the blackcurrant purée into the meringue mixture. Add lemon juice to taste.

9 Fold the blackcurrant-meringue mixture into the whipped cream.

10 Turn the mixture into the loaf tin and freeze for about 24 hours, until firm.

11 If necessary, allow the ice cream to soften slightly in the refrigerator or at room temperature before serving.

Yoghurt Base, All-in-one Method

The fourth type of ice-cream base contains yoghurt and is made by the all-in-one method. This is the simplest type of ice cream to make because all the ingredients are combined together, then frozen and churned. Most ice-cream recipes using yoghurt do not contain any cream, so are considerably lower in fat than other ice creams. For this reason yoghurt-based ice creams tend to be more granular and icy. They feel colder in the mouth and are not as smooth as other ice creams.

Lemon and Passion Fruit Ice Cream (yoghurt base)

SERVES 6

1 large lemon

140 g | 5 oz caster sugar

55 g | 2 oz unsalted butter

2 whole eggs

1 egg yolk

juice and pulp of 4 ripe passion fruit

425 ml | ¾ pint Greek yoghurt

1 Scrub the lemon, then grate the zest, taking care not to remove any of the bitter white pith. Reserve the zest, then juice the lemon.

2 Place the lemon juice, sugar, butter, eggs, egg yolks and passion fruit pulp in a small saucepan. Cook over a medium heat, stirring, until the mixture thickens and one or two bubbles come to the surface. Sieve. (A few passion fruit seeds can be stirred into the mixture if desired.)

3 Stir in the lemon zest, place a piece of greaseproof paper directly on top of the mixture and allow to cool. It can be placed in an ice bath to speed the cooling, if desired.

4 Stir the yoghurt to remove any lumps, then fold into the lemon mixture. Churn if desired following one of the methods described below under *Churning Ice Cream*, then place in the freezer until solid.

5 Before serving allow to stand in the refrigerator for 20–30 minutes to soften slightly if necessary.

Churning Ice Cream

Ice cream is churned by agitating the mixture during the freezing process. The churning process breaks down the ice crystals as they form, making the ice cream smoother, and also aerates the mixture, making it lighter.

Bucket Churn

Prior to the invention of refrigeration, ice cream was made using a bucket churn, invented in the USA by Nancy Johnson in the mid 1800s. The design is much the same today.

The ice-cream mixture is placed in a container that is packed into a second, larger container containing ice and salt. Coarse salt or rock salt is the best type to use because it dissolves more slowly and is less expensive than table salt. The standard proportion of salt to ice is 1:8. Salt lowers temperature, so the more salt there is in proportion to ice, the lower the temperature. However, slower cooling of the mixture is to be preferred as it produces a smoother-textured ice cream.

A hand-cranked paddle is inserted into the ice-cream mixture to churn it. This is a very laborious process and is best tackled by several hungry people. The ice cream is ready when it is no longer possible to turn the crank and should then be scooped into a freezer container and placed in the freezer to harden for at least 30 minutes.

Electric Ice-cream Machine

These machines are very efficient for making ice cream. The least expensive type has a deep bowl that requires freezing before use. The bowl is then placed on to a machine that rotates it. A paddle is attached to the top of the bowl to churn and freeze the ice cream. The process takes 20–30 minutes. Electric ice-cream machines are useful for making small quantities of ice cream, usually about 4 servings at a time. Their main drawback is that the inner bowl needs to be frozen again before another batch of ice cream can be churned. The ice cream is ready when the machine can no longer churn the ice cream. The ice cream should be scooped into another container and placed in the freezer for hardening.

Commercial electric ice-cream machines have a built-in container for the ice-cream mixture. When the machine is operated, the container is chilled while the mixture is churned with a paddle. The machinery in this type of churn is much more sophisticated and much more expensive than the type described above. Although the ice cream will take slightly longer to churn, several batches of ice cream can be made, one after the other, so this machine is suitable for large-scale catering needs.

Still-freezing

For those who do not wish to invest in an ice-cream maker, the simplest method for churning ice cream is the manual method called still-freezing. Place the ice-cream mixture in a shallow container in the deep freeze. As the mixture chills, ice crystals will form around the outside of the container. These need to be broken down with a fork several times during the freezing period and stirred into the unfrozen part of the mixture. Ice cream made by this method needs frequent attention for several hours and produces a rather dense ice cream. It is necessary to use a ★★★ (3-star rated) freezer for this process. These freezers reach a temperature of −18°C|0°F and are suitable for freezing food from room temperature. A freezer compartment inside a refrigerator is not powerful enough to freeze ice cream, being designed to store food that has been previously frozen.

Food Processor

It is also possible to process the fully frozen ice-cream mixture in a food processor. Allow the frozen mixture to soften slightly, then cut into egg-sized chunks. Place in a food processor and process, using the 'pulse' setting, until the mixture is smooth but still icy. Return the beaten mixture to the freezer to harden. Take care not to overprocess a mixture containing cream because this can easily be over-whipped, giving the ice cream a fudgy texture.

Serving Ice Cream

Once the ice cream has been churned it needs to be returned to the freezer for at least 30 minutes to harden before eating.

Ice cream is most enjoyable to eat when it is just on the verge of melting. If it is too cold and hard, the flavours will be dull. Ice cream that has been stored for a longer period of time and has become too hard to scoop easily should be placed in the refrigerator for 20–30 minutes before serving to be allowed to 'come to', that is, to soften just enough to make scooping easy. Alternatively, soften the ice cream in the microwave using the DEFROST setting.

Storing Ice Cream

Most home-made ice cream is best eaten freshly churned. Freezing tends to dull the flavour of the ice cream and ice cream can also easily absorb other flavours from the freezer. Ice cream if stored in the freezer compartment of the refrigerator should be kept for no longer than 24 hours. If kept in a ★★★(3-star rated freezer it should be stored for no longer than 1 week. Place a piece of greaseproof paper directly on the surface of the ice cream in the container before covering it with a lid. This will prevent ice crystals from forming on the surface.

Ice cream should not be allowed to soften and then be refrozen more than once. This ruins the texture of the ice cream and is potentially dangerous with regard to food poisoning. Freezing does not kill bacteria, it only causes them to become dormant, and when the mixture is thawed the bacteria will grow. Ice cream that has been allowed to completely thaw should be discarded.

Ice Cream: What has gone wrong when...

The ice cream has not frozen sufficiently.
- The ice cream has not been in the freezer for long enough.
- The sugar quantity in the ice cream is too high.
- The alcohol quantity in the ice cream is too high.
- The freezer is not cold enough.

The ice cream has a granular, gritty texture.
- The ice cream contains too much milk relative to the amount of cream and the lactose in the milk has frozen.
- The custard curdled when the base was made.

The ice cream has a dense, fudgy texture.
- The ice cream has been over-churned and the fat in the cream has turned to butter.
- The ice cream contains too high a proportion of cream.

The ice cream has a hard, icy texture.
- The mixture has too high a water quantity in relation to the cream.
- The ice cream was insufficiently churned.

The ice cream has a crumbly texture.
- The proportion of cream is too high.

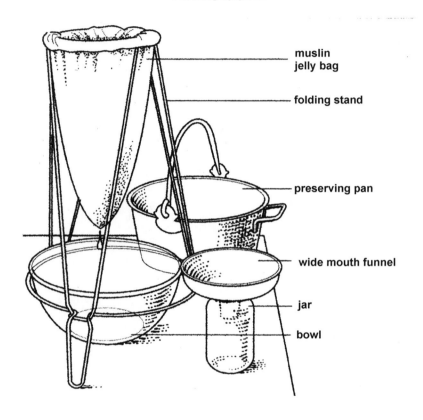

Preserving equipment

muslin
jelly bag

folding stand

preserving pan

wide mouth funnel

jar

bowl

Jams, Jellies and Other Preserves

From the nineteenth century, when a cheap and reliable source of sugar was found in the West Indies, the making and eating of jams and jellies became popular in many homes and their enjoyment was no longer a privilege of the wealthy few. Throughout the countryside, summer's glut of fruit was transformed into rows of shining jars of jams and jellies to be relished through the winter months.

Today, as modern life has become busier and individuals have become, on the whole, wealthier, making jams and jellies is on the wane. However, it is a particularly satisfying way to spend an afternoon, particularly when full-flavoured fruit can be obtained relatively inexpensively from a farmers' market or from a 'pick your own' farm.

Fruit preserves have different names, usually determined by their consistency.

Jam is made from fruit pulp and/or pieces of fruit and syrup made from the fruit juice and sugar. Jam should hold its shape on a plate but should be soft enough to spread.

Conserve traditionally is made from a mixture of fruit, but the term has come to mean a jam with a slightly softer set than jam containing whole fruit or large chunks of fruit.

Marmalade is jam made exclusively from citrus fruit, usually containing pieces of peel.

Jelly is a clear preserve made from the strained juice of the cooked fruit that has been boiled with sugar. Chopped herbs are sometimes stirred into savoury jellies. The jelly should hold its shape on a plate but should not be so firm as to have a rubbery texture.

Fruit butter is made from smooth fruit purée cooked with sugar to the consistency of thick yoghurt. Less sugar is used than for jam.

Fruit cheese is the same mixture as a fruit butter cooked to the point where it is thick and firm enough to cut when set.

Fruit curd, such as *Lemon Curd* (see **Eggs**, page 230), is made from the juice and zest of the fruit along with butter and eggs. Although the high sugar content gives a preserving effect, fruit curd should be refrigerated.

Making Jams and Jellies

Certain types of fruit make a set jam or jelly more successfully than others because some types of fruit are higher in a substance called pectin. Pectin is a carbohydrate that is found in the pulp, skin and cores, but not the juice, of all fruit. It is the pectin that forms the structure of the cells and holds then together. When the fruit is boiled, the pectin, a long stringy molecule, is released. The pectin strands bond with the water present in the fruit juices and/or added water, whilst the acid in the fruit keeps it from separating. The sugar dissolves into a syrup, which in combination with the pectin strands, forms a gel that sets the jam.

Fruit that is at the 'just ripe' stage or is slightly underripe will contain the maximum amount of pectin. When fruit becomes overripe the pectin changes to pectic acid which is unable to gel. Frozen fruit has a slightly lower pectin content than fresh fruit.

Testing for Pectin

All fruit contains pectin to some extent, but certain fruits have enough pectin to set a jam or jelly. The level of pectin in various fruits is given in the table below. To test a fruit for pectin, mix 1 tablespoon unsweetened cooked fruit with 1 tablespoon methylated spirits in a small jar. If the fruit is high in pectin, a jellied lump will form. If it has a medium amount of pectin, a lump will form but will break apart if the jar is shaken. If the fruit is low in pectin, only a few small lumps will be seen.

If the cooked fruit mixture is low in pectin and therefore unlikely to set, the pectin content can be increased in one of the following ways:

- by using a special preserving sugar with added pectin
- by adding a pectin syrup which can be purchased in some supermarkets
- by adding fruit which is high in pectin
- by boiling the fruit with apple cores and seeds, or citrus pips and white pith which have been wrapped in a muslin bag for easy removal

If pectin is added to a fruit, a corresponding percentage of sugar should also be added.

Fruit also contains acids that form a gel in combination with pectin, sugar and heat. In addition to keeping the pectin strands from separating from the syrup, the acid helps to break down the cell walls when the fruit is boiled. Depending on the type of fruit, the acid can be any of the following: citric acid (citrus fruits); malic acid (apples); ascorbic acid (citrus fruits); tartaric acid (certain types of grapes). Scientists have determined that a pH level of between 3.0 and 3.5 is ideal for forming a gel. When making jam or jelly from a fruit low in acid, lemon juice is usually added. The level of acid in different types of fruit is given in the table below.

Fruit	Pectin level	Acid level	Suggested use
Apples, eating	Medium	Varies	Chutney, jelly
Apples, cooking	High	Medium	Jam, jelly, combining with other fruits
Apricots	Medium	Medium	Jam, conserve
Blackberries	Medium	Medium	Jam, jelly, conserve
Cherries	Low*	Medium	Conserve
Crab apples	High	Medium	Jelly
Cranberries	High	High	Jam, jelly
Currants	High	High	Addition to chutney
Damsons	High	High	Jam, cheese
Gooseberries	High	High	Jelly
Grapefruit	High	High	Marmalade
Grapes	Medium	Medium	Jelly
Lemons, Limes	High	High	Jelly, combining with other fruits
Mango	Low*	Low	Chutney
Medlar	Low*	Low	Combine with apple for jelly
Oranges	High	High	Marmalade
Peaches	Low*	Low	Conserve, chutney
Plums	High	High	Jam, conserve
Quinces	High	Medium	Jelly, cheese
Raspberries	Medium*	Medium	Jam, jelly, conserve
Rhubarb	Low*	High	Conserve
Strawberries	Low*	Low	Jam, conserve

* Needs added pectin

The other very important ingredient in jam- and jelly-making is sugar. It is the high sugar content that allows jams and jellies to be stored for periods of up to 3 years. A traditional jam recipe requiring a weight of sugar equal to the weight of the fruit will produce a sweet jam that can be stored for up to 3 years if properly potted. Along with the natural sugar present in the fruit, this ratio of sugar to fruit will result in a jam with a total sugar content of approximately 60 per cent. Jams with a lower sugar quantity will keep for up to 6 months.

Use either granulated sugar or preserving sugar in jam and jelly-making. Granulated sugar, with its larger crystals, dissolves more easily than caster sugar. Caster sugar is likely to set into a solid mass on the bottom of the pan and will take longer to dissolve. Preserving sugar has even larger crystals than granulated, so dissolves very easily and often has added pectin. Brown sugar gives an unattractive colour to preserves so is usually not used, with the exception of chutney. Many recipes call for warming the sugar slightly before adding it to the jam to help it dissolve more easily. Place the sugar in a roasting tin in a low oven.

Equipment

Although most preserving books recommend an extensive list of specialist jam- and jelly-making equipment, it is certainly possible to use everyday cooking utensils. Making an investment in specialist equipment would only be worthwhile if preserving large quantities on a regular basis. All equipment must be scrupulously clean to avoid contaminating the preserves.

- It is necessary to have a heavy stainless-steel stockpot with a capacity of approximately 9 litres | 15¾ pints for processing 1 kg | 2.2 lb fruit. The fruit and sugar mixture should come no more than halfway up the sides of the pan to allow for expansion of the mixture during boiling. A wide stockpot is better than a tall, narrow pot.
- Clean, previously used glass jars, with or without lids, can be used for jams and jellies. Proper bottling jars need only be used if the jars are going to be heat-processed, i.e. boiled after filling. (See *Bibliography and Suggested Further Reading*, page 771, for preserving books giving instructions on heat processing).
- Special wide-mouth funnels are available for filling jars easily without spilling the jam down the sides of the jar. However, if the jam is placed in a clean jug it can be poured into the jars with relative ease.
- For jelly-making, special muslin bags can be purchased for straining the juice from the fruit. The bag needs to be suspended over a clean bowl so that the bottom of the bag does not touch the juice. However, if a jelly bag is not available, the fruit pulp can be strained through layers of boiled muslin placed in a sieve over a bowl.
- It is necessary to weigh the ingredients carefully when making jams and jellies so a set of scales is needed.
- A sugar thermometer is useful but not essential.
- Waxed discs, cellophane covers and rubber bands, if lids are not used, and labels are also required.

Procedure for Sterilizing Jars

To sterilize the jars and lids for bottling jam and jelly, wash the jars and lids well in hot, soapy water and rinse with hot water. Do not dry the jars with a tea towel but place them on their sides on a clean baking sheet in the oven preheated to 160°C | 325°F | gas mark 3 for 10 minutes. Allow the jars to cool slightly before filling with the warm jam or jelly.

Procedure for Making Jam

1 Pick over, wash and dry the fruit. Remove any stones.

2 Soften the fruit over a low heat to the desired texture before adding the sugar. Sugar has a hardening effect on whole fruit.

3 Warm the sugar in a low oven for 10–20 minutes to help it dissolve more quickly, or layer the fruit and sugar together and let stand overnight.

4 Heat the fruit and sugar mixture over a low heat initially to allow the sugar to dissolve completely before bringing the mixture to the boil.

5 Do not stir once the mixture has started to boil as stirring breaks up the fruit.

6 Do not skim the mixture during making because you will waste a lot of the jam: skim once just before potting.

7 When the mixture has started to thicken and begins to look like jam – usually after about 10 minutes – test for setting by using a cold plate (see below).

8 Allow jam and marmalade to stand and thicken for about 15 minutes before potting so the fruit doesn't float to the top of the jar.

9 Fill the jars to 6 mm–1 cm $|$ $\frac{1}{4}$–$\frac{1}{2}$ in from the rim.

10 Seal the jam or jelly when it is hot or cold, never lukewarm. Mildew spores present in the air can be trapped under the seal and will reproduce if warm.

11 Clean the lip of the filled jar with a piece of damp kitchen paper before sealing with well-fitting waxed discs or discs of greaseproof paper dipped in boiling water (see sealing instructions below).

12 Allow the jars to stand undisturbed for 24 hours before storing.

13 Store the jam or jelly in a dark, cool cupboard.

Testing for Setting Point

Setting point occurs when the fruit and sugar mixture reaches a temperature of 105°C $|$ 220°F. This can be tested with a sugar thermometer. Place the thermometer in the mixture before boiling begins or warm the thermometer before inserting it into the boiling fruit.

If you do not have a thermometer, place several small plates into the refrigerator or freezer when you start to cook the jam. After the mixture has been boiling for several minutes, place a teaspoonful on a cold plate and return it to the refrigerator to allow it to cool. Remove the boiling jam from the heat source while you are testing for setting point. Push the cooled jam gently on the plate with your finger. If it wrinkles on the surface and the jam doesn't flow over where you have drawn your finger, setting point has been reached and the jam has been boiled for long enough.

Jelly can also be tested for setting by observing how the jelly runs off the side of a spoon. Before it is ready it will be very liquid and run off the spoon in a single stream. When it reaches setting point it will fall from the bowl and sides of the spoon in 'flakes' or sheets.

Plum Jam

Plums are high in both pectin and acidity so no additional pectin or lemon juice is needed. Damsons can be used for this jam. If the stones are difficult to remove, halve the fruit and cook it with the stones intact. They will float to the surface during boiling and can be skimmed away easily.

MAKES ABOUT 675 g | 1½ lb

900 g | 2 lb barely ripe plums
900 g | 2 lb preserving or granulated sugar

1 Halve and stone the plums. Crack a handful of the stones and remove the kernels. They will impart a slight almond flavour to the jam.
2 Put the fruit and sugar into a glass or plastic bowl and leave to stand overnight.
3 The following day, wash the jars and sterilize them in a low oven (see above).
4 Transfer the fruit and sugar to a preserving pan or a large saucepan and heat slowly until the sugar has dissolved, then boil rapidly for about 7–10 minutes or until the jam reaches setting point (see above). Add the fruit kernels while the jam is still bubbling. Allow the jam to stand for about 10 minutes or until the fruit is evenly suspended. Remove the kernels and any stones.
5 Put the jam into a large jug, then pour into the warm, dry jars, or use a wide-mouth funnel.
6 Cover the jam (see *Sealing Jars of Jam and Jelly*, below) while hot.
7 Leave undisturbed overnight. Store in a cool, dark cupboard.

Procedure for Making Jelly

1 Follow *Making Jam or Jelly: Points to Remember*, above.
2 Cook the fruit according to recipe directions.
3 Place the fruit pulp and juice into a scalded jelly bag.
4 Hang the bag over a sterilized bowl, making sure the bottom of the bag does not touch the surface of the juice.

5 Do not squeeze the jelly bag or the jelly may become cloudy.

6 Do not use more than 1 litre | 1¾ pints juice at a time as larger quantities can have difficulty gelling.

7 Warm the sugar with the juice until the sugar dissolves, then bring to the boil and boil for about 10 minutes.

8 Test for setting point (see above).

9 Bottle in warm jars while still hot. Seal as instructed below.

Apple and Sage Jelly

This jelly is delicious with sausages or roast pork (see **Meat,** *Pork*, page 398) or as an accompaniment to cold meats. Other herbs, such as thyme or tarragon, can be substituted for the sage.

MAKES ABOUT 1–8 KG | 4 LB

2 kg | 4½ lb cooking apples

1.1 litres | 2 pints water

150 ml | ¼ pint cider vinegar

450 g | 1 lb warmed preserving sugar per

570 ml | 1 pint juice

55 g | 2 oz fresh sage leaves

1 Wash the apples and cut them into thick pieces without peeling or coring.

2 Put the apples and water into a saucepan and simmer, covered, for 1 hour.

3 Meanwhile, scald a jelly bag or 2 layers of muslin and a large sieve or colander with boiling water.

4 Add the vinegar to the apples and boil for a further 5 minutes.

5 Hang the jelly bag over a bowl so that the bottom of the bag will not touch the juice.

6 Place the apple pulp in the bag and leave it to drip until it stops. This will take at least 1 hour or the bag can be left overnight. Do not squeeze the bag as this will make the jelly cloudy.

7 Measure the juice and pour into the preserving pan. Add 450 g | 1 lb sugar for every 570 ml | 1 pint juice.

8 Bring to the boil slowly, stirring constantly. Ensure the sugar has dissolved before the juice boils.

9 Boil briskly, uncovered, for about 10 minutes, skimming frequently. Test for setting point (see above).

10 Allow the jelly to cool slightly Finely chop the sage then stir into the jelly.

11 Pour into the warm jam jars and seal as instructed below.

Sealing Jars of Jam and Jelly

The jam or jelly is sterilized by the rapid boiling during cooking. All jars and equipment should be scrupulously clean. Once put into the clean, dry jars, jam is sealed to prevent infiltration of mildew spores and bacteria. Melted paraffin wax poured over the surface of the jam is an old-fashioned and most effective seal but waxed or greaseproof paper discs are easier to manage and nearly as effective. Ideally the jam should be sealed while boiling hot, however, if liquid wax is poured on to liquid jam the surface may be disturbed. Allow the wax to cool slightly so that it thickens but is still clear. Two applications of wax are necessary if the first coating shrinks away from the sides of the jar, leaving a gap.

To seal the jars with waxed paper discs and cellophane covers, fill the warm jars with the hot jam. Wipe any spilt jam from the lip of the jar with a piece of kitchen paper dipped in boiled water. Dip the waxed disc into boiled water and place on top of the jam, waxed side down. Rounds of greaseproof paper dipped in a spirit such as vodka can be used if waxed discs are not available. The disc should cover the surface of the jam completely without folding up the edge of the jar. Smooth any air bubbles from beneath the surface of the disc with your finger. Wipe the cellophane covers on one side with a piece of kitchen paper dipped in boiled water. Place the cellophane over the top of the jar with the moist side uppermost. The heat of the jam will shrink the cellophane, creating a tight seal. If you run out of cellophane covers, greaseproof paper discs dipped in a spirit such as vodka can be used here too.

Perhaps the best method of sealing jam jars is to use metal screw caps with separate metal discs. They should be sterilized and dried thoroughly and new lids should be used for each potting. Check for a tight fit. The jam should be poured up to the shoulder of the jars, leaving a space of 1 cm | ½ in. Screw the caps on tightly. The heat of the jam will create a partial vacuum in the neck of the jars, sealing the lids securely.

Storing Jams and Jellies

Allow the jars to stand undisturbed for 24 hours to cool completely, then store in a cool, dark cupboard. Traditional jams can be stored for up to 3 years. 'Soft-set' jams can be stored for 6 months. If any mould or mildew has grown on the jam when it is opened, the jam should be discarded.

Once a jar of jam or jelly has been opened it is possible for mould to grow on the surface and the jam or jelly may become contaminated with bacteria. This often happens if unclean knives or spoons are dipped in the jam. It is best to keep it refrigerated and to use it within 3 weeks.

Orange Marmalade

The classic marmalade is made from Seville oranges, but as their season is only between the end of January and the middle of February, other tart oranges may be used if Seville are not available. If you find Seville oranges but do not have time to use them immediately, they can be frozen whole for up to 3 months, then defrosted before making the marmalade. The freezing softens the peel, thus reducing the cooking time. This recipe also can be made using a combination of citrus fruits, such as grapefruit, lemons or limes.

MAKES ABOUT 1.5 kg | 3½ lb

900 g | 2 lb Seville oranges

2 lemons

2.8 litres | 5 pints water

1.5 kg | 3 lb warmed preserving sugar

1 Scrub the fruit well, then cut in half and squeeze roughly into a bowl, reserving the pips.

2 Slice the peel finely or thickly, as desired, or chop in a food processor.

3 Tie the pips into a small muslin bag, then place with the peel in a large muslin bag or clean J-cloth. Tie with string.

4 If you have time, place the bag in a bowl with the juice and the water and leave to steep for 24 hours.

5 Transfer to a preserving pan or stockpot and simmer for about 2 hours, until the peel is soft and transparent. You may need to add more water during cooking due to evaporation.

6 Add the sugar to the preserving pan over a medium-low heat and stir whilst bringing to the boil.

7 Boil rapidly until setting point (see above) is reached at 105°C|220°F. This may take up to 20 minutes.

8 Remove the muslin bag and discard the pips. Stir the peel into the marmalade.

9 Allow the marmalade to cool for about 15 minutes to distribute the fruit evenly throughout the jam.

10 Pot in warm jars and seal as instructed above.

NOTE: The peel for marmalade can be softened in a pressure cooker to save time. Process under medium pressure/10 lb for about 10 minutes.

Jam- and Jelly-making: What has gone wrong when...

The jam or jelly has not set firmly enough.

- The fruit/sugar mixture did not reach setting point.
    Reboil the mixture until setting point is reached.
- The fruit was too low in pectin to achieve a set.
    Reboil the mixture with added commercial bottled pectin.

The colour of the preserve is too dark.

- The fruit was cooked for too long.

The fruit has risen to the top of the jar.

- The jam was potted when it was too hot.
    Allow it to cool slightly to thicken so the fruit is held in suspension.

The jam or jelly has crystallized.

- The jam or jelly was not covered properly.
- The jam or jelly contains too much sugar.
- The fruit mixture was boiled before the sugar dissolved.
- The fruit did not contain sufficient acidity.
- The jam or jelly is old.
- The jam or jelly was stored in too cold an environment.
    Add 1 tablespoon boiling water to the top of the jam and allow it to dissolve the crystals, then stir through.

There is mould on the surface of the jam or jelly.

- The jam or jelly was potted in unsterilized jars.
- The jam or jelly was not sealed properly.
- The jam or jelly has been contaminated with dirty utensils.
- The jam or jelly was covered while lukewarm.

    The jam or jelly should be thrown away.

The jam or jelly has fermented.

- The sugar content of the jam or jelly is too low.
- The jam or jelly was stored in too warm an environment.
- The jam or jelly was not boiled sufficiently or the mixture contains insufficient pectin.
- The acid content of the jam or jelly is too low.

    The jam or jelly should be thrown away.

The jelly is filled with lots of tiny air bubbles.

- The jelly was potted when it was too cool.
- The jam or jelly was stirred too much during cooling.

    Reboil and bottle when hot. Do not stir the mixture or shake the jars.

The jelly is cloudy.

- The jelly bag was squeezed, forcing the fruit pulp into the juice.

There is mildew on the surface.

- The jars were wet or cold when the jam or jelly was potted.
- The jam or jelly has not set sufficiently.
- The jam or jelly was stored in a damp place.
- The jam or jelly was lukewarm when covered.

The jam or jelly has set too much.

- The jam or jelly has been boiled for too long.
- Too much pectin has been added to the fruit mixture.

    Melt the jam or jelly, add water and reboil.

Chutney

The word chutney comes from the East Indian word *chatni*. Chutney is the traditional accompaniment for curries but it is also delicious served with meat and cheese.

Chutneys are the easiest preserves to make because obtaining a set is not necessary. Chutney is made from a mixture of fruit and/or vegetables and spices. It can be chunky or smooth but will always have a mixture of sweet and sour flavours.

Both sugar and salt are used in chutneys, but more for flavour than for their preserving qualities. Brown sugar is often used for its slightly caramelized, fuller flavour. As with jams and jellies, boiling the ingredients destroys micro-organisms. Like pickles, chutneys depend on vinegar for its preserving properties.

The ingredients for a chutney should be chopped small enough to be lifted with a teaspoon, but not so small as to be unidentifiable in the mixture. As the ingredients are seldom used whole, bruised or damaged fruit and vegetables can be used if the imperfect parts are removed.

Chutneys improve with keeping. They are usually ready to eat after being stored for 3 months – any sooner and their taste is harsh. Store in a cool, dark place for up to 6 months. Chutney sealed in sterilized jars and heat-sealed (see **Preserving, Bottling**, page 553) will keep for up to 2 years. See the **Bibliography and Suggested Further Reading** (page 771) for specialist preserving books.

Basic Procedure for Making Chutney

1 Wash the fruits and/or vegetables. Cut into pieces, removing any bruised parts.
2 Put all the ingredients except the sugar and vinegar into a non-reactive saucepan.
3 Tie spices into a muslin bag. Place in the saucepan.
4 Add enough good-quality vinegar to cover the ingredients generously.
5 Cook slowly, uncovered, until the ingredients are soft and most of the liquid has evaporated.
6 Add the sugar and the remaining vinegar. Stir until the sugar has dissolved.
7 To test if the chutney is done, scrape a spoon across the bottom of the pan: no liquid should run into the gap. Remove the spices.
8 Pot in sterilized jars as for jam-making above. Do not use metal lids unless they are lined with plastic.

Hot Tomato Chutney

Sterilize the jars as for jam (see above).

MAKES ABOUT 1 kg | 2 lb

2 kg | 4½ lb ripe tomatoes	340 g | 12 oz dark brown sugar
450 g | 1 lb onions, peeled and chopped	290 ml | ½ pint malt vinegar
2 cloves of garlic, crushed	110 g | 4 oz sultanas
5 cm | 2 in piece of fresh root ginger, peeled and grated	2 teaspoons sea salt
6 fresh red chillies, deseeded and finely chopped, or 1 teaspoon cayenne powder	1 teaspoons mustard seeds
	1 teaspoon coriander seeds

1 To peel the tomatoes, place them in boiling water for 10 seconds then plunge them into cold water. Use a knife to peel away the skins.
2 Coarsely chop the tomatoes and place them in a large non-reactive saucepan.
3 Add the remaining ingredients and bring to the boil, stirring constantly.
4 Reduce the heat so that the mixture just simmers. Cook for about 2 hours or until the chutney is thick and syrupy.
5 Ladle into sterilized jars and seal.
6 Store in a cool, dark place for 1 month before using.

Pickles

A pickle has been preserved in a seasoned vinegar mixture or brine. Examples of pickles are gherkins, dill pickles and pickled herrings. The acid preserves the food. Pickles can be sweet, sour and/or hot. Certain spices are characteristic of pickles. These can be any or all of the following: mustard seeds, peppercorns, allspice berries, cardamom pods, ginger, coriander seeds, and cinnamon sticks. The fruit, vegetables or fish to be pickled can be sliced, cut into pieces or kept whole.

Fruit and/or vegetables to be pickled should be of the best quality and slightly underripe. Good-quality cider or wine vinegar is recommended for pickles. Store in sterilized jars as for jam. Pickles do not keep as well as chutneys and should be used within 6 months.

Spiced Fruit Pickle

This pickle has a beautiful crimson colour. It is delicious with cold meats and cheese. The jars should be sterilized as for jam and jelly (see above).

MAKES 1.35 kg | 3 lb

900 g | 2 lb mixed soft fruit, such as plums, rhubarb, apricots, peaches
450 g | 1 lb granulated sugar
425 ml | ¾ pint cider vinegar
grated zest and juice of 1 orange

1 teaspoon ground ginger
4 teaspoons mustard seeds
6 cloves
1 cinnamon stick

1 Wash and dry the fruit, then remove the stalks and stones.
2 Place the sugar and vinegar in a large pan and stir over a low heat until the sugar is dissolved. Add the orange zest and juice, ginger, mustard seeds, cloves and cinnamon stick.
3 Add the fruit, then bring to the boil. Simmer gently for 15 minutes.
4 Strain the fruit, reserving the juice.
5 Boil the juice until syrupy. Mix with the fruit.
6 Pour into warm sterilized jam jars and seal as for jam and jelly (see above).

NOTE: This pickle can be used immediately but it will improve if stored for at least 1 month. Keep in a cool, dark place.

Pickles, Chutneys and Relishes: What has gone wrong when...

The pickles, chutneys or relishes ferment.
- The preserves were not boiled for long enough.
- Not enough sugar or acid was added to the recipe.
- They were stored in too warm a place.

Meat

The French word for meat is *viande*, derived from Latin *vivenda*, meaning 'that which gives life', and is particularly accurate as meat is rich in protein, minerals and vitamins. Meat is relatively expensive and in the past was eaten in smaller quantities than it is today.

Rituals and customs have surrounded the slaughter of animals and the consumption of meat throughout history. Today, these customs are still evident in the tradition of eating roasts for religious celebrations such as Christmas and Easter. For many families in Britain, the Sunday roast remains an important weekly occasion.

Certain religions have customs specifying the method by which animals are slaughtered. Orthodox Jewish people can only eat meat from animals that have cloven hooves and chew the cud. These animals must be ritually slaughtered and prepared to render the meat kosher by a special butcher. Some Muslims only eat meat that has been killed by a licensed halal butcher according to Islamic law.

The Structure of Meat

Muscle tissue is composed of 3 basic materials: water, protein and fat. Meat contains 43–65 per cent water, depending upon the age of the animal (a younger animal will contain more water and less fat), 12–30 per cent protein and 5–45 per cent fat.

Meat contains no carbohydrate as any present in the form of glycogen is broken down into lactic acid when the animal is slaughtered and hanged. This chemical reaction is vital in the maturing process as the lactic acid tenderizes the muscle fibres. The texture and flavour of cooked meat depend on the proportion of water to fat in the meat, the structure of the muscle proteins and the quantity of connective tissue binding the muscle tissue together.

Muscle Fibres

Meat is composed of long, thin cells called filaments that may be as long as the muscle itself. The filaments are bound together to form muscle fibres, which are in turn bound together with connective tissue in bundles. In a young animal, the muscle fibres are fine, but as the animal matures and exercises more, each muscle fibre coarsens and enlarges in diameter due to an increase in the number of muscle filaments. In turn, each bundle increases in width, causing the overall muscle to enlarge. The muscle fibre bundles are aligned in groups to form an individual muscle, which is contained and connected to the bone by tough connective tissue.

The Grain of Meat

The grain of the meat is formed by the groups of muscle fibres running the length of the muscle. It is easier to chew meat along the length of the bundles of muscle fibres than across them. For this reason meat is carved across the grain so that it can be chewed with the grain.

Connective Tissue

Connective tissue is an integral part of muscle as it surrounds the individual muscle fibres and each muscle fibre bundle and sheaths the entire muscle as well as tying the muscle to the bone. Connective tissue varies in structure and distribution with each tissue type. Muscles that get a lot of exercise, as in the neck and shoulders of grazing animals, contain tough, thick membranes running between each muscle section, but these are not as tough as the rubbery, gristly connective tissue that surrounds arteries or forms the tendons that attach muscle to bone. In contrast, muscles that receive little exercise or come from very young animals have small amounts of very fine connective tissue.

Connective tissue is made up of the proteins elastin, reticulin and collagen. Elastin, as its name suggests, has elastic properties and is an important structural component of blood vessel walls and ligaments. Reticulin is a fibrous protein, found between muscle cells and the muscles themselves. It also forms a large part of the initial bone structure in young animals, before the bones calcify and harden. Elastin and reticulin are both very tough to eat and are not broken down or tenderized by cooking.

Collagen is a structural protein found in the skin and the tendons and between muscle cells and muscles. It is also present in large quantities in the bones of young animals. Collagen breaks down into gelatine when cooked slowly in water. Meat containing a large quantity of collagen becomes very tender and improves in flavour as the protein breaks down. As the collagen disintegrates, the muscle fibres start to separate, making the meat easier to chew.

The quality and price of a cut of meat are largely determined by the quantity, distribution and type of connective tissue. Cuts for quick-cooking methods and roasting are the most expensive as they are tender, containing very little connective tissue. Cuts for slow roasting, braising and stewing have a moderate amount of connective tissue and require long, slow cooking in liquid to break it down. The cheapest cuts of meat are rich in connective tissue and require cooking for a long period of time.

Fat

Fat is distributed through and around muscle in the form of adipose fatty tissue as well as under the skin in the form of deposit fatty tissue. Thin streaks and flecks of adipose fat running between muscle fibre bundles are known as marbling.

Marbling is a desirable quality, especially in beef, as the fat tenderizes and enhances the meat's flavour when cooked.

The quantity, distribution and nature of the fat in meat greatly affect its texture, flavour and keeping qualities and determine the way it is prepared for cooking. Fat makes meat succulent by separating the muscle fibres as it melts on cooking and oils the tissue, making it easier to chew and cut. Very lean meat has a tendency to toughen and dry out when cooked as the fibres shrink and pack closely together, squeezing out much of the water in the meat. Deposit fat on the surface of muscles does not tenderize meat in the same way but protects it from excessive moisture loss during cooking.

Fat is present in meat in two different forms: saturated and unsaturated (see *Healthy Eating and Basic Nutrition*, page 17). Unsaturated fat tends to be soft at room temperature, as it does not pack as evenly or densely as saturated fat, which tends to be hard. Pork, poultry and lamb fat contains a higher proportion of unsaturated fat than beef and is therefore much softer, even just out of the refrigerator.

The Colour of Meat

The colour of the meat depends upon the following:

- The quality of the myoglobin, a bright red protein in the muscle tissue that holds the oxygen carried in the blood.
- The amount of exercise the muscle has had. The more exercise a muscle has had, the darker the meat.
- The age of the animal; the younger the animal the paler the meat.
- The species of the animal.
- The diet of the animal.
- The length of time the animal has been hung; the longer the hanging the darker the meat.
- If the meat is packaged in an oxygen-flushed container the colour will be brighter than meat that has not been flushed.

Hanging Meat

Immediately after slaughter the still warm meat is soft but very tough. It is hanged for a period of time to allow the structure of the meat to change and improve its flavour and texture. Much of the structural change in meat is caused by the accumulation of lactic acid, which lowers the pH, causing a proportion of the protein present in the muscle fibres to denature and unravel. This process, occurring several hours after the animal is slaughtered, is the first stage in partially breaking down or tenderizing the muscles so that the meat is easier to cut and eat. The accumulating lactic acid also brings on rigor mortis by activating the proteins responsible for contracting the muscle. The contracting muscle becomes extremely stiff, making the meat too tough to eat even after prolonged cooking. Rigor mortis lasts for up to a day in beef and for approximately 6 hours in pork and chicken. The muscles then begin to relax as the meat proteins continue to change chemically and structurally.

Meat benefits from a period of ageing before it is eaten. It continues tenderize and develops more flavour. The connective tissue is not affected by the accumulation of lactic acid or enzyme activity in the time taken to tenderize meat and therefore remains unchanged.

The hanging time of meat is often limited by the degradation of fat. Fat is susceptible to bacterial growth and becomes rancid quite quickly. Saturated fat is harder and more stable and takes longer to spoil than unsaturated fat. This is one of the main reasons why beef can be hung longer than meats containing a high proportion of unsaturated fats such as poultry, pork, and lamb.

Storage of meat during hanging

To allow the meat to age with the minimum growth of bacteria, it is stored in the dark at very low temperatures: 1–3°C|34–38°F. Beef is aged for 1–3 weeks and lamb for 1 week. The enzymes that degrade the protein components of the meat are also retarded at low temperatures. Cheaper cuts of meat are hung for a minimal amount of time, which may only be as long as it takes to transport it from the abattoir to the butcher's shop.

See also *Factors Affecting the Tenderness of Meat*, below.

Choosing Meat

Although the most expensive cuts of meat are tender, they do not have the strength of flavour of tougher cuts. Provided that tougher cuts have been hung for long enough and are cooked correctly they can be as pleasing to eat as meat from the fillet or loin. See individual types of meat, but in general look for the following:

- The meat should not be too fatty or contain too much gristle.
- The joints should be reasonably small and any exposed bones should be pinkish-blue in colour, indicating a young animal.
- The meat should have a firm, close texture.
- The meat should never be slimy. It should be moist but not gelatinous, with the exception of some veal.
- The meat should not smell.
- The fat should be pale creamy-coloured, not yellow.

Storing Meat

Storing Uncooked Meat

Before the animal is slaughtered most micro-organisms are present only on its skin and hair; they are only present in the muscle if the animal is diseased. The bacteria responsible for meat spoilage are transferred from the skin to the flesh as the meat is cut into portions.

Although meat is usually washed before packaging, a good many bacteria remain on its surface. The concentration of bacteria present on the skin and flesh varies between animals. A piece of pork may have a few hundred bacteria per square centimetre | $\frac{1}{2}$ inch, whereas chicken may harbour many thousands over the same area. As a result, chicken tends to spoil more quickly.

Hygiene when Handling Raw Meat

Due to the high concentration of bacteria present on the surface of raw meat, it is important to prepare it on a work surface that can be washed thoroughly with hot, soapy water. Once the meat has been prepared, first rinse your hands, knives, any other utensils and the chopping board in cold water to remove any loose fragments of protein. If equipment used to prepare meat is immediately dipped into hot water, the protein cooks on to their surfaces, making it harder to remove. Once the equipment has been rinsed in cold water, transfer to hot, soapy water and wash and dry thoroughly.

In the refrigerator: Bacteria thrive on meat unless it is kept below 4°C|40°F in the refrigerator. Cold temperatures reduce the rate at which the bacteria multiply and the rate at which enzymes degrade the meat protein. Nevertheless, the bacteria are still partially active and will spoil the meat if it is stored for too long.

Uncooked meat must be stored separately from cooked food and food that will not be heated before it is eaten. Raw meat loses fluid and blood, containing bacteria while it is stored, and this could drip on to and contaminate other food stored nearby, resulting in food poisoning. For this reason it should always be stored at the bottom of the refrigerator.

To preserve its freshness and colour it is important to allow meat to breathe. If it comes tightly wrapped, pierce the clingfilm or rewrap in oxygen-permeable clingfilm or paper and refrigerate for no longer than 2–3 days. Meat bought in oxygen-flushed sealed containers at a supermarket is best left intact as these are designed to keep meat fresh as long as possible.

In the freezer: Meat can be kept for much longer if it is stored in the freezer at −18°C|0°F. Most bacteria responsible for meat spoilage require water and warmer temperatures to work actively and are therefore inhibited as long as the meat is frozen. The meat can still oxidize when frozen: this is why thawed meat is often dull in colour. It is also important to wrap the meat tightly before storing it in the freezer, to prevent the surface of the meat from drying out, which would affect its taste and texture.

Although meat freezes well, it will be of lower quality than fresh meat. This is due to the formation of ice crystals that rupture the muscle cell walls. When the meat is defrosted, liquid or water contained in it drains away to form a pool of fluid. The loss of fluid results in tougher, drier cooked meat. Meats containing a high proportion of unsaturated fats, such as lamb, pork and poultry, should be eaten within a few months of freezing, as the fats may become rancid. Beef may be frozen for a year or two as its fat is saturated and is less likely to deteriorate.

Storing Cooked Meat

Although cooking meat makes it safe to eat, airborne bacteria soon colonize and multiply on its surface. It is therefore important to keep cooked meat well wrapped to reduce the rate of deterioration.

The flavour of cooked meat deteriorates rapidly in the refrigerator in a matter of hours. This is because during cooking the fat becomes unstable and once cool becomes highly vulnerable to oxidation and bacteria. Meat containing high proportions of unsaturated fat is more vulnerable to flavour deterioration than meat containing saturated fat. To slow the rate of flavour spoilage, reduce the chances of oxidation by wrapping the cooked meat well in clingfilm, making sure that any air bubbles are eliminated. It is also recommended that meat be eaten within 2 days unless it is cured, in which case it can be kept for up to 1 week without its flavour being compromised.

Factors Affecting the Tenderness of Meat

The texture of meat depends not only on the way it is cooked but on the structure of the muscles making up the cut or joint. If the muscle fibres are coarse and there is a high density of connective tissue, the meat will be tougher than if it has a fine grain and the meat is lean.

Age of the animal
The younger the animal and the less exercise it has taken, the more tender its meat will be as the muscle fibres are fine and its flavour delicate. As the animal matures and exercises the muscle fibres coarsen, making the meat tougher to cut and chew.

Amount of exercise
Meat from older animals will remain finer-grained and tender if the animal is not allowed to exercise. The most tender cuts of meat are from muscles that are least used. The fillet, for example, is extremely tender as it runs along the back of the animal and gets little exercise. In contrast, the neck, shoulder, chest and legs are used constantly for supporting the head while grazing, walking and standing and meat from these areas is therefore relatively tough.

Method of rearing
This means the general conditions in which the animal lives, the quality of the feed it is given and whether the animal is able to exercise. These factors are important in determining the flavour and texture of meat. A cheaper cut, such as stewing steak from a high-quality animal, will taste delicious if cooked properly in a casserole. An expensive cut, such as rump steak, from a low-quality animal will be

flavourless and tough. A good butcher will choose meat from reputable suppliers who will know how the animals have been reared. Organic meat should have a better flavour than non-organic, but will not necessarily be more tender. Organic meat is higher in price due to the labour costs incurred during production. The state of the animal prior to slaughter can also affect the tenderness of the meat: for example, if it is relaxed and peaceful, the meat is likely to be more tender.

Storage time before cooking

The carcass should be hung at temperatures no higher than 2°C|35°F for the appropriate amount of time. At this temperature the meat will become increasingly tender as enzymes that partially break down the structure of the proteins are active, while bacterial activity responsible for meat spoilage is retarded.

Distribution of fat in meat

Prime beef, for example, must have a certain amount of marbling to provide flavour, tenderness and succulence when eaten.

Presence of connective tissue

If there is a large amount of connective tissue present, the meat will be tougher and will require longer cooking.

Freezing

Freezing also has a tenderizing effect on meat as some enzymes continue to be partially active and the formation of ice crystals in the meat bruise and partially break down the structure. (See *Storing Uncooked Meat*, above.) However, freezing can result in a loss of moisture in the meat.

Method of cooking

This is probably the most important factor that affects the ultimate tenderness of meat. The method of cooking (see *Methods of Cooking Meat*, below) should be chosen to suit a particular cut of meat, taking into account the coarseness of muscle fibres and the quantity and distribution of fat and connective tissue. These factors are largely determined by the location on the animal of a particular cut.

The most expensive tender cuts of meat, containing very little fat and connective tissue (mainly from the back part of the animal), are suitable for grilling, pan-frying and roasting. Tender cuts are usually cooked until pink in the centre so that the muscle fibres are only partially affected by heat and remain soft and moist. If tender meat is cooked thoroughly to the centre it becomes hard, tough and dry as the muscle fibres shrink in the heat, squeezing the juices out. This explains why it is almost impossible to produce a tender well-done grilled steak.

Although tender cuts are best eaten pink, tougher cuts, containing a high proportion of connective tissue, must be cooked for longer at low temperatures. With gentle, prolonged cooking in liquid heated to just below boiling (100°C|212°F) the protein collagen in connective tissue is broken down into gelatine, a soft-textured substance that is liquid when heated. Also, due to the breakdown of collagen, the muscle fibres are no longer held firmly together and fall apart. As a result of the disintegration of the protein responsible for binding the muscle fibres together and the formation of gelatine, tough meat becomes moist, extremely tender and meltingly easy to eat.

Less expensive cuts containing a small proportion of fat and connective tissue from around the forelegs are suitable for slow-cooking methods using very little liquid, such as braising and pot-roasting. The cheapest cuts contain a high proportion of connective tissue (neck, knuckle, shin, breast and tail) and must be stewed in liquid for a long time to break the connective tissue down into gelatine.

Other Methods of Tenderizing Meat

Tender cuts of meat are usually eaten whole or in portions. Tougher cuts of meat can be tenderized in three ways:

- Long, slow cooking.
- Physically breaking down the structure of meat by pounding, cutting or mincing.
- Chemically by marinating.

Mincing meat
Tougher cuts of meat, especially from beef, veal and pork, are minced to break down the tough muscle fibres and connective tissue. Top-quality mince is obtained from leaner cuts and can contain as little as 5 per cent fat. It is minced coarsely to retain its flavour and juices. Lower-quality mince is from tougher cuts, contains more connective tissue and fat and is often ground very finely as a result. Mince is cooked and used in forcemeats (see page 271), beefburgers and meat sauces.

Marinating meat
Meat is marinated to give it flavour and to soften its texture slightly. A marinade is a combination of acidic ingredients such as wine or lemon juice, oil, and aromatic ingredients such as onions, garlic, herbs and peppercorns. The acidic ingredients will soften the proteins on the exposed surface of the meat.

Aromatic spices and herbs in marinades should be used in moderation as their flavour can become overpowering with time. If the quantity of marinade seems insufficient to cover the meat, place the meat and marinade in a plastic bag and tie it to draw the liquid around the meat.

The longer the meat is left in the marinade, the more pronounced the effect. Tender cuts of meat, such as fillet steak or chicken breast, should be marinated for no longer that a couple of hours. If the meat is left in the marinade for too long, the marinade could overpower the flavour or even break down the structure of the meat, giving it a pasty texture. Tougher cuts of meat, such as chuck steak for a stew or shoulder of venison for a casserole, can be marinated for as long as 2–3 days provided that they are stored below 4°C|40°F.

Meat steeped in marinades should be drained well and wiped dry before cooking because the wet surface of the meat will prevent it from browning.

Marinades may be used as the liquid constituent in braised dishes and stews, or to baste roasting meat. Do not use a marinade that has been in contact with raw meat as a sauce for cooked meat unless it is boiled first to destroy any bacteria.

For examples of marinade recipes see **Poultry**, *Spatchcocked Grilled Poussin* (page 426) and **Game**, *Venison Casserole* (page 472).

Methods of Cooking Meat

When meat is heated, the proteins start to denature at 38°C|100°F, slowly unravelling and coagulating with each other. This effect is visible: when meat is placed in a hot pan it loses its translucency within moments, to become opaque and then dry. Juices from the meat may also accumulate in the base of the pan as the coagulating, shrinking protein squeezes the juices out of the meat. This is why rare meat is so juicy and moist to eat. As the meat reaches a temperature of 55°C|130°F the muscle fibres have shrunk considerably in both width and length. By 77°C|170°F the fibres have shrunk as much as they can and start to separate from each other along their length, and the coagulated proteins have squeezed out most of the liquid contained in the meat, causing it to become firm and dry. Due to the shrinkage of muscle fibres, the coagulation of proteins and the resulting loss of liquid, meat shrinks on cooking.

The colour of meat is also affected by cooking, due to the denaturing of the protein myoglobin, the red pigment in muscle. Myoglobin remains red up to 55°C|130°F but from 60°C|140°F it starts to become a lighter pink which then fades to brown at 77°C|170°F. Thus raw meat is bright red, rare meat is pinkish-red and well-done meat becomes greyish-brown as it increases in temperature.

Fast, Dry Methods

The following fast, dry methods are used to cook tender cuts of meat:

- **Roasting** in the oven, either on a spit or in a roasting pan
- **Frying**, including sautéing and stir-frying
- **Grilling** or barbecuing

Slow, Moist Methods

There are 4 basic techniques for cooking with added liquid. Tough cuts of meat must be cooked by one of these methods in order to become tender. Tender cuts of meat can also be cooked by these methods if care is taken not to overcook the meat.

- **Poaching:** The raw meat is submerged in barely simmering water or flavoured cooking liquor until it is cooked through.

- **Pot-roasting:** The meat is browned first, then cooked with very little liquid in a pot with a tightly fitting lid, either in the oven or on the hob.
- **Braising:** As for pot-roasting, but slightly more liquid is used.
- **Stewing:** The meat is usually browned then immersed in liquid. The meat is simmered in a pot with a tightly fitting lid for a prolonged period of time, 2–3 hours, or until tender.

The important difference between fast, dry and slow, moist cooking methods is not moisture but the characteristic temperatures and rates of heating. Dry cooking methods generally use temperatures of 180°C|350°F|gas mark 4, well above the boiling point of water, to cook the meat by conduction, whereas moist cooking methods are limited to the boiling point of water (100°C|212°F) but are usually carried out at temperatures just below boiling point, thereby cooking the meat slowly and gently. As a result, dry cooking methods are suited to tender cuts of meat and moist cooking methods are generally better for cooking tougher cuts containing a larger quantity of connective tissue.

Browning

Meat may be browned at a high temperature at the initial stages of cooking, not to seal in the juices, as used to be believed, but to brown the surface of the meat to enhance its flavour and colour. Meat is either seared in hot oil or fat in a pan or, for larger cuts, in a very hot oven preheated to 200–220°C|400–425°F for a short amount of time (15–20 minutes). Browned meat will taste more flavourful than poached meat as the surface moisture is boiled off quickly, enabling a crust of concentrated proteins to develop. As these proteins are heated to the temperature of the pan or grill they start to caramelize or brown to a characteristic rich golden-brown colour, enhancing both the flavour and appearance of the meat. This browning reaction is called the Maillard reaction, after the scientist who first described it.

Roasting

Oven-roasting means cooking in an oven with no other liquid than fat, although roasting and grilling used to be virtually the same process carried out in front of an open fire where both large and small cuts of meat were spit-roasted. Provided that the meat was of a uniform shape and thickness, spit-roasting ensured that no part of the meat dried out, because the fat and the meat juices ran over the surface as the meat turned. Today's ovens dispense with the long and arduous job of turning a spit, though some ovens or grills have electrically operated spits, rôtisseries, built into them.

In modern well-insulated and thermostatically controlled ovens, even without rôtisseries, roasts need little attention other than occasional basting to prevent the upper part of the meat from drying out and to enhance their flavour. If the meat has a top layer of fat, basting may not even be necessary. Once the meat is roasted, a simple pan gravy (see **Sauces**, *Savoury, Gravy*, page 592) can be made with the meat juices that collect in the roasting pan during roasting. By skimming off the fat and boiling up with a little stock and/or wine the gravy can be made while the meat 'rests' before carving.

Roasting is mostly used to cook tender joints of meat where the heat will take a relatively long time to reach the centre. The meat may be placed in a very hot oven to initiate the browning process for a short period of time (see *Browning*, above). The oven temperature is then lowered, to ensure that the meat does not dry out or cook too quickly.

Both the cooking time and the roasting temperature are determined by the amount of connective tissue in a cut of meat. A rib roast (see **Beef**, page 357) is a tender cut of meat with very little connective tissue and is roasted for a relatively short period of time. Cheaper cuts of meat, such as chump or rump (see **Beef**, page 357) containing coarser meat fibres and more connective tissue are roasted at a lower temperature. Slow-roasted meat has a tendency to dry out due to the prolonged cooking time and is often moister if pot-roasted (see *Slow-cooking Methods*, below) with a little liquid to retain moisture.

Roasting Meat: Points to Remember

- Bones are good conductors of heat and will transfer heat into the centre of a joint. This should be taken into account when calculating the roasting time as meat on the bone will cook more quickly.
- Lean joints should be basted with fat during roasting to help preserve the meat's moisture as well as form a crisp, browned crust. Alternatively, a layer of pork fat or bacon can be tied around the joint to protect the lean meat beneath, a technique known as barding.
- Stuffed meats should be cooked at around 180°C | 350°F | gas mark 4, giving the stuffed joint long enough to cook through without drying out but not long enough to enable bacteria in the stuffing to flourish.

Method for Roasting Meat

1 Weigh the joint and establish the length of cooking time.
2 Preheat the oven (electric ovens take longer to heat up than gas ovens).
3 Prepare the joint for roasting (see individual types of meat).
4 Heat some dripping in a roasting pan and if the joint is lean, brown it over direct heat so that it is well coloured. Pork and lamb rarely need this but many cuts of beef and veal do.
5 Place the joint in the pan, on a grid if you have one available, as this aids the circulation of hot air and prevents the meat from frying in its own fat.

6 Roast for the time calculated, checking the meat halfway through. Turn it over if it is well browned on top and baste with the melted fat and juices that have collected in the bottom of the pan.

7 When the joint of meat is cooked (see *Testing Roast Meat for Doneness*, below), stand the roast on a warm serving platter and cover loosely with foil. Do not leave it in a warm oven or it will continue to cook.

Roasting Times

A long thin piece of meat weighing 2.3 kg | 5 lb will take less time to cook than a round piece of the same weight, so the times given below are intended only as a guide. The essential point is that meat must reach an internal temperature of 60°C | 140°F to be rare, 70°C | 160°F to be medium pink and 80°C | 175°F to be well done. A joint containing bone will cook more quickly than a boneless joint because the bones conduct the heat.

A meat thermometer inserted into the thickest part of the meat and left there during cooking eliminates guesswork. Do not let the thermometer touch the bone. When using a fan (convection) oven, reduce cooking times by 10 per cent or lower the oven temperature by 10°C | 25°F.

A joint needs to be roasted for a short time at a high temperature to brown the meat for colour and flavour. Then turn the oven down to a lower temperature for the remainder of the roasting time to avoid excessive shrinkage. For specific roasting times see relevant meat sections, **Beef**, page 358, **Pork**, page 398, **Veal**, page 375 and **Lamb**, page 382.

Testing Roast Meat for Doneness

The skewer test: This is a crude but reliable alternative to using a meat thermometer to test the doneness of larger joints of meat.

1 Insert a skewer into the centre of the thickest part of the joint.

2 Leave it there for 10 seconds.

3 Draw the skewer out of the meat and rest the tip of the skewer on the sensitive skin on the inside of your wrist.

- If the skewer is cool, the meat is still uncooked and requires more cooking.
- If the skewer is very warm but bearable on the skin, the meat is cooked rare.
- If the skewer is unbearably hot and cannot be held on the skin for a fraction of a second, the meat is well done.

Resting Roast Meat

Let the roast sit on a warmed serving platter after removing it from the oven. Unless the meat will be standing for longer than 30 minutes, it is not necessary to cover it or place it in in a warming oven. If it is going to stand for longer than

30 minutes, cover it loosely with foil or place in a warming oven no higher than 70°C|150°F|gas mark $\frac{1}{4}$.

The resting time:

- allows intense heat present in the outer layers of meat to penetrate the centre of the joint to cook it more evenly.
- allows the hot juices to redistribute themselves more evenly throughout the joint. In a large roast, the heat drives the juices into the centre, and resting it allows these juices some time to seep back into the outer layers, giving an even colour and juiciness throughout.
- allows the muscle fibres to relax, making the meat easier to carve and more tender to eat.

Roasting Meat: What has gone wrong when...

The meat is underbrowned.

- The initial oven temperature was too low for the surface of the meat to brown. Leaner joints should be browned first by shallow-frying before roasting in the oven.
- The meat was not cooked long enough at the initial higher roasting temperature.

The meat has cooked more quickly than expected.

- Either the oven temperature is too hot or the joint is long and thin and/or is on the bone.

The meat is dry.

- The joint was not basted regularly during roasting. Lean cuts must be basted very regularly or protected by tying on a layer of fat.
- The meat is overcooked.

The meat is tough.

- The meat is overcooked. Alternatively, a cheaper cut has been roasted that would have been better pot-roasted.

Frying

Frying, sometimes referred to as 'shallow-frying', and sautéing are both quick cooking methods suitable for small, not too thick, tender pieces of meat cut into steaks, strips, dice and medallions. The difference between the two methods is the amount of fat used in cooking. For sautéing, an almost dry pan with no more than 1 tablespoon of fat is used; for frying, food is cooked in up to 6 mm|$\frac{1}{4}$ in of fat.

When meat is fried, some of the fat in which it was cooked is eaten with it. For this reason the flavour of the fat – or lack of it – will affect the taste of the dish. Olive oil, butter, bacon dripping, lard and beef dripping all give distinctive flavour to fried foods, while corn, safflower, peanut and most other vegetable oils have little or no flavour.

When choosing fat for frying, remember some fats can be heated to much higher temperatures than others before they break down and start to burn. For example, clarified butter, which is butter with all its milk solids removed (see *Dairy Products*, *Butter*, page 204), can be heated to higher temperatures than whole butter. Pure bacon dripping, lard, beef dripping and solid frying fat can withstand more heat than margarine, butter or vegetable oil.

It is unwise to fry meat in pure butter unless the meat is sliced very thinly, is extremely tender, for example veal escalopes (see *Veal*, page 378) or requires little cooking, as butter contains milk proteins that are likely to burn before thicker slices of meat are cooked. A little butter, however, is often added to vegetable oil for frying, to enrich its flavour. The oil and butter mixture is sufficiently hot for frying when the butter begins to foam. Extra virgin olive oil is not suitable for frying as it has a low smoke point and its characteristic flavour is lost when it is heated to high temperatures.

Frying and Browning: Points to Remember

- Fry in an uncovered wide pan. A lid traps the steam, causing the meat to stew or steam rather than fry crisply.
- Preheat the fat. If the fat is cool when the meat is put into it, it will not brown, will lack flavour, look unattractive and may even absorb some of the cool fat and become greasy. Before adding the meat to the pan, test the temperature of the oil with one piece of meat. If the meat sizzles, the remaining meat can be added, otherwise wait for a few moments before testing the oil temperature again. Carefully regulate the temperature of the pan to prevent the meat from overbrowning before the centre is cooked.
- If the fat begins to smoke before the meat is added, allow the pan to cool a little as the meat is likely to scorch. If the fat is smoking vigorously, remove the pan from the heat and drain the fat off into a metal container as it will taste burnt and spoil the flavour of the meat.
- Fry a little meat at a time spaced evenly over the base of the pan. Adding too much meat at once to hot fat lowers the temperature and again hinders the browning. The meat is also liable to boil in its own juices, becoming tough and unappetizing.
- When the meat is added to the hot pan, it will usually stick to the base. As the surface of the meat browns and dries, it slowly releases itself from the pan and at this point is ready to be flipped over to brown on the other side. It is important not to disturb the meat or prise it from the base of the pan while it is browning as the surface of the meat is likely to tear and the browning process will be compromised and incomplete. Only turn the meat when it is fully released.
- The presentation side of the meat should always be browned first to ensure that it browns evenly.
- The meat should be fried until it is evenly browned on all sides. Once the meat is browned, it may be transferred to a casserole for stewing or braising, to a hot oven for roasting, or the heat may be reduced to medium to complete cooking in the pan.
- Fried meat should be served as soon as possible after cooking otherwise juices will gradually seep out and the meat will toughen on standing, losing its newly fried gloss.

Sautéing

Sautéing is used mainly to brown small cubes, slices or strips of meat, often before they are added to a stew or sauce which is frequently made in the same pan (see **Beef**, *Beef Stroganoff*, page 368). Meats such as pork chops or chicken pieces may be given an initial browning and then cooked with added ingredients that will eventually form a sauce.

Method for Sautéing

1 Brown the meat all over in minimal fat. Remove from the pan and keep warm.
2 *Deglaze* the pan with a liquid such as stock, cream or wine.
3 Add the flavourings for a sauce.
4 If the initial browning has cooked the main ingredients sufficiently, reduce the sauce by rapid boiling and pour it over the dish. Garnish and serve immediately.
5 If the meat needs further cooking, return it to the pan and simmer it in the sauce until tender, then proceed as above.

Stir-frying

The meat is cut into dice, strips or thin slices and fried quickly in a small quantity of hot oil, in a Chinese wok or large frying pan over a high heat. To cook and brown the small pieces of meat evenly, they are moved about constantly with a wooden spoon or Chinese ladle until cooked through. Stir-frying is a fast cooking method and is suited to tender cuts of meat such as poultry breast meat (see **Poultry**, *Stir-fried Chicken with Cashews*, page 438), fillet of beef and pork fillet.

Grilling

Intense heat is the secret of successful grilling. Although this method requires active attention from the cook, the food cooks quickly and the charred surface gives great flavour. To produce succulent, perfectly grilled meat which is crisp brown outside and pink and juicy inside, it is absolutely essential to preheat the grill to its highest setting. It may take 10 or even 20 minutes for the grill on a good domestic cooker to come to the right temperature. Under a cooler grill, the surface of the meat will not brown, in which case it is best to fry the meat instead.

Grilling will not tenderize meat, so only tender cuts should be grilled. They should be no thicker than 5 cm | 2 in because of the high temperatures involved – any thicker and the centre of the meat will remain cold and raw when the outside is black. Unless the cut is fairly thin, once the meat browns it must be moved further away from the heat source so that the interior can cook before the surface burns. Basting with the pan juices, olive oil or butter adds flavour and gloss. Turning is necessary for even cooking and should be done halfway through the cooking time, when the first surface is attractively brown.

Grilling: Points to Remember

- Brush the meat with butter, oil or a mixture of the two to keep it moist and to speed the browning process.
- Do not salt meat in advance as salt draws out moisture. Salt immediately before grilling.
- Avoid piercing the meat, which will allow the juices to escape, by turning it during grilling with tongs or spoons, not a sharp instrument such as a fork.
- Serve immediately. Grilled meat loses moisture, dries up and toughens if kept hot for any length of time.
- The second side cooked is the presentation side.

Char-grilling

The meat is cooked quickly on a ridged cast-iron skillet heated on a hob or on a grill heated by red-hot coals. The skillet or grill rack should be heated over a strong flame, then brushed with oil before the meat is arranged on it. Char-grilled meat blackens where it touches the raised ridges on the skillet or the bars of the grill, to produce a striped effect. The blackened areas give the meat its characteristic char-grilled flavour and appearance.

Lean meat such as poultry is often marinated before char-grilling with a marinade containing oil to protect it from drying out (see *Other Methods of Tenderizing Meat*, above). Alternatively, brush the surface of the meat with oil as it cooks. Use oil with a high smoke point, such as vegetable oil. Char-grilled meat that can be served pink is best served medium-rare but pork and poultry must be cooked through.

Thin portions of poultry, such as the breasts, beef steaks, lamb cutlets and medallions of pork fillet are most suited to char-grilling as the heat can penetrate the meat quickly. Small chickens may also be char-grilled if flattened and spatchcocked (see **Poultry**, *Spatchcocked Grilled Poussin*, page 426). Larger, thicker pieces of meat may be marked on the grill (see below), then transferred to a hot oven to finish cooking.

Char-grilling

Marking Meat on a Ridged Cast-iron Griddle

Diagonal lines: To produce diagonal blackened lines on the meat, place the meat on the heated, oiled griddle at an angle of 45° and grill until it releases itself. Turn the meat over so that it lies at the same angle and cook until the meat releases from the grill, by which time it should be sufficiently cooked or ready to transfer to a hot oven to finish cooking.

Cross-hatching: To form cross-hatch markings on the meat, place it on the griddle at an angle, as above. As soon as the meat releases itself, swing the portion of meat to rest diagonally in the opposite direction at the same angle and leave long enough for the meat to be marked in a pronounced cross-hatched pattern. Turn the meat over and repeat. As the meat must remain on the grill for longer to create the markings, it is best to use this technique for thicker slices of meat such as beef steak that are less likely to overcook (see *Beef*, *Char-grilled Sirloin Steak*, page 366).

Factors Determining Grilling Time for Tender Cuts of Meat

Length of cooking time for steaks varies according to the thickness, density and fat content of the meat as well as the intensity of the heat source, whether that be the base of the pan or grill. When grilling meat, the distance of the meat from the grill will also determine the rate at which the meat browns and cooks, as will the density of the meat. Open-textured steak such as sirloin will cook faster than the same thickness and weight of closer-textured rump. Cooking a steak under the grill will also take longer than in a frying pan or griddle as the meat is not in direct contact with the heat source (see *Beef*, *Cooking Times for Sirloin and Fillet Steak*, page 366).

Testing Grilled and Fried Meat for Doneness

All grilled and fried meats should be well browned on the surface. However, the best guide to whether meat is done is its texture. Feel the meat by pressing it firmly with a finger. Rare meat feels soft, almost raw; medium-done meat is firmer, with some resilience to it, and well-done steak feels very firm (see *The test of the thumb*, below). With practice, there should be no need to cut into the meat to check if it is cooked sufficiently. Try not to cut into the meat until you are fairly sure that it is ready as with every cut juices are lost.

The test of the thumb

A less intrusive method for checking the doneness of small portions of meat is the thumb test, where the cook presses the surface of the meat with the tips of the fingers and compares the texture of the meat to that of the fleshy base of the thumb, held in turn against each finger of the same hand, to discern how well the meat is cooked. Although this method is very accurate, practice is required in order to recognize the changes in texture as the meat cooks from uncooked to rare to medium to well-done.

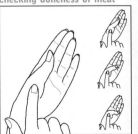

The test of the thumb for checking doneness of meat

When the thumb is relaxed the base of the thumb feels soft and flabby, like the texture of uncooked meat. When the thumb is held against the base of the index finger, the fleshy area becomes softly springy and represents the texture of rare cooked meat. If the tip of the thumb is moved to the middle finger the fleshy area becomes firmer and more like the texture of medium-rare meat. If the tip of the thumb is moved to the ring finger, the fleshy area firms a little more and feels more springy to the touch, like the texture of medium meat. Finally, on moving the thumb to touch the little finger, the fleshy area becomes firm and loses its spring, to represent the texture of well-done meat.

With practice the thumb test can reliably inform the chef of the stage a small joint or sliced portion of meat has reached in cooking without use of a meat thermometer. The thumb test is not suitable for large joints of meat as the outer layers may be quite well cooked whilst the centre may still be rare. Under these circumstances it is best to use a meat thermometer or skewer test (see *Roasting Times* and *Testing Roast Meat for Doneness*, above).

Barbecuing

This is an outdoor cooking method dating back to ancient times, whereby meat is effectively grilled or spit-roasted over burning charcoal. When grilling or roasting over burning charcoal, the embers may take as long as 2 hours to heat before they are flameless yet burn with the necessary intensity. When ready for barbecuing, charcoal glows bright red in the dark and has an ashy-grey appearance in daylight. Due to the intense cooking temperatures involved, barbecued meat will cook quickly – for example, a small lamb cutlet will cook perfectly within 2 minutes. Tender cuts of meat such as beef, pork or lamb steaks and poultry breasts are ideal for barbecuing.

To barbecue portions of meat over charcoal, first brush with oil or clarified butter to prevent them from sticking to the grill and to protect them from drying out. The grill is held in a stand above the charcoal, normally distanced from the embers so that the food can initially be held just above the heat until it is browned, then moved to a higher position to continue cooking more slowly until it is cooked through. It is very important to ensure that pork and poultry in particular are cooked thoroughly to avoid any danger of food poisoning. Small chickens may be grilled on the barbecue if they are flattened and spatchcocked beforehand (see **Poultry**, *Spatchcocked Grilled Poussin*, page 426). Meat and poultry is often marinated before barbecuing to tenderize the meat and enhance its flavour (see *Other Methods of Tenderizing Meat*, above).

Spit-roasting

Chicken, lamb, pork, kid or goat can be spit-roasted. To spit-roast meat it is important to distribute the weight of the meat evenly along the length of the spit, with the limbs tied against the body or on the spit to prevent them from catching and burning. In order to brown the surface of the meat, first brush it with oil and place the spit a short distance from the burning embers. Once an even brown crust has formed, move the meat further away from the heat so that it cooks slowly and evenly to the centre. Baste the surface of the meat periodically with oil to help protect the meat from drying out.

Slow-cooking Methods

The following slow-cooking methods are ideal for cooking tough cuts of meat because the application of heat for a prolonged period of time will cause the collagen in the meat to soften and become sticky. The moisture will help keep the meat from becoming too dry.

The tender-tough-tender principle

These methods of cooking illustrate the tender-tough-tender principle of meat cookery: that is, when meat is rare, it is tender. As it cooks the muscle fibres tighten and the meat becomes tough. With further cooking the connective tissue gelatinizes and the muscle fibres start to separate, giving the meat a tender texture.

The following methods can also be used for tender cuts of meat but cooking should be stopped when the meat is still pink, or just cooked in the case of chicken, or it is likely to become tough and dry due to lack of collagen.

Poaching or Boiling

Poaching is a method of cooking meat by immersing it in liquid, then heating the liquid until the occasional bubble rises to the surface.

Although the term boiling is sometimes used in reference to cooking meat (see **Beef**, *Boiled Silverside of Beef*, page 363), meat cooked by this method is actually poached. This way the meat cooks gently. Meat that is allowed to boil for a prolonged period will become fibrous and dry and will be very hard to slice. The meat fibres will shrink to the extent that almost all the juices in the meat will be squeezed out into the surrounding liquid. When meat is poached, most of its nutrients enrich the surrounding liquid in which it is cooked. As a result, the liquid usually forms a major part of the meal, usually as a broth served either before or with the meat.

Poaching is suited to both tender and tough cuts of meat. Following the tender-tough-tender rule, tender cuts of meat are poached very gently until just cooked to prevent them from becoming tough (see **Poultry**, *Chicken Breasts Stuffed with Grilled Red Pepper Mousseline*, page 435). However, meat containing a great deal of connective tissue is cooked in barely trembling liquid for as long as 3–4 hours, until it falls off the bone as the connective tissue is broken down. The connective tissue gelatinizes and becomes meltingly tender.

Poaching can either take place on the hob or in the oven at 150°C|300°F|gas mark 2. A ham or large piece of bacon is cooked when the meat has shrunk back from the bone or, if boneless, when it has visibly shrunk in size by about one-fifth. The rind or skin will then peel off easily and a skewer will penetrate the meat with little pressure.

Poaching Meat: What has gone wrong when...

The meat is dry and tough.
- The meat has been boiled.
- The wrong cut of meat was used.
- The meat has been overcooked.

The meat is falling apart/off the bone.
- The meat has been overcooked.

Pot-roasting

Pot-roasting is not really roasting but rather baking meat enclosed in a pot, either in the oven or over a low heat on the hob. It involves cooking meat in its own juices and might better be called a simpler version of braising. It is an old, economical method of cooking that was much used to cook tougher cuts of meat, with plenty of connective tissue, in the days before there were many domestic ovens.

Traditionally very little liquid is added to a pot-roast other than the fat needed for browning, as moisture from the meat provides most of the liquid during cooking. With poultry, a few spoons of liquid are usually added after browning.

A casserole with a tightly fitting lid creates a small oven. Steam is formed inside the pot from the moisture given off by the added liquid or by the meat itself, and this tenderizes and cooks it. If the lid does not fit tightly, the steam can escape. To make sure the lid fits tightly, cover the top of the casserole or pan with a piece of greaseproof paper and place the lid on top, jamming it down firmly. If the casserole or pan is too big, the liquid spreads over a large area and is more likely to boil away, so choose one into which the meat will fit snugly.

With a flameproof casserole, you can brown meat on the hob and pot-roast in the oven in the same vessel. Otherwise, brown the meat in a frying pan and transfer it with all the pan juices to a casserole for pot-roasting.

A traditional tip when pot-roasting is to cook the browned meat on a piece of pork rind. This adds flavour and prevents the meat from scorching. A *mirepoix* of coarsely cut vegetables, such as carrot, onion and celery, is sometimes placed under the meat for the same reason. They can be either raw or browned in the same fat as the meat, though the meat should be removed from the pan while browning the vegetables. Once cooked, they can be served with the meat or used as a base for a sauce.

Pot-roasted meat can be tenderized by marinating before cooking (see *Other Methods of Tenderizing* Meat, above) or made more succulent by larding it (see ***Veal,*** *Fricandeau of Veal*, page 377). This is especially important with lean joints. As the meat cooks, the fat partially melts, making the meat juicy and adding flavour and richness to the sauce. As long as the meat cooks slowly, the liquid in the pan is not likely to boil or, more importantly, to evaporate. This liquid becomes a richly flavoured sauce for the meat after cooking. Any vegetables cooked with the meat will help to thicken it.

Transfer the pot-roasted joint to a warmed serving dish or board to carve and remove any strings or skewers. If there is too much liquid left in the pan, simply reduce it by boiling or thicken it with *beurre manié* (see **Sauces, Savoury**, page 580).

Pot-roasting: What has gone wrong when...

The meat and pot are dry.

- The lid did not fit tightly enough, allowing the moisture to escape as steam during cooking.
- The pot may have been too big for the joint or recipe, causing juices to spread and dry up on the base of the pot.

The meat and accompanying juices look grey and unappetizing.

- The meat was not browned thoroughly and evenly before pot-roasting.

Braising

Braising, in the true sense of the word, is a method of cooking meat slowly on a *mirepoix*, a thick bed of finely diced mixed vegetables with the addition of strong stock (see **Game**, *Braised Venison*, page 471). In practice, the term braising is often confused with pot-roasting as in both methods food is cooked slowly in a pan with a tightly fitting lid. The main difference is that pot-roasted food is cooked with little, if any, liquid other than the fat used from browning the ingredients, and braising involves some liquid and at least some cut-up vegetables to add moisture to the pan, even if a true *mirepoix* is not used. A pot-roast should taste roasted and be decidedly fattier than a braise, which is closer to a stew, and depends more on juices and stocks than on fat for flavour.

Meat for braising should be fairly lean and contain a reasonable quantity of connective tissue as this method is ideal for breaking the tissue down into gelatine, which is so important for the final rich flavour and sticky texture of a braised dish. Any fat that melts into the stock should be skimmed off before serving. Poultry may be braised unless it is old and tough, when stewing or poaching are more suitable cooking methods as all the flesh, which will tend to be stringy and dry, is submerged in liquid.

The vegetables for the *mirepoix* should be browned quickly in hot fat and stirred constantly to ensure even colouring, then transferred to a heavy casserole or pan. The meat can be browned in the same fat before it is placed on top of the vegetables and stock is added. As the vegetables cook they will disintegrate, helping to thicken the stock. Making a strong, reduced, well-flavoured stock is time consuming, but is one of the key factors in good braising (see **Stocks**, *Brown Stock*, page 691).

As with pot-roasting, meat may be marinated overnight in the refrigerator and large pieces of exceptionally lean meat may be larded to ensure that they remain moist. Dry the meat well before browning it.

Braising Meat: Points to Remember

- Fry the *mirepoix* of vegetables and a few tablespoons of diced salt pork or bacon slowly in oil and butter, shaking the pan and stirring until the vegetables are evenly browned all over.
- Brown the meat on all sides and place it on top of the vegetable bed in a heavy casserole.
- Add stock to cover the meat. (If the stock is not rich enough and does not set solid with gelatine when cold, the braise will not have the correct melting, sticky texture.) Then stew, without basting, until half-cooked.
- Lift out the meat, strain the stock and discard the mirepoix, which by now will have imparted its flavour.
- Return the meat to the casserole and reduce the stock by rapid boiling until it is thick and syrupy, then pour it over the meat.
- There will no longer be enough stock to cover the meat and there is a danger, even in a covered pan, of the exposed top drying out, so turn the meat every 15 minutes and baste it with the stock. By the end of the cooking time, when the meat is tender, the stock should be so reduced as to provide a shiny coating that will not run off the meat. It will penetrate the flesh, moistening it and giving it the slightly glutinous texture of perfectly braised meat.

Stewing

A stew essentially consists of small pieces of meat that have been cooked slowly and gently in plenty of liquid. Examples of stews are *Family Beef Stew* (see **Beef**, page 362) and *Coq au Vin* (see **Poultry**, page 432). Many stews require preliminary frying of the meat, and sometimes of onions, shallots, carrots or mushrooms as well. This browning gives a richer flavour to the stew and adds colour and flavour to the sauce, which will be made using the browned sediment and dried-on juices sticking to the pan after frying. These are called brown stews. White stews, such as *Blanquette de Veau* (see **Veal**, page 379), are made without the preliminary browning and are less rich, milder in flavour and easier to digest. Both brown and white stews are served in their cooking liquid, which is usually thickened to a syrupy sauce.

Deglazing the browning pan
The principles of browning (see *Sautéing*, above) apply to the preliminary frying for a brown stew. If the sauce is not to taste insipid or be pale in colour, you must

start with a good, even colour on the meat. Deglaze the pan as often as necessary. Deglazing serves 3 essential purposes: it prevents the stuck sediment in the pan from burning; it allows the flavour of the sediment to be captured and incorporated into the sauce and it cleans the pan ready for the next batch of meat.

Due to the large quantity of liquid used to cook the meat, the accompanying sauce may be thin in flavour and texture and may need to be reduced to a syrupy consistency once the meat is tender. The cooking liquor is strained into a clean, wide pan and boiled until it is thick enough to coat the meat and other ingredients lightly.

The meat can be simmered on the hob or cooked in the oven at 150°C | 300° | gas mark 2 until tender. If the meat is a tender cut, it will usually be done within 1 hour, such as *Chicken Sauté Normande* (see **Poultry**, page 433). If a tougher cut is stewed it will need at least 1½ hours if not 2–3 hours until it becomes tender, such as *Lamb Daube* (see **Lamb**, page 386).

Stewing: What has gone wrong when...

The meat is tough.
- The stew has not been cooked for long enough.
- The stew has been allowed to boil.

The meat is dry.
- The stew has been allowed to boil.
- A cut of meat without much connective tissue or marbled fat was used.

Beef

Beef is a term for the meat of cattle. Most of the beef we eat comes from bullocks, castrated male cattle. These animals, known as beef cattle, have a high proportion of muscle and a relatively low proportion of fat. Most beef comes from animals slaughtered at 16–24 months old.

Beef cuts

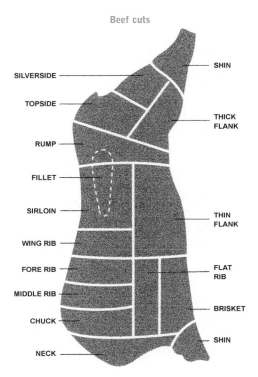

Cuts of Beef

Cut	Best cooking method	Recipe reference
Neck	Stewing Braising	*Family Beef Stew* (page 362)
Chuck/Middle rib	Stewing Braising Pies	*Family Beef Stew* (page 362) *Steak and Mushroom Pie* (page 369) (see also **Steaming**, *Steak and Kidney Pudding*, page 676)

Cuts of Beef—*contd*

Cut	Best cooking method	Recipe reference
Rump steaks	Grilling	Grilled steaks
Sirloin	Roasting	*English Roast Beef* (page 359)
Fore rib/Wing rib	Roasting	*English Roast Beef* (page 359)
Fillet	Roasting	*Fillet of Boeuf en Croûte* (page 360)
	Frying	*Fried Fillet Steak* (page 367)
	Sautéing	*Beef Stroganoff* (page 368)
	Grilling	*Grilled Fillet Steak* (page 366)
Topside/Silverside	Pot-roasting	*Pot au Feu* (page 664)
	Stewing	*Family Beef Stew* (page 362)
	Braising	*Boiled Silverside* (page 363)
Brisket/Thick flank	Pot-roasting	
	Stewing	*Family Beef Stew* (page 362)
	Braising	*Boiled Silverside* (page 363)
	Pies	*Steak and Mushroom Pie* (page 369)
Shin/Thin flank	Stewing	*Family Beef Stew* (page 362)
	Pies	*Steak and Mushroom Pie* (page 369)

Choosing Beef

- Choose deep or dull red meat rather than a bright orange red (see **Meat,** *The Colour of Meat,* page 335). The dull colour suggests that the meat has been hung for a sufficient time to tenderize it. This is difficult in the supermarket because managers assume that their customers want 'bright' meat so there is much use of clever lighting and oxygen-flushed packaging to prolong the red pigment myoglobin's bright red colour.
- The meat should have a slightly moist, shiny appearance.
- The meat should be firm and springy to the touch and have a sweet, light scent.
- Fat should be a pale creamy colour and firm in texture. Tender cuts will be even more succulent, when cooked, if they contain a fine network of fat running through the meat, known as 'marbling'.
- Bones should be pink, sometimes with a blue tinge, and shiny to indicate a young animal.
- There should be few tough lines of the connective tissue known as gristle. A strip of gristle running between the fat and lean layers usually indicates an old animal. (see **Meat,** *Factors Affecting the Tenderness of Meat,* page 338).

Storing Beef

See **Meat**, *Storing Meat* (page 336).

Methods of Cooking Beef

Roasting

Beef is generally roasted at a high oven temperature for 20 minutes to brown the meat or it may be browned in fat on the hob before being transferred to the oven. Whichever the method of browning, calculate the cooking time after the browning has been done, using the *Beef Roasting* Table, below. Roast beef should be served pink and a little bloody to retain its tender succulence.

The best cuts of beef for roasting
Allow 225 g|8 oz of meat on the bone per person; 170 g|6 oz off the bone.

Sirloin: The most expensive roasting joint, sold on the bone or boned and rolled. It is sometimes sold with the fillet attached and this can be cut off and served separately.

Fore rib: One of the larger roasting joints, sold on the bone or boned and rolled.

Wing rib: A large cut close to the sirloin and fillet and one of the most expensive joints of beef as it is the most tender end of the rib. It feeds a large number of people.

Fillet: One of the most expensive cuts of beef as it is extremely tender and requires little preparation before cooking. A whole fillet can be roasted on its own or encased in puff pastry and baked to make *Fillet of Boeuf en Croûte* (see below).

Beef Roasting Table

Meat	Temperature			Cooking time
	°C	°F	Gas mark	per kg/per lb
Brown	220°	425°	7	20 mins+
Rare	160°	325°	3	35 mins|15 mins
Medium	160°	325°	3	45 mins|20 mins
Well done	190°	375°	5	55 mins|25 mins

English Roast Beef

Roast beef is traditionally served with the following:

- Horseradish Sauce
- Gravy: see **Sauces, Savoury** (page 592)
- Yorkshire Pudding: see **Batters** (page 114)
- Roast Potatoes: see **Potatoes** (page 544)

SERVES 10

2.3 kg | 5 lb sirloin or rib roast of beef

a little dry English mustard

salt and freshly ground black pepper

1 Weigh the beef and calculate the cooking according to the *Beef Roasting Table*, above.
2 Preheat the oven to 220°C | 425°F | gas mark 7.
3 Season the beef with a little mustard, salt and plenty of pepper, then place in a roasting pan. Do not season the meat in the tin as this could result in over-seasoned gravy.
4 Roast for 20 minutes to brown the surface of the meat.
5 Turn the oven temperature down to 160°C | 325°F | gas mark 3 and roast for the calculated cooking time.
6 Allow the meat to rest for 20 minutes before carving (see below) to allow the muscle fibres to relax and absorb some of the juices.

NOTE: The beef may simply be served with 'God's gravy', the juices that will run from the meat before and during carving. If thickened gravy is required in addition, see **Sauces, Savoury**, *Gravy* (page 592).

Carving a Large Forerib of Beef

Carving a large forerib of beef

1 Place the meat on its side and make a 5 cm | 2 in cut along the length of the rib.
2 Stand the meat up, rib-side down. Carve several slices and place on a warmed platter.
3 Turn the rib back on its side and make a second 5 cm | 2 in cut along the length of the rib and carve as above.

Carving a small fore rib of beef

1 Cut between the bone and the meat to remove the bone.
2 Place the meat on its side and cut across the width into shorter vertical slices.

Carving a small forerib of beef

Carving a sirloin on the bone

As for *Carving a Large Forerib of Beef*, above.

Roasting fillet of beef

As the fillet is so lean, it should be served pink or rare to ensure that it remains succulent and tender.

Fillet of Boeuf en Croûte

SERVES 8–10

1.8 kg | 4 lb piece of fillet from the thicker central section

freshly ground black pepper

Worcestershire sauce (optional)

30 g | 1 oz beef dripping or 1 tablespoon oil

340 g | 12 oz flour quantity Puff Pastry (see *Pastry*, *Layered Pastries*, page 518)

110 g | 4 oz flat mushrooms, very finely chopped

30 g | 1 oz butter

110 g | 4 oz Chicken Liver Pâté (see *Offal*, page 710)

beaten egg, to glaze

1 Preheat the oven to 230°C | 450°F | gas mark 8.

2 Skin and trim the fillet and season well with pepper and Worcestershire sauce, if using. Heat the dripping or oil in a roasting pan and when hot add the meat and brown on all sides. Roast for 20 minutes.

3 Remove the fillet from the roasting pan and allow to cool.

4 Take one third of the pastry and roll it on a floured board until it is a little more than the length and breadth of the fillet. Place it on a damp baking sheet, prick all over with a fork and bake in the oven for about 20 minutes, until golden-brown. Place the pastry on a wire rack and leave to cool. Do not turn the oven off.

5 Fry the mushrooms quickly in the butter in a frying pan. Place the pastry base on to a baking sheet. Mix the mushrooms with the pâté and spread the mixture over the cooked pastry base. Place the cold fillet on top of this and with a sharp knife, cut away any pastry that is not covered by the fillet.

6 Roll the remaining pastry on a floured board into a 'blanket' large enough to cover the fillet easily. Lift up the 'blanket' and lay it gently over the fillet. Using a sharp knife, cut off the corners of the 'blanket' and reserve these trimmings.

Encasing boeuf en croûte with pastry

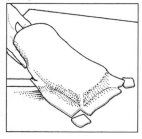

7 Lift one length of the 'blanket' and brush the underside with beaten egg. Using a palette knife, lift the base and tuck the 'blanket' neatly underneath it. Repeat with the other 3 sides.

8 Shape the pastry trimmings into leaves. Brush the pastry-covered fillet with beaten egg. Decorate with the pastry leaves and brush again with beaten egg. Refrigerate until the pastry is firm to the touch.

9 Bake the fillet in the preheated oven for 20 minutes, or until the pastry is golden brown and shiny. This recipe assumes that rare beef is desired, but longer cooking in the first instance, without the pastry, will ensure a more well-done fillet. For medium beef, cook for a further 10 minutes and for well-done beef a further 15 minutes. To check that the beef is cooked, insert a skewer through the pastry into the centre of the meat and leave there for 10 seconds or so, then withdraw it. If the skewer is hot to the touch, the meat is done (see *Meat*, *Testing Roast Meat for Doneness*, *Skewer Test*, page 344).

10 Serve hot or cold. If served hot, the fillet should be carved at the table or the juices will be lost and the meat may become grey and unappetizing in appearance.

NOTE: The dish may be prepared in advance up to the final baking. It should be left ready for the oven on the baking sheet, loosely covered with cling film or kitchen foil to prevent the egg glaze from sticking. If prepared in advance, it is important that the mushrooms and pâté should be completely cold before mixing together and that the meat should be cold before covering with the pastry.

Boeuf en Croûte: What has gone wrong when...

The meat is dry.
- The fillet may have been fried for too long before roasting. Fry in very hot oil to brown its surface as quickly as possible to avoid overcooking.
- The meat was roasted for too long and is overcooked.

The pastry base is soggy.
- The pastry base was undercooked. Ensure the bottom of the base is crisp and an even golden-brown colour before removing from the oven.
- The pastry base was too thick.

The pastry blanket melted before it started to bake.
- The fillet may still have been warm when the pastry was laid over it.
- The oven was not heated to the correct temperature when the Boeuf en Croûte was placed in it.

Stewing

Stewing is a moist cooking method suitable for tougher cuts of meat. The tougher cuts come mainly from the forequarter as this area of the animal is subjected to more rigorous activity because the muscles are involved in supporting the animal's head and much of its weight. These cuts include:

- Topside
- Silverside
- Brisket
- Thick flank
- Chuck
- Shin
- Neck

Before making a stew, read **Meat,** *Frying and Browning: Points to Remember* (page 346), and *Deglazing the browning pan* (page 354).

Preparing meat for stewing
Remove the gristle but not all the fat from the meat as it will add moisture and flavour. Cut the meat into cubes no smaller than 3.5 cm | 1 ½ in. Pieces that are cut too small will fall apart into shreds or become dry and tough during prolonged cooking.

Family Beef Stew

SERVES 4

675 g | 1½ lb chuck steak, trimmed
dripping or oil
2 mild onions, sliced
3 medium carrots, cubed
1 medium turnip, cubed
570 ml | 1 pint Brown Stock (see **Stocks**, page 692)

salt and freshly ground black pepper
1 bay leaf
2 parsley stalks
a pinch of chopped fresh thyme
30 g | 1 oz pearl barley

1 Preheat the oven to 150°C | 300°F | gas mark 2.

2 Remove any gristle and excess fat from the meat and cut it into 4 cm | 1½ in cubes.

3 Melt a little of the dripping or oil in a sauté pan. Brown the beef cubes on all sides, a few at a time, and transfer to a flameproof casserole. After browning each batch of meat, deglaze the pan with a little stock, scraping the sediment from the bottom of the pan. Reserve this liquid (*déglaçage*), heat a little more dripping or oil and continue browning the remaining meat until all is transferred to the casserole dish. Taste the *déglaçage*. If it does not taste burnt add it to the casserole dish.

4 Fry the onions, carrots and turnip in the pan until golden-brown and place them in the casserole dish.

5 Pour the stock into the pan and bring to the boil, scraping any remaining sediment from the bottom. Stir in the seasoning, bay leaf, parsley, thyme and barley and pour on to the meat. Bring to the simmer for 2 minutes.

6 Cover the casserole and cook in the oven for 2–2½ hours or until the meat is tender enough to cut with a fork. Skim off any excess fat.

NOTE: The flavour of the stew improves if kept for a day before eating. The barley also swells up even more to thicken the sauce. The stew may also be frozen for up to 6 months.

Stewing: What has gone wrong when...

The stew looks grey and unappetizing.

- The ingredients were insufficiently browned before the liquid was added. Each surface of sliced or diced meat and vegetables should be evenly and thoroughly browned before adding the liquid. Also make sure that the *déglaçage* from the base of the pan is used in the stew to add its colour and flavour.

The stew looks very dark and tastes burnt.

- The ingredients were overbrowned or the sediment collecting on the base of the pan during browning was not deglazed regularly enough, causing it to burn and taint the flavour of the finished dish.

The sauce is thin in flavour and consistency.

- The sauce was not reduced to a syrupy consistency and seasoned sufficiently before serving the stew.

The stew is fatty.

- The fat that melts into the cooking liquor was not skimmed off before serving or reducing the sauce to a syrupy consistency.

The meat has collapsed into shreds.

- The meat was stewed for too long. Cook the meat until it is tender and the fibres are just beginning to fall apart.
- The meat may have been cut too small.

The meat is tough.

- The meat requires more cooking slowly at a low temperature.

Boiling

When meat is described as 'boiled', it is in fact immersed in liquid and simmered gently. Boiling would cause the meat to overcook and fall apart.

This recipe uses salt beef, beef that has been cured in salt. It is sometimes called corned beef in America.

Boiled Silverside

SERVES 6

1.35 kg|3 lb piece of salt silverside or brisket	4 large carrots, quartered
1 bouquet garni (1 bay leaf, 2 parsley stalks, 6	2 turnips, quartered
peppercorns, 1 small onion, tied in muslin)	12 dumplings (see, **Steaming**, page 679)
6 medium onions	chopped fresh parsley, to garnish

1 Soak the beef in cold unsalted water for about 3 hours to soften the meat.
2 Put the beef into a large saucepan of fresh unsalted water and bring slowly to the boil, skimming as the scum rises to the surface.
3 When the water is simmering, add the bouquet garni and half cover the pan to prevent the water from evaporating too quickly but avoid boiling. Simmer for 3 hours. Remove the bouquet garni and skim off any fat.
4 Now add the vegetables and simmer for a further 1 hour, or until the meat and vegetables are tender.
5 Meanwhile, cook the dumplings: if there is room in the saucepan, float them in the liquid 20 minutes before the end of the cooking time. If not, remove some of the stock from the pan (topping up with boiling water if necessary) and simmer the dumplings in a separate saucepan.

6 Place the beef on a large warmed serving dish. Surround it with the vegetables and the dumplings. Cover and keep warm.

7 Taste the stock. If weak-flavoured, reduce by rapid boiling to concentrate the flavours. Skim if necessary.

8 Ladle a cupful or so of hot liquid over the meat and vegetables, sprinkle with parsley and serve immediately. Serve more of the hot liquid separately in a warmed sauce-boat.

NOTE: Dumplings are always a little soggy when cooked on the hob. For a drier version, they can be baked in the oven.

Grilling

Tender beef, containing very little connective tissue, is mainly cut from the hind quarter. These include the fillet, sirloin, rump, topside and rib of beef, all of which are suitable for roasting or slicing into steaks for grilling or frying.

Steaks are slices of meat of varying thickness cut from the fillet, rump and sirloin. They are lean, contain very little connective tissue or fat and must therefore be cooked quickly by grilling or pan-frying to retain their moist, tender texture. Before cooking, any membranes or excess fat around the edge should be trimmed away.

Timings and cookery methods for different cuts of meat are given below. It is very useful, however, to be familiar with the Test of the Thumb (see *Meat, Testing*, page 349) when cooking a steak. Cooking times will vary depending on the thickness of the meat, the temperature of the meat and the temperature of the grill or pan.

- 'Blue' steak will be dark red and just hot in the centre.
- In rare steak the muscle fibres will be beginning to set, dark red and the juices starting to run freely.
- Medium-rare steak will be a deep pink and well set with fewer free-flowing juices.
- Medium steak is pale pink in the centre with very little free-flowing juice.
- In well-done steak the pink hue will have nearly disappeared to leave firmly set meat, brownish-grey in colour but still moist.

Allow a steak to stand for 5–10 minutes after cooking to allow the muscle fibres to relax and absorb some of the juices. The meat can be covered with foil to help keep it warm but it is best not to place it in a warming oven or it is likely to continue cooking.

Fillet steak

Fillet of beef is a long, lean, boneless cut of meat that runs along the back of the animal. It is subjected to very little activity and therefore contains almost no connective tissue, is finely grained, very lean and extremely tender. It is often roasted whole (see *Fillet of Boeuf en Crôute*, above) or sliced either diagonally or across into steaks of varying thickness for grilling or frying.

Due to the tenderness of the meat, the fillet, and steaks cut from it, should be cooked rare to medium-rare to prevent the meat from drying out. When choosing fillet steak for grilling, look for meat finely flecked with fat as this will help to keep the steak moist. Fillet beef may also be cut across the grain, into strips no thicker than a finger, for sautéing in hot fat to make dishes such as *Beef Stroganoff* (see also *Meat, Sautéing*, page 347).

Steaks cut from the fillet:

- **Tournedos**, cut into neat 2.5 cm $|$ 1 in slices across the tail of the trimmed fillet, weighing 100–125 g $|$ 3–4 oz.
- **Chateaubriand**, cut from the thick end or centre of the fillet into a neat piece serving 2–3 people, weighing approximately 225 g $|$ 8 oz. Due to its size, it may be grilled, spit- or oven-roasted (see *Meat, Browning*, page 343, and *Roasting*, page 342), or pan-fried to brown then roasted in the oven to finish cooking.
- **Medallions** are thin, neat slices of 1 cm $|$ ½ in cut diagonally across the ends of the fillet or across the thicker centre. As they are relatively thin they must be fried quickly in hot fat (see *Meat, Frying*, page 345).

Sirloin steak

Sirloin steak is cut from the upper side of the true sirloin, wing rib and fore rib.

- **Entrecote** is the eye of the sirloin, cut into individual steaks.
- **T-bone steaks** include the bone. The sirloin is on one side and the fillet on the other. This is the largest steak and can serve 2 people.
- **Porterhouse** is a double sized T-bone cut from the wing rib.

Rump steak

These are large, thick slices, about 2 cm $|$ ¾ in, cut across the grain of the rump. For individual servings the steaks are cut into 2–3 smaller neat pieces. Minute steaks are large, thin steaks made by flattening an individual portion of rump steak, and are best fried quickly in hot fat (see *Meat, Frying*, page 345). Rump steak is thinly marbled with fat, which gives it a moist, succulent texture and an excellent flavour when grilled or pan-fried. It is probably the most flavourful of the steaks but is tougher than sirloin or fillet steak. Cook as for sirloin.

Grilled Fillet Steak

The instructions in it is also apply to rump and sirloin steak (see cooking times for sirloin steak below).

SERVES 4

4 fillet steaks

salt and freshly ground black pepper

butter, melted

1 Preheat the grill to its highest setting. Do not start cooking until it the maximum temperature is reached. Brush the grill rack and the steaks with a little melted butter.
2 Season the steaks with pepper. Sprinkle lightly with salt just before cooking to prevent loss of juices from the surface of the meat.
3 Grill the steak quickly on both sides, approximately 2 in | 5 cm from the grill. For a 'blue' or rare steak, keep the heat fierce for the whole cooking time. For well-done steaks, lower the temperature to medium after the initial good browning (see *Grilling times*, below).
4 Allow the meat to stand for 5 minutes before serving to allow the fibres to reabsorb the free-running juices.

NOTE: Serve each steak topped with a slice of *Maître d'Hôtel Butter* (see **Dairy Products**, *Butter*, page 203) or *Béarnaise Sauce* (see **Sauces, Savoury**, page 605).

Grilling times for fillet steaks approximately 2.5 cm | 1 in thick

These suggestions for cooking times, assuming a good, hot grill, should be regarded as guidelines only.

Blue steak:	$2\frac{1}{4}$ mins per side
Rare steak:	$3\frac{1}{4}$ mins per side
Medium-rare steak:	$4\frac{1}{4}$ mins per side
Medium steak:	5 mins per side

Grilling times for sirloin steaks approximately 2 cm | $\frac{3}{4}$ in thick

Sirloin steak is cut slightly thinner than fillet and therefore requires less grilling time.

Blue steak:	$1\frac{1}{4}$ mins per side
Rare steak:	$1\frac{3}{4}$ mins per side
Medium-rare steak:	$2\frac{1}{4}$ mins per side
Medium steak:	$2\frac{3}{4}$ mins per side

Frying

Fried Fillet Steak

The instructions in this also apply to rump and sirloin steak (see *Frying times*, below). Steaks can be fried in a griddle pan following the instructions below. See **Meat**, *Marking meat on a ridged cast-iron griddle* (page 348) for instructions on marking with cross-hatching.

SERVES 4

4 fillet steaks, cut 2.5 cm|1 in thick, or 4 sirloin steaks, cut 2 cm|¾ in thick

salt and freshly ground black pepper

oil or dripping, for frying

1 Season the steaks with pepper. Sprinkle lightly with salt just before cooking.
2 Brush a frying pan with a little oil or dripping and place over a medium heat until it is hot.
3 Cook the steaks on both sides until they are evenly browned. For a blue or rare steak, keep the heat fierce for the whole cooking time. For better-done steaks, lower the temperature to medium after the initial browning.

NOTE: Serve each steak topped with a slice of *Maître d'Hôtel Butter* (see **Dairy Products,** *Butter*, page 203) or *Béarnaise Sauce* (see **Sauces**, **Savoury**, page 605).

Frying times for fillet steak approximately 2.5 cm|1 in thick

The suggestions for cooking times, assuming a good hot pan, should be regarded as guidelines only.

Blue steak:	1½ mins per side
Rare steak:	2¼ mins per side
Medium-rare steak:	3¼ mins per side
Medium steak:	4½ mins per side

Frying times for sirloin steak approximately 2 cm|¾ in thick

Sirloin steak is cut slightly thinner than fillet and therefore requires less frying time.

Blue steak:	1 min per side
Rare steak:	1½ mins per side
Medium-rare steak:	2 mins per side
Medium steak:	2¼ mins per side

Beef Stroganoff

The instructions given below for sautéing strips of fillet beef also apply to all other tender cuts of meat cut into small pieces and cooked by the same method.

The essence of a perfect Beef Stroganoff is the speed at which the beef strips are cooked. If using tougher meat, however, the beef must be stewed gently (after adding the mushrooms and stock) until tender. This alternative can be very good.

SERVES 4

450 g|1 lb fillet of beef	150 ml|¼ pint Brown Stock (see **Stocks**, page 692)
55 g|2 oz butter	1 tablespoon oil
1 medium onion, thinly sliced	2 tablespoons brandy
225 g|8 oz mushrooms, thinly sliced	4 tablespoons crème fraîche
100 ml|3½ fl oz dry white wine	salt and freshly ground black pepper

1 Cut the beef into 5 cm\|2 in strips, the thickness of a finger.

2 Melt half the butter in a frying pan and cook the onion over a low heat until soft and transparent. Add the mushrooms and toss over the heat for 1 minute. Add the wine and stock. Boil rapidly to reduce to about 2 tablespoons. Stir well, then pour into a bowl, scraping the pan.

3 Now heat the oil and the remaining butter in the pan. Once the fat is sufficiently hot to cause a strip of beef to sizzle vigorously, add some of the beef strips. Do not overcrowd the pan. Fry over a high heat to brown the surface without overcooking the middle. Remove the strips to a plate as they are browned, then reduce the heat.

4 Pour the brandy into the hot pan. Set it alight. As soon as the flames subside, pour in the mushroom and stock mixture. Return the beef strips to the pan and stir in half the crème fraîche. Season the sauce to taste with salt and pepper. If the sauce is too thin, remove the beef strips and boil rapidly to reduce to a syrupy consistency.

5 Reheat, then tip into a warmed serving dish and fork the remaining crème fraîche in roughly. If the crème fraîche is very thick, it can be diluted with a little water.

Frying and Sautéing Beef: What has gone wrong when...

The meat starts to boil, rather than fry, when added to the pan.

- The pan and oil are not hot enough when the meat is added, causing it to stew slowly as the meat shrinks and loses most of its juices.
- Too much meat has been added to the pan at one time, causing the pan to cool down.

The meat is sticking and catching to the bottom of the pan.

- The pan is too dry. Add more oil or fat.
- The meat was turned over too soon.

The fat appears to be smoking and burning before the meat is cooked.
- You are using fat, probably whole butter, that burns when subjected to high temperatures for more than a few minutes. Only use whole butter to fry very thin, tender cuts of meat.
- The temperature of the pan is too high.

The surface of the meat is overbrowned before the centre is cooked.
- The pan and oil are too hot. Remove the pan from the heat briefly to allow it to cool a little before adding more meat. If the oil or fat is smoking, clean the pan and start again as it may taint the flavour of the fried food.

The meat looks greasy and underbrowned.
- The meat was added to the pan when the oil was still too cool.

The meat has become tough and dry.
- The meat is overcooked. Once the surface of the meat is evenly browned, turn the heat down to medium so that the centre of the meat can cook more slowly and gently.

The base of the pan has become sticky and blackened.
- Between frying batches of meat, it is important to *deglaze* the bottom of the pan with liquid to loosen fragments of meat stuck to the base of the pan before they catch. This is especially important if the browned sediment is required as a basis for a sauce. Once the sediment has blackened it must be discarded as it may taint the flavour of the finished dish. A blackened pan base may also interfere with the browning abilities of remaining batches of meat.

Making Pies with Beef

The beef is prepared for cooking and browned in the same way as stewing beef. It is then cooked very gently and slowly for at least 2 hours to break down the connective tissue before the pie is assembled. Once the pie is made it is cooked for a further 30 minutes to cook the pastry and to tenderize the meat further.

Steak and Mushroom Pie

SERVES 4

675 g|1½ lb chuck steak
oil or dripping, for frying
1 onion, finely chopped
225 g|8 oz brown mushrooms
30 g|1 oz plain flour
425 ml|¾ pint Brown Stock (see **Stocks**, page 692)

salt and freshly ground black pepper
1 tablespoon chopped fresh parsley
225 g|8 oz flour quantity Rough Puff
 Pastry (see **Pastry,** *Layered Pastries,*
 page 518)
beaten egg, to glaze

1 Trim away the excess fat from the steak and cut the meat into 2.5 cm|1 in cubes.
2 Heat the oil or dripping in a frying pan and fry a few beef cubes at a time until browned all over, putting them into a flameproof casserole as they are done. Fry the onion in the same fat until soft and brown. Add the mushrooms and cook for 5 minutes until soft.

3 Stir in the flour and cook for 1 minute. Gradually add the stock, stirring continuously and scraping any sediment from the bottom of the pan. Bring to the boil, then simmer for 1 minute. Pour over the meat in the casserole, season with salt and pepper and simmer slowly until the meat is tender (about 2 hours). Add the parsley.

4 If the sauce is too greasy, skim off the fat, and if it is too thin, transfer the meat to a pie dish and boil the sauce rapidly until syrupy. Pour the sauce over the meat and leave until completely cold.

5 Preheat the oven to 200°C|400°F|gas mark 6.

6 Roll the pastry out 3 mm|⅛ in thick. Cut a long strip just wider than the rim of the pie dish, brush the lip of the dish with water and press down the strip.

7 Brush the strip with water and lay over the sheet of pastry. Press it down firmly. Cut away any excess pastry.

8 Cut a 1 cm|½ in hole in the centre of the pie-top, to allow the escape of steam, and cover with a leaf-shaped piece of pastry.

9 Decorate the top of the pie with more pastry leaves. Brush all over with egg. Refrigerate until the pastry is firm.

10 Bake in the oven for 30 minutes, or until the pastry is well risen and golden-brown.

Cooking Mince

Mince can be made at home by using a mincer or by chopping the meat with 2 knives (see *Knife Skills*, page 69). Beef mince is made from the tougher cuts of meat such as silverside or stewing beef from the neck. The meat should be reasonably lean or have most of the fat removed before being minced. Although mincing physically breaks down the meat fibres and connective tissue, minced meat requires at least 45 minutes, cooking to tenderize it. Beef mince is used to make Shepherd's *Pie* (see below), meat sauces such as Bolognese sauce, or packed together to make beef burgers or *Meatballs* (see below).

Minced meat carries a high risk of food poisoning, in particular *E. coli*. This is because the many surfaces on the mince can harbour the bacteria, which thrives at low temperatures. To avoid possible food poisoning, always cook minced beef until well done. The interior of a burger should be grey and have reached a temperature of 72°C|160°F. If, however, you mince your own prime cuts of beef, you can then have a rare burger.

The best beef cuts for mince
- Blade (fairly lean)
- Skirt
- Shin
- Silverside
- Neck

Shepherd's Pie

SERVES 4–5

675 g | 1½ lb minced beef

oil, for frying

1 onion, finely chopped

1 carrot, finely chopped

1 stick of celery, finely chopped

2 teaspoons plain flour

570 ml | 1 pint Brown Stock (see **Stock**, page 692)

1 bay leaf

1 teaspoon Worcestershire sauce (optional)

1 teaspoon tomato purée

salt and freshly ground black pepper

For the topping

900 g | 2 lb mashed potato (see *Potatoes*, page 545)

1 Fry half the mince in a little oil, using a large frying pan to avoid over-crowding the pan. Brown well all over, stirring periodically with a wooden spoon or spatula. Remove with a slotted spoon and place in a saucepan. Brown the remaining mince and place in the sieve. Sieve over a bowl to catch the fat.

2 Fry the onion, carrot and celery in the frying pan until just beginning to brown.

3 Add the flour to the fat in the frying pan and cook until brown.

4 Add the stock and bring slowly to the boil, stirring continuously.

5 Now add the bay leaf, Worcestershire sauce, tomato purée, salt and pepper. Mix well with the browned mince.

6 Set the saucepan over a medium heat to simmer. Cover and leave to cook for 45 minutes. Check the pan every so often and add extra water if the mixture becomes too dry.

7 Preheat the oven to 200°C | 400°F | gas mark 6.

8 Remove the bay leaf from the mince and tip the meat mixture into a pie dish, reserving some of the liquid if the mixture is very runny.

9 When slightly cooled, spread the potato over the top. If making in advance, allow the filling to cool completely before topping with the potato.

10 Fork the potato up to leave the surface rough, or draw the fork over the surface to mark with a pattern.

11 Place in the oven for 20–30 minutes, or until the potato is brown and crisp.

Shepherd's Pie: What has gone wrong when...

The mince is not browned sufficiently.

- Too much meat at a time was placed in the pan. The mince has boiled in its own liquid rather than fried in the hot fat.
- The pan and oil were not sufficiently hot to brown the mince.
- The mince was not browned for long enough.

Meatballs

The meat in meatballs is tenderized by mincing rather than by long cooking. Have the butcher mince rump steak for tenderness and flavour. Use a mixture of parsley, basil, rosemary, oregano, sage and/or thyme as you like to season the meat.

Dampening your hands slightly with water makes shaping easier and keeps the meat from sticking to your hands.

Serve the meatballs with spaghetti.

SERVES 4

560 g | 1¼ lb minced good quality beef

55 g | 2 oz fresh breadcrumbs

1 egg, beaten

1 clove of garlic, crushed

2 tablespoons chopped fresh mixed herbs or 2 teaspoons dried herbs

1 × 5 ml spoon | 1 teaspoon salt

freshly ground black pepper

2 tablespoons olive oil

Tomato Sauce (see **Sauces, Savoury**, page 607)

1 Place the meat, breadcrumbs, egg, garlic, herbs and salt in a bowl. Season with pepper and mix together with a fork.

2 Divide the mixture into 20 equal-sized pieces and shape into meatballs.

3 Heat the oil in a sauté pan over medium heat and brown the meatballs in batches on all sides.

4 Place the meatballs in the sauce and simmer for 30 minutes to cook the meatballs through.

Meatballs: What has gone wrong when...

The meatballs fall apart when they are fried.

- The meat was not squeezed firmly enough when the meatballs were shaped.

Veal

Veal is the meat of a calf, no more than a year old, reared for slaughter when weaned. The quality of the veal is directly related to its age, diet and the amount of exercise it is allowed. The Dutch produce veal from calves that are kept in crates, unable to take any exercise. They are fed solely on their mother's milk before being slaughtered at around 2 months old. Their flesh is very pale pink with smooth white fat; it smells of milk and is extremely tender. Despite its melting tenderness, Dutch veal tends to taste mild to the point of insipidity and requires good seasoning: usually plenty of lemon, pepper or a well-flavoured sauce.

The British method of producing veal is kinder as the calves are allowed exercise. The meat is darker pink and more flavoursome as the calves are fed on a diet including cereals or grass and are not slaughtered until they are 3 months old.

The French are very partial to veal, roasted, stewed as in *Blanquette de Veau* (see page 379) or fried and served with a rich sauce, as are the Italians, who serve it in dishes such as Osso Bucco (braised knuckle of veal) and Vitello Tonnato (cold, thinly sliced roast veal with tuna sauce). The British most frequently roast veal or pan-fry it quickly. The less expensive cuts are used for pies.

Veal cuts

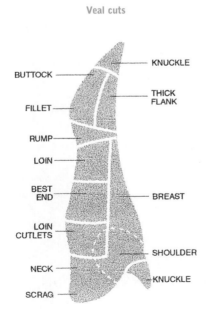

Cuts of Veal

The cuts of veal and their names more closely resemble those of lamb or sheep than those of mature cattle.

Cut	Best cooking method	Recipe reference
Leg	Roasting	*Roast Loin of Veal* (page 375)
	Braising	*Veal Fricandeau* (page 377)
	Stewing	*Blanquette de Veau* (page 379)
Loin	Roasting	*Roast Loin of Veal* (page 375)
	Braising	*Veal Fricandeau* (page 377)
Loin chops	Frying	see **Beef**, *Frying* (page 367)
Best end	Roasting	*Roast Loin of Veal* (page 375)
Best end cutlets	Frying	see **Lamb**, *Frying Cutlets* (page 392)
Breast	Braising	*Veal Fricandeau* (page 377)
	Stewing	*Blanquette de Veau* (page 379)
Shoulder	Braising	*Veal Fricandeau* (page 377)
	Pies	*Veal and Ham Raised Pie* (page 379)
	Stewing	*Blanquette de Veau* (page 379)
Scrag	Stewing	*Blanquette de Veau* (page 379)
Fillet (cushion)	Frying	see **Beef**, *Frying Steak* (page 367)
Escalopes	Frying	*Veal Escalopes with Rosemary* (page 378)
Rump	Frying	
	Braising	*Veal Fricandeau* (page 377)
Buttock	Stewing	*Blanquette de Veau* (page 379)
Knuckle	Braising	
	Stewing	*Blanquette de Veau* (page 379)
	Stock	see **Stocks** (page 685)

Choosing Veal

- The flesh should be pale pink, soft but not flabby, and finely grained.
- Veal should never look bloody or really red as this suggests the animal is much older than 3 months.
- There should be a very little creamy white fat.

- Do not worry if there is a lot of gelatinous tissue around the meat as this is a natural characteristic of a very immature animal. It should, however, be removed before cooking unless the meat is to be braised or stewed, in which case it will break down and help to enrich the flavour and consistency of the cooking liquor.

Storing Veal

See **Meat,** *Storing Meat*, page 336.

Methods of Cooking Veal

Veal can be cooked by most of the methods for cooking meat because it is very tender. Veal is seldom grilled as due to the absence of fat, it becomes too dry. As there is little fat on a calf and a high proportion of water in the meat, care must be taken to moisten veal frequently during cooking to prevent it from excessive moisture loss, shrinkage and dryness. Due to the immaturity of the meat, veal tends to be bland and is usually seasoned well and served with sauces or stuffing for additional flavour.

Veal cuts containing a larger quantity of connective tissue, such as the leg, shoulder and neck, may be cooked slowly and gently by poaching, braising or stewing (see **Meat,** *The tender-tough-tender principle*, page 351).

Roasting

The loin, leg, fillet or the best end of neck are the best joints for roasting.

Roast Loin of Veal

In this recipe, flavoured butter is spread on the lean meat before it is rolled, to flavour and moisten it as it cooks.

SERVES 6

1 kg | 2¼ lb piece of boned loin of veal
30 g | 1 oz butter, softened
2 teaspoons Dijon mustard
chopped fresh mixed herbs (rosemary, thyme and sage)
salt and freshly ground black pepper
1 tablespoon vegetable oil
1 teaspoon plain flour
290 ml | ½ pint Brown Stock (see **Stocks**, page 692)

1 Preheat the oven to 180°C | 350°F | gas mark 4. Weigh the veal and calculate the cooking time at 20 minutes per 450 g | 1 lb.
2 Using a very sharp knife, cut away the rind and most of the fat from the loin, leaving a thin layer of fat about 1 cm | ½ in thick on the joint. Make criss-cross incisions into the outer layer of fat.

3 Spread the butter and half the mustard over the lean side of the joint. Spread the remaining mustard on the fat side, making sure that it penetrates the incisions well. Sprinkle with herbs, salt and pepper. Roll and tie up securely with string.

4 Heat the oil in a roasting pan. When it is hot, put the joint into it and brown the surface evenly. As the veal is roasted at a moderate temperature for a relatively short time, it may not brown sufficiently in the oven (see **Meat,** *Browning,* page 343).

5 Roast in the oven for the calculated cooking time.

6 Remove the joint to a warmed serving dish. Skim the excess fat from the pan. With a whisk or wooden spoon, scrape the bottom of the tin, stir in the flour and cook until the roux is golden-brown, then add the stock. Stir until boiling, then simmer for 2 minutes.

7 Check the seasoning and pour into a warmed sauce-boat. Serve with the joint.

Roasting Fillet of Veal

As veal fillet is so lean and tender it must either be larded (see below) or protected by a layer of fat tied around it (see **Poultry,** *Barding,* page 343). First brown the veal in hot fat over direct heat or roast in the oven for 20 minutes at 200°C|400°F|gas mark 6, then roast, allowing 20 minutes per 450 g|1 lb at 180°C|350°F|gas mark 4.

Braising

Leg, shoulder, breast, and knuckle of veal are the cuts recommended for braising. As veal contains very little fat, the joint is larded with pork fat to moisten it while it cooks. Veal contains gelatinous proteins that break down on slow cooking to enrich the flavour and consistency of the sauce.

Larding

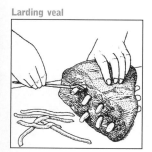

Larding veal

Veal, like other very lean meat, should be larded before roasting. This promotes tenderness and adds flavour. The technique is most commonly used for slow-roasted dishes. A special larding needle that grips the fat with a clamp at the end opposite the sharp end is used. As the meat cooks, the fat partially melts, making the meat juicy and adding flavour and richness to the sauce.

To lard a joint, cut the larding fat (usually rindless back pork fat) into thin strips, longer than the joint or other piece of meat, and put one of them into the tunnel of the needle, clamping down the hinge to hold it in place. The fat should extend a little way out of the needle. Thread the strip all the way through the meat, at 1 cm|½ in intervals, twisting the needle gently to prevent the fat from pulling off. Then release the clamp and trim the 2 ends of fat close to the meat. Repeat with the remaining strips throughout the lean meat at 2.5 cm|1 in intervals.

Veal Fricandeau

This dish has been adapted from a recipe in the *Time Life Veal and Beef* book.

SERVES 8

200 g | 7 oz long strips of pork fat

salt and freshly ground black pepper

1.35 kg | 3 lb piece of rump or loin of veal, cut lengthways along the grain

45 g | 1½ oz unsalted butter

2 onions, thinly sliced

2 carrots, thinly sliced

570 ml | 1 pint White Stock, made with veal bones (see **Stocks**, page 689)

200 ml | 7 fl oz dry white wine

To serve

1.35 kg | 3 lb leaf spinach, destalked and well washed

15 g | ½ oz butter

salt and freshly ground black pepper

freshly grated nutmeg

1 Season the pork fat with salt and pepper.

2 Use the strips of pork fat to lard the meat (see above).

3 Preheat the oven to 180°C | 350°F | gas mark 4.

4 Melt the butter in a flameproof casserole. Add the onions and carrots and cook until softened and lightly browned. Transfer to a plate.

5 Turn up the heat a little, season the veal with salt and pepper, place it in the casserole and brown it lightly all over.

6 Transfer the meat to a plate. Add the stock and wine to the casserole. Bring to the boil and reduce by half. Put the vegetables and veal back into the casserole and cover with a piece of buttered greaseproof paper and a tightly fitting lid. Cook in the oven for 1 hour.

7 Using a ladle, remove half the braising liquid and place in a saucepan. Reduce by boiling rapidly until syrupy. Use this to baste over the fricandeau as it cooks. The surface of the meat should become brown and sticky as the braising liquid evaporates and concentrates.

8 Turn the oven temperature up to 190°C | 375°F | gas mark 5 and remove the covering paper and lid. Cook for 1 further hour, basting the veal frequently with the braising juices to prevent it from drying out.

9 Remove the veal from the casserole. Leave to stand, covered, in the turned off oven while you make the sauce and prepare the spinach.

10 Strain all the meat juices from the casserole into a saucepan. Bring to the boil, then add a dash of cold water. (This will help to bring the scum to the surface.) Skim off all the scum. Repeat this process if necessary.

11 Meanwhile, cook the spinach. Melt the butter in a large sauté pan over medium–high heat until just starting to brown. Add the well-washed spinach and turn in the pan until wilted. Season with salt, pepper and nutmeg.

12 Arrange the spinach on a large warmed serving dish. Place the veal on top of the spinach and hand the sauce separately.

Frying

The fillet, known as the cushion, at the top of the hind leg is most frequently sliced into escalopes. Escalopes are cut with the grain into thin slices not more than 6 mm | ¼ in thick. The fillet contains very little fat or connective tissue and is extremely tender and therefore expensive. The tender cuts from the forequarter from a top-quality milk-fed calf may also be boned out and sliced for escalopes.

Veal Escalopes with Rosemary

Escalopes are often flattened to half their thickness (see *Meat*, *Frying*, page 346) to tenderize them further and ensure they are cooked in the minimum time to prevent the flesh from drying out. Butter is used to fry the veal in this recipe to enrich the flavour of the meat. The butter is unlikely to burn as the veal requires little cooking.

SERVES 4

4 × 140 g | 5 oz veal escalopes
salt and freshly ground black pepper
30 g | 1 oz butter
1 teaspoon chopped fresh rosemary or ½ teaspoon dried rosemary

4 tablespoons dry white wine mixed with 4 tablespoons of water
2 tablespoons double cream or crème frâiche
a squeeze of lemon juice

1 If the escalopes are not very thin, place them between 2 sheets of wet grease-proof paper or clingfilm and beat gently with a meat mallet or heavy-based saucepan. Season with salt and pepper.

2 Melt the butter with the rosemary in a frying pan over a medium heat. When the butter is foaming, fry the escalopes (one or two at a time if they won't fit in the pan together) for 1–2 minutes on each side until a very pale brown (be careful not to overcook them). Remove the veal with a slotted spoon or fish slice and keep warm in a very low oven. Pour any excess fat from the pan.

3 Pour the wine and water into the hot pan and heat, scraping the surface of the pan with a wooden spoon to loosen any sediment. Boil to reduce by half, then add the cream and a few drops of lemon juice. Check the seasoning. Pour over the veal and serve immediately.

Stewing

Most cuts of veal can be used for stewing, although it makes sense to use the more economical cuts.

Blanquette de Veau

Blanquette de Veau is made with cuts of veal suitable for stewing such as shoulder and leg and often known as pie veal. Blanquette de Veau is a white stew, which means that the ingredients are not browned before simmering in white stock or water. Once the meat is cooked, the cooking liquor is thickened with an egg and cream liaison (see **Sauces, Savoury**, page 584) just before the dish is served.

SERVES 4

900 g | 2 lb pie veal
1 slice of lemon
1 bouquet garni (4 parsley stalks, 2 bay leaves,
   1 blade of mace, tied together with string)
salt and freshly ground black pepper
2 carrots, peeled and cut into sticks

2 onions, peeled and sliced
1 teaspoon cornflour
1 egg yolk, or 2 for a very rich sauce
150 ml | ¼ pint double cream
chopped fresh parsley, to garnish

1 Trim the fat from the veal but do not worry about the gristle as much of it will convert to gelatine as it cooks. Put the veal into a saucepan of cold water with the lemon slice. Bring slowly to the boil, skimming thoroughly. Add the bouquet garni and a little salt. Remove the lemon slice and simmer gently for 30 minutes.

2 Add the carrots and onions and continue to simmer until the meat is very tender and the vegetables cooked, and a further 30–40 minutes.

3 Strain the liquid into a jug and skim off any fat. There should be 290 ml | ½ pint liquid. If there is less, add water. If there is more, return the liquid to the pan and reduce by boiling rapidly. Pick over the meat, removing any fat or gristle, and put the meat and vegetables into an ovenproof serving dish. Discard the bouquet garni.

4 Mix the cornflour in a cup with a few spoonfuls of cold water. Stir the mixture into the liquid in the pan and continue to stir while bringing to the boil. You should now have a sauce that is very slightly thickened, about the consistency of single cream. If it is still too thin, do not add more cornflour but boil rapidly until reduced to the correct consistency. Season to taste with salt and pepper.

5 Mix the egg yolks and cream together in a bowl. Add some of the sauce, mix well, and return to the pan (see **Sauces**, **Savoury**, *Egg and Cream Liaisons*, page 584). Reheat gently, stirring, until the egg yolks have thickened the sauce to the consistency of double cream. Do not allow the sauce to boil or the eggs will curdle. Pour the sauce over the meat and vegetables.

6 Serve garnished with chopped parsley.

Raised Pies

Veal can also be used in a Raised Pie (see **Terrines, Pâtés and Raised Pies**, page 714).

Lamb

Lambs are slaughtered between 3 and 15 months old when their meat is pale and tender. There is a difference, however, between baby lamb and the larger animals. Baby lambs have pale, tender flesh before they are weaned and their meat is extremely expensive. A leg from such a lamb would feed only 2 or perhaps 3 people at most. As the animal ages the meat becomes darker in colour, tougher and more strongly flavoured. Animals over a year old, weighing more than 36 kg | 80 lb, are graded as mutton. Mutton is available in speciality butchers' shops.

British lamb is very fine in flavour, but good imported New Zealand lamb is usually cheaper. As a general rule, New Zealand lamb joints come from smaller animals than the full-grown English lambs, but it should be remembered that 3 grades of New Zealand lamb are imported into Britain, ranging from excellent to very tough.

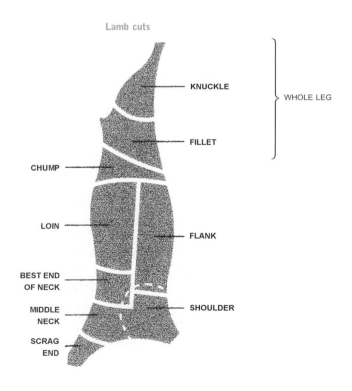

Lamb cuts

KNUCKLE

WHOLE LEG

FILLET

CHUMP

LOIN

FLANK

BEST END
OF NECK

MIDDLE
NECK

SHOULDER

SCRAG
END

Cuts of Lamb

Cut	Best cooking method	Recipe reference
Loin	Roasting	as for *Rack of Lamb* (page 391)
Loin chops/Cutlets	Grilling	as for *Beef Steaks* (page 364)
Noisettes	Frying	as for *Beef Steaks* (page 364)
Best end of neck	Roasting	*Rack of Lamb with Mustard and Breadcrumbs* (page 391); *Crown Roast of Lamb* (page 391); *Guard of Honour* (page 391)
Cutlets/Noisettes	Grilling or frying	*Noisettes of Lamb with Sweet Onion Purée* (page 393)
Collops	Grilling or frying	as for *Beef Steaks* (page 364)
Scrag and middle neck	Stewing	*Lamb Daube* (page 386)
Shoulder	Roasting	*Shoulder of Lamb 'en Ballon' Stuffed with Feta* (page 389)
	Stewing	*Lamb Daube* (page 386)
Leg	Roasting	*Roast Leg of Lamb* (page 383)
	Braising	*Leg of Lamb Braised with Garlic and Spring Vegetables* (page 385)
	Stewing	*Lamb Daube* (page 386)
	Barbecuing/Grilling	*Butterfly Leg of Lamb* (page 387)
Fillet end of leg/Lamb steaks	Grilling	
	Frying	*Lamb Steak à la Catalane with Lentils* (page 394)
Chump/Chops	Braising	as for *Leg of Lamb Braised with Garlic and spring Vegetables* (page 385)
	Grilling	as for *Beef Steaks* (page 364)
	Frying	as for *Beef Steaks* (page 364)
Saddle	Roasting	*Roast Saddle of Lamb* (page 384)
Knuckle	Braising	
	Stewing	*Lamb Daube* (page 386)

Choosing Lamb

- Lamb should be brownish-pink rather than grey in colour, but not bloody. The colour of the meat varies with the age and breed of lamb (see **Meat**, *The Colour of Meat*, page 335). Younger lamb is pale pink and older lamb is redder. However, lambs bred on hilltops and certain rare breeds of lamb have a deeper-coloured flesh due to the amount of exercise taken by the animals.
- The fat should be creamy-white and not oily.
- All joints should be plump and compact rather than long and thin.
- The skin should be pliable, not hard and wrinkled.

Storing Lamb

See **Meat,** *Storing Meat*, page 197.

Methods of Cooking Lamb

Lambs are usually slaughtered young, so most of the cuts are tender enough for grilling, frying or roasting. The fattier, cheaper cuts, such as the middle neck and scrag, are mainly used for casseroles and stews.

Roasting

Best lamb cuts for roasting
- leg
- loin
- best end of neck (rack of lamb), cut from between the middle neck and loin.
- shoulder, from the foreleg cut. Shoulder is cheaper than other roasting joints such as leg as it contains a higher proportion of fat and is more difficult to carve on the bone.
- saddle consists of both loins of lamb, left attached at the backbone. It is cut from the best end to the end of the loins and includes the kidneys. A saddle weighs 2–4.5 kg|4½ –10 lb and feeds approximately 6–8.

Calculating roasting time
To roast, allow 20 minutes per 450 g|1 lb at 190°C|375°F|gas mark 5 for slightly pink lamb, plus 20 minutes for well-done meat. Roast the lamb at 220°C|425° F|gas mark 7 for 20 minutes, then turn the temperature down to 190°C|375°F|gas mark 5. Begin the timing after the initial 20 minutes browning.

If lamb without a trace of pinkness is desired, allow an extra 20 minutes after the calculated time is up.

Remove the pink skin (the bark) if present and cut away any inspection stamps.

Roast Leg of Lamb

The leg weighs 1.35–2.5 kg│3–5½ lb and is relatively lean and easy to carve. It is also available boned and rolled.

SERVES 4

1.8 kg│4 lb leg of lamb
salt and freshly ground black pepper
3 large sprigs of fresh rosemary
200 ml│7 fl oz red wine

For the gravy
2 tablespoons plain flour
290 ml│½ pint Brown Stock, made with lamb
   bones (see **Stocks**, page 683)
1 teaspoon redcurrant jelly
salt and freshly ground black pepper

1 Preheat the oven to 200°C│400°F│gas mark 6.

2 Weigh the joint and calculate the cooking time as above. Wipe the meat, season with salt and pepper and place in a roasting pan, with the sprigs of rosemary on top.

3 Roast in the oven for the calculated cooking time. 30 minutes before the end of cooking, pour the wine over the lamb.

4 When the lamb is cooked, the juices that run out of the meat when pierced with a skewer will be faintly pink. Remove the joint from the oven and place it on a warmed serving dish. Tent loosely with foil while making the gravy, (see **Meat, Roasting**, page 342, and **Sauces, Savoury,** Gravy, page 592).

5 Carefully pour off all but 2 tablespoons fat from the roasting pan. Reserve the meat juices.

6 Add the flour to the remaining fat in the pan and using a wire whisk or wooden spoon, stir it over a low heat until a deep brown. Remove from the heat and stir in the stock, meat juices and redcurrant jelly. Return to the heat, stirring all the time, and simmer for 2 minutes.

7 Check the seasoning and strain into a warmed gravy-boat.

8 Carve the leg of lamb by cutting a 'V'-shaped notch from the middle of the leg and work towards each end, carving slices of meat from both sides of the 'V'.
   Or carve by slicing from the knuckle end of the leg.

NOTE: *Mint Sauce* (see **Herbs**, page 307) is the classic accompaniment to Roast Lamb.

Roast Shoulder of Lamb

Shoulder is also very good roasted. Although it is fattier and more difficult to carve than leg, it is usually less expensive. Follow the recipe for *Roast Leg of Lamb*, above. To carve, cut a wedge-shaped piece from the side of the joint. Carve thin slices towards either end.

Carving leg of lamb from a 'V'-shaped notch in the middle

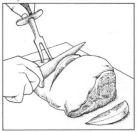

Carving leg of lamb diagonally from the knuckle end

Carving a shoulder of lamb

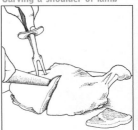

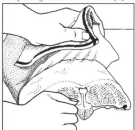

Preparing a saddle of lamb

1 Trim off any excess fat from underneath the saddle and remove the kidneys.

2 Trim away all but 2.5 cm | 1 in of the 2 flaps. Trim off any very large pieces of fat from the edges of the saddle, but leave the back fat. Tuck the flaps under the saddle.

3 Skin the saddle: the best way to do this is to lift the skin at one corner with a sharp knife and hold it tightly in a tea-towel to prevent it slipping out of your grip. Give a sharp tug and pull off all the skin in one piece.

4 Cut out the kidneys but keep them (they can be brushed with butter and attached to the end of the saddle with wooden skewers 30 minutes before the end of the roasting time).

5 Using a sharp knife, score the back fat all over in a fine criss-cross pattern.

6 The pelvic or aitch bone, protruding slightly from one end of the saddle, can be removed, or left in place and covered with a ham frill when the saddle is served.

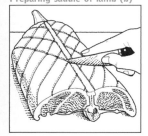

Roast Saddle of Lamb

SERVES 6–8

1 saddle of lamb

dripping

1 clove of garlic, peeled and cut into slivers (optional)

salt and freshly ground black pepper

sprigs of fresh rosemary

For the gravy

425 ml | ¾ pint Brown Stock, made with lamb bones (see **Stocks**, page 683)

2 tablespoons plain flour

1 Preheat the oven to 200°C | 400°F | gas mark 6.

2 Prepare the saddle of lamb as described above. If desired, stick a few slivers of garlic into the saddle near the bone. Season with salt and pepper and a scattering of rosemary. Weigh the joint and calculate the cooking time at 15 minutes per 450 g | 1 lb plus 15 minutes for pink lamb. The saddle cooks in less time than shoulder or leg of lamb due to its shallow shape and large proportion of bone which act as efficient heat conductors.

3 Heat 2 tablespoons dripping in a roasting pan. When it is hot, add the saddle of lamb, tucking the flaps underneath and basting well.

4 Roast for the calculated time. If the saddle is very large, it should be covered with damp greaseproof paper halfway through roasting to prevent it from becoming too brown.

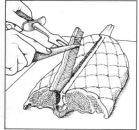

5 Lift the meat on to a warmed serving platter. Pour away all but 2 tablespoons of the fat from the pan. Reserve the juices. Stir the flour into the pan to absorb the fat. Cook over the heat, stirring, until russet brown. Add the stock slowly to make a smooth sauce. Stir until boiling, taking care to scrape up any sediment stuck to the bottom of the pan. Simmer for 2 minutes, then season to taste with salt and pepper.

6 Carve the chump end of the saddle into thin strips across the grain, at right angles to the backbone.

7 Carve the main part of the saddle into thin strips along its length.

Braising

Best lamb cuts for braising
- chump
- chops
- loin
- leg
- shoulder

Leg of Lamb Braised with Garlic and Spring Vegetables

SERVES 6

2 kg│4½ lb leg of lamb

salt and freshly ground black pepper

55 g│2 oz butter

2 cloves of garlic, crushed

290 ml│½ pint dry white wine

290 ml│½ pint Brown Stock (see **Stocks**, page 683)

675 g│1½ lb small new potatoes, scrubbed

450 g│1 lb baby carrots, scraped

340 g│12 oz defrosted or fresh petits pois

2 tablespoons butter, softened

30 g│1 oz plain flour

3 tablespoons double cream

2 tablespoons chopped fresh mint

1 Trim the lamb of all membrane and fat. Season with salt and pepper.
2 Mix together the butter and garlic and spread all over the lamb. Let stand for 30 minutes.
3 Preheat the oven to 180°F│350°C│gas mark 4.
4 Heat a flameproof casserole dish over a medium heat and brown the lamb on all sides.
5 Add the wine and stock and bring to the boil. Add the potatoes.
6 Cover with a lid and cook in the oven for 1½–2 hours or until the lamb is very tender.
7 After 30 minutes add the carrots.
8 After 1 hour add the peas.
9 Remove the lamb and vegetables to a large warmed platter and cover with foil to keep warm.
10 Bring the sauce to the boil in a saucepan.
11 Mix together the butter and flour and whisk bit by bit into the sauce. Boil for 2 minutes. Adjust to coating consistency by boiling further or by adding water.
12 Pass the sauce through a sieve. Stir in the cream and pour over the lamb and vegetables. Sprinkle over the mint and serve.

Stewing

- knuckle
- scrag and middle neck
- leg

Lamb stews are mostly made with middle neck of lamb from between the shoulders, and the scrag end. These cuts have a large proportion of connective tissue, fat and bone and must be trimmed well. Middle neck is sold either whole or ready-cut in pieces. Shoulder and leg of lamb can also be used for stewing.

Lamb Daube

This recipe uses shoulder meat, but leg or middle neck can be used instead.

SERVES 4

900 g | 2 lb boned shoulder of lamb

1 tablespoon oil

110 g | 4 oz streaky bacon, diced

1 onion, chopped

150 ml | ¼ pint Brown Stock (see **Stocks**, page 683)

1 bouquet garni (1 bay leaf, a sprig each of fresh thyme, rosemary and parsley, and a small strip of orange zest, tied together with string)

55 g | 2 oz plain flour

For the marinade

290 ml | ½ pint red wine

1 medium onion, cut into thick slices

1 clove of garlic, bruised

3 whole allspice berries

1 Trim the lamb and cut it into large pieces 3 × 5 cm | 1½ in × 2 in.
2 Prepare the marinade by mixing all the ingredients together. Lay the pieces of lamb in it and leave overnight.
3 Preheat the oven to 170°C | 325°F | gas mark 3.
4 Drain the marinade from the meat. Reserve the marinade.
5 Heat the oil in a heavy frying pan and brown the bacon and onion. Lift out with a slotted spoon and place in a casserole.
6 Brown the lamb in the same pan, a few pieces at a time. Lay them on top of the bacon and onion.
7 Strain the marinade into the empty pan. Add the stock. Bring to the boil, scraping the bottom of the pan to loosen any sediment. Pour over the meat.
8 Immerse the bouquet garni in the liquid in the casserole.
9 Add enough water to the flour to make a stiff dough. Cover the casserole with the lid and press a band of dough around the join of the lid and the dish to seal completely.
10 Cook in the oven for 1½ hours, then remove the bouquet garni.
11 Lift the meat out and place it on a warmed serving dish. Keep warm.
12 Boil the sauce to reduce to a syrupy consistency and pour over the meat.

Preparing Lamb

Boning a leg of lamb (a)

Open Boning: Points to Remember

- Use a boning knife, designed specifically for the purpose with its long, rigid blade and pointed tip (see *Knife Skills*, page 74).
- Hold the knife firmly like a dagger, with the point of the knife down.
- Always cut away from the hands and body to prevent injury if the knife slips.
- Keep the knife as sharp as possible. Blunt knives need more pressure to wield and are therefore more inclined to slip.

Boning a leg of lamb (b)

To Open-bone a Leg of Lamb

1 Cut neatly along the bones on the non-fleshy side of the leg from the tapered bony knuckle end to the hip joint at the fillet end. **(a)**
2 Gradually work out the bones by cutting and scraping the meat away from the bones. **(b)**

Removing the gland (c)

Making a Butterfly Joint

Butterfly jointing is an open-boning technique used to flatten a thick piece of meat, usually the leg, to an even thickness so it can be grilled or barbecued. The leg is opened along its length and the bone removed so that it resembles a pair of butterfly wings. Remove the grey gland, which will be about the size of a hazelnut. **(c)** Slash the thicker section of meat to allow heat to penetrate inside so the joint will cook evenly. **(d)**

Butterfly boning leg of lamb (d)

Butterfly Leg of Lamb

SERVES 6–8

2.7 kg|6 lb leg of lamb, butterfly-boned as described above	2 bay leaves
2 tablespoons soy sauce	3 cloves of garlic, peeled and sliced
½ onion, sliced	2 tablespoons good-quality olive oil
4 sprigs of fresh thyme	salt and freshly ground black pepper
	1 small bunch of watercress, to garnish

1 Weigh the boned leg of lamb and calculate the cooking time at 8 minutes per 450 g\|1 lb plus 20 minutes.
2 Open the leg of lamb and place it skin side down on a large plate. Sprinkle over the soy sauce, onion, thyme, bay leaves, garlic, oil and pepper. Fold the 3 'butterfly' ends inwards to encase the flavourings, cover and leave to marinate overnight.
3 Preheat the oven to 230°C\|450°F\|gas mark 8.

4 Open out the boned leg and lay it flesh side down in a roasting pan. Sprinkle the fatty side fairly liberally with salt and roast in the oven for 20 minutes, then turn down the oven temperature to 200°C|400°F|gas mark 6 and roast for a further 8 minutes per 450 g|1 lb. For example, a 1.8 kg|4 lb leg (boned weight) will require about 50 minutes' cooking.

5 To barbecue or grill, heat the barbecue or grill until very hot (see *Meat, Grilling*, page 350). Grill the meat skin side down first, then turn over and grill the meat side. The length of time on each side will depend on the thickness of the meat (see *Beef, Grilled Steak*, page 364). To test for 'doneness' see *Meat, The Test of the Thumb*, page 349. Allow the lamb to rest for 10 minutes before carving.

6 Garnish the lamb with watercress to serve.

Tunnel-boning

Both leg and shoulder of lamb can be tunnel-boned. Tunnel-boning means to remove the bone without opening out the meat. It is rather more difficult than open boning but it is a useful method as a stuffing can be inserted where the bone was removed so that the meat can be easily carved across its width.

To tunnel-bone a leg of lamb:

1 Loosen the skin and any flesh from the tapered bony knuckle end of the leg.

2 Inserting the knife between the loosened skin and the bone, scrape and cut the flesh away from the bone as far up the knuckle bone as possible, being careful not to pierce the surface of the meat.

3 Turn the leg around and insert the knife between the fillet end and the bone. Again, loosen the meat slowly and carefully away from the bone with a combination of scraping and cutting, keeping the knife as close to the bone as possible and making every effort to keep the meat as intact as possible. Fold the loosened meat down and away from the bone as you go, to allow you to see the course the three bones take through the meat, being especially careful at each joint, until you meet the loosened flesh at the knuckle end.

4 Pull the 3 bones out of the joint. Take care to remove any glands from inside the meat. Look for translucent grey nodules about the size of a hazelnut.

5 The meat can then be stuffed and sewn at each end before roasting.

Boning a Shoulder of Lamb

As shoulder joints **(a)** are difficult to carve they are often open-boned and rolled or stuffed and tied to look like a balloon ('en ballon').

1 Insert the tip of the knife into the shoulder just above and below the blade bone. Scrape the meat away from the flat bone. **(b)**

2 Scrape around the ridge on the blade bone, taking care not to cut through the skin. **(c)**

Tunnel boning leg of lamb

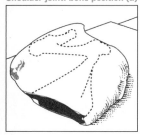

Shoulder joint: bone position (a)

Boning a shoulder of lamb (b)

Boning a shoulder of lamb (c)

3 Continue to scrape the meat from the bone.

4 Starting from the leg end of the bone, cut through the skin where it is attached to the bone on the underside of the shoulder. Scrape the meat from the bone until the 'elbow' is reached. **(d)** The bone should now be released from the meat. Remove it by pulling from the blade end.

5 To stuff the boned shoulder, season the joint inside with salt and pepper and spoon in the stuffing. **(e)**

6 Tie the joint with string to shape into a round. **(f)** To tie the shoulder, turn the shoulder over, skinned side up. Tie the end of a 3 m | 9 ft piece of string firmly around the shoulder, making a knot in the middle at the top. Take the string around again, but this time at right angles to the first line, again tying at the first knot. Continue this process until the balloon is trussed about 8 times. **(g)** The indentations made by the string should resemble the grooves in a melon or the lines between the segments of a beach ball. Tuck in any loose flaps of meat or skin.

Boning a shoulder of lamb (d)

Shoulder of Lamb 'en Ballon' Stuffed with Feta

SERVES 6

1.8 kg | 4 lb boned whole shoulder of lamb (see *Boning a shoulder of lamb*, above).

85 ml | 3 floz red wine

20 g | ¾ oz plain flour

For the stuffing

225 g | 8 oz feta cheese, cut into 1 cm | ½ in cubes

2 teaspoons green peppercorns, rinsed

1 shallot, finely chopped

85 g | 3 oz fresh white breadcrumbs

2 tablespoons thinly sliced sun-dried tomatoes

1 tablespoon fresh thyme leaves

1 egg, beaten

salt and freshly ground black pepper

sprigs of watercress, to garnish

Stuffing the shoulder (e)

Boned shoulder (f)

1 Preheat the oven to 200°C | 400°F | gas mark 6.

2 Trim the lamb of excess fat, leaving a thin layer on the outside to keep the meat moist while cooking.

3 Mix together the stuffing ingredients, beat lightly and season carefully with salt and pepper (the feta can be very salty).

4 Season the inside of the lamb and spread with the stuffing. If the shoulder has been tunnel boned, push the stuffing into the lamb.

5 Using thin string, tie the lamb into a balloon shape.

6 Weigh the lamb and calculate the cooking time. For pink lamb, allow 20 minutes per 450 g | 1 lb plus 20 minutes. For well-done lamb cook for a further 30 minutes.

7 Put the lamb into a roasting pan and roast in the oven for the calculated cooking time.

8 Thirty minutes before the lamb is ready, pour the wine over the joint.

9 When the lamb is cooked, remove it from the oven and place in a warm place to rest for 10 minutes.

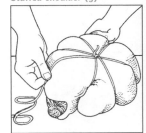
Stuffed shoulder (g)

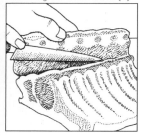

Skinning the Rack of Lamb (a)

Removing the chine bone (b)

Removing the shoulder blade (c)

Removing the paddywack (d)

Cutting through the fat (e)

10　Pour off all but 1 tablespoon of the fat from the roasting pan, place the pan over direct heat and stir in the flour. Cook, stirring, for 1 minute. Add some water and any cooking juices. Bring to the boil, then simmer for 5 minutes.

11　Just before serving, remove the string from the lamb. Carve by cutting wedges from the edge to the centre, like a pie.

12　Garnish with small sprigs of watercress. Serve with the gravy.

Preparing Best End Neck or Rack of Lamb

The best end of neck, also known as rack of lamb, is extremely tender and sweet and is best roasted either on the bone or boned and rolled. Before a whole best end is roasted, both the outer skin and chine bone are removed and the ends of the bones are exposed for presentation by trimming off the fat and meat. A best end can be prepared with an English trim, in which the bones are cleaned 2.5 cm | 1 in from the ends, or with a French trim, in which the bones are exposed to the ends of the bones near the 'eye' of the meat.

An English-trimmed best end of neck can be roasted whole, cut into cutlets by cutting between the bones and grilled or fried or used to make a crown roast or a 'guard of honour' (see below).

Preparing Rack of Lamb

1　Skin the best end: lift a corner of the skin from the neck end with a small knife, hold it firmly, using a cloth to get a good grip, and peel it off. **(a)**

2　Chine the lamb if the butcher has not already done so. This involves sawing carefully through the rib bones just where they meet the chine bone (or spine). Take care not to saw into the eye of the meat. Now remove the chine bone completely, using a sharp knife. **(b)**

3　Remove the half-moon-shaped piece of flexible cartilage found buried between the layers of fat and meat at the thinner end of the best end. This is the tip of the shoulder blade. It is simple to work out with a knife and your fingers. **(c)**

4　Remove the rubbery cream-coloured tendon, known as the 'paddywack', found between the fat and meat at the edge of the eye. **(d)**

5　Chop off the cutlet bones so that the length of the remaining bones is not more than twice the length of the eye of the meat.

6　Make a vertical cut through the fat, to the rib bones, just below the line of the meat for a French trim or 2.5 cm | 1 in from the tips of the bones for an English trim. **(e)**

7　Remove the fat below this line to expose the rib bones. Now cut away the meat between the bones down to the horizontal line to produce a crenellated effect.

8　Scrape the exposed bones clean with a small sharp knife to remove all traces of meat, fat and connective tissue. (Any remaining tissue on the bones will cause them to blacken when the rack is roasted.) **(f) (g)**

9　Now trim the fat covering the eye of the meat until it is no more than 2 mm | $\frac{1}{12}$ in thick, taking care not to cut into the meat. **(h)**

Rack of Lamb with Mustard and Breadcrumbs

SERVES 2

1 rack (best end) of lamb, chined, trimmed and
skinned (see above)

2 teaspoons Dijon mustard

1 tablespoon fresh white breadcrumbs

1 tablespoon chopped mixed fresh herbs, such
as mint, chives, parsley, thyme

salt and freshly ground black pepper

2 teaspoons unsalted butter

1 Preheat the oven to 220°C|425° F|gas mark 7.

2 Trim off as much fat as possible from the meat.

3 Mix together the mustard, breadcrumbs, herbs, salt, pepper and butter. Press a thin layer of this mixture over the rounded, skinned side of the rack of lamb. Refrigerate for 30 minutes.

4 Place the lamb, crumbed side up, in a roasting pan and roast in the preheated oven for 25 minutes for a 7-cutlet rack, less for a smaller one. This will give pink, slightly underdone lamb. Serve with the butter and juices from the pan poured over the top.

5 To carve, cut down between the individual bones.

NOTE: If preparing an English-trimmed rack, double the quantity of topping.

Preparing Crown Roast of Lamb

A crown roast of lamb is assembled using 2 or 3 large best ends. Once the best ends are trimmed (see above):

1 Bend each best end into a semi-circle, with the fatty side of the ribs inside. To facilitate this it may be necessary to cut through the sinew between each cutlet from the thick end to a depth of about 2.5 cm|1 in. Take care not to cut into the fleshy eye of the meat.

2 Sew the ends of the racks together to make a circle, with the meaty part forming the base of the crown.

3 Tie a piece of string round the waist of the crown.

4 Stuff the crown: a crown roast is traditionally stuffed with a non-meat stuffing.

5 Roast as for rack of lamb, above.

6 To carve, cut down between each bone.

Preparing a Guard of Honour

English trim 2 best end racks of lamb as described above.

1 Score the fat in a criss-cross pattern.

2 Hold the 2 best ends, one in each hand, facing each other on a board, with the meaty part of the racks on the board, and the fatty sides on the outside.

3 Jiggle them so that the rib bones interlock and cross at the top.

4 Sew or tie the bases together at intervals.

5 Stuff the arch if required.

6 Roast as for rack of lamb, above.

7 Carve using instructions for rack of lamb (**Meat**, *Carving Meat*, page 359).

Exposing the bones (f)

Scraping the bones (g)

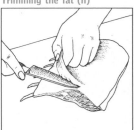
Trimming the fat (h)

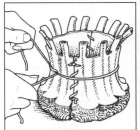
Preparing a crown roast

Preparing a guard of honour

French-trimmed Best End Cutlets

French-trimmed best end cutlets are cut from a skinned, chined and trimmed best end rack of lamb, following the instructions above.

To cut the cutlets from the prepared rack:

1 If thin small cutlets are required, cut between each bone as evenly as possible, splitting the rack into 6–7 small cutlets.
2 If fattier cutlets are required, carefully ease out every other rib bone. Then cut between the remaining bones into thick cutlets.
3 Now trim the fat from the thick end of each cutlet. Cutlets are suitable for grilling and frying and 2–3 cutlets should be served per person.

Lamb Cutlets Grilled with Herbs

SERVES 4

12 French-trimmed lamb cutlets (see above)
30 g|1 oz butter, melted
1 tablespoon oil

mixed chopped fresh herbs, such as thyme,
basil, mint, parsley, marjoram, rosemary
salt and freshly ground black pepper

1 Preheat the grill to its highest setting.
2 Brush the cutlets with the melted butter and oil, sprinkle over half the herbs and season with salt and pepper.
3 Place the cutlets under the grill, about 8 cm|3 in away from the heat (see **Meat**, *Grilling*, page 347), and cook for 3–4 minutes.
4 Turn the cutlets over, baste with the fat from the bottom of the pan and sprinkle with the remaining herbs.
5 Grill for 3–4 minutes (3 minutes per side should give a succulent pink cutlet, 4 minutes a well-done cutlet).
6 Arrange the cutlets on a warmed serving dish and pour over the pan juices. Serve immediately.

Noisettes of Lamb

Noisettes are boneless cutlets, tied into a meat round shape with string. They are made from the loin or best end and are suitable for grilling or frying (see **Meat**, *Methods of Cooking Meat*, page 341).

Preparing noisettes from a best end of lamb

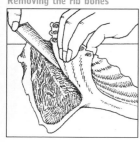

Removing the rib bones

1 Remove the skin from the meat (see *Preparing Rack of Lamb* above).
2 Remove the chine bone and then all the rib bones, easing them out with a short, sharp knife.
3 Remove the half-moon-shaped piece of flexible cartilage found buried between the layers of fat and meat at the thinner end of the best end.

4 Remove the 'paddywack', the tendon found between the fat and the meat at the edge of the eye.

5 Trim off any excess fat from the meat leaving a very thin even layer of fat. Roll it up tightly, starting at the thick meaty side and working towards the thin flap.

6 Tie the roll neatly with separate pieces of string at 4 cm | 1½ in intervals.

7 Trim any ragged ends of the roll to neaten them.

8 Now slice the roll into pieces, cutting accurately between each piece of string.

9 The average 7-bone best end will give 4 good noisettes.

10 Remove the string from the noisette after cooking.

Cutting noisettes of lamb

Noisettes with Onion and Mint Purée

SERVES 4

2 × 6–7 bone best end necks of lamb, chined	a pinch of caster sugar
unsalted butter and vegetable oil	2 tablespoons chopped fresh mint

For the onion purée

55 g | 2 oz butter

1 large Spanish onion, very finely chopped

To garnish

1 small bunch of watercress

1 Prepare the best end of necks as for noisettes, above and slice each into 4 noisettes.

2 Press the noisettes between 2 plates, ideally for 1 hour, and refrigerate.

3 Make the onion purée: melt the butter in a frying pan, add the onion and cook slowly, covered with a piece of dampened greaseproof paper (a *cartouche*), until absolutely soft (this may take 45 minutes). Sprinkle with the sugar, increase the heat and cook until the onions are a very pale brown. Blend to a purée in a liquidizer, then push through a sieve. Stir in the mint.

4 Fry the noisettes in butter and oil for 5 minutes per side, then remove the string and arrange on a warmed serving plate. Garnish with watercress and hand the warm onion purée separately.

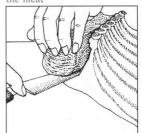
Collops: Seperating the 'eye' of the meat

Collops of Lamb

These are very extravagant small slices of meat taken from best end neck of lamb. They are best pan-fried and can be used in place of noisettes in *Noisettes of Lamb with Onion and Mint Purée*.

Removing the membrane

Preparing collops of lamb

1 Using a sharp knife separate the whole 'eye' of the meat from the bones and fat.

2 Using a sharp, flexible knife, remove all fat and membranes from the meat. Finally slice across the cylinder into neat rounds or collops about 2.5 cm | 1 in thick.

Lamb Steak à la Catalane with Lentils

Like beef steaks, lamb steaks, cut from the upper leg, can be eaten cooked blue to well done, but if overcooked they will become tough. The meat is at its most succulent when cooked until pink in the middle.

SERVES 4

4 lamb steaks, 1 cm | ½ in thick, cut across the upper leg, bones removed

For the marinade

150 ml | ¼ pint olive oil

6 cloves of garlic, crushed

2 tablespoons chopped fresh thyme

1 large onion, sliced

24 black peppercorns, slightly crushed

salt

For the lentils

4 onions, finely chopped

4 cloves of garlic, crushed

olive oil

225 g | 8 oz (raw weight) green or brown lentils, cooked

2 tablespoons tomato purée

4 tablespoons chopped mixed fresh herbs

salt and freshly ground black pepper

sesame oil

1 bunch watercress, to garnish

1 Lay the lamb steaks in a shallow dish. Pour over the oil and add all the other marinade ingredients. Leave the steaks to marinate for at least 8 hours, preferably 24 hours, turning them over 2 or 3 times.

2 To prepare the lentils, sweat the onions and garlic in a little oil until completely soft and transparent.

3 Add the lentils, tomato purée and herbs and season with salt, pepper and a little sesame oil to taste. Keep warm.

4 Meanwhile, get a heavy frying pan or griddle really hot, or preheat the grill for at least 10 minutes.

5 Remove most of the oil from the lamb steaks and put them in the hot pan or under the preheated grill. Fry or grill, turning once, until both sides are a rich brown. Garnish with watercress to serve.

Grilling and Frying

Best lamb cuts for grilling and frying

- best end cutlets
- loin chops
- chump chops
- steaks from fillet end of leg

Cooking Minced Lamb

Best cuts for lamb mince

- scrag
- middle neck
- breast

Cooked lamb left over from a roast is also very good minced and used to make hot dishes such as the traditional cottage pie. These dishes can also be make with beef mince (see **Beef**, *Cooking*, *Mince*, *Shepherd's Pie*, page 371).

Moussaka

Moussaka is a traditional dish found in every village in Greece. There are as many different variations are there are cooks, but the ingredients of tomatoes, onions, garlic and aubergines are universal.

SERVES 4

340 g | 12 oz aubergine

salt and freshly ground black pepper

6 tablespoons olive oil

1 large onion, finely chopped

675 g | 1½ lb lamb or beef mince

150 ml | ¼ pint white wine

150 ml | ¼ pint water

1 clove of garlic, crushed

1 × 400 g | 12 oz can tomatoes or 3 large
    tomatoes, peeled and chopped

2 tablespoons chopped fresh parsley

2 teaspoons chopped fresh oregano or
    1 teaspoon dried oregano

a pinch of ground cinnamon

225 g | 8 oz floury potatoes, peeled

For the topping

200 ml | 7 fl oz Greek yoghurt

1 egg, beaten

4 tablespoons grated Parmesan cheese

1 Remove the stalk from the aubergine, then slice the aubergine into slices 6 mm | ¼ in thick. Salt the slices on both sides, then leave in a colander for 30 minutes for some of the juices to drain out.

2 Place 2 tablespoons of the oil in a small saucepan and sweat the onion over a low heat until soft.

3 Heat 2 tablespoons of the remaining oil in a sauté pan and brown the mince in batches, taking care not to overcrowd the pan. Place the browned mince in a sieve over a bowl to drain away the excess fat.

4 Mix together the wine and water and use a little to deglaze the pan in between batches of meat. Reserve the *déglaçage*.

5 Add the garlic to the onion and cook for 1 minute.

6 Combine the onion, garlic, browned meat, tomatoes, remaining wine/water, parsley, oregano and cinnamon in a large saucepan and simmer for 45 minutes.

7 Boil the potatoes until tender. Drain, cool and cut into slices 6 mm | ¼ in thick.

8 Preheat the grill. Rinse the aubergine slices and pat dry on kitchen paper.

9 Brush the aubergine on both sides with the remaining oil and grill until browned.

10 Preheat the oven to 180°C | 350°F | gas mark 4.

11 Place a thin layer of the meat sauce in a shallow ovenproof dish. Arrange a layer of aubergine slices on the sauce, then add a thin layer of sauce and then a layer of potato slices. Continue layering, finishing with a layer of sauce.

12 Mix together the yoghurt, egg and cheese. Spread over the moussaka. (The dish can be made 1 day in advance and refrigerated at this point.)

13 Bake for 45 minutes until golden-brown on top and hot in the centre.

Pork

Pork is a versatile meat: it may be eaten fresh, cured, salted or smoked. It is also true that there is very little of the pig that cannot be eaten: even the feet and ears are used in a number of dishes. Fresh pork is a rich meat, often flavoured with sage and accompanied with fruit, vegetables flavoured with vinegar (red cabbage or beetroot), rich-tasting sauces, or pulses such as lentils in winter dishes.

Pigs for the fresh meat market are bred for high meat content and are fed on a diet of cereal flours until they weigh 90–100 kg|200–225 lb at around 6 or 7 months old. Pork slaughtered at this age is generally very tender and carries little fat. Fresh pork sold in Britain is mainly cut from the back, leg and shoulder of the pig. Bacon pigs are older and heavier than pigs destined for the fresh pork market and, as a result, the comparable cuts of bacon contain more fat than those of fresh pork (see *Bacon, Ham and Gammon*, pages 408, 410 and 408).

Pork cuts

Cuts of Pork

Cut	Best cooking method	Recipe reference
Trotter	Stewing	
	Braising	See *Offal* (page 451)
Leg	Roasting	*Roast Pork* (page 399)
	Stewing	
	Braising	*Braised Pork with Prunes* (page 401)
	Pies	
Fillet	Roasting	
or tenderloin	Grilling	
	Frying	*Medallions of Pork with Prunes* (page 403)
Loin	Roasting	*Roast Pork* (page 399)
Loin chops	Grilling	See *Meat* (page 341)
	Frying	
Belly	Roasting	
	Stewing	
	Braising	*Braised Pork with Prunes* (page 401)
	Pies	
	Sausages	*Simple Pork Sausages* (page 405), *Boudin Blanc* (page 406)
Hand and spring	Stewing	
	Braising	
	Pies	
	Boiling	
Belly/American spare Ribs	Roasting/Baking	*Chinese Spare Ribs* (page 401)

Choosing Pork

- The flesh should be pale pink, not red or bloody which would suggest an older animal.
- The flesh should be close-grained and firm to the touch.
- The meat should be evenly covered with a layer of fat not more than 1 cm | $\frac{1}{2}$ in thick. The fat should be firm and white, not oily, and without a greyish tinge.
- The bones should be small and bluish-pink in colour, indicating that the meat is from a young animal.
- The skin should be thin, pliable, and free of hair. Older pigs have coarse, thick skin.

Storing Pork

See **Meat**, *Storing Meat*, page 336.

Methods of Cooking Pork

The meat is from young, relatively lean animals, so cuts of pork can be cooked by any cooking method (see **Meat,** *Methods of Cooking*, page oo). Pork is traditionally cooked until it is no longer pink as historically pigs have been associated with eating waste and used to be prone to tape-worms. These days it is unlikely that good-quality pork would be a health risk when eaten pink but it is still usually cooked until well done.

Roasting

Due to the general tenderness of the meat, any part of the pig, bar the head, trotters and knuckle, are suitable for roasting.

- The loin is considered to be superior and is more expensive than leg. The loin is a large joint that is sold either whole or cut into fore loin and hind loin joint.
- Leg of pork is also sold as a large joint weighing 4.5–6.75 kg | 10–15 lb or cut into the upper fillet and the lower knuckle.
- Belly pork is cut from the rear end of the belly and is quite fatty. The best cut is thick belly with a high proportion of meat. Belly pork may be eaten fresh or salted. When eaten fresh it is often boned, stuffed or rolled and roasted.
- Marinated American and Chinese spare ribs are also roasted to promote a crisp finish.
- The fillet can be trimmed of its membrane and roasted whole.
- A suckling pig is roasted whole.

Suckling pigs, as their name suggests, are slaughtered before they are weaned, at around 4–6 months, when their flesh is extremely tender and has a delicate flavour. Weaned piglets older than 6 months are called porkers. A traditional feast food, whole suckling pig is ideally roasted on a spit, but if one is not available, in an oven. During Elizabethan times suckling pig was often served boned and stuffed as a chaudfroid (see **Aspic**, page 93). Today, suckling pig is traditionally served with the head on, with an apple or orange between the jaws.

Pork crackling

Crackling, the roasted skin of pork, is a favourite part of a roast joint with many people.

Using a sharp knife, score through the rind, evenly at 6 mm | ¼ in intervals, then rub with oil and salt. The scored surface allows the heat of the oven and the salt and oil to penetrate deep into the fat, promoting a crisp texture and golden colour. Good crackling is produced when the joint has spent a long time, over 2 hours, in the oven. Scoring the skin makes the crackling easier to cut. Roast in a hot oven.

Roast Pork

SERVES 4–6

2 kg | 4.4 lb loin or leg of pork, with skin intact
oil
salt

For the gravy

20 g | 2 tablespoons plain flour

290 ml | ½ pint Brown Stock (see *Stocks*, page 683)

To serve

1 small bunch of watercress
Apple Sauce (see *Fruit, Apples*, page 279)

1 Preheat the oven to 220°C | 425°F | gas mark 7. Prepare the rind for crackling according to the instructions above.

2 Place the pork in a roasting pan and roast at the top of the oven for 2 hours 15 minutes (25 minutes per 450 g | 1 lb plus 25 minutes). After 30 minutes turn down the oven temperature to 190°C | 375°F | gas mark 5. The initial high temperature is important to promote crisp crackling.

3 Once the pork is cooked, turn off the oven, place the pork on a serving dish and return it to the oven, leaving the door ajar if it is still very hot.

4 Tip all but 2 tablespoons of the fat from the roasting tin, reserving as much of the meat juices as possible.

5 Add the flour and stir over the heat until well browned.

6 Remove from the heat, add the stock and mix well with a wire whisk or wooden spoon. Return to the heat and bring slowly to the boil, whisking all the time. Simmer for a few minutes until the gravy is shiny. Season to taste with salt and pepper. Strain into a warmed gravy-boat.

7 Garnish the pork with watercress and serve with the gravy and Apple Sauce.

8 To carve the pork, cut between the crackling and the meat to remove the crackling. Cut the crackling into small strips. Carve the meat across the grain into slices 6 mm | ¼ in thick.

Carving loin of pork

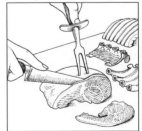

Roast Suckling Pig with Coriander and Lime

A roast suckling pig should be cooked to the point where it is just cooked inside, with a crisp, brown skin. The pig can be eaten hot or cold.

SERVES 8

a 6 kg | 15 lb suckling pig

18 cloves of garlic, peeled

grated zest and juice of 3 limes

4 tablespoons chopped fresh oregano

2 tablespoons capers, rinsed and chopped

4 tablespoons olive oil

1 teaspoon salt

1 teaspoon finely ground black pepper

1 teaspoon curry powder

1 bunch of coriander, stalks removed

2 tablespoons sunflower oil

1 bunch of watercress

1 small apple

1 Using a sharp knife, cut 2 cm | ¾ in slits all over the body, but not the head, of the pig. Slice 5 cloves of garlic thinly and insert into the slits.

2 Crush the remaining garlic and mix with the lime zest and juice, oregano, capers, olive oil, salt, pepper and curry powder.

3 Rub half of the mixture around the cavity of the pig and the remainder over the outside.

4 Place the coriander leaves inside the body cavity. Leave to marinate in the refrigerator for 24 hours.

5 Preheat the oven to 200°C | 400°F | gas mark 6.

6 Place the pig in a large roasting pan with the back facing upwards. Cover the ears and snout with foil to prevent them from burning.

7 Brush with the sunflower oil and rub salt over the skin. Roast for 30 minutes, basting regularly to prevent the skin from cracking.

8 Turn the oven temperature down to 180°C | 350°F | gas mark 4 and continue to roast for 2½ –3 hours or until the juices run clear when the thigh meat is pierced with a skewer.

9 Let the pig stand for 20 minutes before serving garnished with the watercress and the apple placed in the jaws.

NOTE: If you roast the pig on a wire rack the skin will crisp all over as the heat of the oven circulates freely around the pig.

Chinese Spare Ribs

SERVES 4

1.25 kg|2½ lb meaty pork belly pieces
   (American or Chinese spare ribs), skinned

For the marinade
4 tablespoons clear honey

4 tablespoons soy sauce
1 clove of garlic, crushed
juice of 2 lemons
salt and freshly ground black pepper

1 Mix together the ingredients for the marinade. Pour over the spare ribs and leave to marinate for at least 1 hour or up to 48 hours.

2 Preheat the oven to 180°C|350°F|gas mark 4.

3 Put the spare ribs with the marinade into a roasting pan, cover with foil and roast for 1½ hours. Remove the foil and roast, basting occasionally, for a further 30–45 minutes or until the meat is so tender that it falls from the bone and is glazed and sticky.

Braising

All cuts of pork are suitable for braising.

Braised Loin of Pork with Prunes

SERVES 4

1.35 kg|3 lb loin or leg of pork, skinned and fat
   removed
oil, for frying
15 g|½ oz butter
1 onion, finely chopped
290 ml|½ pint Brown Stock (see **Stocks**,
   page 683)

100 ml|3½ fl oz red wine
110 g|4 oz no-need-to-soak prunes
1 tablespoon redcurrant jelly
1 bay leaf
2 sprigs of fresh thyme
150 ml|¼ pint whipping cream
1 small bunch of watercress, to garnish

1 Preheat the oven to 150°C|300°F|gas mark 2.

2 Bone and tie the loin.

3 Heat the oil in a flameproof casserole. Add the butter and when foaming, add the pork. Fry until lightly browned all over (see **Meat**, *Browning*, page 343). Add the onion and fry until golden.

4 Add the stock, wine, one-third of the prunes, the redcurrant jelly, bay leaf and thyme. Bring to the boil, then cover and cook in the oven for 1½ hours.

5 Remove the pork from the casserole and slice neatly. Arrange in overlapping slices on a serving dish and keep warm in the turned-out oven while you make the sauce.

6 Strain the cooking liquor, removing any excess fat. Boil until the sauce has reduced to a syrupy consistency. Add the cream and the remaining prunes.

7 Spoon the sauce over the pork and garnish with watercress to serve.

Tying boned loin of pork

Pork is bred to be lean which means there is little intra-muscular fat. If especially tender cuts such as loin chops and fillet are overcooked, the meat will be dry and tough. As pork should be cooked until it is well done this presents a challenge to the cook. It is difficult to cook the meat until it is no longer pink but is still moist and juicy. Read **Meat,** *The test of the thumb* (page 349) before cooking the recipes for loin chops and pork fillet, below.

Chops are sliced from the loin or spare rib joints, usually 2 cm $|\frac{3}{4}$ in thick. Loin chops are usually cut from either end of the fore loin and have a thick layer of fat running along the outer edge. They are trimmed of rind, and the fat should be snipped or cut across (from the outside towards the meat) at 1 cm $|\frac{1}{2}$ in intervals, because the fat shrinks during cooking, and this tends to curl the chops out of shape. Chump chops are cut from the hind loin and have a bone at their centre.

Spare rib chops are cut from just behind the head. They contain less fat and bone than loin and chump chops and are usually cut more thinly.

Grilled Pork Chops with Caramelized Apples

SERVES 4

4 × 170 g $\|$ 6 oz pork chops	**For the garnish**
a little oil	2 dessert apples
freshly ground black pepper	butter, for frying
3–4 sage leaves, chopped, or a pinch of dried	1 teaspoon sugar
sage	a few sprigs of watercress

1 Preheat the grill to its highest setting.
2 Trim the rind from the chops and snip short cuts through the fat as described above. Brush lightly with oil.
3 Season with pepper and sage.
4 Grill the chops for 5–7 minutes on each side, or until cooked through. Keep warm on a warmed serving platter.
5 Peel and core the apples and cut them into eighths.
6 Melt a knob of butter in a frying pan and when it is foaming add the apples. Sprinkle with a little sugar and fry lightly on both sides until golden-brown but not mushy. The sugar will caramelize, giving a brown, toffee-like coating to the apples.
7 Garnish the chops with the caramelized apples and the watercress.

Preparing a Pork Fillet

The fillet lies along the back of the pig next to the loin. It is the leanest and most tender pork cut. A pork fillet weighs about 340 g | 12 oz and will serve 2 generously.

1 Remove and discard the small 'false fillet' that is sometimes found running the length of the fillet.
2 Using a boning knife or thin fish filleting knife, trim the silver membrane from the fillet.
3 To prepare medallions, cut the fillet across the length, slightly on the diagonal, into 2.5 cm | 1 in slices.
4 Place the slices in a single layer between 2 sheets of clingfilm. Bash with a small heavy saucepan or frying pan to flatten to half the thickness. This helps to tenderize the pork and allows it to cook more quickly.

Removing membrane from pork fillet

Medallions of Pork with Cider

SERVES 4

675 g | 1½ lb pork fillets
salt and freshly ground black pepper
2 tablespoons oil
1 medium onion, finely chopped
1 stick of celery, chopped
2 tablespoons Calvados
150 ml | ¼ pint dry cider

150 ml | ¼ pint white chicken or Vegetable Stock (see **Stocks**, pages 689 or 690)
75 ml | 5 tablespoons double cream
1 teaspoon cornflour
lemon juice to taste
2 tablespoons finely chopped fresh parsley

1 Trim the pork fillets and cut into medallions as described above. Season with salt and pepper.
2 Heat half of the oil in a small saucepan and sweat the onion and celery, covered with a piece of damp greaseproof paper (a *cartouche*), until soft.
3 Heat the remaining oil in a sauté pan and brown the pork medallions on both sides.
4 Add the Calvados and set alight. When the flames subside, add the softened vegetables and the cider and stock. Bring to a simmer, cover and cook for 10–15 minutes or until the pork is just cooked through (see **Meat**, *The test of the thumb*, page 349).
5 Remove the pork from the pan and keep warm. Sieve the juices into a small pan. Remove the vegetables from the sieve and divide then on to 4 plates, then top with the pork.
6 Mix together the cream and cornflour and whisk into the juices in the pan. Bring to the boil to thicken. Season to taste with lemon juice, salt and pepper. Pour over the pork and garnish with the parsley.

Stewing and Pies

Any of the cuts of pork are suitable for stewing or making into pies, but it makes economic sense to use less expensive cuts such as the shoulder.

Sausagemeat

Belly meat is the best cut of pork to use for sausagemeat, a forcemeat mixture (see *Forcemeat*, page 271, and *Terrines, Pâtés and Raised Pies*, page 703) of finely minced pork and minced salted pork fat, flavoured with herbs and spices. Sausagemeat is used with various seasonings and aromatic vegetables to stuff sausage skins, vegetables, the Christmas turkey, meat or poultry paupiettes or encased in puff pastry to make sausage rolls.

To make sausagemeat, weigh out equal quantities of lean pork and fat bacon. Mince finely and add 15 g | ½ oz salt per kg | 2¼ lb mince. Flavour the sausagemeat with chopped onion, mushrooms, garlic, herbs, salt and pepper. 450 g | 1 lb sausagemeat will make 8 breakfast-sized sausages.

Sausagemeat

SERVES 4

450 g | 1 lb minced fatty pork, such as belly pork
1 medium onion, very finely chopped (optional)
4 slices of white bread, crusts removed, crumbed
1 egg, beaten

3 fresh sage leaves, chopped, or 1 teaspoon dried sage
salt and freshly ground black pepper
fat, for frying

1 Mix together the pork and the onion, if using.
2 Stir the breadcrumbs into the mixture with the egg and sage.
3 Add plenty of salt and pepper and mix thoroughly. Fry a little of the mixture in a little oil and taste to check the seasoning.
4 Use as required (see *Simple Pork Sausages*, below)

Sausages

Sausages are forcemeats stuffed into tube-like skins of pig, sheep or beef intestine. The forcemeat or sausagemeat used to make sausages is mostly made with a mixture of finely minced pork and salted pork fat, flavoured with herbs, aromatic vegetables and spices. Sausages may also be made with other meats, fish, game or vegetables.

Sausages are available in fresh, smoked, cured and cooked varieties. Both fresh and smoked (provided you have the equipment) are easy to make in the domestic kitchen as the ingredients are relatively simple to prepare. Cured and cooked sausage varieties are made by specialists and are therefore not covered in this section. Smaller sausages, 10–12.5 cm|4–5 in in length, tend to be eaten for breakfast, and larger ones, up to 15 cm|6 in in length, for supper.

Sausage skins

Two types of sausage skin are used to encase forcemeat: the natural sausage skins and manufactured collagen sausage skins.

Natural sausage skins are lengths of pig, sheep or beef intestine. They are available in different widths, depending upon the animal or area of the intestine used. Pig intestine is used most frequently although sheep intestine is considered superior for making small sausages. Beef casings are much wider in diameter and are used mainly for large sausages originating from Eastern Europe. Most natural sausage skins are available from a good butcher. They are cleaned and salted so must be rinsed in warm water, then soaked in cold water overnight before they are used.

Collagen sausage skins are manufactured and do not need to be rinsed or soaked prior to use. They are inferior to natural sausage skin in both taste and texture and should only be used when natural skins are not available.

Preparing sausages

Sausages are most efficiently made using a sausage stuffing attachment to a mixer but can also be easily made using a heavy-duty piping bag fitted with a wide nozzle.

Simple Pork Sausages

SERVES 4

Use the sausagemeat recipe above and sausage skin measuring 2 cm|¾ in in diameter.

1 Rinse and soak the sausage skin overnight.
2 Cut the skin into a 2 m|6 ft length.
3 Make the sausagemeat: fry a small amount in a little oil to test that it is seasoned sufficiently. Adjust the seasoning if necessary, then refrigerate.
4 Put the sausagemeat into the sausage stuffer or piping bag.
5 Insert the nozzle into one end of the sausage skin. Carefully draw the entire length of sausage skin over the nozzle. Tie a knot firmly in the remaining few inches of sausage skin and pierce the skin a few inches from the end with a skewer to allow trapped air to escape while the sausage skin is stuffed.
6 When using a sausage stuffing attachment, support and guide the casing off the end of the nozzle as the sausagemeat is extruded from the nozzle into the sausage skin. When using a piping bag, squeeze the sausagemeat into the skins with even, constant pressure, supporting the skins with one hand as they are filled (it is helpful to share this job with another person). Do not overfill the sausage skins or they will burst during cooking.

7 If the sausage skin is unevenly filled, gently squeeze the sausagemeat along the skin to redistribute it. Try not to have any air pockets.

8 Once the length of sausage skin is filled, twist at regular intervals into individual sausages. Chipolatas are approximately 5 cm | 2 in in length; traditional breakfast-style sausages are 10–12.5 cm | 4–5 in long. Cumberland sausages are approximately 20–25 cm | 8–10 in long, with the ends of the sausage brought together to form a loop.

9 To ensure that the individual sausages do not untwist, the string of sausages can be twisted together.

10 If the sausages are to be smoked, smoke then once they are twisted together for the required amount of time (see **Preserving**, *Smoking*, *Fish and Meat*, page 549).

Cooking Sausages: Points to Remember

- Fry sausages over a medium heat in a mixture of butter and oil, until they are evenly browned on all sides.
- Sausages will not burst during shallow-frying unless they were overfilled.
- Piercing the sausage skin before cooking can cause it to split as steam accumulates and expands inside the skin.
- The fat in sausages escapes through the skin as they cook; they can therefore be grilled to a golden-brown, basted in their own juices, under a medium to high heat.

Boudin Blanc

MAKES ABOUT 10

Sausages made with a finer mixture, bound with cream and breadcrumbs, must be poached to firm the sausagemeat before frying. This recipe has been adapted from the *Observer French Cookery School*.

1 onion, very finely chopped
15 g | ½ oz butter
150 ml | ¼ pint double cream
100 g | 3½ oz fresh white breadcrumbs
2 m | 6 ft of 2.5 cm | 1 in diameter fresh sausage skin
225 g | 8 oz lean veal
225 g | 8 oz fatty pork
225 g | 8 oz boned chicken breast, or a further
   225 g | 8 oz lean veal

3 eggs
½ teaspoon ground allspice
salt and freshly ground white pepper
oil, for frying
slices of sautéed apple, to serve

For poaching
1.5 litres | 2½ pints water
750 ml | 1¼ pints milk

1 Sweat the onion in the butter until very soft, then cool.

2 Scald the cream by bringing it to a simmer; pour it over the breadcrumbs in a bowl and leave to cool.

3 Soak the sausage skin in cold water.

4 Work the veal, pork and chicken twice through the fine blade of a mincer, adding the onion before the second mincing. Alternatively, work the meat and onion a little at a time in a food processor. Put the mixture into a bowl and stir in the soaked breadcrumbs, eggs, allspice and plenty of salt and pepper. Sauté a small ball of the mixture in a little oil and check the seasoning – the mixture should taste quite spicy. Beat with a wooden spoon or knead with your hand until very smooth.

5 Fill the sausages skin as described above, being careful not to overfill or the sausages may burst while cooking. Twist into 15 cm|6in sausages and tie together to prevent them untwisting as they poach.

6 Pour the water and milk into a large pan and bring to the boil. Lower the string of sausages into the pan. Cover and poach very gently until firm. Do not allow the sausages to boil as this would cause the skins to burst. Remove from the heat and allow the sausages to cool in the liquid until tepid to keep the sausage skins moist, then drain and allow to cool completely. They can be prepared to this stage 24 hours in advance and kept covered in the refrigerator.

7 Reheat by shallow-frying in oil until golden-brown and serve with slices of sautéed apple.

Boudin Blanc: What has gone wrong when...

The sausages have burst.
- The sausage skins were stuffed too tightly.
- The sausages were allowed to boil while poaching.
- The sausage skins were pierced either during stuffing or while they were being cooked.

The sausage skins have dried out.
- The sausages were removed from the poaching liquor before they were completely cold.

Bacon, Ham and Gammon

Pork was originally cured to make bacon, a collective term for all cuts of cured pork, by salting and/or smoking to preserve the meat in the absence of refrigeration. Today pork is turned into bacon mainly for flavour as salting is no longer necessary. Smoked bacon keeps slightly longer than green (unsmoked) bacon, but again, modern smoking is done more for flavour than preservation.

Bacon

To produce bacon, most of the whole pig is salted in brine for up to a week, then matured for a further 7–12 days. At this stage it is known as green bacon, which is characteristically deep pink in colour and slightly salty with a white rind. Once bacon has been salted it may be smoked to increase its shelf life and enhance its flavour. Smoked bacon is hung in cool smoke for up to a month, which gives it a light brown rind and dark pink flesh.

Bacon is either sold thinly sliced as streaky and back rashers, thickly sliced as steaks for frying or grilling, boned and rolled as a whole joint for boiling or roasting, or on the bone as ham and gammon. Commercially produced bacon is generally mild. Bacon cured at home without the use of chemical preservatives is likely to have more flavour and saltiness, but needs soaking before cooking.

Choosing Bacon

Whether the bacon is green or smoked:

- The flesh should be moist and firm.
- The fat should be white or no darker than cream.
- The bacon should not be dry, hard, dark or patchy in colour.

British bacons vary according to manufacturer and price, some being saltier than others, so care should be taken if boiling without prior soaking. It is wise to soak large pieces to be cooked whole, such as gammons or fore hocks. Smaller cuts, steaks and rashers, rarely need soaking.

Danish pigs are all cured in the same manner, giving a good-quality, mild-tasting, not very salty bacon. Avoid buying cheap bacon as the meat is often injected with 'smoke' flavouring, as well as a large quantity of water. This becomes clear when the bacon rashers are placed into a hot frying pan as they boil rather than fry, shrink to half their original length and often taste extremely salty.

Although bacon is cured, it must be stored in the refrigerator. The shelf life of smoked bacon is longer than unsmoked but both types should be eaten within 5 days of purchase unless well sealed and oxygen flushed, in which case be guided by the 'use by' date. Bacon may be frozen for up to 1 year.

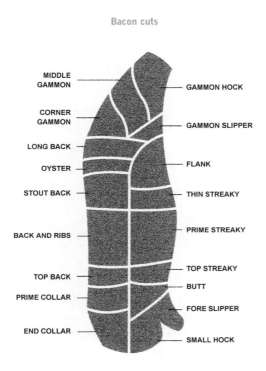

Bacon cuts

Bacon cuts

Cut	Cooking method	Recipe reference
Gammon hock/Fore	Boiling	*Baked Glazed Ham or Gammon Joint* (page 441)
Slipper/Middle hock/ Corner gammon/Gammon slipper/Butt	Baking	
Back and ribs	Frying Grilling	See *Frying Bacon* (page 412)
Prime streaky/Top streaky	Frying Grilling	
Forehock/Gammon/Collar	Stewing	

Gammon

Gammon, the hind leg of a bacon pig, is cured while still attached to the body. The gammon is then cut straight across the top of the leg. A whole gammon may weigh as much as 5 kg|14 lb but is usually sold in smaller portions. It is either boiled or roasted.

Ham

Ham is also bacon from the hind leg, but differs from gammon in the way that it is cut from the body and cured. First, the hind leg of the pig is cut from the carcass so that its top is rounded, often resulting in a ham weighing as much as 6 kg|16 lb. It is then salted, often by dry salting, and may be smoked separately according to local traditions.

Types of Ham

Uncooked ham is sold whole, boned and rolled, or thickly sliced. Cooked ham is available on the bone, boned and rolled, or thinly sliced. English hams are generally cooked before eating hot or cold. The most famous are the Bradenham ham and the sweet milk York ham. Paris ham is similar to English York ham. American Virginia hams owe their sweet flavour to the peanuts and peaches on which the hogs are traditionally fed: they are cured in salt and sugar and smoked over apple and hickory wood for a month. In contrast, Italian Parma ham, German Westphalian ham and French Bayonne ham are salted and smoked but eaten raw, thinly sliced.

Choosing Ham

- The ham should be short and thick with a high proportion of meat to fat and a thin rind indicating that the pig is young.
- The meat should be pale pink and the fat white.

Methods of Cooking Bacon, Ham and Gammon

Boiling and Baking

Most bacon cuts, other than bacon rashers, are suitable for boiling and baking. Due to the density of the meat and the fact that it is salted and maybe smoked, the meat is gently simmered beforehand, with the skin on, in water flavoured with aromatic vegetables, spices and herbs, until just cooked. Roasting or baking the meat from raw would take a long time and would certainly dry it out. After boiling, the meat is baked mainly to improve the appearance of the ham by browning the layer of fat that covers its surface.

Baked Glazed Ham or Gammon Joint

SERVES 4–6

1 ham or gammon joint	black peppercorns
1 onion	2 tablespoons Demerara sugar
1 carrot	1 teaspoon dry English mustard
1 bay leaf	a handful of cloves
fresh parsley stalks	

1 Soak the joint overnight in cold water to remove excess salt. If time does not allow overnight soaking, immerse the joint in cold water and bring to the boil, then simmer for 10 minutes. Drain.

2 Place the joint in a large saucepan of cold water and add the onion, carrot, bay leaf, parsley stalks and peppercorns. Bring slowly to the boil, then turn the heat down to a simmer and cover the pan. Large joints weighing more than 3.5 kg | 8 lb should be simmered for 25 minutes per 450 g | 1 lb. Joints weighing less than 3.5 kg | 8 lb should be simmered for 20 minutes per 450 g | 1 lb. Do not allow the water to boil as the ham may dry out and become grainy (see *Meat, Boiling Meat*, page 351).

3 Preheat the oven to 220°C | 425° F | gas mark 7.

4 Lift the joint out of the poaching liquor and carefully trim off the skin with a sharp knife, leaving a thin coating of fat on the joint. Reserve the liquor for ham stock.

5 Mix the sugar and mustard together and press the mixture evenly all over the fat.

6 Using a sharp knife, cut a diamond lattice pattern across the coated fat. Press any sugar that falls off on again. Stick a clove into the centre of each diamond segment, or into the cuts where the lines cross.

7 Stand the joint upright on a roasting rack in the roasting pan, fat side uppermost. Bake the joint for about 20 minutes or until brown and slightly caramelized.

To make a ham frill

A ham frill is used to cover the bone sticking out of the end of the ham.

1 Fold a piece of greaseproof paper about 20 × 25 cm | 8 × 10 in in half lengthways then loosely in half lengthways again.

2 Make 4 cm | 1½ in cuts, 1 cm | ½ in apart, parallel to the short end of the paper, cutting through from the folded side towards the open sides.

3 Make cuts all along the strip. Now open out one fold of the paper and refold it lengthways in the opposite direction.

4 Wrap the frill round the ham bone and secure with a paste of flour and water.

Frying

Streaky and back bacon, gammon steaks and chops are suitable for frying.

Streaky bacon
To fry streaky bacon, place it in a cold, dry frying pan. Heat over a medium heat, turning the rashers occasionally until they lose their translucency. For crisp bacon, continue cooking until golden-brown. Place on kitchen paper to remove excess fat before serving.

Back bacon
Fry back bacon in a sauté pan with just enough oil to coat the surface of the pan until, very lightly golden on both sides.

Gammon steaks or bacon chops
Before grilling or frying gammon steaks or bacon chops, thick rashers from the prime back, trim off the rind and snip the surrounding thick layer of fat, from the outside towards the meat, at 1 cm | ½ in intervals, to prevent the chops from curling. Bacon chops are sometimes cooked with the rind left on, but snipping is essential as the fat shrinks and curls during cooking, pulling the chops out of shape. Fry or grill until the meat is firm and loses its translucency.

Grilling

Rashers of streaky and back bacon and gammon steaks are suitable for grilling.
1 Preheat the grill to its highest setting until very hot.
2 Place the bacon or gammon steaks on a grill rack over a grill pan.
3 Cook 5–7.5 cm | 2–3 in from the grill for 3–4 minutes per side, until the meat loses its translucency and browns lightly.

Flat Ham Pie

SERVES 4

225 g | 8 oz flour quantity Pâte à Pâte (see
  Pastry, page 518)
55 g | 2 oz Gruyère cheese, finely grated
30 g | 1 oz Parmesan cheese, freshly grated
30 g | 1 oz butter, melted
55 g | 2 oz fresh white breadcrumbs

225 g | 8 oz cooked ham, shredded
2 tablespoons chopped fresh chives
½ clove of garlic, crushed
5 tablespoons soured cream
freshly ground black pepper
beaten egg, to glaze

1 Preheat the oven to 220°C | 400°F | gas mark 6.
2 Roll two-fifths of the pastry into a rectangle about 20 × 15 cm | 8 × 6 in.

3 Place the pastry rectangle on a baking sheet and prick all over with a fork. Refrigerate for 10 minutes, then bake for about 15 minutes until cooked. Allow to cool.

4 Mix together the cheeses, butter and breadcrumbs. Scatter half of the mixture over the baked pastry leaving a border of 1 cm$|\frac{1}{2}$ in.

5 Mix together the ham, chives, garlic and soured cream. Season with pepper. Spread the mixture over the crumbs, then top with the remaining crumb mixture.

6 Roll the remaining pastry into a rectangle slightly larger than the first. Dampen the edge of the baked pastry. Place the uncooked pastry on top and trim the edges to fit. Secure the edges by pressing down with a fork.

7 Glaze the pie with the egg. Decorate with any pastry trimmings, thinly rolled, and cut a steam hole in the top of the pie.

8 Bake for about 30 minutes, until golden brown and no grey or damp patches remain on the pastry. Serve hot or cold.

Poultry

Poultry is the term for birds specifically bred for the table, including chicken, turkey, duck, guinea fowl and goose. The flavour and texture of poultry depends on how it was raised, its diet, when it was drawn (see **Game,** *Drawing Feathered Game*, page 464) and how long it was hung (see **Meat,** *Hanging Meat*, page 335)

The meat of a young bird is tender and therefore is suitable for grilling, frying and roasting. As the bird ages the meat becomes tougher and drier but strengthens in flavour and can be braised or stewed. Most birds are slaughtered very young, so more important than its age is whether or not the bird is free-range. Free-range birds will have been allowed to wander and eat a variety of foods. They will have a more intense flavour and may possibly be slightly tougher than battery birds due to the greater amount of exercise they have taken.

Choosing Poultry

Choose a bird with plump breasts, dry skin and no bruising or blood spots. A pliable breastbone is an indication of a young bird. If the legs are attached, they should be smooth and flexible.

Storing Poultry

Uncooked

If you have bought a bird with giblets, remove them as soon as you get home and store them separately in the bottom of the refrigerator. Unwrap the bird so that air can circulate over the skin. Cover loosely with greaseproof paper. When poultry is wrapped in plastic, moisture tends to condense beneath, creating perfect conditions for bacterial growth (see **Food Safety**, page 21). Store poultry at the bottom of the refrigerator for not more than 2 days.

Cooked

Cooked poultry may be stored near the top of the refrigerator for up to 2 days provided that it is wrapped in clingfilm to prevent it from drying out or being tainted by other ingredients stored nearby.

Frozen

See *Meat* (page 32).

Poultry should be defrosted slowly in the bottom of the refrigerator.

Poultry Defrosting Chart

Weight of bird	Defrosting time in refrigerator
2.25 kg | 5 lb	24 hours
4.5 kg | 10 lb	36 hours
6.75 kg | 15 lb	48 hours
9 kg | 20 lb	64 hours

Types of Poultry

Chicken

Chickens are available in a range of sizes determined by their age. They are usually sold oven-ready, meaning that they are plucked, drawn and often trussed. The more you spend on a chicken, the better it is likely to taste. A frozen supermarket bird, raised on a battery farm and fed fishmeal, is unlikely to taste as good as a free-range bird, however well cooked.

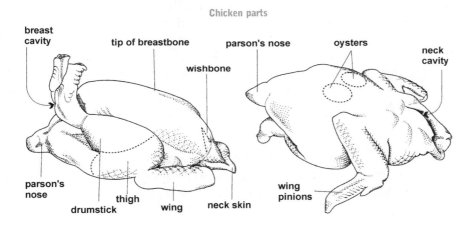

Chicken parts

breast cavity — tip of breastbone — wishbone — parson's nose — oysters — neck cavity

parson's nose — drumstick — thigh — wing — neck skin — wing pinions

Poussin

Poussins come in 2 sizes, termed single and double. Single poussins are 4–6 weeks old, weigh approximately 250 g | 9 oz and serve 1 person. They look attractive on the plate but have very little flavour. To make them more interesting they may be stuffed and/or served with a flavourful sauce. Single poussins are suitable for oven- and spit-roasting or may be flattened (see *Spatchcocking*, below) and grilled.

Double poussins are 6–10 weeks old, weight approximately 350 g | 12 oz, serve 2 people and have a little more flavour than single poussins. Double poussins are often stuffed and roasted, then split in half to serve to 2 people. They are also suitable for spit-roasting or may be spatchcocked and grilled.

Spring chicken
Spring chickens are 10–12 weeks old and weigh approximately 450 g | 1 lb. They serve 2 people and have a similar flavour to that of double poussins. They are best roasted.

Roaster
Roasting chickens are usually over 3 months old and weigh 1.2–1.8 kg | 2½ –4 lb and can have an excellent flavour as long as they have been raised in reasonable conditions. Allow 450 g | 1 lb per serving. Whole chickens are suited to oven-roasting, braising, pot-roasting and poaching. The chickens can be jointed then grilled, baked, fried or stewed.

Corn-fed chicken
This is usually a free-range chicken fed on corn which colours its fat yellow and gives it a distinctive, rich flavour. French corn-fed chickens generally seem to have a slightly gamier flavour than English ones.

Poulet noir
This is a French black-legged chicken. When plucked, it looks more like a guinea fowl, with its larger legs and narrow breast, than a chicken. The texture of the cooked meat is firmer than that of chicken. Poulet noir is more expensive than a conventional chicken as it is reared on pasture from a month old and fed on corn and dairy products in addition to its free-range diet.

Capon
Originally a castrated cockerel which, having lost its interest in sex, ate voraciously and became very plump and tender, weighing as much as 4 kg | 9 lb. They are no longer available.

Boiling fowl
Boiling fowls are very rare today, as there is little demand for older, tougher birds. Boiling fowls may be older than 12 months and contain a high proportion of meat to fat. They require long, slow cooking and have a pronounced flavour.

Duck

Duck is more expensive than chicken as it is unsuited to intensive battery farming and yields a small proportion of meat despite its weight and size. Ducks have a large carcass and farmed ducks contain a high quantity of fat.

Most ducks sold today are ducklings 7–9 weeks old. A 1.8 kg | 4 lb duck feeds only 2–3 people due to the large carcass and high proportion of subcutaneous fat.

Look for a plump breast and skin that is dry, soft and smooth. The duck should not be slimy and should not smell strongly.

Aylesbury and Gressingham ducks are considered to be the best. Due to the high proportion of subcutaneous fat, whole ducks are best oven-roasted, jointed duck is often baked or made into *confit* (see **Preserving**, page 554) and duck breasts are pan-fried. The rich meat stands up to strongly flavoured sauces, often containing fruit.

Goose

Goose is at its best when it weighs about 4.5 kg | 10 lb at around 6–9 months of age. A goose this size and will serve 4–6 people. Goose is more expensive than duck and has an even larger carcass relative to the quantity of meat and a great deal of subcutaneous fat. As a result it has become less popular at Christmas than it was previously and the more economical turkey has become prevalent.

Goose can be delicious, but make sure that you choose a young bird as old geese can be very tough. Fresh goose has a clean white skin which is soft and dry to the touch. The flesh is a cream colour but becomes light brown with a gamy flavour when cooked. Due to its high proportion of subcutaneous fat, goose is best roasted.

Today goose is bred for the Christmas season so fresh goose is more readily available in December.

Turkey

Turkeys are available in many sizes, frozen and fresh, whole or in portions. Their giblets, sold in a bag with the bird or separately, are mainly used for flavouring gravy, for stock, stuffing and pâté.

Try to buy fresh rather than frozen turkey as it will have a better flavour and texture. Size varies enormously depending upon age. Turkeys are at their best at around 8 months, weighing around 4.5–7 kg | 10–14 lb and serving approximately 10–14 people. Allow 450 g | 1 lb of turkey per serving to take account of the weight of the carcass. The flesh should be very white and firm, and the skin dry and soft. Remove all the giblets as soon as possible because they deteriorate quickly, and wipe the bird inside and out before storing.

There are a variety of turkeys available particularly at Christmas time. The quality is usually marked by the price. The Bronze turkey has a particularly good flavour.

Guinea Fowl

This is usually a little smaller than the average-sized chicken, weighing 1–1 ½ kg | 2–3 lb, and has a slightly scrawny appearance. Although guinea fowl is traditionally a game bird and supermarkets often treat it as such, only selling it in the winter months, it is now widely farmed all year round. The taste is that of a very delicious, slightly gamy chicken. Guinea fowl is most suitable for oven or pot-roasting, braising and stewing. As the meat is very lean it must be cooked with great care to prevent it from drying out.

Methods of Cooking Poultry

Roasting

All types of poultry are good for roasting. For instructions on plucking and drawing poultry see **Game**, *Drawing Feathered Game* (page 458).

Stuffing Whole Birds

Roasting chickens and other medium-sized birds can be stuffed in both the neck and body cavity. Turkeys are stuffed only in the neck end due to the risk of salmonella poisoning if the body cavity is stuffed: with a bird as large as a turkey it would take a long time for the stuffing in the body to become hot enough to kill salmonella germs. For this reason it is recommended that stuffing placed in the body cavity of medium-sized birds should not contain meat.

Smaller birds such as poussin are stuffed in the larger body cavity. Do not pack the stuffing in too firmly as it swells with cooking which may cause it to push its way out of the bird as it cooks. When the neck end of a bird is filled, the flap of neck skin is folded over the stuffing and secured with thread or a skewer.

Stuffing birds under the skin: Chickens and smaller birds can be stuffed between the skin and the breast flesh with softened flavoured butters, herbs or soft-textured stuffing, to provide flavour and to help prevent the lean flesh from drying out.

Before the bird can be stuffed in this way, the skin must be loosened away from the flesh. This is done by inserting the first two fingers under the skin at the neck end and sweeping them back and forth to loosen the skin covering the breasts. The stuffing is then inserted, using a piping bag or your fingers. Distribute the stuffing evenly under the skin by moving it about over the breasts, stroking the skin lightly with the fingertips. Only a very thin layer of stuffing should be inserted under the skin or it will cause the skin to split when the bird is cooked.

Trussing

Birds are trussed to maintain a neat, compact shape during roasting. Trussing large birds is not done as it prevents the inside of the thigh from being cooked through by the time the breast is ready. Small birds, especially game birds where underdone thighs are desirable (to prevent toughness), are trussed with their feet left on. The feet may simply be tied together for neatness, and the pinions skewered under the bird. Or they may be trussed in other ways, one of which is described below. If the bird is to be stuffed, stuff it before trussing to get a neater result.

To truss a bird:

1 Arrange the bird so that the neck flap is folded over the neck hole, and the pinions turned under and tucked in tightly. If folded correctly, they will hold the neck flap in place, but if the bird is well stuffed the neck flap may have to be skewered or sewn into place.

2 Press the legs down and towards the bird to force the breast into a plumped-up position.

3 Thread a long trussing needle with thin string and push it through the wing joint, right through the body and through the other wing joint.

4 Push the needle through the body again, this time through the thighs.

5 Tie the 2 loose ends of string together in a bow to facilitate removal later.

6 Then thread a shorter piece of string through the knobbly ends of the 2 drumsticks and tie them together, winding the string round the parson's nose at the same time to close the vent. Sometimes a small slit is cut in the skin just below the end of the breastbone, and the parson's nose is pushed through it.

Trussing a bird

Roasting Poultry: Points to Remember

- Chicken and turkey must be roasted until thoroughly cooked to prevent the risk of food poisoning, in contrast to duck, goose and feathered game, all of which are better roasted until lightly pink to ensure that the meat remains tender and moist.
- Birds for roasting are often stuffed at the neck end. Make sure the weight of the stuffing is taken into account when calculating the cooking time.
- Poultry liable to dry out during cooking can be barded by tying fatty bacon or rindless pork back fat strips over the body of the bird. The barding is removed towards the end of cooking to allow the breasts to brown.
- Fatty birds such as duck and goose should be placed on a wire rack above the roasting pan to allow the large quantity of melted fat to collect below.
- Place the bird breast side down for the first 30 minutes of roasting to encourage the juices to run into the breasts and keep them moist.

Roasting Table for Chicken and Duck

Bird	Temperature			Cooking time	
	°C	°F	gas mark	per kg	per lb
Chicken	200	400	6	35–45 mins	15–20 mins

NOTE: Few chickens, however small, will be cooked in much under 1 hour.

Bird	Temperature			Cooking time	
Duck, small					
(under 2.3 kg│5 lb)	190	375	5	45 mins	20 mins
Large	180	350	4	55 mins	25 mins

NOTE: The same temperatures and timings apply to roast goose.

English Roast Chicken

SERVES 4

1.35 kg|3 lb roasting chicken
15 g|½ oz butter

For the stuffing

30 g|1 oz butter
1 onion, finely chopped
55 g|2 oz fresh white breadcrumbs
1 small cooking apple, grated
2 teaspoons chopped fresh mixed herbs
grated zest of ½ lemon
½ egg, beaten
salt and freshly ground black pepper

To garnish

4 chipolata sausages
4 rindless streaky bacon rashers

For the gravy

1 scant tablespoon plain flour
290 ml|½ pint White Chicken Stock (see
  Stocks, page 689)

To serve

Bread Sauce (see below)

1 Preheat the oven to 200°C|400°F|gas mark 6.
2 To make the stuffing, melt the butter in a saucepan and sweat the onion until soft but not coloured. Allow to cool.
3 Mix the breadcrumbs, apple, herbs and lemon zest together in a bowl.
4 Add the softened onion and enough beaten egg to bind the mixture together. Do not make it too wet. Season to taste with salt and pepper.
5 Stuff the chicken from the neck end, making sure the breast is well plumped. Draw the neck skin flap down to cover the stuffing. Secure with a skewer if necessary. Place in a roasting pan.
6 Smear a little butter all over the chicken and season with salt and pepper. Roast in the oven for about 1½ hours, or until the juices run clear when the thigh is pierced with a skewer.
7 Meanwhile make each chipolata into 2 cocktail-sized sausages by twisting gently in the middle. Cut each bacon rasher in half and roll up.
8 After the chicken has been roasting for 1 hour, put the sausages and bacon rolls into the roasting tin, wedging the bacon rolls together so that they cannot come undone.
9 Baste occasionally and check that the sausages and bacon are not sticking to the side of the tin and getting burnt.
10 When the chicken is cooked, lift it out on to a warmed serving dish. Trim off the wing tips and tops of the drumsticks, surround with the bacon rolls and sausages and keep warm while you make the gravy.
11 Slowly pour off all but 1 tablespoon of the fat from the roasting pan, taking care to keep any juices. Add the flour and stir over heat for 1 minute. Add the stock and stir until the sauce boils. Simmer for 3 minutes. Check the seasoning. Strain into a warmed gravy-boat.
12 Serve the chicken with Bread Sauce and the gravy.

Bread Sauce

This very rich sauce is served with roast chicken and roast turkey. For a lighter sauce, reduce the quantity of butter and omit the cream.

1 small onion, peeled	a pinch of freshly grated nutmeg
6 whole cloves	salt
290 ml|½ pint whole milk	55 g|2 oz fresh white breadcrumbs
1 bay leaf	55 g|2 oz butter
10 peppercorns	2 tablespoons single cream (optional)

1 Cut the onion in half, then stick the 2 halves (*pique*) with the cloves.

2 Place the milk in a saucepan and add the onion, bay leaf, peppercorns, nutmeg and salt. Heat over a medium heat until the milk steams, then remove from the heat and let stand to infuse for 30 minutes. Strain.

3 Reheat the milk. Sieve the breadcrumbs and stir into the milk with the butter and the cream, if using.

4 Heat the sauce gently to thicken. If it becomes too thick, add more warm milk to adjust the mixture to a thick coating consistency.

5 If not serving immediately, dot the surface with butter to keep a skin from forming. Stir in the butter when reheating.

Carving chicken

1 First cut off the legs. Cut through the skin between the breast and the leg and press the thighs down towards the carving dish to expose the hip joint.

2 Cut through the joint and continue to bend the leg back to remove it from the body with the oyster intact. If the bird is very small, the thigh and drumstick are served together.

3 With larger birds, cut through the knee joint to separate the thigh from the drumstick.

4 Remove the wings by cutting diagonally, using the top of the wishbone as a guide, straight through the shoulder joint.

5 With small birds, the breast can be prised from the breastbone in one piece. Larger breasts are sliced thickly diagonally downwards from both sides of the breastbone. Or carve thin slices from each breast by cutting from the top of the breastbone down across the breast towards the leg joint.

Roasting Chicken: What has gone wrong when...

The breast meat is dry.

- The bird was not basted regularly.
- The bird should have been barded to protect the delicate breast meat.
- The bird was small and should have been roasted breast side down for half of the roasting time.
- The bird was cooked for too long.

Roast Duck

SERVES 3

1.8 kg	4 lb oven-ready duck	1 tablespoon plain flour
salt and freshly ground black pepper	290 ml	½ pint Duck or strong White Chicken
1 small onion, peeled and halved	Stock (see *Stocks*, page 689)
1 small orange, halved	Apple Sauce (see *Fruit*, *Apples*, page 279)

1 Preheat the oven to 200°C | 400°F | gas mark 6.
2 Wipe the duck clean inside and out. Season the cavity well with salt and pepper. Place the onion and orange inside the duck (these will enhance the flavour of the duck as well as help to keep the meat moist. Prick the duck skin all over and sprinkle with salt (this will release the fat and crisp the duck skin).
3 Put the duck upside down on a rack in a roasting tin and roast in the oven for 30 minutes (placing the duck breast side down helps to protect the breast meat from overcooking and drying out). Pour off the fat. Turn the duck over and continue roasting for about 1 hour, until cooked. Test by piercing the thigh with a skewer. If the juices run out dark pink, the duck needs further cooking; if the juices are light pink, the duck is ready.
4 Tip the juices from the cavity into a bowl and reserve them. Joint the duck into 6 pieces (see instructions below) and arrange on a serving dish. Alternatively, leave the duck whole for carving at the table (see *Carving duck* below). In any event keep it warm without covering, as this would spoil the crisp skin.
5 To make the gravy, pour off all but 1 tablespoon of the fat in the roasting tin. Stir over a low heat, scraping the bottom of the tin to loosen all the sediment. Whisk in the flour and add the stock and the juices from inside the duck, and whisk until smooth. Simmer, stirring, for 2 minutes. Season to taste with salt and pepper.
6 Strain the gravy into a warmed gravy-boat. Fill a second gravy-boat with hot or cold Apple Sauce and serve with the duck.

Carving duck

1 Remove the wings at the shoulder joints.
2 Carve the breast in slices, starting from the wing and working up towards the breast bone.
3 Once the breast meat is carved the legs can be removed.

Jointing cooked duck into 6 portions

1 Gather the equipment together while the duck is resting. You will need a board, a tray large enough to hold the board, kitchen scissors, a cook's knife and gloves.
2 Place the board over the tray to catch any juices while jointing the duck.
3 Place the duck, breast side down, on the board. Using a pair of scissors, cut out the backbone and discard. **(a)**

Jointing cooked duck (a)
Removing the backbone

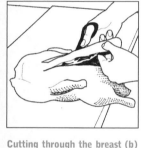

Cutting through the breast (b)

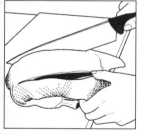

Three pieces of duck (c)

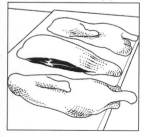

4 Turn the duck breast side up and cut lengthways down the breast, halfway between the breastbone and the wing on both sides. **(b)**

5 There are now 3 pieces of duck: 1 breast and 2 wing-and-leg|thigh pieces. **(c)**

6 Take the breast piece – you will see that the meat is thicker at one end, almost a wedge shape. From the thin end of the breast measure two-thirds of the way up the breast and cut through so that the thicker end of the breast is the smaller piece. **(d)**

7 Take the wing-and–leg|thigh pieces and cut each piece in 2 between the wing and the leg|thigh to ensure that each portion has the same amount of meat. **(e)**

8 There are now 6 portions of duck: 2 breast, 2 wing-and-breast, 2 thigh/leg. **(f)**

9 Trim off any unsightly bones, fat and skin.

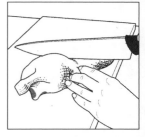

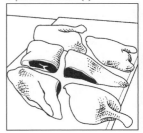

Thawing and Roasting Times for Turkeys

Due to their size frozen turkeys can take a long time to defrost. They should be defrosted slowly to reduce loss of moisture (see table below). Thawing turkey in a warm room (over 18°C|65°F) or under warm water is not recommended, as warmth will encourage the growth of micro-organisms, which might result in food poisoning. It is best to thaw a turkey in the bottom of the refrigerator.

Although the thawing time in the table can be relied on, the cooking times are dependent on an accurate oven. For safety's sake, plan the timing so that the bird will be cooked 1 hour before serving. This will give you leeway if necessary. Remember that the turkey must be weighed to calculate the cooking time after it has been stuffed.

To test if the turkey is cooked, press a skewer into the thickest part of the thigh. The juices should run clear. When the bird is cooked, open the oven door to cool the oven, then put the turkey on a serving dish and return it to the oven to keep warm.

Thawing and Cooking Times for Turkey

Weight of oven-ready bird, including any stuffing	Thawing time in refrigerator 5°C|40°F	Cooking time at 200°C|400°F gas mark 6	Cooking time at 180°C|350°F gas mark 4
4–5 kg|8–10 lb	65 hrs	2½ –3 hrs	–
5–6 kg|10–13 lb	70 hrs	3–3¾ hrs	–
6–7 kg|13–16 lb	75 hrs	30 mins then	3 ¼ –4 hrs
8–9 kg|16–20 lb	80 hrs	30 mins then	4–4½ hrs
9–11 kg|20–24 lb	96 hrs	1 hr then	4–4½ hrs

Roast Turkey

A large square of fine muslin (butter muslin) is needed for this recipe.

SERVES 12

5.35 kg | 12 lb oven-ready turkey (plucked, drawn and trussed)

For the stuffing

30 g | 1 oz butter
1 onion, finely chopped
450 g | 1 lb sausagemeat
225 g | 8 oz fresh white breadcrumbs
1 large egg, beaten
grated zest of 1 lemon
2 teaspoons chopped fresh thyme
1 tablespoon chopped fresh parsley
½ teaspoon salt
salt and freshly ground black pepper

For cooking

170 g | 6 oz butter
giblets

½ onion
2 bay leaves
a few parsley stalks
290 ml | ½ pint water

To garnish

24 chipolata sausages
24 rindless streaky bacon rashers

For the gravy

2 tablespoons plain flour
570 ml | 1 pint Turkey Stock (see **Stocks**, page 691) or vegetable cooking water

To serve

Cranberry Sauce (see **Fruit**, *Berries*, page 00)
Bread Sauce (see page 285)

1 To make the stuffing, place the butter in a saucepan, add the onion and sweat over low heat covered with piece of damp greaseproof paper (a *cartouche*) and a lid until soft. Allow to cool, then tip into a bowl and mix together with the remaining stuffing ingredients.

2 Just before cooking the turkey, stuff the neck end, making sure that the breast is well plumped. Draw the skin flap down to cover the stuffing and secure with a skewer. Shape any remaining stuffing into golf ball–sized balls and refrigerate until required.

3 Preheat the oven to 200°C | 400°F | gas mark 6.

4 Weigh the turkey. Calculate the cooking time according to the table above.

5 Melt the butter and soak a very large piece of butter muslin (about 4 times the size of the turkey) in it until all the butter has been completely absorbed.

6 Season the turkey well with salt and pepper. Place it in a large roasting pan with the giblets (except the liver) and neck. Add the onion, bay leaves and parsley stalks and pour in the water. Completely cover the bird with the doubled buttered muslin and roast in the oven breast side down for the first hour, for the calculated time, turning the oven down after the recommended time. A 5.3 kg | 12 lb turkey should take 3–3½ hours.

7 One hour before the turkey is ready, place the stuffing balls in a baking tin and cook in the oven with the turkey. Turn occasionally while they cook.

8 Meanwhile, prepare the garnishes: make each chipolata into 2 cocktail-sized sausages by twisting gently in the middle. Stretch each bacon rasher slightly with the back of a knife, then cut in half lengthways and roll up. Place the sausages and bacon rolls in a second roasting tin, with the bacon rolls wedged in so that they cannot unravel. Thirty minutes before the turkey is ready, put the sausages and bacon in the oven.

9 The turkey is cooked when the juices that run out of the thigh when pierced with a skewer run clear. Remove the muslin and lift the bird on to a serving dish. Surround with the bacon rolls, sausages and stuffing balls. Keep warm while making the gravy.

10 Place the roasting tin with its juices on the hob and skim off the fat. Whisk in the flour and make up to about 425 ml $|\frac{3}{4}$ pint with stock or vegetable water. Stir until boiling, then simmer for a few minutes. Check the seasoning. Strain into a warmed gravy-boat.

11 Serve the turkey with the gravy, Cranberry Sauce and Bread Sauce.

Carving turkey

Due to the size of the bird, the breast meat can be carved in slices approximately 6 mm $|\frac{1}{4}$ in thick without removing the wings or legs. The drumsticks and thighs may also be sliced and a portion of dark meat served with the breast together with a spoonful of stuffing.

Grilling

(See **Meat**, *Methods of Cooking Meat*, page 341.)

As poultry is prone to drying out, it is important that the meat is regularly basted with melted butter or oil during cooking. The grill must be very hot to brown the surface of the meat sufficiently before or just as the centre of the meat is cooked. Poultry for grilling is often marinated in marinades containing oil, which penetrates the flesh and helps to keep the meat moist during cooking. Although poultry joints may be browned and crisped further under the grill, this cooking method is mostly used for tender cuts of meat from the breast or thigh and very young birds such as spatchcocked poussin which is flattened for grilling (see below).

It is important that the chicken is cooked thoroughly. It is recommended that thicker chicken pieces, such as the breast with the bone, are poached (see *Poaching*, below) before grilling or barbecueing.

Small whole birds such as poussin and spring chicken can be cut in half or *spatchcocked* (see below) and grilled. To grill a small bird, heat the grill or barbecue to its highest setting. Brush the bird with oil.

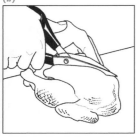

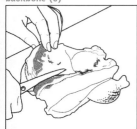

Splitting a small bird in half

1 Place the bird breastbone uppermost on a board.
2 Using a sharp knife, cut through the breast meat as close to the breastbone as possible, from one end of the bird to the other. (a)
3 Using poultry shears or kitchen scissors, cut through the exposed breastbone and the wishbone located at the neck end of the bird. (b)
4 Open out the bird and cut along the length of the backbone on the same side.
5 Cut the backbone away from the other half of the bird. (c)
6 The knobbly ends of the drumsticks and the fleshless tips of the pinions can be cut off before or after cooking.

Spatchcocking a bird

Spatchcocking is a method of flattening a small bird such as poussin or quail before cooking so that it can be grilled or barbecued quickly and evenly and served as a single portion. Spatchcocked birds are often marinated or flavoured with herbs and spices and then grilled, char-grilled (see *Meat*, *Methods of Cooking Meat*, page 341) or barbecued.

1 Place the bird breast side down on a board.
2 Using poultry shears or kitchen scissors, split the bird down one side of the backbone. (a)
3 Cut down the other side of the backbone to remove it.
4 Open out the bird and flatten well on a board by pressing along the breastbone with the heel of your hand. (b)
5 Skewer the bird in position, i.e. flat and open. (c)

Spatchcocked Grilled Poussin

SERVES 4

4 single poussins	lemon juice
salt and freshly ground black pepper	55 g | 2 oz butter
a pinch of cayenne pepper	15 g | ½ oz Parmesan cheese, freshly grated

1 Spatchcock the poussins as described above.
2 Season well with salt, pepper and cayenne and sprinkle with lemon juice. If possible, refrigerate for 1 hour.
3 Preheat the grill to its highest setting. Brush the cut side of the poussins with melted butter. Grill the bird about 5 cm | 2 in away from the heat source until browned on both sides, then move the bird further from the heat to finish cooking through.
4 Grill for about 12 minutes or until a good golden-brown, brushing frequently with the pan juices to keep the meat moist. Turn over, brush again and grill for a further 7 minutes or until the poussin is cooked (when the thickest part is pierced with a skewer, the juices should run clear).
5 Brush once more with the hot butter and sprinkle with the Parmesan cheese. Grill until golden-brown and crisp.

Poaching

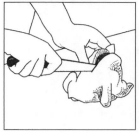
Spatchcocking a bird (a)

(See also **Meat,** *Methods of Cooking Meat*, page 341).

Poaching is a very gentle cooking technique suitable for cooking birds of any age. Older birds will require longer poaching, until the meat starts to fall away from the bone, whereas a younger bird only needs cooking through so that it remains tender and does not dry out. Of the poultry birds, chicken is most frequently poached whole or boned whole and stuffed. Whole poached chicken is used as a basis for a number of classic dishes such as *Chicken Elizabeth* (see below) and *Chicken Chaudfroid* (see **Aspic**, page 93).

Flattening the bird (b)

Poaching is also a perfect cooking method for tender pieces of poultry, such as the breast, which is often stuffed and firmly wrapped in clingfilm or kitchen foil to set its shape while it gently cooks through (see *Stuffing Breast Fillets* and *Chicken Breasts Stuffed with Red Pepper Mousseline*, below). The tender breast meat must be cooked very gently in barely simmering water to avoid overcooking and drying out. Cook the breasts until they are just firm (see **Meat**, *The test of the thumb*, page 349).

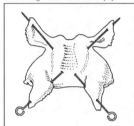
Securing with skewers (c)

Chicken Elizabeth

The Cordon Bleu School devised this dish for the Coronation celebration in 1953 hence its popular name Coronation Chicken.

SERVES 4

1.35 kg | 3 lb chicken, cleaned but not trussed
1 bay leaf
6 peppercorns
1 teaspoon salt
2 parsley stalks
1 slice of lemon
2 teaspoons fresh thyme leaves

225 ml | 8 fl oz Elizabeth Sauce (see **Sauces, Savoury**, page 601)

To serve
Rice Salad (see **Rice**, page 567)
1 bunch of watercress

1 First poach the chicken. Place the chicken breast side up in a large saucepan and add the herbs and flavourings. Pour enough cold water into the pan to leave the breasts standing slightly proud of the water to steam. Cover with greaseproof paper and a lid.

2 Cook gently for $1\frac{1}{4}$–$1\frac{1}{2}$ hours or until the juices from the chicken run clear and the drumsticks feel loose. Remove the chicken from the pan and set aside to cool.

3 Remove the meat from the chicken bones, and when quite cold mix with the sauce, reserving a little of it.

4 Pile the chicken into the middle of a serving dish and coat with the reserved sauce. Garnish with watercress and serve with rice salad.

NOTE: It is easier to remove the meat from the bones while the chicken is still lukewarm. But on no account should the sauce be added to the meat until the meat is completely cold as it is

Jointing a chicken. Cut through the skin along the backbone (a)

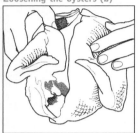
Loosening the oysters (b)

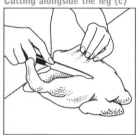
Cutting alongside the leg (c)

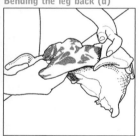
Bending the leg back (d)

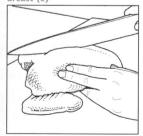
Cutting through the skin and breast (e)

mayonnaise-based and contains raw eggs. If the sauce is allowed to warm beyond 4°C|40°F for any length of time, there could be a danger of food poisoning. (see **Eggs**, *Food Poisoning*, page 215). We recommend using bought mayonnaise or mayonnaise made with pasteurised egg yolks and/or Greek yoghurt if there is a chance that the dish might sit at room temperature for any length of time.

Poaching Chicken: What has gone wrong when...

The chicken is dry.
● The poaching liquor was allowed to boil.

The meat is tender but falling off the bone.
● The chicken is overcooked.

Jointing a Chicken

To joint a medium-sized bird into 8 pieces to serve 4 people
By jointing a chicken into 8 pieces each person will be served with a piece of dark meat and a piece of white breast meat. Before jointing, remove any trussing strings then singe the bird if necessary. Wipe clean with kitchen paper to remove hairs and pin feathers. Use a cook's knife to cut through the flesh and poultry shears or kitchen scissors to cut the bones and cartilage.

1 Place the bird, breast side down, on a board with the parson's nose facing you.
2 Using a large cook's knife, make a cut down the backbone through the skin from one end to the other. **(a)**
3 Locate the soft pockets of flesh called the oysters on either side of the backbone at the top of the legs. Cut round them with the tip of the knife to loosen them from the carcass, then loosen them with the fingertips and thumbs so that they come away freely from the bone. This way, the oyster will remain intact with the legs as they are pulled from the carcass. **(b)**
4 Turn the bird over so that it is breast-side up. Pull the skin covering the breast meat towards the breastbone, then cut through the skin between the breast and the leg, cutting as close to the leg as possible, using the blade of the knife, not the tip. **(c)**
5 Continue cutting the skin around the leg to make a cut perpendicular to the backbone next to the loosened oyster. Bend the leg out from the body and down towards the chopping board to release it from the socket. **(d)**
6 Use a knife to cut the cartilage and tendons around the ball joint.
7 Remove the leg by grasping it firmly and pulling it towards the back of the chicken. Providing the oyster piece is completely loosened it should come away with the leg.
8 Repeat the process with the other leg.

9   Using a sharp knife, cut cleanly through the skin and flesh between the breasts slightly to one side of the breastbone. **(e)**

10 Using poultry shears or kitchen scissors, cut along the length of the breastbone and through the wishbone at the neck end. **(f)**

11 Using scissors, cut along the fat line running along the edge of each breast, cutting through the ribs then around and underneath the wings to the neck of the chicken. **(g)** Do not separate the breast meat from the breastbone as the bone will help to keep the meat moist during cooking. Cut out the wishbone in each piece. Save the carcass for stock.

12 Tuck the wings behind the breasts in the 'sunbathing position'. Place the breasts next to each other to form a heart shape. Using a large, sharp knife, cut through the meat on a slant, from the cleavage of the heart to the elbow joint of the wing. **(h)** You now have 2 wing-breast portions and 2 longer diamond-shaped breast portions. Leave the wing tips (pinions) intact as they help to hold the wing in position while the chicken cooks. They are trimmed at the middle joint once the chicken is cooked (see *Trimming chicken joints*, below).

13 Place the legs skin side up on the board. Locate the joint between the drumstick and thigh by pressing against the meat with your finger to find the notch.

14 Using the large knife, cut down through the joint on both legs. The knife should cut through the joint easily. If it does not, you have hit the bone and you are cutting in the wrong place. **(i)**

15 You now have 8 equal portions of chicken, 4 with white meat and 4 with dark meat. **(j)**

Cutting small birds into portions

Small to medium-sized birds such as spring chicken and guinea fowl are often cut into 4 pieces for cooking. To joint a small bird into 4 pieces, follow steps 1–12 above, then using a large knife, cut off the wing tip through the wing joint on each breast.

Trimming chicken joints after cooking

As the jointed bird cooks, the flesh shrinks, exposing unsightly bone. This should be trimmed off before serving using poultry shears or kitchen scissors.

- Cut the pinion (wing tip) from each wing by cutting through the middle joint.
- Remove the end joint of the drumsticks by grasping the end with kitchen paper, then cutting the skin around the end of the bone just above the joint with a knife. Using kitchen scissors, push the skin back and cut through and remove the bone.

Cutting through breastbone (f)

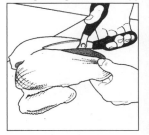

Cutting along the fatline (g)

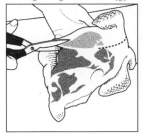

Dividing each breast into 2 (h)

Dividing the thigh and drumstick (i)

Jointing chicken into 8 pieces (j)

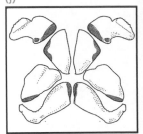

Cooking Pieces of Poultry

Pan-frying and Sautéing

(See **Meat**, *Methods of Cooking Meat*, page 341.)

Jointed poultry is often fried to brown and partially cook it before completing the cooking in liquid (see *Coq au Vin* and *Chicken Sauté Normande*, below). The skin is browned to give colour and flavour to the dish. The skin is left on during cooking to prevent the meat from drying out. The heat under the pan should be adjusted to medium-low so that the fat melts from the skin in the time that it takes to brown. If the chicken is cooked over high heat only the surface of the skin will brown, leaving a thick layer of fat underneath. Thoroughly browned, well-seasoned and crisp skin will also enhance the appearance and flavour of the cooked meat.

Thin pieces of chicken can be browned without the skin but care must be taken not to cook then for too long or over too high a heat or the meat will dry out (see *Stir-frying*, below). Boned chicken is unsuitable for stewing as the meat tends to become tough, dry or stringy with prolonged cooking.

Pan-cooked Chicken Breasts

SERVES 4

1 tablespoon oil

4 chicken breasts with skin and rib bones

salt and freshly ground black pepper

1 Heat the oil in a heavy sauté pan over a medium-low heat.
2 Season the chicken breasts with salt and pepper on the skin side and place them skin side down in the pan in a single layer.
3 Cover the pan with a tightly fitting lid and cook for 30 minutes.
4 Check the chicken by cutting next to the bone to see if the juices run clear. If not, return to the pan and cook for a further 5 minutes before checking again.
5 Serve basted with the pan juices.

Cooking Duck Breasts

Roasting

Due to their substantial covering of fat, duck breasts are well suited to roasting. Duck breasts are often roasted to serve sliced or whole in hot dishes or cold and thinly sliced in salads. Before they can be roasted the subcutaneous fat on their outer surface must be rendered down by frying in a dry pan.

1 Preheat the oven to 200°C | 400°C | gas mark 6.
2 Score the duck skin with a sharp knife and rub with salt and pepper. Lightly season the flesh side.
3 Place the duck breasts, skin side down, in a dry pan over a medium heat. Brown the skin, pouring off the excess fat. This will take 10–15 minutes. Place the breasts in a roasting pan and roast in the oven for 10 minutes or until the meat is medium-rare (see **Meat,** *The test of the thumb*, page 349). If serving hot, allow the breasts to rest for 5 minutes and serve whole, thinly or thickly sliced, or cut in half on the diagonal. If serving cold, allow to cool before slicing to ensure that the meat remains moist and pink.

Pan-frying

Duck breasts can also be pan-fried without the skin, as in the following recipe.

Duck Breasts with Green Peppercorn Sauce

SERVES 4

4 large duck breasts, skinned
45 g | 1½ oz unsalted butter

For the sauce
150 ml | ¼ pint dry white wine
3 tablespoons brandy
8 tablespoons White Chicken Stock (see
 Stocks, page 00)
290 ml | ½ pint double cream
2 tablespoons wine vinegar
1 teaspoon sugar

1 tablespoon port
20 g | ¾ oz canned green peppercorns, well
 rinsed
20 g | ¾ oz red pimiento, cut into tiny dice
salt and freshly ground black pepper

To garnish
30 g | 1 oz unsalted butter
2 firm dessert apples, peeled, cored and cut into
 eighths
a little caster sugar

1 To make the sauce, put the wine and brandy into a large saucepan and boil gently for about 5 minutes or until reduced by two-thirds.
2 Add the stock and boil for a further 5 minutes. Add the cream and boil for about a further 5 minutes, stirring occasionally so that the mixture does not catch on the bottom of the pan, until the sauce has reduced by about a third and is of pouring consistency (i.e. about as thick as single cream).

3 Put the vinegar and sugar into a small saucepan. Boil until the mixture is caramelized and is reduced to about 1 tablespoon. Add to the reduced cream sauce. It may be necessary to replace the pan over the heat to remelt the caramel. Stir well. Add the port, peppercorns and pimiento. Season with salt and pepper. Set aside.

4 To cook the duck breasts, melt the 45 g | 1½ oz unsalted butter in a large, heavy frying pan. When it stops foaming, add the duck breasts and fry quickly on both sides to brown their surface. Reduce the heat and fry slowly for 8–10 minutes or until the meat is medium-done in the centre (see **Meat,** *The test of the thumb*, page 00). Remove from the pan and allow to stand while preparing the garnish.

5 Melt the butter in a second frying pan and add the sugar. Cook until starting to brown then fry the apples until golden-brown.

6 Serve the duck breasts garnished with the apples and hand the sauce separately.

Coq au Vin

If there is time, marinate the chicken joints in the wine with the bouquet garni for a few hours or overnight – this will improve their taste and colour. Dry the joints well before frying or browning will be difficult.

SERVES 4

1.35 kg | 3 lb chicken, jointed into 8 pieces (see above)
290 ml | ½ pint red wine
1 small clove of garlic, peeled and bruised
1 bouquet garni (1 bay leaf, 1 sprig each of thyme and parsley and 1 stick of celery, tied together with string)
8 button onions
110 g | 4 oz rindless bacon, cut into 2 cm × 6 mm | ¾ × ¼ in lardons
55 g | 2 oz clarified butter (see **Dairy Products**, *Butter*, page 204)

12 button mushrooms
salt and freshly ground black pepper
570 ml | 1 pint White Chicken Stock (see **Stocks**, page 689)
1 clove of garlic, crushed
20 g | ¾ oz plain flour

To garnish
1 tablespoon finely chopped fresh parsley

1 Place the chicken pieces in a large plastic bag with the wine, bruised garlic and bouquet garni. Tie the top and marinate in the refrigerator for a few hours or overnight.

2 To remove the skins from the onions, *blanch* them in boiling water for 1 minute, then *refresh* in cold water. Trim the roots level with the bulbs, then peel.

3 Blanch the bacon in boiling water for 30 seconds to remove the excess salt. Drain and dry well.

4 Put half the butter into a large, heavy saucepan and brown the onions, bacon and mushrooms. Remove and reserve.

5 Remove the chicken from the marinade, reserving the marinade and the bouquet garni and discarding the garlic. Pat the chicken dry and season with salt and pepper.

6 Add the remaining butter to the pan and brown the chicken on the skin side over a medium-low heat. Tip off all the fat and reserve.

7 Return the vegetables and bacon pieces to the pan and add the wine from the marinade and enough stock nearly to cover the chicken pieces.

8 Add the crushed garlic and the bouquet garni.

9 Cover with a piece of damp greaseproof paper (a *cartouche*) and a tightly fitting lid and simmer slowly for about 45 minutes, until the onions and chicken are tender. Test each piece of chicken by cutting into the underside near the bone and pressing the meat to make sure the juices run clear.

10 Discard the bouquet garni. Lift out the vegetables and bacon and put them on to a warmed serving dish. Keep warm while you make the sauce.

11 Place the cooking liquid in a jug and reserve.

12 Mix the flour with enough of the reserved fat to make a paste or roux. Cook the roux in a small pan over a medium heat until light brown.

13 Use a bulb baster to remove the liquid from the bottom of the jug, leaving the fat behind. Add the liquid to the roux off the heat, stirring to make a smooth sauce.

14 Return to the heat, bring to the boil and boil for 2 minutes. Adjust the thickness of the sauce to coating consistency either by boiling further or by adding water, as required. Taste and adjust the seasoning.

15 Trim the chicken pieces (see *Trimming chicken joints after cooking*, above), arrange in a warmed deep serving platter and spoon the sauce over the chicken. Garnish with the parsley.

Chicken Sauté Normande

SERVES 4

45 g | 1 oz clarified butter (see **Dairy Products**, *Butter*, page 204)

1.35 kg | 3 lb chicken, jointed into 8 pieces (see above)

salt and freshly ground black pepper

1 tablespoon Calvados or brandy

1 shallot, finely chopped

2 teaspoons plain flour

225 ml | 8 fl oz dry cider

150 ml | ¼ pint White Chicken Stock (see **Stocks**, page 689)

1 bouquet garni (1 × 5 cm | 2 in piece of celery, 1 parsley stalk, 2 sprigs of thyme and 1 bay leaf, tied with string)

2 tablespoons double cream

To garnish

15 g | ½ oz butter

1 tablespoon caster sugar

2 dessert apples, cored and cut into 8 wedges

1 tablespoon chopped fresh parsley

1 Heat the butter in a large sauté pan. Season the chicken skin with salt and brown over a medium heat on the skin side only. Pour off the excess fat and reserve.

2 *Flambé* the chicken: have a lid or baking sheet close at hand in case the flames flare up. Heat the Calvados or brandy in a ladle over a gas flame and set alight. Pour over the hot chicken, pouring it away from you. Shake the pan and allow the flames to subside. If using an electric cooker, pour the Calvados into the hot pan and set a light with a match.

3 Remove the chicken from the pan. Add 1 tablespoon of the reserved fat to the pan. Add the shallot and cook for 2–3 minutes.

4 Add the flour and cook until pale straw-coloured. Add the cider slowly to make a smooth sauce. Add the stock. Bring to the boil and boil for 2 minutes.

5 Return the chicken to the pan with the bouquet garni cover with a damp *cartouche* and a lid and simmer for 30–45 minutes until the chicken is cooked through. Check each piece by cutting on the underside down to the bone and pressing the meat to make sure the juices are clear.

6 Lift the chicken out and trim as described above. Place on a warmed serving dish and keep warm.

7 Sieve the sauce into a clean saucepan and reduce by boiling rapidly to a coating consistency.

8 Add the cream to the sauce in the pan and season to taste with salt and pepper.

9 For the garnish, cook the butter and sugar in a small pan until lightly caramelized. Stir in the apple to coat with the caramel and cook until just tender when pierced with a sharp knife.

10 Pour the sauce over the chicken and garnish with the apple and parsley.

Pan-frying and Sautéing: What has gone wrong when...

The chicken skin is pale and flabby.
- The chicken skin was not browned thoroughly enough.

The sauce is very salty.
- The sauce has been over-reduced or oversalted.
- The bacon was not blanched.

Stuffing a Chicken Breast

The breasts of poultry and feathered game are often stuffed with a soft-textured filling or strong-flavoured ingredients such as truffles. For *Chicken Kiev* (see below), the chicken is stuffed with garlic butter. The stuffing provides added flavour, contrast in texture and enhances the appearance of the sliced breast once it is cooked. Soft stuffings are spooned into a shallow pocket made by cutting into the side of the chicken breast.

Cutting a pocket in breast fillet

Securing the stuffing with the false fillet

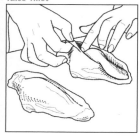

1 Remove the false fillet, the tapered flap of meat on the back of the breast that runs along its length. It is usually only partially attached to the breast and can be removed easily by cutting or pulling.

2 Make a shallow pocket by cutting into the side of the chicken breast.

3 Spoon the stuffing into the pocket.

4 Tuck both ends of the false fillet into the ends of the pocket so that the false fillet secures their stuffing.

Chicken Stuffed with Red Pepper Mousseline

For information about mousselines, see **Mousselines** (page 487), **Forcemeat** (page 271) and **Terrines, Pâtés and Raised Pies** (page 703). To hold the filling in place and help the chicken breast keep its shape, wrap tightly in clingfilm or kitchen foil before poaching. The breasts may also be wrapped in bacon or Parma ham and roasted.

SERVES 4

1 red pepper
½ tablespoon chopped fresh basil
1 teaspoon finely chopped fresh parsley
4 chicken breasts
1 egg white
75 ml | 2 ½ fl oz double cream

1 teaspoon ground mace
salt and freshly ground white pepper
1 tablespoon Tapenade (see, **Sauces, Savoury**, page 610)
Tomato Sauce (see **Sauces Savoury**, page 607), to serve

1 Grill or roast the red pepper until the skin blisters. Place in a plastic bag, to allow the pepper to sweat and the skin to loosen. Remove the skin, membrane and seeds. Cut the flesh into medium dice. Place in a chilled food processor with the basil and parsley.
2 Remove the false fillets from the chicken breasts, chop roughly and add to the food processor.
3 Whizz the mixture briefly, then add the egg white and cream while the machine is still running. The mixture should be smooth, but be careful not to overprocess to prevent it from warming and splitting.
4 Season well with the mace, salt and pepper. Refrigerate until ready to use.
5 Cut a small pocket in the side of each chicken breast (see *Stuffing breasts*, above) and spread a little tapenade inside it. Put a spoonful of the red pepper mousseline mixture into the pocket and pull the edges together to seal.
6 Wrap the breasts in clingfilm and place in a large shallow sauce pan or roasting tin. Pour boiling water then over the chicken then poach for about 15 minutes or until the chicken breasts are firm to the touch. Remove from the pan and allow to set for 10 minutes.
7 Cut the chicken breasts into thick slices and serve with the warm Tomato Sauce.

Making a Supreme

A supreme is a whole chicken breast with the first joint of the wing attached. The wing is cut off at the middle joint, then trim the small bone by scraping it clean with a paring knife. Chicken supremes are used to make *Chicken Kiev* (see below).

Deep-frying

Due to their delicately flavoured, tender flesh, chicken and turkey breast or thigh meat are most suitable for deep-frying. The meat is often cut into strips and protected with a breadcrumb coating or is left whole, as in *Chicken Kiev* (see below). (See also **Deep-frying**, page 206, for techniques and safety information.)

Chicken Kiev

Chicken Kiev is made using chicken supremes (see *Making a Supreme*, above), consisting of the breast and wing. The small wing bone at the shoulder end of the breast can be either removed or left in place. The flavoured butter sealed in the centre of the chicken melts on cooking to moisten and enhance the flavour of the meat.

SERVES 4

110 g | 4 oz butter, softened

1 clove of garlic, crushed

1 tablespoon chopped fresh parsley

a squeeze of lemon juice

salt and freshly ground black pepper

4 chicken supremes

seasoned plain flour

1 large egg, beaten

dried white breadcrumbs

oil, for deep-frying

salt

1 Mix the butter with the garlic, parsley, lemon juice, salt and pepper. Divide into 4 equal pieces, shape into rectangles and chill well in the refrigerator. (Chilled butter will melt more slowly during cooking, allowing the meat to set and any potential cracks to seal before the butter is liquid and likely to leak away.)

2 Remove the skin and breast bone from the chicken breasts. Remove the false fillet and cut into the breast on either side to make a large horizontal, central pocket (see *Stuffing a Chicken Breast*, above).

3 Insert a piece of butter into each horizontal pocket then enclose it by replacing the false fillet, tucking each side of it into the horizontal cuts, along the length of the breast. When the breast is cooked and sliced across, the melted butter should be perfectly in the centre of the meat.

4 To seal the chicken breasts, dust lightly with seasoned flour. Dip into beaten egg, then roll carefully in breadcrumbs. Refrigerate for 30 minutes to set the shape.

5 Brush with more beaten egg and roll again in breadcrumbs. Refrigerate for a further 30 minutes. The second covering of egg and crumbs is to ensure that the chicken is properly sealed to prevent melted butter escaping while the chicken is frying and also to create a crust that becomes firm and crisp fried.

6 Heat oil in a deep-fat fryer until a crumb will sizzle vigorously in it. Fry the chicken pieces in the oil for 12 minutes. Drain well on kitchen paper, sprinkle with salt and serve.

Chicken Kiev: What has gone wrong when...

Most of the butter has disappeared from the centre of the chicken.

- The butter was not chilled sufficiently and melted and escaped before the meat started to set.
- The butter was not encased correctly.

The chicken breast is still rare in the middle and the crust is only lightly coloured after the specified cooking time.

- The oil was not hot enough. Do not place the chicken in the hot oil until it is heated sufficiently to fry a square of bread quickly to golden-brown.
- The chicken was not cooked for long enough.

Boning chicken legs

Legs of chicken can be boned, stuffed and shaped to resemble a miniature gammon as in the following recipe.

Chicken Jambonneaux Stuffed with Wild Mushrooms

SERVES 4

4 chicken drumsticks with the thighs attached

salt and freshly ground black pepper

6 tablespoons dry sherry or Madeira

30 g | 1 oz clarified butter (see **Dairy Products**, *Butter*, page 204)

290 ml | ½ pint White Chicken Stock (see **Stocks**, page 689)

For the stuffing

1 onion, very finely chopped

30 g | 1 oz butter

1 rindless streaky bacon rasher

55 g | 2 oz fresh wild mushrooms, finely chopped

85 g | 3 oz shiitake mushrooms, finely chopped

30 g | 1 oz fresh white breadcrumbs

1 tablespoon finely chopped fresh parsley

1 teaspoon chopped fresh thyme

1 teaspoon dry sherry or Madeira

salt and freshly ground black pepper

Madeira Sauce (see **Sauces, Savoury**, page 595), to serve

small sprigs of watercress, to garnish

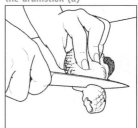
Cutting the knobbly end from the drumstick (a)

1 To make the stuffing, sweat the onion in the half the butter in a small pan covered with a piece of dampened greaseproof paper (a *cartouche*) until soft but not brown. Remove the paper, add the bacon and stir over a medium heat until the bacon is cooked.

2 In a frying pan cook the mushrooms in the remaining butter until all the excess liquid released from them has evaporated. Turn the mushrooms into a bowl and leave to cool. Add the onion and bacon.

3 Cut the knobbly joint off the bottom of each drumstick with a large sharp knife. (a) Using the point of the knife, remove the bones from the leg by cutting around the flesh next to the bone, starting from the thigh end and working to the end of the drumstick. (b) Season with salt and pepper. The skin can either be removed or kept on the chicken.

4 Stuff the chicken legs with the mushroom mixture. Fold the chicken flesh over to encase the stuffing and secure by tying with string.

5 Preheat the oven to 200°C | 400°F | gas mark 6.

Scraping the bone (b)

6 Heat the clarified butter in a sauté pan over a medium heat. If the chicken has the skin on, brown it well on all sides. If the chicken is skinned, brown very lightly, taking care not to scorch the meat.

7 Place the chicken in an ovenproof dish and pour over the sherry or Madeira and the stock. Cover and bake for 30 minutes, or until the juices run clear from the chicken when it is pierced with a skewer.

8 Place the chicken on a warmed serving dish. Add the cooking juices to the Madeira sauce and reduce to coating consistency. Spoon over a little of the sauce and garnish with watercress. Hand the remaining sauce separately.

Stir-frying

(See also **Meat**, *Methods of Cooking Meat*, page 341.)

Poultry meat cut into dice or strips must be fried quickly to brown the surface of the meat before the centre of the meat is overcooked. Use fat or oil with a high smoke point so that the fat may be heated and maintained at a high temperature while the poultry is cooking. Very thin slices or strips of poultry can, however, be browned and cooked briefly in fats such as whole butter as they require very little cooking.

Season poultry just before pan-frying, sautéing or stir-frying otherwise the salt will cause juices to leach from the meat, making the surface damp and difficult to brown.

Stir-fried Chicken with Cashew Nuts

SERVES 4

4 chicken breasts, skinned

2.5 cm|1 in piece of fresh root ginger, peeled and sliced

2 small cloves of garlic, peeled and sliced

2 teaspoons cornflour

1 tablespoon soy sauce

1 tablespoon dry sherry

150 ml|¼ pint White Chicken Stock (see **Stocks**, page 689)

1 tablespoon sunflower or grapeseed oil

55 g|2 oz unsalted cashew nuts

2 spring onions, sliced on the diagonal

1 Trim the chicken of all fat and cut into strips the thickness of your index finger.

2 Put into a bowl with the ginger and garlic, cover and leave to stand.

3 Mix the cornflour with the soy sauce, sherry and stock and set aside.

4 Heat the oil in a wok. Add the cashew nuts and stir-fry until lightly browned. Remove with a slotted spoon.

5 Add the chicken to the wok with the ginger and garlic and stir-fry for 4–5 minutes until the chicken is cooked and tender. Discard the ginger and garlic.

6 Add the cornflour mixture and stir until well blended and thickened. Add a little water if the sauce seems too thick. Check the seasoning. Pile into a warmed serving dish and sprinkle with the cashew nuts and spring onions.

NOTE: For a stronger flavour of ginger and garlic, grate half of the ginger and crush 1 clove of garlic. Add these to the wok 1 minute before the chicken is cooked in step 5.

Stir-frying Chicken: What has gone wrong when...

The chicken is dry.

- The chicken was overcooked.

The chicken is pale.

- The oil was not heated sufficiently before the chicken was added.

Rechauffé Dishes

Cooked poultry is often cut into bite-sized pieces and reheated (*rechauffer*) in a sauce to serve. Poaching or roasting (see above) are the best methods to use for poultry for *rechauffe* dishes.

Chicken Gougère

A gougère is a cheese choux pastry (see **Pastry**, *Choux*, page 525) case which is filled with cooked poultry or fish and/or vegetables, reheated and bound in a sauce.

SERVES 4

For the gougère

105 g | 3¾ oz plain flour
a pinch of salt
freshly ground black pepper
cayenne pepper
85 g | 3 oz butter
220 ml | 7½ fl oz water
3 eggs, lightly beaten
55 g | 2 oz strong Cheddar cheese, cut into
   6 mm | ¼ in cubes
2 teaspoons browned breadcrumbs
1 tablespoon grated cheese

For the chicken filling

30 g | 1 oz butter
1 medium onion, thinly sliced
110 g | 4 oz mushrooms, sliced
20 g | ¾ plain flour
290 ml | ½ pint White Chicken Stock (see
   Stocks, page 689)
salt and freshly ground black pepper
2 teaspoons chopped fresh parsley
340 g | 12 oz cooked chicken, shredded

1 Preheat the oven to 200°C | 400°F | gas mark 6.
2 To make the gougère, sift the flour with the salt, pepper and cayenne. Make the choux pastry as described in **Pastry**, *Choux* (page 525).
3 Stir in the diced cheese. Spoon the mixture round the edge of a 30 cm | 12 in shallow greased ovenproof dish. Bake for 25 minutes.
4 To make the filling, melt the butter in a saucepan and soften the onion over a low heat. Add the mushrooms and cook until soft, about 3–4 minutes.
5 Stir in the flour and cook for 1 minute.
6 Remove the pan from the heat and stir in the stock. Return to the heat and bring to the boil, stirring continuously. Season to taste with salt and pepper.

Simmer for 2 minutes. If the dish is not going to be baked immediately let the sauce cool before adding the chicken.

7 Add the parsley and the chicken.

8 Pile the filling into the centre of the gougère and sprinkle with the breadcrumbs and grated cheese. Return to the oven and bake for about 15 minutes, until the filling is hot.

Boning a Whole Bird

Small to medium-sized birds are often boned and stuffed to serve hot or cold, cut into slices. The following instructions use chicken as an example.

1 Put the chicken breast side down on a board. Cut through the skin to the backbone along the length of the chicken.

2 Feel for the fleshy oyster at the top of each thigh and cut round it against the bone, loosening further with the fingers and thumb (see *Jointing a chicken into 8 pieces*, above).

3 Working down one side of the chicken, cut and scrape the flesh from the carcass with a small sharp knife held as close as possible to the bone. Take care not to cut through the skin.

4 Cut the flesh from each side of the shoulder blade, then, using scissors or poultry shears, cut through the bone at the base of the wing next to the body of the chicken.

5 Continue cutting along one side of the body until the rib-cage is exposed. Once you have reached the centre of the breastbone, start again on the other side of the chicken from step 3 above. **(a)**

6 When the flesh has been scraped from the carcass on both sides, hold the chicken by the carcass, allowing the meat to hang down off the breastbone, and carefully cut the flesh away from the tip of the breastbone. **(b)** Avoid puncturing the skin.

7 Lay the boned chicken skin side down on the board.

8 Using a heavy knife, cut through the skin just above the feet joints to remove the knuckle end of the drumsticks.

9 Working from the inside thigh end, scrape one leg bone clean **(c)**, pushing the flesh down towards the end of the drumstick until you can pull the thigh bone through and remove it. Push the boned skin and flesh of the legs inside the bird. Repeat on the other leg.

10 To bone the wings, cut off the pinions (tips) at the middle joint with a heavy knife.

11 Scrape the wing bones clean from the inside as you did the leg bones.

12 Trim away any excess fat and any remaining bone from inside the bird with sharp knife.

13 Keep the neck flap of skin intact to fold over the end once the chicken is stuffed.

Scraping the meat from the carcas (a)

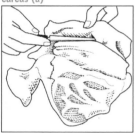

Cutting the carcass from the breastbone (b)

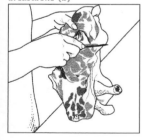

Scraping the thighbone (c)

Ballotines

A ballotine is made from boned poultry (see above), meat or game birds stuffed with forcemeat and either poached, braised with vegetables or roasted and usually served hot with a sauce made from the cooking juices.

The forcemeat is rolled tightly inside the boned flesh and the whole is wrapped securely inside a muslin cloth for poaching and roasting or tied with string for braising.

Ballotine of Chicken Stuffed with Ricotta and Sun-dried Tomatoes

SERVES 6

1.8 kg|4 lb chicken

55 g|2 oz butter, melted

For the stuffing

170 g|6 oz ricotta cheese

1 egg

85 g|3 oz fresh white breadcrumbs

55 g|2 oz sun-dried tomatoes, cut into slivers

30 g|1 oz black olives, pitted

1 tablespoon roughly chopped fresh basil

salt and freshly ground black pepper

fresh basil leaves, to garnish

1 Bone the chicken completely, including the legs and the wings (see *Boning a chicken*, above).

2 Preheat the oven to 200°C|400°F|gas mark 6.

3 To make the stuffing, beat the ricotta cheese, add the egg and beat again. Add the breadcrumbs, sun-dried tomatoes, olives and basil. Season to taste with salt and pepper.

4 Prepare a square of muslin or clean J-cloth sufficiently large to surround the bird with 10 cm|4 in to spare on each side. Dip the muslin or J-cloth in the melted butter as this will encourage the skin of the bird to brown evenly. Open out the cloth on the work top and season generously with salt and pepper.

5 Lay the boned chicken flat, skin side down, on the buttered cloth. Open out the bird and arrange it in a rectangular shape. Separate the false fillets from the breasts and place then on the skin between the leg and breast meat so that the skin is evenly covered with meat.

6 Press the stuffing into a cylindrical shape and place in the central third of the chicken.

7 Enclose the stuffing by firmly folding the surrounding flesh over it. Try not to overlap the flesh as any covered skin along the seam will remain flabby and not very pleasant to eat. Trim away any overlapping skin with kitchen scissors and discard.

8 Secure the ballotine by drawing opposite edges of the muslin together, then folding them down until the muslin holds the ballotine together tightly. Twist the open ends of muslin to form a cracker shape and tie each end with a short length of string.

9 Place the wrapped bird on a wire rack with the fold of the muslin on the underside. Place in a roasting pan. The wire rack raises the bird above the cooking juices, this enabling it to brown evenly on all sides.

10 Roast in the oven for 1 hour. To test that the chicken is cooked, insert a skewer into the centre and leave it there for 10 seconds. Draw the skewer out and place the pointed end on your wrist. If the skewer is too hot to hold against the skin, the stuffing is cooked. If the skewer can be held on the wrist comfortably, return the ballotine to the oven for a further 15 minutes and test again. (See *Meat*, *Testing Roast Meat for Doneness, Skewer Test*, page 344.)

11 Remove the muslin immediately otherwise it might stick to the skin. Using a pair of kitchen scissors, carefully cut the muslin away from the bird, taking care not to damage the crisp, brown skin.

12 Cut into thick slices and serve garnished with basil leaves. To serve cold, wrap the bird tightly in foil to set the shape and make it easier to slice. Allow to cool completely before unwrapping. Once cold, cut into 1 cm | ½ in slices and serve.

Boned Stuffed Duck

Duck is boned in the same way as chicken and the ballotine can be assembled following the instructions for the chicken ballotine recipe above. This stuffing is also delicious in a boned chicken.

SERVES 4

1 duck, boned (see *Boning a Whole Bird*, above)	1 tablespoon mixed chopped fresh tarragon and
1 large chicken breast, boned and skinned	parsley
½ small onion, chopped	30 g	1 oz unsalted pistachio nuts, skinned
110 g	4 oz dried apricots, sliced	salt and freshly ground black pepper

1 Preheat the oven to 200°C | 400°F | gas mark 6.

2 Remove any excess fat from the duck, especially from the vent end.

3 Put the chicken breast and onion together in a food processor and whizz briefly. Add the apricots, tarragon, parsley and pistachio nuts. Mix well and season with salt and pepper.

4 Assemble the ballotine as for *Boned Chicken Stuffed with Ricotta and Sun-dried Tomatoes*, steps 4–8, above.

5 Prick the wrapped bird lightly all over and rub with salt. Place on a wire rack in a roasting pan. The wire rack raises the bird above the cooking juices, thus enabling it to brown evenly on all sides.

6 Roast in the oven for 1¼ hours. To test that the duck is cooked, insert a skewer into the centre and leave it there for 10 seconds. Draw the skewer out and place the pointed end on your wrist. If the skewer is too hot to hold against the skin, the stuffing is cooked. If the skewer can be held on the wrist comfortably, return to the oven for a further 15 minutes and test again (see *Meat*, *Testing Roast Meat for Doneness, Skewer Test*, page 344).

7 Remove the muslin immediately otherwise it might stick to the skin. Using a pair of kitchen scissors, carefully cut the muslin away from the bird, taking care not to damage the crisp, brown skin.

8 Slice thickly and serve with an accompanying sauce, such as *Cumberland Sauce* (see *Fruit, Citrus Fruit*, page 283). To serve cold, wrap the bird (muslin removed) tightly in clingfilm or foil to set the shape and make it easier to slice. Allow to cool completely before unwrapping. Once cold, slice thinly and serve with salad.

Ballotine: What has gone wrong when...

The ballotine does not hold together.
- The ballotine was not wrapped tightly enough when cooked and/or when cooling before serving cold.

The cooking muslin has stuck to the chicken skin.
- The cloth was not oiled sufficiently.
- The muslin sticks to the chicken if it is not removed immediately after cooking.

Galantines

The word galantine is Old French for jelly and refers to the aspic used to decorate galantines (see **Aspic**, page 89). A classic galantine is made with boned chicken stuffed with chicken-based forcemeat to return the bird near to its original shape, or it may be rolled into a cylindrical shape. The galantine is then poached in stock and served cold, sliced and glazed with aspic.

Galantines are also made from game, veal, fish and shellfish where the skin is either inappropriate or non-existent. In such cases the forcemeat is spread on to the boned or cut surface of the flesh and the galantine is then rolled into a cylindrical shape and wrapped in foil, clingfilm or muslin before poaching. The galantine can either be decorated whole or thinly sliced and decorated with garnishing in-gredients and aspic jelly.

Galantine of Chicken with Pistachio and Apricot Stuffing

1 Bone a chicken as instructed above.
2 Prepare the stuffing for *Boned Stuffed Duck*, above.
3 Stuff the boned bird and roll into a sausage shape.
4 Wrap in muslin and tie securely.
5 Submerge in a pan of stock, *court bouillon* (see **Stocks**, page 693) or water and poach for about $1\frac{1}{2}$ hours, until a skewer inserted into the middle of the stuffing comes out piping hot.
6 Remove from the poaching liquid and allow to cool.
7 Chill well, then unwrap. Remove the skin from the bird and discard.
8 Cut into 1 cm|½ in slices.

Offal

The British term offal is derived from 'off falls', referring to those edible internal parts and some extremities of slaughtered pigs, cattle, sheep and poultry, which are removed before the carcass is cut up. These parts have, for the most part, traditionally have been thought of as scraps, so are often cheaper than the meat of animals or poultry. However, offal is often highly nutritious (see *Healthy Eating and Basic Nutrition*, page 13) being low in fat and rich in iron, vitamins and minerals.

Many types of offal are popular in Europe, where they form the basis of many regional dishes. In Scotland, the national dish of haggis consists of a sheep's stomach stuffed with a mixture of the heart, liver and lungs along with oatmeal, spices and fat. Before the BSE crisis in the early 1990s, when the meat of some cattle became infected, a wider variety of offal was eaten in Britain, including calf's brains. These are no longer recommended.

This section covers the most popular types of offal and their preparation.

Poultry Livers

The poultry livers most often used in a wide variety of hot and cold dishes include chicken, duck and sometimes goose. Chicken livers are more widely available than duck or goose and are by far the cheapest. Of the 3 types, goose liver is the largest, most richly flavoured and most expensive, followed by duck and then chicken, but all are sweetly flavoured and have a rich, creamy texture when cooked and served pink. Ducks and geese are force-fed in France to produce the grossly enlarged livers, eaten as the delicacy Foie Gras (see *Foie Gras*, below).

Both chicken and duck livers are sautéed alone or with other flavouring ingredients and served hot, often in warm salads. They are also vital flavouring and texture-improving ingredients in forcemeats for terrines, pâtés and meat pies. They are also used to make savoury mousses and canapés such as chicken livers wrapped in bacon.

Choosing

Goose, duck and chicken livers may be included with the bird, or may be sold with the giblets or in larger numbers in packs. Chicken livers are the most widely available, sold in most supermarkets and butchers. Duck and goose liver may have to be specially ordered from a butcher.

Livers must be bought absolutely fresh as they deteriorate rapidly. Look for:

- A deep red colour. They will become brown then grey as they age.
- The livers must be translucent and shiny. As they age they lose their translucent quality and become cloudy and dull.
- The livers should be wet. They tend to dry out if stored uncovered.
- The 2 halves of each liver should be intact and holding their shape firmly. If they are mushy and shapeless this is a sign that they are deteriorating.

Storing

As with all liver, poultry livers must be stored in the refrigerator and used within 24 hours of purchase. Liver contains a great deal of blood and other fluid which may drip or leak on to other ingredients. To avoid this possibility, store the livers in the bottom of the refrigerator, well covered in clingfilm to prevent them from drying out. Poultry livers may also be frozen in a sealed airtight container for up to 3 months.

Preparing

The livers are surrounded and connected by tough membrane and blood vessels which must be removed before cooking. The livers may also show traces of discoloration where the bitter-tasting, greenish-yellow coloured bile, contained in the gall bladder often left attached to poultry livers, has leaked into the liver. If the gall bladder is still present it must be removed together with any surrounding discoloured tissue. Once the livers are trimmed they are left whole or cut into bite-sized pieces for sautéing or roughly chopped or puréed, by pushing through a drum sieve, for use in terrines, pâtés, forcemeats and savoury mousses.

Sautéing

Livers are sautéed either for serving hot or before puréeing to make smooth pâtés and savoury mousses. It is important to sauté the livers as quickly as possible in hot fat or oil so that the surface is lightly browned before the centre loses its pink colour and creamy texture. Overcooked liver becomes dull brown, dry, grainy in texture and unpleasant to eat. It will also fail to form the smooth, creamy purée that is so important when making smooth pâtés (see *Terrines, Pâtés and Raised Pies*, page 710).

Salade Tiéde

SERVES 4

150 ml | ¼ pint olive oil

110 g | 4 oz piece of rindless bacon, diced

4 slices of white bread, cut into 1 cm | ½ inch
  cubes

salt

225 g | 8 oz chicken livers, cleaned (see above)

5 spring onions, sliced on the diagonal

1 tablespoon tarragon vinegar

1 small frisée lettuce

1 bunch of watercress

1 small radicchio

French dressing (see **Salad Dressings**,
  page 573)

To garnish

1 bunch of chervil, chopped roughly

1 Heat a tablespoon of the oil in a frying pan and cook the bacon until it is evenly
   browned all over. Lift it out with a slotted spoon and keep it warm in a low
   oven.
2 Heat the remaining oil in another frying pan and cook the croûtons until
   golden-brown. Drain well and sprinkle with a little salt. Keep warm in the
   oven.
3 Tip most of the oil out of the frying pan and cook the livers over medium heat
   until slightly stiffened and fairly firm but not hard to the touch. They should be
   golden brown and crisp on the outside and pink in the middle. Add the spring
   onions and fry for 30 seconds.
4 Add the vinegar to the pan and shake the livers and spring onions in it for 10
   seconds.
5 Toss the salad leaves in the dressing and divide them between 4 dinner plates.
6 Scatter the croûtons, bacon, spring onions and livers over the salad. Sprinkle
   with the chervil and serve immediately.

Using Poultry Livers in Forcemeat

See **Terrines**, **Pâtés and Raised Pies**, *Chicken Liver Pâté* (page 710).

Foie Gras

Foie gras, meaning fattened liver, is the grossly enlarged liver of a goose or duck
methodically fattened on a diet of corn. There is a general misconception that foie
gras means goose liver, perhaps because *oie* is French for goose. However, fattened
duck liver is preferred over goose liver. Goose liver is fattened to an average
weight of 675–900 g (1½ –2 lb) and a fattened duck liver usually weighs 300–400 g
(11–14 oz).

Foie gras is served cold in thin slices or used to make terrines, mousses and fine
pâtés, encased in brioche for Pâté en Croûte, sliced and glazed in aspic or potted

and preserved in goose fat. Foie gras may also be served hot, sliced and fried in butter, poached or baked.

Classic garnishes include cornichons, toasted brioche, caramelized orange segments, truffles, Muscat grapes and seafood such as scallops, oysters and lobster. Foie gras may also be coated in aspic or served with a well-flavoured diced aspic jelly, made from its poaching liquor (see *Aspic*, page 89).

Choosing

Although both goose and duck foie gras are considered delicacies, duck foie gras is often preferred as its flavour is more delicate. Raw foie gras should have well-developed lobes that are firm and intact, smooth, putty-coloured and rounded. Do not select over-large foie gras as it may contain an excessive quantitiy of fat in relation to the liver, or foie gras that is yellowish in colour, as it tends to be grainy in texture.

Preparing

1 Chilled raw foie gras is hard and brittle, so remove it from the refrigerator and leave covered until it reaches room temperature and is soft and pliable.
2 Carefully part the 2 lobes so that the artery and veins become visible. Using a long, thin pointed knife, pull the veins away from the liver, taking care not to break the lobes in two. Remove any green parts.
3 Remove any skin covering the liver.
4 The flavour of the foie gras can be enhanced by seasoning the open lobes with finely ground salt and pepper, then closing and wrapping them tightly in clingfilm before refrigerating overnight and/or marinating the liver for 48 hours in port mixed with 10 per cent Armagnac.
5 Weigh before cooking.

Using

When cooking foie gras it is essential that the recipe is followed very accurately. If overcooked, the foie gras simply melts away, leaving a much smaller liver with an unappealing, soggy texture. If undercooked, the liver will taste raw. Cook the foie gras very gently at a constant temperature until the centre of the liver reaches 60°C|140°F. A thermometer to guarantee temperature control during cooking is useful.

Poaching foie gras in stock or goose fat

1 Remove the foie gras from the marinade or wipe excess seasoning from its surface.
2 Weigh the foie gras and calculate the cooking time at 4 minutes per 110 g|4 oz.
3 Heat the stock or fat in a pan to 60°C|140°F, using a thermometer. Add the foie gras to the pan and continue to heat until the stock reaches 65°C|150°F.
4 Poach the liver for the calculated time, constantly regulating the heat source to ensure that the poaching liquor remains at a constant temperature.

5 To check if the liver is cooked, part the lobes: the centre should be warm, slightly pink and have the consistency of lightly set egg white.

6 Using 2 large slotted spoons, carefully lift out the liver and lay it on a large sheet of clingfilm. Reserve the stock or fat in the pan. Wrap the liver firmly to retain its shape, place in a terrine mould, or roll into a cylindrical shape and cool on a wire rack, then refrigerate overnight.

7 Reduce and clear the stock (see *Aspic*, page 90) for jelly to accompany slices of poached foie gras. The fat can also be used for sealing the foie gras in the terrine mould, or for roasting potatoes, or mixed with butter to enrich sauces, meat, fish and vegetables.

8 Serve the foie gras sliced, with toasted brioche.

Slicing foie gras: Slice foie gras with a hot, thin-bladed knife to obtain a clean finish. Clean and reheat the knife in hot water between each slice.

Baking foie gras: Foie gras is baked at a higher temperature for a shorter period of time than foie gras cooked by poaching.

Calves' Liver

After poultry livers, calves' liver is the most popular type of liver, followed by lambs' liver. Calves' liver is rich in flavour and has little, if any, wastage, so 100 g | 3½ oz per serving is usually sufficient. Liver is classically served with sautéed onions, as in the recipe below.

Choosing

The liver should not have a strong smell. It should be bright red, not brown and shiny. Choose pieces of liver that have few tubes running through then.

Storing

Keep in the bottom of the refrigerator for not more than 24 hours. Liver deteriorates rapidly. Freeze for up to 6 months.

Using

Pull the thin membrane from the outside of the liver and cut out any noticeable tubes.

It is important not to overcook liver or it will become tough. It should be pink on the inside, but not bloody, when served.

Frying is the best way to cook liver so that it is browned on the outside and pink on the inside. It can also be grilled, but it is rather more difficult to get it nicely browned without being overcooked.

Calves' Liver Lyonnaise

SERVES 4

55 g│2 oz unsalted butter
1 large onion, thinly sliced
450 g│1 lb calves' liver (prepared as above)
seasoned plain flour
290 ml│½ pint Brown Stock (see **Stocks**, page 692)

1 tablespoon fresh orange juice
1 tablespoon mixed fresh herbs, such as
   rosemary, thyme and sage
salt and freshly ground black pepper

1 Heat half the butter in a frying pan and slowly cook the onion until golden-brown. This will take up to 40 minutes. Place in an ovenproof dish and keep warm.

2 Dip the liver into the seasoned flour, shaking off any excess.

3 Heat the remaining butter in a sauté pan over a medium heat until foaming.

4 Fry the liver for about 2 minutes on each side, until golden-brown. Place on top of the onions and keep warm.

5 Add a teaspoon of the seasoned flour to the pan and cook until brown. Stir in the stock and the orange juice. Boil for 2 minutes.

6 Add the herbs and season with salt and pepper. Pour over the liver and serve.

Calves' Liver: What has gone wrong when...

The liver is tough and rubbery.
- It has been overcooked.

The sauce is pale.
- The liver was not browned sufficiently during cooking.

Lambs' Liver

Lambs' liver is darker in colour than calves' liver. Choose, store and use as for calves' liver.

Pigs' Liver

Pigs' liver is darker and stronger in flavour than lambs' liver. It is usually used in terrines (see **Terrines, Pâtés and Raised Pies**, page 703). Choose and store as for calves' liver.

Ox and Calves' Kidneys

Choosing

These kidneys are multi-lobed, resembling a bunch of grapes. The best kidneys are from the youngest animals. Kidneys are sold either ready prepared or still encased in their white fat (suet).

The kidneys should be plump and a deep red-brown colour. Due to their strong flavour kidneys are usually served with a strong sauce, such as a mustard sauce.

Storing

Store as for liver.

Using

Remove the suet, then peel away the thin membrane. Cut into bite-sized pieces, discarding the central core. Ox and calves' kidneys are used for *Steak and Kidney Pudding* (see **Steaming**, page 676).

Lambs' Kidneys

Lambs' kidneys are single, rather than multi-lobed, and are shaped like a kidney bean. They are often sold covered in the white fat (suet).

Storing

Store as for liver.

Using

Lambs' kidneys are highly regarded and are often served grilled. Peel away the suet and the thin membrane. Cut in half. Use kitchen scissors to remove the fatty core and blood vessels. The kidneys should only be cooked enough to become brown on the outside whilst remaining pink on the inside or they will be tough and rubbery. Thread on a skewer to grill (see **Meat,** *Grilling*, page 347).

Kidneys can also be braised. The long, slow cooking tenderizes them. They can also be sautéed over high heat.

Lambs' Kidneys with Mushrooms in Mustard Sauce

SERVES 2

6 lambs' kidneys
30 g | 1 oz butter, clarified (see **Dairy Products**, *Butter*, page 204)
110 g | 4 oz large flat mushrooms, cut into thick slices
4 tablespoons double cream

2 teaspoons Dijon mustard
salt and freshly ground black pepper
lemon juice
1 tablespoon chopped fresh parsley, to garnish

1 Prepare the kidneys as described above, then cut into 2.5 cm | 1 in chunks.
2 Melt the butter in a frying pan until foaming, then fry the kidneys over a high heat to brown all over. Place in a sieve to drain. Discard the juices.

3 Cook the mushrooms in the pan for 3 minutes, then return the kidneys and cook for about 2 minutes, until pale pink on the inside.

4 Stir in the cream and mustard. Taste and season with salt, pepper and lemon juice. Garnish with the parsley.

Sautéed Kidneys: What has gone wrong when...

The kidneys are tough and rubbery.
- The kidneys are overcooked.

The sauce tastes bitter.
- The kidney juices were used in the sauce.
- The kidneys were not drained.

Tongue

Ox, sheep's and lambs' tongue are the most readily available. Tongue is usually salted, pressed and served cold accompanied by a piquant sauce.

Sweetbreads

Sweetbreads are the thymus and the pancreas glands of calves and lambs. Thymus sweetbreads are long and irregular in shape. The pancreas sweetbreads are spherical. Calves' sweetbreads are the superior of the two. Sweetbreads are blanched to whiten, then poached, braised or sautéed.

Tripe

Tripe is obtained from the first and second stomachs of ox, calves and sheep. The first stomach, called the blanket, is smooth-textured. The second, inner stomach, known as honeycomb tripe, is textured. Tripe is simmered in milk.

Feet and Trotters

Although the feet of calves, sheep and lamb are available, pigs' trotters are the most widely used for cooking. Calves' feet are generally used split for stocks (see *Stocks*, page 688).

Pigs' trotters are purchased scalded, dehaired and dehooved. Sometimes they are brined and in ethnic markets they can be coloured a vibrant red. They can be cooked whole stewed in a well-flavoured stock, grilled or braised. They can also be boned and stuffed with forcemeat before roasting, braising or crumbing and frying. Pig's trotters contain a large quantity of connective tissue and are often boiled to make jellied stock and brawns. Hot pigs' trotters are traditionally served with mustard sauce or cold with vinaigrette.

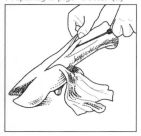

Preparing a pigs' trotter (a)

Preparing Pigs' Trotters

1 Buy blanched pigs' trotters. Singe off any remaining hairs.
2 Place in a large pan and cover with water and aromatic vegetables. Bring to a simmer and cook for 4 hours or until tender.
3 Weight the trotters under a chopping board to press out excess water.
4 Slit the underside of each trotter, starting at the ankle end.
5 Using a sharp knife, cut the main tendon and then start to work off the skin by cutting around it close to the bone.
6 Pull the skin right down and cut through the knuckle joint at the first set of toes. Snap and twist off the bones and discard.

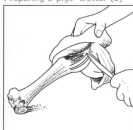

Preparing a pigs' trotter (b)

Pigs' Trotters with Wild Mushrooms

SERVES 4

55 g | 2 oz dried porcini mushrooms
340 g | 12 oz lean pork
110 g | 4 oz pork fat
1 teaspoon salt
fresh ground white pepper
a pinch of ground allspice
1 teaspoon finely chopped fresh sage

4 pigs' trotters, prepared as above
55 g | 2 oz butter, melted
55 g | 2 oz dry white breadcrumbs

To serve
Sauce Robert (see **Sauces, Savoury**, page 595)
mashed potatoes (see **Potatoes**, page 545)

1 Place the mushrooms in a bowl and pour over enough boiling water to cover. Set aside.
2 Process the pork meat and fat in a food processor, then pass through a sieve.
3 Drain the mushrooms, reserving the liquid. Chop finely and add to the meat.
4 Season with the salt, pepper, allspice and sage. Add 1 tablespoon of the mushroom liquid. Poach a small piece of the mixture to check the seasoning.
5 Stuff the trotters with the mixture, then wrap each trotter tightly in a square of kitchen foil, forming each parcel into a sausage shape. Refrigerate until firm.
6 Preheat the oven to 180°C | 350°F | gas mark 4.
7 Place the trotters on a baking sheet and bake for 45–60 minutes or until the stuffing is piping hot when tested with a skewer.
8 Preheat the grill.
9 Brush the trotters with the melted butter, then roll in the breadcrumbs. Grill until well browned and crisp. Serve with Sauce Robert and mashed potatoes.

Oxtail

Oxtail was not sold during the BSE crisis but has now started to reappear in the shops. Oxtail is usually sold skinned and jointed. Due to the large quantity of connective tissue the tails produce a high-quality gelatine when cooked very slowly so are ideal for a braise or a stew. Substitute oxtail for lamb in the *Lamb Daube* recipe (see **Lamb**, page 386) and cook for 6–8 hours.

Seasonal Table for Game

Feathered Game

Grouse	12 August–10 December
Partridge	1 September–1 February
Pheasant	1 October–1 February
Pigeon and squab	In season all year round
Quail	Available all year round
Snipe	August–January
Wild duck, teal and wigeon	Various, starting September and finishing 20 February
Woodcock (Scotland)	1 September–31 January
(England and Wales)	1 October–31 January

Furred Game

Venison	Seasons are complicated

(see *Statutory deer close seasons*, below), but frozen wild venison is often available all year round and farmed venison is available throughout the year.

Statutory deer close seasons

		England and Wales	Scotland
Red	Stags	1 May–31 July	21 October–30 June
	Hinds	1 March–31 Oct	16 February–20 Oct
Sika	Stags	1 May–31 July	21 October–30 June
	Hinds	1 March–31 Oct	16 February–20 Oct
Fallow	Bucks	1 May–31 July	1 May–31 July
	Does	1 March–31 Oct	16 February–20 Oct
Roe	Bucks	1 Nov–31 March	21 Oct–31 March
	Does	1 March–31 Oct	1 April–20 Oct

Muntjac and Chinese water deer have no statutory close seasons. The British Deer Society recommends that to avoid orphaning muntjac fawns dependent upon the mother's milk, only immature and heavily pregnant females (at which time a previous fawn will be independent) should be culled.

Hunting seasons

Staghunting	Autumn stags	early August–end October
	Hinds	1 November–end February
	Spring stags	March–end April
Rabbit	Wild or farmed available all year	
Hare	September–March	

Game

The term game refers to all wild animals and birds hunted for sport and cooked for the table. Due to an active life and diet in the wild, game tends to be lean, often darkly coloured, and has a stronger flavour than farmed animals or birds.

Game is divided into 2 major groups: furred and feathered. Furred game is subdivided into large game, including deer, roebuck and wild boar, and small game such as wild rabbit and hare. Feathered game includes a wide variety of bird species such as woodcock, grouse, pheasant, partridge, duck and wild pigeon.

Game is low in fat so it must be cooked carefully to prevent it from becoming dry and tough. The meat is often marinated to help tenderize it. Tender cuts of larger game such as haunches, saddles and loins of venison, and of hare and rabbit are roasted; noisettes and cutlets are either fried or sautéed. Tougher cuts containing more connective tissue, such as the breast, shoulder and neck, are slow-cooked in casseroles and braised dishes.

Feathered game is generally cooked by the same methods used for poultry (see **Poultry**, page 418). Due to the strong flavour of furred and feathered game, both are usually accompanied with highly flavoured sauces often containing fruit and nuts. Game is also used to make terrines, pâtés and game pies (see **Terrines, Pâtés and Raised Pies**, page 703).

Game Seasons

The game season for furred and feathered game is determined by breeding season. For purposes of conservation, it is important that each species should breed uninterrupted and their offspring grow to a sufficient size to enable them to breed or at least to be worth hunting and eating (see table below).

Hanging and Storing Game

Game is usually matured or 'hung' to tenderize the muscle fibres and strengthen the meat's characteristic flavour (see **Meat,** *Factors Affecting the Tenderness of Meat*, page 338). Furred game is hung by the hind legs, to give the haunches a good shape, and feathered game by the neck. Game is not skinned or plucked before hanging as this would encourage deterioration. During hanging, the flavour of the meat develops from mild to 'gamy' to 'high'. It is important not to overhang game, to prevent the risk of food poisoning. It is also worth knowing that the fresher a bird the easier it is to pluck and draw as the skin and flesh is firmer and less likely to tear (see *Plucking* and *Drawing*, below).

The period of time for which game is hung is determined by a number of factors:

- **The animal or bird's age and size:** Older and large game requires longer hanging than young or small game as the muscle fibres are coarser and take longer to tenderize. Younger, smaller game will be reasonably tender without hanging and is hung for a short period of time mainly to develop its flavour.
- **Variety:** Feathered game generally requires less hanging than furred game.
- **Storage facilities:** The hanging room should be dry, cool and well ventilated. In warm, humid weather game will reach the required maturity in half the time it would take to mature in cold, dry conditions.
- **Personal taste:** Many people are unused to the flavour of well-hung meat.

If the game is already prepared, i.e. drawn, skinned or plucked, it should be stored loosely wrapped in the bottom of the refrigerator.

The hanging times in the table opposite vary depending on the hanging conditions and the required gaminess of the meat.

Tenderizing Game Further Following Hanging

Larger and older game is often marinated to partially break down the meat fibres, using acidic ingredients such as wine, lemon juice or vinegar. Marinades also contain oil to prevent the lean meat from drying out as it cooks. Young animals and birds rarely require marinating, as they are relatively tender after hanging. If a marinade is used, be careful that it enhances rather than overpowers the flavour of the meat (see **Meat,** *Factors Affecting the Tenderness of Meat*, page 338).

Hanging Times for Game

Game	Hanging time	Number per person	Notes
Feathered Game			
Grouse	2–10 days	1	After 2 days grouse does not have a strong flavour but after 10 days it will be very gamy. Red or Scottish grouse is best.
Partridge	3–4 days	1	At Leiths partridge, particularly the grey British, as opposed to the French red leg, is considered the best of all game birds.
Pheasant	3–8 days	Allow 1 pheasant for 2 people	As with most game birds, the hen is juicier than the cock. Pheasant is fairly mild in terms of gaminess.
Pigeon and squab	Eat fresh	1 whole bird or 2 breasts	These are in season all year round. Squab are fledgling pigeons. Pigeon breast meat should be moist and a glistening dark red. It is difficult to judge the age of pigeon by its appearance so you need to buy it from a reliable game dealer.
Quail	Eat fresh	2	Most quails today are farmed and should look plump for their size. They have a slightly gamy flavour.
Snipe	4 days	2	Snipe is a small bird with a long bill which is sometimes served pushed into the body of the bird like a skewer, drawing the head through the legs before roasting. It is traditionally roasted ungutted and served on a croûte.
Wild duck **Teal** **Wigeon**	Eat fresh Eat fresh Eat fresh	1 2 3–4	Wild duck varies in size from the large mallard to the tiny teal. It tends to be rather dry and can have a fishy flavour. This can be overcome by stuffing the cavity with an orange, by marinating or by parboiling the plucked bird.
Woodcock	2 days	1–2	Like snipe, woodcock is roasted undrawn. It is very rarely available in shops.
Furred Game			
Rabbit	24 hours	a 1 kg|2¼ lb rabbit feeds 2–3	Wild and farmed rabbit are available all year round. Rabbit must be paunched and gutted as soon as it is killed.
Hare	5–6 days	A good-sized hare feeds 4, a leveret 3	Unlike rabbit, hare is hung unpaunched.
Venison	3–10 days	see *Venison*, below	Farmed venison is available all year round, unlike wild venison, the game seasons of which are strictly controlled. Farmed venison is not as strongly flavoured as its wild counterpart.

Feathered Game

Choosing

As with poultry, when choosing feathered game it is important to be able to distinguish young from old birds.

- Young birds have soft, pliable feet and a flexible breastbone and beak.
- Older birds have a hard breastbone and hard, scaly feet with pronounced spurs.

Preparing Feathered Game for Cooking

Plucking

Some birds are easier to pluck than others, ducks being notoriously tedious. All birds are easier to pluck if still warm, as the feathers pull out more easily and cleanly without tearing the skin.

1 Place a chopping board supporting the bird in a bin liner and work away from draughts to help prevent the feathers from flying about while plucking. Rub some washing-up liquid around the opening of the bin bag; it will attract small feathers.
2 Tug the feathers, working from the tail to the head, pulling against the direction of growth.
3 At the breast, however, pluck the feathers in the direction of growth, supporting the skin with the fingers of your other hand to avoid tearing the flesh. Do not pluck the wings. Cut them off at the first joint from the body.
4 Cut off the head next to the body and remove the neck. Watch out for a swollen pouch in the neck called the 'crop'. It often contains recently ingested corn and is messy if cut into.
5 Singe the bird over a flame to remove any down, hairs and parts of feathers still attached to the skin. This can be done directly over a burning taper or gas flame. Take care to singe only the down and small feathers and not blacken the flesh.
6 If any quills remain embedded in the skin, they can be removed with tweezers after singeing.
7 Rub the bird clean with kitchen paper to remove any remaining stubble.

Drawing Birds

The cooling time for feathered game is little affected by the removal of the innards. Birds actually keep better if they are hung with their innards intact as they are less likely to attract flies. However, woodcock and snipe are not drawn. Their gizzards are removed before cooking, then the cooked innards are spread on toasted bread (croûtes) and served with the roasted bird. Once eviscerated, they must be cooked within 1–2 days. When you are ready to cook the bird, take it down and proceed as follows:

1 Pluck the bird as described above.

2 Cut round the feet at the drumstick joint, but do not cut right through the tendons.

3 Pull the legs off the bird, drawing the tendons out with them. If the bird is small this is easy enough – just bend the foot back over the edge of a table until it snaps, and pull. Turkeys are more difficult; snap the feet at the drumstick joint by bending them over the edge of the table, then hang the bird up by the feet from a stout hook, and pull on the bird. The feet plus tendons will be left on the hook. All too often birds are sold with the tendons in the legs, making the drumsticks tough when cooked.

4 Put a finger into the neck hole, to the side of the stump of neck left on the bird. Move the finger right round, loosening the innards from the neck. If you do not do this you will find them difficult to pull out from the other end.

5 Using a sharp knife, slit the bird open from the vent to the parson's (or pope's) nose, making a hole large enough just to get your hand in. Covering the gutting hand with a cloth or wearing a rubber glove helps extract the intestines in one piece. Insert your hand (or the first 2 fingers if the bird is small), working so that the back of the hand is up against the arch of the breastbone, and carefully loosen the entrails from the sides of the body cavity, all the way round. Pull them out, taking care not to break the gall bladder, the contents of which would make any flesh they touch taste bitter. The first time you do this, it is unlikely that you will get everything out in one motion, so check that the lungs and kidneys come too. Once the bird is empty, wipe any traces of blood with a clean damp cloth.

The neck and feet can be used to make stock with the heart and cleaned gizzard. To clean the gizzard, carefully cut the outside wall along the natural seam so that you can peel it away from the inner bag of grit. Throw the grit bag away, along with the intestines and the gall bladder.

Do not include the liver when making stock: it may make it taste bitter. Instead, it may be trimmed of membranes and any bitter-tasting discoloured areas where it lay against the gall bladder, before cutting into small pieces to fry and add to a sauce or gravy. Alternatively it may be frozen until enough poultry liver has been collected to make pâté (see **Offal,** *Chicken Livers,* page 444).

Cooking Feathered Game

The rules and procedures for preparing and cooking feathered game are much the same as for poultry (see **Poultry,** *Methods of Cooking Poultry,* page 418). Feathered game contains very little subcutaneous fat and must be cooked carefully to prevent the meat from drying out. Provided that the bird is cooked correctly, the breast meat is almost always tender but the legs are often very tough and require long, slow cooking to tenderize them.

Young feathered game is sufficiently tender for roasting, grilling, sautéing and serving pink. The exception to the rule is guinea fowl which must be cooked through to prevent the risk of salmonella poisoning. Tougher, older birds are often marinated to tenderize the flesh, then casseroled or braised until the meat is beginning to fall away from the bone.

Roasting

(See also **Poultry, Methods of Cooking Poultry**, page 418.)

Roast the bird upside down or on its side to protect the tender breast meat from the fierce heat of the oven. Alternatively, the bird may be barded (see **Poultry, Barding**, page 343) with strips of streaky bacon. A soft stuffing or flavoured softened butter can be stuffed under the skin to keep the breasts moist or a quartered apple placed in the body cavity will help to prevent the bird from drying out. The bird should also be basted regularly while roasting.

Roast game birds are traditionally served with game chips and Bread Sauce (see **Poultry, English Roast Chicken**, page 420) or fried breadcrumbs. Smaller birds such as woodcock and snipe are served on a croûte, a circular piece of toasted bread spread with the birds' innards or 'trails'.

Larger birds like pheasant and grouse are drawn before roasting as the innards are not suitable for eating, but the liver may be returned to the body cavity to cook with the bird. This, plus any scrapings from the inside of the bird, is spread on the uncooked side of the croûte, which is then cut in half on the diagonal, and served as a garnish with the whole roast bird.

Roasting Table for Feathered Game

Bird	Temperature			Cooking time
	°C	°F	gas mark	
Grouse	190	375	5	20–30 mins
Guinea fowl	190	375	5	70 mins
Partridge	190	375	5	20–25 mins
Pheasant	190	375	5	45–60 mins
Pigeon	200	400	6	25–35 mins
Quail	180	350	4	20 mins
Snipe	190	375	5	15–20 mins
Wild duck	200	400	6	40 mins
Woodcock	190	375	5	20–30 mins

Roast Pheasant

Roast pheasant is traditionally accompanied by *Fried Crumbs* and *Game Chips*.

SERVES 4

2 medium oven-ready pheasants

salt and freshly ground black pepper

4 rashers of streaky bacon

For the gravy

1 teaspoon plain flour

1 tablespoon ruby port

1 teaspoon redcurrant jelly

To serve

Fried Crumbs (see below)

Game Chips (see below)

1 Wipe the pheasants and remove any remaining feathers.
2 Preheat the oven to 200°C | 400°F | gas mark 6.
3 Season the birds inside with salt and pepper.
4 Tie the bacon over the breasts with string to prevent the breasts from drying out during cooking. Season with salt and pepper.
5 Place the pheasants in a roasting pan and pour 6 mm | ¼ in water into the pan. Roast for 40–50 minutes, basting frequently.
6 When the pheasants are cooked, lift them out of the pan and keep warm.
7 Sprinkle the flour into the roasting juices and add the port and the jelly. Bring to the boil, stirring. Boil for 2 minutes, then sieve into a warmed sauce-boat and serve with the pheasant.

Fried Crumbs

SERVES 4

55 g | 2 oz butter

2 tablespoons dried white breadcrumbs

1 Melt the butter in a frying pan and fry the crumbs very slowly until they have absorbed most of it and are golden and crisp.
2 Serve in a warmed bowl, handed with the sauce or sauces.

NOTE: Fresh white breadcrumbs can also be used, but rather more butter will be needed as they are very absorbent. Great care should be taken to fry slowly so that the crumbs become crisp as well as brown.

Game Chips

Before attempting Game Chips, see *Deep-frying* (page 211).

SERVES 4

450 g | 1 lb potatoes (each potato should be roughly the same size)

oil, for deep-frying
salt

1 Peel the potatoes and shape them into cylinders of similar diameter.
2 Slice very thinly into rounds, using a mandolin or a very sharp cook's knife (see *Knife Skills*, page 68).
3 Soak the potato slices in cold water for 10 minutes to remove some of the surface starch, as this will improve their crispness.
4 Dry thoroughly in a clean tea towel as water will cause the fat to spit as the potato slices fry.
5 Heat the oil in a deep-fryer to test the temperature with one or two potato slices. If the potatoes rise to the surface within a minute or so, the oil is ready.
6 Lower the first batch of potato slices into the hot oil and gently move them around with a metal slotted spoon to prevent them from sticking to one another. As the potato slices cook and dry out they will rise to the surface. Allow them to cook a little longer until they are crisp and light golden.
7 Using a metal slotted spoon, remove the potato slices from the hot oil and drain on kitchen paper. Sprinkle lightly with salt.
8 The game chips should be served immediately or placed in a warm oven to remain crisp until they are to be served.

Grilling and Pan-frying

(See *Poultry*, *Methods of Cooking Poultry*, page 418.)

As with roasting, it is best to use young birds to ensure that the meat is tender. The breasts are most suited to grilling or pan-frying and are best served pink in the centre to prevent the meat from becoming dry. The breasts are often separated from the carcass, which is used to make stock for an accompanying sauce. As with poultry, the tender meat must be grilled under or pan-fried over a high heat to allow the surface of the meat to brown before the centre of the meat overcooks. The breasts are served whole, sliced in half diagonally or sliced thinly and fanned on the plate.

Warm Pigeon Breast and Cracked Wheat Salad

Pigeon is a dark purple-coloured meat and should be sautéed or grilled until 'blue' (rare) or, at most, pink (medium-rare) as the meat will toughen with overcooking. In this recipe the pigeon breasts are marinated to enhance their flavour rather than tenderize them. 4 duck breasts can be substituted for the pigeon breasts, if desired.

SERVES 4

8 pigeon breasts, skinned

110 g | 4 oz bulghur or cracked wheat (see **Grains**, page 301)

2 tablespoons sesame oil

½ red chilli, deseeded and finely chopped

2.5 cm | 1 in piece of fresh root ginger, peeled and grated

110 g | 4 oz shiitake mushrooms, sliced

110 g | 4 oz Parma ham, sliced

140 g | 5 oz plum jam

5 spring onions, sliced on the diagonal

55 g | 2 oz sun-dried tomatoes in oil, drained and sliced

salt and freshly ground black pepper

lemon juice

30 g | 1 oz pine nuts, toasted

½ cucumber, deseeded and finely chopped

2 tablespoons oil

2 tablespoons chopped fresh chives, to garnish

For the marinade

2 tablespoons Chinese five-spice powder

1 tablespoon light soy sauce

1 Mix together the marinade ingredients and coat the pigeon breasts on both sides. Place in a shallow dish, cover and leave to marinate for at least 30 minutes or overnight in the refrigerator.

2 Put the cracked wheat into a bowl and cover with boiling water. Leave to stand for 15 minutes. Drain thoroughly, squeeze out any remaining water and spread out to dry on kitchen paper.

3 Heat the sesame oil in a wok or large frying pan, add the chilli, ginger, mushrooms and Parma ham and stir-fry over a high heat for 2–3 minutes. Ad the jam, spring onions and sun-dried tomatoes and bring to the boil. Add the cracked wheat and season to taste with salt, pepper and lemon juice. Heat thoroughly and stir in the pine nuts and cucumber. Keep warm.

4 Heat the oil in a frying pan. Season the pigeon breasts with salt, then add to the pan in batches and fry for 3 minutes. Turn and cook for a further 2 minutes until browned but pink inside.

5 To serve, place 2 pigeon breasts on each of 4 dinner plates and spoon a portion of the cracked wheat salad beside them. Sprinkle with the chives.

Braising and Stewing

(See **Poultry**, *Methods of Cooking Poultry*, page 418.)

Due to the small size of feathered game and the lack of fat covering the lean meat, the birds retain their moisture best when they are casseroled or braised whole. Jointed or carved just before serving. In the recipe below the partridges are trussed (see **Poultry**, *Trussing*, page 418) to maintain a compact shape.

Partridge with Lentils

SERVES 2

2 partridges, drawn, trussed and larded

salt

30 g | 1 oz lard or 2 tablespoons oil

30 g | 1 oz rindless unsmoked bacon, chopped

30 g | 1 oz onion, chopped

110 g | 4 oz Puy lentils, soaked in cold water for 1 hour and drained

grated zest of ½ lemon

1 bay leaf

110 g | 4 oz Gyula sausage or similar dried, smoked pork sausage

290 ml | ½ pint White Chicken Stock (see *Stocks*, page 689)

85 ml | 3 fl oz crème fraîche

1 Preheat the oven to 170°C | 325°F | gas mark 3.

2 Sprinkle the partridges with salt. Melt the lard or place the oil in a large frying pan and fry the partridges until they are golden-brown all over. Remove from the pan.

3 Fry the bacon and onion in the same pan until golden-brown.

4 Put the lentils into a large casserole with the lemon zest and bay leaf. Add the partridges, sausage, bacon and onion. Pour over enough stock just to cover the ingredients. Cover with a lid and cook in the oven until the partridges are tender, about 45 minutes. If partridges are ready before the lentils remove the partridges and the sausages from the pan and continue to cook the lentils.

5 When the lentils are tender, pour over the crème fraîche and bring the liquid to the boil.

6 Carve the partridges and cut the sausages into thin slices. Place the lentils in a deep serving dish, put the partridge pieces on top, and garnish with the sliced sausage.

Preparing and Cooking Furred Game

Drawing Game

Most large game, such as venison, is drawn, which means the innards are removed as soon as the animal is killed to allow the carcass to cool down quickly and delay the onset of deterioration. Rabbits, though much smaller, the same treatment. In this case drawing is referred to as 'paunching', as their digestive juices quickly cause the surrounding meat to deteriorate.

Rabbit

The flesh of wild rabbit is gamier and less tender than farmed, whose pale flesh is rather like chicken. If the rabbit has not been skinned, look for smooth, sharp claws and delicate, soft ears. Rabbit is a lean, tender meat and is suitable for roasting, grilling, sautéing or cooking slowly by braising and stewing. The meat should be cooked through and is often served with sauces flavoured with mustard. When roasted, rabbit may be stuffed with any stuffings suitable for poultry and must be basted well to prevent the lean meat from drying out. Before cooking, rabbit is often soaked in cold salted water or water with a little vinegar added to whiten the rabbit's flesh.

Preparing Rabbit for the Oven

To skin a rabbit:

1 Cut off the 4 feet above the knee.
2 Place the rabbit on the work surface with the tail nearest to you.
3 Make a 2.5 cm|1 in cut across the belly of the rabbit in line with the thighs.
4 Pull the skin towards the thighs and then turn the thighs out of the skin, almost like pulling a glove inside out.
5 Pull the skin towards the tail, until the whole lower body is skinned.
6 Turn the body over so that the head is nearest to you and firmly pull the skin towards the head end. Turn out the legs, working on one at a time. Pull the skin off towards the head end.
7 Cut off the head with the skin.

To joint a rabbit:

1 Remove the hind legs by cutting through the joint between the legs and the body. Cut the fore legs away from the ribs.
2 Chop the saddle into 2 pieces, across the width.

Mustard Rabbit

Preparation for this dish begins a day in advance.

SERVES 4

1 rabbit, skinned and cleaned
2½ tablespoons French mustard
1 teaspoon chopped fresh tarragon
45 g|1 ½ oz butter or bacon dripping
85 g|3 oz bacon or salt pork, diced
1 onion, finely chopped

1 clove of garlic, crushed
1 teaspoon plain flour
570 ml|1 pint White Chicken Stock (see ***Stocks***, page 689)
2 tablespoons chopped fresh parsley, to garnish

1 If the rabbit's head has not been removed, cut it off with a sharp, heavy knife. Then joint the rabbit into 6 neat pieces, following the instructions above.
2 Soak the rabbit in cold salted water for 3 hours.
3 Spread 2 tablespoons mustard mixed with the tarragon over the rabbit pieces and refrigerate overnight.

4 The following day, preheat the oven to 170°C|325°F|gas mark 3.

5 Heat the butter or dripping in a frying pan and brown the rabbit pieces all over. Remove them with a slotted spoon and place in a casserole.

6 Add the bacon or salt pork and onion to the pan and cook over a low heat until the onions are soft and just browned. Add the garlic and cook for 1 minute. Stir in the flour and cook for 1 minute.

7 Remove the pan from the heat and stir in the stock. Return to the heat and bring the sauce slowly to the boil, stirring continuously.

8 Pour this sauce over the rabbit. Cook in the oven for about 1½ hours, or until the rabbit is tender.

9 Lift the rabbit on to a warmed serving dish. Add ½ tablespoon mustard to the sauce and check the seasoning. Boil for 1 minute. If the sauce is now rather thin, reduce it by boiling rapidly until it is shiny and rich in appearance. Pour the sauce over the rabbit pieces.

10 Sprinkle with the parsley.

Hare

If the hare has not been skinned, look for smooth, sharp claws and delicate, soft ears. Dry, ragged ears and blunt claws are a sign of age. A leveret (young hare) has a hardly noticeable harelip – this becomes deeper and more pronounced in an older animal. Once the hare has been hung, skin it, collecting any blood as this is used to thicken the gravy or sauce when the hare is roasted or 'jugged'. If the hare has been skinned, look for deep claret flesh.

Only tender joints of young hare, i.e. the back and hind legs, are suitable for stuffing and roasting, and require much basting. The joints from an old animal are best jugged, casseroled or used in pies.

Preparing Hare for the Oven
Skin the hare in the same way as described for rabbit above.

To joint a hare:
1 Cut off the hind legs at the hip joint and chop them in two at the knee.
2 Cut off the fore legs at the shoulder joint and chop them in two at the knee.
3 The back (saddle) can be left intact for roasting or may be cut into 4–6 pieces for slow cooking.
4 Trim off any surplus skin.

To flavour and tenderize the meat, hare is often marinated for up to 2 days before roasting or stewing. Roast hare is often stuffed and served with gravy thickened with its blood and flavoured with redcurrant jelly.

Jugged Hare

This is a traditional English dish where the hare is cooked slowly in brown stock. The stock is made into a sauce, flavoured with port and redcurrant jelly and thickened with the hare's blood (see **Sauces, Savoury**, *Thickening Sauces*, page 585) at the end of cooking. The sauce requires the hare's blood to thicken it. If very little blood (less than 150 ml|¼ pint) comes with the hare, the basic stock must be thickened with a little beurre manié (see **Sauces, Savoury**, *Thickening Sauces*, page 583). This must be done before the addition of the blood, which curdles if boiled.

SERVES 6

1 hare, skinned and jointed, with its blood
2 tablespoons oil
225 g|8 oz mirepoix of carrot, onion and celery
1 bouquet garni (1 bay leaf, 2 parsley stalks,
    1 sprig of fresh thyme, tied together with string)

570 ml|1 pint Brown Stock (see **Stocks**,
    page 692)
salt and freshly ground black pepper
1 tablespoon redcurrant jelly
3 tablespoons port

1 Wash and wipe dry the pieces of hare, removing any membranes. Heat the oil in a large saucepan and fry the joints until well browned, adding more oil if the pan becomes dry. Lift out the joints and brown the mirepoix.
2 Return the hare to the pan. Add the bouquet garni, stock, salt and pepper. Cover and simmer for 2 hours, or until the hare is very tender.
3 Place the joints in a casserole and keep warm.
4 Strain the stock into a saucepan. Add the redcurrant jelly and port and simmer for 5 minutes. Remove the pan from the heat.
5 Mix the blood with a cupful of hot stock. Pour back into the pan without allowing the sauce to boil. The blood will thicken the sauce slightly.
6 Check the sauce, for seasoning. Pour over the hare joints in the casserole and serve.

Venison

Venison, the meat of deer, used to be available only during the close hunting seasons listed in the table at the beginning of this section. Since the 1960s venison has been farmed successfully for all-year-round availability. The animals are fed on a diet of grass, hay, potatoes and apples and are slaughtered at around 18 months old. Farmed venison is usually sold ready prepared for cooking.

Venison is exceptionally lean and often requires a relatively lengthy hanging period to tenderize the meat and develop flavour. Venison is hung for 3–10 days, depending on the hanging conditions and the required gaminess. Venison hung for 3 days tastes rather like beef that has been hung for 3 weeks. Venison hung for 10 days becomes extremely gamy. As with all game, older venison will be tougher and more strongly flavoured than young venison and will require a longer period of hanging to tenderize the tough muscle fibres. As a result, older venison, when it is suitably hung for eating, will taste much stronger than meat from a young animal.

Choosing

- The meat should be dark red with a firm texture and fine grain. It should be moist but not slimy or gelatinous and with very little fat.
- The small amount of fat under the skin should be firm and white. Fat does not marble venison meat as with beef.

Preparing Venison for Cooking

When preparing venison, remove as much of the membrane surrounding the meat as possible as this will toughen on cooking and distort the shape of the meat. Tougher, older venison, despite being hung for a relatively long time, may require marinating to tenderize the meat fibres further.

Methods of Cooking Venison

The tenderest cuts of venison are from the loin and haunch and are suitable for grilling, frying, roasting and braising. They are best served pink. The other cuts benefit from marinating and slow cooking until the meat fibres start to fall apart. Venison is traditionally accompanied by redcurrant jelly, poivrade sauce, cranberries and braised chestnuts. Bitter chocolate is sometimes added to sauces served with venison to enhance the rich flavour of the meat.

Venison Cooking Table

Venison cut	Best cooking method	Recipe reference
Haunch/leg	Roasting	
	Braising (haunch of older animal)	
		Braised Haunch of Venison (page 471)
Whole saddle	Roasting	
	Frying	
Saddle chops	Grilling	
Fillet	Roasting	
Fillet steaks	Frying	*Peppered Venison Steak* (page 470)
	Grilling	
Shoulder	Braising	
	Stewing	*Venison Casserole* (page 472)
Neck	Stewing	*Venison Casserole* (page 472)
	Mincing	
Flank	Stewing	*Venison Casserole* (page 472)
	Mincing	

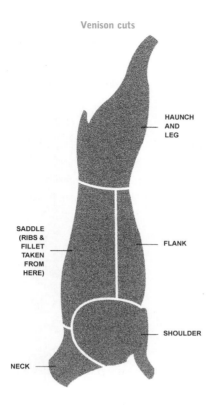

Venison cuts

HAUNCH
AND
LEG

SADDLE
(RIBS &
FILLET
TAKEN
FROM
HERE)

FLANK

SHOULDER

NECK

Roasting

Whole haunch and saddle, or the fillet are the best cuts of venison for roasting. To protect the lean meat while roasting, large joints of venison (weighing more than 3.5 kg | 8 lb) are often barded with streaky bacon (see **Poultry**, *Barding*, page 343) or larded with strips of pork fat (see **Veal**, *Larding*, page 376).

Season the venison with salt and freshly ground black pepper. Brown in a little oil, then place in the oven preheated to 200°C | 400°F | gas mark 6 and roast for the calculated cooking time. Allow 45 minutes per kg | 1½ lb, 20 minutes per 450g | 1 lb.

To ensure the venison remains moist and juicy it is best eaten pink. A large joint of venison also benefits from resting for up to 30 minutes, before carving (see **Meat**, *Resting Meat After Roasting*, page 344), covered in foil or in a plate-warming oven. This resting period allows the meat to reabsorb some of the free-running juices released during cooking, before it is carved.

Grilling and Frying

(See **Meat**, *Methods of Cooking Meat*, page 341.)

Although venison steaks and chops are suitable for both grilling and frying, the meat is so lean that it becomes dry if cooked beyond medium-rare. If less pink meat is required it should be browned well until medium-rare, then transferred to a low oven which will allow the meat to continue cooking very slowly for a few more minutes. This way, the meat is able to relax and will remain tender and juicy. (See **Meat,** *Grilling and Pan-frying Beef Steaks,* page 364.)

Peppered Venison Steak

If the venison is very fresh and you want a gamier taste, marinate it for 2 days in equal quantities of red wine and oil, flavoured with a sliced onion, 6 juniper berries and a bay leaf. Dry well with kitchen paper before frying.

SERVES 4

4 × 140 g⎮5 oz venison collops (steaks), cut from the fillet	30 g⎮1 oz unsalted butter
2 tablespoons black peppercorns	2 tablespoons brandy
1 tablespoon olive oil	150 ml⎮¼ pint double cream
	salt

1 Wipe the venison steaks and trim off any gristle.

2 Crush the peppercorns coarsely in a mortar or under a rolling pin and press them into the surface of the meat on both sides.

3 Cover the steaks and refrigerate for 2 hours at room temperature for the flavour to penetrate the meat.

4 Heat the oil in a heavy pan, add the butter, and when it is foaming fry the steaks as fast as possible until done to your liking (about 2 minutes per side for blue, 3 minutes for rare, $3\frac{1}{2}$ minutes for medium and 4 minutes for well-done).

5 Pour in the brandy and set alight. Add the cream and a pinch of salt. Mix the contents of the pan thoroughly, scraping up any sediment stuck to the bottom.

6 Place the steaks on a warmed serving platter.

7 Boil the sauce to a syrupy consistency and pour over the meat. Serve immediately.

Braising

The shoulder and the haunch of venison are the best cuts for braising. Before cooking tougher cuts of venison, remove as much gristle as possible as it will not soften with cooking.

Braised Haunch of Venison

SERVES 6–8

2.7 kg|6 lb haunch of venison	1 tablespoon chopped fresh thyme
salt and freshly ground black pepper	1 teaspoon chopped fresh sage
30 g|1 oz butter	290 ml|½ pint red wine
1 tablespoon oil	425 ml|¾ pint Brown Stock (see **Stocks**,
2 onions, sliced	page 692)
225 g|8 oz carrots, sliced	30 g|1 oz butter
4 sticks of celery, sliced	30 g|1 oz plain flour
1 bay leaf	1 tablespoon cranberry jelly

1 Preheat the oven to 150°C\|300°F\|gas mark 2.

2 Prepare the venison by trimming away any tough membranes, sinews and gristle. Season with salt and pepper.

3 Heat the butter and oil in a large flameproof casserole and brown the venison well on all sides. Remove from the casserole.

4 Add the onions, carrots and celery, and fry until lightly browned.

5 Add the bay leaf and the thyme and sage. Lay the venison on top of the vegetables. Add the wine and enough stock to come about a quarter of the way up the meat.

6 Bring to simmering point, then cover tightly and cook in the oven for 1½ hours, or until tender. Check the meat after 1 hour to ensure there is still liquid in the casserole. If not, add 290 ml\|½ pint water.

7 When cooked, lift out the meat, carve it neatly and place on a warmed serving dish. Keep warm, covered with a lid or aluminium foil.

8 Strain the liquid from the vegetables into a saucepan. Skim any fat from the surface.

9 Mix the butter and flour together to make a beurre manié. Add this to the liquid bit by bit, stirring, and bring to the boil. Boil until syrupy. Stir in the cranberry jelly and check the seasoning.

10 To serve, spoon a thin layer of sauce over the venison to make it look shiny and appetizing; serve the remaining sauce in a warmed sauce-boat.

Braising: What has gone wrong when...

The braised dish looks grey and unappetizing.

- The ingredients were insufficiently browned before the liquid was added.

The braised dish looks very dark and tastes burnt.

- The ingredients were overbrowned.

The sauce is thin in flavour and consistency.

- The meat contained too little connective tissue.
- The stock was not sufficiently gelatinous and strongly flavoured.

The dish is fatty.

- The fat that melts in the cooking liquor was not skimmed off before serving or reducing the sauce to a syrupy consistency.

The meat is tough.

- The meat requires more cooking, slowly at a low temperature.

Stewing

The best cuts of venison for stewing are the neck, flank and shoulder, although any cut other than the saddle is suitable. The meat benefits from marinating as well as slow cooking to tenderize the meat. (See **Meat,** *Browning*, page 343.)

Venison Casserole with Chestnuts and Cranberries

SERVES 4

675 g | 1lb 8 oz shoulder, neck or flank of
   venison

For the marinade
5 tablespoons sunflower oil
1 onion, sliced
1 carrot, sliced
1 stick of celery, peeled and sliced
1 clove of garlic, crushed
6 juniper berries, slightly crushed
1 slice of lemon
1 bay leaf
290 ml | ½ pint red wine
2 tablespoons red wine vinegar
6 black peppercorns

For the casserole
2 tablespoons sunflower oil
30 g | 1 oz butter
110 g | 4 oz button onions, peeled
1 clove of garlic, crushed
110 g | 4 oz whole button mushrooms
2 teaspoons plain flour
150 ml | ¼ pint Brown Stock (see **Stocks**,
   page 692)
1 tablespoon cranberry jelly
salt and freshly ground black pepper
55 g | 2 oz fresh cranberries
15 g | ½ oz sugar
110 g | 4 oz cooked whole chestnuts
chopped fresh parsley, to garnish

1 Cut the venison into 5 cm | 2 in cubes, trimming away any tough membranes sinews or gristle.
2 Mix the ingredients for the marinade together in a bowl and add the venison. Mix well, cover and refrigerate overnight.
3 Preheat the oven to 170°C | 325°F | gas mark 3.
4 Remove the venison from the marinade and pat dry with kitchen paper. Strain the marinade and reserve.
5 Heat half the oil in a heavy saucepan and brown the venison cubes a few at a time. Place them in a casserole. If the bottom of the pan becomes brown or too dry, pour in a little of the strained marinade and swish it about, scraping off the

sediment stuck to the bottom, then pour over the browned venison cubes. Then heat a little more oil and continue browning the remaining meat.

6 When all the venison has been browned, repeat the *déglacage*, boiling up a little marinade and scraping the bottom of the pan.

7 In the remaining oil fry the onions until golden-brown. Add the garlic and cook for a further minute. Add the mushrooms and continue cooking for 2 minutes.

8 Melt the butter in a saucepan, stir in the flour and cook for 1 minute. Remove from the heat and add the reserved marinade and the stock. Return to the heat and stir until boiling, again scraping the bottom of the pan.

9 Add the cranberry jelly to the sauce. Season to taste with salt and pepper. Pour the sauce over the meat.

10 Cover the casserole and cook in the oven for about 2 hours or until the venison is very tender.

11 Meanwhile, cook the cranberries briefly with the sugar in 2–3 tablespoons water until just soft but not crushed. Strain off the liquor, reserving the cranberries.

12 Using a slotted spoon, lift the venison, mushrooms and onions into a warmed serving dish.

13 Boil the sauce fast until reduced to a shiny, almost syrupy consistency. Add the cranberries and chestnuts and simmer gently for 5 minutes.

14 Pour the sauce over the venison and serve garnished with chopped parsley.

Mincing

Tougher cuts of venison, such as flank and neck, may be tenderized by mincing, which breaks up the meat fibres and connective tissue (see **Meat, *Mincing Meat*,** page 340). Venison mince may be used to make venison burgers and sausages or combined with pork mince in forcemeats for terrines, coarse pâtés and raised pies (see **Terrines, Pâtés and Raised Pies**, page 703).

Making Meringues: Points to Remember

- Use clean, grease-free equipment. Do not use plastic bowls or spatulas as they tend to retain traces of grease on their surfaces.

- Ensure the whites are free from yolk.

- If possible, do not make meringues on a damp or rainy day. The humidity makes it difficult to dry them out sufficiently.

- Older egg whites are easier to whisk than fresh egg whites. Egg whites can be kept in the refrigerator for up to 3 weeks. However, if they start to smell, throw them away.

- Allow egg whites to come to room temperature before using them. They will whisk more easily.

- If the whites are very fresh, add a tiny pinch of salt before beginning to whisk, to help break the thread of the whites.

- Begin by whisking slowly, then increase your speed as the egg whites begin to foam.

- Do not add any sugar before the egg whites are very stiff. This can be tested by holding a small amount of white upright on the end of your whisk; the white should stand straight up without bending.

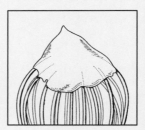

- Avoid overwhisking egg whites or they will lose their elasticity and will not expand well when cooked. If whites are overwhisked their volume will begin to decrease. A sign that the whites have been whisked too much is a lumpy, cottonwool-like texture around the edge of the bowl. Continuing to whisk can lead to collapse.

- Acid, often in the form of cream of tartar, can be added to stabilize the foam. Although it has no effect on the volume of foam produced, it makes it less prone to overwhisking and collapse. Only a tiny amount is needed to make a significant difference – about $\frac{1}{16}$ teaspoon per egg white.

- Use baking parchment to line the baking sheets and tins.

Meringues

Meringues, the snowy confection of egg whites and sugar, were first made in Europe in the 1600s. Some cookery historians believe that a Swiss pastry chef, Gasparini, who practised his art in the small town of Meringen, invented meringues, hence the name. Meringues were soon adopted by the French court.

There are three types of crisp meringue: Swiss Meringue, Italian Meringue and Meringue Cuite, or cooked meringue, in addition to the soft meringue which is used principally as a topping for pies, such as lemon meringue pie.

The first part of this section covers crisp meringues.

Meringue is a combination of egg white foam and sugar which has been dried in a low oven until the moisture content has been reduced enough to stabilize the mixture. As the egg whites are whisked, the proteins stretch. When the egg whites are stiff and the proteins have been stretched as far as possible, the sugar is beaten in. The sugar attracts the water in the egg whites and forms a syrup which coats the stretched proteins. When the meringue is baked the water evaporates, leaving a dry coating of sugar on the coagulated egg protein. Egg whites are notoriously temperamental so it is necessary to abide by the rules at the beginning of this section when making meringues (see also *Eggs*, *Whisking Whites*, page 233).

Using Copper Bowls to Whisk Egg Whites

Egg whites whisked in a copper bowl will be more stable and have more volume when baked. The foam will have a greater elasticity, which will give a lighter result. This is due to the chemical reaction between the egg whites and the copper.

The bowl must be cleaned before each use. To do this, rub the inside of the bowl with the cut edge of half a lemon and a teaspoon of salt until any oxidation disappears. Rinse with clean water and dry with kitchen paper.

Swiss Meringue

Swiss meringue is used for making individual meringues sandwiched together in pairs with cream, for Petits Fours and for Vacherin, which is assembled from 2 or 3 discs of piped meringue layered together with cream. It is named after the French cheese vacherin, which it resembles in shape and colour.

Swiss meringue is made with twice the weight of caster sugar to egg white. One medium egg white weighs 30 g | 1 oz with a volume of 30 ml | 1 fl oz, so for each egg white use 55 g | 2 oz caster sugar. If whisking by hand it is relatively easy to whisk up to 4 whites at a time; more than that becomes very tiring. Standard electric mixers can usually whisk up to 8 whites. Refer to the manufacturer's instructions for capacity.

Swiss meringue will liquefy if left to stand for any time, so be prepared to use the mixture as soon as it is ready: have the oven preheated and the baking sheets lined with baking parchment.

Swiss Meringue

SERVES 8

4 egg whites
225 g | 8 oz caster sugar

For the filling

200 ml | 7 fl oz double cream, lightly whipped

1. Preheat the oven to 110°C | 225°F | gas mark ½.
2. Line 2 baking sheets with baking parchment.
3. If using a copper bowl, clean as noted above. Place the whites in the bowl.
4. Start whisking slowly, increasing the speed as the whites increase in volume.
5. When the whites have reached a stiff peak gradually add 4 heaped tablespoons of the sugar (this should be approximately half of the total quantity) a little at a time while whisking. This process should take no more than 2 minutes.
6. Fold in the remaining sugar, using a large metal basting spoon.
7. Using a piping bag and nozzle or a spoon, immediately shape the meringue on to the prepared sheets. Place the piping bag in a jug to make it easier to fill. Fill the bag about half full, then twist the top to prevent the meringue from spilling out. Hold the bag in one hand with your thumb and index finger around the twisted part. Hold the bag vertically to pipe, using your other hand to guide the nozzle.
8. Place in the lower third of the oven for 1 hour for small meringues or 1½ hours for a Vacherin or larger meringues. The meringues are done when they will peel easily from the paper and feel firm to the touch on the underside.
9. Cool on a wire rack. The meringues can be stored, unfilled, in an airtight container for up to 2 weeks.
10. To fill the meringues, whisk the cream until it holds its shape and use to sandwich the meringues together. The meringues can be stored in the refrigerator, but after an hour or so they will start to soften.

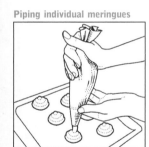

Piping individual meringues

Swiss Meringues: What has gone wrong when...

The egg whites will not whisk to a stiff peak.

- The whites contain oil or yolk or the equipment was not clean of grease.

The meringue mixture is too soft.

- The sugar was added before the whites came to a stiff peak.
- The mixture was beaten for too long once the sugar was added.
- The mixture was overfolded when the sugar was added and started to collapse.

Melted sugar oozes from the cooked meringues (the meringues weep).

- The meringues were cooked for too long.
- The meringues were cooked at too high a temperature.

The meringues do not dry out.

- The meringues have not been cooked for long enough.
- The weather is too damp.

Flavouring Meringues

Finely ground nuts, such as almonds or hazelnuts, are traditionally added to a Swiss Meringue mixture and baked in round, flat discs to produce a Dacquoise or a Hazelnut Meringue. The discs are layered with whipped cream and the confection is served as a cake, usually with a sharp fruit coulis (see *Sauces, Sweet*, page 617). Cocoa powder or coffee essence can be folded into a meringue mixture before baking it.

It is important to add the flavouring ingredients after all the sugar has been incorporated. Fold the ingredients into the meringue mixture quickly and avoid overfolding: the added ingredients tend to break down the egg white foam and could cause the meringue to collapse. 30 g | 1 oz finely ground nuts per egg white is recommended. Mix 1 tablespoon of the sugar with the nuts when grinding to absorb some of the oils and make the nuts more free-flowing.

Hazelnut Meringue Cake with Raspberry Coulis

Toasted almonds can be used in place of the hazelnuts in the following recipe to make a Dacquoise.

SERVES 6–8

110 g | 4 oz skinned, toasted hazelnuts (see *Nuts*, page 494)
225 g | 8 oz caster sugar
4 egg whites
a drop of vanilla essence
½ teaspoon white wine vinegar

To serve
200 ml | 7 fl oz double cream, lightly whipped
290 ml | ½ pint Raspberry Coulis (see *Sauces, Sweet*, page 617)

1 Preheat the oven to 180°C | 350°F | gas mark 4.
2 Line 2 × 20 cm | 8 in sandwich tins with lightly oiled aluminium foil.
3 Set aside 6–8 whole hazelnuts for decoration if desired. Grind the remaining hazelnuts to the texture of breadcrumbs in a nut grinder or food processor. Add 1 tablespoon of the caster sugar to the nuts before grinding if using a food processor (see *Nuts*, page 494).
4 Stir half the sugar into the nuts.
5 Whisk the egg whites to stiff peaks and add the remaining caster sugar, 1 teaspoonful at a time, while whisking.
6 Carefully fold in the nut and sugar mixture, vinegar and vanilla.
7 Turn into the prepared tins, smoothing the surface with a spatula.
8 Bake in the middle of the oven for 40 minutes, or until the foil peels easily from the meringue. The meringue will still be mallowy in the centre due to the nuts and the vinegar.
9 Allow the meringues to cool in the foil on wire racks.
10 Carefully peel away the foil and sandwich together with the cream. Decorate the top with rosettes of cream and reserved whole hazelnuts if desired. Serve with the raspberry coulis.

Pavlova

This favourite meringue was named after the famous ballerina Anna Pavlova. There is an on-going debate between the Australians and the New Zealanders as to who invented it first. It is made with Swiss Meringue to which cornflour and vinegar are added. This keeps the interior of the meringue mallowy.

SERVES 6–8

4 egg whites
225 g | 8 oz caster sugar
1 teaspoon white wine vinegar
1 teaspoon vanilla essence
1 teaspoon cornflour

For the filling

200 ml | 7 fl oz double cream
450 g | 1 lb raspberries or a mixture of soft
   fruits

1 Preheat the oven to 140°C | 275°F | gas mark 1.
2 Line a baking sheet with baking parchment and mark with a 20 cm | 8 in circle.
3 Turn the paper over to avoid marking the meringue.
4 Whisk the egg whites to stiff peaks in a clean, grease-free bowl. Gradually add half the caster sugar, a teaspoonful at a time, while whisking. The mixture should be very stiff and satiny.
5 Mix together the vinegar, vanilla and cornflour and fold into the meringue along with the remaining sugar.
6 Spread half the meringue over the marked circle to form a base, then heap the remainder around the edge of the base to make a rough bowl.
7 Bake in the lower third of the oven for 1–1½ hours. Turn off the oven and leave the meringue in the oven until it is cool. Store in an airtight container until required.
8 To fill, whip the cream to soft peaks, then layer the cream and fruit into the centre of the meringue.

Italian Meringue

Italian Meringue uses the same proportions of sugar to egg white as Swiss Meringue but the sugar is made into a syrup which is brought to the firm ball stage (see *Sugar, Sweetners and Sugar Syrups, Stages of Sugar Syrup,* page 701) before being added to the stiffly whisked egg whites. This method produces a meringue mixture that is very stable once mixed and can be stored uncooked tightly covered with clingfilm, in the refrigerator for up to 2 days.

Italian Meringue cooks more quickly than Swiss Meringue and produces a chalkier, more powdery, brilliant white meringue. It is excellent for making piped meringue baskets because it holds its shape well during cooking and is sturdy enough to hold up well when filled. Italian Meringue is also used as a base for ice cream (see *Ice Creams,* page 315).

Italian Meringue

225 g | 8 oz granulated or lump sugar   4 egg whites
6 tablespoons water

1 Put the sugar and water into a heavy saucepan over a low heat.
2 If using, place a sugar thermometer in the pan. Bring slowly to the boil stirring gently to help the sugar dissolve. Wash down the sides of the pan with a pastry brush dipped in water to remove any sugar crystals sticking to the sides of the pan.
3 The syrup is ready when the temperature reaches 120°C | 248°F. Alternatively test for the firm ball stage (see *Sugar, Sweetners and Sugar Syrups*, *Stages of Sugar Syrup*, page 701).
4 While the sugar is boiling, whisk the egg whites to stiff peaks.
5 Pour the boiling sugar syrup on to the whites in a thin, steady stream while whisking. Take care not to allow the syrup to pour on to the beaters as it could stick if it comes in direct contact with them.
6 Once all the syrup has been added, continue to whisk until the mixture is stiff, shiny and stable and when the whisk is lifted, the meringue does not move.
7 Keep covered with clingfilm or a damp cloth if not using immediately.

Italian Meringue: What has gone wrong when...

The mixture fails to thicken or increase in volume.
- The sugar syrup was not hot enough when poured onto the whites.

The mixture collapses.
- The mixture was overwhisked.
- The sugar syrup was boiled to too high a temperature.

Meringue Cuite

Meringue Cuite, or cooked meringue, is a professional chef's meringue used for icings, cake fillings, and meringue baskets. Meringue Cuite is finer and chalkier-textured than Italian Meringue or Swiss Meringue. Like Italian Meringue, Meringue Cuite is very stable in the oven, hardly swelling at all, and is unlikely to cook out of shape.

Meringue Cuite can be kept for up to 4 hours in the refrigerator before baking, if closely covered. The proportion of sugar to whites is the same as for most meringues, i.e. 55 g | 2 oz sugar per egg white, but the sugar used is icing (confectioner's) sugar, rather than caster sugar.

An electric hand-held whisk is necessary to make this type of meringue as it can require up to 15 minutes of whisking.

Meringue Cuite

4 egg whites   3 drops of vanilla essence
225 g | 8 oz icing sugar, sifted

1 Place the whites into a heatproof bowl that will fit snugly over a saucepan of simmering water. The base of the bowl should not come into contact with the water. Whisk the egg whites to stiff peaks.

2 Sift the icing sugar over the whites, then set the bowl over the pan of water. Whisk slowly at first to avoid the icing sugar billowing out of the bowl.

3 Continue whisking until the mixture is thick and stable and feels just warm to the touch.

4 Remove the bowl from the water and continue whisking for up to 5 minutes until the mixture and the bowl feel cool. The meringue should be thick enough to hold a teaspoon vertically.

5 Whisk in the vanilla. Keep covered with a damp cloth or clingfilm if not using immediately.

Meringue Cuite: What has gone wrong when...

In addition to the problems listed above under *Swiss Meringue* and *Italian Meringue*, the following can occur:

The meringue does not become stiff enough during whisking.
- The mixture has not been whisked enough or it has been overwhisked.
- The water under the bowl was not hot enough.

Strawberry Meringue Basket

This recipe uses Meringue Cuite because it is the most stable of the three types of crisp meringue. Make one large basket for a spectacular centrepiece for a buffet or make individual baskets for a smart dinner party.

Two quantities of Meringue Cuite (see recipe above) are needed. Make the second batch while the first batch is baking.

SERVES 8

For the filling   450 g | 1 lb strawberries, hulled and sliced in
425 ml | ¾ pint double cream, highly whipped   half lengthways

1 Preheat the oven to 140°C | 275°F | gas mark 1.

2 Line 2 baking sheets with baking parchment. For a large basket, mark 3 × 18 cm | 7 in circles on the underside of the paper. For individual baskets, mark 24 × 8 cm | 3 in circles.

3 Make the first batch of Meringue Cuite as directed in the recipe above.

4 Using a 1 cm | ½ in plain nozzle for the large basket or a 6 mm | ¼ in nozzle for the small baskets, pipe a circular base for each of the baskets. Start piping in the centre of the circle. Hold the piping bag vertically and allow the meringue to drop from the nozzle on to the paper while guiding the meringue into the correct shape. If there are any gaps between the lines, gently lift the edge of the paper to tilt the lines together. Cover half the paper circles with piped meringue.

5 Pipe hoops over the remaining circles.

6 Bake the meringue bases and hoops for 45–60 minutes, or until dry and crisp. Cool on a wire rack.

7 Make up the second batch of Meringue Cuite.

8 Place the cooked base on a baking sheet. Use the uncooked meringue to glue the hoops over the base. Don't worry if the hoops break, just stick them together with the uncooked meringue.

9 Fit the piping bag with a 1 cm | ½ in star nozzle for the large basket or a 6 mm | ¼ in nozzle for the small baskets.

10 Pipe in straight lines from the base of the meringue over the top edge. Carefully trim the points from the inside of the basket with a knife to make a smooth edge. If desired, pipe scrolls over the top edge of the meringue.

11 Bake for 45–60 minutes until set and crisp.

12 Cool on a wire rack, then carefully remove the paper.

13 Layer strawberries and cream in the basket no more than 1 hour before serving. Reserve the best strawberries and use to decorate the top. The strawberries can be glazed with cooled melted redcurrant jelly if desired.

Soft or Pie Meringue

Soft meringue is used to top pies such as Lemon Meringue Pie and for Baked Alaska, which is a concoction of meringue-coated ice cream on a sponge cake base. For each egg white use 30 g | 1 oz caster sugar. See *Making Meringues: Points to Remember*, above.

In the following recipe for Lemon Meringue Pie, a gel made from cornflour and water is whisked into the whites to stabilize the meringue and help prevent it from beading.

Lemon Meringue Pie

For information on fillings set with eggs, see **Eggs**, *Use of Eggs in Cooking* (page 224).

SERVES 8

170 g | 6 oz sweet rich shortcrust pastry (see
   Pastry, page 512)

For the filling

4 level 15 ml spoons cornflour

225 g | 8 oz caster sugar

290 ml | ½ pint water

4 egg yolks

juice and zest of 2½ large unwaxed lemons

For the meringue

3 tablespoons water

2 teaspoons cornflour

4 egg whites

110 g | 4 oz caster sugar

a little extra caster sugar

1   Make the pastry and use to line a 20 cm | 8 in flan ring. Chill until firm then bake blind (see page 509). Turn the oven temperature to 180°C | 350°F | gas mark 4.
2   Place the cornflour and sugar in a saucepan. Stir in the water.
3   Place over medium heat and cook, stirring, until the mixture boils. It will become thick and translucent.
4   Whisk in the egg yolks into the hot mixture then pass through a sieve to remove any eggy threads.
5   Whisk in the lemon juice and zest.
6   Pour the hot filling into the warm pastry case and place in the middle of the oven for 5 minutes.
7   For the meringue topping: place the water and cornflour in a small saucepan and whisk over medium heat until the mixture is thick and translucent. Remove from the heat.
8   Whisk the whites until stiff peaks form then gradually whisk in the caster sugar. Whisk in the warm cornflour gel.
9   Pile the meringue on top of the filling starting at the edge next to the pastry case then moving towards the middle. Mound the filling slightly in the centre.
10   Use a fork to make peaks on the meringue then sprinkle with a little extra sugar.
11   Place in the oven for 15 minutes until the topping is light brown.
12   Allow to cool before serving or refrigerate if keeping overnight.

Soft Meringue: What has gone wrong when...

Droplets of sugar syrup form on top of the meringue.

- The meringue was overbaked.
- The oven was too hot.

There is a wet layer underneath the meringue.

- The meringue was underbaked.
- The filling was not hot when the meringue was piled on top.

Microwave Cookery

In conventional oven cooking the air is heated and the heat is passed slowly into the centre of the food by conduction. In microwave cooking, the microwaves cause the moisture molecules in the food to vibrate, causing friction, which results in heat.

The microwaves are reflected off the metal cavity of the oven and form criss-cross patterns. The food absorbs waves from all directions. As microwaves only penetrate about 5 cm|2 in into food, the microwave oven is most efficient for cooking small pieces of food. With pieces of food thicker than 5 cm|2 in, the centre will cook by the conduction of the heat nearer the surface. The waves pass through china, glass and paper. Metal must not be used as the waves are reflected and bounce off. Arcing may occur and damage the oven.

For information on microwave cooking see also **Kitchen Equipment,** *Microwave ovens* (page 63).

Cooking in a Microwave Oven: Points to Remember

- Do not use metal containers or dishes with metal decorations. Food should be placed in a microwave proof container (see list below) and covered with clingfilm.
- Instructions will call for microwave time and standing time. The standing time is important: the food is still cooking during this time.
- Take care when removing the clingfilm as steam often escapes and can cause burns.
- Containers should not be filled more than half full with liquid due to the risk of boiling over.
- Turn the food once or twice during cooking.
- Stir liquids, such as soups and stews, once or twice during cooking and reheating.
- Take care when stirring liquids; they can boil up without warning.

There is no need to preheat the microwave oven but the colder the food, the longer it will take to cook. Larger pieces of food and several pieces of food take longer than small or single pieces. The shape of the food needs to be taken into account – the more even it is, the more evenly the food will cook. Very dense foods, such as Shepherd's Pie, will take longer to heat than foods with a light, open texture such as a sponge pudding. Unless the microwave oven has a grill element at the top, the food will not brown during cooking.

Microwave ovens are good for defrosting moist foods such as soups, but for large, denser foods, such as chicken, defrosting in the microwave is not recommended. The food usually starts to cook on the outside before the inside is defrosted.

Do not use the following in the microwave oven:

- Metal containers that reflect the waves.
- Dishes with gold or silver decorations.
- Packets with a gold line, which gets hot causing the paper to burst into flames.
- Anything containing glue.
- Pottery, which often has a high iron content or a metallic glaze.
- Melamine or similar plastic which will absorb the microwaves.
- Crystal glass, which contains lead.
- Thin-stemmed glasses, which may break.

Microwave ovens are available in different strengths, so it is best to consult the manufacturer's handbook for cooking instructions. As a general guideline, however, microwave ovens can be used for the following:

Boiling vegetables
The microwave oven is very useful for cooking vegetables that would normally be boiled, and are particularly good for cooking up to 4 servings of cauliflower, broccoli or carrots (see *Vegetables*, page 717). Cut the vegetables into bite-sized pieces and place in a microwave proof container with $3 \text{ mm} | \frac{1}{4}$ in water. Cover with clingfilm. Microwave on HIGH for 3 minutes. Stand 2 minutes. If further cooking is needed, cook for a further 1–2 minutes on HIGH.

Sweating onions
Combine 1 chopped onion with 1 tablespoon oil in a microwave proof dish. Cover with clingfilm and microwave for 3 minutes on HIGH. Stand for 3 minutes.

Potatoes
The microwave oven can also be used for 'baking' potatoes, although the potatoes will taste boiled and have soft rather than crisp skins. Pierce the potatoes in several places with a skewer to prevent them from exploding. Wrap in a piece of kitchen paper and microwave on HIGH for 5 minutes. Stand for 3 minutes, then microwave on HIGH for a further 3 minutes. Check that the potatoes are tender and repeat the process if necessary.

Bacon
Streaky bacon cooks particularly well in the microwave oven. Fold a double layer of kitchen paper around 4–6 rashers in a single layer. Microwave on HIGH in increments of 1 minute until the bacon is cooked as desired.

Fish
See *Fish* (page 262).

Melting and softening butter
Microwave on the DEFROST setting in increments of 10 seconds.

Melting chocolate

Place the chopped chocolate in a glass or ceramic bowl. Do not cover. Microwave in increments of 30 seconds on DEFROST, stirring in between cooking sessions.

Chestnuts

Pierce the tops and place on kitchen paper. Cook on HIGH for 2 minutes and peel while warm.

Caramel

To make caramel for *Crème Caramel* (see **Eggs**, page 227), place 110 g | 4 oz caster sugar and 4 tablespoons water in a glass or ceramic dish. Cover with clingfilm and microwave for 2 minutes on HIGH. Stir and microwave for about a further 6 minutes. As the sugar starts to brown, remove it from the oven and swirl carefully around the dish. The sugar will continue to brown in its own heat.

Reheating cooked food

Microwave ovens are particularly good for reheating 1–2 servings of food. Microwave for 2–3 minutes on HIGH. Stir and repeat. Always ensure food is piping-hot all the way through before serving.

Mousselines

Mousselines are delicate forcemeats made from pounded fish or shellfish mixed with cream and seasoning. Mousselines can also be made with veal, poultry, pork or feathered game. A mousseline is used as a stuffing for fish (see **Aspic**, *Chaudfroid of Salmon*, page 93) and poultry, shaped into fish 'sausages' or formed into quenelles. When poached or baked, mousselines are usually served hot, but they can be served cold, particularly when part of another dish, such as in *Chaudfroid of Salmon*.

The meat or fish is enriched and lightened with cream and bound with eggs. The proportions are very important: too much egg and the mousseline will be rubbery; too little egg and the mousseline will not hold together when cooked. If too much cream is added the mousseline will be too soft and may fall apart during cooking; too little cream and the mousseline will be dry and have a grainy texture. The standard proportion is 1 kg | 2¼ lb fish/1 litre | 1¾ pints double cream/4 egg whites.

Preparing Mousseline Forcemeat

All the principles of preparing a forcemeat are detailed in the **Forcemeat** section (page 271). In addition, it is particularly important to beat the cream into the puréed fish or meat over ice.

Fish Quenelles

Fish that contains natural gelatine, such as sole, whiting and pike, work particularly well when making mousselines.

SERVES 4

675 g | 1½ lb skinned fish fillets, such as sole, salmon or pike
3 egg whites
570 ml | 1 pint double cream
salt and freshly ground white pepper
cayenne pepper

570 ml | 1 pint Fish Stock or *court bouillon* (see **Stocks**, page 693)

To serve
Fish Beurre Blanc (see **Sauces, Savoury**, page 605)
sprigs of fresh chervil

1 Process the fish in a food processor until smooth.
2 Add the egg whites through the feed tube while the motor is running.

3 Place a tammy or drum sieve over a bowl set into a second bowl filled with ice water. Pass the fish through the sieve.

4 Beat the cream into the fish a little at a time, keeping the fish cool over the ice. Make sure the mixture stays fairly firm.

5 Season and poach a small amount of the mixture to taste. Adjust the seasoning if necessary.

6 Heat the stock or *court bouillon* until the surface just trembles.

7 Using 2 wetted spoons of the same size, form the fish mixture into quenelles. Carefully scrape each quenelle as it is formed into the poaching liquid.

8 Cook for 3–5 minutes, turning the quenelles over halfway through the cooking time. When done they will be firm to the touch.

9 Flood the base of 4 plates with the *Fish Beurre Blanc* (see page 605). Arrange 3 quenelles on each plate. Garnish with chervil.

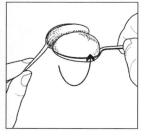
Shaping quenelles

Shaping quenelles

1 Place a mound of the mixture on one spoon. Hold the second spoon at a 30° angle at the far side of the first spoon.

2 Scrape the mixture towards you and into the second spoon.

3 Hold the second spoon flat and repeat the scraping with the other spoon.

Fish Quenelles: What has gone wrong when...

The quenelles fall apart when cooking.

- The mixture contains too little egg white.
- The mixture contains too much cream.
- The poaching liquid was boiling.

The quenelles are rubbery.

- The quenelles have been overcooked.
- The mixture contains too much egg white.
- The mixture contains too little cream.

The quenelles are dry and grainy.

- The mixture contains too little cream.
- The quenelles are overcooked.
- The mixture was not sieved through a fine enough sieve.

Mousses

Mousse is a French term meaning froth or foam which can be used to describe any rich, airy dish, sweet or savoury, hot or cold. A mousse is similar to a soufflé but is usually heavier and richer in texture (see **Soufflés**, *Cold Soufflés*, page 652). The light texture of both mousses and soufflés results from the stretching of the proteins in the eggs and the cream to create a foam. A series of foams are created which are then carefully folded into one another. Sometimes a mousse is set with gelatine (see **Gelatine**, page 294) and can be served in a dish or turned out.

Before making a mousse, familiarize yourself with the information given in the following sections:

- **Eggs,** *Whisking Whites* (page 233)
- **Dairy Products,** *Whipping Cream* (page 201)
- **Gelatine** (page 294)

Mousse carries the risk of salmonella poisoning because uncooked or partially cooked eggs are used. Recipes that require boiling sugar syrup to be poured on to both the egg yolks and the whites are considered safer than those made with uncooked eggs. Pregnant women, very young or very old people or people with impaired immune systems are advised not to eat mousse.

Mousse: Points to Remember

- Use very fresh eggs from a reputable supplier.
- Ensure clean equipment is used and good hygiene practices are followed.
- Prepare your serving dishes before starting to cook. For a mousse which will be turned out, lightly oil the mould with a flavourless oil and allow to drain on to a piece of kitchen paper to remove the excess.
- When combining 2 mixtures of different consistencies, fold the thinner mixture into the thicker.
- Whip cream only until it starts to mound and holds its shape. It will be worked further when added to the mixture.
- Fold carefully with a metal spoon, using a figure-of-eight motion. Turn the bowl while folding to ensure all parts of the mixture are combined.
- Keep the mousse either hot or cold and consume as soon as possible. Cold mousse should be eaten within 24 hours.

Dessert Mousses

For *Chocolate Mousse*, see **Chocolate** (page 192).
For *Raspberry Parfait*, see **Ice Creams** (page 314).

Dessert mousses may be served chilled, as for *Chocolate Mousse*, or frozen, as for *Raspberry Parfait*.

Caramel Mousse

This is a delicious, sophisticated mousse that is tricky to make well. The final result depends very much on cooking the caramel to a rich, dark caramel (see **Caramel**, page 174). If the caramel is not dark enough the mousse will be sickly sweet.

SERVES 4

170 g 6 oz granulated sugar	150 ml ¼ pint double cream
1 tablespoon lemon juice	
2 teaspoons powdered gelatine	**To decorate**
3 eggs	55 g 2 oz caster sugar
45 g 1½ oz caster sugar	100 ml 3½ fl oz double cream, whipped

1 Melt the granulated sugar with 3 tablespoons warm water over a low heat, stirring occasionally, until the sugar is dissolved.
2 Have 5 tablespoons water ready in a cup by the saucepan. Wash the sides of the saucepan with a pastry brush dipped in water to remove any sugar crystals. Boil the sugar syrup until it reaches a deep caramel colour, then quickly and carefully tip in the water.
3 Warm the caramel over a low heat until any lumps are dissolved. Cool to lukewarm.
4 Place the lemon juice with 2 tablespoons water in a small saucepan and sprinkle over the gelatine.
5 Using an electric hand-whisk, whisk the eggs with the caster sugar in a heatproof bowl set over a bowl of simmering water until the mixture leaves a ribbon trail when the beaters are lifted. Remove from the heat and continue to whisk until the bowl feels cool and the mixture no longer feels warm.
6 Dissolve the soaked gelatine over a low heat until clear.
7 Fold the liquid gelatine into the caramel then fold in the egg mixture, and place in a cold bain-marie. Stir occasionally until beginning to set.
8 Whip the cream until it just holds its shape, then fold into the mousse.
9 Turn into a serving dish and refrigerate for about 4 hours until set.
10 To make the decoration, lightly oil a heatproof tray or baking sheet. Make a dry caramel with the caster sugar by melting it over low heat until dissolved, then boiling until it reaches a deep caramel. Pour immediately on to the tray or baking sheet. When cool, break into chips.
11 Decorate the mousse with rosettes of whipped cream and the caramel chips.

Caramel Mousse: What has gone wrong when...

The mousse separates into layers.

- The mixture was not stirred frequently enough before setting point was reached.
- The cream was added before setting point was reached.

NOTE: For further information on problems in making caramel mousse, see **Gelatine** (page 294).

Savoury Mousses

A savoury mousse is most often made from cooked, well-flavoured fish lightened with whipped cream. If the mixture is baked after being prepared with the raw ingredients it is called a mousseline (see **Mousselines**, page 487). Some pâtés, such as *Chicken Liver Pâté*, are similar preparations to a mousse, but are heavier in texture because the cream is not whisked before being added to the base.

Basic Fish Mousse

If you whisk to turn the mousse out, make it in one large mould or in individual timbale moulds. The mousse can also be set and served in individual ramekins. Serve with Melba Toast (see **Fish**, *Smoked Trout Pâté*, page 264).

SERVES 6

2 tablespoons white wine or water

3 teaspoons powdered gelatine

450 g | 1 lb cooked fish, such as salmon or tuna, or smoked haddock or trout

200 ml | 7 fl oz Mayonnaise (see **Sauces, Savoury**, page 599)

2 tablespoons chopped mixed fresh herbs, such as dill, parsley and/or chives

2 teaspoons grated horseradish (optional)

lemon juice to taste

salt and freshly ground black pepper

200 ml | 7 fl oz double cream

1 If you wish to turn the mousse out, lightly brush a large mould or individual moulds with a flavourless oil. Place upside down on a piece of kitchen paper to drain.
2 Place the wine or water in a small saucepan and sprinkle over the gelatine.
3 Place the fish in a large bowl and break it into small flakes with a wooden spoon.
4 Stir in the mayonnaise and season with the herbs, horseradish sauce, lemon juice, salt and pepper.
5 Dissolve the gelatine over a low heat until it is clear. Stir into the fish mixture.
6 Whisk the double cream until it just holds its shape. Fold into the fish mixture.
7 Pour into the mould or moulds and refrigerate for about 4 hours until set.
8 To turn out, dip the mould in a bowl of hot water until it softens slightly at the edges. Invert on to a serving plate, then give the dish a sharp downward shake.

Nuts

Nuts are dry edible kernels enclosed in a shell. Nutritionally dense with a high fat content, most nuts are delicious eaten as a snack. In addition, they are used extensively in cooking to add texture and flavour to both sweet and savoury dishes.

As a good source of protein, nuts play a particularly important part in the vegetarian diet and are also high in calcium, magnesium, potassium, folic acid, Vitamin E, and fibre. As most nuts are high in fat, however, the quantity consumed should be limited if calories are being counted. About half of the fat in nuts is of the monounsaturated variety, which is now thought by nutritionists to help to lower the level of LDL cholesterol (see **Healthy Eating and Basic Nutrition**, page 13) See table below for fat content of individual nuts.

Choosing Nuts

Nuts are usually purchased dried but occasionally they are sold fresh when they are known as green or wet nuts. Nuts in the shell should be heavy for their size and should not rattle if shaken. If shelled, the nuts should be firm, not soft, and have a uniform colour. Nuts are expensive, so buy in small quantities from a shop with a rapid turnover and use quickly. Because of their high fat content they become rancid relatively quickly. Rancid nuts smell and taste 'off' and will spoil the flavour of any food.

Storing Nuts

Wet nuts should be used within a few days of purchase or picking. Dried nuts have a low water content so they keep well. Nuts in their shells keep best of all but are laborious to use.

   All nuts should be stored in an airtight container in a cool place. If packaged, consume by the 'use by' date, otherwise use within 4 months. Nuts can be frozen for up to 6 months. To freeze, double wrap in plastic bags, excluding as much air as possible.

Toasting Nuts

A light toasting in the oven enhances the flavour of most nuts.
1 Preheat the oven to 180°C | 350°F | gas mark 4.
2 Place the nuts in a single layer in a roasting tin or on a baking sheet.
3 Bake for 8–10 minutes until lightly browned, stirring once or twice. Allow to cool.

Skinning or Blanching Nuts

The skins of nuts can be bitter so blanching is usually recommended.

To remove the skin from hazelnuts:
1 Roast at 180° | 350° | gas mark 4 for 8–10 minutes until the nuts are light brown.
2 Rub the nuts in a tea towel to remove the skins.

To remove the skin from almonds:
1 Immerse the nuts in boiling water to which 3 tablespoons bicarbonate of soda has been added.
2 Turn off the heat and allow the nuts to stand for 3 minutes. Drain.
3 Squeeze the nuts out of their skins.
4 Dry in a single layer for 30 minutes or toast as above.

Grinding Nuts

Nuts that have been freshly ground will always have a better flavour than purchased ground nuts. A food processor is excellent for this job. Allow toasted nuts to cool before grinding. Place the nuts in the bowl and process in short bursts until the nuts are of a fine, uniform texture rather like fresh breadcrumbs. Take care not to over-process the nuts or they will become oily. If over-processed nuts are used in cakes or pastry they will make them greasy and heavy. If processing for a recipe using sugar, add a couple of tablespoons of the sugar to the nuts while processing. It will absorb some of the oil and help keep the nuts free-flowing.

Nuts can also be ground with a small hand-held grater or can be chopped finely with a large cook's knife, using the cross-chopping technique as for chopping parsley (see **Knife Skills**, page 69).

Small grater for grinding nuts

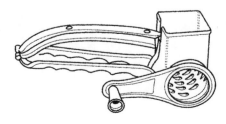

Nut Table

Type	Approximate fat content of raw nut	Use in cooking
Almond	50–54%	Baking, marzipan, praline, meringues
Brazil nut	65–70%	Baking
Cashew	46–47%	Chinese stir-fries, Indian dishes
Chestnut	2–3%	Baking, ground into flour, desserts, garnishing Brussels sprouts
Hazelnut	60–65%	Baking, meringues (see **Meringues**, page 477)
Macadamia nut	70–75%	Baking
Peanut (a)	48%	Peanut butter, satay sauce, garnishing Thai and Chinese food
Pecan	70%	Baking, can replace walnuts
Pine nut (b)	50%	*Pesto Sauce* (see **Sauces, Savoury**, page 610), salads
Pistachios	46–50%	Garnishing terrines (see **Forcemeat**, page 274) and flavouring ice cream
Walnuts	60–64%	Baking, sauces, pickling

(a) Although peanuts are actually legumes they are included here for comparative purposes

(b) Although pine nuts are seeds they are included here for comparative purposes

Almonds

Sweet almonds are the most widely used nut in cooking. The almond tree prefers a moderate climate; almonds are grown extensively in the Mediterranean, California, South Africa and Australia. The other type of almond, bitter almonds, are used to flavour the Italian biscuits Amaretti and to make Amaretto liqueur. Bitter almonds are toxic when eaten raw so their sale is prohibited in some countries.

Almonds are available in the shell, unblanched in their brown skins, blanched, flaked and ground. Almonds are the main ingredient in marzipan, which is used for modelling and to cover fruit cakes (see **Cake Icings and Decoration**, page 160) and to make the confection of caramelized nuts called *praline* (see **Caramel**, page 178).

Almonds are also used in *frangipane*, the filling for Tarte Normande (see below) and Gâteau Pithiviers, the French pâtisserie made from puff pastry filled with frangipane.

Normandy Apple Tart

This tart can be frozen after baking, wrapped in foil. Warm through in the oven before serving.

SERVES 8–10

225 g | 8 oz flour quantity Rich Shortcrust
  pastry (see **Pastry**, page 512)
4 large dessert apples

For the frangipane

200 g | 7 oz blanched almonds
200 g | 7 oz butter, softened
200 g | 7 oz caster sugar

2 eggs, beaten
2 egg yolks
1 tablespoon Calvados or Kirsch
4 tablespoons plain flour

To finish

250 gl | 9 oz warm apricot glaze (see **Pâtisserie**,
  page 533)

1. Use the pastry to line a 25 cm | 10 in tart tin. Bake the pastry case blind (see *Pastry*, page 509)
2. Grind the almonds to a fine, even texture (see *Grinding Nuts*, above), adding 2 tablespoons of the sugar if using a food processor. Set aside.
3. Beat the butter and the remaining sugar until light. Gradually add the whole eggs and yolks, beating well after each addition.
4. Beat in the Calvados or Kirsch.
5. Fold in the ground almonds and the flour.
6. Spread the frangipane into the pastry case.
7. Preheat the oven to 180°C | 350°F | gas mark 4.
8. Core the apples and slice them very thinly. Arrange the apple slices on the frangipane like the spokes on a wheel, pressing them down into the frangipane until they touch the base of the pastry.
9. Place the tart on a baking sheet and bake for 45 minutes, or until the frangipane is set. Use a knife to prise up the apple in the centre of the pastry to check.
10. Place the tart on a wire rack to cool. While still warm, brush with the apricot glaze. Serve warm or at room temperature.

Fanning a sliced apple

Pine Nut Tart

SERVES 6–8

For the pastry

170 g|6 oz flour

pinch of salt

110 g|4 oz butter

1 tablespoon caster sugar

1 egg yolk mixed

For the filling

2 tablespoons cherry or raspberry jam

100 g|3½ oz butter, softened

100 g|3½ oz caster sugar

½ teaspoon vanilla essence

100 g|½ oz ground almonds

2 tablespoons plain flour

55 g|2 oz pine nuts

½ tablespoon icing sugar

1 Sieve the flour with a pinch of salt into a bowl. Cut the butter into small pieces then chop into the flour with two knives. Rub in the butter until the mixture resembles fresh breadcrumbs. Stir in the sugar.

2 Mix the egg yolk with 1 tablespoon cold water then add enough of the mixture to the flour to bring it together into a dough.

3 Roll the pastry thinly and use to line a 22 cm|9 in shallow tart tin. Chill until firm.

4 Preheat the oven to 200°C|400°F|gas mark 6.

5 Line the pastry with paper and baking beans and *bake blind*. Allow to cool.

6 Turn the oven temperature down to 180°C|350°F|gas mark 4.

7 Spread the jam over the pastry base.

8 To make the filling: beat the butter and sugar together until light. Stir in the vanilla, almonds and flour. Spread into the pastry case.

9 Sprinkle with the pine nuts.

10 Bake for about 25 minutes or until golden brown and set.

11 Cool on a wire rack. Sieve over the icing sugar to serve.

Frangipane: What has gone wrong when...

The frangipane is liquid in the centre.

- The frangipane is undercooked.

The frangipane is greasy.

- The frangipane is overcooked.
- The almonds were over-processed.

Common Pasta Shapes

Pasta comes in a variety of shapes, each suited to a different sauce. Some of the more usual shapes are described below.

Agnolini: A half moon shaped stuffed egg pasta bent into a ring from Emiglia-Romano, often served in broth.

Cannelloni: Rectangular noodles about the size of a dinner plate, used to roll around a cooked filling such as ricotta and spinach.

Capellini: Otherwise known as 'Angel Hair', the thinnest of the spaghetti type, used with light sauces or oil.

Conchiglie: Ridged shells, useful for chunky sauces.

Farfalle: Shaped like butterflies or bow-ties. Used wih thick sauces.

Fettucine: Ribbon pasta, about 1 cm/ $\frac{1}{2}$ in wide, used for cream or oil-based sauces.

Fusilli: Corkscrew spirals, used for chunky sauces.

Lasagne: Wide, flat sheets of pasta used for layering with thick sauces to create dishes that are baked.

Linguine: Similar to spaghetti but with a slightly flattened strand, usually served with a seafood sauce.

Maccheroni or macaroni: Elbow-shaped tubes with a small diameter, often baked with cheese or meat sauces.

Orecchiette: Small pasta, shaped like little ears.

Pappardelle: Short, broad pieces of flat pasta, traditionally served with a chunky game sauce.

Penne: Tubular quill shaped pasta, used with thick, chunky sauces.

Ravioli: Filled pasta of various sizes, usually square or round.

Rigatoni: Tubular pasta wider in diameter than maccheroni and with a ridged outer surface, used with chunky sauces.

Spaghetti: Long round strands of pasta of varying diameter, originally made by pulling the dough but now made by machine.

Tagliatelli: Ribbon pasta similar to fettucine but slightly narrower.

Tortellini: Stuffed pasta, usually a round which is folded over a filling to make a half-moon shape. The points are pressed together and the rounded edge is then folded over like a collar.

Pasta

Pasta is a generic word meaning dough. The origins of pasta can be traced back to about 1000 BC in China. Today many countries have their own versions of pasta. Pasta provides complex carbohydrates, which are an excellent source of energy (see *Healthy Eating and Basic Nutrition*, page 13).

Pasta can be purchased in many different sizes and shapes (see list). Generally the pasta should be matched to the sauce it is served with: lighter sauces demand a finer, more delicate pasta, whilst heavy, chunky sauces are used for the sturdier types of pasta.

Making Pasta

Pasta is made from semolina flour, a high-protein, strong flour made from durum wheat (see *Flour*, page 269). This flour, called 'OO' flour in Italy, is very finely milled and will produce a smooth, silky pasta. Bread flour and plain flour can also be used to make pasta, but it will be inferior to pasta made from 'OO' semolina flour. Commercial pasta is usually made with unbleached flour and water. Pasta made with egg has a tendency to crack and crumble, so it is more often sold as fresh pasta.

No salt is added to the dough because it attracts moisture, resulting in white spots on the cooked pasta. The pasta is seasoned through the addition of salt to the cooking water.

The dough can be rolled with a rolling pin or with a pasta machine. The best type of rolling pin to use is a long thin rolling pin that tapers at both ends, called a *laganatura*. This type of rolling pin allows you to put a lot of pressure on the dough in order to stretch it as thinly as possible.

A pasta machine consists of two metal rollers that are turned by a hand crank or motor. The space between the metal rollers can be adjusted by moving a small lever from one notch to the next. If using a manual machine it is helpful to have another person to work with; one person can feed the dough into the machine and the other can catch it when it comes through the rollers.

Egg Pasta

FOR EACH SERVING
100 g | 3½ oz pasta flour   1 teaspoon olive oil
1 medium egg, beaten

1 Sift the flour on to a work surface and make a well in the centre.

2 Place the egg and oil in the well and slowly draw the flour into the egg, using the fingertips of one hand.

3 When the flour is combined with the egg, knead the dough on a work surface, adding a little more flour if necessary. If the dough is too stiff, add a little more beaten egg or egg yolk. Knead for about 5 minutes or until the the dough is smooth and silky.

4 Wrap the dough in clingfilm and allow to rest at room temperature for at least 30 minutes.

5 Roll the dough on a lightly floured work surface as thinly as possible or pass through a pasta machine (see instructions below).

6 Hang the pasta to dry over the handle of a clean rolling pin placed between the backs of 2 chairs or place on lightly floured greaseproof paper.

7 Cut to the shape required as soon as the pasta no longer feels tacky.

8 The pasta is ready to cook when the surface feels leathery. If not cooking immediately, dust the pasta with a little flour and store in a plastic bag. Do not coat the pasta with too much additional flour. The flour becomes slimy when the pasta is cooked.

Cutting Pasta by Hand

When the surface of the pasta no longer feels tacky, dust it lightly with flour and roll up loosely. Cut across the roll with a sharp knife. Unroll each piece of pasta and lay out to dry until it feels leathery.

Using a Pasta Machine

Work with a small amount of dough at a time, about a 55 g | 2 oz flour quantity. Keep any remaining dough tightly covered with clingfilm to prevent it from drying out.

1 Set the rollers to their widest setting. If the dough is sticky, flour it lightly.

2 Shape the pasta into a slightly tapered oval and feed through the rollers.

3 Fold the pasta in half across its width and feed through the rollers again. Repeat 3 or 4 times until the pasta is smooth, then reduce the width of the rollers by one notch.

4 Feed the pasta through the rollers again and reduce the setting. Repeat the rolling. After each rolling reduce the setting until the pasta has been rolled as thinly as required. If the pasta becomes too long to manage easily, cut it in half across its width.

5 Pass through the cutting roller, if desired. To dry, hang the pasta, as in *Egg Pasta*, step 6, above, or place on a lightly floured piece of greaseproof paper.

Making Pasta in a Food Processor

A food processor can be used to make pasta very quickly. Because the machine works the dough it will require little kneading.

1 Using the *Egg Pasta* recipe above, place all the ingredients in a food processor.

2 Process until the mixture resembles breadcrumbs. Squeeze a little of the paste with your fingertips. It should come together easily without being sticky or cracking. Add more flour or beaten egg or yolk to adjust the consistency.

3 Turn the dough on to a work surface and knead lightly to bring together. It should be smooth and silky.

4 Wrap in clingfilm and rest for at least 30 minutes.

5 Roll by hand, as in *Egg Pasta*, or by machine as detailed in *Using a Pasta Machine*.

Pasta: What has gone wrong when...

The pasta is difficult to roll and cracks when put through a pasta machine.

- The dough was made too dry.

  Place the dough in a food processor and whizz with a little additional egg.

The pasta sticks to the pasta machine/rolling pin.

- The dough was made too wet.

  Flour the dough well before passing through the machine or rolling out.

The cooked pasta is tough.

- The wrong type of flour was used.
- The dough was made too dry.
- The pasta is undercooked.
- The dough was not rested for long enough.

Storing Pasta

Egg pasta is best cooked within a few hours of making because it becomes very brittle when it dries. However, it can be stored for 24 hours in the refrigerator in a large plastic bag if it has been blanched in boiling water for 1 minute. Store with as much air as possible excluded. Blanched pasta can also be frozen for up to 1 month in a plastic bag. Cook from frozen.

Flavoured Pasta

Add any of the following along with the eggs when making fresh pasta. These additions are for a 4-egg quantity of pasta. A little additional flour might be needed if the dough is too sticky.

- **Black Pepper Pasta:** Add 2 teaspoons cracked black peppercorns.
- **Tomato Pasta:** Add 2 teaspoons tomato purée.
- **Saffron Pasta:** Add a large pinch of saffron strands infused in 1 tablespoon boiling water.
- **Spinach Pasta:** Use 225 g | 8 oz cooked spinach in place of 2 eggs.
- **Beetroot Pasta:** Add 1 small cooked puréed beetroot.
- **Herb Pasta:** Add finely chopped fresh herbs with the eggs for a speckled effect or place the leaves of soft herbs such as flat-leaf parsley between the sheets of dough in *Using a Pasta Machine*, Step 3, above.

Cooking Pasta

Pasta must be cooked in a large quantity of boiling salted water to prevent it from sticking together. Pasta has been made without salt so the water must be well salted: allow 1 tablespoon salt per 1 litre | 1¾ pints water. Stir the pasta during the first minute of cooking to prevent it from sticking together and keep the water at a rolling boil. Fresh pasta will take 1–4 minutes to cook, depending on its thickness and how fresh it is. Dried pasta will take 8–15 minutes to cook, depending on its shape.

There is much discussion as to whether to put oil in the water or not. Some say that the oil helps to prevent the pasta from sticking together, but as the oil floats on the surface of water it seems unlikely that it has much effect.

How to Tell When Pasta Is Done

The most reliable way is to bite into a piece of pasta. It should be cooked through so there is no white core, but should still have some 'bite'. This is called *al dente* in Italian and the term has been widely adopted.

It is best not to rinse pasta once it has cooked; instead, toss it with a little of the sauce with which it is to be served or a little olive oil. Tossing the pasta with a little oil once it has drained will mean that it will soak up less of the sauce.

To keep pasta warm for up to 20 minutes, drain it, then cover with lukewarm water. Drain again before serving.

If the pasta is to be served cold as part of a salad, rinse it with cool water, then toss with olive oil or the salad dressing.

Filled Pasta

Ravioli and tortellini are both filled pasta shapes. The filling is made either with cooked ingredients or with raw ingredients in the case of fillings made from fish. It is important that the filling is well seasoned, as the pasta covering is bland. The ingredients must be finely minced so that no air is trapped in the filling. Any air trapped inside the filled pasta will expand upon cooking and cause the pasta to burst open. Once shaped, the filled pasta must be allowed to dry until the surface feels leathery to keep the shapes from sticking together during cooking.

Ravioli

The word *rabiole* is an Italian word meaning 'thing of little value'. It is thought that these pouches of filled pasta got their name because the chefs on sailing ships filled their ravioli with scraps and leftovers. For instructions on filling ravioli, see *Shaping ravioli: Methods 1, 2 and 3*, below. Ravioli varies in size from very tiny to the size of a saucer.

Crab and Prawn Ravioli

Save the shells from the crab and prawns for the sauce.

SERVES 4

4-egg quantity *Egg Pasta* dough (see above)

For the filling

110 g | 4 oz shelled, cooked prawns
110 g | 4 oz cooked crabmeat
1 egg white
2 teaspoons finely chopped fresh chives
2 teaspoons lemon juice
salt and freshly ground black pepper

For the sauce

1 tablespoon oil
1 small onion, roughly chopped
½ bulb of Florence fennel, chopped
1 clove of garlic, crushed
45 ml | 3 tablespoons brandy
2 tomatoes, chopped
1 bay leaf
1–2 teaspoons tomato purée
1 litre | 1¾ pints White Shellfish or Fish Stock
  (see **Stocks**, page 690)
150 ml | ¼ pint double cream
chopped fresh chives, to garnish

1 Make the pasta, wrap in clingfilm and leave to relax for at least 30 minutes.
2 To make the filling, put the prawns and crabmeat into a food processor and whizz until smooth.
3 Add the egg white, chives, lemon juice, salt and pepper and process to combine. Check the seasoning, then chill until required.
4 To make the sauce, heat the oil in a sauté pan and fry the shells, onion and fennel until beginning to brown. Add the garlic and cook for a further 30 seconds.
5 Add the brandy, tomatoes, bay leaf, tomato purée and stock. Simmer for 20 minutes.

6 Fill the ravioli following one of the methods described below.

7 Pass the sauce through a sieve and return to the sauté pan.

8 Boil the sauce to reduce to 150 ml|¼ pint.

9 Add the cream and continue to boil until the sauce has the consistency of single cream. Season to taste.

10 Cook the ravioli for 3–4 minutes in simmering water until *al dente*.

11 Place the ravioli in a warmed serving dish, pour over some of the sauce and garnish with the chives.

Shaping ravioli: Method 1

1 Roll the dough to the thinnest setting on a pasta machine or as thinly as possible by hand.

2 Cut out 2 identically sized pieces of dough.

3 Dampen one piece of dough around the edge with a little water.

4 Place the filling in the centre, then place the second piece of dough on top, taking care to exclude any air from in between the pieces of dough.

5 Place the ravioli on a tray lined with greaseproof paper or a floured tea towel and leave to dry until the surface feels leathery.

Shaping ravioli: Method 2

1 Roll long strips of dough to the thinnest setting on a pasta machine or as thinly as possible by hand.

2 Working with 2 strips of dough at a time, place spoonfuls of filling on one piece of dough, leaving enough space between each spoonful to seal the parcels.

3 Dampen the dough around each spoonful of filling.

4 Place a second long strip of dough on top, and working from one end to the other, press the top piece of dough around the filling to exclude air and seal the dough.

5 Cut into individual ravioli, using a pasta wheel (see **Kitchen Equipment**, page 49) or a sharp knife.

6 Place the ravioli on a tray lined with greaseproof paper or a floured tea towel and leave to dry until the surface feels leathery.

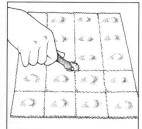
Cutting ravioli

Shaping ravioli: Method 3

1 Roll the dough to the thinnest setting on a pasta machine or as thinly as possible by hand.

2 Flour a ravioli mould and place a strip of dough over the top. Gently press the dough into the depressions.

3 Fill each depression with the filling.

4 Brush a little water on the dough between each mound of filling.

5 Place a second strip of dough on top of the mould, pressing down to seal.

6 Roll across the surface with a rolling pin to cut the pasta into individual ravioli. Use a sharp knife or pasta wheel if necessary.

7 Invert the mould on to a tray lined with greaseproof paper or a floured tea towel. Remove the mould and leave the ravioli to dry until the surface feels leathery.

Tortellini

The shape of tortellini is meant to resemble a young girl's navel.

Shaping tortellini

1 Roll the dough to the second thinnest setting on a pasta machine or by hand.
2 Cut out rounds of dough. A plain biscuit cutter is useful for this.
3 Dampen the edge of each round with a little water.
4 Place the filling in the centre and fold over the edges to make a semi-circle.
5 Wrap the semi-circle around your finger and overlap the points, pressing down gently to seal.
6 Roll the curved edge of the semi-circle back, rather like a collar.
7 Remove the tortellini from your finger and place on a tray lined with greaseproof paper or a flour tea towel. Leave to dry until the surface feels leathery.

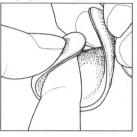

Cooking Filled Pasta

1 Bring a large saucepan or sauté pan of salted water to the boil.
2 Place the ravioli or tortellini in the water so that each piece has enough space to cook without being crowded.
3 Reduce the heat to a simmer. If filled pasta is boiled vigorously it is likely that the pieces will break open and the filling will spill out.
4 Simmer until *al dente* (see above) and the thickest part of the pasta is cooked through.
5 Remove from the pan, using a large slotted spoon.
6 Dress with sauce or oil and serve immediately.

Filled Pasta: What has gone wrong when...

The pasta breaks open when it is cooked.

- Air was trapped inside the filled pasta.
- The pasta was boiled too vigorously.

The pasta is hard around the edges yet the centre and filling are cooked.

- The pasta was not rolled thinly enough so where it is doubled it is too thick.

Types of Pastry

Shortcrust Pastry is a basic pastry of half fat to flour made by the rubbing-in method. It is used for savoury flans, such as quiche. This pastry contains a small proportion of lard or vegetable shortening for crispness.

Rich Shortcrust Pastry is similar to Shortcrust Pastry but is made entirely with butter and includes a little extra butter and an egg yolk for extra richness. It is used for sweet and savoury tarts.

Sweet Rich Shortcrust Pastry is the same as Rich Shortcrust Pastry with the addition of sugar. It is used for sweet tarts.

Suet Pastry is made using beef or vegetable suet as the fat and with self-raising flour. It is used to line pudding basins for steamed puddings such as *Steak and Kidney Pudding* (see page 676). It has a spongy texture.

Hot Water Crust is made with a high proportion of boiling water which gelatinizes the starch in the flour. It is used for containing moulded meat pies and has a chewy texture.

Pâte Sucrée is a French pastry enriched with egg yolks and sugar. It has a crisp, biscuit texture and is used for fruit tarts.

Pâte Frollée is a French pastry enriched with egg yolks, sugar and ground almonds. It is used to make a flat base for fresh fruit or for almond biscuits.

Pâte à Pâte is a French pastry made with a high proportion of butter and enriched with egg yolks. This rich and crumbly pastry is used for encasing savoury meat pâtés.

Flaky Pastry, Rough Puff Pastry and Puff Pastry are all layered pastries, used for pie toppings, cooking meat and fish 'en croute', feuilletée cases and other pastry cases.

Choux Pastry makes light, crisp, hollow buns that are filled to make *Profiteroles* and *Eclairs* (see page 525).

Strudel or Filo Pastry is stretched into thin sheets. Several layers are used to encase both sweet and savoury fillings.

Pastry

Pastry is a combination of flour, fat and in most cases liquid to make a dough which, when baked, is used to hold or cover other ingredients. With a few exceptions, the fat content of pastry is at least half the weight of the flour, making pastry relatively high in fat. Few pastries are leavened, with the exception of yeasted layered pastries such as croissants and Danish pastries (see *Pâtisserie*, page 534).

For many centuries in the Western world, the principal function of pastry was as a container in which meats, pâtés or fruit were baked. Usually the pastry was discarded after baking, having served its purpose of protecting the meat or fruit from the fierce heat of the oven and keeping the contents moist. In the fifteenth century, pastry-making techniques were refined and pastry was promoted, in France particularly, both as an art and a comestible in its own right. Today the maker of pastry, the pâtissier, has a separate section in the restaurant kitchen and a pâtisserie shop in the high street.

The different types of pastry and the methods for making them are described in detail below. Although the proportions of fat to flour as well as the methods of preparation vary quite considerably, certain basic principles need to be followed for successful pastry-making (see below).

How Much Pastry to Make

To determine the amount of pastry required to line a flan ring the general rule is to subtract 2 from the diameter of the flan ring as measured in inches. This will give you the amount of flour to use in ounces. Thus a 15 cm|6 in flan ring will require a 110 g|4 oz flour quantity of pastry, a 20 cm|8 in flan ring will require a 170 g|6 oz flour quantity of pastry and so on.

If baked pastry is refrigerated it will lose its crisp texture. However, once the pastry case has been filled, the filling will determine the method and length of storage.

Preparing a Pastry Case

Specific procedures are common to the types of pastry used for lining tart tins, as follows:

Rolling Out Pastry

To roll out pastry, sprinkle a work surface lightly with flour and rub the rolling pin with flour. Gently tap the surface of the pastry to ridge it, then roll using gentle strokes away from you. Give the pastry a quarter turn to ensure that it is not sticking to the surface and to keep the pastry round. If necessary, use a palette knife to release the pastry from the work surface. Repeat the procedure until the pastry is the desired thickness. Generally, the smaller the pastry case, the thinner the pastry should be. A thickness of 3 mm | $\frac{1}{8}$ in, about the thickness of a £1 coin, is recommended for a 15–20 cm | 6–8 in flan ring.

To make rolling out easier, place the pastry between 2 sheets of clingfilm or baking parchment. Roll as described above to the desired thickness.

Lining a Flan Ring with Pastry

Metal flan rings or tins produce crisper pastry than ceramic flan dishes. To line a flan ring or tart tin, place the ring or tin on a baking sheet, then drape the rolled pastry over a rolling pin. (a) Gently lower the pastry into the flan ring, placing the side that was against the work surface uppermost. (b) Allow the pastry to drape over the sides of the flan ring. With the side of your finger, ease the pastry into the edges of the flan ring, then gently press the pastry against the side of the ring, taking care to avoid creasing or stretching the pastry. (c)

Use the rolling pin to remove the excess pastry by rolling from the centre of the ring to the edge. The sharp edge of the ring will cut through the pastry. (d)

Run the side of your thumb along the top edge of the pastry and the ring to straighten the sides of the pastry case and ease the edge from the ring. (e) If the pastry overlaps the edge of the ring it will be impossible to remove the ring after the pastry is baked without breaking the pastry case.

Refrigerate the pastry case until it is firm. This will take up to 30 minutes if the pastry is very soft and the kitchen is warm.

Very soft pastry can be rolled between clingfilm. After rolling, chill the pastry. When firm enough to handle remove the film from one side of the pastry and use the other side to help guide the pastry into place.

Baking Blind

If a recipe calls for baking the pastry blind, this means that the pastry needs to be baked completely before the filling is added. Preheat the oven to the required temperature and place the oven shelf in the top third of the oven. Make a *cartouche* by cutting a round of greaseproof paper a little larger than the diameter of the pastry case. Crumple the paper to help it mould to the shape of the pastry, then line the pastry with the cartouche. Fill the pastry with enough baking beans to support the sides of the pastry in the oven until the sides are firm. Baking beans are either small ceramic beans or dried haricot beans used exclusively for the purpose of baking pastry cases blind. The base of the pastry case only needs a thin layer of beans, about 1 cm|½ in, to keep it from puffing up.

Place the pastry on the baking sheet in the top third of the preheated oven and bake for about 15 minutes or until the sides of the pastry have cooked through. The pastry will lose its grey tinge and become opaque and sand-coloured when cooked.

Using a large spoon, remove the beans from the pastry case and transfer them to a bowl to cool. Remove the greaseproof paper and return the pastry to the oven, placing it on the middle shelf. Continue to bake the pastry for about 5–10 minutes until the base is a pale golden-brown and feels sandy to the touch. The pastry will have lost its grey appearance.

Lining a flan ring with pastry (a)

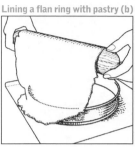
Lining a flan ring with pastry (b)

Easing the pastry up the sides to avoid creases (c)

Rolling off extra pastry (d)

Easing pastry from edge (e)

If the pastry base forms a hump, it means that some air was trapped underneath the pastry when the flan ring was lined. Gently press the hump with the back of a spoon to flatten the pastry against the baking sheet.

Storing Pastry

Uncooked pastry can be stored in the refrigerator for 24 hours if tightly wrapped or may be frozen for up to 1 month if closely wrapped in a double layer of clingfilm. Freeze uncooked pastry in preference to baked pastry. However, baked pastry can be stored in an airtight container for up to 3 days or frozen for 1 month. To freeze, wrap tightly in clingfilm, then overwrap. Pastry will absorb other flavours from the freezer.

Shortcrust Pastry (Rubbing-in Method)

The basic pastry in the European kitchen is shortcrust pastry (Pâte Brisée) which is made by the rubbing-in method. The texture of good shortcrust can be described as both tender and crumbly, or 'short'.

Blackberry and Apple Crumble

Making a crumble is a good way to learn the rubbing-in method. It doesn't matter if the mixture is slightly overworked because it still remains short and crumbly because it doesn't need water. Other fruit can be used instead of the apples. Plums make a very good crumble, as do pears. The crumble topping can be prepared in advance and frozen for up to 3 months.

SERVES 4

For the crumble

170 g | 6 oz plain flour
a pinch of salt
110 g | 4 oz butter, cut into 1 cm | ½ in cubes
55 g | 2 oz caster sugar

For the fruit

900 g | 2 lb Bramley apples

110 g | 4 oz blackberries
110 g | 4 oz caster sugar
½ teaspoon ground cinnamon
1 teaspoon cornflour

For the topping

1 tablespoon Demerara sugar

1 Preheat the oven to 190°C | 375°F | gas mark 5.
2 Sift the flour with the salt into a large bowl. Use two knives scissor-fashion to cut the butter into pea-sized pieces.
3 Rub the mixture between your fingertips and thumb until the mixture resembles breadcrumbs. Stir in the sugar then place in the refrigerator until the fruit is ready.

4 Peel and core the apples and cut into chunks. Place in a bowl with the blackberries.

5 Combine the sugar, cinnamon, and cornflour. Toss with the fruit. Place the fruit into an ovenproof dish large enough to leave a 2.5 cm|1 in space from the top.

6 Tip the crumble mixture over the fruit. Do not pack it down. Sprinkle with the Demerara sugar.

7 Place on a baking sheet in the oven and bake for 40–45 minutes or until the crumble is golden brown and the fruit is soft when tested with a skewer.

VARIATION

Apple and Orange Crumble: Substitute 1 orange, segmented, for the blackberries. Omit the cinnamon.

Basic Shortcrust

This is a basic pastry recipe using half the amount of fat to flour. It is usually used for savoury fillings because of the lard content (see **Eggs,** *Quiche,* page 228). The lard makes the pastry crisper and flakier than a pastry made entirely with butter. For vegetarians a similar pastry can be made by substituting solid vegetable fat for the lard.

FOR A 20 CM|8 IN FLAN RING

170 g|6 oz plain flour
a pinch of salt
55 g|2 oz cold butter

30 g|1 oz lard
about 3 tablespoons ice-cold water

1 Sift the flour with the salt into a large bowl. Cut the fat into 1 cm|½ in pieces and toss into the flour. Cut the fat into the flour until it is the size of small peas, using 2-table knives scissor-fashion.

2 Rub the fat into the flour by dipping your fingertips into the flour and gently rubbing the small pieces of fat in the flour between the tips of your thumbs and fingers to flatten them and incorporate them with the flour. Pull the flour up above of the bowl as you do this to aerate it and keep the mixture cool as it falls back into the bowl. Continue this procedure until the mixture resembles fresh breadcrumbs.

3 Shake the bowl occasionally to bring the pieces of fat to the surface of the flour. If at any point during the rubbing-in process the mixture starts to feel greasy or becomes yellow in colour, the fat has become too warm and the pastry will be greasy if it is not chilled. Place the bowl in the refrigerator to chill.

4 When the mixture resembles fresh breadcrumbs, sprinkle half the water over the surface of the flour/fat mixture, then stir quickly with a table knife. The pastry will start to form lumps. If any dry flour remains in the bowl, sprinkle a little more water over the dry part only and stir again with the flat blade of the table

Chopping in fat with 2 knives (a)

Rubbing the fat into the flour (b)

knife. It is important to add just enough liquid to bring the pastry together; too much liquid will result in a hard pastry which will shrink when baked.

5 Using a wiping motion, bring the mixture together with your fingertips and squeeze gently to form an even-textured dough. If it is very soft, flatten it into a disc 1 cm|½ in thick, then wrap it closely with clingfilm and refrigerate for at least 10 minutes. The dough should have the texture of plasticine for easy rolling. Line a flan ring as described above and chill until firm.

6 Preheat the oven to 200°C|400°F|gas mark 6.

7 Bake the pastry case blind (see above). Use as required.

Using a food processor to combine fat and flour

The fat can also be rubbed into the flour using a food processor, in a fraction of the time. It also means that the fat is kept cool, a real bonus if you have hot hands. Use the steel blade and the pulse button to chop the fat into the flour. The mixture should then be turned into a bowl and rubbed in by hand for about 30 seconds, to coat the flour grains with the fat. This helps to prevent gluten development when the liquid is added.

The liquid should also be added by hand as this makes it much easier to control the quantity and less likely that the paste will become too wet and overworked.

Rich Shortcrust

This pastry is richer and more tender than the Shortcrust Pastry above. It has a slightly higher fat content. It can be used with either sweet or savoury fillings (see **Nuts,** *Normandy Apple Tart,* page 496)

FOR A 20 CM|8 IN FLAN RING

170 g|6 oz plain flour	1 egg yolk
100 g|3½ oz butter	2 tablespoons ice-cold water

Make the pastry by the same method described above. The egg yolk must be mixed with the water to avoid making the pastry streaky. A tablespoon of the combined mixture is added in place of the water. Additional liquid is added if required.

Sweet Rich Shortcrust

For a sweet pastry suitable for desserts, add 2 tablespoons caster sugar to the flour in the above recipe after the butter has been rubbed in. Bake as directed for the Shortcrust Pastry recipe but be aware that the sugar in the pastry will make it brown more quickly. The edges of the pastry case can be protected with strips of kitchen foil, if necessary.

Shortcrust Pastry: What has gone wrong when...

The pastry has shrunk during baking.
- The pastry wasn't chilled until firm before baking.
- There was too much water in the pastry.
- The oven temperature wasn't hot enough.
- The pastry was stretched when the flan ring was lined.

The pastry has a grey appearance.
- The pastry has not been cooked for long enough.
- The uncooked pastry has been kept for too long in the refrigerator.

The pastry has a greasy appearance.
- The pastry has been overcooked.
- The pastry was overworked and the fat became oily.

The pastry is hard and tough.
- Too much water was added to the pastry.
- The pastry has been overworked and the gluten has been developed.

Savoury Pastries

Suet Pastry

Suet pastry is most often used for steamed savoury puddings (see **Steaming**, *Steak and Kidney Pudding*, page 676).

Self-raising flour is used to make a lighter pastry, so it needs to be placed in the prepared pudding basin and used as soon as it is mixed to benefit from the raising agent.

Beef suet is the fat surrounding the kidneys of the animal. If fresh suet is used, it should be chilled then grated. If packaged suet is used, allow it to soften slightly at room temperature before using.

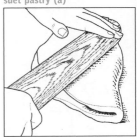
Lining a pudding basin with suet pastry (a)

butter, for greasing
340 g | 12 oz self-raising flour
salt

170 g | 6 oz shredded beef suet
ice-cold water, to mix
extra flour, for rolling

1 Grease a pudding basin with butter.
2 Sift the flour with 2 pinches of salt into a large bowl. Stir in the suet, then rub in with your fingertips to combine slightly with the flour.
3 Sprinkle with enough cold water to bring together into a dough.
4 On a floured work surface, roll two-thirds of the pastry into a round.
5 Flour the uppermost surface of the pastry, then fold in half to make a semi-circle. Roll the rounded side of the pastry to make a bag shape. **(a)** Brush away any excess flour.
6 Place the pastry in the pudding basin **(b)** and fill with meat.
7 Roll the remaining pastry into a round for the lid. Brush the inner lip of the pastry with water to seal the lid in place.
8 Trim with a knife. Steam as directed in **Steaming** (page 675).

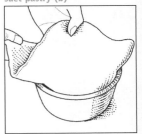
Lining a pudding basin with suet pastry (b)

Suet Pastry: What has gone wrong when...

The pastry is tough and hard.

- Too much water was used.
- The pastry was overworked.
- The pastry was not placed in the pudding basin and steamed quickly enough.

The surface of the pastry is speckled or has small holes.

- The suet was not rubbed in thoroughly enough.
- The water was not evenly distributed in the flour.

Making a raised pie (a)

Hot Water Crust

This pastry is used to encase raised pies (see **Terrines, Pâtés and Raised Pies**, *Veal and Ham Raised Pie*, page 714).

40 g | 1¼ oz butter
40 g | 1¼ oz lard
85 ml | 3 fl oz water

225 g | 8 oz plain flour
½ teaspoon salt
1 egg, beaten

Removing the clingfilm (b)

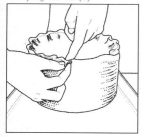

crimping the lid (c)

1 Wrap a soufflé dish approximately 15 cm | 6 in in diameter with clingfilm and then a double band of baking parchment secured with a paper clip.
2 Cut the butter and lard into small pieces and place with the water in a small saucepan. Bring to the boil.
3 Meanwhile, sift the flour with the salt into a large bowl and make a well in the centre. Place the egg in the well and cover over with the flour.
4 Pour the boiling water and fat around the edge of the bowl and quickly stir in with a table knife.
5 Knead lightly until the pastry loses its streakiness and becomes smooth. Wrap in clingfilm and chill for 20–30 minutes.
6 Reserve one-third of the pastry for the lid. Keep wrapped in clingfilm.
7 Roll the remaining pastry into a circle 5 cm | 2 in larger than the base of the dish.
8 Invert the dish, place the pastry over the base and gently press the pastry down over the sides of the dish to a thickness of 6 mm | ¼ in. **(a)** Take care that the corners of the pastry do not become too thin.
9 Refrigerate the pastry, uncovered, until firm and dry to the touch.
10 Carefully remove the pastry from the dish. Place the pastry on a baking sheet and wrap the baking parchment around the outside of the pastry to support it. Secure with a paper clip. Remove the clingfilm from inside the pastry. **(b)**
11 Fill the pastry with the meat.
12 Dampen the inside of the top edge of the pastry, then roll out the remaining pastry 6 mm | ¼ in thick. Place the pastry lid on top of the meat, bringing the lid pastry up the edge of the outer pastry. Trim to a depth of 1 cm | ½ in. Save the trimmings for decoration. Crimp the edge of the lid. **(c)**
13 Glaze with beaten egg and decorate the top of the pie with the pastry trimmings. Glaze again and refrigerate.

Hot Water Crust: What has gone wrong when...

The pastry is stretchy.

- Too much liquid was added to the flour.

The pastry is stiff, hard to mould and cracks when cooked.

- Not enough liquid was added to the flour.

The pastry is tough.

- Too much liquid was added to the flour.
- The paste was overworked.

French Flan Pastries

Pâte Sucrée, Pâte Frollée, Pâte Sablée, and Pâte à Pâte are all types of French pastry that are used for tarts and biscuits. These are rich pastries that bake to a thin, crisp biscuit texture. They are nearly always baked blind (see *Baking Blind*, above) before being filled. Pâte Sucrée, Pâte Frollée and Pâte Sablée are sweet and are usually filled with fruit and/or cream or pastry cream (see ***Pâtisserie***, *Crème Pâtissière*, page 532) or rich custard-type fillings which require only a very short baking time.

The method for making these French flan pastries is described below in the recipe for Pâte Sucrée.

French Flan Pastries: Points to Remember

- Use good-quality unsalted butter that has been allowed to come to room temperature. Do not allow the butter to become oily.
- If your hands are warm, touch the pastry as little as possible. Use a food processor if available.
- Roll the pastry very thinly, about 2 mm$\left|\frac{1}{12}\right.$ in thickness for a large tart case, thinner for individual serving-sized tins and canapé tins. (See ***Kitchen Equipment***, *Barquette Tins*, page 55.)
- Watch the pastry carefully during baking because it will colour quickly due to the high proportion of butter and sugar.
- For the best flavour, do not allow the pastry to take on any more than the palest colour during baking.
- After removing the baking beans from the pastry case, cover the sides of the pastry with strips of foil if they are beginning to brown.
- Remove the pastry from the tin while it is still warm. It becomes crisp as it cools and will break if removed from the tin when cool.

Pecking the eggs, butter and sugar (a)

Ensuring there are no lumps of butter (b)

Scooping the flour over the butter mixture (c)

Chopping the flour into the butter mixture (d)

Fraiser the paste (e)

Pâte Sucrée

Pâte Sucrée is used for lining tart cases, large or small, that are baked blind then filled with pastry cream and fruit. It is also used for Tarte au Citron or Tarte au Chocolat. It is not suitable for fillings that require a long baking time. It can be cut with a biscuit cutter to make small biscuits to accompany a dessert mousse, fruit salad or ice cream.

170 g | 6 oz plain flour

a pinch of salt

85 g | 3 oz unsalted butter, softened

3 egg yolks

85 g | 3 oz caster sugar

2 drops of vanilla essence

1. Sift the flour with the salt on to a work surface. Scrape the flour away from the centre to make a circle of flour about 25 cm | 10 in in diameter.
2. Place the butter in the centre of the well, then place the yolks on top of the butter and the sugar and the vanilla on top of the yolks. **(a)**
3. Using a pecking motion with the fingertips of one hand, combine the butter, yolks and sugar until the mixture is completely smooth. **(b)**
4. Using a palette knife, scoop the flour on to the butter mixture. **(c)**
5. Hold the palette knife with each hand at either end and use the side of the knife to chop the flour into the butter. Continue chopping until there are no floury patches remaining and the mixture begins to stick together in larger lumps. **(d)**
6. Gather the pastry into a long narrow rectangle. Use the side of the palette knife again to smear the pastry on to the work surface to bring it together into a smooth dough. This smearing is called to *fraiser* the pastry. **(e)**
7. Wrap the pastry in clingfilm, pressing it into a flat disc.
8. Refrigerate until pliable but not sticky then roll out and press into the tart tin. Refrigerate until firm.
9. Meanwhile, preheat the oven to 190°C | 375°F | gas mark 5.
10. Line the pastry case with crumpled tissue paper and sufficient beans or uncooked rice to support the sides. Bake the pastry case blind as directed above, protecting the edges of the pastry with strips of foil if they show signs of browning.
11. Allow the pastry to cool for about 5 minutes before removing it from the tin.

Pâte Frollée (Almond Pastry)

Pâte Frollée is a French flan pastry made with the addition of ground almonds. The almonds make it slightly less crisp than Pâte Sucrée. It is most suited for making a flat pastry disc to be covered with glazed soft fruit or for making biscuits.

110 g | 4 oz plain flour
a pinch of salt
45 g | 1½ oz ground almonds
85 g | 3 oz unsalted butter, softened

45 g | 1½ oz caster sugar
1 egg yolk
2 drops of vanilla or almond essence

The method is the same as for Pâte Sucrée, above, up to step 7 except that the almonds are scattered over the top of the flour at the end of step 1.

Proceed as follows:

1 Refrigerate the pastry, then roll it into a 22–25 cm | 9–10 in round, about 1 cm | ½ in thick. Place the round on a baking sheet and crimp the edge. Place one forefinger on the surface of the pastry at the edge, without pressing down. Squeeze the pastry on either side of the forefinger, using the thumb and forefinger of your other hand, to make a point. Repeat this action all the way round the edge of the pastry.

2 Prick the centre of the pastry through to the baking sheet and within 2.5 cm | 1 in of the edge. Refrigerate until firm.

3 Preheat the oven to 190°C | 375°F | gas mark 5. Bake the pastry until it is pale golden-brown in the centre and slightly darker around the edges.

4 Run a palette knife under the pastry immediately after it is removed from the oven otherwise it will stick to the baking sheet. After 5 minutes transfer it to a wire rack to finish cooling.

Crimping the edge of pâte frollée

Pâte Sablée

Pâte Sablée is a crisp, delicate pastry, much like very thin shortbread. It is particularly good made into biscuits, then layered with soft fruit and cream to make an elegant dessert.

140 g | 5 oz plain flour
a pinch of salt
110 g | 4 oz unsalted butter, softened

1 egg yolk
55 g | 2 oz icing sugar
2 drops of vanilla essence

The method is the same as for Pâte Sucrée, above.

To assemble into Sable au Fraises, make Pâte Sablée biscuits 5 cm | 2 in in diameter. Layer with sliced strawberries macerated with a small amount of *Raspberry Coulis* (see **Sauces, Sweet**, page 00). Decorate with additional coulis, cream and a sprig of fresh mint.

Pâte à Pâte

This is a savoury pastry made by the French method. It is used for tarts with savoury fillings and for raised pies (see **Bacon, Ham and Gammon,** *Flat Ham Pie*, page 412).

225 g|8 oz plain flour
½ teaspoon salt
165 g|5½ oz unsalted butter, softened

2 small egg yolks
2–3 tablespoons cold water

Make as for Pâte Sucrée, above, sprinkling the water over the flour after it has been scooped over the butter (step 4) but before you *fraiser* the pastry (step 5). Use as required. Do not be tempted to leave out the water because otherwise the pastry will be too crumbly when baked.

French Flan Pastries: What has gone wrong when...

The pastry is hard and tough.
- The pastry has been overworked at the *fraiser* stage.
- The pastry is overbaked.

The pastry is greasy.
- It has been overworked during the pecking stage and the butter has become too warm.

Layered Pastries: Basic Method

Flaky Pastry, Rough Puff Pastry and Puff Pastry are all known as layered pastries or laminated pastries. This type of pastry, where layers are formed during making through a process known as rolling and folding, became popular in France during the time of Catherine de Medici. Marzipan pastries made with Flaky Pastry were reputedly a favourite of Louis IV.

The Détrempe

The base of each of these pastries is a mixture of flour, a little fat and water, called a 'détrempe'. The détrempe is made with plain flour (see **Flour**, page 268) and is manipulated very lightly to avoid gluten development which would make the pastry tough.

The greater part of the fat is incorporated into the détrempe during the rolling and folding process. It is important that the fat is pliable, but not greasy, so that it can be rolled out thinly when the pastry is rolled.

Although the recipes for each type of pastry differ slightly and the method of incorporating of the fat varies, several common factors and techniques are used to make layered pastries.

Rolling and Folding to Produce Layers

The technique of rolling and folding is used in these pastries to produce the crisp layers. When these pastries are baked, the water in the pastry turns to steam and the air trapped between the layers expands, causing them to separate and rise up. Puff Pastry, which is given a total of 6 rolls and folds, will have a total of 730 layers.

Ridging a layered pastry (a)

Rolling a layered pastry (b)

The Technique of Rolling and Folding

1 Gently tap the pastry with the rolling pin to produce slight ridges. (a)
2 Lightly roll the pastry away from you. (b)
3 Run the palette knife under the pastry and tap the sides to keep them straight and the corners square.
4 Alternate the ridging and rolling until the pastry is 3 times as long as it is wide, about 12 × 35 cm|5 × 15 in.
5 Fold the bottom third of the pastry up and the bottom third down to make a parcel, rather like a business letter. This is 1 roll and fold. (c)
6 Press the edges of the pastry gently with the rolling pin to seal the air inside the layers.

Folding a layered pastry (c)

Using Layered Pastry

These points should be followed whether the pastry is home-made or bought.

- Once all the rolls and folds have been completed, the pastry can be rolled from side to side and front to back in the same directions in which it was rolled to make the layers. If a large, round shape is needed, roll the pastry into a square and cut out the round.
- Allow the pastry to sit for 5 minutes after rolling to relax before cutting into shapes.
- When cutting layered pastry, cut straight down through the pastry with a sharp knife. Do not drag the knife along the edge of the pastry as this would seal the layers together.
- Before baking a layered pastry, knock up the sides by cutting lightly into the edge of the pastry in the direction of the layers.
- When glazing layered pastry, do not let the glaze run down the edges of the pastry, as this would seal the layers together.
- Never gather the pastry into a ball, you will ruin all your carefully made layers. Any left over pieces can be piled up and brought together with a further roll and fold.

Flaky Pastry

Flaky pastry is used primarily for encasing a filling, as for Eccles Cakes, or to make a crisp pastry shell, as for Cream Horns. The fat is added to the détrempe in small pieces, producing a tender, flaky pastry. The pastry should rise to double its original thickness.

225 g|8 oz plain flour
a pinch of salt
85 g|3 oz butter, cut into 1 cm|½ in pieces

6–8 tablespoons|90–120 ml cold water
85 g|3 oz lard, cut into 1 cm|½ in pieces

1 Sift the flour with the salt into a large bowl. Toss in half the butter.
2 Using 2 table knives scissor fashion, cut half the butter into the flour until the pieces are the size of a small pea. Use your fingertips to rub the butter into the flour until the mixture resembles breadcrumbs.
3 Sprinkle 6 tablespoons water over the flour and quickly stir with a knife until it starts to clump together. If necessary, sprinkle a little additional water over any dry flour remaining in the bowl.
4 Use your fingers to bring the pastry together into an even-textured dough.
5 This is the détrempe (see above). It should have a soft, pliable texture without being sticky. If it is too firm it will be difficult to roll out and the pastry will not rise well. Shape the pastry into a rectangle 2 cm|¾ in thick, then wrap closely with clingfilm or greaseproof paper and refrigerate for at least 10 minutes to allow the gluten in the flour to relax.
6 Flour a work surface lightly, then roll the pastry into a long rectangle about 12 × 35 cm|5 × 15 in. Dot half the lard over the top two-thirds of the pastry.
7 Fold the bottom third of the pastry up over the middle third, then fold again to make a parcel, rather like folding a business letter. Give the pastry a quarter

turn so the closed edge is to your left, rather like a book. Gently seal the open edges of the pastry parcel with the rolling pin.

8   Give the pastry a roll and fold as detailed above in *The Technique of Rolling and Folding*. This roll and fold is called a blind roll and fold because no fat has been added to the pastry in this roll and fold. Wrap the pastry again and refrigerate it for at least 10 minutes to allow the gluten to relax and the lard to firm slightly.

9   Ridge and roll the pastry again until it is 3 times as long as it is wide. Dot the remaining butter pieces over the top two-thirds of the pastry. The butter should be pliable so that you can gently smear the lumps on to the pastry.

10 Fold the bottom third of the pastry up over the middle third, then again over the top third. Press the edges to seal.

11 Rotate the pastry a quarter turn and ridge and roll the pastry until it is 3 times as long as it is wide. Dot the remaining lard over the top two-thirds of the pastry and fold as before.

12 Give the pastry another roll and fold without adding any fat. If the pastry is streaky with butter, make another roll and fold, but more than one additional roll and fold is not recommended because the layers of dough would then become too thin to keep the layers of fat separate.

To use the pastry for Eccles Cakes or Cream Horns, roll it to a thickness of about 3 mm | ⅛ in. For a pie top, roll the pastry 6 mm | ¼ in thick. The pastry must be refrigerated until firm before baking. It can be glazed with beaten egg or with frothed egg white and sprinkled with a little sugar (see *Using Layered Pastry*, above).

Rough Puff Pastry

Rough puff pastry is a quick method for producing a layered pastry. It is often used for topping a savoury pie (see **Meat,** *Beef, Steak and Mushroom Pie*, page 369). It is important that the butter is is cool yet pliable enough to be flattened when pressed. This pastry should rise to double in thickness when baked. The rise is likely to be somewhat uneven.

225 g | 8 oz plain flour
a pinch of salt

140 g | 5 oz pliable butter, cut into 1 cm | ½ in cubes
6–8 tablespoons | 90–120 ml ice-cold water

1   Sift the flour with the salt into a large bowl. Using a table knife, toss the butter cubes with the flour.
2   Sprinkle 6 tablespoons water over the flour and stir quickly with a table knife so that the pastry clumps together.
3   Gather the lumps together with your fingertips, leaving any dry mixture in the bottom of the bowl.
4   If necessary, sprinkle additional water over any remaining dry flour to make a soft but not sticky dough.
5   Bring all the pastry together and knead it lightly once or twice to bring it together into a smooth, even-textured dough.

6 Form the pastry into a rectangle 2 cm | ¾ in thick and wrap it in clingfilm, or greaseproof paper. Refrigerate for at least 10 minutes to allow any gluten formed to relax and for the pastry to achieve an even texture. The butter must not be allowed to become hard or it will tear the pastry when it is rolled out.

7 Give the pastry a total of 4 rolls and folds following the instructions under *The Technique of Rolling and Folding* above. If the pastry still looks streaky after 4 rolls and folds it can be given one more before being used. Allow the pastry to relax for at least 10 minutes before using.

Puff Pastry (Pâte Feuilletée)

Of all the layered pastries, puff pastry is the most exacting and difficult to make. The amount of fat added can vary between 140 g | 5 oz and 200 g | 7 oz to a 225 g | 8 oz quantity of flour. The greater the quantity of butter used, the trickier it is to make this pastry.

Due to the large proportion of butter in puff pastry, unsalted butter is traditionally used because it is thought to be fresher than salted butter and has a milder flavour. However, if you are confident of its freshness, either salted or unsalted butter can be used. Choose butter with a flavour that you like. If using salted butter, decrease the amount of salt added with the flour to 1 pinch.

225 g | 8 oz plain flour
3 pinches of salt
30 g | 1 oz lard

6–8 tablespoons | 90–120 ml iced water
140–200 g | 5–7 oz unsalted butter, at room temperature.

1 Sift the flour and salt into a large bowl. Cut the lard into small pieces and toss into the flour. Rub in the lard with your fingertips or process in a food processor (see *Shortcrust Pastry*, above).

2 In one addition, sprinkle 6 tablespoons of the water over the flour. Quickly stir the water into the flour, using the blade of a table knife.

3 As the pastry forms into clumps, pull them to one side, leaving any dry flour in the bottom of the bowl.

4 Sprinkle a little additional water over the dry flour to bring it together if necessary.

5 Using your fingers, pull the clumps of moistened flour together and fold the paste over, doubling 4–5 times to make a smooth dough. The détrempe should be soft but not sticky.

6 Shape the détrempe into a rectangle about 10 × 15 cm | 4 × 6 in. Wrap the détrempe in greaseproof paper on clingfilm and leave in a cool place for about 30 minutes to allow the gluten to relax and the moisture to become evenly distributed.

7 The butter needs to be the same texture as the détrempe so that it can be easily incorporated into the pastry. The butter should bend without breaking. If it is too firm, place it between 2 sheets of greaseproof paper and bash it with a rolling pin to soften it. The butter should not be oily, however. If it looks oily it has become too soft and needs to be refrigerated.

8 To incorporate the butter, roll the détrempe into a rectangle about 15 × 30 cm | 6 × 12 in. Use a table knife to shape the butter so that is a little less than half the size of the détrempe.

9 Place the butter on one half of the détrempe, leaving a margin of about 1 cm | ½ in round the edge of the détrempe. Fold these edges over the butter, then fold the other half of the détrempe over the top of the butter to encase the butter completely. **(a) (b)**

10 At this point, do not turn the pastry. Give the pastry 2 rolls and folds as directed under *The Technique of Rolling and Folding*, above. If at any time the butter breaks through the pastry because it has become too soft, wrap the pastry and refrigerate it immediately until the butter is firmer but still pliable. If the pastry is chilled for too long the butter will become hard and will break when the pastry is rolled and folded again. If at any time you can feel hard lumps of butter in the pastry, leave it at room temperature until the butter softens so that it is pliable.

11 Give the pastry a total of 6 rolls and folds. If streaks of butter still show in the pastry, give it a 7th roll and fold, but no more than 7 or the layers of flour will become too thin to keep the layers of butter separate.

13 To use the pastry, see *Using Layered Pastry*, above. Roll to the thickness specified in the recipe and trim the pastry about 1 cm | ½ in from the edges to avoid an uneven rise at the edges. Shape the pastry as required, chilling well before baking in the top third of the oven, preheated to 200°C | 400°F | gas mark 6.

Encasing the butter (a)

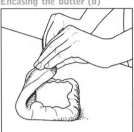
Encasing the butter (b)

Feuilletée Case (a)

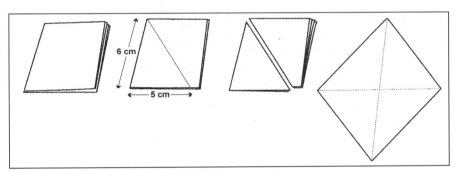

Feuilletée Cases

These boxes of puff pastry are classically served filled with poached seafood (see **Shellfish**, *Seafood Feuilletées*, page 637) and a Beurre Blanc sauce (see **Sauces, Savoury**, page 605).

MAKES 4

225 g | 8 oz flour quantity Puff Pastry (see above)

To glaze
1 egg beaten with a pinch of salt, then sieved

Cutting around template (b)

1 Cut a template from paper. **(a)**

2 Roll the pastry just big enough to cut 4 cases from the pastry after trimming the edges. When cutting puff pastry, do not drag the knife, cut straight down, using a very sharp knife, to prevent the layers from sealing together. **(b)**

3 Glaze the top of the pastry cases, taking care not to let the glaze drip down the sides, which could seal the layers together.

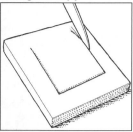

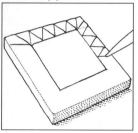

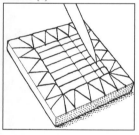

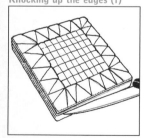

4   Cut a lid in the box, using a small sharp knife and cutting halfway through the thickness of the pastry. (c)

5   Mark the edges of each box in a diamond pattern, using the back of the knife. Mark the lid of the box into a grid pattern. (d) and (e)

6   Knock up the edges of the cases with a knife to help separate the layers. (f)

7   Refrigerate the pastry cases until very hard before baking, to set the shape of the cases.

8   Preheat the oven to 200°C | 400°F | gas mark 6.

9   Glaze the tops of the pastry cases again before baking.

10 Bake in the top third of the oven for 25–30 minutes. Do not open the oven door until 20 minutes have elapsed as any draughts could cause the cases to collapse.

11 Before removing the cases from the oven, gently squeeze the sides to ensure that they are firm. If they still feel flexible, allow the pastry to cook for a further 5 minutes. If the cases are removed from the oven before the sides are set if is likely that they will fall.

12 When the cases are well risen and golden-brown, with firm sides, remove them from the oven and use a sharp knife to cut out the lids.

13 Scrape the uncooked pastry from inside the cases, taking particular care to remove it from the corners. The pointed end of a teaspoon or the tines of a table fork are useful for this purpose.

14 Return the cases and the lids to the oven to dry out and crisp. The lids will need to be removed from the oven after a minute or two as they tend to dry out more quickly. The cases should take about 5 minutes to dry out. If fat starts bubbling from the pastry, it is starting to overcook.

Layered Pastries: What has gone wrong when...

The pastry has not risen very much and the texture is crumbly rather than flaky.
- The butter broke through when rolling and folding so the layers have been lost.
- The lard was rubbed in too much at the beginning.
- The pastry has been rolled and folded too many times and the layers have been lost.

The layers are visible in the pastry but it has not risen very much.
- The pastry was removed from the oven before the sides had baked enough to hold its shape.
- The oven door was opened during the first 15 minutes of baking.

Fat has seeped out of the pastry.
- The pastry has been overbaked.
- The pastry was not chilled for long enough prior to baking.

The pastry is tough.
- Too much water was added when making the détrempe.
- The détrempe was overworked.
- The pastry was not allowed to rest long enough between rolls and folds.

Choux Pastry

Choux is the light, crisp, hollow pastry used for *Profiteroles* and *Eclairs*. It may be so called because the individual buns look like little cabbages (*choux* in French), but it is possible that the term choux is a corruption of the word *chaud* (French for hot) – the pastry was originally called Pâte à Chaud.

Choux pastry can be used for either savoury or sweet dishes. It is the pastry used for Gougère, a French dish consisting of a ring of choux pastry filled with soft fruit and whipped cream, served as a dessert, or with a sauced meat or vegetable preparation in a savoury version (see **Poultry,** *Chicken Gougère*, page 439). Tiny choux buns with a little cheese added to the pastry make an easy canapé base.

Choux is one of the easiest types of pastry to make because it involves little handling and is not greatly affected by the temperature in the kitchen. Careful measuring of ingredients and control of oven temperatures and timings will ensure successful results.

The method for making choux pastry is quite unlike that for any other pastry. The water and butter are brought to the boil and then the flour is stirred in to make the base of the pastry, called the *panade*. It is this mixture of flour and water that forms sheets of gluten (see **Flour**, page 118). Eggs are then beaten into the *panade*, a little at a time, to make a soft, silky paste which should be of a reluctant dropping consistency. This means that a small amount placed on the end of a wooden spoon will fall off if the spoon is sharply jerked, and still hold a mounded shape. It is the eggs that cause the paste to puff up to 3 times the original size before the flour bakes to a thin, crisp shell (see **Eggs**, page 224).

Choux pastry is baked in a hot oven so that the incorporated water quickly turns to steam, which also leavens the paste. The egg bound to the gluten framework traps the steam to form a pastry-coated bubble. It is important that the oven door is not opened prematurely and that the pastry is not removed from the oven before it is completely firm or there is a danger that the pastry will collapse.

Choux Pastry

85 g | 3 oz butter, cut into small cubes
220 ml | 7½ fl oz water
105 g | 3¾ oz plain flour

a pinch of salt
3 eggs, beaten

1 Place the butter and water in a saucepan over a low heat and allow the butter to melt.
2 Meanwhile, sift the flour 3 times on to greaseproof paper to aerate it and ensure it is free of lumps.
3 When the butter has melted, turn the heat to high and bring the mixture to the boil.
4 As soon as the water comes to a fast boil, so that the liquid climbs the sides of the pan, turn off the heat and quickly tip the flour all at once into the liquid.

5 Using a wooden spoon, stir the flour into the liquid to form a firm, smooth paste. Beat the paste until it comes away from the edges of the pan, forming a ball. Do not beat it any longer than it takes to come away from the sides of the pan or the baked choux will have a cracked, crazy-paving appearance.

6 Tip the paste on to a cold plate and smooth it into a thin layer. Leave it to cool for about 10 minutes, until it feels just warm to the touch.

7 Return the paste to the pan and beat in the eggs, a tablespoon at a time, beating well after each addition.

8 Continue adding the egg until the mixture is of a reluctant dropping consistency, holds its shape and has a slight sheen.

9 The pastry can now be used immediately or it can be refrigerated for 24 hours if tightly covered, or frozen for up to 1 month.

10 To bake choux buns or eclairs, preheat the oven to 200°C|400°F|gas mark 6. For buns, pipe or spoon walnut-sized lumps on to lightly greased baking sheets. Bake in the top third of the oven for 20–30 minutes.

11 When the buns are golden-brown and firm, remove them from the oven. Make a small hole in the underside of each bun, using the tip of a small knife or the end of a teaspoon. Lay the buns on the baking sheets so that the holes are uppermost and return then to the oven for a further 5 minutes to allow the interiors to dry (out) and become crisp. Remove from the oven and place on a wire rack to cool completely before filling.

Piping an éclair

Piping an éclair

Using a piping bag fitted with a plain 1 cm|½ in nozzle, pipe a line of choux pastry to the desired length of the éclair. Without stopping, pipe back over the line twice more, to create a flattened 'S' shape. Push down any pastry that is sticking out with a dampened finger.

Chocolate Profiteroles

MAKES ABOUT 18

Profiteroles and éclairs can be filled with whipped double cream sweetened with icing sugar or with *Crème Patissière* (see **Pâtisserie**, page 532). If desired, the filling can be flavoured with vanilla, coffee or chocolate.

290 ml|½ pint double cream	110 g|4 oz plain chocolate, chopped
1–2 tablespoons icing sugar	15 g|½ oz butter
1 recipe Choux Pastry (see above)	2 tablespoons water

1 Whip the cream in a bowl until it just holds its shape. Sift the icing sugar over the cream and fold in.

2 Using a piping bag fitted with a plain 6 mm|¼ in nozzle, pipe the cream into the choux buns, using the hole made during baking (see *Choux Pastry*, Step 11, above). Fill the buns until the cream begins to squeeze out of the hole.

3 Place the chocolate, butter and water in a small heatproof bowl over, but not touching, simmering water. Melt the chocolate, stirring occasionally.

4 Hold a choux bun by its base and dip the top in the melted chocolate, rotating the bun to coat as much as possible without coating your fingers. Repeat until all the buns are coated, then place them on a serving plate.

5 Serve as soon as possible. Do not refrigerate unless absolutely necessary as the chocolate coating will lose its sheen and the pastry will become soggy.

Choux Pastry: What has gone wrong when...

The choux pastry is badly risen.
- The oven door was opened before the pastry had set, or the pastry was removed from the oven too soon.
- Not enough egg was beaten into the pastry.
- The *panade* was too warm when the egg was added.

The surface of the choux pastry is crazed with many small cracks.
- The *panade* was beaten for too long after the flour was added.

Filo Pastry

This type of pastry, made sheet by sheet and containing little fat, can be traced back to the Romans. Although excellent filo pastry can be purchased, it is fascinating to make. Whether making your own filo or using the bought pastry, work quickly and keep the pastry covered and/or brushed with oil or melted butter because it quickly dries out and cracks. Filo pastry is used to make Apple Strudel.

Apple Strudel

SERVES 4

140 g | 5 oz plain flour
a pinch of salt
½ medium egg
75 ml | 5 tablespoons water
½ teaspoon oil

For the filling
450 g | 1 lb cooking or dessert apples
caster sugar to taste

1 teaspoon ground cinnamon
grated zest of ½ lemon
4 tablespoons dried white breadcrumbs
55 g | 2 oz raisins

To finish
2 tablespoons melted butter
2 tablespoons icing sugar

1 Sift the flour with the salt into a large bowl. Make a well in the centre.

2 Mix together the egg, water and oil. Stir enough of the liquid into the flour to make a soft dough.

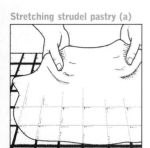
Stretching strudel pastry (a)

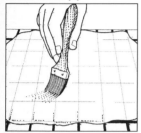
Brushing strudel pastry with melted butter (b)

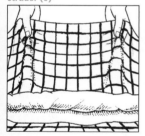
Using the cloth to roll the strudel (c)

3 Knead by throwing the dough on to a work surface from shoulder height for 15 minutes until it loses its stickiness and is so elastic that it can be stretched from one hand to the other to a length of about 50 cm|20 in.

4 Wrap the pastry in clingfilm and leave at room temperature for at least 30 minutes or up to 4 hours to allow the gluten to relax.

5 Make the filling before stretching the dough: peel and core the apples. Cut into 2 × 1 cm|1 × ½ in chunks. Toss with caster sugar to taste, cinnamon and lemon zest. Stir in 2 tablespoons breadcrumbs and the raisins.

6 When ready to use the pastry, cover a work surface measuring about 1.5 × 1 m|60 × 39 in with kitchen paper or tea towels liberally dusted with flour.

7 The stretching is best done by 2 people working together. Before stretching the dough, remove any watches or rings. Pull the pastry gently, using the back of your hand and the tips of your fingers to stretch it. **(a)** When it becomes transparent in the centre, place it on the floured work surface and continue to stretch it until it is thin enough to read newsprint through. Take care not to tear the pastry, but if it does, it can be patched with a little extra pastry. Work quickly so the pastry doesn't become too dry.

8 Brush the pastry all over with the melted butter. **(b)** Trim the thick edges with kitchen scissors to make a neat rectangle. Sprinkle with breadcrumbs.

9 Preheat the oven to 200°C|400°F|gas mark 6. Place the filling along the edge of the pastry in a rectangle about 30 × 10 cm|12 × 4 in.

10 Roll up using the kitchen paper or tea towel to help. **(c)** Place on a baking sheet and curve into a horseshoe shape.

11 Bake for 30–40 minutes, until the apple is tender when pierced with a skewer. Dust with the icing sugar to serve.

Filo Pastry: What has gone wrong when...

The pastry will not stretch to a transparent sheet.

- The dough was too dry.
- The dough was not worked for long enough.
- The dough was not rested for long enough.

The pastry pulls into shreds.

- The dough has been stretched a little then left to stand. The gluten strands have broken down and the pastry cannot be pulled out thinly.

The pastry tears when stretched.

- A certain amount of tearing is likely. It will not usually show when the pastry is used. Take greater care when stretching the pastry.

The pastry cracks when it is rolled up.

- The pastry has become too dry. Keep it brushed with oil or butter or covered with clingfilm.

Types of Pâtisserie

The following list describes many of the items often found in a pâtisserie and where to find the recipes in this book:

- Eclairs, Profiteroles: See **Pastry,** *Choux* (page 525)
- Glazed fruit tarts: See **Pastry,** *Pâte Sucrée* (page 516)
- Custard Tarts: See **Pastry** (page 515) and **Eggs,** *Baked Custard* (page 226)
- Cream Slices (Millefeuille): See **Pastry,** *Puff Pastry* (page 522)
- Meringues, Dacquoise (nut meringue): See **Meringues** (page 474)
- Filled speciality cakes: See **Cakes,** *Génoise* (page 147) and **Cake Icings and Decoration** (page 155)
- Brioche, Chelsea Buns: See **Bread, Yeast**, *Breads, Enriched* (page 132)
- Croissants, Danish Pastries: See below (page 534)
- Bread of all descriptions: See **Bread,** *Yeast* (page 116)
- Muffins and loaf breads: See **Baking**, *Quick Breads* (page 105)

Petits Fours

In addition to miniature versions of pâtisserie, the following are suitable for serving as after-dinner Petits Fours.

- Truffles: See **Chocolate** (page 196)
- Tiny tartlets: See **Pastry,** *Pâte Sucrée* (page 516) and **Eggs,** *Lemon Curd* (page 230)
- Fudge: See **Sugar** (page 699)
- Brandy Snaps: See **Sugar** (page 698)
- Tuiles: See **Biscuits** (page 101)
- Brownies: See **Biscuits** (page 100)

Pâtisserie

Pâtisserie is a French word that is used for the art of pastry and cake-making and also the shop in which the pâtisserie can be purchased, often along with a cup of *café au lait, chocolat chaud* or tea. The chef who produces the pâtisserie is called the pâtissier and in France is represented by the Guild of Pastry Cooks, where pâtisserie is considered a specialist art.

The famous French chef La Varenne wrote the first book of pastry-making in 1655. Before this, cakes and pastries were baked almost as an afterthought in the large ovens used for baking bread. Small ovens, called *petits fours*, began to be used to bake the pastries. Today the miniature forms of pâtisserie are still called Petits Fours, after the ovens. These bite-sized pastries are served at the end of a formal meal (see box opposite).

The craft of pâtisserie ranges from the making of a simple éclair to fancifully decorated, complex assemblages of meringue and spun sugar. See opposite for different types of pâtisserie and where to find them in this book.

Crème Pâtissière (Pastry Cream)

Crème Pâtissière is a custard (see **Sauces, Sweet**, page 611) thickened with flour or cornflour to a smooth, heavy consistency. Crème Pâtissière is spread thickly on the base of blind-baked tart shells before decorating the tart with glazed fresh fruit, or spread thinly between wafer-thin layers of puff pastry for millefeuille. Crème Pâtissière is also piped into choux buns and meringues or spread on to enriched sweet doughs, such as Danish Pastries, before they are baked.

The following recipe makes a very thick Crème Pâtissière. It is best lightened with a equal quantity of lightly whipped cream and/or flavoured with liqueur, chocolate, coffee or the zest of citrus fruits. Crème Pâtissière can also be lightened with whisked egg whites to make Crème St Honoré, a filling for the choux pastry dessert Gâteau St-Honoré.

The starch in the mixture allows it to boil without curdling, but it is necessary to stir it continuously to prevent lumps from forming. It is important to boil the mixture or an enzyme in the egg yolks (see **Eggs**, page 226) could make the mixture runny.

Crème Pâtissière

290 ml | ½ pint milk
2 egg yolks
55 g | 2 oz caster sugar
150 ml | ¼ pint double cream, lightly whipped

20 g | ¾ oz plain flour
20 g | ¾ oz cornflour
vanilla essence

1 Scald the milk by bringing it to just below boiling point in a saucepan.
2 Cream the egg yolks with the sugar. Add a little of the hot milk to the yolks to warm them gradually, then mix in the flours. Pour on the remaining milk and mix well.
3 Rinse out the pan to remove the coagulated milk proteins, pour the mixture into the pan and bring slowly to the boil, stirring continuously.
4 Boil for 1 minute to thicken while stirring. Pass through a sieve into a cold bowl.
5 Stir in the vanilla to taste.
6 Place a piece of dampened greaseproof paper directly on the surface to prevent a skin from forming and allow to cool.
7 The Crème Pâtissière will become very stiff when cold. To use, place it in a food processor and whizz for about 30 seconds, or pass through a sieve, then fold in lightly whipped cream.

VARIATIONS

Crème Pâtissière can be flavoured with melted chocolate, liqueurs, dissolved coffee powder, ground macaroons or almonds. The flavouring ingredient is added once the custard has thickened.

Storing Crème Pâtissière: Refrigerate, covered with greaseproof paper then clingfilm, for up to 2 days. Freezing is not recommended.

Crème Pâtissière: What has gone wrong when...

The Crème Patissiere is lumpy.
- The mixture was not stirred sufficiently when it started to thicken.
  To correct, pass through a sieve or whizz in a food processor.

The mixture becomes thinner upon standing.
- The mixture was not brought back up to the boil to denature the enzyme found in egg yolk which breaks down the thickening properties of starch.
  Discard the mixture.

The Crème Pâtissière is too thin.
- The Crème Patissiere was not brought to the boil.
  To correct, return to the saucepan and bring to the boil while stirring.

Glazing Tarts and Other Pâtisserie with Jam

Warmed jam is used to glaze fruit tarts and certain other types of pâtisserie. The jam glaze adds sweetness and flavour to the tart and helps keep the fruit from drying out.

Apricot jam glaze is used to glaze yellow, orange, and green fruit. Either apricot jam or redcurrant jelly is used to glaze red fruit. It does not make sense to use good-quality jam that is full of fruit for glazing because the fruit is sieved from the jam before it is used.

Apricot Glaze

SUFFICIENT FOR A 25 CM|10 IN FRUIT TART

250 g|9 oz apricot jam   1 strip of lemon peel
2 tablespoons water   lemon juice, to taste

1 Place the jam in a heavy-based saucepan together with the water and the lemon peel.
2 Warm over a low heat to melt.
3 Pass through a fine sieve into a clean saucepan. Discard any fruit left in the sieve.
4 Add lemon juice to reduce the over-sweet jam flavour.
5 For a fruit tart, the jam glaze should have a thick coating consistency but be runny enough to flow off a pastry brush. As the glaze cools it will thicken. Rewarm the glaze over a low heat or in a microwave. It must not be too hot or it will cook the fruit.
6 The fruit must be dry or the glaze will run off.
7 Starting in the centre of the tart and working towards the edges, dab the fruit with a pastry brush loaded with the glaze. Be sure to cover the fruit completely but do not glaze the fruit twice or the glaze is liable to form lumps. Do not glaze the pastry.
8 Unused glaze can be kept indefinitely in the refrigerator as long as it does not contain crumbs.

Redcurrant Glaze

SUFFICIENT FOR A 25 CM|10 IN RED FRUIT TART

250 g|9 oz redcurrant jelly
lemon juice, to taste

1 Melt the jam over a low heat.
2 Add lemon juice to reduce the over-sweet jam flavour.
3 Do not boil or the colour will become murky.
4 Pass through a fine sieve and use as required.

Glazing: What has gone wrong when...

The glaze runs off the fruit.
- The fruit is wet.
- Too much water has been added.

The glaze is lumpy.
- The glaze is too cool.
- The glaze has not been sieved.
- The glazed areas have been reglazed.

Yeasted Layered Pastries

Croissants and Danish Pastries are known as yeasted layered pastries. They are made using a combination of bread-making and pastry-making techniques and are considered to be among the most difficult types of pâtisserie to make well. They are terrifically rewarding to make but are very time-consuming and require great skill and care. The home-made product is invariably much richer and fresher-tasting than most store-bought equivalents.

Before attempting either Croissants or Danish Pastries the cook should have made puff pastry and bread successfully. The **Pastry** and **Bread**, **Yeast** sections should be read as a reminder of the principles of yeast cookery and the making of layered pastries.

Yeasted Layered Pastries: Points to Remember

- Work in a cool kitchen to prevent the yeast from working too rapidly and to keep the butter from oozing out of the pastry.
- The butter needs to be soft in order to form a layer between the dough. It should be the same texture as the dough.
- If the butter starts to ooze out between the layers of dough or breaks out from the dough, chill the pastry immediately.
- Allow the shaped pastries to prove in a cool environment. Normal room temperature of about 20°C|70°F is ideal. If the pastries are proved in too hot an environment, the butter will seep out of the pastries, making them greasy.
- Chill the pastries after proving and before baking to set the shape and chill the butter so it is less likely to run out during baking.

Danish Pastries

The technique of interleaving a yeasted dough with butter and folding it to create layers is thought to have originated in Turkey. The technique spread throughout the Austro-Hungarian empire before being brought to Denmark by an Austrian chef in the 1800s, which is why these pastries are called wienerbrot or Vienna Bread in Denmark. The pastries can be eaten for breakfast or for a snack at any time of day with a cup of tea or coffee.

Plain flour is used in this recipe to give the pastries a cake-like, tender texture. Strong flour can be used for a more open, chewy texture.

It is best to spread the making of the pastries over 2 days. It takes about 6 hours to complete the process.

Danish Pastries are can be filled with an almond paste filling or a cinnamon filling. Dried fruits, such as apricots or prunes, are sometimes placed inside the pastries. The pastries can be decorated with toasted flaked almonds. The glacé icing should not be made up until the pastries are baked.

Danish Pastries

MAKES 6 LARGE OR 12 SMALL PASTRIES

15 g | $\frac{1}{2}$ oz fresh yeast
1 tablespoon caster sugar
110 ml | 4 fl oz warm milk
225 g | 8 oz flour (use half strong and half plain)
a pinch of salt
1 egg, beaten
110 g | 4 oz unsalted butter, softened
1 egg, beaten, to glaze

For the almond paste filling

45 g | $1\frac{1}{2}$ oz butter, softened
45 g | $1\frac{1}{2}$ oz icing sugar
30 g | 1 oz ground almonds
2 drops of vanilla essence

For the glacé icing

110 g | 4 oz icing sugar
boiling water, to mix
55 g | 2 oz toasted flaked almonds to garnish

1 Cream the yeast with 1 teaspoon of the sugar and 2 tablespoons of the milk.

2 Sift the flour and the remaining sugar with the salt into a large bowl and make a well in the centre. Pour the yeast mixture, the remaining milk and the egg into the well and stir to make a soft dough.

3 Turn the dough on to a work surface and knead once or twice to make a smooth dough. Roll into a rectangle about 1 cm | $\frac{1}{2}$ in thick, 12 cm × 36 cm | 5 × 15 in. Cover with clingfilm and refrigerate for at least 30 minutes to rest.

4 Lightly sprinkle the work surface with flour, then place the chilled dough on the work surface. Divide the butter into hazelnut-sized pieces and dot it over the top two-thirds of the dough, smearing it into the dough slightly but leaving gaps between the pieces of butter.

5 Fold the dough into 3, bringing the bottom third up, then folding the middle third to encase the butter. Press the edges together lightly.

6 Give the dough a quarter turn so that the folded edge of the dough is on your left, like the binding on a book.

7 Repeat steps 5 and 6, then wrap the pastry in an oiled plastic bag and refrigerate for 10 minutes.

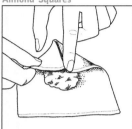

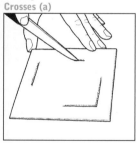

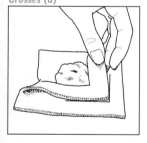

8 Repeat steps 5 and 6 twice more so that the pastry has had a total of 4 rolls and folds. The pastry should not look streaky. If it does, give it another roll and fold. Refrigerate for 15 minutes.

9 Roll the pastry into a 20 × 60 cm | 8 × 24 in rectangle. Place on a lightly floured baking sheet, cover with clingfilm and refrigerate until firm or overnight.

10 To make the almond paste, beat the butter with the icing sugar, then stir in the almonds and the vanilla. Refrigerate.

11 The following day, cut the well-chilled pastry to the desired size and shape, as shown in the diagrams below.

12 Shape the pastries as illustrated. Cover the pastries with oiled clingfilm.

13 Allow the pastries to rise up until they are very soft and pillowy, then refrigerate them for 20 minutes before baking.

14 While the pastries are chilling, preheat the oven to 200°C | 400°F | gas mark 6.

15 Glaze the pastries with beaten egg and bake for 20 minutes or until golden-brown. Cool on a wire rack.

16 To make the Glacé Icing, sift the icing sugar into a bowl. Add boiling water a little at a time to achieve the consistency of single cream. Make a piping bag out of greaseproof paper (see *Chocolate*, page 194) and use it to drizzle the icing over the pastries in a zig-zag motion. Sprinkle with toasted flaked almonds if desired.

Almond Squares
1 Put a spoonful of filling into the centre of each square.
2 Bring each corner to the middle of the filling and press down lightly to seal.

Crosses
1 Cut through 2 opposing corners at right angles, about 1 cm | ½ in from the edge. (a)
2 Bring the outside edge of the 2 strips to match the edge of the central square. (b)
3 Place a little filling in the hollow in the centre of the cross. (c)

Pinwheels
1 Place a spoonful of filling in the centre of each square.
2 Cut a diagonal from each corner to meet the filling in the centre. (a)
3 Bring the right point of each triangle to meet in the centre of the filling. (b)
4 Press the point down lightly to seal.

Comb
1 Place a line of filling down the centre of each pastry square.
2 Fold the edges over like a book.
3 Cut several slits from the open edge towards the filling. Curve the pastry backwards to open out the cuts.

Cinnamon Wheels

MAKES 8

55 g | 2 oz butter, softened
55 g | 2 oz caster sugar
2 teaspoons ground cinnamon

2 tablespoons chopped mixed peel and mixed
dried fruit

1 Cream the butter with the sugar, then stir in the cinnamon.
2 Roll the Danish Pastry dough into a 25 cm × 20 cm | 12 × 8 in rectangle.
3 Spread the cinnamon paste over the pastry, then sprinkle with the fruit.
4 Roll up the pastry from the short end, then pinch the edges to seal.
5 Cut the roll into 8 rounds. Place them on a baking sheet, then press them lightly with a floured hand to flatten them to 10 cm | 4 in rounds.
6 Allow to prove, then refrigerate for 20 minutes.
7 Bake as for Danish Pastries above.

Danish Pastries: What has gone wrong when...

The pastries are flat and greasy.

- The dough was rolled too thinly.
- The butter broke through the layers during rolling and folding.
- The pastries were overproved and collapsed.
- The pastries were overbaked.
- The pastries were underproved.

The pastries are tough.

- The dough was overworked when it was mixed together.
- Too much flour was used during rolling and folding.

Croissants

The French word *croissant*, meaning crescent, describes the shape of these yeast-raised layered pastries. Although the making of pastries in crescent shapes can be traced back to Turkey, it is thought that the croissant as we know it was developed in France in the twentieth century.

The quality and flavour of croissants vary dramatically depending on the amount of butter layered into the dough. With the recent popularity of filled croissants, bakers have started using less butter or substituting margarine for butter. Two types of croissant are now available in the shops, *croissant au beurre*, which must be made with butter, and croissants containing vegetable fat. The version with less butter tends to have a more bread-like texture that makes it ideal for dunking into coffee or hot chocolate.

To make croissants the cook must be familiar with the techniques of bread-making and the making of layered pastries. Read the notes above under *Yeasted*

Pinwheels (a)

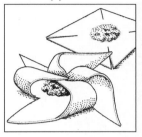
Pinwheels (b)

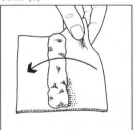
Making Danish Pastries: Comb (a)

Making Danish Pastries: Comb (b)

Layered Pastries: Points to Remember. The texture of the détrempe should be slightly softer than the détrempe for puff pastry. The butter must be very malleable and of the same texture as the détrempe.

It is recommended that the making of croissants be spread over a period of 2–3 days.

Croissants

The détrempe should be made 12–24 hours in advance to allow the flavours to develop.

MAKES 10 CROISSANTS AND 4 *PAINS AU CHOCOLAT*

15 g|½ oz fresh yeast
300 ml|½ pint cold milk
500 g|1 lb 2 oz strong white flour
1 teaspoon salt
45 g|1½ oz caster sugar
285 g|10 oz unsalted butter

For the glaze

1 egg yolk, beaten with 1 tablespoon milk

For the pains au chocolat

30 g|1 oz plain chocolate

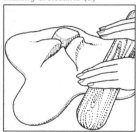

Making croissants (a)

Folding over the détrempe (b)

Cutting croissants using a template (c)

1 Whisk the yeast into the milk.
2 Sift the flour and salt into a large bowl and stir in the sugar. Mix to a smooth, soft dough with the water mixture but do not knead.
3 Cover the dough with lightly oiled clingfilm and leave in a warm place until doubled in size, about 1 hour.
4 Knock back the dough by patting it firmly. Do not work the dough. Place it in a lightly oiled plastic bag and refrigerate for 4 hours or overnight.
5 Shape the dough into a ball and cut a cross into the top halfway through the centre of the dough. Pull each quarter lobe away from the dough ball and roll into a thin flap. **(a)**
6 Place the butter in the centre, then fold over the flaps to encase the butter. **(b)**
7 Lightly flour a work surface, then ridge the dough to form a 40 × 75 cm|16 × 30 in rectangle. Brush off the excess flour and fold the dough into 3 like a business letter.
8 Give the dough a quarter turn so that the folded edge of the dough is on your left. Repeat step 7.
9 Wrap the dough in clingfilm and refrigerate for 20 minutes.
10 Repeat steps 7 and 8 until the dough has had 4 rolls and folds and is no longer streaky.
11 Roll the dough out into a rectangle 25 cm|10 in wide and ½ cm|¼ in thick. Place on a baking sheet covered with greaseproof paper, then cover the dough with lightly oiled clingfilm. Refrigerate until firm or overnight.
12 Using a large knife, trim the edges of the dough. Using a triangular template 15 × 17.5 cm|6 × 7 in, cut the dough into triangles. Save the trimmings for the *Pains au chocolat.* **(c)**

13 Place the triangles one at a time on the work surface with the longer point towards you. Stretch out the 2 shorter points, **(d)** then roll the triangle up loosely. **(e)** The tip should fold over the top of the croissant and touch the baking sheet but it should not be underneath the croissant.

14 Place the shaped croissants on a baking sheet curving them into a crescent shape **(f)** and leaving enough space for them to double in size without touching. The points should be facing towards the middle of the baking sheet to help prevent them from burning. **(g)**

15 Cover them croissants with lightly oiled clingfilm and prove at normal room temperature, 20°C|70°F, until they are very puffy. Refrigerate for 20 minutes to set the shape.

16 Meanwhite, preheat the oven to 250°C|450°F|gas mark 8.

17 Glaze the croissants with the egg yolk and milk and bake in the hottest part of the oven for 10 minutes, then turn the oven down to 190°C|375°F|gas mark 5 and bake for a further 20 minutes or until the croissants are a deep brown. If they are becoming too brown, cover with greaseproof paper. Cool on a wire rack.

Pains au chocolat

1 Layer the trimmings on top of one another, and give the pile a roll and fold.

2 Roll pastry out to ½ cm|¼ in thick. Cut into 4 rectangles.

3 Divide the chocolate between the rectangles and fold the pastry in three over the chocolate, like a letter.

4 Place on the baking sheet seam side down.

5 Proceed as for Croissants, Step 15.

Croissants: What has gone wrong when...

The croissants are badly risen.
- The dough was rolled too thinly.
- The butter broke through the layers when rolling and folding.
- The croissants were not proved for long enough.
- The croissants were overproved and collapsed in the oven.

The croissants are greasy.
- The butter was too soft when added to the détrempe.
- The croissants were not chilled for long enough before baking.
- The croissants were proved at too high a temperature.
- The croissants were overbaked.

The middle of the croissants is doughy.
- The croissants were underbaked.
- The croissants were underproved.

Stretching the corners (d)

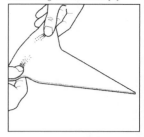

Rolling the croissant (e)

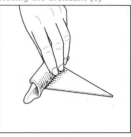

Curving into a crescent (f)

Croissants on baking sheet (g)

Types of Potato

Potato Variety	Season	Type	Use
Arran Pilot	New/First early	Waxy	Salad, boil
Belle de Fontenay	New/Early maincrop	Waxy	Salad, boil
Cara	Early maincrop	Floury	Bake, boil, chip
Charlotte	New/second early	Waxy	Salad, boil
Desiree	Early maincrop	Floury	Boil, chip, mash, roast
Duke of York	First early	Waxy	Boil
Estima	Second early	Floury	Boil, mash
Fianna	Maincrop	Floury	Bake, chip, roast
Golden Wonder	Late maincrop	Floury	Bake, roast, chip
Jersey Royal	First early	Waxy	Salad, boil
Kerr's Pink	Maincrop	Floury	Bake, roast, mash
King Edward	Early maincrop	Floury	Roast, chip, mash
Linzer Delikatess	First early	Waxy	Salad, boil
Marfona	Second early	Floury	Boil, bake
Maris Bard	First early	Floury	Boil, bake
Maris Peer	Second early	Floury	Chip, roast
Maris Piper	Early maincrop	Floury	Boil, chip, roast
Nadine	Second early	Waxy	Salad, boil
Nicola	New/early maincrop	Waxy	Salad, boil
Pentland Dell	Early maincrop	Floury	Bake, chip
Pink Fir Apple	New/late maincrop	Waxy	Salad, boil
Premiere	First early	Floury	Boil, chip
Ratte	New/early maincrop	Waxy	Salad, boil
Rocket	First early	Waxy	Salad, boil
Romano	Maincrop	Floury	Boil, roast
Sante	Early maincrop	Floury	Boil, bake
Saxon	Second early	Floury	Boil, bake, chip
Wilja	Second early	Floury	Boil, chip, roast, mash
Yukon Gold	Second early	Floury	Bake, roast

Guide to Potato Seasons

Most varieties of potatoes store well, so we are fortunate to be able to buy a variety of potato types throughout the year. However, most potatoes taste better when in season, rather than having been stored for several months, as anyone who has tasted a new potato in June then again in December might notice.

As a guide, in this country, it is recommended that potatoes be planted by late April. The harvest time for the different varies is as follows:

First earlies:	10 weeks from planting
Second earlies:	13 weeks from planting
Early maincrop:	15 weeks from planting
Late maincrop:	20 weeks from planting

Potatoes

The potato is a tuber, the tip of an underground stem. Indigenous to Central and South America where it was cultivated more than 4,000 years ago, the potato was brought to Europe by the Spaniards around 1570. Regarded with suspicion, it was not widely consumed until A. A. Parmetier, a pharmacist, persuaded Louis XVI to serve potatoes to his court. Today the potato is a dietary staple for much of the world. Being a complex carbohydrate (see **Healthy Eating and Basic Nutrition**, page 13), the potato is an excellent source of energy as well as supplying Vitamin C and fibre.

Types of Potatoes

Many varieties of potatoes are available in supermarkets today and the gardener with some land to spare can grow an even greater variety. Gardening catalogues often classify potatoes according to when they are ready for harvesting, i.e. early, second early, main crop, etc. but often all these types will be found on the supermarket shelves at the same time. Potatoes can also be classified by colour – red or white – or by texture – i.e. waxy or floury when cooked. It is the texture of the potato that most often determines the cooking method. New or early potatoes are usually waxy and main-crop potatoes are usually floury.

Preparing Potatoes

Green on a potato indicates that it has been exposed to light and chlorophyll has formed. Exposure to light also aids the production of the alkaloids solanine and chaconine. These alkaloids are toxic when consumed in large quantities, so any green on a potato should be cut away and discarded due to the presence of toxins. The toxins are also naturally concentrated around the eyes of potatoes so it is recommended that they are removed before cooking.

New Potatoes / Waxy Potatoes

New potatoes are small, with a waxy texture when cooked and a skin that rubs off easily. They are best cooked by boiling and are excellent for salads because they hold their shape without breaking up. The season for new potatoes is traditionally May–July, although they can now be found in the supermarkets all through the year.

New potatoes do not keep as well as old potatoes. Store them in a cool, dark place and use within 1 week of purchase.

The skins of new potatoes are very thin and can be easily scraped off using a small, sharp knife. The potatoes can also be cooked and eaten with the skins left on. Any small spots or eyes in the potatoes or any green spots should be removed.

Boiled New Potatoes

SERVES 4

450 g | 1 lb new potatoes

2 sprigs of fresh mint

30 g | 1 oz butter or 2 tablespoons olive oil

sea salt

2 tablespoons chopped fresh parsley or mint

1 Bring a large saucepan of salted water to the boil.

2 Add the potatoes and simmer for about 15 minutes depending on their size. The potatoes are done when they are tender when pierced with a sharp knife. They will also start to float in the water, if the pan is large enough.

3 Drain the potatoes in a colander, then return to the pan, place the sprigs of mint over the top, cover and leave to steam-dry for about 5 minutes.

4 Before serving, discard the mint sprigs. Toss the potatoes with melted butter or oil. Season with sea salt and sprinkle with the chopped herbs.

Potato Salad

To serve as a salad, allow to steam-dry. Do not toss with butter. Toss with olive oil and sea salt. Allow to cool. If desired, dress with Mayonnaise (see *Sauces*, *Savoury*, page 599).

Preparing potatoes en papillote (a)

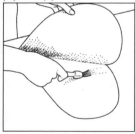

New Potatoes en Papillote

SERVES 4

450 g | 1 lb new potatoes, washed and dried

1 tablespoon sunflower oil

salt and freshly ground black pepper

4 cloves of garlic, unpeeled

1 Preheat the oven to 200°C | 400°F | gas mark 6.

2 If necessary, cut the potatoes so they are all the same size. Turn the potatoes in the oil in a bowl, and season with salt and pepper.

3 Cut a large piece of greaseproof paper cut into a heart shape and brush with oil. (a) Add the garlic.

4 Twist the edges of the paper together to seal the parcel. (b)

5 Place on a baking sheet in the top third of the oven and bake for about 45–60 minutes, or until the potatoes feel tender when pressed with your finger on top of the paper.

6 Serve in the paper parcels or turn into a warmed serving dish with the garlic.

Preparing potatoes en papillote (b)

Roast New Potatoes with Rosemary

SERVES 4

4 tablespoons olive oil	450 g│1 lb new potatoes
4 sprigs of fresh rosemary	sea salt

1 Place the oil in a roasting tin with 2 sprigs of the rosemary and heat in a 200°C│400°F│gas mark 6 oven.

2 Cut the potatoes into 2 cm│¾ in pieces.

3 Toss in the hot oil and roast, turning occasionally, for about 1 hour. Discard the rosemary.

4 Chop the remaining rosemary and sprinkle on the potatoes along with some sea salt.

Old Potatoes / Floury Potatoes

Floury potatoes are also known as main-crop potatoes because they are harvested later than new potatoes, usually in August and September. When these potatoes are cooked the cells separate from each other, giving the potato a dry, floury texture. It is this texture that makes them ideal for baking, roasting and mashing.

Occasionally potatoes will develop black spots when boiled. This is due to a reaction of iron with phenolic substances in the potato. It can be reduced by acidifying the cooking water, adding ½ teaspoon cream of tartar to each 570 ml│1 pint cooking water halfway through cooking.

Floury potatoes keep well and can be stored in a cool, dry, dark place for several months, however, it is best not to refrigerate them. If the storage place is too warm, the potatoes will soften and sprout. If the potatoes are exposed to light they will develop green spots (see *Preparing Potatoes*, above).

Peeling Potatoes

A high proportion of the nutritional value of the potato lies in the layer just underneath the skin, so it is wise to peel potatoes as thinly as possible. Use a vegetable peeler or a small, thin-bladed knife. Have a large bowl of cold water to dip the potatoes into while peeling, to wash them and keep the soil from being rubbed in. Place the peeled potatoes in a saucepan with enough cold water to cover them to keep them from oxidizing (turning brown).

If peeling the potatoes in advance of cooking, wait until just before you are ready to cook to cut them into smaller, even-sized pieces. If the pieces are too small they are likely to break down when cooked and the more cut surfaces exposed to water, the more the water-soluble nutrients are lost in the cooking liquid.

Boiled Potatoes

The potatoes can be peeled either before or after boiling.

SERVES 4

675 g|1½ lb floury potatoes

1 teaspoon salt

30 g|1 oz butter, melted (optional)

salt and freshly ground black pepper

1 Wash the potatoes thoroughly and remove any eyes and green spots. Peel if desired (see above). Cut into even-sized pieces no smaller than 4 cm|1½ in.

2 Place the potatoes in a large saucepan with enough cold water to cover them by about 4 cm|1½ in. Add the salt. Cover and bring to the boil.

3 When the water boils, turn down the heat and cook the potatoes at a simmer. If the water boils too quickly, the surface of the potatoes will become water-logged and they are likely to break apart. Leave the lid on the pan but cover it only partially so that the steam can escape.

4 Simmer until the potatoes are cooked through. If a table knife is inserted into a piece of potato the texture should feel the same all the way through and if the knife is lifted the potato should fall off the knife.

5 Drain the potatoes, saving the water for soup or gravy, if required. Allow the potatoes to steam-dry in the colander for about 5 minutes. Peel at this point if wished.

6 Toss with the butter and season with salt and pepper.

Boiled Potatoes: What has gone wrong when...

The potatoes fall apart.
- The potatoes were boiled too vigorously.
- The potatoes were overcooked.

Roast Potatoes

Potatoes can be roasted at a wide range of oven temperature, from about 160°C|325°F|gas mark 3 to 225°C|425°F|gas mark 7. Obviously the cooking time will vary accordingly.

SERVES 4

1 kg|2 lb 4 oz floury potatoes

sunflower oil

30 g|1 oz butter

salt

2 tablespoons chopped fresh parsley

(optional)

1 Preheat the oven to 200°C|400°F|gas mark 6.

2 Prepare the potatoes as instructed above for *Boiled Potatoes*. Once the water has come to the boil, simmer the potatoes for 5 minutes only.

3 Place oil in a roasting tin to a depth of 6 mm|¼ in and place in the top third of the oven to heat.

4 Drain the potatoes, saving the water for gravy or soup, if required.

5 Return the potatoes to the warm pan and toss over a medium heat for about 10 seconds to dry the potatoes and roughen their surface slightly.

6 Remove the roasting tin from the oven, then carefully tip the potatoes into the hot oil. Baste the potatoes with the oil and return to the oven.

7 Roast the potatoes for 1 hour, turning them every 20 minutes.

8 Add the butter to the roasting tin and turn the potatoes in the fat. Roast for a further 30 minutes or until the potatoes are crisp and well browned on all sides.

9 Sprinkle the potatoes with salt and the parsley, if using. Place in a warmed shallow serving dish. If keeping the potatoes warm, do not cover them or they will become soggy.

Roast Potatoes: What has gone wrong when...

The potatoes are not crisp.
- The potatoes were not roasted for long enough.
- The potatoes were covered.
- The potatoes were roasted round a joint.
- The wrong type of potato was used.
- The fat wasn't hot when the potatoes were added to the pan.

Mashed Potatoes

Potatoes for mashing must be floury or the texture will be gluey. It is important to mash the potatoes while they are still warm and to use warm milk, never cold, otherwise the starch in the potatoes will set and the texture will be gluey. The amount of milk needed will vary depending upon the type of potato as well as personal preference.

The potatoes can be mashed with a potato masher or a mouli sieve or they can be pushed through a metal sieve one at a time, using a wooden spoon. When potatoes are boiled the starch granules absorb liquid and swell. A gluey texture will result if these starch granules are broken by mashing in a food processor or by overworking. The potatoes must be mashed when hot because the starch granules separate, resulting in light, fluffy potatoes.

SERVES 4

1 kg|2 lb 4 oz floury potatoes	85–150 ml|3–5 fl oz warmed milk
1½ teaspoons salt	salt and freshly ground white pepper
55 g|2 oz butter, melted	

1 Cook the potatoes with the salt as instructed in the recipe for *Boiled Potatoes*, above. After draining the potatoes, return them to the saucepan and place over a low heat to steam-dry for about 1 minute.

2 Mash using one of the methods described above.

3 Stir in the butter and enough warm milk to give the required texture. Season with salt and pepper. Take care not to stir the potatoes too much or the texture will become sticky.

4 Turn the mashed potatoes into a warmed serving dish. If not serving immediately, flatten the surface of the potatoes, dot with additional butter and flood with a little milk. This will prevent a crust from forming. Stir the milk and butter into the potatoes just before serving.

VARIATIONS:

Garlic and Olive Oil Mash: Add 2 peeled cloves of garlic to the cooking water when boiling the potatoes. Mash the garlic in with the potatoes. Substitute 4 tablespoons olive oil for the butter.

Parsnip and Potato Mash: Substitute peeled parsnips for half of the potatoes.

Mashed Potatoes: What has gone wrong when:

The potatoes are gluey.

- The wrong type of potato was used.
- The potatoes were mashed too vigorously or were mashed in a food processor.
- The potatoes were mashed when cold.
- Cold milk was added to the potatoes.

Baked Potatoes

Use old, floury potatoes for baking. Cara, Desiree and Marfona are particularly good varieties to bake. Potatoes can be baked at almost any temperature but for a good thick skin, a hot oven is best. Rubbing the potatoes with oil will also help the skin to crisp. Wrapping the potatoes in foil will produce a soft skin. The potatoes must be cut into or pierced before baking or they may explode in the oven.

SERVES 4

4 large floury potatoes	sea salt
olive oil	

1 Preheat the oven to 200°C | 400°F | gas mark 6.

2 Scrub the potatoes well with a stiff brush and remove any eyes and green spots. Pierce the potatoes with a skewer and cut a cross in the top about 1 cm | $\frac{1}{2}$ in deep.

3 Brush the potatoes with oil and sprinkle with salt.

4 Place the potatoes directly on the oven shelf. Bake until tender all the way through when pierced with a skewer.

5 To serve, squeeze the potatoes gently to open the cross.

Sautéed Potatoes

The nicest sautéed potatoes have absorbed a lot of butter and have crisp, brown, crumbly edges.

SERVES 4

1 kg | 2 lb 4 oz floury potatoes
1 ½ teaspoons salt
55 g | 2 oz butter

2 sprigs of fresh rosemary
1 tablespoon chopped fresh rosemary

1 Boil the unpeeled potatoes with the salt, as for *Boiled Potatoes*, above.
2 Peel the potatoes while they are still hot. The easiest way to do this is to insert a fork into the potato to hold it firmly, then peel it with a small knife.
3 Break the potatoes into irregular chunks of about 4 cm | 1 ½ in. Do not cut them with a knife or the edges will not crumble.
4 Melt the butter with the rosemary sprigs in a large sauté pan over a medium low heat.
5 When the butter foams, add the potatoes and turn them to coat in the butter. Do not allow the butter to brown.
6 Cook the potatoes, turning them frequently, for about 45 minutes. They should soak up the butter, and their edges should crumble and turn an even golden-brown.
7 Sprinkle with salt and the chopped rosemary.
9 Turn the potatoes into a warmed shallow serving dish. If keeping warm, do not cover or they will become soggy.

Sautéed Potatoes: What has gone wrong when...

The potatoes are not crumbly.
- The butter was too hot when the potatoes were added.
- The potatoes were too cool when added to the butter and the starch set.
- The wrong type of potato was used.
- The potatoes were not cooked for long enough.

Pommes Dauphinoise

This creamy potato dish is always a favourite. It is important to use floury potatoes and to slice them thinly. Do not soak the potatoes in water: the starch is necessary to thicken the cream. The potatoes can be sliced with a mandolin to save time.

Using a mandolin to slice potatoes

SERVES 4–6

30 g | 1 oz butter, plus extra for greasing
1 onion, thinly sliced
290 ml | ½ pint milk
100 ml | 3½ fl oz crème fraîche

290 ml | ½ pint double cream
salt and freshly ground black pepper
1 kg | 2 lb 4 oz floury potatoes
1 clove of garlic, crushed

1 Melt the butter and stir in the onion. Cover with a piece of damp greaseproof paper (a *cartouche*) and a lid. Sweat for about 20 minutes until tender, stirring occasionally.
2 Meanwhile, heat the milk and the cream and season with salt and pepper.

3 Peel the potatoes and slice them about 3 mm | ⅛ in thick. Drop them into the milk as they are sliced to prevent them from browning.

4 When the onion is soft, add the garlic. Cook for a further minute, then add to the potatoes.

5 Cook the potatoes at a simmer, until they have started to soften.

6 Preheat the oven to 160°C | 325°F | gas mark 3.

7 Turn the potatoes into a buttered ovenproof dish, arranging the top layer neatly. (The potatoes can be made in advance to this point. Refrigerate when cool if keeping for more than 1 hour before cooking.)

8 Bake the potatoes for 1 hour (1½ hours if they have been refrigerated), or until they are tender when tested with a knife and browned on the top.

Pommes Dauphinoise: What has gone wrong when...

The cream has curdled.

- The potatoes were cooked at too high a temperature.
- The onion was not softened enough, so the acid in the onion curdled the milk.
- Single cream was used instead of double cream.

Rösti Potatoes

Rösti means crisp and golden, which is exactly what these fried cakes of grated potato, a speciality of Switzerland, should be. This recipe is best made with potatoes that hold together when boiled and do not become too fluffy, such as Maris Piper or large new potatoes.

SERVES 4

1 onion, finely chopped	salt and freshly ground black
45 g	1½ oz butter	pepper
675 g	1lb 8 oz potatoes peeled and cut into large chunks	4 tablespoons oil

1 Sweat the onion in half the butter.

2 Place the potatoes in a saucepan with 1 teaspoon salt. Cover with cold water and simmer the potatoes for 5 minutes.

3 Drain in a colander. When the potatoes are cool enough to handle (protect your hands with rubber gloves), grate them coarsely and toss with salt, pepper, butter and onion.

4 Place 2 tablespoons of the oil in a 25 cm | 10 in sauté pan over a medium heat. When hot, add half the remaining butter and heat until foaming.

5 When the foaming subsides, press the grated potato into the pan. Fry over a low heat until the potato is golden and crusty on the underside, about 15 minutes.

6 Slide the potato cake out of the pan on to a plate. Add the remaining oil and butter to the pan and heat until foaming. When the foaming subsides, slide the potato cake back into the pan, uncooked side down.

7 Cook for a further 15 minutes until the underside is golden and crusty.

8 Serve hot, cut into wedges like a cake.

VARIATION

Grated raw carrot, celeriac or parsnip can be substituted for one-third of the potatoes.

Preserving

Although the word preserves is often taken to mean jams, jellies and marmalades, preserves are in fact any food that has been treated in some way in order to keep it longer than it would untreated. Frozen food, dried food, salted food and smoked food are all preserved foods.

Prior to the invention of refrigeration man had to be inventive in his storage of food. Many of the following techniques are ancient methods used for preserving the surplus of the summer for a time when food might not be available in sufficient quantity.

Spoilage of food is caused by natural deterioration due to enzyme activity as well as the growth of yeasts, moulds and bacteria. In order for these to grow they need warmth, moisture and a source of nourishment, so preserving methods have evolved to retard the spoilage of food, by changing its environment, whether chemically or through dehydration.

Drying

Drying was one of the earliest methods used to preserve food. Man quickly learned that strips of meat, fruits and berries would all keep longer if they were dried in the air.

Hot, dry air is essential as humidity encourages bacterial growth and rotting. Drying dehydrates food so the yeasts, moulds and bacteria cannot grow. An additional benefit to ancient man was that food became easier to store and transport when dried.

Examples of dried foods are beef and venison jerky, Parma ham, sun-dried tomatoes, wild mushrooms, apricots, prunes and raisins. Most of these are consumed in their dried state but mushrooms need to be rehydrated. Place them in a bowl and pour over enough boiling water to cover. Allow to stand for 20 minutes, then remove the mushrooms with a slotted spoon. Keep the liquid for use in soups, stews or risotto as it has a lot of flavour. Decant the liquid to leave any gritty sediment on the bottom of the bowl. Packaged sun-dried tomatoes also require rehydrating by soaking; those packed in oil in jars do not need to be soaked, simply drained.

Smoking

Smoking is another ancient method of preserving, originally applied to fish and meat. Food can be either hot- or cold-smoked. Smoking is an effective preserving technique as it partially dehydrates the food, whilst the toxins produced by the smoke inhibit the growth of bacteria. Smoking is traditionally used to flavour pork products such as ham, bacon and sausages, as well as fish such as salmon, trout, mackerel, herring and haddock.

Cold-smoking is done at a temperature of 10–30°C|50–85°F and takes up to 1 month. Meat, poultry, game, fish, shellfish, cheese, nuts and some vegetables can be successfully cold-smoked. Most cold-smoked pork products are salted or soaked in brine before smoking to allow the saltpetre to give the meat an attractive pink colour. The salting and brining also help to preserve the food as well as making it more porous so that the smoke penetrates it easily. The food remains uncooked after the cold-smoking process. Kippering is the process by which herrings are salted, dried, then cold-smoked.

Hot smoking is done at temperatures of 45–75°C|120–180°F and takes a much shorter time – 20 minutes to several days – to impart a smoky flavour and 'cook' the food. Cuts of meat, mainly pork/poultry, game, sausages and some fish are exposed to thick smoke from a fast-burning fire covered with sawdust. The smoking process acts as a preservative and imparts flavour.

Originally smoking was done on a very small scale over an open fire but today commercial smokehouses can process large quantities of food.

Home Smoking

Cold-smoking at home is not recommended because the process takes several hours, during which time the food is held at a temperature just above room temperature, providing an ideal environment for the growth of harmful bacteria.

Hot-smoking can be done very easily at home using a kit or by making a smoker with 2 identical roasting pans and a wire rack. Thin, tender food such as trout fillets or prawns can be smoked most successfully.

The smoking must be done in a well-ventilated area. Dry wood chips are needed and can be purchased from specialist cookware shops or garden centres.

Place enough wood chips over the base of one of the roasting pans to cover the bottom, then place the wire rack on top of the pan. The food to be smoked is placed on the wire rack, then the second pan is placed on top, to create an oven. Wrap tightly in aluminium foil. Heat over a medium heat until the wood chips catch fire. Turn off the heat and allow the food to smoke for 10–15 minutes. Fish is cooked when it turns from translucent to opaque and feels firm to the touch.

Hot-smoking can also be done with a barbecue. Use lumps of wood about the size of a baking potato. Soak the wood in water for about 20 minutes before placing it on the fire. The wood should smoulder, not burn.

Salting

Salting is a method of preserving fish that has been used since biblical times. Salt cod was a staple of many Mediterranean countries and in the Middle Ages salted herring was the only source of protein during Lent, when meat was forbidden. In ancient times, salt was a precious commodity, hence the saying 'worth his salt'. In another saying, 'below the salt', a person's social rank was measured according to where they were seated in relation to the salt cellar.

Gravad Lax

This Swedish dish preserves the salmon by salting. Freeze the fish for 24 hours to kill any parasites before preserving.

SERVES 10–12

1 kg | 2 lb 4 oz middle-cut fresh salmon, scaled, filleted into 2 sides and pinboned (see *Fish*, page 246)

30 g | 1 oz granulated sugar

30 g | 1 oz coarse sea salt

2 tablespoons cracked black peppercorns

2 tablespoons brandy

30 g | 1 oz chopped fresh dill

sliced brown bread and butter, to serve

For the mustard sauce

1 tablespoon Dijon or wholegrain mustard

2 tablespoons wine vinegar

6 tablespoons vegetable oil

1 tablespoon chopped fresh dill

salt and freshly ground black pepper

2 teaspoons caster sugar

1 Place one of the salmon fillets skin side down in a glass or ceramic serving dish.

2 Sprinkle the fish with the sugar, salt, peppercorns, brandy and dill.

3 Place the other piece of salmon, flesh side down, on top.

4 Cover with clingfilm. Place a second dish on top of the fish and weight it down with several cans.

5 Refrigerate for 12 hours then turn the fish over and weight again. Refrigerate for a further 12 hours. The fish can be kept refrigerated for a further 24 hours. Turn it every 12 hours, pouring off any liquid.

6 To make the mustard sauce, put the mustard into a small bowl and whisk in the vinegar. Gradually whisk in the oil. Stir in the dill and season with salt, pepper and sugar.

7 To serve the salmon, pour off the juices, then scrape away the marinade and discard. Slice the salmon thinly across the grain as for smoked salmon (see *Fish*, page 263). Serve with the Mustard Sauce and brown bread and butter.

Dry-salting

Moist vegetables are usually dry-salted before pickling to remove excess juices that would dilute the vinegar (see *Pickling*, below). To dry-salt, slice the vegetables or pierce whole tough vegetables such as shallots. Layer the vegetables with rock salt or sea salt and allow to stand for 24 hours. Drain away the liquid, rinse off the salt and pat dry. Table salt is not recommended because it contains additives that might make the pickle cloudy.

The salting process known as degorging is also used to dehydrate food slightly before cooking. It was traditionally used to remove the bitter juices from aubergine before frying. Sliced cucumber is also often degorged to soften it and remove some of the juices before mixing with yoghurt or vinegar for a salad.

To degorge vegetables, slice and sprinkle with a thin layer of salt. Place on a wire rack and allow to stand for 1 hour. Rinse the slices and pat dry.

Brining

Brine is heavily salted water used for pickling and preserving foods. Both meat and fish are cured in brine, often before smoking. A brine can be prepared by heating 55 g | 2 oz rock or sea salt with 570 ml | 1 pint water to dissolve the salt, then allowing the mixture to cool. Sometimes the brine is sweetened slightly with sugar or molasses.

Some food items undergo several types of cure. For example, the American version of smoked salmon called lox is prepared from salmon that has been cured in brine then cold-smoked. Some hams are soaked in brine before they are smoked. Parma ham is salt-cured then air-dried.

De-salting

Many foods that have been salted or brined need to be de-salted before they are cooked. Hams and salt cod are two examples of these. To de-salt large pieces of food, soak in several changes of cold water over a period of 24–48 hours. To test if the food has been de-salted sufficiently, cut a small piece from the food and poach it before tasting. Small pieces of food, such as lardons of bacon, can be de-salted by blanching in boiling water for 30 seconds, then draining and rinsing in cold water.

Pickling

All manner of fruit, vegetables, eggs, fish, and nuts can be preserved in a solution with high acidity. Vinegar is an essential preserving ingredient along with salt and sugar. Fruit for pickles is usually cooked in sugared vinegar and bottled in sweetened vinegar syrup before bottling. Vegetables are usually but not always pickled raw, and are generally dry-salted (see above) or steeped in brine before being immersed in vinegar and bottled.

Pickling vinegar should be strong, containing at least 5 per cent acetic acid. Most brand vinegar contains sufficient acid, but home-made or draught vinegar is not suitable. Brown malt vinegar is the best for flavour, especially if the pickling liquid is to be highly spiced or used to preserve strong-tasting foods. White vinegar has less flavour but will produce a good, clear pickle. Wine vinegar is suitable for delicate, mild-tasting foods. Commercial cider vinegar is good for preparations using apples.

The vinegar may be spiced and flavoured to taste by the addition of cayenne pepper, ginger or chillies, or aromatic spices such as cardamom seeds, cloves, nutmeg or cinnamon sticks. It is best to use whole spices as they can be removed easily and will not make the vinegar cloudy.

Most pickles and chutneys need to be stored for about 3 months in a cool, dark place to allow their flavours to mellow and develop (see *Jams, Jellies and Other Preserves*, page 332).

Bottling

Bottling is a method of preserving food by heating and boiling in jars with a airtight seals. The food is heated sufficiently to destroy any bacteria and the heat develops a vacuum in the jar so that any remaining bacteria cannot grow, as no oxygen is available. However, there is still the possible danger of botulism poisoning due to anaerobic bacterial growth. Food that does not contain sufficient sugar or acid to stop this growth needs to be bottled. The bottling times given in specific recipes should be followed precisely and fastidious hygiene during food preparation is essential (see *Bibliography and Suggested Further Reading*, *Preserving*, page 771, for specialist books).

Freezing

This is a method of preserving food by chilling it until it is frozen. A 3-star freezer which freezes to a temperature of $-18^{\circ}C(0^{\circ}F)$ is recommended if frozen food is stored for longer than 1 week.

Jam- and Jelly-making

A high concentration of sugar will prevent bacterial growth. Fruit is preserved by the high sugar content in jams and jellies (see *Jams, Jellies and Other Preserves*, page 553). From the twelfth century, when sugar was brought to Europe by the Crusaders, sugar has also been used in curing meat because it counteracts the toughening effect of salt.

Preserving in Fat or Oil

Fat in the form of oil or a solid fat such as butter or duck or goose fat is used to preserve food for short periods of time by preventing it from being exposed to the air. Confit of duck or goose is an example, where the meat is packed into jars with layers of its own fat. The fat is scraped from the meat before serving cold or reheating for use in composite dishes.

The old-fashioned preparation of potted meat is a similar example of meat being preserved through the use of fat. Vegetables, such as sun-dried tomatoes, artichoke hearts and herbs, are bottled in olive oil. Vegetables bottled in this way in particular carry a risk of botulism poisoning. The surface of pâtés is often sealed with a layer of clarified butter to prevent oxidation.

Confit de Canard

Confit is a traditional dish from south-west France made with goose or duck.

The confit takes 2 days to prepare. The fat will preserve the goose or duck if the confit is kept refrigerated for up to 1 month.

SERVES 4

4 duck legs or 1 whole duck, jointed (see **Poultry**, page 422)

4 sprigs of fresh rosemary, chopped
2 bay leaves, crushed

For the marinade

4 tablespoons brandy
30 g | 1 oz sea salt
1 tablespoon black peppercorns, cracked
2 cloves, crushed

For the confit

675 g | 1lb 8 oz duck or goose fat
1 head of garlic, divided into cloves, unpeeled
15 g | ½ oz sprigs of fresh thyme

1 Place the duck pieces fat side down in a single layer in a non-corrosive dish. Sprinkle with the brandy.
2 Mix together the salt, peppercorns, cloves, rosemary and bay leaves. Sprinkle over the duck.
3 Cover with clingfilm and weight down. Refrigerate for 24 hours.
4 Preheat the oven to 150°F | 300°C | gas mark 2.
5 Pour off any liquid from the duck and scrape off the marinade.
6 Heat the fat over a low heat in a heavy flameproof casserole.
7 Layer the duck with the garlic and the thyme in the casserole. The duck should be entirely submerged in the fat.
8 Bake for 3½ –4 hours, or until the meat is very tender when pierced with a skewer and the fat in the skin is totally rendered.
9 Remove from the oven and allow to cool, uncovered.
10 Remove the duck from the fat and trim off any exposed bone.
11 Boil the cooking fat then strain a little of it into the bottom of a clean ceramic dish. Refrigerate to set.
12 Place the duck pieces in the dish, making sure they do not touch the sides. Strain over the liquid fat to cover. Allow to cool. Refrigerate until required. Scrape the fat from the duck before using either cold or reheated.

NOTE: Confit can be reheated under the grill to crisp the skin or it can be reheated in the oven with parboiled potatoes.

To reheat confit

1 Preheat the oven to 200°C | 400°F | gas mark 6.
2 Scrape the fat from the meat and place the meat in a roasting tin.
3 Bake for 40 minutes, or until heated through.
4 To crisp the skin, sprinkle it with a little salt and grill at the highest setting until crisp and brown.

Pressure Cooking

The pressure cooker, invented by the French physicist Denis Papin in 1647, is a special cooking pot with a locking, airtight lid and valve system to regulate the internal pressure. Large pressure cookers continue to be used most frequently in large catering units such as schools and hospitals, where they are also known as autoclaves. In the domestic kitchen, the pressure cooker is a useful piece of equipment because it reduces cooking time by up to two-thirds while preserving the nutritional value of the food. It is particularly useful for dried pulses, stews and root vegetables, such as beetroot.

The basic principle of pressure cooking is that the ingredients and liquid are enclosed in a pressure-tight vessel and the steam which would escape freely from a traditional saucepan is controlled and released slowly, thereby raising the pressure inside the pressure cooker. The rise in pressure increases the temperature of the boiling liquid inside the cooker and therefore raises the temperature at which the food is cooked. It is this high temperature, as well as the steam that is forced through the food, that cooks and tenderizes at the same time, which makes for rapid cooking.

Pressure cookers are especially useful for foods that would normally be cooked with moist heat. They can also be used for bottling. Traditional models are equipped with detachable pressure regulators.

The more kg|lb of pressure, the higher the internal temperature and the quicker the food cooks. The chart below gives the pressure required for certain types of cooking:

Pressure		Boiling point raised to	Use
LOW	2.3 kg|5 lb	108°C|226°F	Steaming puddings Bottling fruit
MEDIUM	4.6 kg|10 lb	115°C|239°F	Blanching vegetables Marmalade
HIGH	6.9 kg|15 lb	122°C|252°F	Boiling Stewing Braising

Safety Features

Modern pressure cookers have a safety valve which will automatically vent steam should there be a malfunction or if the cooker boils dry. However, a pressure cooker should never be left unattended over the heat. If the cooker boils dry, do not attempt to move it. You will know this has happened if steam is no longer being released from the steam value, i.e. the hissing stops. Switch off the heat and leave the cooker to cool down for at least 1 hour before attempting to open it.

Using a Pressure Cooker

For safety purposes, check the following before use:

- the pintle moves freely
- the rubber seals have not deteriorated around the edge or pintle
- the handles lock securely

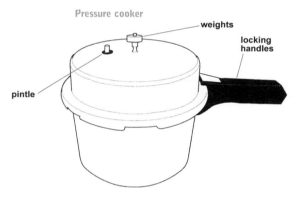

Pressure cooker

weights

locking
handles

pintle

Pressure cooking relies on steam, so enough liquid must be added to produce steam during the cooking time. The manufacturer's instructions should be followed. Water, stock or juice can be used, but oil, melted fat or butter are not suitable. Use at least 290 ml|½ pint liquid for the first 15 minutes of cooking. A further 150 ml|¼ pint of liquid is needed for each additional 15 minutes of cooking time. Calculate the amount of liquid required, then add it before starting to cook. Place the food in the liquid. The total volume (liquid plus food) should not exceed the following:

Cereals, pulses, dried peas and lentils	Not more than one-third full
Liquid-foods such as rice, pasta, stews	Not more than half full
Milk and foods that may froth up when cooking	Not more than half full
Solid foods, joints, vegetables	Not more than two-thirds full

Never cook food such as dumplings that may swell and block the safety valves.

Cooking in a Pressure Cooker

If the food requires browning, brown it in a little fat before adding the liquid. After placing the food and the liquid in the pressure cooker, secure the lid. Place over a high heat and bring to the boil. When the pintle rises, blocking the hole in the lid, wait for 10 seconds, then reduce the heat to maintain a steady low hiss of steam. Add the required weights, then steam as specified in the recipe. Start timing from this point. Refer to the manufacturer's directions for cooking times. Otherwise cook for one-third of the conventional cooking time before depressurizing the cooker (see below) and checking the food to see if it is done. If the food is not done, add more liquid if necessary and repressurize.

If at any time during cooking the hiss of steam disappears, the cooker has boiled dry. Turn off the heat to depressurize (see below), then open the cooker and add more liquid.

To depressurize, turn off the heat and wait for the pintle to drop before opening the lid. Some newer models have manual|automatic choice for depressurization. See the manufacturer's instructions. Before removing the lid, ensure all pressure has been released. Never try to force open a pressure cooker as the ingredients might spray all over the kitchen.

Sauces that are too thin should be reduced after cooking once the lid has been removed.

Pulses

Pulses are the dried seeds of the category of plants called legumes. A legume is any one of 1,000 plant species that have seed pods that split along both sides when ripe. The pulses that are important in the human diet are lentils, beans and peas. These inexpensive high-protein pulses are a staple throughout much of the world, particularly in areas where animal protein is scarce. Although the protein is incomplete (see *Healthy Eating and Basic Nutrition*, page 13), when served with rice pulses make a complete, usable protein. Pulses also contain Vitamin B, thiamin, complex carbohydrates, fibre, fats and minerals.

Soaking Pulses

Pulses are usually cooked by boiling to rehydrate them and to gelatinize their starch, making them soft enough to eat. Cooking makes pulses more nutritious as the heat destroys certain components that cause problems with digestion. Salt is not added to the cooking water as it is thought to toughen the skins. Soaking beans and peas in cold water for about 4 hours can shorten the cooking time. Pulses can be soaked overnight but soaking for a longer period than 4 hours has little effect on cooking time. Lentils cook in a relatively short time so do not require soaking, although soaking for up to 1 hour will shorten the cooking time

Cooking Pulses

Enough cold water should be added to pulses to cover them by 2.5 cm | 1 in and they should be boiled uncovered. Depending on the type of pulse, the pan might need topping up with boiling water from a kettle during cooking. See individual types of pulse, below, for cooking times.

Dried beans and peas need to be boiled vigorously for 10 minutes, uncovered to drive off toxins. They are then drained, covered with cold water and boiled again until soft. If prepared in a slow cooker (see *Kitchen Equipment*, page 63) the beans and peas must be boiled first before they are placed in the cooker. Pressure cooking is an ideal method for cooking pulses (see *Pressure Cooking*, page 555).

An acidic cooking environment keeps the pulses from softening so it is recommended that they are boiled to the required degree of softness before any sauce is added. Some recipes call for a small amount of bicarbonate of soda to be added to the water to help soften the pulses. Although this practice can reduce the nutritional value, a small amount of bicarbonate of soda, $\frac{1}{8}$ teaspoon per 170 g|6 oz pulses, has been found to speed the cooking time without having a marked effect on the nutritional value.

Pulses double in weight and volume when cooked.

Storing Pulses

All dried legumes should be stored in an airtight container and will keep for up to 1 year.

Types of Pulse

Lentils

The lentil is probably the oldest cultivated legume. It can be traced back to 7000 BC. The word lentil comes from the Latin word *lens*, which describes the shape of the lentil. With one of the highest protein contents of all vegetables, lentils remain especially popular in the Middle East and India and parts of Europe.

French or Puy lentil: This lentil is small, with a greyish green seed coat and a yellow inside. It maintains its shape and has a firm texture when cooked so is useful for salads as well as a starchy accompaniment for meat. Boil for about 35 minutes. (See *Meat*, *Game, Partridge with Lentils*, page 464.)

Red lentil: This lentil, often used in Indian cooking, is small and round with a reddish–orange colour. It is sold without its seed coat. It becomes mushy when cooked so it is good for soups. When puréed, it has a slightly grainy texture. Boil for about 20 minutes.

Yellow lentil and green lentil: These pea-sized lentils break down when cooked. They are good for purées such as dhal, the Indian curried lentil dish, and soups. Boil for about 45 minutes.

Brown lentil: This small, dusky lentil is popular in Egypt. Boil for about 40 minutes. (See *Meat*, *Lamb*, *Lamb steak à la Catalane with Lentils*, page 394.)

Beans

Beans can be purchased in their dried form or in tins. Tinned beans need to be drained and rinsed: they do not require any further cooking. If used in salads, cooked beans should be eaten within 24 hours as they have a tendency to ferment.

Dried beans take a long time to cook, so soaking (see above) is recommended. Some beans contain toxins and must be boiled vigorously for 10 minutes, uncovered, at the beginning of their cooking time. Drain the beans after boiling, then cover again with cold water and simmer until tender for the time given for each type of bean.

If cooking in a pressure cooker (see *Pressure Cooking*, page 555), the first boiling must be done with the lid off. The second boiling can be done under pressure for a third to half the times given below.

Adzuki and **mung** beans usually feature in Chinese and Japanese cuisine. They are also used for sprouting and the sprouts are eaten raw. Boil for about 40 minutes.

Black-eyed beans are a relative of the mung bean. These small, buff-coloured beans have a tiny black spot on the side. They are used in African and Caribbean cooking. Boil for about 1 hour.

Broad beans or fava beans: These beans can produce a reaction in people of Mediterranean descent sensitive to the toxin vicine. Boil for 1 hour.

Butter beans are large, somewhat flat, starchy beans used in purées and as a starchy accompaniment for meat. Boil for about $1-1\frac{1}{2}$ hours.

Cannellini beans are Italian white, kidney-shaped beans used in soups, stews and purées. Boil for about $1\frac{1}{4}$ hours.

Flageolet beans are pale green with a thin kidney shape. In French cuisine they are popular for salads and stews. Boil for about $1\frac{1}{2}$ hours.

Haricot beans are oval, buff-coloured beans, familiar to most people as the bean in baked beans. They are also used for the French dish, Cassoulet. Boil for about $1\frac{1}{2}$ hours.

Pinto beans are pinkish-brown and are used in Mexican cookery. Boil for about 40–50 minutes.

Red kidney beans are used in salads and stews such as the well-known Mexican dish, Chilli. Boil for about $1-1\frac{1}{2}$ hours. Kidney beans must be boiled rapidly for 10 minutes to destroy their toxins before cooking until tender (see above).

Soy beans are an important crop throughout the world. Native to South-East Asia where they are a staple part of the diet, they are consumed as bean curd, sprouts, boiled beans, milk and ground into flour. Soy beans have the highest protein content of all the beans. They are also pressed to obtain soy bean oil. Soy sauce is made by fermenting the beans.

Peas

The pea is another ancient legume that was particularly important during the Middle Ages. Today, 2 types of pea are cultivated: a high-starch variety which when dried produces split peas, and a high-sugar variety which is harvested when immature, to eat as a green vegetable.

Split peas are used for making soups and purées. Soak them overnight if possible.

Yellow split peas are used for purées such as Indian dhal and for Pease Pudding.

Green split peas are used for soup and as an accompaniment for boiled ham.

Chickpeas are important in the Mediterranean, Middle East and India where they are eaten boiled, roasted and deep-fried, made into purées and ground into flour (besan) for bread. Chickpeas are the basis for the popular Middle Eastern dip, *Hummus* (see below). Soak the chickpeas overnight, then boil for $1\frac{1}{2}$ hours.

Hummus bi Tahini

Hummus is traditionally served with warm pitta bread.

SERVES 4

225 g | 8 oz cooked chickpeas

1–2 cloves of garlic, crushed

3 tablespoons lemon juice

1 tablespoon tahini paste (sesame seed paste)

$\frac{1}{2}$ teaspoon ground cumin

$\frac{1}{4}$ teaspoon ground cayenne

salt, to taste

110 ml | 4 fl oz olive oil

2–3 tablespoons boiling water

To garnish

1 tablespoon olive oil

paprika

1 Purée the chickpeas in a food processor with the garlic, lemon juice, tahini, spices and salt.
2 Add the olive oil through the feed tube while the machine is running.
3 Add enough water to thin the paste to a dipping consistency, about the texture of thick yoghurt.
4 Pile into a dish, drizzle with oil and sprinkle with paprika.

Rice

Evidence of rice cultivation in China dates back to at least 5000 BC. Today, rice is cultivated in more than 100 countries as the staple grain for over half the world's population. Rice is a more reliable crop than its starchy competitors, wheat and barley. With its low moisture content, rice stores particularly well and will keep for several years.

Nutritionally rice is an excellent source of energy, consisting of 80 per cent starch which, when digested, becomes glycogen, a complex carbohydrate which provides sustained muscular energy. Although protein makes up 9 per cent of the grain, it is an incomplete protein (see *Healthy Eating and Basic Nutrition*, page 13). This means that rice needs to be accompanied by another source of protein, such as meat, eggs or beans, to make a complete protein that can be used by the body for cell growth and repair.

With the exception of brown rice and some types of red rice, the husk, bran and germ are removed from the rice grains prior to sale. Although brown rice is more nutritious than white, for many people the whiteness of rice is prized. In the past this has resulted in nutritional deficiencies in some countries, with the removal of the bran responsible for the disease beriberi, a disease of the nervous system caused by lack of thiamin in the diet.

Rice can be cooked by a number of different methods, but steam or boiling water is always required to break down the cell walls and gelatinize the starch. The 2 starches in rice are called amylose and amylopectin. It is amylopectin that makes the rice sticky. All rice contains at least 70 per cent amylopectin but sticky rice has up to 83 per cent. The two main techniques of rice cooking are open boiling and the absorption method. Recipes for both these methods are given below.

There are thousands of varieties of rice as it cross-breeds easily. Certain types of rice predominate in different rice-consuming areas. The following categories of rice are those most commonly available in England.

Long-grain Rice

Long-grain rice is sometimes referred to as Patna rice. A grain of this rice will be 4–5 times as long as it is wide. It has less amylopectin than short-grain rice and will cook to separate, dry grains. Both brown and white rice come in the long-grain form.

Long-grain rice is higher in the starch amylose, which makes the rice harden when it cools. When the rice is reheated the starch will become soft again. If using long-grain rice for rice salad it is important to add the dressing while the rice is still hot. This added moisture helps keep the rice from hardening when cold.

Basmati Rice

This is a long-grained rice grown primarily in the foothills of the Himalayas and also in the USA. The grains are aged to give them a characteristic nutty, fragrant smell and flavour. Basmati rice is the traditional accompaniment to curries. It is also the rice to use for Biryani, Kedgeree and Pilafs.

Thai Fragrant Rice or Jasmine Rice

This rice, produced in Thailand, has a flowery fragrance. It is a slightly sticky, long-grain rice and is used throughout Asia.

Converted Rice or 'American' Rice / Carolina Rice / Easy-cook Rice

All these are names for long-grain rice which has been 'converted' or parboiled, a process in which the unhulled rice is soaked then steamed before milling. The process gelatinizes the starch and concentrates the nutrients into the centre of the rice. This makes the rice slightly more nutritious than other types.

Converted rice has a yellowish, waxy colour before it is cooked. It cooks into separate, fluffy grains with a slightly chewy texture. The cooking time is slightly longer than for untreated rice but the rice is less likely to become mushy if overcooked.

Converted rice has a bland flavour that is suitable for making pilaf, salads or an accompaniment to casseroles.

Quick-cooking Rice

Quick-cooking rice has been partially cooked. The grains have been fissured to allow the heat to penetrate more easily when the cooking process is resumed.

Wild Rice

Wild rice is not actually a rice but a type of grass native to the Great Lakes region of North America. It has long, thin dark brown grains with a nutty flavour. It is best cooked by boiling. It will take longer to cook than white rice. It is done when it is tender and the grains have just started to split open. It can be served as an accompaniment to stews and other meat dishes or in salads. Wild rice is often paired with dishes using duck.

Wild rice is expensive so is frequently sold mixed with white rice. The wild rice sold in this way has been 'scarified' or scratched on the outside to make it cook more quickly so that it cooks in the same amount of time as the white rice.

Medium-grain Rice

Medium-grain rice has a slightly shorter grain than long-grain and has a lower amylose content, so does not harden when it cools. It is primarily grown in Italy, Spain and California. This type of rice can be cooked by either of the methods for cooking rice, below. It is particularly suitable for rice salads and rice pudding.

Italian Arborio Rice

This is a fat medium-grain rice grown in the Po Valley in northern Italy. The centre of each grain has a small area of undeveloped starch which, when used for risottos, results in a firm bite to the rice. The Italians refer to this texture as *al dente*, whilst the outer part of the rice becomes soft.

A risotto is made by adding boiling stock a ladleful at a time to the rice while stirring continuously. The rice should absorb up to 5 times its volume in liquid. There are several different types of risotto rice, each reputed to be best for certain types of risotto, although it is possible to substitute one for the other. Some risotto rices have short, nearly round grains (see *Mushroom Risotto*, below).

Arborio is also the best rice to use for rice cakes.

Paella Rice

This rice has a medium grain and gives a somewhat creamy finish to Paella. It is also marketed as Valencia or Bomba rice. Italian Arborio rice can be substituted for Spanish rice in recipes.

Camargue Red Rice

This attractive brownish-red rice is the result of an accidental cross-breeding in the south of France. It has a nutty flavour and a firm texture. It can be used in place of brown rice as an accompaniment to meat dishes and for rice salad.

Short-grain Rice

Short-grain rice is only a little longer than it is wide. It is high in the starch that makes it sticky so when it is cooked the grains tend to stick together. Because of this, it is the favoured rice in Asia where the stickiness makes it easier to eat with chopsticks. It is the rice used for making Sushi.

Risotto Rice

The Italian rices Carnaroli and Vialone Nano have short grains and can be used for risotto or rice pudding.

Pudding Rice

Pudding rice is a short-grain rice which is used for making into rice pudding. The rice is baked or simmered with sweetened milk and spices. Pudding rice is not suitable for cooking by the boiling or absorption methods.

Glutinous Black Rice

This rice from South-East Asia is used primarily for desserts, cooked with coconut milk, sugar and lemon grass.

Methods of Cooking Rice

55–85 g | 2–3 oz uncooked rice is the amount recommended per person at a Western meal where rice is the accompaniment to a meat dish.

Rice is cooked when the starch has gelatinized all the way through the grain. To see if it is done, break a grain in half. The white core should have disappeared. If the rice is not cooked through it will be hard to the bite. Recipes for risotto often require the rice to be cooked until *al dente*, an Italian expression meaning 'to the tooth'. Each grain will be cooked though but it will have some texture rather than being mushy. Brown rice will always take longer to cook than short-grain rice.

Boiling Rice

This method is most suitable for cooking long-grain rice to give fluffy, separate grains. It is not good for cooking short-grained rice because the grains have a tendency to become soggy. It is not necessary to soak the rice to remove the starch before cooking when using this method.

Cook the rice in a large quantity of simmering salted water: 1 litre | 1¾ pints water and 1 teaspoon salt per 110 g | 4 oz rice is sufficient. Do not boil the rice vigorously or the grains will break up and the rice will become waterlogged. Leave uncovered while boiling.

When the rice is done (see above), drain it in a sieve and rinse with a little cold water from the tap to stop the cooking process and wash away any remaining starch. Allow the rice to stand in the sieve for a few minutes to steam-dry.

To keep the rice warm, place it in a warmed covered serving dish in a low oven, 80°C | 175°F | gas mark ¼, for up to 30 minutes.

Approximate cooking times

Basmati and Thai rice	10 minutes
American long-grain	12 minutes
Easy-cook long-grain	15 minutes
Brown and red rice	30 minutes
Wild rice	45–55 minutes

Rice Salad

Almost any vegetables can be added to rice to make a salad, but it is important to have approximately equal quantities of rice and vegetables, or the result will be lifeless and stodgy. Add the dressing to the warm rice for the best flavour. The dressing should moisten, not soak, the rice.

SERVES 8

225 g|8 oz long grain rice
110 g|4 oz frozen peas
1 red pepper, cored, deseeded and diced
1 small stick of celery, chopped
¼ cucumber peeled, deseeded and chopped
1 tomato, peeled and cut into strips
2 tablespoons finely chopped fresh herbs, such
   as paisley, mint, chives or dill

For the dressing

4 tablespoons vegetable oil
1 tablespoon vingar
½ small onion very finely chopped
salt and freshly ground black pepper

1 Put all the dressing ingredients into a screw-top jar and shake to combine.
2 Boil the rice in plenty of salted water until just tender, about 10 minutes. About 4 minutes before the end of cooking, add the frozen peas.
3 Rinse the rice in cool water and leave to drain well.
4 Stir the dressing into the rice.
5 When the rice is completely cool, stir in the vegetables. Season with salt and pepper if necessary.

Absorption Method

This is the classic method of cooking all types of rice. It will give very different results depending on the type of rice used. To produce a fluffy rice with separate grains, use a long-grain rice. The rice must first be soaked and/or washed to remove excess starch which would cause the grains to clump together on cooking.

Some recipes call for soaking the rice in cold water for various lengths of time from 30 minutes to overnight. Others specify rinsing the rice in several changes of cold water until the water is clear. However, if separate grains of rice are desired, washing the rice until the water is clear is vital. Soaking the rice will slightly reduce the cooking time.

The rice can be cooked in stock instead of water and aromatic flavourings such as cinnamon stick, cardamom pods, saffron strands and/or peppercorns can be added to the pot. The rice will absorb the flavours during cooking.

The absorption method of cooking is used for rice Pilaf (see *Saffron Rice Pilaf*, below), a dish of Turkish origin, and Biryani, an Indian dish.

Place the washed rice in a heavy-based saucepan and cover with double the volume of water or stock. Add $\frac{1}{2}$ teaspoon salt unless the rice is to be served with Chinese food, in which case omit the salt. Bring to the boil, uncovered. Turn the heat down so that the water simmers, then cover the pan and cook for a further 8 minutes or until the surface of the rice is covered with little holes and the liquid has been absorbed by the rice. Turn off the heat. Place a tea towel under the lid of the pan, wrap it over the top and replace on the saucepan. The tea towel will catch any condensation and help to dry the rice. Leave to stand for 10 minutes, then fluff the grains with a fork to separate.

Saffron Rice Pilaf

SERVES 4

225 g | 8 oz Basmati rice

1 tablespoon ghee or butter

I small onion, finely chopped

2.5 cm | 1 in piece of fresh root ginger, peeled and grated

1 cinnamon stick, broken into 2.5 cm | 1 in pieces

6 cardamom pods, bruised

6 black peppercorns

4 whole cloves

570 ml | 1 pint White Chicken or Vegetable Stock (see **Stocks**, pages 689–90)

a large pinch of saffron strands

$\frac{1}{2}$ teaspoon salt

To garnish

1 small onion, thinly sliced

1 tablespoon ghee or oil

1 Place the rice in a large bowl and cover with cold water. Allow to stand for 30 minutes.

2 Heat the ghee or butter in a saucepan and stir in the onion. Cover the onion with a piece of damp greaseproof paper (a *cartouche*) and a lid and sweat until soft.

3 Remove the cartouche and stir in the ginger. Cook for a further 5 minutes.

4 Add the cinnamon, cardamom pods, peppercorns and cloves. Cook, stirring, for 1 further minute.

5 Drain the rice in a sieve and rinse under cold water until the water runs clear.

6 Add the rice to the saucepan and cook for about 2 minutes, stirring, until it turns opaque.

7 Stir in the stock, saffron strands, and salt and bring to the boil. Turn the heat down to a simmer, then cover the pan and cook for 20 minutes.

8 Meanwhile, fry the onion for the garnish in the ghee or oil until browned. Set aside.

9 Turn off the heat. Wrap a clean tea towel under the lid of the pan and replace the lid. The tea towel will absorb extra moisture from the rice. Allow to stand for a further 5 minutes.

10 Fluff the rice with a fork and remove the whole spices, if wished. Turn into a warmed serving dish and garnish with the fried onions.

Using a Rice Cooker

Most people for whom rice is a staple part of their diet cook their rice using a rice cooker. The rice cooker is particularly useful for cooking rice for a large number of people. Other advantages are that it needs little attention and will keep the rice warm for up to 1 hour.

The rice must first be washed, as above, to remove any excess starch. It is then placed in the rice cooker along with the liquid as specified in the manufacturer's instructions and the timer is set. Add a generous pinch of salt. Other flavourings such as ground spices or cinnamon sticks, cardamom pods or bouillon powder can be added.

Asian cooks use what they call 'the finger method' for measuring the water. After washing the rice, place it in the cooker and cover with enough water to come up to the first joint on your index finger when your finger is placed on the surface of the rice. Allow the rice to stand for about 10 minutes, then turn on the cooker. Cooking will take about 20 minutes. When the rice it is done, stir it through, using the handle of a wooden spoon to fluff up and separate the grains.

Mushroom Risotto

A good risotto should be creamy from the starch of the rice whilst the grains should have some texture (*al dente*). It is necessary to use an Italian rice specifically suited to making risotto (see above). The rice cooks by absorbing most of the stock, however constant stirring is required to emulsify the starch from the rice in the remaining stock.

SERVES 4

55 g｜2 oz butter	100 ml｜3 ½ fl oz white wine
1 large onion, finely chopped	about 1.2 litres｜2 pints boiling well-seasoned
55 g｜2 oz dried wild mushrooms	White Chicken or Vegetable Stock (see
1 clove of garlic, crushed	***Stocks***, pages 689–90)
225 g｜8 oz fresh mushrooms, wiped and sliced	55 g｜2 oz Parmesan cheese, freshly grated
300 g｜10 oz risotto rice	2 tablespoons finely chopped fresh parsley

1 Melt the butter in a sauté pan and gently cook the onion until soft.

2 Meanwhile, pour 100 ml｜3 ½ fl oz boiling water over the dried mushrooms and allow to stand for 20 minutes.

3 Stir the garlic into the onion and cook for 1 further minute.

4 Add the fresh mushrooms to the pan with the onion and cook, stirring, for 5 minutes.

5 Drain the dried mushrooms, adding the soaking liquid to the stock. Chop the mushrooms if necessary, then add to the risotto pan.

6 Stir the rice into the onion mixture to coat the grains with butter and cook for 2 minutes.

7 Gradually stir the stock into the rice, a ladleful at a time. Keep the heat under the pan hot enough so that the mixture continues to bubble gently. As the stock is absorbed by the rice, add another ladleful, stirring continuously. Continue adding stock in this way until the rice is cooked but still has a slight bite (*al dente*) and the mixture is of a creamy consistency. This process will take about 20 minutes.

8 Stir in all but 2 tablespoons of the Parmesan cheese. Let stand for 3 minutes then serve garnished with the parsley and the remaining Parmesan.

Storing Rice

Cooked rice is a potential source of food poisoning. It is a high protein food with a high moisture content, ideal conditions for bacterial growth. Refrigerate as soon as it is cold, within 1 hour, and use within 24 hours.

Rice Products

Rice flour is a fine powder made from plain rice. It is used in biscuits and cakes. It is slightly finer than ground rice. Substitute for ground rice.

Glutinous rice flour is made from glutinous rice and is used for thickening sauces and desserts in Asian cooking.

Ground rice is made by grinding long-grain rice to a powder. It has a slightly gritty texture and is used in baked goods.

Rice bran is the layer on the outside of the rice grain under the husk. It is high in soluble fibre. It has been found to be effective in lowering cholesterol.

Rice noodles are translucent noodles made from rice flour. They can be deep-fried to use as a garnish or as part of a dish, or they can be soaked to use in soup or as an accompaniment to stir-fries.

Rice paper is an edible, translucent paper made from the pith of an Asian shrub. It is used for baking confections such as macaroons and meringues. The paper sticks to the base of the confection. It can also be used to wrap delicate foods before deep-frying.

Rice wine is a sweet wine made from fermenting steamed glutinous rice. Japanese rice wine is known as Sake or Mirin wine. There are many varieties of Chinese rice wine. Rice wine is used for drinking and in cooking.

Oils for Salad Dressings

- **Extra virgin olive oil**

Extra virgin oil is extracted from olives by cold pressing, a process which retains the rich, fruity taste of the olive, often described as 'grassy' or 'peppery', and should be used for special salads and in dressings accompanying Mediterranean food. More refined olive oils are not as flavoursome and salad oil, a half-and-half mixture of extra virgin olive oil and vegetable oil, does equally well for basic salad dressing. Extra virgin olive oil is most often emulsified with white wine vinegar, red wine vinegar or balsamic vinegar. Top-quality olive oil is expensive and should be used for dressings where its flavour will be noticed and appreciated. Store olive oil in a cool, dark cupboard for up to 1 year. If refrigerated the oil will become cloudy but this will dissipate if allowed to come to room temperature.

- **Nut oils**

Walnut and hazelnut oils are strongly flavoured and highly scented so are usually diluted with a neutral oil such as groundnut (peanut) or sunflower in the proportions of 1 part flavoured oil to 2 parts neutral oil. They are best combined with aromatic vinegar such as sherry vinegar or balsamic vinegar. Nut oils have a tendency to become rancid very quickly. Store in a cool, dark cupboard for not more than 6 months.

- **Sesame seed oil**

Before the oil is extracted the sesame seeds are toasted, a process that dramatically strengthens the flavour of the oil. Sesame oil is extremely pungent and should be used in small quantities or diluted in the proportions of 1 part sesame oil to 3 parts neutral oil. Vinaigrettes scented with sesame oil are usually used to dress salads and foods of Asian origin. Suitable vinegars include rice wine vinegar and sherry vinegar. Store as for nut oils, above.

- **Neutral-flavoured oils**

Oils with a neutral taste are refined, with the result that their characteristic flavours and scent have been removed. The most commonly used neutral oils include groundnut, sunflower, safflower, corn, vegetable and grapeseed. Neutral oils provide a suitable background for flavoured vinegars. Equally, they are commonly emulsified with red and white wine vinegar. Store as for olive oil.

- **Salad oil**

For most vinaigrettes, salad oil is used. It is made up of half vegetable oil and half olive oil. Due to its neutral taste, salad oil provides a suitable background for most vinegars. Store as for olive oil.

- **Infused oil**

There are many varieties of flavoured oils available in the supermarkets, such as lemon, truffle and chilli oil. They can be used in combination with neutral flavoured oils, or alone if a stronger flavour is desired. Store as for nut oil.

Salad Dressings

Vinaigrette Dressings

Vinaigrette is a cold emulsion of a thin coating consistency, originating in France, hence its other common name, French dressing. It is made from a mixture of vinegar, oil, salt and pepper to which various flavourings may be added: finely chopped shallot and fresh herbs, garlic, mustard, honey, anchovies and capers. Lemon juice may often be used in place of vinegar or as an additional flavouring ingredient. Vinaigrettes are used mainly to dress green salads although they are also used for warm salads and other salads containing a variety of ingredients: cold vegetables such as tomatoes, asparagus, leeks, potatoes, artichoke hearts and avocado, and various kinds of boiled offal, chicken and seafood.

Dressings made with white wine vinegar are suitable for seasoning strong-flavoured leaves, such as endive, cos lettuce and chicory, whereas red wine vinegar dressings are preferable for seasoning delicate or rather flavourless salad leaves such as butter lettuce and mâche as it has a stronger, more complex taste.

Richer-tasting Vinaigrettes made with sherry or balsamic vinegar and nut oils are often used with strong, bitter-tasting leaves such as watercress or rocket. Dressings made with vinegar, infused with rosemary, tarragon or garlic or flavoured with fruit or vegetable purée, may be used to dress salads garnished with meat or fish.

The standard ratio of oil to vinegar in Vinaigrette is 3–4 parts oil to 1 part vinegar or lemon juice; however, the precise ratio will vary depending on the acidity of the vinegar and the oil, as well as personal preference.

Vinaigrettes are made by whisking oil and vinegar together to form a temporary, unstable emulsion. At room temperature the emulsion will separate into its 2 components within 15 minutes. If the Vinaigrette is chilled in the refrigerator, the emulsion will last longer as the oil becomes more viscous. Oil and vinegar emulsions can be stabilized with the addition of finely powdered dried mustard as it increases the attraction between the droplets of oil and vinegar.

A salad made from soft leaves should only be dressed immediately before serving, as the addition of the dressing will cause the leaves to wilt. Toss the salad leaves with the dressing in a large bowl, then transfer the dressed salad to a serving bowl. This keeps the serving bowl clean and grease-free.

Vinaigrette Dressing

1 tablespoon vinegar

a pinch of dry English mustard

salt and freshly ground black pepper

3–4 tablespoons oil

1 Combine the vinegar and seasonings in a small bowl.
2 Whisk together with a small sauce whisk to dissolve the seasonings.
3 Add the oil to the bowl in a steady stream, whisking constantly to establish the emulsion.
4 Taste the dressing on the food it will accompany and add more seasoning if necessary. If the dressing is too acidic, add more oil. If the dressing is too oily, add more salt.

Vinaigrette: What has gone wrong when...

The oil and vinegar have separated.
- Vinaigrette is an unstable emulsion and will separate on standing. Whisk again to bring it back together.

The dressing is bland and oily.
- Insufficient salt or vinegar was added to the dressing.

The dressing is very acidic.
- Too much vinegar/not enough oil was added to the dressing. Add more oil.

Salt crystals remain undissolved.
- They were both added after the oil or were not mixed with the water-based ingredients for long enough before the oil was added.

Dijon Mustard Dressing

Used to dress a wide variety of salads ranging from tomato salad to bitter-leaf salad.

SERVES 4

1 tablespoon red wine vinegar

1 teaspoon Dijon mustard

salt and freshly ground black pepper

3 tablespoons vegetable oil

1 tablespoon olive oil

1 Whisk the vinegar, mustard and seasoning together in a bowl until the salt has dissolved.
2 Whisk in the vegetable oil, followed by the olive oil. Taste and adjust the seasoning if necessary before serving.

Storing Vinaigrette

Vinaigrette is best freshly made but it can be stored in the refrigerator for up to 1 week.

Flavouring Vinaigrette

Fresh ingredients most often used to flavour dressings include finely diced shallot, crushed garlic and chopped fresh herbs. Acidic fruit juice such as lemon juice or puréed and strained soft fruit and vegetables can also be used with or in the place of vinegar to add colour and a fresh, sweet flavour. Flavoured Vinaigrette is often used to accompany warm or cold salads garnished with vegetables, meat or fish.

- The flavour and texture of finely chopped onion or shallot and crushed garlic should be softened by marinating in the dressing for at least 1 hour before it is required.
- Immediately before using, whisk the dressing to re-emulsify the ingredients.
- Add any freshly chopped herbs immediately before the Vinaigrette is to be used. If fresh herbs are added too far in advance they will discolour and lose their flavour.

Storing flavoured Vinaigrette
Flavoured dressing should be used within 24 hours.

Garlic and Herb Dressing

Used to dress Mediterranean salads such as Salade Niçoise, a composed salad of tuna fish, hard-boiled egg, tomatoes, cooked French beans, boiled new potatoes and anchovies.

SERVES 4

1 tablespoon wine vinegar
salt and freshly ground black pepper
½ clove of garlic, crushed

3–4 tablespoons olive oil
1 tablespoon finely chopped fresh mixed herbs

1 Put the vinegar, salt, pepper and garlic into a bowl and whisk until the salt has dissolved.
2 Whisk in the oil and leave to stand for at least 30 minutes in the refrigerator.
3 Just before serving, whisk the dressing to re-establish the emulsion and add the fresh herbs.

Garlic and Herb Dressing: What has gone wrong when...

The garlic tastes overpowering and has a crunchy texture.
- The dressing was not allowed to stand for long enough to soften the flavour and texture of the garlic.

The herbs have lost their fresh green colour.
- The herbs were added to the dressing too early and were discoloured by the vinegar.

Using Dairy Products to Stabilize Vinaigrette

Vinaigrettes may be stabilized and thickened with the addition of double or soured cream. The milk proteins act as weak emulsifiers, increasing the attraction between the oil and vinegar. Vinaigrettes made with the addition of cream are, as a result, richer and thicker and coat the salad ingredients more evenly. The cream may thicken in the presence of acidic ingredients such as vinegar and can be thinned with water. Do not use single cream as it will curdle in the presence of vinegar.

Soured Cream and Herb Dressing

SERVES 4

1 tablespoon white wine vinegar

salt and freshly ground black pepper

3 tablespoons oil

2 tablespoons soured cream

1–3 tablespoons chopped fresh mixed herbs

1 Whisk the vinegar and seasonings together until they have dissolved.
2 Whisk in the oil and then the cream until thickened and emulsified.
3 Add the herbs, taste and add more seasoning if necessary.

Storing Vinaigrette with added cream
The cream will thicken and deteriorate if the dressing is not used within an hour or so of making if not refrigerated. If refrigerated use with 48 hours.

Emulsified Vinaigrettes

An emulsified Vinaigrette is a basic Vinaigrette emulsified with whole eggs (see **Sauces, Savoury**, *The Emulsifying Properties of Egg Yolks*, page oo). Emulsified Vinaigrette dressings are thinner and lighter than cream-based or Mayonnaise-based dressings but are heavier and creamier than basic Vinaigrette. Its flavour is similar to that of Vinaigrette but it will not separate and coats salad leaves more evenly. Emulsified dressings are mainly used to dress leaves with a crisp texture or strong flavour. Dressing containing raw or partially cooked eggs should not be served to pregnant women, the very young, old or infirm.

Caesar Salad Dressing

This dressing is traditionally used to dress cos lettuce. If chunks of anchovy are preferred, add the anchovies to the salad when it is tossed with the dressing. Because of the partially cooked egg yolk, the dressing should be stored in the refrigerator for no longer than 24 hours and should not be served to pregnant women, the very young, old or infirm.

SERVES 4

1 small clove of garlic, crushed

1 tablespoon white wine vinegar

a pinch of dry English mustard

freshly ground black pepper

2 anchovy fillets, rinsed and finely chopped

1 egg, boiled in its shell for 1 minute

6–8 tablespoons olive oil

2 tablespoons freshly grated Parmesan cheese

squeeze of lemon juice

1 Place the garlic, wine vinegar, mustard, pepper, and anchovies in a liquidizer and whizz until smooth.

2 Crack the egg into the liquidizer bowl and scrape the cooked egg from inside the shell into the liquidizer. Whizz until smooth.

3 Drizzle the oil into the liquidizer, with the motor running, to establish the emulsion.

4 Add the cheese and process briefly.

5 The dressing should be of single-cream consistency. If it is too thick, add water, lemon juice or vinegar, depending on acidity.

Caesar Salad Dressing: What has gone wrong when...

The dressing has not thickened.

- The dressing has not emulsified properly as the oil was added too quickly.

Mayonnaise-based Dressings

Mayonnaise can be used as a base for thicker salad dressings or may be thinned with water and/or lemon juice to the consistency of double cream (see *Sauces, Savoury, Mayonnaise*, page 599). Mayonnaise-based dressings can be flavoured with strongly flavoured ingredients such as garlic, herbs, mustard, spices, capers, anchovies and blue cheese. These dressings are rich and heavy and are best used for Potato Salad (see *Potatoes, Boiled New Potatoes*, page 542) and Coleslaw (see below) or to dress crisp salad leaves such as iceberg, cos, curly endive and radicchio.

Mayonnaise can be used as a base for thicker salad dressings or may be thinned with water and/or lemon juice to double cream consistency (see *Sauces, Savoury, Mayonnaise*, page 599). Mayonnaise-based dressings can be flavoured with strongly flavoured ingredients such as garlic, herbs, mustard, spices, capers, anchovies and blue cheese. They are rich and heavy and are best used to dress potato salad, coleslaws or crisp salad leaves such as iceberg, cos, curly endive and radicchio.

Storing Mayonnaise-based Dressings

Mayonnaise-based dressings are stable emulsions and can be stored in the refrigerator for up to 2 days.

Coleslaw with Raisins and Walnuts

SERVES 4

225 g|8 oz firm white cabbage, very finely shredded

3 small carrots, peeled and coarsely grated

3 tablespoons Mayonnaise (see page 000)

1 teaspoon French mustard

1 teaspoon sugar

salt and freshly ground black pepper

a little cold water

1 tablespoon raisins

1 tablespoon chopped walnuts

1 Toss the cabbage and carrots together in a bowl.

2 Mix the Mayonnaise with the mustard and sugar, stir approximately half a tablespoon of water into the Mayonnaise to thin it to coating consistency (see **Sauces, Savoury**, page 599). Season with salt and black pepper to taste.

3 Combine the mayonnaise dressing with the cabbage and carrots.

4 Refrigerate for an hour before serving to allow the vegetables to soften slightly.

5 Stir in the raisins and walnuts: just before serving.

Flavoured Vinegars

Infused vinegars are used to add complexity to a dressing. Rosemary, tarragon and garlic flavoured vinegars are the most widely used and are made by simply immersing a few blanched sprigs of herb or one or two cloves of garlic in a bottle of white or red wine vinegar and leaving it to infuse for several weeks.

Herb vinegar

1 Blanch a selection of herbs (rosemary, thyme, tarragon, parsley) for 30 seconds.

2 Cool in iced water, wipe them dry in absorbent paper and place in a bottle of red or white wine vinegar.

3 Leave to macerate for at least a month before using.

Sauces, Savoury

A sauce is a hot or cold seasoned liquid usually thickened and served with or used as an integral part of a dish. The word comes from the Latin *salsus* (salted). The function of a sauce is to moisten, enhance and add flavour to the other ingredients making up a dish. Larousse defines a sauce as 'liquid seasoning for food'. A sauce can be anything from the juices in the frying pan or melted butter to sauces requiring more skill, such as mayonnaise. The 3 most important properties of an appetizing sauce are consistency, flavour and colour.

Although there are several different types of sauce, categorized later in this section, many have certain properties and preparation methods in common. These general techniques are described in the first part of this section, followed by recipes for individual sauces.

Making Sauces: Points to Remember

- Use heavy-based saucepans to ensure the even distribution of heat and to prevent the cooking sauce from burning or curdling.
- Use the best and freshest ingredients in season. Wine or alcohol used in sauces should be good enough to drink.
- Stocks and meat and fish glaces must be well flavoured.
- The consistency and viscosity of a sauce should enhance the texture of the food it accompanies.
- To enhance the sauce's shine, strain through a sieve, quickly whizz in a blender or mount it with a little extra diced butter, shaken in piece by piece.
- The sauce can be kept warm in a bain-marie (see *Sauce-making Terms*, above, and individual recipes).

Sauce-making Terms

Roux: A mixture of equal quantities of fat and flour used to thicken white, blond and brown sauces. There are three colours: white, blond and brown; the longer the roux is cooked, the darker its colour will be. To make it easier to incorporate the liquid into the roux, the fat quantity can be slightly higher, by about 10 per cent, than the flour quantity. This will produce what is called a 'slack roux'.

Flowing or syrupy: A sauce is described as flowing or syrupy when it moves like a thin syrup or single cream. It should drip freely from the tip of a spoon. If a finger is drawn along the back of a spoon coated in a flowing sauce, the mark made will disappear slowly as the sauce flows. This is also described as a light coating consistency. A flowing sauce is often used to flood the base of a plate.

Coating consistency: Most classic sauces are made to coating consistency with a body and texture similar to that of double cream. The sauce should coat the food to a depth of 2–3 mm | $\frac{1}{8}$ in without running off (see *napper*, below). When a spoon is dipped into the sauce, a thin, even coating of sauce will cover the back of the spoon. If a finger is drawn through the coating, the mark will remain and the sauce will not flow into the mark.

Another way to test the coating consistency of a sauce is to pour a little on to the base of a plate. Tip the plate at a shallow angle and watch the sauce move. It should flow slowly, like thick syrup, coating the base of the plate thinly and evenly. If the sauce is too thick, it will form a skin, which wrinkles when the plate is tipped, or worse, solidify as it cools.

Masking sauces are used to coat food evenly to a depth of 4–5 mm | $\frac{1}{6}$ in. The sauce will not flow. A masking sauce has the consistency of unset natural yoghurt and will cover the back of a spoon thickly: an indent will be left when a finger is passed through it. If a trail is made over the top of the sauce it will not flow together. Food is coated with a sauce of masking consistency by using the *napper* method.

Napper: To coat food evenly with a layer of sauce. Use a large basting or serving spoon. Hold the spoon near the bowl of the spoon with your hand over the top of the handle and fill it with the sauce. Pour the sauce from the side of the spoon whilst moving the spoon across the food being coated. The food should be coated with an even layer of sauce without any gaps.

Beurre manié: Literally, 'kneaded butter'. A stiff paste made from softened butter and flour that is whisked into a sauce then boiled to cook the flour and thicken the sauce. Beurre manié is used for thickening unmeasured quantities of liquid, such as the gravy for a stew.

Reduction: Liquid that has been boiled to concentrate the flavour and lessen the quantity.

To reduce: To boil a liquid rapidly to lessen the quantity, to concentrate the flavour and sometimes to thicken.

To deglaze: To add water or other cold liquid to a hot pan in which meat and/or vegetables have been browned to remove the brown colour from the pan. The liquid is called the *déglaçage* and is used to add colour and flavour to a sauce.

Glace: Stock that has been reduced until syrupy and allowed to cool to a rubbery paste.

Monter au beurre: To whisk small pieces of unsalted, cold butter into a hot but not boiling sauce, to thicken it slightly, to add richness and to make it shine.

Pass: To put through a sieve to remove any solid particles.

Slake: To mix a dry powder with a small amount of cool liquid, usually water, so that it will combine easily with a hot sauce.

Equipment used in sauce-making

Bain-marie or double boiler: A saucepan half filled with water with a bowl fitted over the top so the bottom of the bowl does not touch the water. A bain-marie is used for cooking heat-sensitive sauces such as Hollandaise. A bain-marie can be made using a roasting tin half-filled with water placed directly over the hob. The water should be held at a simmer. The sauce can be made in a porcelain pudding basin placed in the water but not directly over the heat source.

Bulb baster: A 20 cm|8 in tube with a bulb at the end, used for degreasing sauces. Squeeze the bulb to expel the air, push the tube into the liquid below the fat, then slowly release the pressure on the bulb to suck the liquid from below the fat.

Conical chinois or tammy sieve: A cone-shaped sieve made of very fine mesh. It is used to make sauces glossy and perfectly smooth by passing them through the sieve. If a sauce is to be mounted with butter (see *monter au beurre*, above) it should be passed through the chinois before the butter is beaten in.

Sauce whisk: a small whisk with a coiled loop used to whisk sauces and to add butter and *beurre manié* (see above) to sauces.

General Sauce-making Techniques

Thickening Sauces

Reduction

Reduction is the process of boiling a liquid in order to concentrate the remaining ingredients by evaporation. Reducing a sauce by boiling deepens its flavour and colour and improves its consistency and appearance, increasing its viscosity. By reduction, a sauce can be thickened without the addition of starches or emulsifying ingredients. Reduction sauces are either made from the cooking liquor in which meat, fish or vegetables have been steamed, poached, or simmered, or by deglazing the brown sediment (*déglacage*) from the bottom of a sauté pan with water, stock or alcohol following pan-frying. Reduction sauces include red and white wine sauces, pan sauces and many cream sauces.

To reduce a liquid: Use a wide, shallow pan placed over a high heat to boil the liquid most efficiently. The liquid remaining after boiling is termed the reduction. A recipe may ask the cook to reduce the sauce by half. This means that one half of the original volume should remain and will be twice as concentrated. Frequently the recipe will require the sauce to be reduced until it is *syrupy*. This means the sauce will have the consistency of a light syrup and will coat the back of a spoon lightly. A sauce must not be reduced too far or it will distract from the food it accompanies, either because it is too thick and cloying or because it is too strongly flavoured. If this happens, let it down (thin) with a little water.

Although reducing the water content of a sauce will improve the complexity of its flavour, the process also affects other compounds contained in the sauce. Some acids; and other strong-tasting compounds, such as alcohol and tannins in wine, have low boiling points and are boiled off with the water, improving the balance and softening and refining the flavour of the remaining sauce. These compounds, however, can also reduce the stability of a finished sauce, by curdling enriching ingredients such as cream.

To reduce a liquid to a highly concentrated essence, the pan will be almost dry (*au sec*). Stocks reduced until they have the consistency of a thick syrup are called a *glace*.

Recognizing the consistency of sauce by the way it boils: It is also possible to gauge the viscosity of a sauce made by the reduction technique by watching the bubbles on its surface as it boils. As the sauce becomes more concentrated, the bubbles become larger and move more slowly as the viscosity increases.

Seasoning: Reduction sauces are seasoned and flavoured in stages. Once the cooking liquor has been reduced it may be made more complex by adding wine or a spirit. The sauce is then reduced again, to evaporate the additional liquid as well as to boil off the alcohol and any other sharp-tasting compounds. When reducing a small quantity of wine or spirit, such as brandy, it is best to add a little water with it to prevent the wine or spirit from boiling away altogether. Once the sauce has become syrupy and glossy again, it can be served as it is, or the concentrated flavours may be softened with the addition of cream and reduced once more until the sauce reaches the required consistency (see *Cream Sauces*, below). Once the sauce has reached the required consistency and basic flavour it should be seasoned to taste. Never season a reduction sauce before it is fully reduced to prevent the risk of overseasoning.

Cream Sauces Made by the Reduction Method

Cream is often added to a reduced sauce and boiled briefly to balance and soften the flavour of the sauce, as well as to thicken it. Only double and whipping creams contain a sufficiently high proportion of butter fat to prevent curdling at high temperatures. The butterfat in cream forms a stable emulsion with water-based ingredients to thicken the sauce. Once double or whipping cream is added and brought to the boil, the sauce will thicken rapidly and reach coating consistency in a very short time. Low-fat alternatives such as yoghurt or single cream, on the other hand, split almost immediately.

Although double and whipping creams are relatively stable when subjected to heat, they will curdle if added to a sauce before the alcohol is boiled off or if the sauce reduction is very acidic. It is therefore important to reduce any alcoholic or other strongly flavoured ingredients fully to prevent the cream from curdling or over-reducing. Double cream or whipping cream can be made more stable before it is added to the reduction, by boiling it vigorously in a separate pan until it is reduced by half. This increases the butterfat-to-water ratio in the cream, so that it emulsifies more densely when it is stirred into the sauce.

Cream will also split if it is over-reduced as the butterfat no longer contains sufficient water to form an emulsion. If a cream sauce becomes too thick and starts to look oily around the sides of the pan, add water and stock to restabilize the emulsion and to thin and lighten the sauce once again. A sauce may also be thickened and made glossier with the addition of a small quantity of double cream although it will lose its clarity due to the higher proportion of milk solids present.

Thickening Sauces with Beurre Manié (Kneaded Butter)

Beurre manié is made by blending equal quantities of flour and softened butter together to form a paste. This is stirred into the boiling sauce in small pieces then boiled until the sauce reaches the required consistency. The flour provides the starch necessary for thickening the sauce while the butter enriches it, adds flavour and separates the flour granules, to facilitate their even dispersal through the liquid, thus preventing lumps of half-cooked flour from forming in the sauce. Beurre manié is mostly used to thicken stock-based sauces and hot stews.

Using beurre manié to thicken hot sauces:

1 Make 30 g | 1 oz beurre manié by thoroughly blending 15 g | ½ oz plain flour and 15 g | ½ oz softened butter to a thick paste.

2 Whisk small pieces of the beurre manié into the simmering sauce and continue to whisk until the sauce begins to thicken.

3 Continue to simmer the sauce for 2 minutes to lose the taste of raw flour and to develop the thickened consistency as the starch granules in the flour swell in the hot liquid. Strain to remove any lumps of beurre manié that have not been incorporated.

Thickening and Enriching Sauces with Egg Liaisons

Sauces can also by thickened and enriched with a combination of egg yolk and cream, called a liason. Liaisons are used mainly to thicken cream-based or roux-based sauces, such as velouté sauces. The sauce for the classic white stew, *Blanquette de Veau* (see **Meat**, *Veal*, page 379) is thickened with an egg and cream liaison. Sauces bound with egg yolks have a velvety texture.

The protein in the egg partially coagulates and binds with liquid when gently heated above $55°C | 130°F$. However, if the thickened sauce is allowed to get too hot it will curdle, with the protein coagulating into solid lumps and squeezing the liquid back into the sauce. This process is clearly visible as the sauce will become thin once again and lumps of egg will appear on the surface. As egg protein is so heat-sensitive, sauces thickened with egg yolks must be cooked with great care.

Using an egg and cream liaison:

Combining the egg yolk with cream raises the temperature at which the yolk proteins coagulate, making it easier to incorporate them into a sauce without curdling. Egg yolks start to coagulate at $55°C | 130°F$. Mixing them with cream raises the coagulation temperature to $82–85°C | 180–185°F$.

Use 2 egg yolks and $150 ml | \frac{1}{4}$ double or whipping cream to thicken $570 ml | 1$ pint sauce.

1 Whisk the egg yolk and cream together. Warm the egg yolks gently by slowly adding a small amount of the hot sauce while stirring continuously.
2 Stir the warmed liaison mixture into the sauce.
3 Warm the sauce, stirring, until it steams and thickens. Do not allow it to boil or the egg yolks will cook and the sauce will become grainy.
4 Pass through a fine chinois (see above) to catch any particles of cooked egg. Keep warm in a bain-marie (see above).

Thickening and Enriching Sauces with Butter (Monter au Beurre)

Monter au beurre (to mount with butter) refers to the process of swirling or whisking cold butter into a hot sauce to lighten and enrich its flavour, to provide gloss and to thicken its consistency. Brown, flour-based and pan sauces are most frequently finished with unsalted butter, used for its pure, delicate flavour. It is important to avoid cheap salted butters as they contain a high percentage of salted buttermilk and are likely to over-season the sauce.

To monter au beurre:

1 Chill the butter and cut into small dice. Keep cold.

2 Remove the boiling sauce from the heat.

3 Holding the pan firmly, whisk, shake or swirl a piece of butter into the hot sauce until it is fully incorporated. Agitating the butter and sauce in this way will allow the butter and sauce to thicken as it forms an emulsion.

4 Add the remaining butter piece by piece until all the butter is incorporated. The finished sauce should be smooth, glossy and of light coating consistency.

5 Do not return the sauce to the heat as this would cause the sauce to split.

6 Serve as soon as possible.

Thickening Sauces with Crème Fraîche

Crème fraîche is often used to thicken and add body to sauces. Full-fat crème frâiche has a delicious, slightly nutty flavour and can be used interchangeably with double or whipping cream. It is lightly acidulated and therefore tastes less rich than cream.

Low-fat crème fraîche is less stable and contains less butterfat than double cream, so cannot be heated above 80°C|175°F or it will separate. To use it in a hot sauce, whisk it in off the heat, without further cooking.

Thickening Sauces with Yoghurt

Yoghurt separates if heated above 80°C|175°F but can be whisked into a sauce, a spoonful at a time, to give a delicate acidity and creaminess. It is widely used in Indian curries. A teaspoon of cornflour dissolved in a little water and stirred into 150 ml|$\frac{1}{4}$ pint yoghurt will stabilize it before it is added to a hot sauce. Yoghurt is very useful to bulk out stiff cold mayonnaise sauces and cream sauces to reduce their calorie content.

Thickening Sauces with Blood

Blood is mainly used to thicken sauces served with game such as venison and hare. Blood used for cooking usually comes from pigs, rabbit or poultry. It is important that the blood is prevented from coagulating by adding a few drops of vinegar as soon as it is purchased. 150 ml|$\frac{1}{4}$ pint blood will thicken 1 litre|$1\frac{3}{4}$ pints sauce to a coating consistency, or a little more can be used if a thicker sauce is required. Blood, like egg yolk, contains a large quantity of protein and binds and thickens in exactly the same way. It must also be used with the same amount of care to prevent the protein from coagulating and the sauce from curdling.

Using blood to thicken sauces:

1 Slowly add enough hot sauce to warm and acclimatize the blood to the change in temperature and stir well.

2 Slake the warm blood and sauce mixture into the remaining hot sauce off the heat and stir well.

3 Replace the pan over a medium heat and cook the sauce until it thickens, stirring all the time.

4 As soon as the sauce begins to simmer, remove from the heat immediately and pass through a fine chinois into a clean pan. Keep it warm in a bain-marie and serve as soon as possible.

Thickening Sauces with Fécules

The term fécule is used to describe pure starch in the form of a fine flour, derived from corn (cornflour), the roots of tropical plants (arrowroot), rice or potatoes. Fécules are used widely, especially in Asian cooking, to thicken hot sauces and soups as they leave the liquid clear and glossy.

Fécules are used to thicken sauces at the end of cooking once they have been seasoned. Fecules thicken sauces by the gelatinization of starch, the process whereby starch granules absorb moisture when they are added to a liquid and heated. The sauce thickens as the liquid is absorbed. The cook does not want the sauce to reduce any further so requires a thickening agent that will work almost immediately.

Using fécules to thicken sauces:

Fecules must first be mixed with cool liquid. This process of mixing a powder with a liquid is known as 'to slake'. The solution is known as a slurry. The cool liquid separates the grains of starch and allows them to begin absorbing liquid without becoming lumpy. The starch slurry is added to either hot or cold liquid, depending on the fécule. Do not reheat or cook fécule-thickened sauces for a prolonged period as the starch granules break down and lose their thickening power.

- **Cornflour** must be slaked with a cold liquid which is then added to a hot liquid (or sauce) and boiled to thicken the liquid and to remove the floury taste. Stirring must be continuous as when the slurry is incorporated it thickens almost immediately on contact with hot liquid. Once the cornflour slurry is fully incorporated, the sauce must be cooked gently for about 5 minutes to remove the raw starch flavour.
- **Potato starch** thickens boiling sauces almost immediately and must be stirred rapidly to avoid lumps. On standing, the sauce will continue to clear, which may or not be an advantage, depending on the dish.
- **Arrowroot** must be slaked with a cold liquid. The slurry must only be added to cold liquids to avoid any risk of it becoming stringy. Once it is combined with the liquid to be thickened, heat the liquid and boil for 1 minute. Do not boil for longer or the starch might lose its thickening ability. Arrowroot is ideal for thickening dessert sauces where a clear syrupy finish is required: for example, a red wine sauce accompanying poached pears.

Thinning Sauces with Water or Stock

If a sauce is too thick or strong-tasting, the addition of water or unseasoned stock will soften the flavour and thin the sauce to the required viscosity. Once a reduction sauce is finished and removed from the heat a little water should be added to prevent it from thickening further as the sauce will continue to reduce due to the heat in the pan.

Finishing Sauces

To finish a sauce means to adjust the final consistency using the methods described above and to adjust the seasoning. To obtain a perfectly smooth, shiny sauce of coating consistency, strain the finished sauce through a fine chinois into a clean pan, serving dish or directly on to the plate. Thicker sauces with a masking or binding consistency should be pressed through a wire mesh sieve with the back of a ladle.

Seasoning and Balancing the Flavour of a Sauce

Although the basic ingredients that make up a sauce are often seasoned at the start of the cooking process, it is important to adjust the seasoning only once the sauce has reached the required finished consistency and any garnishing ingredients have been added. Before the finishing stages a sauce should only be tasted for its complexity and richness of flavour. Once the sauce is finished it should not be taken for granted that seasoning is necessary, especially with reduction sauces where the concentrated ingredients containing natural salts and sugars may provide sufficient seasoning. Before seasoning a sauce taste a full dessertspoon, moving it around the tongue in order to decide accurately which seasonings are required and in what quantities.

If the finished sauce tastes too bland, too sour, too sweet or too creamy, it is at this point that seasoning ingredients are added in small quantities, between tastings, until the required flavour is obtained. The 5 main seasonings used to enhance the flavour of a sauce are salt, pepper, sugar, vinegar and lemon juice

Seasoning a savoury sauce: If the sauce is too
- **bland:** Add salt, pepper, and/or lemon juice.
- **sweet:** Add salt or lemon juice or vinegar.
- **creamy and cloying:** Add a little water, lemon juice or vinegar to cut through the fat.
- **acidic:** Monter au beurre or add cream, sugar and salt.

If a finished sauce tastes too salty, it may be difficult to correct this without diluting and adding thickening ingredients, which in turn will dilute the other flavouring ingredients. Slight saltiness may be counteracted with a few drops of lemon juice or vinegar. To avoid making over-salty stock-based sauces, always use home-made stock as it does not contain salt.

The sauce might taste rounded and balanced but require a kick. The addition of freshly ground pepper just before serving will make the most of its lively flavour. A few drops of vinegar or lemon juice, added to a characterless sauce, especially one made with cream or butter, is effective for pepping up the taste.

Keeping Sauces Warm

Although sauces are often at their best when used or served immediately, many can be made in advance and kept warm for an hour, using a bain-marie. Instructions for keeping a sauce warm and for storage are given with each recipe.

Serving Sauces

A warm sauce is served by flooding the base of a warmed plate, or in a warmed sauce-dish or sauce-boat. Be careful not to overheat the plate or sauce-boat as the sauce may catch at the edges, lose excessive liquid, thicken further or, worse still, curdle.

Classification of Sauces

Many of the classic hot sauces are divided into mother and daughter sauces. The six principal sauces, collectively known as mother sauces, are White Sauce, Blond or Velouté Sauce, Brown or Espagnole Sauce, Mayonnaise, Hollandaise and Beurre Blanc. These base sauces or mother sauces can be used on their own or flavoured with a wide variety of ingredients to create daughter sauces. Other sauces, referred to as combination sauces, do not use the 'mother and daughter' categorization.

The Flour-thickened Sauces

White Sauce, Velouté Sauce and Brown Sauce are flour-thickened sauces. These are mother sauces, or bases, to which flavourings are added to create more complex sauces. They are made with a roux (see *Sauce-making Terms*, above). When liquid is added to the roux and the mixture is boiled, the roux thickens the sauce. In most cases a cold liquid is added to a warm roux. In instances where the liquid is hot, it is easier to combine the liquid with the roux if the roux is cooled before adding the liquid. A hot liquid added to a hot roux is likely to turn lumpy because the heat cooks the flour into lumps before they are beaten out.

The Thickening Properties of Roux

The following proportions of roux to liquid stand for white and blond roux. Flour browned to nut-brown for use in brown roux will lose much of its thickening property.

- 40 g | 1½ oz flour-quantity roux will thicken 570 ml | 1 pint liquid to a light coating consistency.
- 60 g | 2 oz flour-quantity roux will thicken 570 ml | 1 pint liquid to a coating consistency.

- 80 g|3 oz flour-quantity roux will thicken 570 ml|1 pint liquid to a heavy binding consistency.

The White Sauces

White sauce is a mother sauce made with a white roux, a mixture of nearly equal proportions of butter and flour, cooked without colour, and milk. Due to the plain taste of a basic white sauce it is rarely used without the addition of other flavouring ingredients. See the Sauce Table below.

White Sauce

20 g|¾ oz butter	290 ml|½ pint milk
20 g|¾ oz plain flour	salt and freshly ground white pepper

1 Melt the butter, then remove the pan from the heat and stir in the flour to make a smooth paste.
2 Place the pan over a medium heat and stir for about 1 minute, until the roux bubbles. Remove the pan from the heat and allow to cool for about 1 minute.
3 Gradually add the milk, about 1 tablespoon at a time, stirring vigorously and constantly to remove lumps. When half the milk has been added and the mixture is smooth, add the remaining milk in one addition.
4 Return the pan to the heat and cook over a medium heat, stirring continuously until boiling.
5 Boil for 2 minutes to cook the flour and make the sauce shine.
6 Season with salt and pepper.

Daughter Sauces of White Sauce

Mornay Sauce

Mornay sauce is a cheese sauce used for Cauliflower Cheese, Macaroni Cheese, etc. It is made by adding ½ teaspoon dry English mustard and a pinch of cayenne pepper to the roux in the above recipe for White Sauce. After the sauce has boiled, add 55 g|2 oz finely grated cheese, such as Cheddar or Gruyère, and 15 g|½ oz freshly grated Parmesan. Do not boil the sauce once the cheese has been added or the cheese might become stringy and make the sauce greasy.

Béchamel Sauce

Béchamel is a variation of White Sauce made using milk infused with onion, mace, cloves, parsley stalks and bay leaves. It can be used on its own or can be flavoured with additional ingredients. Béchamel Sauce should be rich, creamy and absolutely smooth, with a shine and no hint of graininess. The flavours of onion and clove should be apparent but not overwhelm the clean, milky taste of the sauce. It should be the consistency of double cream so that it is thick enough to coat or bind foods lightly but not so thick that it tastes of the roux. Béchamel Sauce is used for egg, vegetable, pasta and gratin dishes.

Béchamel Sauce is made by heating the milk until it steams with 1 slice of onion, 1 blade of mace, a few fresh, bruised parsley stalks, 4 white peppercorns, and 1 bay leaf. Allow to stand for 10 minutes for the flavours to infuse. Strain the milk and use in the White Sauce recipe above.

The sauces listed in the table below are made with White Sauce or Béchamel Sauce. Due to the aromatic flavouring ingredients used to make Béchamel, the sauces listed below made with Béchamel will be more complex than those made with a plain White Sauce. The flavouring ingredients are added to the finished sauce.

White Sauce: Daughter Sauces

Daughter sauce	Flavouring ingredients	Served with
Anchovy	Anchovy butter	Fish poached in court bouillon, fish quenelles
Béchamel	Onion, bay leaf, mace, peppercorns	Fish, pasta, vegetables
Crème	Cream	Chicken, fish, eggs, vegetables
Egg	Sieved hard-boiled egg yolk, finely diced egg white, finely chopped fresh parsley	Fish, chicken, ham, potatoes
Green	Blanched watercress	Fish, chicken
Cheese (Mornay)	Strong-tasting cheese: Cheddar, Gruyère and/or Parmesan	Eggs, vegetables, gratins, fish, pasta and gnocchi
Onion (Soubise)	Onions sweated in butter	Lamb, vegetables, gammon
Parsley	Finely chopped fresh parsley	Boiled ham and poached chicken

The Velouté Sauces

Velouté sauce is made by thickening White Stock, made from fish, veal or chicken bones (see *Stocks*, page 689), with a blond roux. The ivory-coloured sauce should have a mild flavour of meat or fish from the stock. It should be thick enough to coat food lightly.

A blond roux is made by cooking the flour and butter mixture while stirring for about 5 minutes over a medium heat until the flour turns straw-coloured and smells faintly biscuity.

Velouté Sauce

20 g | ¾ oz butter
20 g | ¾ oz plain flour
290 ml | ½ pint White Stock, strained and well skimmed (see **Stocks**, page 689)

2 tablespoons double cream
salt and freshly ground white pepper
a few drops of lemon juice

1 Melt the butter in a heavy saucepan.
2 Remove from the heat and stir in the flour to make a smooth paste. Cook the paste over a low heat, stirring, until the flour turns straw-coloured and smells nutty. Remove from the heat.
3 Gradually stir the cool stock into the roux to make a smooth sauce.
4 Return to the heat and bring to the boil, stirring. Boil for 2 minutes until slightly syrupy.
5 Stir in the cream and season with salt, pepper and lemon juice.
6 Pass through a chinois or fine sieve.

Velouté Sauce: Daughter Sauces

Name of sauce	Flavouring ingredients	Garnished with	Finished with	Served with
Aurore	Meat stock, tomato purée		Butter	Eggs, white meat, poultry
Poulette	Chicken stock, mushroom liquid reduction, lemon juice	Parsley		Chicken
Mushroom	Meat or fish stock	Mushrooms		Chicken or fish
Supreme	Chicken stock		Cream	Chicken

Egg yolk and cream liaison
Sauces of the Velouté family are sometimes finished with a liaison of egg yolk and double cream that is added to a sauce to enrich and slightly thicken it. When this liaison is added to Velouté Sauce along with lemon juice, the resulting sauce is called an Allemande Sauce. (See *Methods of Sauce-making*, above.)

Storing White Sauces

Sauces can be an excellent medium for the growth of bacteria. If they are to be kept warm before serving they should be held above 65°C | 170°F. Ladle a little melted butter over the surface of the sauce to prevent a skin from forming. Flour-thickened sauces can be made up to 2 days in advance if kept in the refrigerator. Place a piece of greaseproof paper directly on the surface to prevent a skin from forming. Boil the sauce for 2 minutes upon reheating. Sauces of the White Sauce family tend to become grainy when frozen. Velouté Sauces freeze well as long as they do not contain a large proportion of dairy products.

Gravy

Gravy is made from the pan juices (known as God's Gravy) of poultry, beef, lamb or pork after roasting. Gravy is often thickened with blond or brown roux made from flour and some of the dripping collected in the roasting pan and stock. In Britain, pork gravy is traditionally the thickest, made to the consistency of double cream, followed by lamb, then chicken, made to the consistency of single cream, then beef, which is the thinnest. Properly made pan gravy should have a strong, meaty taste.

The flavour of gravy is often enhanced with the addition of red or white wine and other ingredients, such as herbs or redcurrant jelly for lamb gravy. Season the meat with salt and pepper on the work surface, before placing it in the roasting pan. This is to avoid seasoning collecting in the roasting pan and over-seasoning the roasting juices used to make the gravy.

Although gravy is traditionally thickened with roux in Britain, the French prefer to deglaze the roasting pan with a little stock or wine and reduce the juices and other liquid ingredients to a syrupy consistency. Dishes served with this sauce are described as '*au jus*'.

Gravy

SERVES ABOUT 4

1 onion, sliced	290 ml ½ pint Stock (see **Stocks**, page 682)
20 g 2 tablespoons plain flour	salt and freshly ground black pepper

1 45 minutes before the end of the roasting time, add the onion to the bottom of the roasting tin.
2 When the meat is cooked, remove it to a warmed serving platter and keep warm by tenting loosely with aluminium foil.
3 Pour off all but 2 tablespoons of fat from the roasting tin, leaving the onion and any brown sediment in the pan. If there is not enough fat, add vegetable oil as required.
4 Stir in the flour, then place over a medium heat and cook, stirring with a wooden spoon, until the flour takes on a medium-brown colour. Always cook it to a darker colour than that required of the finished gravy.
5 Remove from the heat, then stir in the stock.

6 Return to the heat and bring to the boil for 2 minutes to cook the flour, then simmer for at least 10 minutes.

7 Adjust the consistency by boiling or by adding water.

8 Season, then pass through a sieve and serve in a warmed gravy-boat.

VARIATIONS

To add wine to gravy: Boil 100 ml | 3½ fl oz wine in a small saucepan until reduced by half. Stir into the gravy after the stock has been added.

To add recurrant jelly: Whisk in 1–2 tablespoons jelly while the gravy is simmering.

To add fresh herbs: Chop the leaves of the herbs and stir into the gravy after sieving.

Gravy for roast chicken: Make as above but only cook the roux until it is straw-coloured. Use White Chicken Stock (see **Stocks**, page 689).

Flour-thickened Sauces: What has gone wrong when...

The sauce is lumpy.

- The liquid was added to the roux too quickly.
- The sauce was not stirred thoroughly enough.

    To correct, whisk vigorously with a sauce whisk, whizz in a blender or pass the sauce through a sieve, then bring back to the boil for 1 minute, stirring constantly.

The sauce is too thick.

- The sauce has reduced excessively while cooking.
- Too much flour was used.

    To correct, slowly stir more water or stock to the sauce.

The sauce is too thin.

- Too much liquid was added.
- The sauce has not boiled for long enough.
- Not enough flour was used.

    To correct, boil while stirring to reduce, or add a spoonful of beurre manié (see *Sauce-making Terms*, above) to the hot sauce, or make another roux in a clean pan and add the sauce to it. Simmer for 2 minutes to cook the newly added flour.

The Brown or Espagnole Sauces

Brown Sauce, also known as Espagnole Sauce, is the mother sauce of the Brown Sauce family. As with the White and Velouté Sauce families, it is made using a roux of equal proportions of flour and fat. However, the roux for a Brown Sauce is cooked until it becomes a deep brown colour. This takes 6–8 minutes over a low heat. Oil or clarified butter is used for this roux because ordinary butter would burn during the time it takes for the flour to become brown. When flour is browned it loses much of its thickening power, so brown roux is used mainly to add a smooth, velvety texture to Brown Sauces which are then reduced to the required consistency. When a thicker sauce is required, twice as much brown roux as white may be necessary to thicken a given volume of liquid.

A *mirepoix* of vegetables – cubed carrot, onion and celery – is cooked in the oil until golden-brown and a little tomato purée is added for a more complex flavour and deeper colour in the finished sauce. Brown Stock (see **Stocks**, page 692) is used for the liquid component of the sauce.

Espagnole Sauce should have a syrupy consistency, a deep brown colour and a complex meat and vegetable flavour without sweetness.

Espagnole Sauce

A small amount of flour is added to this sauce for texture. Brown the flour by placing it in a baking pan in the oven preheated to 150°C│300°F│gas mark 2 for about 20 minutes, stirring occasionally, until the flour is light brown.

SERVES ABOUT 2

2 tablespoons oil

1 tablespoon carrot, cut into 1 cm│½ in dice

1 tablespoon celery, cut into 1 cm│½ in dice

2 tablespoons onion, cut into 1 cm│½ in dice

2 teaspoons plain flour, browned

½ teaspoon tomato purée

570 ml│1 pint Brown Stock (see **Stocks**, page 692)

a few button mushrooms

1 bouquet garni (2 parsley stalks, 2 bay leaves and 1 blade of mace, tied together with string)

1 Heat the oil in a sauté pan. Add the carrot and celery and fry over a medium-low heat until they begin to soften and shrivel. Add the onion and continue to fry until the vegetables are evenly cooked to a pale brown.

2 Stir in the flour and continue to cook slowly, stirring continuously, until the vegetables are a deep brown. Add the tomato purée and cook to caramelize.

3 Remove the pan from the heat. Stir in three-quarters of the stock to make a smooth sauce. Add the mushrooms and bouquet garni.

4 Return to the heat and bring to a simmer. Skim thoroughly to remove any fat and scum. Add a splash of cold stock to the boiling liquid to help bring the scum and fat to the surface.

5 Transfer the sauce and vegetables to a small saucepan and simmer for about 2 hours, skimming as required. The vegetables should be covered with liquid at all times. Add more stock as necessary.

6 Pass through a chinois. Do not press the vegetables or they might break up and make the sauce cloudy.

7 Boil to reduce as required. See *General Sauce-making Techniques*, above.

Storing Espagnole Sauce

Espagnole Sauce can be kept in the refrigerator for up to 2 days. Place a piece of clingfilm or greaseproof paper directly on the surface. Boil before using. Espagnole Sauce can also be frozen. Daughter sauces should be stored in the same manner unless their added ingredients would spoil.

Demi-glace

Demi-glace is made up of equal quantities of Espagnole Sauce and Brown Stock (see **Stocks**, page 692), reduced to a syrupy consistency. It can be finished with a small quantity of reduced Madeira to make a Madeira Sauce.

Espagnole Sauce: Daughter Sauces

Many of the daughter sauces in the Brown Sauce family are made with a base of Demi-glace Sauce to give them a more pronounced flavour of roasted meat.

Brown Sauce: Daughter Sauces

Name of sauce	Flavouring ingredients	Garnished with	Finished with	Served with
Bordelaise	Red wine, shallots	Poached sliced beef marrow	Butter, parsley	Roast fillet of beef, tournedos, game, pigeon
Chasseur (Hunter's Sauce)	White wine	Sautéed shallots, mushrooms and tomato concassé	Chopped fresh parsley, tarragon	Sautéed chicken, kidneys, veal chops, medallions and escalopes
Poivrade		Cracked peppercorns	Butter	Marinated meat and game
Madeira	Dry Madeira		Port	Veal, pork, chicken
Périgueux	Dry Madeira	Finely diced truffles		Individual portions of game, poultry and meat
Mushroom	Dry Madeira	Sautéed mushroom caps or sliced mushrooms	Butter	Grilled meat or sautéed meat
Robert	Sweated onion, Dijon mustard, dry white wine		Parsley, cream	Roast pork, grilled pork chops and kidneys
Reforme	Cracked black pepper, reduced vinegar	Finely diced gherkins, hard-boiled egg white, button mushrooms, pickled tongue and truffles	Butter	Lamb cutlets or to fill an omelette

Espagnole Sauce: What has gone wrong when...

The sauce is cloudy.

- The sauce was boiled vigorously while the vegetables were in the sauce and they have broken down.
- The sauce was not skimmed adequately.
- The vegetables were pressed when the sauce was sieved.

The sauce has a sweet flavour.

- Too much carrot was used.
- Too much tomato purée was used.

The sauce has an orange colour.

- Too much tomato purée was used.

The sauce has a bitter flavour.

- The vegetables burnt during browning.

The sauce has a pale colour and an insipid flavour.

- The vegetables were not adequately browned.
- The roux was not adequately browned.
- The stock was of poor quality.

Jus Lie

A properly made jus lie is rich, smooth and of syrupy consistency so that it clings lightly to food. Jus lie should also be dark brown with a glossy shine resulting from its high gelatine content. Jus lie is used instead of Espagnole or Demi-glace Sauce when a Brown Sauce with a lighter consistency is required. Jus lie is easier to make than Demi-glace, but will only be as good as the stock used to make it. It can be made in 3 ways:

Jus Lie: Method 1

A rich Brown Stock (see *Stocks*, page 692) can be thickened with cornflour or arrowroot. Mix 1 teaspoon cornflour or arrowroot with 1 tablespoon cold water per 290 ml|½ pint stock. Mix into the reduced stock and boil (see *General Sauce-making Techniques*, above).

Jus Lie: Method 2

Reduce a rich Brown Stock (see *Stocks*, page 692) made with bones high in gelatine such as pig's feet, calves feet and veal bones. The natural gelatine will help to thicken the jus, giving it a syrupy texture. Sauces made from reduced stock tend to have a richer flavour.

Jus Lie: Method 3

If you do not have a good brown stock available to use as above, the following recipe using white stock makes a delicious jus.

Chicken and Thyme Jus

SERVES 6–8

450 g | 1 lb chicken wings	4 sprigs of fresh thyme
2 tablespoons sunflower oil	1 bay leaf
1 leek, sliced	1 sprig of fresh parsley
1 small carrot, sliced	6 black peppercorns
1 stick of celery, sliced	290 ml | ½ pint dry white wine
2 shallots, sliced	425 ml | ¾ pint dry red wine
2 tomatoes, halved and de-seeded	3 litres | 5¼ pints well flavoured White Stock,
2 cloves of garlic, bruised	made with chicken bones

1 Brown the chicken wings thoroughly in the oil in a large saucepan. Lift out and set aside.

2 Add the leek, carrot, celery and shallots to the pan and fry over a low heat until golden-brown. Add the tomatoes and garlic and cook for a further 2–3 minutes. Add the herbs and peppercorns. Remove any excess oil.

3 Pour over the white wine, bring to the boil and allow to simmer slowly until the wine is reduced to 1–2 tablespoons. Return the browned chicken wings to the pan.

4 Add the red wine to the pan and bring to the boil, then lower the heat, add the stock and cook very slowly for 2–3 hours, skimming frequently. On no account allow the liquid to boil.

5 Strain into a clean saucepan, discarding the bones and vegetables. Bring to the boil, then lower the heat and allow to simmer until the liquid is reduced until syrupy. Strain through a chinois and season to taste with salt and pepper.

Making a Gastrique

A gastrique may also be used to give a sweet-and-sour flavour and a deeper brown colour to sauces made with stock. Caramelize a small amount of sugar to a dark brown colour (see *Caramel*, page 174). Add a splash of vinegar and stir until the caramel has dissolved. Reduce by half to boil off the sharp-flavoured compounds in the vinegar. Add as required to a Brown Sauce.

Emulsified Sauces

Mayonnaise, Hollandaise, and Beurre Blanc are emulsified mother sauces. They are made by forming a suspension of tiny droplets of fat such as oil or melted butter in a liquid such as water, vinegar or lemon juice. Depending upon the ingredients and techniques used to form the suspension, Emulsified Sauces vary widely in stability and consistency.

Emulsified Sauces of flowing consistency, such as salad dressings (see *Salad*

Dressings, page 572) tend to fall out of suspension in a matter of minutes. These emulsions are described as 'unstable'. Sauces, such as Mayonnaise and Hollandaise, however, with thick coating or even masking consistency, can be held in suspension for hours or even indefinitely and are termed 'stable' emulsions.

The Emulsifying Properties of Egg Yolks

Mayonnaise and Hollandaise Sauce depend upon egg yolks to form stable emulsions. Egg yolks contain water, fat and a large quantity of an emulsifying protein called lecithin. An emulsifier helps other substances that would not normally combine, such as oil and water, to come together. Lecithin has the unique ability to combine with both oil and water, binding to and coating each oil droplet and attaching itself to the surrounding aqueous liquid. The oil droplets are thus held in suspension, evenly distributed in the liquid to create a stable emulsion. One egg yolk will form a stable emulsion with up to 200 ml | 7 fl oz oil or 55 g | 2 oz melted butter. The balance of lecithin, vinegar and oil, as well as the action of whisking, is crucial to achieve an emulsion. The higher the proportion of oil to vinegar, the thicker the sauce will be. The higher the proportion of vinegar to oil, the thinner the sauce will be. If the proportion of oil to liquid becomes too great, the emulsion will split, i.e. the oil and liquid will separate.

Emulsified Sauces: Points to Remember

- Use fresh eggs.
- Have all ingredients at room temperature.
- Use clean equipment.
- Do not mix a fresh sauce with an old sauce.

Mayonnaise

Mayonnaise is made with egg yolks so it is a stable emulsion. The egg yolks are not cooked so there is a risk of salmonella infection. The very young, old, pregnant women, and people with impaired immune systems should not consume Mayonnaise made with fresh eggs. Dried pasteurized eggs can be used to avoid the risk of food poisoning.

The formation of an emulsion can be helped by using room-temperature ingredients as well as a little salt and dried English mustard. The addition of salt thickens the egg-yolk base and assists the formation of an emulsion. Dry mustard is a fine powder that coats the oil droplets and helps to keep them apart, in fact it is the only 'dry' emulsifying ingredient.

Mayonnaise is a thick sauce. It should be thick enough to hold its shape in a mound. It is used as a spread in sandwiches, as a dip or as a binding ingredient. It is thought that it originated in the town of Mahón, in Minorca. Mayonnaise can be served just as it is with cold poached or roast chicken, cold crab, lobster, prawns and langoustines, or with poached fish such as salmon, hake and cod. Alternatively, strong-flavoured ingredients such as capers, cornichons, shallots, garlic, finely chopped fresh herbs, blanched celeriac, curry spices, tomato sauce or mustard can be added to make a wide range of cold classic daughter sauces.

A neutral-flavoured vegetable oil or salad oil (half vegetable oil, half olive oil) is most often used to make classic Mayonnaise. Olive oil alone tends to make very viscous, strong tasting Mayonnaise and contains substances that reduce the emulsifying properties of lecithin. As a result, Mayonnaise made entirely with olive oil can be oily and unstable. White wine vinegar is used for a basic Mayonnaise but tarragon vinegar is often used to add flavour to the sauce. The lecithin will emulsify most efficiently if the eggs are as fresh as possible and at room temperature. The seasoning ingredients, vinegar and/or lemon juice, salt, pepper and dry English mustard, must be used carefully so that the Mayonnaise tastes delicate and no one ingredient dominates the flavour of the sauce. Mayonnaise tends to be more highly flavoured with lemon juice when served with fish and should contains more vinegar when served with vegetables.

Mayonnaise

MAKES 290 ML $\vert$ ½ PINT

2 egg yolks	up to 1 tablespoon white wine vinegar
salt and freshly ground white pepper	150 ml $\vert$ ¼ pint each olive oil and vegetable oil
1 teaspoon dry English mustard	a squeeze of lemon juice

To make by hand:

1 Put the yolks into a small bowl with a pinch of salt, half the mustard and a few drops of vinegar. Beat well with a wooden spoon.
2 Add the oil, literally drop by drop from the prongs of a fork, beating continuously with the wooden spoon. Beat the mixture until the oil is no longer visible on the surface or on the sides of the bowl.
3 When the mixture has thickened, trickle the oil into the bowl, using a teaspoon, beating constantly to incorporate the oil. If the mixture looks oily on the surface, beat in a drop or two of lemon juice or water. Continue to beat the Mayonnaise until all the oil has been incorporated.
4 Season to taste with salt and pepper and add the remaining vinegar or lemon juice if necessary.
5 If the mixture starts to split (separate), beat the split mixture into a new yolk. Increase the amount of oil in the recipe accordingly.

To make by machine:

Mayonnaise can be made in a food processor or with an electric hand-held whisk. A machine is recommended for making larger quantities of Mayonnaise. For this technique to be successful there must be sufficient egg yolks to cover the rotary blade in the machine. Use 1 whole egg in place of 2 egg yolks per 290 ml|½ pint oil.

1 Place the egg, dry mustard, a drop of vinegar and a pinch of salt in the bowl of a food processor (using the metal rotary blade) or blender.
2 Whisk on high speed until frothy.
3 Add a small amount of lemon juice or vinegar to the egg mixture and whisk to combine.
4 With the processor on high, very slowly trickle in the oil until the mixture thickens and an emulsion is established.
5 Pour the oil into the bowl in a slow, steady stream. The Mayonnaise can now be whipped at a slightly slower speed so that its consistency can be watched more clearly. A small amount of liquid can be added if the Mayonnaise becomes too thick.
6 Once all the oil has been added to the Mayonnaise, switch the machine off and taste and adjust the seasoning if necessary.

Storing Mayonnaise

Mayonnaise should be stored in the refrigerator as it contains uncooked eggs. If the refrigerator is a little too cold it may slightly reduce the stability of the egg and oil emulsion. This can be seen as an oily film on the surface of the Mayonnaise and is easily rectified by briefly beating the Mayonnaise to re-emulsify the small quantity of separated oil. Although the vinegar content will inhibit the growth of bacteria, Mayonnaise should be consumed within 24 hours. To avoid the risk of salmonella poisoning use pasteurized egg yolks.

Mayonnaise: What has gone wrong when...

The Mayonnaise is too thick and appears oily on the surface.
- Insufficient liquid was added. Add a little water or vinegar.
- The Mayonnaise has become too cold. This can happen when Mayonnaise is refrigerated. To correct, allow the mayonnaise to warm until it is just below room temperature, then beat it vigorously. Beat in a little lemon juice, vinegar or water, depending on the flavour.

The Mayonnaise has split or curdled into coagulated flecks of egg and oil.
- The oil was added too quickly.
- The mixture wasn't beaten vigorously enough.
- Cold ingredients were used.

Rescuing curdled Mayonnaise
If the mayonnaise curdles and water will not re-emulsify it, start again with a new yolk in a clean bowl. Using a fresh egg yolk, trickle the curdled mixture on to the beaten yolk, adding water if the Mayonnaise becomes too thick and oily. Adjust the quantity of oil in the recipe accordingly.

Mayonnaise: Daughter Sauces

Name of sauce	Flavouring ingredients	Garnished with	Served with
Aïoli	Crushed garlic		Raw vegetables or fried fish, fish soup
Elizabeth	Curry powder, apricot chutney or jam, sweated onions, tomato purée	Cream or plain yoghurt	Cold poached chicken
Green	Blanched watercress		Cold poached salmon or trout
Marie Rose	Tomato ketchup, creamed horseradish, Worcestershire sauce, Tabasco, lemon juice		Prawns
Remoulade	Tarragon, chervil, Dijon mustard	Chopped capers, gherkins and anchovy fillets	Cold chicken
Rouille	Crushed garlic, red chilli, puréed red pepper		Fish soup
Tartare	Chopped capers, gherkins, shallots, parsley, lemon juice		Fried fish

Elizabeth Sauce

This sauce was invented by the staff at the Cordon Bleu School for the Coronation of Queen Elizabeth II in 1953 and has become a classic. At Leiths we often substitute 150 ml|¼ pint Greek yoghurt for half of the mayonnaise to make a lighter version of the sauce.

If making the sauce in large quantities, cut the water amount by half. The cooking time for the sauce will be longer. Make sure the paste is thick or the sauce will be too runny to adhere to the chicken.

SUFFICIENT FOR 1 1.8 KG|4 LB CHICKEN, POACHED

1 small onion, finely chopped

2 teaspoons oil

2 teaspoons curry powder (see **Spices**, page 671)

½ teaspoon tomato puree

3 tablespoons water

1 small bay leaf

4 tablespoons red wine

2 teaspoons apricot jam

1 slice of lemon

1 teaspoon lemon juice

290 ml|½ pint mayonnaise

2 tablespoons double cream

salt and freshly ground black pepper

1 Place the onion in a small saucepan with the oil. Cover with a piece of dampened greaseproof paper (a *cartouche*) and a lid. Cook the onion over low heat until softened.

2 Add the curry powder and fry gently for 1 minute.

3 Add the tomato puree, water, bay leaf, wine, jam, lemon slice and juice and simmer until the mixture becomes a thick paste, about 10 minutes. Stir frequently.

4 Strain the mixture, pushing as much as possible through the sieve or process in a food processor until smooth. Leave to cool.

5 Use the cold paste to flavour the mayonnaise to the desired strength.

6 Half whip the cream and fold into the sauce.

Hollandaise Sauce

Hollandaise Sauce is a warm emulsion of egg yolks and butter. Hollandaise is classically flavoured with a reduction, which is made from white wine vinegar boiled with a bay leaf, a blade of mace and peppercorns until the quantity is reduced by two-thirds. The reduction process boils off sharp-tasting compounds in the vinegar and allows the aromatics to infuse the liquid with their flavour. A properly made Hollandaise Sauce is smooth, with a thick coating consistency. It should show no signs of oiliness or curdling. Hollandaise Sauce forms the basis for daughter sauces such as Béarnaise and Maltaise Sauce. On its own, Hollandaise traditionally accompanies poached, steamed and grilled fish, poached eggs, and fresh asparagus.

Hollandaise Sauce can be made by several different methods. Each depends upon vigorous beating to break down the fat molecules to a very tiny size, and gentle heat to partially coagulate the egg proteins in order to stabilize the emulsion of fat, liquid and egg yolk. By beating the egg yolks vigorously while slowly adding melted butter, the lecithin from the egg yolk coats the individual butterfat droplets and holds them in suspension in the vinegar. It is critical not to overheat this mixture or the egg yolks will cook, giving the sauce a curdled appearance. Egg yolks begin to coagulate at 55–$60°C \mid 130$–$140°F$. The cooked protein contracts and squeezes out the oil and water it has attached to, breaking the emulsion. This process is known as splitting.

As the sauces in the Hollandaise family are made with partially cooked eggs, they provide ideal conditions for bacterial growth. Pasteurized egg yolks can be used to reduce the risk of salmonella poisoning or the sauce can be made by the Sabayon method, in which the egg yolks are poached before the butter is added.

Hollandaise Sauce

MAKES 290 ML| ½ PINT, SERVES ABOUT 8

6 tablespoons white wine vinegar	4 egg yolks
12 black peppercorns	salt
2 bay leaves	225 g|8 oz unsalted butter, cut into dice
2 blades of mace	lemon juice, to taste

To make the reduction, place the vinegar, peppercorns, bay leaf and mace in a small saucepan and reduce slowly, by simmering, to $1\frac{1}{2}$ tablespoons. Strain the reduction into a cold bowl.

Method 1 (the cold butter method):

1 Cream the egg yolks with a tiny pinch of salt, $\frac{1}{2}$ teaspoon reduction and a nut of the butter in a small heatproof bowl until thick.

2 Set over, not in, a saucepan or roasting tin of gently simmering water and stir continuously until the egg mixture has thickened slightly. If using a roasting pan for a bain-marie, place half on the heat, half off, with the bowl over the end away from the heat. The water must be maintained at a very gentle simmer to prevent the sauce from overheating.

3 Using a wooden spoon, beat in the butter piece by piece, adding another piece when the previous one has nearly melted. As the sauce thickens and grows in volume, the butter can be added more quickly. Watch the sauce carefully. Remove from the heat if it is getting too thick and oily and add a little cold reduction (or water, if sufficient reduction has been added). Return to the heat and beat in the remaining butter. Turn up the heat slightly and continue to cook if the Hollandaise is too thin. The mixture should be thick enough to leave a trail across the surface when the spoon is drawn across it.

4 Remove from the heat and beat in the last piece of butter.

5 Check the seasoning. Because unsalted butter is used, the sauce will need to be seasoned with salt, finely ground white pepper and lemon juice.

6 Keep warm by standing in a warm but not simmering bain-marie. Serve warm.

Hollandaise Sauce can be also made using warm melted butter. Although it is more difficult to control the temperature, this method is much quicker and is used for making larger quantities of sauce with at least 4 egg yolks as the yolks need to cover the blades of the processor. The butter needs to be hot enough to partially cook the egg yolks. If the sauce tastes of raw yolk it will need to be heated in a heatproof bowl in a bain-marie (see *Method* 1, above), while beating until it is warm enough to partially cook the yolks. If the butter is too hot, the yolks will cook completely, giving a grainy sauce. If the butter is added too quickly, the emulsion will break and the sauce will split. Rescue a split sauce by beating the sauce into a new egg yolk, using *Method* 1, above.

1 Put the egg yolks, a pinch of salt and 1 teaspoon reduction into the machine and process to combine.
2 Melt the butter until it is hot but not boiling.
3 With the motor running, pour the warm butter on to the yolks in a slow, steady stream.
4 Season and keep warm in a bain-marie.

Method 3 (the Sabayon method):

The Sabayon method, in which the yolks are poached in a sauté pan before the butter is whisked in, is used when making Hollandaise Sauce with more than 4 egg yolks. It is the method most frequently followed in restaurants and can be used with up to 10 yolks.

1 Put the egg yolks into a sauté pan with 1 tablespoon water per yolk. For 4 yolks, substitute 1 tablespoon reduction for 1 tablespoon water, i.e. 1 tablespoon reduction, 3 tablespoons water.
2 Whisk the yolks and liquid to combine.
3 Place over a low heat and cook, whisking continuously, until the yolks thicken.
4 Whisk in the butter piece by piece, adding another piece when the previous one has nearly melted.
5 Season.

Storing Hollandaise Sauce

Hollandaise Sauce should be made just before serving. However, it can be kept warm in a closely regulated bain-marie at a temperature of 60°C | 140°F. If the sauce exceeds this temperature it will become too thick then split as the water content evaporates and the sauce gets too hot. Add a few drops of water from time to time and stir to maintain the correct consistency. It is not advisable to keep Hollandaise Sauce for more than 1 hour before serving.

Hollandaise Sauce: What has gone wrong when...

The Hollandaise Sauce has curdled.

- The sauce has got too hot.

    Beat in a splash of cold water and turn the sauce into a cold bowl.

    If the sauce has split only slightly, place a new yolk in a clean bowl over a bain-marie and slowly add the sauce to form an emulsion.

The sauce has not thickened.

- The sauce was not beaten vigorously enough.
- The mixture was not heated enough.
- Too much liquid has been added.

    If the sauce is too cool, reheat it gently in a bain-marie.

The sauce looks oily.

- Not enough liquid was added.
- The sauce is too hot.

    To correct, beat in a few drops of cold water.

Hollandaise Sauce: Daughter Sauces

Name of sauce	Flavouring ingredients	Garnished with	Served with
Béarnaise	Tarragon, chervil, *glace de viande*	Tarragon	Steak, chicken
Choron	Tarragon, *glace de viande*, tomato purée, cream	Tarragon	Grilled or sautéed meat, poached eggs, vegetables
Sauce Maltaise	Blanched julienne or grated zest and juice of blood orange		Steamed asparagus, grilled Dover sole
Sauce Mousseline	Hollandaise lightened with softly whipped double cream just before it is served		Nappéed over steamed fish, boiled or steamed vegetables and browned under the grill
Sauce Moutarde	French mustard		Grilled herrings, mackerel and sautéed rabbit

Beurre Blanc

Beurre Blanc is an Emulsion Sauce made with butter and a small amount of liquid. The milk proteins in butter contain a small quantity of the emulsifying protein lecithin, so when whisked into a liquid, they form an emulsion with the liquid and the butterfat. Butter contains only a small amount of protein, which means the sauce can separate and curdle easily if excessively heated or if the butter is added too quickly. The emulsion is much less stable than that of the Hollandaise Sauce family. Whipping or double cream is often added to Butter Emulsion Sauces to increase the proportion of milk proteins that stabilize the sauce. With or without the addition of double cream, Beurre Blanc should be made just before serving to avoid separation.

Although butter sauces are made using the same principles as Hollandaise, they are thinner and lighter. Their consistency is similar to double cream and they are less rich in taste. Beurre Blanc is made with a reduction of white wine vinegar and shallots. The reduction should be simmered slowly to allow the sweet flavour to be released from the shallots. (See also **Dairy Products,** *Beurre Noir*, page 205.)

Beurre Blanc

225 g | 8 oz unsalted butter
1 tablespoon very finely chopped shallot
45 ml | 3 tablespoons white wine vinegar

45 ml | 3 tablespoons water
salt and freshly ground white pepper
a squeeze of lemon juice

1 Cut the butter into 3 lengthways, then across into thin slices. Keep refrigerated.
2 Put the shallot, vinegar and water into a shallow heavy-based pan. Boil until reduced to about 2 tablespoons. Strain and return to the pan.
3 Lower the heat under the pan. Using a wire whisk, gradually add the butter, piece by piece, whisking vigorously and continuously. The process should take about 5 minutes and the sauce should become thick, creamy and pale.
4 Season to taste with salt, pepper and lemon juice.

VARIATION
Beurre Rouge is made in the same way, substituting red wine vinegar for the white wine vinegar.
Chicken and Fish Beurre Blanc are made by substituting the appropriate stock for the water then stirring a small nut of *glace* into the finished sauce.

Storing Beurre Blanc

The reduction can be made in advance, sieved and stored indefinitely. Storage of Beurre Blanc is not recommended.

Beurre Blanc: Daughter Sauces

Name of sauce	Flavouring ingredients	Garnished with	Served with
Chicken Beurre Blanc	Chicken stock		Chicken
Fish Beurre Blanc	Fish stock		Fish
Orange Beurre Blanc	Orange juice	Orange zest julienne	Chicken, fish
Saffron Beurre Blanc	White wine, saffron	Cream	Fish, chicken

Beurre Blanc: What has gone wrong when...

The sauce has turned grey.

- The sauce was made in an aluminium pan. The pan reacts with the vinegar reduction and discolours the sauce. Use a heavy-based stainless-steel or galvanized-copper pan that distributes the heat well.

The sauce has separated into an oily and liquid layer.

- The sauce has overheated.
  To correct, add a small amount of cold water and beat vigorously.

The sauce tastes sweet.

- Too much reduction was used.
- Too much shallot was used in the reduction.
  To correct, add lemon juice and/or salt.

Combination Sauces

The Combination Sauces are made from and sometimes thickened with vegetables or fruit. (See **Fruit**, *Apples*, *Apple Sauce*, page 279.)

Tomato Sauce

MAKES 570 ML | 1 PINT

1 large onion, finely chopped

3 tablespoons olive oil

10 tomatoes, roughly chopped, or 2 × 400 g | 14 oz cans plum tomatoes

salt and freshly ground black pepper

a pinch of caster sugar

150 ml | ¼ pint White Chicken or Vegetable Stock (see **Stocks**, page 689)

1 tablespoon chopped fresh thyme basil or oregano

1 Sweat the onion in the oil in a saucepan covered with a piece of damp greaseproof paper (a *cartouche*) and a lid until soft.

2 Add the tomatoes, salt, pepper and sugar and cook uncovered for 25 minutes.

3 Add the stock and cook for a further 5 minutes. Bash the tomatoes with a wooden spoon to break them down.

4 Liquidize the sauce and push though a sieve. If it is too thin, reduce it by boiling rapidly to the desired consistency. Take care as it has a tendency to spit and catch on the sides of the pan.

5 Add the thyme or basil. Check the seasoning.

NOTE: To use dried herbs substitute 1 teaspoon dried thyme, basil or oregano for the fresh herbs Add the dried herbs with the tomatoes in step 2.

Tomato Sauce: Daughter Sauces

Name of sauce	Flavouring ingredients	Garnished with	Served with
Provençal Sauce	Garlic, bouquet garni, white wine and white stock	Chopped fresh parsley or basil	Poultry, fish, vegetables, eggs, pasta
Spanish Sauce		Finely diced red peppers	Soft-boiled or poached eggs, pasta
À la Grecque	Garlic, crushed coriander seeds, chopped fresh fennel	Chopped fresh parsley	Binds vegetables such as aubergine, courgette and mushrooms
Pizzaiola Sauce	Dried oregano, dried basil and bay leaves		Used to cover pizza bases, pasta
À la Niçoise		Capers and chopped black olives	Grilled fish, pasta

Coulis

The term coulis most often refers to a liquid purée of vegetables and/or fruit. It is used to enhance the flavour and colour of sauces, or as a sauce in its own right. Both vegetable and fruit coulis should be vivid in colour and have the consistency of single cream. The flavour and colour of a coulis should be that of the main ingredient, enhanced by the other flavouring ingredients. For fruit coulis, see **Sauces, Sweet** (page 617).

Vegetable Coulis

Coulis is often made from a single vegetable base such as tomato or red pepper, cooked with aromatic herbs, vegetables and spices, then puréed and thinned with stock, water or cream. Due to its low fat content, vegetable coulis is often served hot or cold as an alternative to the richer classic sauces with vegetables, rice, pasta, meat, poultry, fish or shellfish.

Tomato Coulis

Serve hot with grilled fish, add to Beurre Blanc or Fish Velouté or use with Béchamel Sauce in a gratin of fresh pasta.

MAKES ABOUT 570 ML | 1 PINT

675 g | 1lb 8 oz ripe tomatoes
30 g | 1 oz carrots, peeled and finely chopped
30 g | 1 oz onions, finely chopped
1 tablespoon vegetable oil

1 teaspoon caster sugar
1 bouquet garni
salt and freshly ground black pepper

1 Peel the tomatoes by immersing them in boiling water for 10 seconds, then in cold water. Deseed and finely dice the tomatoes.
2 Place the carrot, onion and oil in a shallow pan and sauté until brown.
3 Add the tomatoes, sugar and bouquet garni to the pan and season with salt and pepper. Stir and bring to the boil, then cover, lower the heat and cook until the mixture is reduced to a purée.
4 Pass through a sieve and reheat to reduce to the desired consistency if necessary. Season to taste and serve hot or cold.

Contemporary Sauces

Pan Sauces

A pan sauce is a quick sauce made from the juices left in a pan after meat has been cooked. It requires familiarity with the *General Techniques of Sauce-making* described earlier in this section.

1 To make a pan sauce, after browning meat deglaze the hot sauté pan with 55 ml | 2 fl oz water, wine or stock. Scrape the bottom of the pan with a wooden spoon to remove the browned juices.
2 Boil the *déglaçage* until reduced to half its original volume.
3 Add 290 ml | ½ pint appropriately flavoured stock to the pan. Boil until reduced to syrupy. Taste and adjust the seasoning. If the sauce is very strongly flavoured it can be thinned with water. Beurre manié can be whisked into the liquid to thicken it.
4 Pass the sauce through a chinois or fine sieve, then rewarm gently.
5 The sauce can be enriched with a couple of tablespoons of double cream or crème fraîche. A small knob of butter can be whisked into the warm sauce off the heat for shine and flavour.

Salsas

Salsas are a mixture of fresh uncooked, finely diced vegetables and fruit, flavoured with Vinaigrette (see *Salad Dressings*, page 572), lime or lemon juice, spices, salt and herbs. The resulting flavour is intensely, fresh, cool, hot, spicy and sweet all at once. Salsas are extremely easy to prepare and contain very little fat. Their lively colours and flavours complement Mediterranean and South American dishes of grilled fish, shellfish, poultry and meat (see *Fish*, *Ceviche*, page 248). Salsa is also served on toasted bread for Italian bruschetta.

Salsas: Points to Remember

- Finely dice the ingredients to the same size.
- Toss all the ingredients together and refrigerate for at least 30 minutes before serving to allow the flavours to combine, but for no longer than 4 hours.
- Chopped raw garlic, shallot and onion will mellow in flavour and soften in texture if mixed with any oil or acid ingredients included in the recipe for 10 minutes before the other ingredients are added.
- Add salt to a salsa just before serving to prevent the salsa becoming watery.

Pesto

Pesto is an Italian sauce made from fresh basil, garlic, pine nuts, Parmesan cheese and olive oil (see *Herbs*, page 307).

Tapenade

Tapenade can be used as a dip, a spread or as a stuffing for chicken breasts (see *Chicken Stuffed with Red Pepper Mouseline*, page 435).

110 g | 4 oz black olives, pitted
2 tablespoons capers
1 clove of garlic, chopped

85 ml | 3 fl oz olive oil
freshly ground black pepper

1 Put the olives, capers and garlic into a food processor and process until smooth.
2 Add the olive oil gradually through the feed tube while the motor is running.
3 Season with pepper.

Sauces, Sweet

Dessert sauces provide contrasting flavour, colour and texture for the dessert they accompany. Sweet sauces, with a few exceptions, can be divided into custards, sabayons, fruit sauces, chocolate sauces and caramel sauces. The simplest sweet sauce can be made by flavouring double or whipping cream with sugar and vanilla.

Sweet sauces may have liqueur added to them to enhance their flavour. Unlike savoury sauces, the alcohol content of the liqueur is required to give sweet sauces added character. The alcohol is usually added towards the end of cooking so that it does not evaporate, and retains its fiery taste.

Custard/Crème Anglaise

Custard is a sauce made from milk or cream and sugar that is thickened with egg yolks and sometimes cornflour or plain flour. Custards are usually served at coating consistency, the thickness of unwhipped double cream. The basic custard is flavoured with vanilla but custard can also be flavoured with coffee, chocolate or caramel.

Crème Anglaise is served hot or cold in place of fresh cream with hot desserts such as apple pie or steamed pudding. Chilled Crème Anglaise is more suitable as an accompaniment for cakes, fresh fruit tarts, ice creams and other cold desserts. Cold Crème Anglaise is also used to decorate dessert plates (see below) and forms the base of custard-based ice creams (see **Ice Creams**, page 312).

Before making a custard read **Eggs**, *Custards* (page 226). If an egg mixture is heated slowly over a low heat and stirred continuously, the protein in the eggs denatures slowly to increase the viscosity of the liquid at around 70°C|160°F. Heating custard quickly retards the thickening properties of egg protein until the liquid reaches 80°C|175°F, at which point the protein denatures to thicken the liquid before quickly packing densely together to form coagulated lumps of scrambled egg at 82°C|180°F. If custard appears to be thickening too quickly it can be saved from overcooking by immediately removing the pan from the heat and passing the custard through a sieve into a bowl.

Sweetening Custard Sauces

It is important not to use too much sugar to sweeten custards as it reduces the thickening properties of the eggs. The large sugar molecules interfere with the binding sites of denatured egg protein, inhibiting its ability to thicken or set custard. Acidic ingredients such as citrus juice have the opposite effect, causing egg protein to denature at a lower temperature, increasing the rate at which custards thicken or set.

Thickening and Stabilizing Custard Sauces with Cornflour

Custard sauces are stabilized and thickened with the addition of starch in the form of cornflour. Custard sauces thickened with starch, including Crème Pâtissière (see *Patisserie*, page 531), must be boiled. The added starch coats the egg proteins, preventing them from denaturing, binding to one another or coagulating, even at $85°C|185°F$. Above this temperature the protein molecules are forced into close contact and partially coagulate, thickening the sauce. When the sauce boils the starch cells absorb the surrounding liquid and swell to form a gel that increases the density of the custard.

Egg yolk contains the enzyme amylase, which breaks down starch. Boiling denatures this enzyme. If the custard is not boiled, the amylase enzyme will break down the starch and the custard will become runny once again.

The thickness of Crème Anglaise depends on the proportion of egg yolks to milk or cream. The more yolks used, the richer and thicker the custard will be, due to the increased concentration of protein in the liquid. Used as a sauce that evenly coats the back of a spoon, it is made in the proportions of 2 egg yolks to $150\,ml|\frac{1}{4}$ pint milk. The classic dessert Crème Brûlée (see *Caramel*, page 176) is made with Crème Anglaise enriched with extra egg yolks and double cream that sets to a thick cream when cool.

Crème Anglaise

MAKES 290 ML $|\frac{1}{2}$ PINT

290 ml $|\frac{1}{2}$ pint milk

1 vanilla pod, split lengthways, or a few drops of vanilla essence

2–3 egg yolks

2–3 tablespoons caster sugar

1 Heat the milk and vanilla pod, if using, until steaming. Leave to stand for 20 minutes to allow the flavours to infuse, then scrape the seeds from the vanilla pod and stir into the milk.
2 Beat the egg yolks in a bowl with the sugar. Pour the milk slowly on to the eggs in a thin stream, stirring constantly. Rinse out the pan to remove the coagulated milk proteins, then return the milk to the pan.
3 Stir over a medium–low heat until the mixture thickens sufficiently to coat the back of the spoon (when the custard starts to steam it is almost cooked). Do not boil or the egg will coagulate into lumps.
4 Strain into a chilled bowl to remove any fragments of cooked egg and stir from time to time to help the custard cool quickly and prevent it from cooking further or forming a skin.

5 Add the vanilla essence if using.

VARIATIONS
Cinnamon Crème Anglaise: Infuse the milk with a stick of cinnamon as it heats. Remove before pouring the milk on to the egg yolk and sugar mixture.

Orange Crème Anglaise: Infuse the milk with the finely grated zest of 1 orange and 1 vanilla pod as it is brought to the boil. Remove the vanilla pod and make the custard as described above. Strain into a chilled bowl and allow to cool. Lemon Crème Anglaise is made in the same way, using lemon zest.

Coffee Crème Anglaise: Flavour the milk with 2 teaspoons instant coffee granules and heat until it begins to steam. Make the custard as above.

Chocolate Crème Anglaise: Add 55 g | 2 oz plain dark chocolate to the milk. Bring to steaming point and stir to melt the chocolate completely. Make the custard as above.

Flavouring Crème Anglaise with Liqueurs: To enhance Crème Anglaise with spirits or liqueurs such as rum or Grand Marnier, add 1 tablespoon to the basic recipe above at the end of cooking.

Storing Crème Anglaise
Once the Crème Anglaise is completely cold, cover with clingfilm or place in an airtight container and refrigerate for a maximum of 48 hours. Crème Anglaise is unsuitable for freezing.

Serving Crème Anglaise
Crème Anglaise is served separately in a sauce-boat, by flooding the base of a plate, or drizzling it around the edge of the plate before placing the dessert on top. Often 2 Crème Anglaise sauces of different colour and flavour are used to decorate the dessert plate.

Crème Anglaise: What has gone wrong when...

The custard sauce is lumpy.
- The custard sauce was overheated and coagulated. If the sauce contains only a few lumps it should be passed through a fine sieve or it can be liquidized in a blender. If the sauce is very lumpy, start again.

The custard sauce is too thin.
- The custard sauce has not been heated sufficiently. Return to the pan and heat gently, stirring continuously, until the custard starts to steam and thicken.

The custard sauce has become lumpy after it has been removed from the heat.
- The custard sauce has been left in a hot pan and has continued to cook.

The custard sauce is too thick.
- Too much time was taken to cook the custard. Add a little milk or cream.

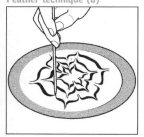

Decorating a dessert plate with
elongated hearts (a)

Decorating a dessert plate with
elongated hearts (b)

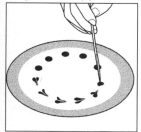

Decorating a Plate with a Dessert Sauce

Flooding the base of a plate

Place 2 tablespoons of sauce on the centre of the plate. Slowly swirl the sauce over the base by tipping the edge of the plate in a smooth, circular motion. Tap the plate gently on the work surface to level the sauce.

Feather technique, using 2 sauces that contrast in colour

Flood the base of the plate with one of the sauces as above. Use a triangle of baking parchment to make a paper piping bag (see diagrams opposite). Fill with a little of the second sauce and use to quickly and smoothly draw concentric circles in the centre of the plate. (a) If the sauce runs out before the circle is completed, repeat the action. Trail another circle of the sauce $1-2\,\text{cm}\,\big|\,\frac{1}{2}-\frac{1}{4}$ in inside the first and repeat again with a third smaller circle near the centre of the plate. Using the tip of a cocktail stick, a small knife or a teaspoon handle, draw lines at even intervals through the sauces from the outer circle to the centre of the plate. (b) This action will cause the circular lines to merge in a feather pattern at equal intervals around the plate.

Elongated hearts, using 2 sauces that contrast in colour

Flood the base of the plate with one of the sauces as above. Using a teaspoon, drip spots of the second sauce at equal intervals around the edge of the plate. (a) Place the tip of a cocktail stick, a small knife or a teaspoon handle in the centre of one of the spots and draw the circle out into an elongated heart shape with a smooth, short stroke. Repeat in the same direction with the remaining spots. (b)

Drizzling sauce across the plate

Use one, or two Crème Anglaise sauces of contrasting colour. Dip a teaspoon into the sauce and quickly flick the sauce back and forth in a thin trail across the plate. Repeat with the second Crème Anglaise sauce, if using.

Creme Chantilly

Crème Chantilly is whipped cream (see **Dairy Products**, page 201), sweetened with sugar and flavoured with vanilla. It is served with fresh fruit desserts, waffles and crêpes or as a filling for choux buns and meringues or to decorate cakes and iced desserts.

SERVES 4

150 ml | ¼ pint double cream
1–2 teaspoons icing sugar

2 drops of vanilla essence
30 ml | 2 tablespoons iced water

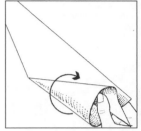

Making a paper piping bag (a)

1 Chill the ingredients and equipment before starting to make the Crème Chantilly, to slow down the rate at which the milk proteins coagulate as the cream is whipped. The resulting cream will be lighter and whiter.

2 Put the cream into a chilled bowl and whisk with a balloon whisk, steadily but not too fast, for about 2 minutes or until the cream starts to thicken.

3 Add the icing sugar and the vanilla.

4 Whisk faster until the mixture is very fluffy and forms soft peaks. It is important not to overbeat or the cream will become grainy and eventually curdle. If the cream becomes too thick, fold in a few tablespoons of milk.

Making a paper piping bag (b)

VARIATIONS

Coffee Crème Chantilly: Dissolve 2 teaspoons instant coffee powder in 1 tablespoon hot milk and allow to cool. Add the cooled coffee to the sweetened cream before beating.

Liquer Crème Chantilly: Add 1 tablespoon liqueur instead of the vanilla. Do not add excessive quantities of liqueur to the cream, as the alcohol will cause it to curdle.

Making a paper piping bag (c)

Serving Crème Chantilly

Crème Chantilly is served in large spoonfuls either on or to the side of a desserts, or is used as a filling, piped into choux buns (see page 525) and meringues (see page 474).

Storing Crème Chantilly

Crème Chantilly is best used as soon as it is made. It can, however, be stored in an airtight container in the refrigerator for up to 24 hours or frozen for up to 1 month. Lightly whip again once defrosted.

Sabayon Sauce

Sabayon Sauce is a light and foamy custard that is served warm, poured over hot sponge and fruit desserts, or cold as a chilled dessert or sauce with fruit jellies, pastries, ice cream and sorbet. It is made by whisking eggs, sugar and sweet wine or liqueur over a pan of simmering water. A certain amount of skill is required to make Sabayon Sauce as the yolks must only partially coagulate and thicken to a light froth.

The egg proteins coagulate as they are heated, whilst whisking incorporates air to lighten the thickened mixture. The Sabayon mixture contains a high proportion of sugar, which reduces the ability of egg proteins to bind to one another. Both the heat and the action of whisking reduce the inhibiting effect of the sugar and allow the Sabayon to become thick and creamy. Because the egg proteins are only partially cooked and not firmly set, the Sabayon will gradually lose its volume within 30–40 minutes unless it is thickened and stabilized with whipped cream and/or gelatine. Sabayon may also be lightened with whisked egg whites.

Sabayon Sauce

SERVES 4

4 egg yolks
55 g | 2 oz caster sugar
150 ml | ¼ pint sweet white wine
30 ml | 2 tablespoons Marsala wine

150 ml | ¼ pint double cream, whipped to soft peaks (see **Dairy Products**, page 201) (optional)

1 Place the egg yolks, sugar and wine in a large bowl over a saucepan of simmering water.
2 Whisk with an electric hand whisk for about 15 minutes or until the mixture is thick and mousse-like. When the beaters are lifted, a trail of the mixture should remain on the surface without recombining.
3 Remove from the heat and continue to whisk for about 5 minutes, until the mixture feels cool.
4 Fold in the Marsala and the cream, if using.
5 Serve immediately.

Serving Sabayon Sauce

Sabayon Sauce made without stabilizing ingredients is served warm and must be served immediately as the partially coagulated foam will collapse within minutes. Sabayon Sauce stabilized with cream must be used within 1 hour.

Sabayon Sauce: What has gone wrong when...

The sauce is thin and loses its foam almost immediately.

- The sauce was cooked at too low a temperature or for too short a time.

  Make sure the foam leaves a definite ribbon trail when the whisk is held above the mixture. Return to the heat and cook until thickened and frothy.

The sauce is lumpy and has lost volume.

- The sauce was cooked at too high a temperature or for too long. The coagulated egg is no longer sufficiently elastic to hold bubbles of air.

Coulis

A coulis is a sauce made from puréed, usually uncooked, fruit. Fruit Coulis are smooth, tangy and vividly colourful sauces made with the puréed flesh and juice of ripe soft fruit. The fruit is either puréed raw or cooked first before puréeing if it is likely to oxidize and discolour.

Fruit Coulis is usually made with only one fruit to obtain the purest possible flavour and colour. There are some exceptions to this rule as mango and passion fruit combine well in both colour and flavour, as do raspberry and strawberry. The intense colours and smooth consistency of Fruit Coulis make them ideal for decorating dessert plates (see above). Two or three different coulis contrasting in colour but compatible in flavour may be used to decorate a dessert plate before the dessert is arranged on top.

Raspberry Coulis (1)

250 g | 9 oz fresh or thawed raspberries
55 g | 2 oz icing sugar

lemon juice, to taste

1 Place the raspberries and sugar in a small saucepan and bring to the boil.
2 Pass through a sieve to remove the pips.
3 Season with lemon juice and additional sugar if needed.

NOTE: The coulis should be of thin coating consistency. If the sauce is too thin, reduce it by boiling in a heavy-based saucepan. If it is too thick, thin with a little water, sugar syrup (see **Sugar**, page 699) or fruit juice.

Raspberry Coulis (2)

This coulis is made with sugar syrup.

250 g	9 oz fresh or thawed raspberries	55 ml	3 tablespoons water
55 g	2 oz granulated sugar	lemon juice, to taste

1 Place the raspberries in the bowl of a food processor or liquidizer.

2 Place the sugar and water into a small pan over medium heat until dissolved then bring to the boil.

3 Boil the syrup for 2 minutes and pour over the raspberries.

4 Purée the raspberries in the machine then pass them through a fine sieve to remove the seeds.

5 Adjust the seasoning with lemon juice or additional sugar, if required.

VARIATIONS

Any soft fruit is suitable for making a coulis. Water, fruit juice or sugar syrup can be used to thin the sauce.

Serving Coulis

Flood the base of the plate or drizzle the coulis across or around the edge of the plate before arranging the dessert on top. Alternatively, Fruit Coulis may be served separately in a sauce-boat.

Storing Coulis

Fresh Fruit Coulis can be stored for up to 3 days in the refrigerator, covered in clingfilm or sealed in an airtight container. Freeze for up to 3 months.

Jam Sauce

Jam sauce is served hot with steamed puddings. Melt the jam over a low heat with enough water to make a pouring consistency. The sauce can be sieved if desired. Jam sauce can be stored covered in clingfilm or in an airtight container in the refrigerator for up to 3 days.

Caramel Sauce

Caramel Sauce is served with hot autumnal fruit puddings. It is also used to macerate oranges in the classic dessert Caramel Oranges (see *Caramel*, page 175) and to flavour ice creams. Caramel sauce is used to flood the base of the plate before placing the dessert on top, or it may be drizzled around the edge of the plate to frame the dessert. Alternatively it may be served separately in a sauce-boat.

Caramel Cream Sauce

In the recipe below, cream is added to the caramel to make a creamy, smooth sauce for ice cream, cakes or fruit desserts.

110 g | 4 oz granulated sugar   150 ml | ¼ pint whipping or double cream
5 tablespoons water

1 See **Caramel** (page 174), for detailed instructions on making caramel. Place the sugar and the water in a small heavy-based saucepan and heat over a low heat until the sugar dissolves.
2 When the sugar has dissolved completely, wash down the inside of the pan with a pastry brush dipped in cold water.
3 Bring the mixture to the boil and cook until it turns a deep caramel colour.
4 Protecting your hand with an oven glove, pour in the cream to stop the caramel cooking.
5 Heat gently to dissolve the caramel if necessary.
6 Sharpen with a little lemon juice if desired. Serve warm or cold.

Chocolate Sauce

For a rich chocolate sauce see **Chocolate** (page 193).

Categories of Shellfish

Edible shellfish can be divided into 2 categories: crustaceans and molluscs.

Crustaceans

Crustaceans are shellfish with an external, hinged shell and have 5 pairs of legs, including a pair of claws. With the exception of crayfish, they are all found in the sea.

- Crabs
- Crayfish
- Langoustines
- Lobsters
- Prawns
- Shrimps

Molluscs

Molluscs can be divided into 3 groups.

Gastropods (univalves) are single-shelled:

- Whelks
- Winkles

Bivalves are double-hinged. The bivalves are also known as filter-feeders:

- Clams
- Mussels
- Oysters
- Scallops

Cephalopods have tentacles and a modified internal shell:

- Squid
- Octopus
- Cuttlefish

Shellfish

Shellfish is the collective term for the group of aquatic animals that have a shell, usually on the outside of their body, that is, an exoskeleton rather than an internal skeleton. The 2 main types of shellfish are crustaceans and molluscs (see above).

Shellfish, a readily available source of protein found throughout the world, has been consumed by man for thousands of years. The meat of shellfish is tender and delicate because the muscle fibres are short and any connective tissue is thin. Although the fat content is low in comparison with meat, the cholesterol content of shellfish is relatively high, so it is recommended that people who are limiting their cholesterol intake do not consume large quantities of shellfish.

Buying Shellfish

All shellfish have a very short shelf-life. Once shellfish dies, the flesh deteriorates rapidly due to the enzymes that work at cool temperatures. If possible, buy live shellfish from a reliable source with a high turnover and cook it within 24 hours of purchase. Cooked shellfish must be refrigerated and consumed within 24 hours of purchase.

In Britain, in accordance with EU regulations, molluscs and other shellfish can only be marketed and sold commercially if harvested from an area that has met with government approval and has been designated safe by scientific research. It is unwise to gather shellfish yourself from any area you are not completely confident about. This is particularly important where bivalves or filter-feeders are concerned as they filter a considerable amount of water through their systems each day and in so doing can pick up toxins and bacteria in the water. This does not affect the shellfish, but eating contaminated shellfish could have adverse effects on the consumer.

Storing Shellfish

Store live shellfish in the refrigerator for up to 24 hours, covered with crushed ice in a tray that allows the melted water to drain away. Do not store covered in water. Discard any shellfish that has died.

Freeze cooked and uncooked shellfish for up to 6 months. Freezing, however, tends to give the meat a rubbery texture. If buying frozen shellfish, the quality will be better if it has been frozen raw rather than cooked.

Cooking Shellfish

Shellfish needs only very short, gentle cooking to coagulate the protein at 41°C|105°F. Beyond this point the tissue tends to dry out and toughen or even disintegrate. It is not a good idea to keep cooked shellfish warm because if the temperature is high enough to prevent bacterial growth, the shellfish will continue to cook and the quality will deteriorate.

With a few exceptions such as mussels, uncooked shellfish has translucent flesh. Once cooked, the flesh becomes opaque and firm to the touch. The exoskeletal shellfish, such as crab, lobster and prawns, have shells that turn an intense orange-pink colour when heated. This change in shell colour is another way of telling when the shellfish is cooked.

Recommended methods of cooking are described below under each category of shellfish.

Crustaceans

Crab

There are many different varieties of crab, ranging from the tiny Stone Crab to the giant King Crab, which grows to a width of 1 m|39 in.

Choosing

Purchase crab alive or ready-cooked. It is also possible to buy prepared (dressed) crab. Buy only from a shop with a quick turnover. The larger the crab, the more meat it will contain. Small crabs are best for making soup, such as *Shellfish Bisque* (see **Soups**, page 659).

Choose a crab that is heavy for its size with a hard shell.

The Blue Crab is a soft-shell crab, sold when it has just moulted. These crabs are in season in the late spring on the eastern coast of the USA. They are rarely found in Britain because they are highly perishable. Soft-shell crabs must be purchased alive.

The crab most often found in the Britain is the Common or Brown Crab which can be over 60 cm|24 in wide. Its powerful claws will give a painful pinch, so are usually secured with tough elastic bands.

The female crab is called a hen and has sweeter flesh than the male, but the male crab has larger claws and it is the claw meat of the crab that is the most prized. Apart from the size of the claws, the sex of a crab can be determined by the width of its tail. Turn the crab over to find the tail tightly curled underneath its body. The tail of the females is wide and that of the males is narrow.

Storing

Keep live crab in the bottom of the refrigerator in a container covered with a damp tea towel for up to 24 hours.

Once cooked, store in the refrigerator for up to 24 hours.

Cooking

The following is a classic method of preparing Common or Brown Crab to be served as a first course or as part of a light lunch.

Dressed Crab

SERVES 3

a 900 g | 2 lb live crab or 3 smaller crabs

fresh white breadcrumbs

lemon juice

freshly ground black pepper

Mayonnaise (see *Sauces, Savoury*, page 599), to bind

1 egg, hard-boiled (see *Eggs*, page 217)

2 tablespoons chopped fresh parsley

To serve

Mayonnaise (see *Sauces, Savoury*, page 599)

6 slices of buttered brown bread

1 Kill the crab by inserting a skewer in between its eyes and moving it back and forth.

2 Place the crab in a pan of well-salted water. Add 1 tablespoon salt per litre | 1¾ pints. Cover, then simmer, allowing 15 minutes per 450 g | 1 lb crab. Remove from the pan and allow to cool.

3 Lay the crab on its back and twist off the legs and claws. (a) Scrub the shell.

4 Crack around the natural shell line by tapping it gently with a rolling pin. Remove the belly shell and discard it. (b)

5 Remove and throw away the small sac at the top of the crab's body and the spongy lungs that line the edge. These look rather like grey fish gills and are sometimes referred to as 'dead man's fingers'. (c)

6 Have 2 bowls ready, one for the white meat and one for the dark meat. Lift out the crab's body and using a lobster pick or a cocktail stick, pick out all the white meat. This is a very fiddly job and can take up to 15 minutes.

7 Scrape the brown meat from the shell into the second bowl. Mix with the breadcrumbs, lemon juice and pepper to taste. Refrigerate.

8 Wash the shell.

9 Crack the large claws, using a lobster cracker, or by wrapping the claw in a tea towel and tapping with a rolling pin. Remove the meat and place with the white meat.

10 Using a lobster pick, cocktail stick or the end of a teaspoon, remove the meat from the legs and place with the white meat.

11 Mix the white meat with a little Mayonnaise to bind. Season with lemon juice.

12 Pile the brown meat in the centre of the shell and the white meat on either side.

13 Separate the egg yolk and white and sieve each separately. Use to garnish the crab in neat lines along with the parsley. Keep refrigerated until ready to serve. Serve with Mayonnaise and brown bread and butter.

Preparing crab
Twisting off legs (a)

Removing belly shell (b)

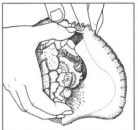

Removing dead man's fingers

Crayfish

Crayfish look like miniature lobsters. They are the only crustaceans to be found in fresh water. They have dark brownish-green shells that turn red when cooked.

Choosing

It is important to buy these crustaceans alive as their flesh disintegrates quickly. The flesh of crayfish is sweet, but there is only a little in each one, so 8–10 are needed per serving.

Storing

Place in a large box covered with damp tea towels in the bottom of the refrigerator for up to 24 hours. The cold makes the crayfish sleepy, but once they warm up they can become very lively. Their little claws can give you a nasty nip.

Cooking

Prepare a *court bouillon* (see **Stocks**, page 693) and allow to cool. Place the crayfish in the liquid, cover and bring to a simmer. Cook for about 5 minutes, or until the shells turn a deep orange-pink.

To remove from the shell, gently twist off the tail. Peel off the tail shell from one side to the other. Remove the black intestinal track from along the top of the back. The shells can be used for shellfish stock and soup.

Langoustines / Dublin Bay Prawns / Scampi

These shellfish resemble small lobsters and can measure up to 25 cm|10 in, although the more usual size available in the market is 10 cm|4 in. They are found in the Adriatic, the Atlantic coast of Britain and in the western Mediterranean. The colder the water they come from, the sweeter and firmer the flesh. Langoustines are often served as a part of a *plateau de fruits de mer*.

Choosing

Langoustines are most often found as frozen scampi tails and have already been cooked. If found in the shell, the larger the langoustine, the more meat it will contain.

Live langoustines have a pinkish-orange shell which turns red on cooking.

Storing

As for crayfish, above.

Cooking

As for crayfish, above. See also *Seafood Feuilletées*, below under *Scallops*.

Lobster

Lobster, with its firm flesh and sweet flavour, is the most prized of shellfish today, although less than 100 years ago it was poorly regarded.

Choosing

Lobsters are found throughout the world, with the best coming from colder waters. There are 2 species of lobster, the American and the European, that look quite similar with a large pair of claws. American lobsters are more plentiful and are therefore usually cheaper than European.

The colour of a live lobster ranges from dark blue-green to nearly black, depending on its habitat. Lobster should be bought alive or freshly cooked, as for crab. By the time it is large enough for the table it is over 6 years old. It is very labour-intensive to catch, hence its high price.

Allow a lobster weighing at least 450 g | 1 lb per serving. Lobsters over 1 kg | 2 lb 2 oz can be tough.

Lobster should be heavy for its size. Give the lobster a shake: if it makes a sloshing sound this means it is filled with water and should be avoided.

Like crabs, lobsters shed their shells every few years. Avoid buying a lobster with a soft shell as this means it has recently moulted and will have soft, watery flesh.

When buying live lobster, choose an energetic lobster with a tail that springs back when unfolded. Avoid lobster with broken antennae, which can be a sign of being 'tank stale': this results in deterioration in flavour.

Lobster can also be bought freshly boiled. Buy from a shop with a high turnover or directly from a fish market. Store in the refrigerator and use within 24 hours.

Storing

As for crab, above.

Using

Lobster is delicious boiled and is traditionally served with drawn or clarified butter, butter that has been melted and had the whey skimmed off. Serve the lobsters with lobster claw crackers and a lobster pick for removing the meat from the legs (see **Kitchen Equipment**, page 49).

If lobster flesh is going to be cooked as part of a recipe, the lobster should first be killed and the raw flesh removed (see below).

To boil: Place the lobster in the freezer for 2 hours before boiling, to subdue it. Only use a deep-freeze for this purpose, the small ice box in a refrigerator is not suitable.

Bring a large pot of salted water to the boil. Drop the lobster into the pot and boil, allowing 8 minutes per 450 g | 1 lb. Up to 2 lobsters at a time may be cooked in the same pot. Once the lobster is cooked, the pigments in the shell turn it a deep terracotta colour.

Killing a lobster (a)

Killing a lobster (b)

Cutting through the shell (c)

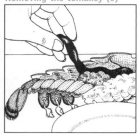

Removing the stomach sac (d)

Removing the tomalley (e)

Killing lobster

1 Subdue the lobster by chilling it well, then place it on a chopping board.
2 Place a tea towel over the tail and hold the tail down.
3 Insert a large cook's knife down through the cross on the back of the lobster's head. The nerve centre lies below this cross, so the lobster is killed instantly.

Preparing lobster

1 To split the lobster in half, cut down through the tail, starting from the cut through the head.
2 Once the lobster has been cut in half, remove the greenish-black roe, the stomach sac and the thread-like intestine.

NOTE: The roe (or coral) can be used in sauces (see recipe below). When cooked it turns bright red and has an excellent flavour. The grey-green paste near the head of the lobster is the tomalley or the liver. Many people like to eat it cooked and spread on toast.

Grilled Lobster with Red Butter Sauce

SERVES 4

4 small live lobsters
unsalted butter, melted
cayenne pepper
watercress, trimmed, to garnish

For the red butter sauce
1 shallot, finely chopped
150 ml | ¼ pint dry white wine

150 ml | ¼ pint white fish or Shellfish Stock
    (see **Stocks**, page 689)
110 g | 4 oz unsalted butter, chilled and diced
the coral from the lobster
3 tablespoons double cream
salt and freshly ground white pepper

1 Begin to prepare the Red Butter Sauce: put the shallot into a small saucepan with the wine and stock. Cook slowly until the liquid is reduced to 4 tablespoons. Strain into a clean saucepan and set aside.
2 Next kill the lobsters: push a sharp, strong knife through the nerve centre of each lobster. (a) This is the well-defined cross on the back of its head. (b) When the middle of the cross is pierced the lobster will die instantly, although it will still move alarmingly.
3 Lay the lobster out flat and split it in half lengthways. (c) Remove the stomach sac from near the head and remove the threadlike intestine running the length of the body. (d) Do not mistake the roe (or coral), which may or may not be present, for the intestine, which is tiny. Remove the tomalley. (e) Scoop out the roe and reserve for the sauce together with the tomalley. (f)
4 Preheat the grill to high.
5 Brush the lobster with melted butter and season with cayenne. Place in the grill pan, cut side uppermost, and grill for 5–10 minutes on each side, depending on size, until the lobster is a good bright red.

6 Meanwhile, continue with the butter sauce: mix 1 teaspoon of the butter with the lobster coral.

7 When the lobsters are cooked, crack the claws, without removing them from the body if possible, with a claw cracker or by bashing them with a rolling pin. Keep the lobsters warm while finishing the sauce.

8 Heat the reduced wine and stock. Using a sauce whisk, whisk in the butter piece by piece to make a thick emulsion (see **Sauces, Savoury**, page 584).

9 Whisk in the coral, tomalley, cream and any juices from the grill pan. Heat, whisking, until the the sauce turns a pale red. Season to taste with salt and pepper.

10 Arrange the lobsters on a plate. Garnish with the watercress and hand the sauce separately.

Flat Lobster

These lobsters, which are found in warm waters, do not have a large pair of front claws like American and European lobsters. There are more than 50 different species of flat lobster, called by various names such as Balmain Bugs and Moreton Bay Bugs in Australia, and *cigales* in France. Their meat, which is in the tail, is firm and sweet in flavour. Choose, store and use as for lobster, above.

Prawns and Shrimps

The terms prawn and shrimp are often confused and used for the same creature, depending upon which side of the Atlantic you are from. It is safe to say that in Britain the term prawn is applied collectively except for the very small (1½ cm|¾ in) brown shrimps.

Many different varieties of prawn are found throughout the world. Prawns from colder waters are thought to have a sweeter flavour than warm-water prawns, although the large Mediterranean Prawn is delicious and in recent years the Tiger Prawn from the Indo-Pacific has become particularly popular.

Choosing

The majority of prawns are cooked at sea, then deep-frozen before being shipped around the world. It is best to buy uncooked prawns if they are going to be cooked further. Using cooked prawns in a recipe will almost always result in overcooking of the prawns, giving them a rubbery texture. Buy the size or type of prawn specified in the recipe.

Storing

Store frozen prawns in the freezer at −18°C|0°F for up to 6 months or until the 'use by' date on the package. Defrost as described below.

Uncooked fresh prawns should be stored in the refrigerator and cooked within 24 hours of purchase.

Store cooked prawns in the refrigerator and eat within 24 hours.

Using

Prawns can be served in the shell or peeled. They are a popular first course served with *Mayonnaise* or *Sauce Marie-Rose* (see **Sauces, Savoury**, page 599).

If using frozen prawns, defrost by placing in a single layer on a tray or plate in the refrigerator. They should thaw within 4 hours. Never defrost prawns by immersing them in warm water. The risk of food poisoning is high with shellfish and it must be kept as cool as possible.

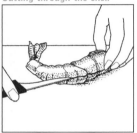

Cutting through the shell

To peel prawns:

1 Pull off the head.
2 Grasp the edge of the shell on one side of the legs and peel away the shell around the width of the body. This procedure might need to be repeated 2–3 times for a large prawn.
3 Pull off the remaining tail piece.
4 A thin intestinal tract runs down the curved side of the prawn. To remove, use a knife to make a shallow slit along the back. Hook the thread-like intestinal tract in the middle with the tip of the knife and pull it out.

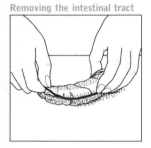

Removing the intestinal tract

Cooking

Prawns need only a little heat to coagulate the proteins and turn the flesh from translucent to opaque. The flesh becomes a creamy pink-white colour when cooked and the body of the prawn curls up. It is important not to overcook prawns as they will become rubbery. If the prawns are still in their shell, the shell will turn orange-pink when heated. This change in colour is a good indication that the prawn is cooked through.

Dry-fried Prawns with Coriander

This has been adapted from a recipe by Yan-Kit So.

SERVES 4

450 g | 1 lb raw, medium, shell-on prawns, weighed without heads
5 cloves of garlic
2.5 cm | 1 in piece of fresh root ginger
3–4 tablespoons oil
1 tablespoon dry sherry
3 spring onions, chopped
1 tablespoon chopped fresh coriander

For the marinade

½ teaspoon salt
1 teaspoon sugar
1–2 tablespoons light soy sauce
2 teaspoons Worcestershire sauce
2 teaspoons oil
freshly ground black pepper

1 Using a small sharp knife, slit along the back of each prawn and remove the black vein. Cut off the legs. Wash and pat dry.
2 Mix together all the marinade ingredients in a dish and add the prawns. Leave to stand for at least 30 minutes.

3 Bruise the garlic with a rolling pin, remove the skin and leave the cloves flattened but whole. Peel the ginger and bruise it with a rolling pin.

4 Heat a wok or heavy sauté pan until it is very hot. Add the oil and swirl it about. Fry the garlic and ginger for about 1 minute then remove and discard.

5 Add the prawns. Spread them out into a single layer and fry for about 1 minute. Reduce the heat if they show signs of beginning to burn. Turn over and fry on the other side for about 1 minute. Turn up the heat if necessary.

6 Splash in the sherry. The prawns are cooked when they have turned red and curled up. Sprinkle with the spring onions and coriander. Stir once or twice and serve immediately.

Molluscs (Gastropods)

The gastropods listed below are in season from September to April.

Whelks and Winkles

These are usually sold ready-cooked in their shells or ready-shelled to be eaten as a snack with vinegar and bread.

Winkles are smaller than whelks and are removed from their shells with a pin.

Cooking

Wash in several changes of water, then soak for 2–3 hours. Boil in salted water for 15–20 minutes.

Cockles

These are usually sold cooked and shelled. They can be used in place of mussels.

Using

Cook in a saucepan with a little water for 4–5 minutes until the shells open. Using a pin, remove from the shells, discarding any that have not opened. Cook for a further 4–5 minutes until tender.

Bivalve Molluscs

Clams

Clams are found throughout the world. They range in size from very tiny to the giant clam that grows to a length of over 1 m|39 in. Clams are very popular in America where they are eaten raw on the half-shell, steamed, made into chowder, battered and deep-fried. Clams have a sweet flavour and a rubbery texture.

In Europe clams are farmed, so are widely available. The Italians use them in a tomato-based sauce for linguine.

Choosing

It is best to buy live clams. Choose as for mussels (see below).

Of the varieties of clams available, Cherrystone and Littleneck are used for eating raw, steaming and sauces. The Quahog Clam is the best for chowder.

Storing

As for mussels, below.

Cooking

As for mussels, below.

Cockles

The small, pale brown cockle has 2 equal-sized heart-shaped shells. Although cockles are found throughout the world, they are primarily associated with Britain where pickled cockles are widely available.

Cockles can also be used like clams for soups and sauces.

Choosing

The colour of the flesh will be similar to that of the shell, so choose the palest cockles.

Storing

As for mussels, below.

Cooking

Soak cockles in cold water for several hours to remove any sand from inside the shellfish. Steam as for mussels (see below). Remove from the shell and add to soups, sauces and risotto.

Mussels

Mussels are hinged-shell bivalve molluscs and are filter-feeders. Several species are found in the sea and in fresh water throughout the world. The shell middens, mounds of ancient shells, found near the northern coasts of France and Belgium provide evidence of the consumption of mussels reaching back to prehistoric times. Mussels have remained particularly popular in Europe where they are cultivated widely.

The most abundant mussel is the Blue or Common Mussel that is found worldwide. These range in size from 3.5 to 10 cm $|$ $1\frac{1}{2}$ to 4 in: the smaller mussels have a sweeter flavour, the larger ones have a meatier flavour.

The New Zealand Green Lip Mussel has become popular in recent years. Green Lip is the trade name for this large species of mussel found in the Pacific. It has a shell about 7 cm $|$ 3 in long. It is often frozen for the UK market and is good for topping with breadcrumbs and baking (see recipe below).

Choosing

Cultivated mussels can be eaten throughout the year. Wild mussels should only be eaten during the colder months as during the summer months they can be affected by algae growth.

Mussels should smell of the sea. Discard any with broken or cracked shells or that are heavy for their size as they might be filled with mud. The shells should be tightly closed. Any mussel that does not have a tightly closed shell should be discarded as it is probably dead.

Storing

To store uncooked mussels overnight, place in a colander over a bowl and cover with a damp tea towel. Do not immerse them in water. Store in the bottom of the refrigerator.

Once the mussels have been cooked, it is best to consume them right away. Do not attempt to keep them warm. However, if the mussels are refrigerated immediately after cooking they can be kept in a cold refrigerator for up to 24 hours. Any mussel that dies before cooking should be discarded. Mussels that are not fresh can cause food poisoning.

Freeze mussels for up to 1 month.

Cleaning

Pulling away the beard

Pull off any beards. These are the wiry tendrils that the mussels use to attach themselves to the ropes or rocks on which they grow. Often the beards have been removed prior to sale so don't worry if you don't find any. Scrape off any barnacles attached to the shells, using a short, sturdy knife, then scrub the shells with a stiff brush.

Cooking

Mussels should be cooked gently, for as short a time as possible, to coagulate the proteins. They will not change colour but will become firm when cooked. If they are overcooked they will become rubbery.

If you wish to use the mussels for a recipe where they need to be used opened but uncooked, prise open the mussel shell by inserting a paring knife or oyster knife between the top and bottom shells at the back of the mussel next to the hinge. Gently work the knife around to the front of the mussel, twisting the knife slightly.

Poaching: Mussels can be poached for soup. Place the raw shelled mussels in the simmering broth. Cook for 2–3 minutes or until the mussels feel firm when pressed.

Steaming: Blue or Common Mussels are good to steam.
1 Place the mussels in a large covered pan with a small amount of boiling water flavoured with chopped shallot and white wine.
2 Cover with a tight-fitting lid, then steam for 4–5 minutes, shaking the pan occasionally. Once the mussels are cooked, the shells should open wide. If not, cook them a little longer and discard any that have not opened.

3 Turn the mussels into a large colander placed over a bowl. Save the steaming liquor, as it is full of flavour.

4 Carefully pour off and reserve the top part of the liquid, leaving behind the sandy sediment on the bottom of the bowl.

Moules Marinière

Recipes for *moules* vary from port to port in Europe. The fennel in the recipe below can be omitted, if preferred. The cream can also be omitted and the broth thickened with butter or a *beurre manié* (see **Sauces, Savoury**, page 583) if desired.

Sometimes the top shells of the mussels are removed when serving. It is a good idea to give each person an empty bowl to collect the discarded shells.

SERVES 4

1 medium onion, chopped	parsley stalks
1 small bulb of fennel	900 g | 2 lb live mussels
2 cloves of garlic, peeled and chopped	4 tablespoons double cream
150 ml | ¼ pint dry white wine	1 tablespoon chopped fresh parsley, to garnish
150 ml | ¼ pint water	

1 Place the onion in a large saucepan.

2 Reserve the fennel fronds, then chop the bulb. Add the fennel to the onion along with the garlic, wine, water and parsley stalks.

3 Bring to the boil and simmer for 10 minutes.

4 Pull the beards off the mussels, scrape off the barnacles and scrub the shells (see *Cleaning mussels*, above).

5 Place the mussels in the pan, cover and simmer for about 5 minutes, until the shells open, shaking the pan from time to time.

6 Place a colander over a bowl and tip the mussels into the colander.

7 Place the mussels in a warmed serving dish and cover with aluminium foil.

8 Sieve the cooking liquid back into the saucepan, discarding any sandy sediment.

9 Boil the liquid to reduce by half, then whisk in the cream.

10 Pour the mixture over the mussels and garnish with the fennel fronds and parsley.

Steaming Mussels: What has gone wrong when...

The mussels haven't opened very much.
- The mussels were not cooked for long enough.
- The heat was too low.

The mussels are rubbery.
- The mussels were overcooked.

Baking: Mussels on the half-shell can be topped with a flavoured breadcrumb mixture and baked until the crumbs are browned and the mussel is firm. Mussels can also be hot-smoked (see **Preserving**, *Smoking*, page 549).

Baked Mussels Provençal

These baked mussels make a delicious first course.

SERVES 4

32 live Common Mussels or 20 Green Lip Mussels

freshly ground black pepper

For the topping

55 g | 2 oz fresh breadcrumbs

4 tablespoons olive oil

1 clove of garlic, crushed

2 tablespoons finely chopped sun-dried tomatoes

1 tablespoon chopped fresh basil

30 g | 1 oz Parmesan cheese, freshly grated

To serve

1 lemon, cut into wedges (see **Food Presentation**, *Garnishes*, page 12)

1 Pull off the beards, then remove the top shells of the mussels as directed above. Place the mussels in a single layer on a baking sheet. Season with pepper.

2 Preheat the oven to 220°C | 425°F | gas mark 7.

3 Mix together the topping ingredients, then divide over the mussels.

4 Bake in the top third of the oven for 5–10 minutes, or until the mussels feel firm when pressed and the breadcrumbs are golden. Serve with lemon wedges.

Baked Mussels: What has gone wrong when...

The mussels are tough and rubbery.

- The mussels have been overcooked.

The mussels are soft.

- The mussels are undercooked. Do not eat.

Oysters

The oyster is now the most prized of the bivalves, perhaps because of its reputation as an aphrodisiac. Oysters are also among the most expensive of the bivalves.

Of the several species of oysters found throughout the world the two most widely available in Britain are the Native Oyster and the imported Pacific or Gigas Oyster. The Native Oyster is not available from 14 May to 4 August. The saying

'Never buy oysters when there is an "r" in the month' is a good recommendation because during this time the oysters are breeding and their flesh becomes soft. The Gigas Oyster, however, is framed and so is available all year round. Oysters have been farmed since Roman times.

There has been a decline in numbers of Native Oysters harvested as the result of a harmful virus that has destroyed many of the oyster beds. This has resulted in the increase of imported Pacific Oysters which are not affected by the virus.

Choosing

Native Oysters, of which the Colchester and the Whitstable are the best known, are the most prized by oyster aficionados. They are slightly smaller than the Gigas Oyster and have a richer flavour. Native Oysters have a nearly round shell that is flat on one side. The shell of the Gigas Oyster is an elongated oval shape.

Buy live oysters from a reputable supplier with a high turnover.

Storing

As for mussels, above.

Using

Oysters are most often eaten raw on the half-shell. The flatter top shell is removed in a procedure known as *shucking* and the oyster is served on the cupped shell. The oysters are usually placed on a bed of rock salt to keep them from tipping over. Serve the oysters accompanied by lemon wedges (see **Food Presentation**, *Garnishes*, page 12) and Tabasco sauce.

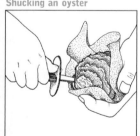

Shucking an oyster

Shucking oysters (opening)

Shucking oysters is notoriously difficult. It requires practice and can be dangerous, as the oyster knife is prone to slipping. The oyster or shucking knife has a short, sturdy blade with a rounded tip.

1 Hold the oyster in a thick cloth to protect your hand.
2 Insert the knife into the hinge of the shell.
3 Hold the oyster over a bowl to catch any juice.
4 Twist the knife to prise open the shell.

If the oysters are going to be cooked, the shells can be opened by placing the oysters in the oven preheated to 200°C|400°F|gas mark 6 for 5–10 minutes. This kills the oysters and the shells pop open slightly. The oysters must be cooked through immediately, however, as there is a risk of food poisoning if they are only partially heated.

Cooked oysters feature in the well-known first course, *Oysters Rockefeller*, below.

Oysters Rockefeller

This dish is named after the wealthy American industrialist.

SERVES 4

450 g | 1 lb coarse sea salt

20 medium oysters on the half-shell (see above)

55 g | 2 oz butter

225 g | 8 oz fresh baby spinach, stalks removed

4 tablespoons finely chopped fresh parsley

4 spring onions, very finely chopped

1 stick of celery, very finely chopped

55 g | 2 oz fresh breadcrumbs

salt and freshly ground black pepper

Tabasco sauce

2 tablespoons Pernod

To serve

lemon wedges (see ***Food Presentation,***
   Garnishes, page 12)

1 Place the salt in a shallow ovenproof dish or tray, then place the oysters on the salt in a single layer.

2 Preheat the oven to 220°C | 425°F | gas mark 7.

3 Melt half the butter in a sauté pan and sauté the spinach for 2–3 minutes until it wilts.

4 Drain the spinach in a sieve and squeeze dry. Chop finely and place in a bowl.

5 Melt the remaining butter and stir into the spinach along with the parsley, spring onions, celery and breadcrumbs. Season with salt, pepper and Tabasco.

7 Pile the mixture on top of the oysters. Sprinkle with the Pernod.

8 Bake for 8–10 minutes, or until the oysters feel firm when pressed and the crumb mixture is golden-brown. Serve with lemon wedges.

Scallops

Scallops are the one of the most delicious types of shellfish, with a sweet flavour and meaty texture. The round pale cream nugget with a half-moon-shaped orange coral attached is sometimes available in its fan-shaped shell. The coral is both the male and female reproductive parts of the scallop. It is considered a delicacy in Europe but is not eaten in the USA.

Choosing

The best scallops are diver-caught fresh scallops that are bought alive in the shell. These are very expensive. Live scallops are also harvested by dredging. These scallops are also very good but the shells may contain mud.

In the UK market, King and slightly smaller Queen Scallops are the most widely available.

Scallops should be a pale cream colour but have often been soaked to make them whiter.

Frozen scallops are readily available. They are ice-glazed, which means that they have been dipped in water to create a thick coating of ice. This protects the delicate flesh.

Storing

Store live scallops in the bottom of the refrigerator. Place on a bed of ice in a perforated tray so that the water can drain away. Cover with a tea towel. Use within 24 hours.

Store previously frozen scallops in the bottom of the refrigerator. Use within 24 hours of defrosting (see below).

Keep frozen scallops for up to 6 months in the freezer.

Defrosting: To defrost scallops that have a thick ice coating, stand on a perforated tray set over another tray and leave to thaw, which can take several hours. Do not pull the ice from the scallop as will tear the meat, and do not immerse in cold water as scallops which have been soaked can be watery.

To open scallops: Place the scallop on a board, flat side down, and insert a fish filleting knife between the top and bottom shells. Press down hard against the bottom shell and cut the scallop from the bottom shell. Use a spoon to scoop out the scallop.

Cleaning scallops: Cut the white muscle from the side of the scallop and peel away the thin membrane that encircles the scallop. If required, separate the coral from the scallop.

Cleaning a scallop

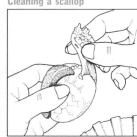

Cooking

Scallops to be used in sauced dishes can be poached in *court bouillon* (see **Stocks**, page 693). *Coquilles St Jacques* (see below) is one of the classic scallop dishes. Do not overcook scallops or they will become rubbery.

Scallops au Gratin

This dish, also known as Coquilles St Jacques, requires the curved scallop shells. These can be purchased or the fresh shells can be used if they are boiled for 10 minutes to destroy any toxins. Alternatively the individual servings can be prepared in small, shallow overproof dishes.

SERVES 4

150 ml | ¼ pint dry white wine
150 ml | ¼ pint water
1 bay leaf
1 slice of onion
8 large or 12 small scallops
450 g | 1 lb mashed potatoes (see **Potatoes**, page 545)
45 g | ½ oz butter

30 g | 1 oz plain flour
2 tablespoons double cream
salt and freshly ground black pepper
lemon juice
4 tablespoons dried breadcrumbs

To serve
4 scallop shells

1 Put the wine, water, bay leaf and onion into a saucepan and bring to the boil.
2 Turn down the heat so that the liquid barely trembles, add the scallops and poach gently for 2 minutes or until they feel firm when pressed. Lift the scallops from the liquid and slice horizontally into 2–3 pieces. Keep the coral whole or discard if preferred. Reserve the cooking liquid.

3 Divide the scallops between the 4 shells.

4 Pipe or spoon the mashed potato around the edge of the shells.

5 Preheat the grill to its highest setting.

6 Heat 30 g|1 oz of the butter in a saucepan and stir in the flour. Cook for 1 minute, then remove from the heat and slowly add the reserved cooking liquid to make a smooth sauce.

7 Strain the scallop cooking liquid into the saucepan and bring to the boil.

8 Boil for 2 minutes, then stir in the cream. Season with salt, pepper and lemon juice.

9 *Napper* the scallops with the sauce. Sprinkle over the crumbs, and dot with the remaining butter, then brown under the grill. Serve immediately.

Searing or Pan-frying: Scallops are often seared before adding to other dishes. The outside of the scallop caramelizes and turns crusty in a delicious contrast with the smooth interior.

Fresh live scallops are best for searing. Frozen scallops can be too watery to sear well.

1 Heat a dry frying pan or griddle over a high heat until it just starts to smoke.

2 Wipe the scallops to dry the surface and sprinkle with salt.

3 Cook the scallops for 30–60 seconds on each side. The surface of the scallop should be golden-brown and the centre should just be turning from translucent to opaque.

Seafood Feuilletées with Spinach

SERVES 4

4 feuilletée cases made from Puff Pastry (see **Pastry**, *Puff Pastry*, page 522)

For the filling

450 g|1 lb baby spinach leaves

30 g|1 oz butter

290 ml|½ pint White Fish or Shellfish Stock (see **Stocks**, page 689)

85 g|3 oz raw langoustines or scampi, preferably in their shells

340 g|12 oz cooked, peeled prawns

3 small single sole fillets, cut into goujons

110 g|4 oz scallops, cleaned as above

salt and freshly ground black pepper

freshly grated nutmeg

For the sauce

2 shallots, finely chopped

225 g|8 oz cold unsalted butter

100 ml|3 ½ fl oz dry white wine

1 tablespoon double cream

juice of ¼ lemon

salt and freshly ground white pepper

1 To make the filling, wash the spinach well and remove the stalks. Melt half the butter in a sauté pan and quickly cook the spinach until just beginning to wilt.

2 Put the stock into a large shallow pan. Heat until it is just starting to tremble, then add the langoustines. Poach for 1 minute, then add the sole fillets and prawns and poach for 1 further minute. Remove the fish from the pan with a slotted spoon and keep warm in a low oven.

3 Reduce the fish cooking liquid to a syrupy glaze and reserve.

4 To make the sauce, sweat the shallots very slowly in 15 g | ½ oz of the butter until very soft. Add the fish glaze and the wine, then strain. Discard the shallots.

5 In a small dry pan, sear the scallops on both sides until nearly cooked through. Keep warm in the oven.

6 Preheat the oven to 150°C | 300°F | gas mark 2.

7 Add the cream to the pan and reduce again until syrupy.

8 Cut the remaining butter into thin slices and whisk piece by piece into the hot reduction, using a small sauce whisk, so that the butter thickens the sauce without melting. Season with the lemon juice, salt and pepper.

9 Place the feuilletée cases in the oven to warm through.

10 Reheat the spinach in the remaining 15 g | ½ oz butter and season with salt, pepper and nutmeg.

11 Divide the spinach between the pastry cases and top with the seafood. *Napper* the seafood with the sauce, then place the tops of the cases on at an angle. Serve any remaining sauce separately in a sauce-boat or ramekin.

Grilling: Scallops can also be grilled until they feel firm to the touch. This will take 5–8 minutes, depending on the heat of the grill. Press the scallops with your finger; they should feel firm, not squidgy. Do not overcook the scallops or they will become rubbery.

Grilled Scallops with Bacon

Sweet scallops and salty bacon have a wonderful affinity. Serve this dish for breakfast, brunch or as a first course, accompanied by a small salad.

SERVES 4

12 large scallops, cleaned as described above	6 rashers of streaky bacon
salt and freshly ground black pepper	30 g	1 oz butter, melted

1 Preheat the grill to its hottest setting.

2 Season the scallops with salt and pepper.

3 Stretch the bacon slices with the back of a knife and cut in half.

4 Wrap each scallop around the edge with a piece of bacon and push on to a skewer.

5 Brush the scallops with the melted butter and grill for 3–4 minutes on each side, until the bacon is browned and the scallops are firm to the touch.

Steaming: Scallops can be steamed by the indirect method (see *Steaming*, page 675), in or out of their shells. Cook until firm when pressed.

Cephalopods

The name cephalopod is from the Greek, meaning 'head with feet', which aptly describes the appearance of these shellfish. Although cephalopods are descended from snails, they no longer have an outside shell. All cephalopods have an elongated sac for a body, tentacles and an ink sac which they use to protect themselves from predators.

Allow 225 g|8 oz for each serving.

Squid

Several species of squid are found throughout the world. Squid is particularly popular in the Mediterranean countries and in Japan.

Choosing

Buy squid that smell fresh and are slippery. Avoid any that have broken bodies or ink sacs. Squid range in size from a few centimetres to over 30 cm|12 in long. The smaller squid are the most tender.

Storing

Store in the bottom of the refrigerator for up to 24 hours.

Store frozen squid for up to 6 months.

Cooking

Squid needs to be cooked only briefly to coagulate the proteins in the flesh, turning it from translucent to opaque. If it is cooked longer than this it becomes tough and rubbery. Should this happen, however, if it is cooked long and slowly it will become tender again.

Preparing squid

Most squid comes prepared but if the tentacles are still attached it needs to be cleaned. It is a messy but simple procedure.

1 Clean the squid in the sink. Pull the tentacles from the body sac to remove the entrails and the ink sac. (a)
2 Pull out the clear, plastic-like quill from the inside of the body and discard. (b)
3 Rinse the body sac under the tap.
4 Cut through the head just below the tentacles. (c)
5 Squeeze the base of the tentacles to remove a bony piece called the beak (it resembles a bird's beak).
6 Cut the flaps from the body sac and set aside. Scrape the membrane from the body. (d)
7 Wash all the pieces of squid well. (e)

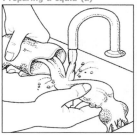

Removing the cartilage (b)
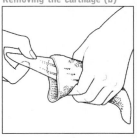

Cutting off the tentacles (c)

Pulling off the membrane (d)
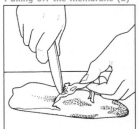

Cleaned squid (e)
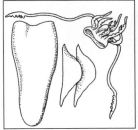

Italian Seafood Salad

SERVES 6 AS A FIRST COURSE

450 g | 1 lb fresh squid

a few slices of onion

a few parsley stalks

1 bay leaf

2 slices of lemon

salt

1 medium leek

1 medium carrot

55 g | 2 oz peeled, cooked prawns

55 g | 2 oz cooked cockles

55 g | 2 oz button mushrooms, thinly sliced

For the dressing

1 tablespoon good-quality olive oil

2 tablespoons sunflower oil

1 teaspoon white wine vinegar

1 teaspoon lemon juice

salt and freshly ground black pepper

1 small clove of garlic, crushed

1 tablespoon finely chopped fresh parsley

1 Clean and skin the squid, as described above. Cut into 6 mm | $\frac{1}{4}$ in strips.

2 Place the squid in a saucepan and just cover with water. Add the onion, parsley stalks, bay leaf, lemon slices and a pinch of salt. Simmer for about 1 minute, until the squid turns opaque. If the squid is large, however, it might need to be simmered for a long time, up to 1 hour, to tenderize. Drain and discard the vegetables. Allow the squid to cool.

3 Cut the leek into julienne strips (see *Knife Skills*, page 71), then wash well. Blanch in boiling water for 30–60 seconds until just tender, then refresh in cold water. Drain and reserve.

4 Peel the carrot and cut into thin ribbons, using a potato peeler. Reserve.

5 Make the salad dressing by whisking all the ingredients together.

6 Toss the dressing with the squid, prawns, cockles, mushrooms, leek and carrots.

7 Chill well in the refrigerator before serving.

VARIATIONS

The following shellfish can be used in the salad in place of the cockles.

Mussels: Prepare and cook as described above. Remove the mussels from their shells, discarding the rubber-band-like piece surrounding the mussel.

Raw scampi: Simmer in a *court bouillon* (see *Stocks*, page 693) for 3–4 minutes. Cool.

Stuffed Squid Provençal

SERVES 4

750 g | 1¾ lb small squid with bodies about
   5 cm | 2 in long
2 tablespoons olive oil
Tomato Sauce (see **Sauces, Savoury**, page 00)

For the stuffing
1 clove of garlic, crushed
1 tablespoon chopped sun-dried tomatoes

100 g | 3½ oz mozzarella cheese, shredded
100 g | 3½ oz fresh white breadcrumbs
2 teaspoons chopped fresh oregano
1 tablespoon chopped fresh parsley
grated zest of 1 small lemon
1 egg, beaten
salt and freshly ground black pepper

1 Prepare the squid as described above.

2 Mix the stuffing ingredients together.

3 Fill the squid with the mixture, securing the tops with cocktail sticks.

4 Preheat the oven to 150°C | 300°F | gas mark 2.

5 Heat the oil in a sauté pan over a medium heat and brown the squid lightly on both sides. Transfer to a casserole dish.

6 Cover the squid with the Tomato Sauce and a lid and bake for 45–60 minutes, or until the squid is tender.

Cooking Squid: What has gone wrong when...

The squid is rubbery.

- The squid has been overcooked but not long enough to tenderize it.

Squid ink

Squid ink can be obtained from inside the squid or purchased separately from fishmongers. It is used to give colour and a salty, fish flavour to risottos and home-made pasta. Dilute the ink with a little water and use immediately.

Octopus

Octopus does not have an internal skeleton like squid.

Choosing

Octopus can be purchased fresh or frozen. Look for octopus with 2 rows of suckers on the tentacles. Those with one row are not as good.

In some countries fresh octopus will have been tenderized by flailing on a concrete surface at least 100 times to soften it. Some anglers do not consider this necessary.

Storing

As for squid.

Octopus needs long slow cooking to tenderize it. The ink has a very strong flavour so is usually discarded.

Preparing

1 Remove the head from the body by twisting. Discard.
2 Rinse out the body to remove the entrails.
3 Bash the octopus with a mallet to tenderize it.
4 Cut the body and tentacles into strips. Simmer for 1 hour or until tender.
5 Dress with a lemon and olive oil Vinaigrette (see **Salad Dressings**, page 573).

Cuttlefish

Cuttlefish look similar to squid but have a squat body and stubby legs. They are popular along the Mediterranean coast.

Choosing

The smallest cuttlefish will be the most tender.

Storing

As for squid, above.

Cooking

Boil the body for a few minutes, then scrape away the brown membrane. Prepare as for squid, above.

Cuttlefish benefit from beating with a mallet to tenderize and long slow cooking, as for octopus. Substitute cuttlefish for squid in the *Stuffed Squid Provençal* recipe, above.

Sorbets

Sorbet is the French word for a water ice made from sugar syrup and flavourings, usually fruit juices and purées. The sorbet was introduced in Europe at the same time as ice cream (see *Ice Creams*, page 310) and shares its history. The Italian equivalent of a sorbet is a sorbetto. The granita is another Italian ice with a higher proportion of water which gives it a grainy texture and a fast melt. A sorbet does not contain milk or other dairy products. A similar ice, called sherbet, which is popular in America, is distinguished from a sorbet by its milk content.

Sorbet

Sorbet is most often served for dessert although it is sometimes served between courses to refresh the palate, when it is called an *interdit*. Sharp sorbets, such as lemon, grapefruit or champagne, are served in this way.

Sorbet is made with a combination of sugar syrup and fruit juice or purée. The ingredients must be in a specified ratio to each other or the sorbet will not have the correct texture: too much sugar and it will be oversweet, syrupy and too soft to hold its shape; too little sugar and it will be icy and hard. Liqueurs are sometimes added to a sorbet to enhance the flavour. The alcohol will inhibit the freezing of the sorbet so not more than 2 tablespoons per 570 ml | 1 pint of liquid should be added.

Chefs use a saccharometer (*pèse-syrop*), a specially designed hydrometer to measure the density of a syrup, to ensure they have the required ratio of ingredients. A saccharometer is an enclosed glass tube that looks rather like a fat thermometer. It has a weight enclosed at one end and gradations marked along the shaft. The saccharometer will either be delineated in the Baume scale, named after the French chemist, Antoine Baume (1728–1804), who invented the system, or in a decimal scale. Another measuring system, called Brix, is used in the USA.

To use a saccharometer, fill a second tube, either a deep jug or a measure called an éprouvette, with enough sorbet syrup to allow the saccharometer to float. Place the saccharometer in the syrup and take the reading on the saccharometer at the level of the syrup. The reading for a sorbet should be:

Without alcohol	17–20° Baume	1.13–1.16° decimal
With alcohol	14–17° Baume	1.11–1.13° decimal

A granita should be about 9 Baume without alcohol or 8 Baume with alcohol to give a truly icy result. Saccharometers and éprouvettes can be obtained from professional chef supply shops or from wine-making accessory shops.

Good results can be obtained if the sorbet mixture contains about one-third sugar and two-thirds other ingredients. Bearing this figure in mind, the cook can make almost any sorbet with 2 parts unsweetened liquid and 1 part sugar, bringing the sugar slowly to the boil to dissolve the sugar, then cooling and freezing it, whisking as necessary. Before freezing, the sorbet base should be very sweet and intensely flavoured as freezing dulls its flavour.

Churning Sorbet

Sorbets are churned in the same manner as ice cream (see *Ice Creams*, page 310). Churn until the sorbet holds its shape like lightly whipped cream. If it is overchurned it will have a fluffy, mousse-like texture and will lack flavour.

Storing Sorbet

Sorbet is at its best freshly made, but can be stored in the freezer for up to 1 week. After a day or two it will become more icy and granular. Many restaurants melt and rechurn their sorbets on a daily basis. Sorbet that contains egg white should be consumed within 24 hours of making and should never be rechurned.

Adding Egg White to Sorbet

If the sorbet is going to be still-frozen it is best to add 1 tablespoon egg white per 570 ml | 1 pint sorbet mixture at the end of the freezing process. After the addition of the egg white, refreeze the sorbet to firm the texture. The egg white coats the ice crystals, helping to prevent the formation of large crystals, slows the melt and gives the sorbet a smoother 'mouth-feel'.

To add egg white to a sorbet using a food processor, cut the sorbet into egg-sized chunks. Whizz, using the pulse button, until it is smooth. Whip the egg white with a fork to break it up, then add it to the sorbet through the feed tube of the food processor while the motor is running. This should take about 5 seconds. Do not overprocess or the sorbet will melt too much and will have a granular texture when frozen.

The addition of uncooked egg white carries a health risk associated with raw eggs, so sorbets to which egg white has been added should not be eaten by the very young, old, infirm, or pregnant or lactating women. Once the egg white has been added the sorbet should be consumed within 24 hours.

Mango and Passion fruit Sorbet

SERVES 4–6

140 g|5 oz granulated sugar
270 ml 9 fl oz water
2 ripe mangoes

3 ripe passion fruit
1 tablespoon lime juice
1 egg white (optional)

1 Place the sugar in a saucepan with the water and heat over a low heat, stirring occasionally, to dissolve the sugar. Turn up the heat to bring the syrup to the boil and boil for 1 minute.

2 Purée the mango flesh and the passion fruit pulp and seeds in a food processor. Do not use a liquidizer because it will break up the passionfruit seeds.

3 Sieve the purée. You should have 290 ml|½ pint. Stir in the lime juice.

4 Add the syrup to the fruit purée and allow to cool.

5 Churn in a machine or still-freeze (see **Ice Creams**, *Churning*, page 310).

6 If adding egg white, see above.

Sorbets: What has gone wrong when...

The sorbet will not freeze solidly enough.

- The mixture contains too much sugar.
- The mixture contains too much alcohol.

The sorbet freezes too solidly.

- The mixture contains too much water.
- The mixture contains too high a quantity of fruit solids.
- The mixture has not been churned sufficiently.

The sorbet has a grainy, icy texture.

- The mixture does not contain enough fruit solids.
- The mixture has not been churned sufficiently.

Granitas

A granita is similar to a sorbet with an icy, granular texture. Granitas contain a higher proportion of water and are best made by stirring frequently with a fork during the freezing process. This method will produce a traditional granita, which has an even texture of visible icy granules.

The ideal density of a granita is 9° on the Baume scale or 8° if it contains alcohol. Most sorbets can be made into a granita by increasing the water quantity to 375 ml|12 fl oz water to a standard recipe making 1 litre|1¾ pints sorbet.

A tiny dish of granita is particularly suitable for serving as an *interdit* between courses at formal dinners, to freshen the palate.

Freezing a Granita

Place the unfrozen mixture in a shallow container or several containers so that the depth of the liquid is no more than 2.5 cm|1 in. Place the containers in the freezer for 30 minutes, then remove and scrape the frozen mixture from the edges into the middle, using a table fork. Return the containers to the freezer. Repeat the scraping procedure every 30 minutes for about 2½ hours or until the mixture is completely frozen with an even, grainy texture. Serve immediately or return to the freezer. If the mixture becomes solid, allow to stand at room temperature for about 15 minutes before scooping into small glasses or bowls.

Melon and Champagne Granita

This granita is deliciously refreshing but the melon needs to be very ripe and full of flavour. It can be served between courses or as a low-fat dessert.

SERVES 4–6

340 g|12 oz granulated sugar
570 ml|1 pint water
juice of 1 lemon

290 ml|½ pint champagne or sparkling wine
1 large ripe Ogen or Galia melon

1 Place the sugar and the water in a saucepan and dissolve the sugar over a low heat, stirring occasionally.
2 Bring the syrup to the boil and boil for 1 minute. Add the lemon juice and the wine and allow to cool.
3 Cut the melon into quarters and discard the seeds. Cut the flesh into small chunks, then purée in a food processor or liquidizer.
4 Combine the puréed melon with the sugar syrup and freeze as directed above.

Soufflés

A soufflé is often considered to be the premier example of classic French cooking. Soufflés can be savoury or sweet. Technically a soufflé should be a hot preparation; however, there are recipes for cold soufflés. As well as being the name of a dish, the term soufflé is used to describe a dish that has risen up. The French word *souffler* means to puff.

Hot soufflés have been prepared in France since the late 1700s. Although soufflés have an undeserved reputation for being difficult to prepare, they are little more than a thick base that has been lightened with egg whites. They are quick to make and once the principles are mastered, should present little difficulty to the cook.

A hot soufflé is a delicate dish, being held together by no more than the lightly cooked proteins in the egg foam. A roulade is a soufflé baked flat in a thin layer which, when cool, is rolled around a filling.

Cold soufflés are much like a mousse in ingredients and texture and are usually called soufflés when they are served in a dish like a hot soufflé. Gelatine is used to give stability to the egg and cream foams in a cold soufflé. These soufflés are described in detail below (see also **Mousses**, page 489).

Hot Soufflés

Before making a soufflé, read the sections on **Eggs,** *Whisking Whites* (page 233) and **Sauces, Savoury,** *White Sauce* (page 589).

Soufflés can be savoury for a first course or sweet for a dessert. The base of a soufflé is called a *panade*. The *panade* should be thick enough to hold its shape when mounded, rather like Greek yoghurt. If it is too thick, the soufflé will be badly risen. If it is too thin, the soufflé will puff up too easily in the oven and will flow over the sides of the dish.

A successful soufflé will be light and well risen, almost double its original volume. It should be well flavoured. An individual soufflé should have about 1 tablespoon undercooked (*baveuse*) mixture in the centre; a larger soufflé should have a little more.

Hot Soufflés: Points to Remember

- Weigh all ingredients accurately.
- Heat a baking sheet for additional 'bottom heat', while preheating the oven.
- Place the oven shelf in the top third of the oven, taking care to leave enough room for the soufflé to rise.
- Prepare the dishes before beginning to cook.
- Do not add the egg yolks to a hot *panade* (base) or they will cook and loose their elasticity.
- Overseason the *panade*.
- Whisk the egg whites to the medium peak stage.
- Take care not to overfold the whisked whites or volume will be lost.
- Turn the oven up one setting when putting the soufflés into the oven. The increase in temperature helps them rise up.
- Do not open the oven door until the soufflés are nearly done.
- Serve the soufflés immediately. They do not hold.

Cheese Soufflés

SERVES 4

40 g | 1½ oz butter, plus extra melted butter for greasing

2 tablespoons dried white breadcrumbs, for coating

30 g | 1 oz plain flour

½ teaspoon dry English mustard

a pinch of cayenne pepper

290 ml | ½ pint milk

85 g | 3 oz strong Cheddar or Gruyère cheese, finely grated

4 eggs, separated

salt and freshly ground black pepper

1 Preheat the oven to 200°C | 400°F | gas mark 6. Place the oven shelf in the top third of the oven or in the position nearest the hottest part, allowing space for the soufflé to rise. Place a baking sheet in the oven. Lightly butter 4 ramekins and coat with the breadcrumbs.

2 To make the *panade*, melt the butter in a small saucepan. Remove the pan from the heat and stir in the flour, mustard and cayenne. Return the pan to a medium heat and cook, stirring, until the mixture bubbles. Remove from the heat.

3 Gradually stir in the milk to make a smooth sauce. Return to the heat and bring to the boil, stirring. Allow to boil for 2 minutes. The mixture will be very thick and will leave the sides of the pan. Remove from the heat.

4 Stir in the cheese and egg yolks. Taste for seasoning. The mixture should be very well seasoned because the flavour will be diluted by the addition of the egg whites. If making ahead, cover the *panade* with a disc of greaseproof paper.

5 Whisk the egg whites until just stiff. Mix a spoonful of the whites into the *panade* to loosen it. Using a large metal spoon, fold in the remaining whites.

6 Fill the ramekins three-quarters full.

7 Place on the heated baking sheet. Turn the oven up to 225°C|425°F|gas mark 7 and bake for 8–10 minutes until the soufflés are well risen with only a slight wobble in the centre. Do not test to see if the soufflés are done for at least 8 minutes. Serve immediately.

Preparing a Ramekin for a Sweet Soufflé

This method works particularly well for sweet soufflés when the egg whites have been stabilized by whisking in some of the sugar.

1 Lightly rub the inside of each ramekin with the softened butter, then leave a band of butter about 1 cm|1½ in deep and 0.5 mm thick around the top edge of the ramekin.

2 Fill the ramekin to the top with the soufflé mixture and level the surface with a palette knife.

3 Use the edge of your thumb or the end of a teaspoon to scrape the butter and the soufflé mixture from the rim of the ramekin.

Seville Orange Soufflé

This is a recipe of Sophie Grigson's that was published in the *Evening Standard*.

SERVES 4

softened butter for the soufflé	15 g|½ oz butter
110 g|4 oz caster sugar	finely grated rind and zest of 2 Seville oranges
30 g|1 oz plain flour	4 egg yolks
150–200 ml|5–7 fl oz milk	5 egg whites
1 vanilla pod, split	icing sugar to dust

1 Prepare the soufflé dish(es) as instructed above.

2 Preheat the oven to 200°C|400°F|gas mark 6. Place a baking sheet in the oven to heat.

3 Mix half the sugar with the flour in a saucepan. Pour in a little of the milk to make a smooth paste then gradually stir in the remaining milk.

4 Add the vanilla pod and heat over a medium-low heat, stirring, until the mixture comes to the boil. Boil for 1 minute. The mixture should be the consistency of thick yoghurt. Add more milk if necessary.

5 Remove from the heat. Scrape the seeds from the vanilla pod and add them to the mixture. Discard the pod.

6 Beat in the butter and stir in the zest and juice and finally the egg yolks. Transfer to a large mixing bowl.

7 Whisk the egg whites until stiff then gradually whisk in the remaining sugar. Fold gently into the orange mixture.

8 Spoon in to the soufflé dish(es) filling them to the brim. Use the edge of your finger to scrape the mixture away from the top ½ cm|¼ in of the inside rim.

9 Bake in the top third of the oven for 20–25 minutes for a large soufflé or 12–15 minutes for individual soufflés.

10 Test by giving the soufflés a 'shake'. If it wobbles alarmingly return to the oven for another few minutes.

11 Dust with icing sugar and serve immediately.

Hot Soufflés: What has gone wrong when...

The soufflé falls dramatically upon removal from the oven.

- The soufflé is undercooked. Return it to the oven for a couple of minutes.

The soufflé mushrooms out of the dish and runs down the sides.

- The mixture contains too high a proportion of egg whites.
- The *panade* was too soft.

The soufflé doesn't rise very much.

- The *panade* was too thick.
- The egg whites were overfolded.
- The egg whites were over/underwhisked.
- The recipe does not contain enough egg whites.
- Heavy ingredients were added to the *panade*.
- The *panade* was too warm when the whites were added.

Twice-baked Soufflés

Twice-baked soufflés are an exception to the rule that soufflés must be served immediately. Twice-baked soufflés are made in advance then reheated. The reheating process gives them a second puff but also results in a heavier, denser soufflé.

Twice-baked Spinach Soufflés

These soufflés are made by the same method as the soufflé above but they are baked in a bain-marie. After the first baking they can be set aside then reheated up to 24 hours later.

SERVES 4

melted butter for greasing
150 ml | ¼ pint milk
1 small slice of onion
100 g | 3½ oz fresh spinach
20 g | ⅔ oz butter
15 g | ½ oz plain flour
1 egg yolk
30 g | 1 oz Gruyère cheese, finely grated

grated fresh nutmeg
salt and freshly ground black pepper
2 egg whites

To serve

4 tablespoons single cream
4 tablespoons finely grated fresh Parmesan cheese

1 Preheat the oven to 180°C|350°F|gas mark 4. Grease 4 timbale moulds generously with melted butter.

2 Heat the milk with the onion until it steams. Leave to stand for 10 minutes to infuse.

3 Bring a saucepan of water to the boil. Trim the stems from the spinach and discard. Wash the spinach leaves very well to remove any grit.

4 Immerse the spinach in the boiling water for about 30 seconds, until wilted. Rinse under cold running water, then squeeze dry and chop finely.

5 Melt the butter in a small saucepan over a medium heat. Stir in the flour to make a roux. Allow to bubble, then cook for 30 seconds. Remove from the heat.

6 Remove the onion from the milk. Gradually add the milk to the roux to make a smooth, thick sauce. Return to the heat and cook until it boils. Boil for 1 minute. Cool to tepid.

7 Stir the sauce into the egg yolk. Stir in the spinach and cheese. Season with nutmeg, salt and pepper.

8 Whisk the egg whites until just stiff. Fold in 1 tablespoon of the whisked egg white to loosen the mixture, then fold in the remainder, using a large metal spoon.

9 Turn the mixture into the prepared timbales and place in a bain-marie.

10 Bake the soufflés in the oven for 12–15 minutes, until well risen, lightly browned on top and with only a very slight wobble in the centre. Remove from the oven and the bain-marie and allow to sink. Turn out into an ovenproof dish. Refrigerate if holding for more than 1 hour before serving.

11 To serve, preheat the oven to 220°C|425°F|gas mark 7. Top each soufflé with 1 tablespoon of the cream and sprinkle with 1 tablespoon of the Parmesan. Bake for 10 minutes or until lightly browned and puffed. Serve immediately.

Chocolate Roulade

Chocolate Roulade, a favourite dessert, is actually a soufflé that has been allowed to fall after baking. It is baked in a roasting tin or Swiss Roll tin.

SERVES 6

225 g|8 oz plain chocolate, chopped	140 g|5 oz caster sugar
85 ml|3 fl oz water	icing sugar, to dust
1 teaspoon instant coffee powder	200 ml|7 fl oz double cream
5 eggs, separated	

1 Line a 27.5 × 32.5 cm|11 × 13 in roasting tin or Swiss Roll tin with baking parchment.

2 Preheat the oven to 200°C|400°F|gas mark 6.

3 Put the chocolate, water and coffee into a saucepan and melt over a low heat. Allow to cool to room temperature.

4 Beat the egg yolks with all but 1 tablespoon of the caster sugar until pale and mousse-like. Fold in the melted chocolate.

5 Whisk the egg whites until just stiff, then beat in the remaining caster sugar.

6 Fold 1 tablespoon of the whisked egg whites into the chocolate mixture to loosen, then carefully fold in the remainder, using a large metal spoon.

7 Turn the mixture into the prepared tin and bake for 15–20 minutes, or until the cake feels cooked when pressed in the centre. You will have to press hard enough to break the crust on the top of the cake. Do not overcook the cake or it will break apart when rolled.

8 Remove the cake from the oven and cover with a clean tea towel or piece of damp kitchen paper to help soften the crust.

9 Lift the cake and parchment out of the baking tin and place on a wire rack to cool.

10 Place a sheet of greaseproof paper large enough to hold the cake on a work surface and sift over enough icing sugar to coat the paper.

11 Remove the tea towel from the top of the cake, then quickly turn the cake on to the icing sugar.

12 Whisk the cream until soft peaks form.

13 Trim the edges from the cake. Spread the cake with the cream and roll up from the short edge, using the paper to help. Place on a serving dish.

NOTE: The roulade can be stored in the refrigerator for up to 24 hours or frozen for 1 month.

Roulades: What has gone wrong when...

The roulade cracks when rolled.

- Some cracking is a characteristic of a roulade but if it breaks apart when rolled it has been overcooked.

  Spread additional cream over the outside of the cake. It will still taste delicious.

The roulade is very flat/badly risen.

- The egg whites were underwhisked or were overfolded.

There are lumps of egg white visible in the cake.

- The egg whites were overwhisked.
- The egg whites were underfolded.

Cold Soufflés

Cold or iced soufflés are mixtures that have been set with gelatine and lightened with whisked egg whites and sometimes whipped cream. Although similar in texture to a mousse (see **Mousses**, *Caramel Mousse*, page 490), they are lighter and are usually sweet rather than savoury. The serving dish for a cold soufflé is sometimes tied with a paper collar that is removed before serving, giving a 'risen' appearance similar to that of a hot soufflé.

To make a cold soufflé you will need to be familiar with the techniques in the following sections:

- **Gelatine** (page 294)
- **Eggs**, *Whisking Egg Whites* (page 233)
- **Dairy Products**, *Double Cream* (page 201)

Cold Lemon Soufflé

SERVES 4

3 tablespoons water

scant 1½ teaspoons powdered gelatine

3 medium eggs, separated

grated zest and juice of 2 washed large lemons

140 g|5 oz caster sugar

icing sugar (optional)

150 ml|¼ pint double cream

To decorate (optional)

150 ml|¼ pint double cream, whipped

55 g|2 oz flaked almonds, toasted

1 If desired, prepare a large soufflé dish or each of 4 ramekins with a collar of doubled baking parchment by securing with a paper clip a band of paper extending 5 cm|2 in above the edge of the dish.

2 Place the water in a small saucepan and sprinkle over the gelatine. Allow to sponge.

3 Place the egg yolks, lemon juice and sugar in a large bowl set over a saucepan of simmering water. Whisk with an electric hand whisk until the mixture is very thick. When the beaters are lifted, it should form a *ribbon trail*. Remove from the pan of hot water and continue whisking until the mixture feels lukewarm and the bottom of the bowl is cool.

4 Whisk in the lemon zest.

5 Dissolve the gelatine over a low heat until it is clear. Fold it into the lemon mixture. Taste the mixture, adding more lemon juice if it is too sweet or sifted icing sugar if too tart.

6 Rest the bowl of lemon mixture in a cold bain-marie. Stir the mixture occasionally until setting point (see **Gelatine**, page 294) is reached.

7 Whisk the cream until it is just holding its shape, then fold into the lemon mixture.

8 Whisk the egg whites to the medium peak stage (see **Eggs**, *Whisking Whites*, page 233). When the lemon mixture reaches setting point, fold in the whisked whites, using a large metal spoon.

9 Turn the mixture into the serving dish(es) and refrigerate for 2–3 hours, or until set.

10 To remove the paper collar(s) heat a metal spatula under hot running water, then dry it. Carefully run it between the paper and the soufflé while peeling the paper away from the soufflé.

11 Decorate the soufflé(s) with rosettes of cream and almonds, if desired.

Cold Soufflés: What has gone wrong when...

The soufflé contains lumps of rubbery gelatine.
- The soufflé base was too cold when the gelatine was added.
- The gelatine was not warmed sufficiently before it was added to the base.

The soufflé contains lumps of cream.
- The cream was overwhipped.
- The cream was not folded in sufficiently.

The soufflé has separated into a lemon layer and a frothy layer.
- The egg whites were added to the base before setting point was reached so the gelatine sank to the bottom of the dish.

The soufflé is dense and heavy.
- The mixture was overfolded when the cream and/or egg whites were added.
- The lemon base was not whisked sufficiently.
- The base was stirred too frequently/too briskly while waiting for setting point.
- Too much gelatine was used.

Categories of Soup

Puréed Based on ingredients first cooked in stock, water or milk, puréed and then strained to produce a smooth soup of thin to medium coating consistency. Made with vegetables, meat, fish and fruit (see *Simple Vegetable Soup*, below).

Cream Soups based on puréed vegetables, fish, shellfish or chicken, enriched and thickened with whipping or double cream, or egg and cream liaison, or Béchamel Sauce.

Bisques Cream soups made with the puréed shells and flesh of shellfish flavoured with cognac and thickened with cream to medium coating consistency (see *Prawn Bisque*, below).

Chunky Soups consisting of a liquid base of varying thickness, cooked with one or a number of flavouring ingredients cut into uniform dice or in less formal larger pieces. These include Bouillabaisse, chowders and *Minestrone* (see below).

Broths Thin soups based on plain, unclarified, unthickened stock made from boiling meat or fish with vegetables. Either served plain or as broth-based chunky soups, made more substantial by garnishing the broth with some of the meat or fish and vegetables and substantial ingredients such as pulses or grains, e.g. the Scottish soup *Cock-a-Leekie* (see below).

Consommés Thin, clear soups based on richly flavoured, fat-free, clarified stock made from beef, poultry and game bones. Either served cold and jellied, or hot garnished with vegetables, small pasta shapes and dumplings, or thickened with egg and cream liaison (see *Beef Consommé* below).

Potages or Regional French Unthickened stews, based on traditional French recipes. Made with a high proportion of meat, seafood, vegetables, rice or grains gently cooked in broth, stock or flavoured water. Often so substantial that they are served as a meal in their own right (see *Pot au Feu* and *French Onion Soup*, below).

Cold Smooth or chunky soups, served very chilled. Sometimes enriched with cream or garnished with vegetables, croûtons, herbs or a small quantity of the main flavouring ingredient (see *Iced Vichyssoise* and *Gazpacho*, below).

Soups

The term 'soup' originates from the medieval word *sop*, describing a slice of bread placed in the bottom of a bowl before broth or the contents of the cooking pot, termed *potage*, were poured on to it. The broth or potage was made with various vegetables, grains, pulses and meat boiled in water or stock and was eaten as the main meal of the day by the poor and rural population. By the end of the seventeenth century, *soupe* was recognized as a course in its own right and was eaten at the beginning of the meal, often without bread, to titillate the palate. During the eighteenth century the word soup was used to describe chunky, wholesome regional soups thickened with bread or grains, and potage came to describe smooth, elegant soups with a more delicate flavour. The word soup is now used as a comprehensive term for both chunky and smooth soups served at the beginning of a meal or as a meal in their own right (see *Categories of Soup*, above).

Puréed Soups

Puréed soups are smooth in texture and vary from thin to medium coating consistency depending upon the thickening agent used and the style of soup. Puréed soup can be thickened solely with its puréed ingredients or with roux, breadcrumbs, egg and cream liaison, fécules or cream (see **Sauces, Savoury**, page 657).

The purée is made by blending the ingredients in a food processor or liquidizer or by passing through a fine sieve. Although food processors will purée the ingredients adequately, the end result may be grainy and it may be necessary to press the purée through a fine sieve. Soups containing acidic ingredients are best passed through a nylon sieve as a wire sieve may taint their flavour.

To pass soup through a sieve, first pass the liquid through it into a bowl, holding the vegetables back, then rest the sieve over a clean pan and with a ladle or wooden spoon gently rub or push through a little of the cooked vegetable at a time. Once the vegetables are puréed, gradually add the liquid until the soup reaches a coating consistency. When puréeing potatoes, make sure that they are pressed through quickly to prevent them from becoming gluey.

Vegetable and fruit soups made from puréed vegetables are sometimes thickened with starchy ingredients such as potato, rice or pulses. If making a soup with a green vegetable, take care not to overheat the vegetable or it might turn a drab olive colour. The best way to preserve the bright green colour is to cook and cool the green vegetable entirely, cool the stock and then purée the two together. Reheat briefly just before serving.

Simple Vegetable Soup

SERVES 8

45 g|1½ oz butter	225 g|8 oz potatoes, chopped
225 g|8 oz onions, chopped	860 ml|1½ pints water
450 g|1 lb carrots, chopped	salt and freshly ground black pepper
110 g|4 oz celery, chopped	425 ml|¾ pint milk

1 Melt the butter in a large, heavy-based sauce pan with 2 tablespoons water. Add the onions, carrots, and celery, stir and cover with a lid. Cook over a low heat, stirring occasionally, for about 45 minutes, until the vegetables soft but not coloured.

2 Add the potatoes and water. Season with salt and pepper and simmer, uncovered, for 15 minutes.

3 Strain the vegetables, reserving the cooking liquor. Purée the vegetables in a food processor or liquidizer until smooth, then pass through a sieve.

4 Add the milk and as much cooking liquor as required to bring the soup to a coating consistency.

5 Pour into the rinsed-out pan, adjust the seasoning and reheat carefully.

Puréed Soups: What has gone wrong when...

The soup has a grainy texture.

- The soup was not puréed until completely smooth and the sieve was not sufficiently fine to hold back the grainy lumps.

The soup has a metallic taste.

- The soup contained acidic ingredients and was passed through a metal sieve which has tainted its flavour.

The soup is too thin.

- The cooking liquor and vegetables were puréed together. Add the strained cooking liquor to the puréed vegetables once they have been passed through the sieve until the required consistency is achieved.

The puréed vegetables have become gluey in consistency.

- The vegetables included potato that was overworked while being passed through the sieve.

Cream Soups

Cream soups are similar to puréed soups in texture but are richer. They are enriched and thickened with Béchamel Sauce or egg and cream liaison (see **Sauces, Savoury**, pages 589 and 584), or whipping or double cream.

Bisque

Bisque is a cream soup thickened and flavoured with the shells of crustaceans, such as prawns, lobster or crab. The shells are cooked in stock, then pounded to a thick paste and passed through a fine sieve to remove any remaining fragments of shell membrane.

With harder-shelled varieties of shellfish such as lobster or crab, the shell must first be smashed in a plastic bag with a rolling pin and the large, hard pieces removed. The remaining pulverized shell can then be liquidized and pressed through a heavy fine-holed conical sieve with a heavy wooden spoon.

Prawn Bisque

In this recipe the prawn shells are not puréed and added to the soup but are used to make a flavourful stock which is strained and added to the puréed shelled prawns.

SERVES 4

900 g|2 lb shell-on cooked prawns	1 bay leaf
2 tablespoons oil	1 parsley stalk
110 g|4 oz butter	1 blade of mace
2 shallots, chopped	45 g|1½ oz plain flour
juice of ½ lemon	salt and freshly ground white pepper
3 tablespoons brandy	Tabasco sauce
1 litre|1¾ pints well-flavoured White or Brown Fish or Shellfish Stock (see **Stocks**, pages 689 and 693)	3 tablespoons single cream

1 Peel all but 4 of the prawns and reserve the shells. Wash the prawns, remove the dark veins (see **Shellfish**, page 627) and reserve any roe.

2 Heat the oil in a large, heavy-based saucepan, add 30 g\|1 oz of the butter and fry the prawn shells for 2 minutes. Add the shallots, lemon juice and brandy and cook for a further 2 minutes. Add the stock, bay leaf, parsley stalk and mace and cook for 30 minutes (this will help to give the bisque flavour and colour).

3 Meanwhile, blend or pound together all the peeled prawns with about 45 g\|1½ oz of the remaining butter and any reserved roe.

4 Melt the remaining butter in a saucepan. Add the flour and cook for 30 seconds. Strain in the stock and bring slowly to the boil, stirring constantly. Simmer for 2 minutes, then strain in the pan juices and whisk in the prawn butter.

5 Season with salt, pepper and Tabasco. Add the cream and the reserved prawns.

NOTE: If no roe is available, whisk 1 teaspoon tomato purée into the bisque to enhance its colour.

Bisque: What has gone wrong when...

The soup has a grainy texture.

- Some of the shells were left on the prawns before pounding them to a purée.
- Some or all of the prawns were not deveined before pounding them with the butter.
- The shells were not washed properly before cooking and peeling, causing the stock to be gritty.

Chunky Soups

Chunky soups consist of a liquid base of varying thickness cooked with one or a number of flavouring ingredients cut into uniform dice or less formal, larger pieces. Chunky soup may be sufficiently substantial to be eaten as a meal in its own right, as it often contains a high proportion of starchy ingredients such as noodles, pasta, rice, barley or bread as well as fish, vegetables and meat added to flavour it. Such soups are eaten all over the world as hearty national and regional dishes; examples include Bouillabaisse, chowders and Minestrone. Alternatively, chunky soup may also be lighter and more refined, containing a lower proportion of solid ingredients, to serve as a first course.

Minestrone

Minestrone is made with a wide variety of ingredients in season. These include green vegetables, aromatic vegetables, dried beans, potato, sometimes sausage, bacon or a little meat, but minestrone always contains small pasta shapes or broken-up spaghetti or macaroni. The liquid base is either stock or water. Minestrone is served with Parmesan cheese and sometimes Pesto (see **Herbs**, page 307).

Minestrone

SERVES 6

85 g | 3 oz dried haricot beans

1 tablespoon oil

3 rashers of rindless streaky bacon, diced

2 cloves of garlic, crushed

1 large onion, sliced

2 carrots, diced

1 stick of celery, chopped

2 medium potatoes, peeled and diced

1.1 litres | 2 pints Ham Stock or Vegetable Stock (see **Stocks**, page 690)

1 bouquet garni (3 fresh basil leaves, 2 parsley stalks and 1 bay leaf, tied together with string)

1 tablespoon tomato purée

110 g | 4 oz white cabbage

3 large tomatoes, peeled and chopped

55 g | 2 oz broken spaghetti or other small pasta

salt and freshly ground black pepper

freshly grated Parmesan cheese

1 Soak the beans in cold water for 3–4 hours, then drain.
2 Heat the oil in a heavy-based saucepan, add the bacon, garlic, onion, carrots and celery and cook for 2 minutes, stirring. Add the potatoes and cook until the oil

has been absorbed and the vegetables are soft, skimming off any fat and scum that rise to the surface.

3 Add the stock and bring to the boil, then add the bouquet garni, tomato purée and drained beans. Simmer for 45 minutes.

4 Add the cabbage, tomatoes and spaghetti and continue to simmer for a further 15 minutes, or until the beans are soft and the spaghetti is tender.

5 Just before serving, remove the herbs and check the seasoning. Serve sprinkled with Parmesan cheese.

Minestrone: What has gone wrong when...

The minestrone has become cloudy.

- The soup was allowed to boil while cooking, causing the ingredients, especially the potatoes, to overcook and break up.
- The soup was not skimmed sufficiently to remove fat and scum accumulating on the surface.

Broth-based Soups

Broth-based soups are thin and watery but are made more substantial with the addition of filling ingredients such as rice, barley or pulses. Broth-based chunky soups should also contain the diced vegetables and meat used to flavour them. Broth-based soups are mostly made with the cooking liquor of ham, chicken, lamb and beef.

French Onion Soup

This is a classic French broth-based soup. To obtain the maximum sweetness and flavour from the onions, sweat them extremely slowly until they are completely soft and a deep brown. The sweated onions must then be slowly simmered in well-flavoured stock to create the rich, sweet flavour characteristic of this soup.

SERVES 4–6

55 g | 2 oz butter
450 g | 1 lb onions, sliced
½ clove of garlic, crushed
1 teaspoon plain flour
1.1 litres | 2 pints well-flavoured stock, preferably Brown Stock (see **Stocks**, page 692)

salt and freshly ground black pepper
55 g | 2 oz Gruyère cheese, grated
1 teaspoon dry English mustard
4 slices of French bread

1 Melt the butter in a large, heavy-based saucepan and slowly sweat the onions for at least 1 hour, until the onions are a deep brown and very soft.

2 Add the garlic and cook for 1–2 minutes.

3 Stir in the flour and cook for 1 minute.

4 Add the stock and stir until boiling. Season with salt and pepper, then simmer for 20–30 minutes.

5 Preheat the oven to 200°C | 400°F | gas mark 6.

6 Mix the cheese with the mustard and season with pepper. Spread the mixture on the bread slices and place them on the bottom of an earthenware tureen. Ladle over the soup. The bread will rise to the top. Put the soup (uncovered) in the oven until well-browned and bubbling.

French Onion Soup: What has gone wrong when...

The soup is pale and lacks flavour.
- The onions were not browned for long enough.

The soup tastes bitter.
- The onions or garlic were burnt.

Consommés or Clear Soups

Clear soups are based on richly flavoured, fat-free, clarified broth or stock, served with or without garnishing or flavouring ingredients. The stock is richly flavoured with a large proportion of bones and aromatic vegetables as it provides most or all of the soup's flavour. Garnishing ingredients tend to be added just before the soup is served and have little chance to enhance its flavour (see *Soup Garnishes*, below).

Clear soups, such as Consommé, are not designed to be filling but are watery in consistency and are traditionally served to excite the taste-buds at the beginning of a dinner where a large number of courses may be served. Consommé is time-consuming to make and needs a large quantity of ingredients to flavour it. It also requires a certain amount of skill as the flavoured stock must be entirely fat-free and clarified with egg whites until a crystal clear liquid is obtained (see ***Aspic***, page 90).

Meat-based stocks for clear soups are mainly made with the bones of beef, poultry and game as well as bones that provide a rich gelatinous quality, such as veal bones, and rich flavour, such as marrow bones. The stock may also be flavoured with mushroom stock and fortified wine like sherry, port or Madeira.

Consommés are based on meat stock as fish stock is harder to clear without removing almost all of its flavour. Consommé soups are served either hot or cold, set to a delicate jelly that melts in the mouth. The jellied quality is obtained either by making the stock with gelatinous bones like veal knuckle or by adding a small quantity of gelatine to the clarified stock. It may also be thickened and enriched to a smooth velvety consistency with egg and cream liaison (see ***Sauces, Savoury***, page 584).

Beef Consommé

SERVES 6

1.75 litres|3 pints very well-flavoured Brown
   Stock, made from beef, veal or chicken bones
   (see **Stocks**, page 692)

225 g|8 oz lean shin of beef, minced (this will
   flavour the stock further as well as assisting
   the clarifying process)

salt and freshly ground black pepper

3 egg whites

3 egg shells, crushed

5 tablespoons medium sherry or Madeira

1 Place the stock, beef and sherry in a large saucepan. Season very well with salt and pepper. Add the egg whites and crushed egg shells.

2 Clarify the stock, using the technique described under **Aspic**, *Clearing* (page 90).

3 Fix a double layer of fine muslin or white kitchen paper over a clean basin. Place a spoonful of crust into the sieve. Carefully strain the soup through it. Do not try to hurry the process by squeezing the cloth as this will produce a murky soup: it must be allowed to drip through at its own pace. The consommé is now ready for serving.

4 Garnish as required (see *Garnishes for Consommé*, below).

NOTE: To serve Consommé en Gelée (Jellied Consommé), pour the liquid into a shallow pan or tray and refrigerate until set. Chop roughly with a knife and spoon into ice-cold soup cups. Serve with a wedge of lemon and toast.

Consommé: What has gone wrong when...

The soup is cloudy.

- The equipment used to make the consommé was not perfectly clean.
- The stock was not sufficiently skimmed or properly clarified.
- The clarifying stock was forced through the straining cloth.
- The crust was whisked into the stock.

The soup tastes bland.

- The stock was not sufficiently flavoured or seasoned well enough before it was clarified and strained.

The soup will not set to a jelly.

- The clarified stock contained insufficient gelatine to set. The bones used did not contain enough gelatine or too little extra gelatine was added to the clarified stock.

Garnishes for Consommé

Consommé is named depending upon the garnish used.

Aux pointes des asperges: Place cooked asparagus tips at the bottom of a warmed tureen and pour the soup over.

À la julienne: Add mixed carrot, turnip, leek and celery cut into julienne strips to the consommé and cook until tender. Chopped fresh chervil or parsley is sometimes added just before serving.

Lady Curzon: Chill the consommé in ovenproof cups. Flavour 2 tablespoons double cream with curry powder, salt and pepper and pour over each serving. Place under a hot grill to brown the top. Put into a warm oven to heat the soup.

Aux vermicelli: Cook vermicelli in stock until tender. Rinse well, place in a warmed tureen and pour the soup over. Other small-size pasta can also used.

Consommé Royal: To garnish 6 bowls of consommé, mix 1 egg white with 4 tablespoons double cream and season with salt and freshly ground white pepper. Place in a heatproof dish and stand in a pan of gently simmering water until just set. Cool, cut into neat strips and add to the consommé just before serving.

Potages or Regional French Soups

Potages may be described as unthickened stews as they are made with a high proportion of solid ingredients gently cooked in broth, stock or flavoured water. Potages are mainly based on traditional French recipes made with meat, seafood, vegetables, rice or grains, depending upon availability in a particular region. As they are generally substantial and highly nutritious, potages are usually served as a meal in their own right, with bread, the vegetables used to flavour the soup and traditional sauces.

Of the potages, Pot au Feu, traditionally made with beef, and the Mediterranean fish soup Bouillabaisse are probably the best-known. Pot au Feu, a hearty broth, was eaten almost daily by the rural population in France and is still served as a wholesome meal at home and in restaurants.

Bouillabaisse originates from the time when fishermen simmered any fish left behind in the nets in a pot on their boats to make a filling stew. Although the seafood used to make Bouillabaisse varies enormously, depending upon the catch of the day and the vegetables in season, it is always made with a mixture of shellfish and unfilleted white fish found along the French Mediterranean coast, such as gurnard and rascasse. Bouillabaisse is best made with a well-flavoured Fish Stock made with the bones of white fish and the shells of shellfish (see *Stocks*, page 689). Other typical flavouring ingredients include olive oil, tomatoes, garlic, fennel, chilli and saffron.

Chowders

The word chowder originates from *chaudière*, the French term for an iron cauldron used by fishermen on their boats to make soup. The term has since come to describe the wholesome soup traditionally served in New England. Chowders are milk-based and flavoured with chunks of fish or shellfish, such as clams, mussels and oysters, potatoes and bacon. Chowder may also be made with vegetables, usually including sweetcorn.

Cold Soups

Cold soups are mainly eaten in warm weather as a refreshing start to a meal. Classic cold soups described as tangy include chilled Borscht, Spanish *Gazpacho* and Tomato and Basil Soup. Delicate-tasting cold soups include Cucumber and Yoghurt, Pea and Lettuce, and Vichyssoise, a leek and potato soup enriched with double cream. Like hot soups, cold soups are garnished with herbs, cream, croûtons, diced or julienne of vegetables or a small quantity of the main flavouring ingredient.

Iced Vichyssoise Soup

Iced Vichyssoise was created in New York in the 1920s by a French chef called Louis Diat who refined the basic leek and potato soup regularly eaten in France by adding milk and cream and chilling it.

SERVES 4

55 g│2 oz butter

1 medium onion, finely chopped

the white parts of 3 large or 5 small leeks, chopped, about 285 g│10 oz

110 g│4 oz floury potatoes, peeled and sliced

290 ml│½ pint White Chicken Stock (see **Stocks**, page 689)

salt and freshly ground white pepper

290 ml│½ pint creamy milk

2 tablespoons single cream

To garnish

chopped fresh chives

extra cream (optional)

1 Melt the butter in a heavy-based saucepan and add the onion and leeks. Cover with a piece of damp greaseproof paper (a *cartouche*) and a lid.
2 Sweat the vegetables for about 15 minutes, until softened but not crisp or browned.
3 Add the potatoes, stock, salt and pepper. Simmer until the potatoes are soft.
4 Liquidize the soup in a food processor or blender. Strain it through a sieve.
5 Gradually add the milk and cream until the soup has a coating consistency.
6 Check the seasoning, then refrigerate until well chilled.
7 Add the chives just before serving and perhaps a swirl of cream, if liked.

NOTE: The soup is also good hot. Reheat without boiling.

Iced Vichyssoise: What has gone wrong when...

The leek and potato purée becomes gluey.

- The potato was overworked as the soup was puréed. Potatoes are best puréed by pushing them one at a time through a fine sieve.

Gazpacho

Gazpacho, originating from Andalucia in Spain, is an iced soup made with cucumber, tomato, onion, red pepper, crushed bread, olive oil, garlic, vinegar and Tabasco. It is served chilled, often with crushed ice added. Individual bowls of diced vegetables and croûtons are handed separately. There are numerous recipes for Gazpacho; this is one of our favourites.

Gazpacho must be thickened to coating consistency with the bread and the emulsified oil, and is best made in a food processor or liquidizer. If the soup becomes too thick, dilute it with iced water or tomato juice.

SERVES 6

900 g | 2 lb fresh, very ripe tomatoes, peeled
1 large mild Spanish onion
2 red peppers
1 small cucumber, peeled and deseeded
1 thick slice of white bread, crust removed
2 large cloves of garlic
6 tablespoons olive oil
1 tablespoon tarragon vinegar

450 g | 1 lb canned tomatoes or peeled deseeded ripe tomatoes
1 tablespoon tomato purée
sea salt and freshly ground black pepper

To serve
large bowl of croûtons (see *Soup Garnishes*, below), accompanied by small bowls of diced vegetables

1 Finely dice a small amount of the fresh tomato, onion, red pepper and cucumber to the same size and put into separate bowls for the garnish. Roughly chop the remaining vegetables.
2 Put the bread and garlic into a food processor or liquidizer. Turn on the machine and add the oil in a thin, steady stream while the motor is running. You should end up with a thick, Mayonnaise-like emulsion.
3 Add the vinegar, then gradually add all the roughly chopped vegetables, the vinegar, tinned or deseeded tomatoes and the tomato purée and blend until smooth.
4 Sieve the soup to remove any tomato seeds and season to taste with plenty of sea salt and pepper. Hand round the croutons and chopped vegetables seperately.

Gazpacho: What has gone wrong when...

The soup has not thickened.

- The oil was added to the bread and garlic too quickly to form a stable emulsion.

Soup Garnishes

Smooth-textured soups benefit in appearance and taste when garnished with ingredients finely chopped or diced, with fresh herbs or a drizzle of flavoured oil. Other garnishes, such as croûtons, provide contrast in texture to enhance a soup that might otherwise be rather dull. Chunky soups are usually served with a garnish of chopped fresh herbs. French regional soups are often garnished with croûtes of bread served either in or with the soup.

Chopped Fresh Herbs

Chopped fresh herbs are used to flavour and add colour contrast to a wide variety of soups. They are added just before serving to ensure that their bright green colour and fresh flavour are not lost in cooking. Finely chopped parsley and chives are most commonly used to garnish soups. Parsley can be used to garnish almost any soup but chives, with their powerful onion taste, should be used with a little more caution. Finely sliced basil is often used to garnish tomato soups, as is coriander with spicy soups and dill with fish soups.

Whole leaves of herbs such as parsley, basil and sage may be deep-fried in vegetable oil until crisp, then sprinkled with salt and drained on kitchen paper and used to garnish the soup immediately before serving.

Sauces made with basil, garlic and olive oil, such as Pesto (see **Herbs**, page 307), are used to garnish chunky Mediterranean peasant soups.

Vegetables

Leafy vegetables such as sorrel, watercress and rocket are often finely shredded before adding to soups made of the same ingredients or to fish soups. Finely diced or sliced vegetables, used as a main ingredient in the soup, may also be blanched or lightly sautéed and added just before the soup is served. Thinly shredded leek, carrot and ginger may be deep-fried until crisp and used as a garnish.

Soured Cream or Crème Fraîche

Cream, soured cream, crème fraîche and yoghurt are often swirled or spooned into the centre of smooth-textured, thin or chunky soups to provide colour contrast and a cool, creamy texture.

Rouille

Rouille (meaning 'rust' in French) is a spicy emulsion of crushed chillies, garlic, breadcrumbs and oil (see **Sauces, Savoury**, *Mayonnaise: Daughter Sauces*, page 601), served with croûtes (see below) and sometimes grated Gruyère cheese as a garnish for the French fish soup Bouillabaisse.

Pastry

Simple bistro-style soups may be served under a lid of Puff Pastry (see **Pastry**, page 522). Pour the cold soup into large ovenproof soup bowls. Roll out the pastry very thinly and cut out circles a little larger than the rim of the bowl, allowing about 1 cm | ½ in extra). Brush a little beaten egg around the edge of each circle and attach the pastry to the bowl, pressing firmly to make a good seal. Trim off any uneven edges. Brush the pastry with the remaining egg glaze and chill the covered bowls well in the refrigerator. Place the soup bowls on a baking sheet and bake near the top of the oven preheated to 220°C | 425°F | gas mark 7 for 20 minutes, until well risen and golden-brown.

Bread: Croûtons or Croûtes

Croûtons are made by uniformly dicing stale bread and either deep-frying the cubes in oil or shallow-frying them in butter until crisp and light golden in colour. For a low-fat alternative, croûtons can also be made by tossing bread cubes in a few tablespoons of oil and baking them in a moderate oven until crisp and lightly browned.

Croûtons are sometimes flavoured with garlic by infusing the oil with cloves of garlic before frying them. They may also be seasoned with salt, or rolled in finely grated fresh Parmesan cheese once fried. Croûtons will keep for a week provided they are stored in an airtight container. Sprinkle on to the soup just before serving to make the most of their crisp texture.

Croûtes are thin slices of French bread, either shallow-fried in oil or drizzled with oil and baked in the oven. Like croûtons, they are usually added to the soup just before serving as they absorb the liquid quickly and become soggy.

Croûtes are often topped or flavoured with other ingredients. Garlic croûtes are made by rubbing the cut surface of a garlic clove on each side of the cooked croûte. Alternatively, croûtes may be topped with strong-flavoured cheeses such as Parmesan or mature Cheddar or Gruyère. Cheese croûtes traditionally garnish the classic *French Onion Soup* (see above).

Quenelles Made from Fish and Shellfish Mousseline

Small mousseline quenelles, shaped with teaspoons, may be poached in delicate-tasting fish soups or clear soups immediately before serving (see **Mousselines,** *Fish Quenelles*, page 487).

Spices

Spices are strongly flavoured and/or aromatic substances of vegetable origin widely used for seasoning both sweet and savoury food. Although most spices originate in the tropics, demand for them is worldwide. The search for spices from the fifteenth century resulted in the discovery of the Americas.

Choosing

Buy spices in small quantities from a shop with a high turnover. To obtain the maximum flavour, buy whole spices and roast and grind using a coffee grinder or mortar and pestle.

Storing

Ground spices should be stored in an airtight container in a cool, dark place. Once ground, spices lose their potency very rapidly. They are best used within 6 months.

Using

In cooking, spices are used in their whole form to infuse liquids or as a garnish and in their ground form as part of the recipe. Some spices, such as mustard seed, are made into pastes to use as condiments.

Ground spices have a harsh, raw taste and should be cooked to extract and soften their flavour. Fry in a little oil over a medium heat for 30–60 seconds, until the fragrance is released. If spices are to be added to a dish at the end of cooking, dry-fry in a pan without oil for 30–60 seconds. Their colour will darken slightly when cooked but take care not to scorch them or they will become bitter.

Roasting

Roast whole spices in a sauté pan in a little oil, stirring to cook evenly or place in a roasting tin and bake for 8–10 minutes in the oven preheated to at 180°|350°|gas mark 4.

Grinding

Grind roasted spices when cool in a mortar and pestle or a small electric coffee grinder. Use a pastry brush to clean the grinder of any excess spice or process a little bread. Alternatively, use the end of a wooden rolling pin and a deep metal bowl as a makeshift mortar and pestle.

Bruising

Bruising means to crush lightly. This helps the flavour to escape from the spice by releasing its essential oils and bringing more surface area in contact with the liquid or mixture to which it is added.

Spice Table

Spice	Uses
Allspice	Strong spice similar to cinnamon, used in pickles, meat terrines and spice cakes
Aniseed	Liquorice-flavoured seed, used in Indian cookery
Caraway	Mild anise-flavoured seed, used in English seed cake, biscuits, rye bread
Cardamom	Pale green or white pods containing 4–5 small black seeds, used in Middle Eastern, North African and Indian cookery; also for milk puddings. Bruise pods to use
Celery seed	Used for vegetable dishes, often mixed with salt
Cinnamon	Dried bark of tropical tree used whole to infuse milk, or ground in baking, fruit dishes, Middle Eastern meat dishes
Cloves	Used whole to infuse milk and sugar syrups, in pickles and baked ham; ground for Christmas baking
Coriander	Small beige seeds, used whole in Indian and North African cookery and pickles: ground in Scandinavian baking
Cumin	Predominant flavour in many curries. Used whole and ground in Indian cookery
Dill seed	Strongly flavoured seeds, used for pickles
Fennel seed	Strongly flavoured seeds similar to dill seeds, classically used for Mushrooms à la Grecque
Fenugreek	Hard, musty, lemon-flavoured seeds, used whole in Indian cookery
Ginger	Fresh ginger used in Indian and Asian cookery (see below). Peel the thin beige skin with a vegetable peeler or by scraping with the edge of a teaspoon, then grate or finely chop the hard flesh. Fry lightly with onions when making curry. Use slices of ginger to infuse milk and sugar syrups. Dry ground ginger used in baking
Juniper	Berries used in marinades and to flavour gin
Lemon grass	White middle part chopped finely for Thai and South-East Asian cookery
Mace	Outer coating of the nutmeg, used to infuse liquids for sauces
Mustard seed	Used whole for pickles, salad dressings
Nutmeg	Best to buy whole and grate as needed for Christmas baking, egg custard, seasoning spinach
Paprika	Orange to burnt-red spice, used in Hungarian cookery and for garnishing
Pepper, cayenne	Very hot ground pepper, used to give heat to curries and as a general seasoning
Peppercorns	Used for general seasoning for savoury dishes
Saffron	Medicinally flavoured bright yellow-orange spice from the crushed stamens of the saffron crocus. The world's most expensive spice. Used for rice dishes (see *Rice, Saffron Rice Pilaf*, page 568), also Spanish, Moroccan, Indian cookery. Buy the whole stamens rather than the ground spice which is often adulterated. The whole stamens are strong-flavoured, so only a small quantity is needed. Use to infuse stock to flavour Risotto Milanese
Star anise	Flower-shaped seed pods with a strong anise flavour, used in Asian cookery, desserts
Szechuan peppercorns	Spicy berries resembling black peppercorns, used in Chinese cooking. Watch out for thorns
Tumeric	Rhizome similar to ginger but very small and hard. Used for its bright yellow colour in Moroccan and Indian dishes, also as a colour substitute for saffron when saffron flavour not needed
Vanilla pod	The fruit of a tropical orchid. Buy whole vanilla pods, 1 or 2 at a time, as they don't keep well. Cut in half lengthways to infuse milk for custards and ice cream. Scrape the tiny black seeds from the pod and stir into the custard for additional flavour. Put used pods in a sugar canister to perfume the sugar with vanilla. Buy natural vanilla essence or extract only. Imitation or artificial vanilla essence tastes only of chemicals. Used to flavour milk puddings, sauces and in baking. Avoid vanilla flavouring

Spice Mixes

Chilli powder is a mixture of ground dried chillies, garlic, oregano, ground cumin, ground coriander and cloves. It is available in both mild and hot versions to use in Mexican recipes.

Chinese five spice is a combination of equal portions of cinnamon, cloves, fennel seed, star anise and Szechuan peppercorns. It is used in Chinese cooking.

Curry powder is a mixture of spices which varies from region to region as well as from dish to dish. It is best made from whole spices that have been freshly roasted and ground. The most usual base ingredients are turmeric, ground coriander, cumin and cayenne.

Garam masala is a mixture of dry roasted spices from the northern part of India. The most usual ingredients are ground coriander, cumin, cayenne, black pepper, cinnamon, cloves and nutmeg (see recipe below).

Mixed spice is a combination of cinnamon, cloves, nutmeg and sometimes ground coriander and allspice, used in baking, especially for fruit cake and Christmas pudding (see **Cakes**, *Black Sticky Gingerbread*, page 141).

Quâtre épices is a French blend of ground black peppercorns, ground cloves, ground ginger and ground nutmeg used for seasoning meat mixtures and in baking.

Spice rub is a term referring to a mixture of spices, generally coriander, cumin, cinnamon and chilli, used to rub on to meat before pan-frying, barbecueing, or roasting.

Lamb Curry

Use the individual ground spices as indicated in the recipe, using a level 5 ml spoon = 1 teaspoon, or make the recipe for garam masala and use 2 level tablespoons.

SERVES 4

30 g | 1 oz clarified butter or ghee (see **Dairy Products**, *Butter*, page 204)

1 large onion, finely chopped

2.5 cm | 1 in piece of fresh ginger, peeled and finely chopped (see above)

1 clove of garlic, crushed

1 tablespoon ground coriander

1½ teaspoons ground cumin

1 teaspoon ground turmeric

½ teaspoon ground cayenne

¼ teaspoon ground black pepper

675 g | 1½ lb boneless lamb, preferably shoulder, cut into 4 cm | 1½ in cubes

a pinch of sugar

1 teaspoon salt

570 ml | 1 pint Brown Stock (see **Stocks**, page 692) or water

To serve

Saffron Rice Pilaf (see **Rice**, page 568)

1 Heat the clarified butter or ghee in a large sauté pan and stir in the onions. Cook over a low heat until lightly browned, adding the ginger just as the onions start to brown.

2 Add the garlic and cook for 1 further minute.

3 Combine the spices in a small bowl, then tip into the onions. Cook for 30–60 seconds until the fragrance rises from the pan.

4 Stir in the lamb and sprinkle with the sugar and salt.

5 Add the stock and bring to a simmer. Cover and cook for 1½–2 hours until the lamb is very tender.

6 Serve with *Saffron Rice Pilaf* (see **Rice**, page 568).

Garam Masala

1 tablespoon coriander seeds

1 teaspoon cumin seeds

1 teaspoon black peppercorns

½ teaspoon cardamom seeds, measured after removing from the pod

2.5 cm | 1 in piece of cinnamon stick, roughly crushed

1 Place the spices in a dry frying pan over a low heat and cook, stirring, for 1–2 minutes, or until the spices turn slightly brown and fragrant.

2 Turn on to a plate and allow to cool completely.

3 Grind to a fine powder in a coffee grinder or a mortar and pestle.

4 Store in an airtight jar in a cool, dark place.

Steaming

Steaming is a gentle method of cookery primarily used for fish and chicken, vegetables and steamed puddings. There are two methods of steaming food, direct and indirect.

Direct Method of Steaming

In the direct method the food is placed in a perforated basket over steaming liquid, usually water. The food cooks in the hot vapours. The food does not come into contact with the cooking liquid, unlike boiling, so the loss of vitamins and minerals is minimal. The moist environment created by the steam helps to keep the food from drying out. The direct method of steaming is used to cook delicate foods such as fish and vegetables quickly. Direct steaming is a useful method of cooking for invalids because no fat is added to the food during cooking and the nutrients in the food are preserved. It is a method widely used in Chinese cookery.

Equipment

A variety of equipment is available for food cooked by the direct method of steaming. Most common are round or oval steamers, which are like double saucepans, except that the top pan has holes in the base. Steam from the lower pan rises through the holes to cook the food, whilst the lid on the upper pan keeps in the steam (see *Kitchen Equipment*, *Steamers*, page 46).

Another popular device is a stainless-steel basket with folding sides and short legs (see *Kitchen Equipment*, *Steamers*, page 46). The basket fits down inside a saucepan. The legs keep the base of the basket elevated above the steaming liquid. It is particularly suitable for foods that do not need a long cooking time, otherwise the liquid will need to be topped up frequently. The saucepan must have a tight-fitting lid.

The tiered wicker steaming baskets available in Chinese supermarkets are also good for the direct method of steaming. The food is placed inside the baskets with the most delicate food in the top basket. The tier of baskets is then placed in a sauté pan of boiling water so that the water comes about halfway up the sides of the bottom basket. Alternatively, the steamer can be placed in a wok instead of a sauté pan.

Vegetables are often steamed because they cook quickly (see also *Vegetables*, page 716). Steaming vegetables preserves their nutritional content. Careful timing is important because overcooked steamed food is tasteless.

Vegetables should be cut into even-sized pieces so that they all take the same length of time to cook. Root vegetables should be cut into small, even pieces so that the cooking time is short. Both new and floury potatoes can be successfully steamed. The vegetables should not fill the steamer by more than half, to allow the steam to circulate freely. If the vegetables are too close to the lid the condensation from the steam will drip on to them, making them wet and, in the case of green vegetables, discoloured.

Steam vegetables until they are tender when pierced with a sharp knife. Take care when testing the vegetables as contact with the steam can cause nasty burns.

Fish fillets and small steaks can be steamed quickly. The moist heat helps keep the fish from drying out so steaming is a particularly suitable method for cooking white fish, which has a tendency to be dry. It is important that the fish is not overcooked or it is likely to disintegrate. Oil the base of the steamer or place the fish on a piece of greaseproof paper cut to size, to prevent it from sticking to the steamer. The heat of the steam causes the delicate proteins in the fish to denature and coagulate in a matter of minutes. Cook the fish only until it turns from translucent to opaque.

Plate steaming is an excellent method of cooking small quantities of fish in their own juice. Plate steaming is an indirect method of steaming (see below) because the food does not come into contact with the steam. Place the food to be cooked on a lightly buttered overproof plate and season well. Cover the plate with a matching buttered overproof plate or with buttered kitchen foil. Set the plates over a saucepan of gently boiling water or on a trivet inside a large frying pan. Cook for 8–10 minutes per 2.5 cm | 1 in thickness of fish.

Whole fish can also be steamed. Place the fish on a rack inside a fish kettle (see **Kitchen Equipment,** *Pots and Pans*, page 44). Ramekins can be used to keep the rack elevated from the bottom of the kettle. Steam the fish for about 8 minutes per 450 g | 1 lb.

Poultry pieces can be cooked by steaming if the pieces are no more than 2.5 cm | 1 in thick and of even thickness. Small quail can also be successfully steamed. As steaming does not impart any flavour to the food, add flavour by marinating the meat before cooking or by serving it with a sauce. Poultry must be cooked through completely to avoid the possibility of food poisoning. See **Poultry** (page 423) for instructions on how to tell if poultry is cooked.

Chinese cooking traditionally involves a lot of steaming. Fish, shellfish and tender cuts of meat, often wrapped in pastry or vegetable leaves, are quickly steamed in wicker baskets. Chinese dumplings are also steamed. The dumplings are placed on rice paper then steamed. The rice paper is then trimmed to fit the dumpling and is eaten as part of the dumpling.

Indirect Method of Steaming

The indirect method of steaming is used for steaming puddings, such as *Steak and Kidney Pudding*, *Christmas Pudding* and *Treacle Sponge* (see recipes below). Cooking in a closed container gives the food a soft, open texture because the steam produced when the water in the food vaporizes is trapped in the container.

The food is placed in a sealed container, such as a pudding basin. The container is then covered and placed on a trivet in a large saucepan of boiling water so that the water comes at least halfway up the sides of the container. Steaming in this manner takes a considerable length of time because the heat reaching the food is very low.

Pleating greaseproof paper (a)

To prepare a pudding basin for steaming:

1 Grease the inside of the pudding basin with a thick layer of softened butter. Cut a double layer of greaseproof paper to cover the pudding and fold it so that it has a pleat in the middle. (a)
2 Cut a piece of aluminium foil to cover the basin, leaving about 5 cm|2 in excess around the edge.
3 Cut a piece of string 4 times the circumference of the pudding basin.
4 Fill a saucepan large enough to hold the pudding basin half full with water. Cover and bring to the boil.
5 Fill the pudding basin, leaving about 2.5 cm|1 in space below the rim of the basin to allow the food to expand.
6 Cover with the buttered greaseproof paper and foil. (b) Tie with the string, making a loop over the top for a handle.
7 Using kitchen scissors, trim the greaseproof paper just below the string.
8 Wrap the foil over the greaseproof paper.
9 Use the string handle to lower the pudding into the boiling water. (c)

Covering a pudding basin (b)

Steamed Puddings

Steamed puddings such as *Christmas Pudding* and *Treacle Sponge* are made with a cake mixture which is placed directly into the prepared pudding basin then steamed for the required length of time. The pudding is done when it is well risen and springs back when pressed in the centre. A skewer inserted into the middle of the pudding should come out clean.

Pudding basins can also be lined with pastry (usually Suet Pastry) then filled with meat to make the traditional *Steak and Kidney Pudding* (see recipe below). Sussex Pond Pudding is a sweet pudding in which the basin is lined with pastry, then filled with whole lemons, butter and sugar.

Lowering pudding into boiling water (c)

Steak and Kidney Pudding

SERVES 4

675 g | 1lb 8 oz chuck steak
225 g | 8 oz ox kidney
340 g | 12 oz flour-quantity Suet Pastry (see
   Pastry, page 513)

salt and freshly ground black pepper
plain flour, for coating
2 tablespoons finely chopped onion
2 tablespoons finely chopped fresh parsley

1 Cut the steak into 2.5 cm | 1 in cubes.

2 Cut the kidney into 1 cm | 1½ in pieces, discarding any sinew.

3 Make the pastry and use to line the pudding basin (see *Pastry*, page 513).

4 Place a trivet in the bottom of a saucepan, then add enough water to come half way up the sides of the pudding basin. Bring to the boil.

5 Place the steak and kidney in a large sieve and season with salt and pepper. Sprinkle with flour to coat.

6 Mix the meat with the onion and parsley and fill the pudding basin with the mixture.

7 Cover the pudding and place in the boiling water, as described above. Turn the heat down to bring the water to a gentle boil, then cover the saucepan tightly with a lid.

8 Steam for 5–6 hours. The pudding is done when the meat is tender when pierced with a skewer and the pastry is lightly browned.

9 Serve from the pudding basin wrapped in a white napkin or turn out on to a serving dish.

Christmas Pudding

Christmas Pudding is steamed by the indirect method. Do not allow the aluminium foil to come into contact with the pudding or the acid in the fruit will eat into the foil and eventually the cover will no longer be watertight. Christmas Pudding is best made several months in advance to allow the flavours to mellow and mature. A fish kettle (see **Kitchen Equipment**, page 44) is ideal for steaming several puddings at once.

MAKES 2.3 KG|5 LB

170 g|6 oz raisins

110 g|4 oz currants

200 g|7 oz sultanas

85 g|3 oz chopped mixed peel

225 g|8 oz mixed dried apricots and figs, chopped

290 ml|½ pint brown ale

2 tablespoons rum

grated zest and juice of 1 orange

grated zest and juice of 1 lemon

110 g|4 oz prunes, stoned and soaked overnight in cold tea, then drained and chopped

1 dessert apple, grated

225 g|8 oz butter, softened

340 g|12 oz soft dark brown (muscovado) sugar

2 tablespoons treacle

3 eggs, beaten

110 g|4 oz self-raising flour

2 teaspoon ground mixed spice

1 teaspoon ground cinnamon

a pinch of freshly grated nutmeg

a pinch of ground ginger

a pinch of salt

225 g|8 oz fresh white breadcrumbs

55 g|2 oz chopped toasted hazelnuts or almonds

1 Soak all the dried fruit except the prunes overnight in the ale, rum, orange juice and lemon juice.

2 The following day, mix in the prunes and apple.

3 Grease the pudding basin(s) and put saucepan(s) of water on to boil.

4 Cream the butter with the sugar, treacle, orange and lemon zests until fluffy. Gradually beat in the eggs.

5 Sift together the flour, spices and salt, then fold into the creamed mixture.

6 Fold in the breadcrumbs, nuts, dried fruit and soaking liquor.

7 Divide between greased pudding basins, leaving a 2.5 cm|1 in space between the pudding and the rim. Cover as described above.

8 Steam, using the table below to calculate the time required.

9 When cool, cover with fresh greaseproof paper and foil, then store in a cool, dry, dark cupboard.

NOTE: To reheat Christmas pudding, place the sealed pudding on a trivet in a saucepan with enough water to come halfway up the sides of the pudding basin. During steaming, add boiling water from time to time to ensure the saucepan does not boil dry.

Size of pudding basin	Cooking time	Reheating time
570 ml | 1 pint	5 hours	2 hours
900 ml | 1¾ pints	7 hours	3 hours
1.2 litres | 2½ pints	9 hours	3 hours

Serving Christmas Pudding

Turn the pudding on to a heatproof serving dish. If the pudding is going to be flamed, the serving dish should have a lip. To flame a Christmas Pudding, heat 2 tablespoons brandy from a new bottle with 1 teaspoon caster sugar in a small saucepan until the mixture steams. Light it with a match, then pour it over the pudding, taking care to keep well away from the flames. The sugar keeps the flames burning for a longer time. Serve with Brandy Butter (see **Dairy Products**, *Butter*, page 203) or lightly whipped cream flavoured with brandy.

Treacle Sponge

SERVES 4–6

30 ml \| 2 tablespoons golden syrup
2 teaspoons fine white breadcrumbs
110 g \| 4 oz butter, softened
110 g \| 4 oz caster sugar
grated zest of 1 lemon
2 medium eggs, beaten
110 g \| 4 oz self-raising flour

a pinch of salt
1 teaspoon ground ginger
3 tablespoons milk

To serve
custard (see **Sauces, Sweet**, page 612) or
  cream

1 Prepare a 1 litre \| 1¾ pint pudding basin as described above. Place a trivet in a deep saucepan and half-fill with water. Bring to the boil.
2 Measure the syrup with a warm, wetted 15 ml measure. Place the syrup in the bottom of the pudding basin and sprinkle over the breadcrumbs.
3 Cream the butter with the sugar and lemon zest then gradually beat in the eggs (see **Cakes**, *Creaming Method*, page 142).
4 Sift together the flour, salt and ginger and fold into the creamed mixture with the milk.
5 Turn into the pudding basin and cover as described above.
6 Place in the saucepan so that the boiling water comes halfway up the sides of the pudding basin.
7 Steam for 1½ hours.
8 Turn out and serve with custard (see **Sauces, Sweet**, page 612) or cream.

Steamed Puddings: What has gone wrong when...

The pudding is heavy and has not risen.

- The pudding was not put into the steamer quickly enough.
- The water was not boiling when the pudding was put into the steamer.
- The pudding was allowed to boil dry.
- The lid was taken off the pudding before it had cooked enough to hold its shape.

The top of the pudding (after inverting for serving) is too brown or burnt.

- The pudding was allowed to boil dry.

The bottom of the pudding (after inverting for serving) is soggy.

- The pudding was not adequately covered and the water and/or steam got into the pudding basin.

Dumplings

Dumplings are made from a mixture rather like a scone. They are cooked on the top of a thick soup or stew by a combination of poaching and steaming. They are risen by chemical raising agents (see *Baking*, page 139). Dumplings can function as the carbohydrate component of a meal in place of bread, rice or potatoes. The dumplings can be flavoured with herbs, grated cheese and/or spices.

As for all baking, the ingredients for dumplings must be measured accurately. Too much flour or liquid will give a heavy result. Mixing needs to be quick and light. The soup or stew should be at a *poach*, that is, the surface should be just trembling and an occasional bubble should pop on the surface.

When placing the dumplings on to the surface of the stew, leave a few centimetres of space between each one to allow for expansion and for the steam from the stew to escape. The stew should fill the saucepan about halfway to allow enough room for the dumplings. Use a pan with a diameter of at least 20 cm | 8 in. To test for doneness, it is necessary to break a dumpling open.

Dumplings

These dumplings can be flavoured with chopped fresh herbs or grated fresh horseradish, if desired.

SERVES 4

200 g | 7 oz plain flour
3 teaspoons baking powder
½ teaspoon mustard powder
¼ teaspoon ground cayenne pepper
½ teaspoon salt

55 g | 2 oz lard, suet or solid vegetable
   shortening
about 150 ml | ¼ pint iced
   water

1 Sift the flour, baking powder, mustard powder, cayenne, and salt into a large bowl. Add the fat.

2 Using 2 table knives scissor-fashion (see **Pastry**, page 511), cut the fat into the flour until each piece is no bigger than a small pea. Mix in any herbs or horseradish.

3 Stir in enough water to make a soft dough, taking care not to overwork the dough.

4 Divide the dough into 8 pieces and place on to the hot stew or soup, spacing them evenly. Cover and simmer for about 15 minutes. Do not lift the lid during cooking or the dumplings will be heavy.

5 When the dumplings feel firm to the touch, remove the lid and cook for a further 5 minutes to dry the surface of the dumplings. Break one open to check that it is cooked through. There should not be any uncooked, doughy mixture left in the centre.

Dumplings: What has gone wrong when ...

The dumplings are heavy.

- Too much flour or too little liquid was used.
- The dumplings were not placed quickly enough on top of the stew.
- The stew was not hot enough.
- The lid was lifted before the raising agent had a chance to work.

Notes

Stock Cooking Times

Fish	20–30 minutes
Shellfish	30–40 minutes
White vegetable	30 minutes
Brown vegetable	30 minutes
White chicken and veal	2–4 hours
Brown chicken	4–6 hours
Brown beef, lamb and veal	6–8 hours
Game	3 hours

Stocks: Points to Remember

- Do not use salt.
- Use fresh ingredients and raw bones.
- Cover the ingredients with cold water.
- Skim frequently. Stock that is not skimmed properly will be greasy.
- *Depouiller*. Add cold water to the stock. Bring to the poach again to bring scum to the surface. Skim with a ladle.
- Heat so that the surface just trembles: Do not allow to boil. Boiling will make the stock become cloudy.
- Use *non*-starchy root vegetables.
- Cook for the recommended time, do not overcook.

Stocks

The French term for stock is *fond*, meaning foundation, which clearly describes its role in cooking. Stock is a clear, fat-free, flavoured liquid base for soups, stews, braised dishes and sauces. Making stock is simple, inexpensive and well worth the effort. If made correctly, stock is highly nutritious and should taste good enough to eat as a broth. Even the most superior bouillons or stock cubes cannot compete with the depth of fresh flavour of home-made stock. Stocks do take a long time to make, but as the Roux brothers say, 'If you are serious about cooking, good stock is essential.' In classic French restaurants, the quality of the stock is thought to be so important that a chef is often employed purely to make and tend to the stocks.

White Stock

White Stock is characteristically colourless and mild in flavour. It is made by gently simmering the raw bones of poultry, veal, or fish with aromatic herbs and vegetables in water. It is used as a base to enhance other subtle-flavoured ingredients in white sauces, soups, blanquettes and fricassées, poached chicken and fish dishes.

Brown Stock

Conversely, Brown Stock has a strong, rich flavour and deep colour. It is used as a base in brown sauces, gravies, robustly flavoured soups, braised dishes and casseroles. The brown colour is obtained by either shallow-frying or roasting the bones of veal, beef, poultry, lamb and game or the shells of crustaceans and molluscs and vegetables, until they reach an even deep caramel colour. The ingredients are then submerged in cold water and simmered for the required length of time.

Brown Fish Stock is not a classic stock but is used when a more powerful flavour is required in rustic Mediterranean recipes such as Paella. The shells of prawns, crabs and lobsters are packed with flavour and make a rich-tasting stock.

Stock Glaces

Stock glace is a concentrate obtained by boiling down well-strained, well-skimmed white or brown stock to approximately one-tenth of its original volume. Glace is characteristically syrupy in consistency, feels sticky when rubbed between the thumb and forefinger and sets to a firm jelly when chilled. It is used as an essence to add strength of flavour and colour (if made from brown stock) to sauces, stews and gravies. Alternatively, glace can be reconstituted with water to use as a basic stock. As stock glace is so concentrated, it contains a large proportion of natural sugars and salt, so should be tasted before adding to a dish to avoid over-flavouring.

Stock glace can be made from almost all stocks (with the exception of ham stock, due to its large salt content). Glace made from meat and poultry stocks is known as Glace de Viande and glace made from fish stock is called Glace de Poisson.

Glace de Viande

Glace de Viande is classically made from reduced Brown Stock made with beef bones. It is used in small quantities to flavour *Béarnaise Sauce* (see **Sauces, Savoury**, page 605), to add depth of flavour and colour to meat, poultry and fish dishes or to enrich brown sauces. Well-browned chicken bones, however, may also be used.

Glace de Poisson

Glace de Poisson is made from reduced white Fish Stock and is used as a flavourful base for butter-mounted sauces (see **Sauces, Savoury**, page 584) to be served with fish, as well as fish stews and soups.

Equipment for Making Stock

Use a deep, narrow pot to ensure that the stock ingredients are fully submerged to extract maximum flavour. Exposed stock ingredients will not add flavour to your stock. Using a narrow pot will reduce the rate at which the liquid evaporates from the surface during the long cooking period. Skim the stock with a ladle and collect the scum in a clear bowl placed next to the hob. Any clear stock removed with the scum may be returned to the pan, using a bulb baster. Keep a large jug of cold water close by to add to the stock before skimming, use a fine sieve to strain the stock and collect any remaining fragments left in the liquid once the stock is cooked.

Ingredients for Making Stock

Only use the freshest ingredients to make stock, otherwise it will taste dull and stale. As Alice Walters from the Californian restaurant Chez Panisse says, 'A stock made with garbage will taste like garbage.'

Meat Bones

Try to use very fresh raw meat bones as they will make a stronger, fresher-tasting stock than one made with cooked bones from a roast. Raw bones are very often free from the butcher, or can be bought very cheaply. Ask the butcher to cut the bones into small, manageable-sized pieces. Choose bones that are covered in a little meat, the bloodier the better, as they will provide more flavour and help to produce a clear stock. As the stock heats up, the blood will coagulate, locking in a good deal of the impurities that cause cloudy stock. The coagulated blood then rises to the surface as scum, which can be skimmed off.

Traditional brown stock is made with raw beef bones as they impart a rich, balanced flavour that will enhance rather than overpower the other ingredients in a recipe. Veal bones are often added to stocks as they contain a large quantity of gelatine, which provides body and richness. Veal bones do not themselves contain much flavour and are best used together with flavoursome bones of beef or game. Chicken carcasses produce a more delicately flavoured stock and can be browned and sometimes used in preference to beef bones to make a brown stock. Lamb bones have a very distinctive flavour and are used to make stock to add to lamb dishes only. Similarly, stock made from pork bones is only suitable for pork pies or other pork dishes.

Fish Bones

The best Fish Stock is made with very fresh fish bones, heads and skin that still smell of the sea. Fish heads provide a rich source of gelatine and contribute body and depth of flavour to stock. If you are unable to obtain them, however, fish bones and skin alone will make a good stock. The best bones for stock are those from fish with mild-tasting white flesh, such as sole, sea bass, snapper or cod. Avoid using bones of oily fish such as salmon, mackerel or trout as these have too strong a flavour.

Fish bones must be clean as fish blood tastes extremely bitter and causes cloudiness if allowed to simmer through the stock. To clean the fish bones, pull off any remaining viscera, roe and bloody membranes, then rinse under running water to remove all traces of blood before blanching briefly in boiling water. The bones can then be broken into pieces small enough to fit easily into the stock pan. If using fish heads, ensure the gills are removed as they are especially rich in blood.

Crustacean Shells

The shells of both cooked and uncooked prawns, lobster, crab and mussels contain a great deal of flavour for making stocks for shellfish soups, sauces and stews.

Before making stock with uncooked raw shells, rinse them under cold running water to remove any loose fragments of flesh, fine grit or sand. Hard shells of lobsters and crabs will be clean after cooking. Break the large shells into smaller pieces to extract maximum flavour from them.

Vegetables

When making stock it is important to include vegetables that enhance rather than overpower the flavour of the bones. The principal stock vegetables are onion, white of leek (a mildly flavoured alternative to onion, especially in vegetable stock), carrot (for sweetness and colour), celery stalks (for body and sweetness) and button mushrooms (for their rich flavour), collectively termed 'aromatic vegetables'. Turnips and celeriac also add additional aromatic flavour to rich meat stocks. Carrot is most likely to overflavour stock with its natural sweetness so is used in smaller quantities than the other basic stock vegetables. Onion skins are sometimes added to brown stocks to deepen their colour.

Fish stocks are often flavoured with additional aromatics such as Florence fennel for its delicate aniseed flavour and a slice of lemon or strip of lemon zest for a hint of citrus. Tomato skins are also added to provide a delicate acidic flavour and reddish tinge in Mediterranean fish recipes.

Tomato purée
Tomato purée may be added to the browning vegetables, to provide a richer colour and a little acidity. Be careful not to add too much tomato purée, however, as it can easily overpower the other flavours and colour the stock orange.

Vegetables to avoid when making stock
Starchy vegetables such as potato or parsnip, or the flesh of tomato are unsuitable as they break up during long cooking which can make the stock cloudy and rough-textured. Also avoid green vegetables such as broccoli, courgettes and green beans, all of which have a pungent, unpleasant flavour and smell, reminiscent of school meals, when simmered for too long. Shredded cabbage, asparagus stalks and pea pods are good for vegetable stock which is simmered for only 20–30 minutes.

Preparing vegetables for stock
The vegetables should be diced uniformly, the size of the dice depending on both the length of time required to cook the stock and the pot size. Fish stock is cooked for a short time so it is important that the vegetables are cut small enough (ideally around 1 cm | $\frac{1}{2}$ in thick) to present as much surface area to the water as possible and draw out the maximum amount of flavour. However, if the vegetables are cut too small they have a tendency to float and may be lifted out each time the stock is skimmed. As meat stocks are cooked for much longer, the vegetables are ideally cut into large dice (approximately 2.5 cm | 1 in thick), to prevent them from disintegrating, providing the pot can accommodate them.

The flavour of meat and poultry bones, shellfish shells and vegetables is strengthened by browning and caramelizing the natural sugars and proteins on their surface. The rich colour and flavour of browned bones or shells and vegetables give stock an intense rich flavour and appetizing colour, which in turn lends great character to the dishes in which it is used.

Meat bones are browned to a deep russet colour by roasting them in a hot oven for approximately 1 hour. To ensure that the bones brown evenly they should be turned periodically. Vegetables are cut into equal-sized pieces and gently fried in oil until softened to concentrate the natural sugars, then browned over a medium to high heat until they are a deep brown. Shellfish shells are shallow-fried in vegetable oil until golden-brown. It is very important not to burn the ingredients or add any burnt pieces to the stockpot after browning as they will taint the flavour of the stock. Just 1 burnt carrot will ruin 4.5 litres|8 pints stock.

Herbs

Parsley stalks, sprigs of thyme and bay leaves play an important role in stock-making. Like aromatic vegetables, they greatly enhance the flavour of the bones. It is traditional to use the stalks of parsley for stock, leaving the leaves available for some other purpose. Thyme and bay leaves should be used sparingly as they are pungent in flavour. Other herbs are often used to give stock a distinctive flavour, such as tarragon in Fish Stock and rosemary and mint in Lamb Stock. The herbs are added to the stockpot with the vegetables, either tied together with a stick of celery into a bouquet garni or simply thrown in, as the stock will be strained once it is cooked.

Spices

Spices are always used whole as they are easily strained from the finished stock and provide a more subtle flavour than ground spices. Black peppercorns are most commonly used for their bold, rich, aromatic quality. White peppercorns are sometimes used for white fish stock but are less powerful and have a slightly hotter, floral flavour. Cloves are also used to flavour ham stock and juniper berries are often added to game stock.

Water

The water must be cold. If it is hot the fat in the bones will melt immediately and when the stock begins to boil much of the fat will be bubbled through the stock. Cold water encourages the fat to rise to the surface where it can be skimmed off.

Salt

Never add salt to a stock. Stock ingredients contain natural salt and sugars, which are dissolved in the water. These will become concentrated if the stock is reduced and additional salt would render the resulting stock too salty. Stock is used as a base for dishes to which other flavours are added, so it should never taste overpowering in its own right. If the stock is to be used without reducing, say for soup, use as the recipe specifies and then taste and season if necessary.

Flour

Never use flour to thicken stock as it will spoil its clarity and pure flavour. Stock should only be thickened by reduction.

Jellied Stock

Veal bones produce a particularly good stock that sets to a jelly. At Leiths a split calf's foot is often added to stock to produce the gelatinous quality required for rich stews, sauces and aspic. Pig's trotters have the same effect.

Storing Stock

To prevent bacterial growth, home-made stock should be chilled as quickly as possible by placing the uncovered pan in the sink of cold running water, without the plug. When cold, cover and refrigerate. Stock will keep for 1 week in the refrigerator, providing it is reboiled for at least 5 minutes every 2–3 days to kill any bacteria that may have developed. Jellied stocks tend to keep better than thin stocks, providing they are kept well covered with clingfilm in the refrigerator.

Reducing stock to a glace is the most efficient method for storage as the glace can be stored in small pots in the refrigerator for several weeks or in ice-cube trays in the freezer for up to 1 year.

Basic White Stock Method

1 Peel and dice the vegetables to the same size, about 2.5 cm | 1 in.
2 Trim excess fat from meat bones and bloody tissue from fish bones.
3 Place the prepared bones in a deep, narrow pot. Cover with cold water and slowly bring to a poach.
4 Skim off the scum and fat that rise to the surface, using a ladle.
5 When the water starts to boil, *dépouiller*. Pour cold water into the pan to solidify the fat and scum and skim well to remove the fat and scum, to ensure that the remaining liquid is as clear as possible.

6 Add the vegetables, herbs and peppercorns to the pot and cover all the ingredients with cold water.

7 Bring back to a poach, then regulate the heat so that the stock gently simmers throughout the cooking period. Poach the ingredients for the required period of time defined by the type of bones used (see *Stock Cooking Times* above), skimming occasionally.

8 Make sure that the ingredients remain covered with water. As the liquid evaporates, top the pan up with cold water as this will help to draw any remaining fat and scum to the surface.

9 Once the stock is cooked, strain carefully through a fine sieve, to remove all remaining fragments, into a storage container or a clean wide pan for reducing. Never force the liquid through the sieve by pressing the ingredients as this may result in a cloudy stock.

10 Reduce the stock to the required strength, skimming regularly to remove any further impurities that collect on the surface. To store the stock, continue to reduce it to a glace, then cool. Store as above.

White Chicken Stock

MAKES 1 LITRE|1¾ PINTS

2 onions, cut into 2.5 cm|1 in dice

1 medium carrot, cut into 2.5 cm|1 in chunks

2 sticks of celery, cut into 2.5 cm|1 in chunks

1 leek, green leaves removed, cut into
   2.5 cm|1 in chunks

55 g|2 oz button mushrooms

a handful of parsley stalks

1 bay leaf

½ teaspoon black peppercorns

2 chicken carcasses, broken up

1 veal knuckle bone

1 sprig of fresh thyme

1 bay leaf

about 2 litres|3½ pints cold water

Follow the *Basic White Stock* Method, above, simmering the stock for 3–4 hours.

White Fish Stock

Fish stock becomes bitter if the bones are cooked for too long. Once strained, however, the flavour can be strengthened by further boiling and reducing.

MAKES 1 LITRE|1¾ PINTS

1 onion, peeled and cut into 1 cm|1½ in dice

1 small carrot, peeled and cut into 1 cm|½ in dice

1 stick of celery, cut into 1 cm|½ in dice

1 leek, cut into 1 cm|½ in dice

1 slice of lemon

a handful of parsley stalks

1 bay leaf

1 spring of fresh thyme

6 white peppercorns

1–450 g|1 lb white fish bones, skin, heads
or tails

2 litres|3½ pints cold water

Follow the *Basic White Stock Method*, above, simmering the stock for 20–30 minutes.

White Shellfish Stock

This is used as a base for shellfish soups and sauces or clarified for making aspic to decorate cold shellfish dishes.

MAKES 1 LITRE | 1¾ PINTS

a selection of prawn, mussel, lobster or crab shells

1 onion, peeled and cut into 1 cm | ½ in dice

1 small carrot, peeled and cut into 1 cm | ½ in dice

1 stick of celery, cut into 1 cm | ½ in dice

1 bouquet garni

6 black peppercorns

1 Clean the shells under cold running water to remove fragments of flesh, sand and grit.
2 Put all the ingredients into a saucepan. Cover with water and bring to the boil, then reduce the heat and simmer for 30 minutes. Skim regularly.
3 Strain and reduce to two-thirds of the original volume by boiling rapidly. Use as required.

White Vegetable Stock

MAKES 1 LITRE | 1¾ PINTS

1 kg | 2¼ lb aromatic vegetables or trimmings, to include:

  2 onions, cut into 1 cm | ½ in dice

  2 carrots, peeled and cut into 1 cm | ½ in dice

  1 leek, green leaves removed and cut into 1 cm | ½ in dice

  2 sticks of celery, cut into 1 cm | ½ in dice

  a few mushroom stalks

2 litres | 3½ pints cold water

a handful of parsley stalks

1 spring of fresh thyme

1 bay leaf

½ teaspoon black peppercorns

Place all the ingredients in a saucepan and simmer for 30 minutes, skimming regularly, then strain.

Ham Stock

The best-flavoured ham stock is generally the well-skimmed liquor from boiling a ham or gammon, but can be made almost as successfully using a cooked ham bone. Ham stock is generally salty and should not be reduced. It is used mainly as a flavourful base for winter soups.

1 ham or gammon bone

1 onion, cut into 2.5 cm | 1 in dice

1 carrot, cut into 2.5 cm | 1 in dice

1 bay leaf

1 stick celery, cut into 2.5 cm | 1 in dice

a handful of parsley stalks

½ teaspoon black peppercorns

1 Place all the ingredients together in a large saucepan. Cover with cold water and bring to a gentle simmer.
2 Simmer for 2–3 hours, skimming frequently and adding more water if necessary.
3 Strain and use as required.

Turkey Stock

Ideally all stocks are made with raw bones, but turkey stock is most frequently made from the cooked bones of the roast Christmas turkey. This recipe may also be used with the cooked bones of chicken, goose or a game bird and is ideal for making soups and casseroles. Never add the bird's liver to the stockpot as it will make the stock taste bitter.

MAKES 1 LITRE|1¾ PINTS

1 turkey neck

turkey giblets, well washed, without the liver

1 turkey carcass, cut into pieces

1 onion, sliced

1 stick of celery, sliced

1 carrot, sliced

a handful of parsley stalks, bruised

1 sprig of fresh thyme

2 bay leaves

10 black peppercorns

2 litres|3½ pints cold water

Follow the *Basic White Stock Method*, above, simmering the stock for 2–3 hours.

Basic Brown Stock Method

For brown stocks made with beef, veal, lamb or chicken bones:

1 Trim the bones of excess fat and roast in at 225°C|425°F|gas mark 7 for approximately 1 hour to brown them to a rich russet-brown. Turn them occasionally to ensure that they roast and brown evenly on all sides. During the browning process most of the remaining fat will melt and collect in the roasting tray.

2 Meanwhile peel and dice the vegetables to the same size, 5 cm|2 in.

3 Brown the vegetables by shallow-frying them in vegetable oil until they are caramelized to a rich golden-brown. It is essential that they do not burn.

4 Add the tomato purée to the vegetables just before they are fully browned to caramelize it to a deeper red-brown colour.

5 Remove any burnt vegetables pieces as they will taint the stock with a bitter flavour.

6 Place the bones and vegetables in a deep, narrow pot and cover with cold water.

7 Bring slowly to the boil, skimming off the scum as it rises to the surface. There should be little fat as most of it was rendered down during the roasting and browning process.

8 When the water comes to a poach, pour cold water into the pan to solidify the fat and scum and skim well to remove the fat and scum, ensuring that the remaining liquid is as clear as possible.

9 Add more cold water, to cover all the ingredients, then bring back to the boil. Poach the ingredients for the required period of time defined by the type of bones used (see *Stock Cooking Times*, above), skimming occasionally.

10 Continue as for white stock, above.

Brown Stock

MAKES 1 LITRE | 1¾ PINTS

1 kg | 2¼ lb beef or veal marrow bones
    or chicken carcasses, cut into 5 cm | 2 in pieces
2 medium onions, unpeeled, cut into 2.5 cm | 1 in
    dice or into eighths through the root
2 tablespoons beef dripping or oil
2 medium carrots, peeled and cut into
    2.5 cm | 1 in slices
2 sticks of celery, cut into 2.5 cm | 1 in slices
½ small celeriac, peeled and cut into
    2.5 cm | 1 in dice

110 g | 4 oz button mushrooms
1 bulb Florence fennel
1 teaspoon tomato purée
a handful of parsley stalks
1 bay leaf
½ teaspoon black peppercorns
1 spring of fresh thyme
about 2 litres | 3½ pints cold water

Follow the *Basic Brown Stock Method*, above, simmering the bones for 6–8 hours or the chicken carcasses for 4–6 hours.

Brown Vegetable Stock

MAKES 1 LITRE | 1¾ PINTS

2 tablespoons vegetable oil
2 onions, unpeeled
2 carrots
2 sticks of celery
1 small parsnip
55 g | 2 oz mushrooms or mushroom stalks and
    peelings

1 clove of garlic
1 teaspoon tomato purée
a handful of parsley stalks
1 bay leaf
1 sprig of fresh thyme
12 black peppercorns
2 litres | 3½ pints cold water

1 Heat the oil in a large, heavy-based saucepan and brown the vegetables slowly and evenly on all sides to a russet-brown colour. If you are making a large quantity of stock, do not overcrowd the pan with vegetables on they will sweat rather than brown. Instead, brown the vegetables in batches and return them to the pan before adding the remaining ingredients.
2 Remove any overbrowned or burnt pieces of vegetable before adding all the remaining ingredients to the pan.
3 Cover with water and stir. Bring to the boil, then simmer for 1 hour, skimming occasionally.
4 Strain and reduce to the required strength.

Brown Fish Stock

This is not a classic stock but can be used when a stronger flavour is required.

MAKES 1 LITRE | 1¾ PINTS

2 tablespoons oil

2 shallots, peeled and cut into 1 cm | ½ in dice

½ bulb of Florence fennel, cut into 1 cm | ½ in dice

½ carrot, peeled and cut into 1 cm | ½ in dice

1 stick of celery, cut into 1 cm | ½ in dice

1 litre | 1¾ pints cold water

fish bones, skins, fins, crustacean and mollusc shells, cleaned and cut into 5 cm | 2 in pieces

1 bouquet garni

1 clove of garlic

½ teaspoon tomato purée

1 Heat the oil in a large saucepan and add the vegetables. Cook over a very low heat until the vegetables are soft and evenly browned. Do not allow them to burn.

2 Remove the pan from the heat and add the fish bones, trimmings and shells, the bouquet garni, garlic and tomato purée. Cover with cold water.

3 Bring to the boil, then simmer for 30 minutes, skimming regularly.

4 Strain and use as required.

Court Bouillon

Court Bouillon is an acidulated cooking liquor flavoured with aromatic vegetables, herbs and seasonings. It is used to poach and enhance the flavour of delicately flavoured foods such as fish, shellfish, white offal and white meats such as chicken and veal. Court bouillon differs greatly from stock, not only in the way it is made but also in its role. Although, like stock, it is used to enhance the flavour of foods cooked in it, Court Bouillon is too acidic to be used as a base for a sauce or reduced to an essence.

MAKES 1 LITRE | 1¾ PINTS

Whole fish are usually placed into cold court bouillon and brought slowly to simmering point, to prevent the flesh shrinking. Portions of fish, however, can be placed directly into hot court bouillon.

150 ml | ¼ pint white wine vinegar

1 carrot, thinly sliced

1 onion, peeled and thinly sliced

1 stick of celery, thinly sliced

12 white peppercorns

2 bay leaves

½ lemon, sliced

1 tablespoon oil

1 teaspoon salt

1 litre | 1¾ pints cold water

1 Place all the ingredients in a large saauepan with half of the water and bring to the simmer.

2 Simmer for 20 minutes, then allow to cool. Strain and discard the vegetables.

3 Add the remaining water. Use as required.

Sugar, Sweeteners and Sugar Syrups

(See also **Caramel**, page 174.)

Sugar, a simple carbohydrate, is a chemically stored energy source for all plants and animals. Although many different types of sugar are found in nature, only 3 are used in the kitchen: these are sucrose, glucose and fructose. Sucrose, the refined product of sugar cane or sugar beet, is the most widely used. Table sugar is 99 per cent pure sucrose. Glucose and fructose are the major components of honey.

Honey is nature's sweetener and has been widely used in cooking and religious ceremonies for centuries. From 2500 BC when bees were first domesticated by the Egyptians, honey was widely used as the primary sweetener until the more easily stored cane sugar became available in the sixteenth century.

Although the process of pressing the syrup from sugar cane and boiling it until it crystallizes into dark crystals was developed in India as early as 500 BC, sugar did not reach Europe until it was brought from the Americas by Columbus in the 1500s. Sugar cane continued to be the only source of sugar until the nineteenth century when it was discovered that sugar could be produced from beets. Napoleon promoted the use of sugar beet when the blockade of France during the Napoleonic wars meant that supplies of cane sugar stopped. Sugar from beets now accounts for 40 per cent of world sugar production.

The process of refining sugar cane produces different kinds of cane sugar and syrups. However, the refining of sugar beet produces only white sugar. Although the white and brown sugars can often be substituted for each other in recipes, the different flavour of each type will affect the flavour of the finished dish.

Sugars and Sweeteners

Brown Sugars

Muscovado or Barbados sugar is the darkest of the brown sugars. It has a high proportion of molasses residue and a strong caramel flavour. It is moist and hygroscopic, meaning that it absorbs moisture from the air, and will make cakes and biscuits soft and moist, improving their keeping qualities. All moist brown sugars should be tightly wrapped in plastic, then stored in an airtight container. If they dry out they become hard and unworkable. A piece of damp kitchen paper or a slice of apple can be stored with the sugar for a short time to rehydrate the sugar.

Demerara sugar is more refined than Muscovado sugar. Originally made in Demerara, Guyana, it has harder crystals than Muscovado sugar. Much of what is sold today as Demerara sugar is made by adding a little molasses to white sugar, resulting in a product with an insipid taste. It is used primarily as a sweetener for coffee.

Light brown sugar is further refined sugar with a much smaller proportion of molasses syrup remaining in the crystals. It has small crystals, a moist texture and a subtle caramel flavour. It is used for biscuits and cakes. Store as for Muscovado sugar.

Refined White Sugars

Refined white sugars are the result of a manufacturing process to remove the molasses and any impurities. These sugars have been washed with lime and clean syrups to whiten them. All flavours have been removed other than the sweetness. White sugars should be stored in an airtight container to keep them free from moisture.

White sugars are marketed in different crystal sizes: for the most part, the size of the crystal will determine the sugar's use.

Preserving sugar has the largest crystals and will dissolve fastest when added to a liquid. It is used for making jams and jellies. Pectin is sometimes added to the sugar so it is best to check the label (see ***Jams, Jellies, and Other Preserves***, page 323).

Granulated sugar has medium-sized crystals and is used for making sugar syrups as it dissolves readily in liquid. Lump sugar is granulated sugar formed into lumps through the addition of a little moisture.

Caster sugar/Superfine sugar (USA) has very small crystals. It is known as caster sugar because it was designed to be used in a sugar caster (shaker). It is the most widely used sugar for baking and meringues. It is also used for making dry caramel and praline.

Icing sugar/Confectioner's sugar (USA) has been ground until it is a white powder. Cornflour is often added to keep it free-flowing. It is used primarily for icings but is also useful for adding to sweet sauces where a granular texture is undesirable.

Cane Sugar Syrups

Cane sugar syrups are used for cooking in England, mostly for cakes and biscuits. These include black treacle, light treacle, a refined version of black treacle, and glucose syrup. These syrups will keep indefinitely.

To measure syrups accurately for use in cooking, warm the spoon in very hot water, then dry it before measuring the syrup. For larger quantities, warm the syrup gently in a bowl placed over a pan of simmering water, then measure by weighing.

Black treacle or Blackstrap molasses is a dark, sticky syrup with a strong, slightly bitter caramel flavour that is a by-product of sugar refining. It is the least refined sugar product and is used in gingerbreads (see *Cakes*, *Gingerbread*, page 141) and cakes.

Light treacle/Golden syrup is a clear, golden, sticky syrup that is slightly more refined than black treacle. It is used to drizzle on to pancakes and for making treacle sponge, tart and flapjacks.

Glucose syrup is a clear syrup that is used in confectionery to help avoid crystallization. It has no flavour other than its sweetness. Golden syrup can be substituted for glucose syrup in most instances, although golden syrup has a slight caramel flavour.

White and dark corn syrups are sugar syrups made from maize in the USA. Golden syrup is similar to dark corn syrup and can be used as a substitute for it. White corn syrup has no flavour other than its sweetness.

Honey

Honey is a thick golden liquid made by bees from flower nectar. The flavour of honey varies depending upon the blossom, so choose a honey with a flavour you particularly like. The darker the colour of the honey, the stronger the flavour will be. In addition to its use as a sweetener, honey is still used to make many traditional foods, such as Baklava (Greece) Lebkuchen (Germany), Nougat (France) and Halvah (Middle East).

Honey is available in the waxy comb and in both a clear or runny form and a set or cloudy form. Cloudy honey has some of the comb stirred into it and is not usually used for cooking.

Clear honey is often pasteurized to help prevent crystallization. Store tightly sealed honey in a cool, dry place for up to 1 year. Refrigerated honey will crystallize. Honey can be liquefied by placing it in a bowl over a pan of warm water or by heating gently in a microwave oven.

One measure of honey is equal to $1\frac{1}{4}$ measures of white sugar. However, honey is hygroscopic, meaning that it attracts moisture from the environment.

Maple Syrup

Maple syrup is made in the USA and Canada from the sap of the maple tree. It has a distinctive flavour and a golden colour. It is used to pour over pancakes, waffles and as a flavouring for fudge and ice cream. As the natural product is expensive, it is often made from a corn syrup with a little added maple flavouring. This should be labelled 'maple-flavoured' syrup and is best avoided.

Brandy Snaps

Brandy Snaps can be served as small biscuits with ice cream or can be moulded over a timbale or ramekin to form a cup for ice cream, sorbet or fruit salad.

The mixture has a high proportion of sugar and golden syrup. The ratio of the ingredients to each other is important, so be sure to measure carefully. To measure golden syrup, dip the measuring spoon into very hot water then into the syrup. Make sure the syrup is level in the spoon. It should slide off the spoon easily.

The mixture can be kept overnight in the refrigerator. It will become firm but will melt when baked. Shape the firm mixture into cherry-sized balls and place on baking parchment.

110 g | 4 oz caster sugar	2 tablespoons lemon juice or brandy
110 g | 4 oz butter	110 g | 4 oz plain flour
4 tablespoons golden syrup	a large pinch of ground ginger

1 Preheat the oven to 190°C | 375°F | gas mark 5. Cover a baking sheet with baking parchment, then cut the paper into 4 equal squares. This will make shaping the Brandy Snaps easier.
2 Melt the sugar, butter and syrup together. Stir in the lemon juice or brandy and allow to cool to room temperature.
3 Sift together the flour and the ginger. Stir into the sugar mixture.
4 Bake one test biscuit to see if the mixture is the correct consistency.
5 Place a teaspoonful of the mixture on the centre of each square of paper and bake for 5–7 minutes until golden-brown. Remove the baking sheet from the oven.
6 Use the paper to lift the biscuits from the baking sheet and immediately drape over a rolling pin. Alternatively, the biscuits can be wrapped around the handle of a wooden spoon or can be draped over an upturned ramekin to make a cup for ice cream or fruit. Allow the biscuits to cool. They will firm as they cool.
7 Store in an airtight container.

NOTE: If the biscuits become too hard to shape, return them to the oven for a few seconds. They will become pliable again.

Brandy Snaps: What has gone wrong when...

The Brandy Snaps are too thick.
- Too much flour was added to the mixture.
- The sugar mixture was not allowed to cool before the flour was added.
  Add a little additional golden syrup and bake a test biscuit.

The Brandy Snaps are too thin and fall apart when moulded.
- Too much golden syrup or butter was added.
  Add a little additional flour and bake a test biscuit.

Fudge

oil, for greasing
310 g|11 oz caster sugar
15 ml|1 tablespoon glucose syrup
290 ml|½ pint double cream

110 g|4 oz unsalted butter
1 vanilla pod, split (optional)
1 tablespoon icing sugar, sifted

1 Prepare a 20 × 30 cm|8 × 12 in baking tin by oiling lightly.
2 Place the sugar, glucose, cream and butter in a large, clean, heavy saucepan. If desired, add a vanilla pod.
3 Bring to the boil slowly, stirring to dissolve the sugar.
4 When the mixture boils, reduce the heat so it boils gently and cook to 117°C|243°F.
5 Remove from the heat and carefully pour into a large bowl. Remove the vanilla pod if used, and sift in the icing sugar. Scrape the seeds from the pod and add to the mixture. Allow to stand for 10 minutes.
6 Slowly beat the mixture with an electric hand-whisk until it becomes very firm. This will take about 10 minutes.
7 Pour into the prepared tin and smooth the surface.
8 Allow to cool and set, preferably overnight. Cut into small pieces and store in an airtight container.

Fudge: What has gone wrong when...

The fudge does not set.
- The mixture was not taken to a high enough temperature.
- The fudge is too warm.

The fudge is hard and granular.
- The mixture was taken to too high a temperature.
- The mixture was boiled before the sugar dissolved.
- The fudge has not been stored correctly and has dried out.
- The fudge was not allowed to stand before beating.
- The fudge was beaten for too long.

Sugar Syrup

Sugar syrups are used in cooking for ice creams, sorbets, meringues and fruit coulis. In a sugar syrup, the sugar is dissolved in water or other liquid so that it is held in its dissolved state, in suspension. The more sugar in the suspension relative to the amount of liquid, the thicker the syrup.

Chefs often keep a supply of sugar syrup in the refrigerator, ready for use. This is known as stock syrup or light syrup and is usually made with a ratio of 1:2: that is, 1 part sugar to 2 parts water. This consistency of syrup is used for fruit coulis and fruit salads. It can also be boiled down (reduced) to make a thicker syrup for meringues, ice creams and sorbets.

Granulated sugar is the best sugar to use for a sugar syrup. The larger crystals dissolve more easily than those of caster sugar so it is quicker to make.

Making Sugar Syrup: Points to Remember

- Make sure the saucepan is clean.
- Use warm water from a kettle to help the sugar dissolve more quickly.
- Place the saucepan over a low heat to dissolve the sugar.
- Stir gently with a wooden spoon while the sugar is dissolving.
- Do not allow the water to boil before the sugar has dissolved entirely.
- Do not stir once the water starts to boil.
- Wash any crystals from the sides of the pan, using a pastry brush dipped in water.

Stock Sugar Syrup

This stock syrup can be flavoured with aromatics such as a vanilla pod or slices of peeled root ginger, strips of lemon or orange peel, cinnamon sticks, bruised stalks of lemon grass or star anise pods. Add as desired after the sugar has dissolved completely. Remove before refrigerating.

150 g|5 oz granulated sugar
290 ml|½ pint warm water

1 Place the sugar in a clean saucepan and pour over the warm water from a kettle.
2 Brush the sides of the saucepan with a pastry brushed dipped in clean water to rinse away any sugar crystals that may have stuck to the sides.
3 Place the pan over a low heat. Stir the sugar gently with a wooden spoon to help it dissolve.
4 When all the sugar has dissolved and no crystals can be seen on the bottom of the pan, turn the heat to high. Brush the sides of the pan again, as described above. Boil the syrup for 2 minutes, then cool. Store in the refrigerator.

To use in a fruit coulis, purée the fruit and pass through a sieve. Gradually stir in enough stock syrup to the desired consistency. Adjust the flavour with lemon juice if required. See **Sauces, Sweet** (page 00) for specific recipes.

Sugar Syrup: What has gone wrong when...

The sugar syrup is cloudy.
- The mixture was boiled before the sugar dissolved.
- The sugar and/or the pan was not clean.

Stages of Sugar Syrup

As sugar syrup boils, the liquid evaporates, the sugar becomes more concentrated and the mixture becomes more viscous. The more concentrated the solution, the higher the boiling point (temperature). At the point where the sugar molecules are in balance with the water molecules, the sugar syrup is said to be saturated. Although there is a risk of a sugar syrup crystallizing at almost any time, at this point the risk is particularly high.

When sugar syrup crystallizes it turns within seconds from a clear liquid to a cloudy, grainy mass. Any grain of sugar, a stir from a spoon or debris from the side of the pan, can act as a 'seed' and cause the sugar to crystallize around it. Occasionally the mixture can be saved by putting the pan over a very high heat to melt it or by adding enough water to cover, then melting the sugar over a low heat before attempting to boil it again.

To prevent crystallization, a small amount of acid is added to the sugar, usually in the form of powdered cream of tartar. The addition of this acid causes the sugar to become 'inverted', which means that it has been broken down into its 2 components, glucose and fructose. Inverted sugar slows the process of crystallization, giving the cook more time to proceed with the recipe.

Glucose or corn syrup can also be used to inhibit crystallization altogether. Both hard and fine-textured fudge (see recipe above) are made using corn syrup or glucose in either its powdered or liquid form.

To make sugar syrup that will be boiled to a particular viscosity, use granulated sugar and just enough warm water to cover the sugar. Proceed as described above.

Sugar syrups are used at particular viscosities for different recipes:

Stages in Sugar Syrup Concentration

Type of sugar syrup	Boiling point	Uses
Vaseline	104°C 219°F	Syrup and sorbets
Short thread	108°C 227°F	Syrup and sorbet
Long thread	110°C 230°F	Syrup and sorbet
Soft ball	115°C 235°–240°F	Fondant, fudge
Firm ball	120°C 248°–250°F	Italian meringue, mousse-based ice creams
Hard ball	124°C 255°–265°F	Marshmallows
Soft crack	138°C 280°F	Soft toffee
Spun sugar	155°C 310°F	Hard toffee and some nougat
	160°C 318°F	Nougat
Hard crack	152°C 305°F	Spun sugar

A sugar thermometer (see **Kitchen Equipment**, page 61) is a very useful tool to test the temperature of the sugar. Place the thermometer in the syrup before it boils to allow it to reach the desired temperature slowly. Ensure that the base of the

thermometer is covered to the point indicated on the gauge 'level of liquid', about 3 cm | 1¼ in from the end, to ensure an accurate reading.

If you do not have a sugar thermometer you can test the sugar by placing a small amount on to a teaspoon. Dip your finger into cold water, then into the sugar. When sugar is at the Vaseline stage, the syrup will have an oily feel when rubbed between your finger and your thumb. As it becomes slightly hotter and more concentrated, the syrup will feel tacky and a short thread, about 1 cm | ½ in in length, will form between your wetted finger and thumb when they are pulled apart. A thread of about 2 cm | ¾ in in length is considered a long thread.

After this point is reached it is best to drip the syrup from the spoon into a jug of cold water. At the soft ball stage the syrup will clump into a little ball that will flatten on to the bottom of the jug. It will feel soft and pliable.

Stages of sugar syrup: long thread

A firm ball will still have a little 'give' but will hold its round shape. At the hard ball stage, the sugar will form into a round clear ball like a boiled sweet. If tapped on the side of the jug, it will make a sharp sound. At the crack stage the sugar will begin to take on a little colour and will form into hard threads rather than a ball. From this point the sugar can be used for spun sugar and other decorative garnishes.

Spun Sugar

Soft ball stage

Sugar work should be done on a dry day in a draught-free room. Use a clean, heavy-based saucepan. Professional pâtissiers who work with sugar use unlined copper pans for melting sugar. All equipment must be scrupulously clean.

To use sugar for decorative garnishes it is a good idea to add a little glucose or cream of tartar to the sugar before melting it. Add 1 teaspoon glucose, syrup or a pinch of cream of tartar to 250 g | 9 oz of granulated sugar with enough warm water to cover the sugar. This will slow down the crystallization of the sugar, giving you a longer time to use the syrup.

Boil the sugar to 152°C | 305°F, following the directions for making sugar syrup, above. Dip the base of the pan momentarily into cold water to halt the cooking, then allow the syrup to stand for a few minutes to becomes viscous. Dip the prongs of 2 forks held back to back into the sugar or use a special sugar whisk. Shake the forks back and forth over a clean, lightly oiled broom handle that has been suspended between the backs of 2 chairs. Lining the floor below the broom handle with old newspaper will make clearing up easier. Gather the spun sugar into balls and store in an airtight container. If keeping for more than 1 hour, place silica gel packs in the storage container to keep it dry.

Spun sugar: springs

For sugar springs, oil a round sharpening steel or the handle of a wooden spoon. Cool the sugar until it will pull a thread when dripped from the end of a small teaspoon. Wrap this thread around the steel or handle until the spring is the desired length, then snap the end of the thread. Tip the spring on to a tray. Store as for spun sugar, above.

For sugar cages, turn a soup ladle upside down and lightly oil the base. Drizzle the sugar from the teaspoon over the ladle to form an open lattice. Finish by encircling the bottom of the cage with several threads of sugar to strengthen the structure. Store as for spun sugar, above.

See also **Caramel** (page 174).

Spun sugar: cage

Terrines, Pâtés and Raised Pies

Terrines, pâtés and raised pies as well as other products such as sausages (see **Meat**, page 404), and galantines (see **Poultry**, page 443) are made of or stuffed with forcemeat (see **Forcemeat**, page 271).

The terrine is named after the mould in which it is baked, derived from French *terre*, meaning earth, as terrine moulds are traditionally made from glazed earthenware although they are also available in enamelled cast iron, porcelain, metal and glass. A terrine mould is rectangular or oval with a tightly fitting lid and handles at each end.

Terrine forcemeat (see **Forcemeat**, page 271) is made from highly flavoured meats, pork fat and garnishes. The meat, usually including pork or veal, mixed with a predominant flavouring meat such as poultry or game, after which the terrine is named, is often marinated first in alcohol, to tenderize and enhance its flavour. The meat is then coarsely minced and/or coarsely chopped or cut into small dice or strips and highly seasoned with spices and herbs. The forcemeat is then mixed or layered with garnishes, pressed into a terrine mould and baked in a bain-marie. Terrines are served cold.

Terrines

Preparing a Terrine Mould

Lining a terrine mould with bacon

Use thinly sliced pork back fat or streaky bacon rashers. The slices must be sufficiently long enough to run from the centre of the terrine base and up one side of the mould and droop over the edge of the terrine by at least 2.5 cm | 1 in so that the slices meet comfortably over the forcemeat once the terrine is filled.

Lining a terrine with bacon

Remove any rind from the bacon. Stretch each rasher by running the back of a knife along its length. Place one strip of pork fat or bacon tightly against the corner of the terrine mould so that the strip extends from just past the centre of the base to 2.5 cm | 1 in above the rim of the mould. Now place another strip in the mould, making sure that the first strip is overlapped by 6 mm | $\frac{1}{4}$ in on the base of and also extends above the rim.

To line the ends, arrange strips of pork fat or bacon along the short end of the mould, placing them tightly against the corner. The end of each strip should overlap the bacon running across the base of the mould by 1 cm $|$ ½ in. The other end of the strip should extend above the rim of the terrine by 2.5 cm $|$ 1 in.

Filling the terrine mould

Once the mould is lined, carefully fill the base of the terrine by firmly pressing the forcemeat against the sides and into the corners with the back of a wooden spoon to ensure that the edges of the terrine are sharp and clean.

More formal, layered terrines are made by lining the mould with pork back fat, bacon or blanched leafy vegetables, as described above, before layering the forcemeat with other garnishing ingredients or a second forcemeat of another colour to create a striped or mosaic effect.

If making a layered terrine, evenly press each layer down and against the sides of the terrine mould with the back of a wooden spoon.

Periodically tap the base of the terrine mould on a solid work surface to remove any air pockets as these cause unsightly holes in the cooked forcemeat.

Make sure that the forcemeat is slightly domed along the centre of the terrine before covering it with the ends of the lining ingredients. This is to ensure that the finished terrine has a satisfying, full shape. If the lining ingredients do not meet, add some short strips to ensure the top of the forcemeat is completely covered. Alternatively, a thin layer of fat may be poured on the surface of the forcemeat and garnished with spices and herbs before baking.

Baking the terrine

Cover the forcemeat with a piece of greaseproof paper cut to fit. Place the lid on the terrine mould and/or encase the mould in kitchen foil folded loosely above the mixture to prevent water from penetrating the terrine while it bakes in the bain-marie. Place the terrine in a bain-marie, to prevent the sides from catching, and bake in the oven preheated to 140°C $|$ 275°F $|$ gas mark 1 for fish and vegetable forcemeats and 180°C $|$ 350°F $|$ gas mark 4 for forcemeat made with meat.

Pressing the terrine

To ensure that coarse meat terrines or layered terrines slice well, a second terrine mould should be placed on top of the hot cooked terrine. Weights such as unopened cans are placed in the empty mould and left there until the terrine has cooled fully.

Garnishing the terrine

Rustic terrines made with coarse forcemeat are served from their mould so are often decorated with a thin layer of fat, herbs and spices. As the terrine cooks, fat in the forcemeat melts and settles on the surface. As the fat cools, the garnishing ingredients are set in place.

Terrines, Pâtés and Raised Pies

Serving the terrine

Meat terrines are served either in the container they are cooked in or cut into thin slices and served with sharp-flavoured garnishes such as pickled gherkins, pickled onions, chutney (see **Jams, Jellies and Other Preserves**, page 330) and bread or toasted brioche. Fish and vegetable terrines are served warm with a butter sauce (see **Sauces, Savoury**, page 605) or cold with a tomato sauce (see *Terrine Nicoise*, below) or a herb sauce.

Storing the terrine

Cool the terrine with the lid off, then store the terrine in the refrigerator, ideally in the terrine dish, covered in clingfilm, for up to 5 days. The flavour of a terrine will continue to improve for up to 2 days after it is made. Once the terrine has been sliced, eat within a couple of days, as the forcemeat will discolour as it oxidizes on contact with air. If the terrine is to be eaten over 2 days, wrap the cut terrine very tightly in clingfilm and return to the refrigerator as quickly as possible to slow the rate of oxidation. The cooked terrine may also be frozen for up to 3 months provided it is tightly wrapped in clingfilm.

Pork and Liver Terrine

Make this terrine the day before serving.

SERVES 6

225 g | 8 oz rindless belly of pork, minced	2 teaspoons brandy
225 g | 8 oz lean veal, minced	a pinch of ground allspice
110 g | 4 oz pigs' liver, minced	salt and freshly ground black pepper
2 shallots, finely chopped	225 g | 8 oz thin rashers of rindless streaky bacon
1 clove garlic, crushed	110 g | 4 oz chicken livers, cleaned

1 Chill all the ingredients and equipment thoroughly to below 4°C | 40°F.
2 Mince the pork, veal and pigs' liver once through the largest sized disc of a mincer and again through the next size for rough-textured pâté.
3 Mix the minced meats together with the shallots, garlic, brandy and allspice. Season with pepper and marinate overnight in the refrigerator.
4 Preheat the oven to 170°C | 325°F | gas mark 3.
5 Line a medium terrine mould or loaf tin with the bacon (see above).
6 Season the forcemeat with salt. Fry off a small portion of the forcemeat to check the seasoning before using. Add more seasoning if necessary.
7 Tip half the mixture into the prepared mould or tin and spread it flat.
8 Trim any discoloured parts from the chicken livers, then place them over the mixture in an even layer and top with the remaining mixture. Lay the bay leaves on the surface.

9   Cover with greased greaseproof paper and kitchen foil cut to fit. Twist the edges of the foil over the edge of the mould or tin to seal. Stand the terrine in a roasting tin half-filled with hot water (a bain-marie) and bake in the preheated oven for 1–1 $\frac{1}{4}$ hours. The terrine is done when it feels fairly firm to the touch and a skewer inserted into the centre for 10 seconds feels hot. The juices will still be pink, however, due to the nitrates in the bacon.

10 Remove from the roasting tin, place a weight on the terrine (see above) and leave overnight to cool and harden. Refrigerate up to 2 days. Turn out on to a plate to serve.

NOTE: This is good served with *Cumberland Sauce* (see **Fruit**, *Citrus Fruit*, page 283).

Pork Terrine: What has gone wrong when...

The terrine is full of air pockets and unsightly holes.

- The terrine was incorrectly filled with forcemeat. Make sure the corners are well filled before filling the base of the terrine and press the remaining forcemeat firmly into the terrine to remove air pockets. Periodically tap the base of the mould on a work surface to remove any trapped air bubbles. If garnishing ingredients are added to the forcemeat, make sure they are precooked if they are liable to shrink on cooking, otherwise air pockets will form around them.

The cooked terrine is very shallow.

- Insufficient forcemeat was used to fill the terrine. Make sure there is enough forcemeat to form a domed shape once the mould is filled. The domed surface will be flattened when the terrine is pressed with weights.

The cooked terrine is very dry and crumbly.

- The terrine mould was not sealed properly during cooking, causing moisture in the forcemeat to escape.
- The terrine has been overcooked.

The base and sides of the terrine are browned or burnt and the forcemeat is dry and crumbly.

- The terrine has been overcooked. The water level of the bain-marie was too low. Make sure the bain-marie is topped up throughout cooking to provide sufficient protection against the dry heat of the oven.

The terrine is loose-textured and hard to slice.

- The terrine was not pressed following cooking.
- The terrine was weighted too lightly.

Varieties of Terrine

Not all terrines are made with traditional forcemeat or contain any forcemeat, yet they are still called terrines as they are moulded and cooked in a terrine mould. These include foie gras terrines (see **Meat**, *Offal, Foie Gras*, page 446), layered vegetable terrines, brawns (otherwise known as aspic terrines), mousses, rillettes and confits.

Vegetable Terrines

As well as being low in fat, vegetable terrines are very colourful and attractive. They are made either by lining the mould with blanched leaf vegetables, such as spinach (see below), then setting a number of separately prepared vegetables of contrasting colour and flavour in aspic, or suspending brightly coloured vegetables in a vegetable mousseline to create a mosaic effect when sliced. The layered vegetables need to be cooked until soft before layering in the terrine. If they are too firm the terrine will not slice easily. Use a knife with a serrated edge.

Lining a terrine mould with leafy vegetables such as spinach, cabbage or lettuce: Remove any tough stems and veins from the leaves, being careful to keep the leaves as intact as possible. Blanch the leaves by immersing them in boiling water, then in cold water to fix their colour. Dry on kitchen paper.

Place the leaves in the terrine mould, starting from one end, making sure that they overlap, with the smooth upper surface of the leaf against the side of the mould and any remaining veins and stems facing inwards. Due to the irregularity of their shape and the fact that they are so thin, the leaves may be arranged less precisely than strips of bacon (see above).

Lining a terrine mould with clingfilm: If the lining ingredients, such as leaves, or delicate forcemeats might stick to the terrine, first line the oiled mould with clingfilm.

Terrine de Ratatouille Niçoise

This is a delicious, colourful vegetable terrine that is excellent as a first course in warm weather. Make sure the vegetables for layering are cooked until they are very soft otherwise the terrine is difficult to slice neatly.

SERVES 10–12

For the mousse

½ onion, chopped

3 red peppers, chopped

2 tablespoons olive oil

2 cloves of garlic, crushed

2 tomatoes, chopped

2 tablespoons tomato puree

1 tablespoon caster sugar

150 ml | ¼ pint dry white wine

290 ml | ½ pint water

12 fresh basil leaves

1 sprig of fresh thyme

6 leaves of gelatine

For the vegetables

2 green peppers

20 large spinach leaves, blanched and refreshed

2 red peppers

2 yellow peppers

2 aubergines

olive oil

1 bulb of Florence fennel

2 medium courgettes

salt and freshly ground black pepper

For the Basil Sauce

25 fresh basil leaves

150 ml | ¼ pint mayonnaise

150 ml | ¼ pint single cream

lemon juice to taste

salt and freshly ground black pepper

1 To prepare the mousse: sweat the chopped onions and red peppers in the olive oil, covered with dampened greaseproof paper (a *cartouche*), until soft. Stir in the garlic and cook for a further minute.

2 Add the tomatoes, tomato purée, sugar, wine and water. Cook until thick and reduced by half, about 20 minutes. Add the herbs and cook for a further 5 minutes. Measure the sauce. You should have 725 ml | 1¼ pints.

3 When the sauce is cooked soak the gelatine in cold water until soft then add to the hot sauce. Allow to cool to room temperature then purée in a liquidizer. Pass through a fine sieve into a bowl placed in a ice-bath.

4 Prepare the vegetables while the sauce is cooking. Preheat the oven to 220°C | 425°F | gas mark 7.

5 Line a 900 g | 2 lb terrine with clingfilm then the spinach leaves as instructed above.

6 Place the whole peppers in a roasting pan and bake for 20–25 minutes, or until they collapse. Cool, then remove the skins and seeds.

7 Trim the tops from the aubergines then cut into 1 cm | ½ in thick slices lengthways from top to tail. Brush with olive oil then bake for 20 minutes.

8 Trim the stems and the root from the fennel then divide into layers. Blanch for about 6 minutes until tender. Refresh in iced water and pat dry.

9 Trim the tops from the courgettes then slice lengthways into quarters. Blanch for 1–2 minutes then refresh and pat dry.

10 Assemble the terrine: place a thin layer of the mousse over the base, then a layer of vegetables, trimming the vegetables to fit. Season the vegetables are you go. Continue layering the vegetables with the mousse in the following sequence: yellow pepper, aubergine, courgette, red pepper, fennel, green pepper aubergine, yellow pepper until the top of the terrine is reached. Finish with a layer of mousse.

11 Fold over the spinach leaves to cover then cover with clingfilm. Place a second tin over the top of the terrine and weight lightly. Refrigerate for 8–24 hours.

12 For the Basil Sauce: place all the ingredients in a liquidizer and purée. Season.

13 To serve, slice the terrine into 1 cm|½ in slices and garnish with a sprig of basil and a little sauce.

Savoury Mousse Terrines

Savoury mousse terrines are made from cooked meats, poultry, fish, shellfish or vegetables, which are puréed and mixed with Béchamel or other binding sauce (see **Sauces, Savoury**, page 589), set with gelatine and lightened with whipped cream. The mixture is then left to set in a terrine or individual moulds lined with aspic or clingfilm (see **Mousses**, page 89).

Foie Gras Terrines

Foie gras terrines are made from the lobes of foie gras pressed into a terrine mould or from traditional pork forcemeat layered with lobes of fresh foie gras and encased in fat from the liver during cooking. The foie gras can also be puréed with eggs, cream and seasoning then baked in a terrine. This preparation is known as a *parfait* (see **Meat**, *Offal, Foie Gras*, page 446).

Brawns

Brawns are rustic terrines made by simmering gelatinous cuts of meat, such as pig's head, feet and tongue, in a rich stock flavoured with wine, spices and herbs. The meat is cooked until it pulls away from the bone easily. It is then diced and packed into a terrine mould with chopped fresh herbs. The stock, enriched further by the gelatine and flavours extracted from the meat, is clarified with egg white (see **Aspic**, page 90) and reduced to concentrate its gelatine content before pouring it over the meat. Once the terrine has cooled and set it can be turned out and sliced. Brawns are thinly sliced and traditionally served with Cumberland Sauce (see **Fruit,** *Citrus Fruit*, page 283).

Rillettes

Rillettes, a speciality of Touraine in central France, are prepared by cooking well-seasoned pork or fatty poultry, such as goose or duck, very slowly in its own fat until the meat falls off the bone. The warm meat is then shredded and combined with some of the cooking fat. The mixture is packed into a terrine and covered with more of the cooking fat to seal it. Provided the rillettes remain sealed in fat and are stored in the refrigerator, they will keep for several weeks. Rillettes are served cold, cut directly from the mould, and eaten with rustic bread or toast.

Confit

A speciality of south-western France, confit, like rillettes, is made most frequently with pork, duck or goose covered in a thick layer of fat (see **Preserving**, page 553). The meat is first cut into portions before salting to remove some of its moisture. The portions are cooked gently in their own fat until tender. The meat is then lifted out and placed into an earthenware jar or terrine mould. The fat is strained and poured on to the portions of meat and left to cool and harden, sealing the meat and thus preserving it for several weeks provided it is kept in the refrigerator.

Pâtés

Pâté is a general term to describe forcemeat consisting of marinated, minced or diced ingredients that have been mixed with spices, herbs and aromatic vegetables. Pâté forcemeat tends to have a finer texture and a richer flavour than terrine forcemeat and when cooked in a terrine mould is known as Pâté en Terrine. When the forcemeat is cooked in a pastry crust it is called Pâté en Croûte. Pâté is served hot or cold. See *Pâtés*, below.

For information in choosing and preparing chicken livers, see **Meat**, *Offal*, page 444.

Chicken Liver Pâté

For a stronger flavour, replace half the chicken livers with duck livers.

SERVES 6

225 g | 8 oz unsalted butter
1 onion, very finely chopped
1 large clove of garlic, crushed
450 g | 1 lb chicken livers
2 tablespoons brandy

110 g | 4 oz clarified butter (see **Dairy Products**, *Butter*, page 204)
salt and freshly ground black pepper
extra clarified butter, to seal

1 Melt half the butter in a large, heavy frying pan and fry the onion over low heat until soft and transparent.
2 Add the garlic and cook for 1 further minute.
3 Cut any discoloured or bloody parts from the liver together with any fibrous tissue and discard.
4 Add the livers to the pan and cook over a medium heat, turning occasionally, for about 5 minutes, until the livers are pink but not bloody.

5 *Flamber* the brandy and add to the livers. Allow to cool until just tepid.

6 Process the livers in a food processor or liquidizer with the remaining butter.

7 Pass through a sieve for a fine pâté. Season with salt and pepper. Pack into ramekins or a terrine.

8 Top with a layer of melted, cooled clarified butter to seal the pâté and prevent the surface from oxidizing. Store in the refrigerator for up to 3 days or freeze for up to 1 month.

Chicken Liver Pâté: What has gone wrong when...

The pâté is dry and crumbly.

- The livers were overcooked.
- Not enough butter was used.

The pâté is bitter.

- The livers were not thoroughly cleaned.
- The livers were overcooked.

Pâté en Terrine

Pâté en terrine is usually made with meat, game, offal or fish forcemeat moulded in a terrine, lined with bacon, before baking in the oven. It is therefore technically a terrine (see *Terrines*, above) and can only be distinguished by its finer texture and richer flavour. Pâtés en Terrine are always served cold and are often glazed with aspic and garnished with herbs, spices, vegetables and fruit.

Pâté en Croûte

Pâtés en Croûte are made with a forcemeat based on pork and flavoured with another meat, game or fish, and baked in a pastry crust to serve hot or cold. Pâtés en Croûte are baked either in a terrine (for rustic-style forcemeats) or in highly decorative hinged moulds with deep sides when the forcemeat is finer or contains expensive ingredients.

While the Pâté en Croûte bakes the forcement shrinks away from the pastry. In order to fill the resulting space, a sauce is often poured through a hole made in the pastry lid (the chimney) if the Pâté en Croûte is to be served hot. If the Pâté en Croûte is to be served cold, cool aspic jelly (see **Aspic**, page 89) is poured through the chimney once the pâté is cool and it is then left to set overnight before slicing.

The pastry crust: The type of pastry used to encase pâté depends on the forcemeat used. In the past the pastry was used only to encase the meat and was not eaten. *Hot Water Crust Pastry* (see **Pastry**, page 514), made with lard, is used to encase heavy forcemeat mixtures as it is sufficiently durable to withstand the long baking time required to cook the forcemeat as well as to hold in the juices that escape as it cooks. Streaky bacon or thinly sliced pork back fat is often used to line the inside of the pastry case to protect it from the liquid released by the forcemeat during cooking.

Finer forcemeats such as *mousselines* (see page 487) and those containing delicate ingredients such as foie gras require less cooking and are enhanced by a more delicate, richer-tasting pastry crust such as Pâte à Pâte, made with butter and eggs. Puff Pastry (see **Pastry**, page 522) and savoury brioche dough (see **Bread,** *Yeast*, page 134) can also be used.

Preparing Pâté en Croûte: Prepare the forcemeat ingredients as directed above. Prepare the pastry, either Hot Water Crust, Pâte à Pâte or Puff Pastry. Pig's caul can be used to line the pastry. Use the recipe for *Pork and Liver Terrine* without the lining bacon, above, for the filling.

Method 1: Making a Rustic Pâté en Croûte without a mould

1 Reserve a long strip of the rolled pastry, 10 cm | 4 in wide, for the top. Place the remaining rectangle of pastry on a baking sheet.
2 Lay the pigs' caul over the pastry to cover it entirely.
3 Arrange the meat filling in a neat rectangle about 20 × 7.5 cm | 8 × 3 in on the pastry.
4 Cut the corners out of the pastry, wet the edges and lift the pastry up to the sides of the meat, forming a terrine shape. Seal at the corners and crimp (see **Pastry**, page 520). Cut the reserved strip of pastry down to the exact size and lay over the top. Decorate the edges by crimping. Make 4 steam holes in the top of the pastry at the sides.
5 Glaze the pastry all over with beaten egg. Garnish with pastry trimmings cut into decorative shapes, such as leaves or flowers. The decorative details must be brushed with water on their underside to stick them firmly to the pastry lid. Chill in the refrigerator for 30 minutes, then glaze again.
6 Bake for 15 minutes in the oven preheated to 200°C | 400°F | gas mark 6 to brown the crust, then cover in kitchen foil and reduce the oven temperature to 150°C | 300°F | gas mark 2. Bake the Pâté en Croûte until the temperature, taken through the chimney from the middle of the forcemeat with a meat thermometer, has reached 66°C | 150°F for meat or 60°C | 140°F for fish and vegetable pâtés (alternatively the skewer test can be used, see, **Meat**, page 344). The cooking time is generally calculated at 15–18 minutes per 450 g | 1 lb forcemeat.
8 Allow the pâté to cool slightly in the mould or tin before turning it out on to a wire rack. Leave to cool completely overnight.
9 Make up the required quantity of aspic jelly and allow to cool but not set.
10 Check the pastry crust for any holes or cracks on the base or along the sides. If any are found, plug them with soft butter and refrigerate the Pâté en Croûte before progressing to the next stage, to allow the butter to harden.
11 Fill the baked Pâté en Croûte with aspic jelly (see **Aspic**, page 89).
12 Refrigerate overnight to ensure the aspic is thoroughly set.
13 To serve, cut the Pâté en Croûte into thick slices, using a ham or salmon knife, with long downward strokes.

Method 2: Making Pâté en Croûte in a terrine mould

Pâté en Croûte made in a terrine mould will be more elegant than Pâté en Croûte made by Method 1.

1 Using a terrine mould as a template, first mark the pastry lightly with a knife into lengths to line the base and sides of the mould, leaving enough to fold over the top of the forcemeat. Once you are happy that the marked areas will fit the mould correctly, cut the pastry just outside the marks to allow for error. Cut a second rectangle slightly larger than the top of the mould for the lid.

2 Lightly butter the inside of the mould.

3 Dust the surface of the rolled pastry with flour, carefully fold in half length-ways and lower into the mould.

4 Using your thumbs and a ball of pastry dough, made from pastry trimmings, press the pastry tightly into the corners and sides of the mould.

5 Trim the pastry dough so that 2.5 cm|1 in hangs over the ends of the mould and there is enough to cover the top of the terrine along the sides.

6 Line the pastry case with thin slices of pork fat, streaky bacon or ham, allowing 2.5 cm|1 in extra to hang over the sides of the mould. The extra lining of fat promotes a crisp finish to the crust by preventing liquid squeezed from the cooking forcemeat from making the pastry soggy.

7 Start to fill the pastry crust, pressing the forcemeat into the corners and against the sides to follow the shape of the mould and to avoid air pockets forming. Layer and garnish as appropriate but stop about 2 cm|1¾ in below the rim of the mould.

8 Fold the fat or bacon lining over the top of the forcemeat. Use additional pieces if necessary to cover the entire surface of the forcemeat.

9 Fold the pastry hanging over the sides of the mould over the fat, starting with the 2 short ends.

10 Brush the pastry with egg wash and carefully lay the pastry lid on to it. Press any overlapping areas of the pastry lid down the sides of the mould, using a palette knife.

11 Make a neat hole (chimney) either in the centre of the Pâté en Croûte or at each end, depending on the length of mould used, to allow steam to escape during cooking. To prevent liquid from escaping through the chimney, which might mark the pastry lid, place a narrow strip of pastry around its edge.

12 Decorate the lid with roses, leaves or other shapes made from the pastry trimmings, sticking each piece on to the surface of the Pâté en Croûte with egg wash. Once the lid is finished, brush the entire surface, including the decorations, with egg wash.

13 Bake: See Method 1.

14 Fill with aspic, if serving cold: See Method 1.

15 Serve: See Method 1.

Raised Pies

Traditional meat pies, such as pork pie or game pie, are made with a forcemeat (see *Forcemeat*, page 271) or diced pieces of lean meat seasoned with herbs and spices. The heavy pie mixture is encased in Hot Water Crust Pastry (see *Pastry*, page 514) before it is baked. Once cool, it is filled with aspic jelly to keep the meat moist (see *Aspic*, page 89).

Veal and Ham Raised Pie

SERVES 6–8

225 g | 8 oz flour quantity Hot Water Crust Pastry (see *Pastry*, page 514)

450 g | 1 lb boned shoulder of veal

110 g | 4 oz ham

salt and freshly ground black pepper

3 tablespoons very finely chopped onion

2 tablespoons chopped fresh parsley

1 egg, beaten

150 ml | ¼ pint aspic, flavoured with tarragon (see *Aspic*, page 89)

The pastry case should be made at least 1 hour in advance of the filling or overnight.

1 Prepare the Hot Water Crust as instructed in the recipe in *Pastry* (page 514) and use two-thirds of it to line the pie dish.
2 Cut the veal and ham into 2.5 cm | 1 in cubes, trimming away most of the fat and all the skin and gristle. Season with salt and pepper. Mix in the onion and parsley.
3 Fill the pastry case loosely with the filling, mounding it slightly in the centre.
4 Use the reserved third of pastry to make the lid, wetting the rim of the pie case to stick it down firmly. Trim and crimp the edges.
5 Make a neat hole (chimney) in the middle of the lid for steam to escape.
6 Decorate the lid with pastry trimmings shaped into leaves. Brush with beaten egg.
7 Secure a lightly buttered double piece of greaseproof paper around the pie with a paper clip to support the sides of the pastry case. Refrigerate until firm.
8 Preheat the oven to 190°C | 375°F | gas mark S.
9 Bake the pie in the oven for 15 minutes, then reduce the temperature to 170°C | 325°F | gas mark 3 and bake for 1 further hour.
10 Thirty minutes before the end of cooking, if the sides of the pastry are firm and are starting to brown, remove the paper collar, brush the pastry evenly all over with beaten egg and return to the oven.
11 Test that the pie is cooked with a skewer (see *Meat*, page 344). The meat should feel tender and if the skewer is inserted into the centre of the pie for 10 seconds it should come out hot. Allow the pie to cool on a wire rack.
12 Once the pie is cold, inspect the crust for holes or cracks and fill any with softened butter.
13 Fill the pie with aspic (see *Aspic*, page 89) and refrigerate until set.

Vegetables

Vegetables are an important source of A, B and C vitamins and fibre in the diet (see **Healthy Eating and Basic Nutrition**, page 13). The vitamin content of vegetables declines markedly over a short period of time, particularly at room temperature, so if they are not going to be eaten within a few days of purchase it is better to cook and consume frozen vegetables which have been frozen quickly within hours of picking. Frozen vegetables will have a higher nutritional content than vegetables that have been stored for a long time. In their natural state, vegetables are low in fat, making them an ideal food for those on a diet. To home-freeze vegetables, see the charts at the end of this section.

The Structure of Vegetables

Vegetable cells are comprised of up to 96 per cent water. The cell walls of vegetables are made of cellulose, a substance that is not digestible by man. This is the fibre in the vegetables that is important for a healthy digestive system. The cells are held together by pectic substances which soften and gel when cooked.

Older plants develop an amorphous substance called lignin, which hardens the cell walls. This can be seen very dramatically in a stalk of asparagus. The end of the stalk is tough and woody whereas the tip is moist and green. As the asparagus ages, the tough woody part advances towards the tip.

The pigment in green plants is called chlorophyll. To preserve this, it is important not to cook green vegetables for more than 7 minutes because after this, the chlorophyll loses its bright green colour. Overcooked vegetables also release acids that turn the vegetables an unattractive olive–green. Sometimes these acids noticeably affect the flavour of the vegetable too, as anyone who has eaten overcooked spinach will know.

Along with the preservation of the nutritional content, this is the reason why quick cooking methods are recommended for green vegetables. Occasionally recipes call for the addition of bicarbonate of soda to the vegetable cooking water. This advice dates back to Apicius, the first Roman cookery writer. This alkali preserves the green colour of the vegetables but it also softens the cells, turning the vegetables mushy and adversely affecting the nutritional content, so it is not a recommended practice.

Methods of Cooking Vegetables

Boiling: vegetables that grow above the ground
Vegetables that grow above the ground are placed in just enough boiling salted water to cover them and cooked with the lid off. It is particularly important to cook green vegetables uncovered, since once boiling begins the acids in the steam collect on the lid of the pan then drop back on to the vegetables, causing their bright green colour to turn to an unappetizing khaki. Cook until the vegetables are tender when pierced with a knife, then drain in a sieve or colander and pass briefly under cold running water. This is called *refreshing* and is done to stop the cooking and set the colour of the vegetables. If the vegetables are to be served immediately refresh them for only a few seconds.

Boiling: roots and tubers
Roots and tubers are vegetables that grow below the ground. They are usually dense and hard and therefore require longer cooking to soften them. These vegetables are placed in just enough cold, salted water to cover them and boiled with the lid on until tender when pierced with a knife. Drain in a colander. Vegetables that grow below the ground do not need to be refreshed unless it is vital to stop the cooking if they might otherwise overcook.

If possible, it is sound practice to save vegetable cooking water to use in soups, stews and gravies.

Blanching
The term blanching means to cook vegetables by boiling, as above, but only for long enough to half cook them. Blanching is done prior to freezing (see *Charts*, page 000) to de-activate the enzymes in the vegetables that might cause spoilage. Vegetables can also be blanched and refreshed in advance, then reheated in boiling water to finish cooking just before serving.

Sweating
To sweat a vegetable means to cook it in a little oil or melted butter but no liquid until it is very soft. First finely chop or thinly slice the vegetable, then stir it into the fat. Place a piece of dampened, crumpled greaseproof paper, called a *cartouche* (see below), directly on top of the vegetables. Cover with a lid and stir occasionally. The cartouche traps the steam from the vegetables as they cook, helping to soften them. The process is most frequently used for softening onions and cooking off their acidity before using them in a recipe.

Sautéing
A few types of vegetables, such as mushrooms, are cooked by sautéing. Melt a small amount of butter in a sauté pan over a medium heat and, add the vegetables, then cook until tender, stirring occasionally.

Stir-frying
Stir-frying is a good method for cooking most vegetables because it is quick and it preserves the nutrients of the vegetables. All types of vegetable are suitable for stir-frying with the exception of potatoes, which would break up with the constant stirring.

The vegetables need to be cut into small even-sized pieces or julienne (see **Knife Skills**, page 71). Heat a little oil in a wok or sauté pan. Sunflower or groundnut oil is recommended. The oil can be flavoured with thinly sliced garlic or root ginger (see **Spices**, page 670). Add the aromatic at the beginning of heating, then remove it with a slotted spoon just before starting to cook.

Add the vegetables to the pan and cook, stirring continually, over a high heat for 2–3 minutes or until tender enough to eat.

Steaming

Vegetables are steamed by placing them over boiling water either in a folding steaming basket (see **Steaming**, page 673) or in a sieve or colander. For the steam to cook the vegetables the pan needs to be covered with a lid. The liquid must continue to boil during cooking. This closed method of cooking will cause green vegetables to turn olive-coloured if they are too close to the lid.

Baking or roasting

Baking or roasting, to use the popular term, is a good method of cooking root and other hard vegetables that require a longer cooking time. Potatoes are excellent baked, as are squashes, fennel and onions. Tender vegetables or thinly cut root vegetables can be baked *en papillote* (see **Potatoes**, page 542). Tomatoes are often roasted to concentrate their flavour.

Chunks of root vegetables can be tossed in a little oil and baked. See individual vegetables and recipe under *Turnips*, below.

Braising

Some vegetables can be braised, that is, cooked in a covered pan with a small amount of liquid over a low heat. Vegetables such as celery, cabbage, fennel, leeks and endive are suited to braising. (See recipes under *Cabbage* and *Endive*, below.)

Grilling/Griddling

Cooking vegetables by grilling and griddling has become very popular recently. The vegetables need to be thin in order to cook through by the time the outside of the vegetables has charred slightly. Peppers, sliced aubergine and sliced courgette are all well suited to this method. (See recipe under *Peppers*, below.)

Microwaving

The microwave is useful for cooking certain vegetables. It is particularly good method for cooking broccoli, Brussels sprouts, carrots, cauliflower, onions, sliced and chopped, swede and turnips. (See **Microwave Cookery**, page 483.)

Vegetable Terms

To top and tail: To trim the ends off the vegetables.

Cartouche: A *cartouche* is a dampened piece of greaseproof paper placed directly on top of the vegetables when sweating or softening. The *cartouche* traps the steam from the cooking vegetables and helps to cook them more quickly. The moisture also helps to keep them from burning.

Aromatic vegetables: Onions, carrots, celery and leeks are often termed aromatic vegetables because they are used to flavour soups, stews, stocks and sauces.

Blanch: To half cook by boiling.

Refresh: To place the vegetables briefly under cold water to stop the cooking and set the colour.

Organic Vegetables

Organic enthusiasts argue that organic vegetables taste better than non-organic. In many cases we believe this to be true. However, we do not believe that this is the only strength of the organic case. You will often find that organic vegetables produced locally are fresher than some of the non-organic alternatives. And organic production is of course good for the environment and for this reason should be encouraged.

'Organic' vegetables must be produced without using artificial fertilizers, pesticides or fungicides. Only natural equivalents are allowed. The ground in which crops are grown must be free of any non-organic residues, which is why there is a three-year transition period before a farm can be registered as organic.

Not surprisingly, organic products are more expensive than non-organic. Without the use of artificial fertilizers and pesticides, yields are lower and costs higher.

Types of Vegetable

There are more than 200 different types of vegetable available worldwide. The vegetables more commonly found in the UK are listed below. Although most vegetables can now be found in the shops year round, the UK harvest seasons are listed below. Vegetables that are in season should be less expensive than vegetables that have travelled from abroad and, hopefully, should be fresher. Vegetables taste better and are better for you when freshly picked.

Artichokes, Globe

UK season: June–August
Artichokes are the flower of a plant of the thistle family. They are eaten for the fleshy part at the bottom of each leaf and for the prized heart, which lies at the base of the globe. Serve as a first course with *Hollandaise Sauce* (see **Sauces, Savoury**, page 602) or melted butter and lemon juice, or remove the hearts to use in salads.

Choosing
Choose bright green globes that are heavy for their size. Avoid any that seem dry or are starting to blossom in the centre.

Storing
Seal in a plastic bag and store in the refrigerator for up to 2 weeks. The hearts can be blanched and frozen.

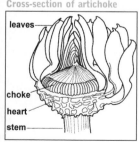
Cross-section of artichoke

leaves

choke
heart
stem

1 Half fill with water a saucepan large enough to hold the artichokes. Add salt and 1 teaspoon vinegar or lemon juice. Bring to the boil.

2 Trim the stem from each artichoke by making a cut around the stalk at the base. Lay the artichoke on its side with the stalk protruding over the edge of the work surface, then put downwards pressure on the stem to snap it off and pull out the strings running into the heart. Trim the bottom of the artichoke so it will sit flat.

3 Use scissors to cut 1 cm $|$ ½ in from the top of the artichoke, then trim each leaf by 6 mm cm $|$ ¼ in. Rub the cut edges with lemon juice.

4 Place the artichokes stem end down in the boiling water in the saucepan. Place a saucer on top of the artichokes to keep them submerged.

5 Simmer for about 35–45 minutes until a leaf pulls easily from the artichoke and the heart is tender when pierced with a sharp knife.

6 To serve, drain the artichokes upside down in a colander and allow to cool slightly. Wearing rubber gloves to protect your hands from the heat, open the centre of the artichoke. Pull out the pale purplish leaves in the centre to expose the strands of silky choke. Use a teaspoon to scrape the choke from the heart.

7 Serve with Hollandaise Sauce (see **Sauces, Savoury,** *Hollandaise*, p. 602) or melted butter and lemon wedges (see **Food Presentation**, *Garnishes*, page 12).

Artichokes, Jerusalem

UK season: January–February

These knobbly vegetables make a wonderful cream soup. Jerusalem artichokes are also delicious made into a gratin (see **Potatoes,** *Pommes Dauphinois*, page 547).

Choosing

The gnarled tubers look very similar to small salad potatoes. Choose tubers that are firm with unwrinkled skin.

Storing

Place in a paper bag and store in the refrigerator for up to 1 week.

Cooking

Peel the tubers and boil as for root vegetables. Serve seasoned with butter, salt and pepper, or mash with potatoes.

Asparagus

UK season: May–June

Asparagus is traditionally served as a first course with melted butter or *Hollandaise Sauce* (see **Sauces, Savoury**, page 602). For formal occasions it is served on a linen napkin. A finger bowl can be placed to the side of the diner. People traditionally eat asparagus with their fingers, leaving the woody end of the stalks.

Choosing

Look for firm spears with tightly closed, undamaged tips.

Storing

Stand the asparagus with the stem ends in water or wrap the stem ends in damp kitchen paper, then in clingfilm, and store in the refrigerator for up to 2 days. Wash just before using.

Cooking

The thick ends of asparagus stalks are often woody and are best made into a cream soup. To trim the woody stems, bend the asparagus stalk, then trim where it snaps naturally. The lower third of the shortened stalk can be peeled with a vegetable peeler to help the asparagus cook evenly.

Cook asparagus by steaming either in a tall narrow pot especially made for asparagus or using a vegetable steamer or colander. Asparagus can also be baked *en papillote* (see **Potatoes**, page 542).

To boil asparagus bring a sauté pan containing 2.5 cm | 1 in salted water to the boil. Place the woody ends of the asparagus stalks in the water and rest the tips on the sides of the pan. Cook until nearly tender. Tip the entire stalk into the water to finish cooking for the final minute. Drain, refresh and season.

Aubergines

UK season: August–October

Aubergines are widely used in Italian and Greek cooking. They are also part of the popular Provençal dish, *Ratatouille* (see below), and of *Moussaka* (see **Meat**, Lamb, page 395).

Choosing

Look for relatively slender, glossy aubergines that are heavy for their size and without any soft spots. Fat aubergines tend to be old and contain many bitter seeds.

Storing

Store unwrapped in the refrigerator for up to 5 days.

Cooking

Many recipes for aubergines call for them to be *degorged*, which means to sprinkle the sliced or cubed vegetable liberally with salt then allow to stand in a colander for 30–60 minutes before rinsing and using.

This process was said to remove the bitter juices. Aubergines today have been bred without the bitter juices, but the process can still be carried out because it dehydrates the cells on the cut surface of the aubergine and helps prevent the absorption of oil during cooking. Aubergines soak up oil like a sponge, so it is important to try to prevent this.

Aubergines can be baked whole in a hot oven for about 20 minutes until they collapse, then used as the base for a dip.

They are also delicious griddled and simply dressed with a little balsamic vinegar and olive oil. Degorge the aubergine as described above before griddling.

Ratatouille

SERVES 4

2 small aubergines, about 450 g | 1 lb
salt
85 ml | 3 fl oz olive oil
1 large onion, diced
1 clove of garlic, crushed
2 courgettes, about 340 g | 12 oz
1 green pepper, cored, deseeded and diced
   (see *Peppers*, below)

1 red pepper, cored, deseeded and diced (see
   Peppers, below)
6 large tomatoes, peeled, quartered and
   deseeded
a pinch of ground coriander
1 tablespoon shredded fresh basil
salt and freshly ground black pepper

1 Wash the aubergines and cut them into 2.5 cm | 1 in chunks. Sprinkle with salt and leave to stand in a colander for at least 30 minutes.
2 Place 1 tablespoon of the oil in a saucepan and stir in the onion. Cover with a piece of damp greaseproof paper (a *cartouche*) and a lid and cook over a low heat until soft, stirring occasionally.
3 When the onion is soft, stir in the garlic and cook for 1 minute. Set aside.
4 Wash the courgettes and cut them into 1 cm | ½ in chunks or thick slices.
5 Rinse the aubergine and pat dry. Heat 2 tablespoons of the remaining oil in a sauté pan and brown half of the aubergine on all sides. Repeat with the remainder. Set aside.
6 Brown the courgettes lightly in the remaining oil.
7 Place all the ingredients except the basil in a large sauté pan and cook, covered, over a medium-low heat, stirring occasionally.
8 When the vegetables are soft, stir in the basil and season to taste with salt and pepper.

Ratatouille: What has gone wrong when...

The vegetables have disintegrated.
- The ratatouille was overcooked.
- The vegetables were cut too small.

The aubergine is spongy.
- The aubergine is undercooked.

The dish is greasy.
- The ratatouille is overcooked.
- Too much oil was used.

Bean Sprouts

UK season: Year Round

Bean sprouts make a crunchy addition to salads and stir-fries.

Choosing

Bean sprouts should be firm and pale cream to white in colour, without any brown tips.

Storing

Wrap in kitchen paper, then place in a plastic bag and store in the refrigerator for 1 day.

Using

Bean sprouts can be eaten raw or briefly warmed by adding to a stir-fry near the end of cooking. Wash before using.

Beans, Broad

UK season: May–June

Broad beans are in season for a very short time and are delicious when young and tender. Old broad beans are starchy and bitter. They are served as a vegetable accompaniment or as part of a salad.

Choosing

Look for firm, moist pods without any brown spots.

Storing

Place the pods in a plastic bag and store in the refrigerator for up to 3 days.

Cooking

Remove the beans from the pods and blanch in boiling water, as for *Vegetables That Grow Above the Ground*, above. Unless the beans are very small, peel the wrinkled grey skin from each bean and discard. To serve, reheat briefly in boiling water.

Beans, French

UK season: July–August

French beans are usually served as a vegetable accompaniment or as part of a salad. They are a traditional accompaniment for lamb.

Choosing

The beans should be firm, with a bright green colour and no softening or mould at the tips.

Place in a plastic bag and store in the refrigerator for up to 3 days.

French beans are topped and tailed before cooking. They are most often boiled, see *Vegetables That Grow Above the Ground*, or steamed or stir-fried.

Beans, Runner

UK season: July–August

Runner beans are one of the main-stay vegetables of the home gardener. They are most often served as a vegetable accompaniment.

Choose firm slender pods without any developing seeds.

Place in a plastic bag and store in the refrigerator for up to 3 days.

Many home kitchens will have little gadgets to pass the beans through to remove the strings and cut the beans into thin strips. These are hard to find in the shops, so if you do not have one, the easiest way to prepare the beans is to run a vegetable peeler down each edge of the bean, then, using a roll-slice action (see **Knife Skills**, page 67), cut the beans into thin slivers on the diagonal. This is called Frenching. Boil as for *Vegetables That Grow Above the Ground*, above.

Beetroot

UK season: August–February

Beetroot are most often served as a part of a salad or as a vegetable accompaniment. They are the main ingredient in the Russian soup Borscht. Beetroot can be pickled in vinegar and bottled.

Small beetroot, no larger than a walnut, are best because they taste sweet when fresh. As beetroot becomes larger it develops a woody texture, but is still good for soups. Stems of about 2.5 cm|1 in should be left on the beetroot before cooking otherwise the colour will bleed when it is cooked.

The leaves of small beetroot are delicious eaten raw in salads or sautéed briefly as for *Spinach*, below. The leaves wilt quickly so should be used within 24 hours.

Place in a plastic bag and store in the refrigerator for up to 2 weeks.

Using

Beetroot can be peeled and grated to use raw in a salad or boil as for *Boiling Roots and Tubers*, above, or cook in a pressure cooker (see **Pressure Cooking**, page 555).

Bok Choy

UK season: July–September

Bok choy and its relative pak choy are small heads of dark green leaves with thick white stems. They are used widely in Chinese cooking as part of a stir-fry or steamed and served with oyster sauce as a vegetable accompaniment.

Choosing

Look for firm white stems and crisp dark green leaves. Avoid any that are brown or wilted.

Storing

Wrap in kitchen paper, then place in a plastic bag and store in the refrigerator for up to 2 days.

Cooking

Steam whole or separate the leaves and use whole or shredded in a stir-fry.

Broccoli

UK season: November–August

Broccoli is most often served as a vegetable accompaniment. It is particularly delicious served with Hollandaise Sauce (see **Sauces, Savoury**, page 602). It can also be served cold when lightly cooked and tossed with a salad dressing such as a *Vinaigrette* or *Caesar Dressing* (see **Salad Dressings**, page 577).

Choosing

Look for firm, deep green, tight heads without any sign of flowering or yellowing.

Storing

Wrap in kitchen paper, then place in a plastic bag and store in the refrigerator for up to 5 days.

Cooking

Divide the head of broccoli into small, even-sized florets, leaving about a 4 cm | 1½ in stem. Trim the stem of its thick outer coating so it will cook in the same length of time as the floret. The large stem of the broccoli head can be peeled and cut into batons (see **Knife Skills**, page 72).

Boil gently as for *Vegetables That Grow Above the Ground*, above, or microwave. Broccoli can also be cut into small florets and stir-fried.

Broccoli, Purple Sprouting

UK season: February–March

This vegetable is one of the treats of the early spring. It has a delicious nutty flavour that is enhanced by stir-frying. Serve as a vegetable accompaniment. It has a pronounced flavour so is best served with other strong-tasting food.

Choosing

Look for small, firm, purple heads with a minimum amount of green leaf and stem. Avoid any that are brown or wilted.

Storing

Wrap in kitchen paper, then place in a plastic bag and store in the refrigerator for up to 2 days.

Cooking

Trim the broccoli of any large, thick stalks and divide into even-sized florets and leaves. Stir-fry or boil the florets until nearly tender, then add the leaves and cook for a further 30 seconds.

Brussels Sprouts

UK season: September–January

Brussels sprouts are the traditional accompaniment to roast turkey. They combine well with chestnuts as a special seasonal dish.

Choosing

Choose small, firm, bright green sprouts. Avoid any that are starting to yellow or have brown spots.

Storing

Place in a plastic bag and store in the refrigerator for up to 2 days.

Cooking

Brussels sprouts are usually boiled as for *Vegetables That Grow Above the Ground*, above. They can also be microwaved or steamed. It is important not to overcook them or they will become bitter.

Trim the hard stem level with the vegetable. Do not make a cross-cut in the stem because it allows water to permeate the sprouts, making them soggy.

Cabbage

Different types available year round

Cabbage is shredded and served raw as in the ubiquitous salad, Coleslaw, or can be steamed, braised, stir-fried or boiled.

Choosing
There are many different types of cabbage (see below). Look for heads that are heavy for their size without any brown or yellowing leaves. Avoid any that appear to be trimmed.

Storing
Store in the refrigerator for up to 1 week.

Using
Chinese cabbage has a white, oblong head with pale green edges. It is usually served raw as part of an Asian-style salad or is added to a stir-fry at the end of cooking. See *Mangetout, Stir-Fried Vegetables*, below.

Green cabbage or Dutch cabbage really looks more white than green. It is used for Coleslaw and boiling.

Red cabbage can be used in a salad but being a bit tougher than green cabbage it is often braised (see recipe below).

Savoy cabbage has beautiful dark green leaves and a nutty flavour. It is good for boiling or stir-frying.

Braised Red Cabbage

The vinegar ensures the cabbage stays a deep red colour. Serve with pork.

SERVES 4

30 g │ 1 oz butter	2 tablespoons dark brown sugar
1 red onion, thinly sliced	2 tablespoons red wine vinegar
1 small red cabbage	a pinch of ground cloves
1 red dessert apple, grated	salt and freshly ground black pepper

1 Melt the butter in a small saucepan and stir in the onion. Cover with a damp *cartouche* and a lid. Cook over a low heat until softened.

2 Remove the hard stalks from the cabbage and slice thinly (see **Knife Skills**, *Julienne*, page 72).

3 Combine all the ingredients in a large, heavy-based saucepan, season with salt and pepper and cook over a low heat, stirring every 15 minutes, for about 2 hours, until the cabbage is very soft. A little water might need to be added during cooking.

4 Taste and season with additional salt, pepper or sugar.

Braised Cabbage: What has gone wrong when...

The cabbage is hard.
- The cabbage is undercooked.

The cabbage is mushy.
- The cabbage is overcooked.

The cabbage scorched.
- The heat was too high.
- The cabbage wasn't stirred frequently enough.
- Water should have been added to the pan.

The cabbage has turned blue.
- The mixture has become too alkaline. Add a tablespoon of wine vinegar.

Carrots

UK season: Baby Carrots May–June; Large Carrots July–February

Carrots are an important source of Vitamin A. They store well and are available for most of the year.

Choosing

Look for firm, bright orange carrots without any brown spots or wilted tips. Carrots with their frond-like leaves will be the freshest.

Storing

Remove any leaves by cutting the stems 2.5 cm|1 in above the carrot before storing. Store in the refrigerator for up to 2 weeks.

Using

Carrots can be eaten raw, grated into a salad or as part of a crudités platter (see *Canapés*, page 172).

Carrots are most often boiled but they can also be roasted as part of a root vegetable combination (see recipe under *Turnips*, below). Carrots also make a very good purée (see recipe below).

Carrot Purée

Other vegetables such as swede or parsnips can be substituted for the carrots. Green vegetables do not make good purées because they are too watery and fibrous.

SERVES 4

450 g | 1 lb carrots

290 ml | ½ pint crème fraîche or double cream

salt and freshly ground black pepper

a pinch of ground mace

1 Top, tail and peel the carrots. Slice thinly.
2 Boil as for *Boiling Roots and Tubers*, above, until very soft when pierced with a knife. Drain.
3 Purée the carrots in a food processor or push through a sieve. Place in a saucepan. Stir over a medium heat until dry.
4 Bring the cream to the boil in another saucepan. Reduce by half.
5 Gradually beat the cream into the carrots to make a smooth purée. The purée should just hold its shape.
6 Warm through gently and season to taste with salt, peppers and mace.

Vegetable Purée: What has gone wrong when...

The purée is grainy.
- The vegetables were not cooked for long enough.
- The vegetables were not sieved.

The purée splits into a greasy mass.
- The purée has been heated for too long. Beat in some water.

Vichy (Glazed) Carrots

This is a traditional method for making glazed carrots. Originally the carrots were cooked in mineral water from Vichy, France.

Turning a carrot

SERVES 4

450 g | 1 lb carrots

2 teaspoons butter

½ teaspoon salt

1 teaspoon caster sugar

freshly ground black pepper

1 teaspoon each chopped fresh mint and parsley

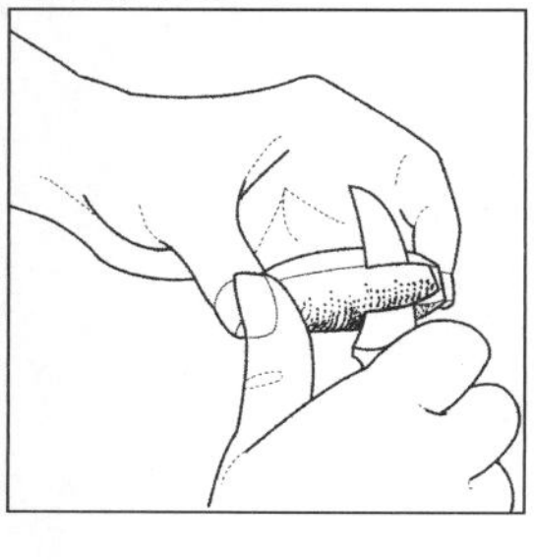

1 Top, tail and peel the carrots. Cut into batons or shape by turning (see **Knife Skills**, page 75, and diagram below). Leave them whole if they are very young.
2 Put all the ingredients except the pepper and the herbs into a saucepan and half cover with water.

3 Boil until the water has almost evaporated and the carrots are tender, then turn down the heat and allow the carrots to caramelize slightly in the remaining butter and sugar.

4 Season with pepper and toss with the mixed herbs.

Glazed Carrots: What has gone wrong when...

The carrots are shrivelled.
- The carrots are overcooked.

The carrots are very brown.
- The carrots were left to caranelize for too long at the end of cooking.

The carrots are hard.
- The carrots are undercooked.

Cauliflower

UK season: June–January

Cauliflower can be served plainly boiled as a vegetable accompaniment or baked with a cheese sauce (see **Cheese**, page 589) as a supper dish or as an accompaniment to roast pork or gammon. It is also delicious served raw, grated as part of a salad.

Choosing
Look for a bright white to creamy-white colour without any browning, mildew or signs of trimming. The florets should be tightly packed. Choose heads that are heavy for their size. Any leaves should be bright green without any signs of wilting or yellowing.

Storing
Wrap in kitchen paper, place in a plastic bag and store in the refrigerator for up to 5 days.

Cooking
Divide into florets of even size. Boil as for *Vegetables That Grow Above the Ground*, microwave or steam.

Celeriac

UK season: September–January

Celeriac is a root vegetable with a mild celery flavour. It can be substituted for potatoes in most recipes.

Look for small knobs without too many roots or any signs of sprouting. Large knobs are woody.

Storing

Store in the refrigerator for up to 1 week.

Cooking

Celeriac is most often used in soups (see **Soups**, page 656) or for mashing either on its own or in combination with potatoes. Boil as for *Boiling Roots and Tubers*, above, drain, then mash with a fork. Celeriac is too stringy to pass though a sieve.

Celeriac can also be roasted (see recipe under *Turnips*, below). It can be cut into julienne (see **Knife Skills**, page 72) and blanched for use in salads. The classic salad Celeriac Remoulade is made with blanched, julienned celeriac combined with a Remoulade Sauce, a daughter sauce of *Mayonnaise* (see **Sauces, Savoury**, page 601).

Celery

UK season: October–November

Celery is available both blanched (whitened) and in its natural green form. Green celery has a stronger flavour.

Choosing

Look for firm stalks without any sign of wilting or browning.

Storing

Wrap in kitchen paper, then place in a plastic bag and refrigerate for up to 5 days.

Using

Celery is used in a *bouquet garni* and in a vegetable *mirepoix* in cooking to add flavour to soups and stews. It is also served raw in salads and is used as a vegetable for a *Crudités* platter (see **Canapés**, page 172).

Chillies

UK season: July–October

Chillies come in many different varieties. Their colour ranges from green to orange to red and their heat from mild to very hot.

Choosing

Often supermarkets will have a chilli heat guide, but as a very general rule, the smaller the chilli, the hotter it will taste. Look for chillies that are firm without any sign of browning.

Storing

Place in a plastic bag and store in the refrigerator for up to 1 week.

Using

Chopping chillies

Try not to touch the chillies with your fingers. The pungent oil will stay on them for a long time and will sting your eyes if you happen to rub them. The hottest part of the chilli is the placenta, the white membrane inside the chilli that supports the seeds.

To deseed and chop a chilli, cut it in half lengthways. Use a fork to hold the chilli near the stem end, then slice the chilli into long strips. Roll-slice (see **Knife Skills**, page 67) across the chilli to cut it into dice.

Courgettes

UK season: July–August

Courgettes are available in green and yellow varieties. They taste similar, with the green variety being slightly stronger in flavour. Courgettes are usually served as an accompaniment or as part of a salad. They can also be grated and stirred raw into muffin and quick bread batters.

Choosing

Look for small, firm vegetables with a bright colour.

Storing

Store in the refrigerator for up to 5 days.

Cooking

Boil courgettes as for *Vegetables That Grow Above the Ground*, above, or stir-fry, griddle or steam. Courgettes can also be griddled (see *Methods of Cooking Vegetables*, above). They have a high water content and cook quickly, turning to mush if not watched carefully.

Courgette flowers

Courgette flowers can be dipped in batter and deep-fried to serve as an appetizer or a first course. The slender male flowers on their sturdy stalks are the best to use because the female flowers are too open and tend to absorb a lot of oil when fried. See **Batters** (page 111) and **Deep-frying** (page 206). Courgette flowers can also be stuffed with a variety of fillings and either baked or fried.

Cucumbers

UK season: August–September

Cucumber is usually served raw on its own, in sandwiches or as part of a salad.

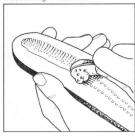

Choosing

Choose firm, slender cucumbers. The ends should not be soft.

Storing

Cucumbers are often sold tightly wrapped in plastic. They will keep in the refrigerator for up to 5 days uncut. Once cut, they will keep for 2 days in the refrigerator.

Using

If cucumber has been waxed it should be peeled, otherwise it can be peeled or not as required. Sprinkle thin slices of cucumber with salt and allow to stand for 30 minutes (degorge) before using in sandwiches.

Slices of deseeded cucumber 6 mm $\frac{1}{4}$ in thick can also be blanched as a garnish for fish dishes.

Endive (also known as chicory)

UK season: November–December

Endive has a bitter flavour and crisp texture. It is widely used in Europe where it is served as part of a salad. It can be braised as a vegetable accompaniment.

Choosing

Look for small, firm, white heads without any browning or wilting.

Storing

Keep wrapped in the blue paper it is usually sold in, or wrap in a paper bag and store in the refrigerator for up to 3 days.

Using

Wash and slice thinly to serve raw. To braise, cut in half lengthways and place in a heavy saucepan containing 1 cm $\big|\frac{1}{2}$ in water. Season with salt and pepper and dot with butter. Cover and cook over a low heat until tender, turning occasionally. It should be slightly caramelized. Braised endive is sometimes served with a Cheese Sauce (see **Sauces, Savoury**, page 589) as an accompaniment to gammon.

Fennel

UK season: June–August

A popular vegetable in Italy, these fist-sized white bulbs with dill-like fronds have a strong scent of anise and a crunch like celery. Fennel is delicious eaten raw and crunchy in salads or briefly blanched as an accompaniment to fish. Fennel can also be cut in half and baked or braised as for *Endive*, above.

Choosing

Choose small, heavy bulbs without any browning. Look for fresh green feathery leaves.

Storing

Place in a plastic bag and refrigerator for up to 3 days.

Using

Cut the stems and fronds off near the bulb. Reserve any feathery fronds for garnish. Remove any brown spots from the outside layer and peel away any thick strings, using a vegetable peeler. Cut the bulb in half from top to bottom, then cut out the hard core. Slice thinly.

To eat raw, immediately toss with lemon juice or *Vinaigrette* (see **Salad Dressings**, page 57) or the fennel will discolour. Blanch in boiling water for 30 seconds, then refresh in cold water.

Garlic

Dried garlic available all year round. Fresh garlic is available from June to October.

Garlic is used to flavour all kinds of savoury dishes, from soups and sauces to casseroles, roasts, stir-fries and salads.

Choosing

Look for firm bulbs that are heavy for their size and show no sign of sprouting.

Storing

Keep unwrapped in a cool, dark, well-ventilated place for up to 2 weeks, or store in the refrigerator for up to 1 month.

Bruising garlic

Using

Garlic is usually crushed before use. It should never be added to onion to cook for a long time as it will burn and taste bitter. Garlic only needs to be fried for 30–60 seconds.

To bruise and peel garlic easily, place the flat blade of a knife over the top of the clove and whack it with the heel of your palm. The papery skin should come away easily.

If there is a green sprout in the centre, remove it. It can taste bitter. Chop the garlic finely, then mash to a purée with a little salt.

Alternatively, use a table knife to scrape the peeled clove into a paste. See also **Knife Skills**, *Bruising/peeling garlic* (page 70).

Reducing garlic to a purée

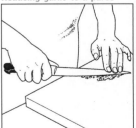

Baked garlic

Garlic is also delicious when baked. Baking gives it a mellow, smoky flavour, making it particularly good for garlic bread and *Pesto* (see **Herbs**, page 307). Cut off the very top of the garlic to expose the tips of the cloves. Drizzle with 1 tablespoon of olive oil and place in the oven preheated to 180°C|350°F|gas mark 4 for about 20 minutes or until tender when pierced with a skewer. Keep in the refrigerator for up to 1 week.

Kohlrabi

UK season: August–November

This pale green bulbous stalk with a few flag-like leaves protruding from the sides is occasionally seen in markets. It has a mild, turnip-like flavour.

Choosing
Choose small bulbs without any soft spots or browning.

Storing
Store in the refrigerator for up to 3 days.

Using
Remove the thick skin with either a vegetable peeler or a knife. Cut into chunks and boil as for *Vegetables That Grow Above the Ground*, above, or cut into julienne (see **Knife Skills**, page 72) and use in a stir-fry.

Leeks

UK season: October–January

Leeks usually form part of a dish rather than being served on their own, although they are good served with a White Sauce (see **Sauces, Savoury**, page 589) as an accompaniment. They make a delicious soup with potatoes (see **Soups,** *Iced Vichyssoise*, page 665).

Choosing
Look for slender, firm bulbs without any browning.

Storing
Place in a plastic bag and store in the refrigerator for up to 5 days.

Cooking
Leeks can be boiled as for *Boiling Roots and Tubers*, above, braised or steamed.

Cut off the green tops and discard as they are tough and stringy. Trim the root end of any roots but leave the root end intact. Cut the leek in half from one end to the other. Rinse well under cold running water to remove any dirt or grit. Slice as required (see **Fish**, *Noisettes of Salmon Braised with Leeks and Mustard*, page 260).

Lettuce

UK season: May–September

There are many varieties of lettuce available in the market year round. Lettuce is most often served as a salad (see also **Salad Dressings**, page 572).

Choosing

Look for lettuces that are heavy for their size and show no sign of wilting or browning.

Storing

The firmer, crisper lettuces, such as iceberg and radicchio, keep for up to 5 days in the refrigerator if wrapped in kitchen paper then stored in a plastic bag. Tender leaves such as lamb's lettuce should be stored in the same manner but can be kept for only 1 day. Wash just before using.

Using

Slightly limp lettuce can be refreshed by soaking in cold water for 10 minutes then drained and dried in a salad spinner (see **Kitchen Equipment**, page 53).

Tear into bite-sized pieces no larger than 5 cm|2 in. Toss with dressing only just before serving or the the lettuce will become limp. Toss in one bowl, then transfer to the serving bowl to avoid having a greasy serving bowl.

Mangetout

UK season: May–June

These bright green, flat pea pods need only minimal cooking. Serve as a vegetable accompaniment, as part of a stir-fry or as part of a salad.

Choosing

Fresh mangetout are bright green and firm. Avoid any with brown spots or those that are very large.

Storing

Place in a plastic bag and store in the refrigerator for up to 3 days.

Using

Top and tail, then pull the strings from the edges. Boil as for per *Vegetables That Grow Above the Ground*, above, or stir-fry (see recipe below).

Stir-fried Vegetables

2 tablespoons sunflower oil or groundnut oil

a 2.5 cm|1 in piece of fresh root ginger, peeled and sliced

110 g|4 oz mangetout, topped and tailed

110 g|4 oz baby sweetcorn, cut in half lengthways

1 red pepper, cut into julienne (see **Knife Skills**, page 72)

1 clove of garlic, peeled and crushed

110 g|4 oz bean sprouts, rinsed

85 g|3 oz Chinese leaves, cut into julienne

2 tablespoons soy sauce

2 teaspoons sesame oil

3 spring onions, diagonally sliced

1 Heat the oil in a wok or large sauté pan.
2 Add the ginger and heat until lightly browned. Remove with a slotted spoon.
3 Add the mangetout, sweetcorn and red pepper to the pan and cook, tossing and turning the vegetables, for 2–3 minutes.
4 Add the garlic, bean sprouts and Chinese leaves and cook for 1 further minute.
5 Add the soy sauce and sesame oil, garnish with the spring onions and serve immediately.

Stir-fried Vegetables: What has gone wrong when...

The vegetables are too crunchy.

- The vegetables have not been cooked for long enough. The heat could have been too low.

The vegetables are scorched.

- The heat was too high.

The vegetables taste bitter.

- The garlic was overcooked.

The vegetables are soft.

- The vegetables have been cooked for too long.

Mushrooms

UK season: September–November

Mushrooms come in many different varieties. If picking mushrooms in the wild, be sure you can positively identify them; some are deadly poisonous.

Mushrooms are usually sautéed in butter before adding to sauces or stews. Mushrooms can also be baked.

For instructions on using dried mushrooms, see **Preserving** (page 549).

Choosing

Look for firm caps that are even in colour without any sign of shrivelling or becoming slimy, particularly underneath the caps.

Storing

Mushrooms should be stored in a paper bag in a cool, dark place for up to 3 days. Storing in the refrigerator tends to dehydrate them.

Using

Only very large mushrooms need to be peeled because their skins are tough. Pull the skin off the cap by peeling the edge back towards the centre. Wipe mushrooms with damp kitchen paper to clean them or stroke them with a mushroom brush. Never soak them in water as they are like sponges and will absorb a lot of water, which will ruin their flavour.

Remove the tough part of the stalks, then cook the mushrooms whole or sliced. Sauté in butter until lightly browned and the water they give out has evaporated.

Onions

UK season: October–November

Choosing

Onions come in many different varieties (see below); choose onions that are heavy for their size. They should not have any soft or wet patches nor should they show any signs of sprouting.

Storing

Keep in a cool, dry, dark place. Onions need to have air circulation to keep them dry and free from rot. Keep for up to 4 weeks.

Using

Onions are widely used in cooking, as one of the main flavouring ingredients for soups and stews. For instructions on slicing and chopping onions, see **Knife Skills** (page 70).

Most recipes will call for the onions to be cooked in order to soften them before using. See the instructions under *Sweating* in *Methods of Cooking Vegetables* above. Sweating diminishes the acidity in the onions and brings out their sweetness. Onions can also be baked, pan-fried and deep-fried in batter.

Onion Sizes

1 large onion = 250 g|9 oz
1 medium onion = 170 g|6 oz
1 small onion = 110 g|4 oz

Red onions have a sweet flavour and are one of the best the best onions to eat raw. They are widely used in Italian cookery and are delicious baked with a sprinkling of olive oil, balsamic vinegar and rosemary or sweated as a topping for *Olive Oil Bread* (see **Bread**, page 128). The layer of onion just beneath the skin of red onions needs to be removed if it has dried out.

Spanish onions are large onions with a brown skin. They have a mild flavour and are a good all-purpose onion.

Shallots are small members of the onion family, about 2.5 cm | 1 in in diameter, with a slightly sweeter flavour. They are used to make sauce reductions (see **Sauces, Savoury**, *Beurre Blanc*, page 605). Shallots are also used whole in many dishes such as casseroles.

To remove the skins, immerse the shallots in boiling water for 1 minute, then plunge them into cold water. The skin should peel off easily.

Pickling onions are another small variety of onion. They are about the same size as shallots but have a sharper flavour. They can be substituted for shallots or pickled.

Spring onions are also called salad onions, scallions or green onions. They are used as garnishes and in Chinese dishes. See *Mangetout, Stir-fried Vegetables*, above.

Choosing
Look for firm, crisp onions without any signs of wilting. Avoid any with brown and/or slimy skin on the white bulbs.

Storing
Place in a paper bag and store in the refrigerator for up to 3 days.

Using
Trim off the tough green tops and remove any wilted layer from the outside of the onion. Roll-slice thinly on the diagonal (see **Knife Skills**, page 67).

Parsnips

UK season: November–February

Parsnips need a frost to bring out their sweetness so they are at their best in late autumn. They are excellent for roasting or mashing with potatoes (see **Potatoes**, page 546). They can also be used in soups or cooked as for *Vichy Carrots*, above, using orange juice in place of water.

Choosing
Look for small to medium plump parsnips without any brown spots or signs of wrinkling.

Cut off any leaves, then place in a plastic bag and store in a cool, dark place for up to 7 days.

Cooking

Parsnips are usually cut into baton-sized pieces (see **Knife Skills**, page 72). Parsnips can be roasted like potatoes (see **Potatoes**, page 544) or boiled as for root vegetables. (see *Methods of Cooking Vegetables*, above).

Peas

UK season: May–June

Most peas are purchased frozen; however, there is a short season when fresh peas in their pods are available.

Choosing

Look for moist, firm pods no more than 5 cm | 2 in long without any wrinkling or signs of wilting at the tips. Avoid swollen pods. Peas are best when freshly picked as their natural sugars begin to turn to starch once picked.

Storing

Place in a plastic bag and store in the refrigerator for up to 1 day.

Cooking

Shell the peas by squeezing the pod at one end to make it pop open. Run your finger along the length of the pod to remove the peas.

Boil as for *Vegetables That Grow Above the Ground* (above) with a little sugar added to the water instead of salt. Salt toughens the skins of the peas.

Peppers, Sweet

Imported all year round.

Peppers are delicious eaten raw in salad or cooked as part of another dish. Griddled peppers make a delicious salad (see recipe below).

Choosing

Look for firm, shiny, brightly coloured (red, yellow, orange or green) peppers without any wrinkling or soft spots.

Storing

Store unwrapped in the refrigerator for up to 5 days.

Using

Remove the core and seeds from the pepper, then cut from top to bottom along the corners to produce 4 flat sides.

Grilling peppers

1 Deseed and quarter the peppers, then place skin side up under a hot grill or on a barbecue until the skins have blackened.
2 Place in a plastic bag to cool. The steam will soften the peppers and help remove the skins.
3 Peel and use as required.

Griddled Vegetable Salad

SERVES 4

1 small aubergine, sliced and degorged

2 small courgettes, sliced diagonally

4 tablespoons olive oil

2 red or yellow peppers, deseeded, quartered and grilled (as above)

2 tablespoons balsamic vinegar

salt and freshly ground black pepper

4 sprigs of fresh basil

1 Brush the aubergine and the courgette slices with a little of the oil.
2 Heat a griddle pan over a medium–high heat and griddle the aubergine and courgette slices until soft.
3 Peel then cut the peppers into 2.5 cm|1 in wide strips.
4 Toss all the vegetables with the remaining oil and the vinegar. Season with salt and pepper.
5 Tear the basil leaves and scatter over the vegetables.

Griddled Vegetables: What has gone wrong when...

The vegetables are too mushy,

● The vegetables have been overcooked.

The vegetables do not have brown lines from the griddle pan.

● The pan was not hot enough.

The vegetables are too hard.

● The vegetables have not been cooked enough.

Sweating Peppers

Peppers can be cooked in this way for use in sauces or to add to other dishes.

1 Remove the core from the peppers and de-seed as above.
2 Cut the peppers into quarters, then roll-slice into thin strips (see **Knife Skills**, page 67).
3 Place the peppers with a little olive oil in a saucepan and cover with a *cartouche* and a lid. Sweat until soft.

Potatoes

See **Potatoes** (page 541).

Pumpkin

UK season: October–November

Pumpkin is a large orange round squash, widely available in the autumn. Pumpkin is dense and starchy. It makes an excellent cream soup (see **Soups**, *Cream*, page 659). In Italy it is added to risottos and used to fill ravioli. The American dessert pumpkin pie is usually made with canned pumpkin.

Choosing
Look for a pumpkin that is heavy for its size, without any bruising or soft spots.

Storing
Keep in a cool, dry place for up to 2 weeks, or store in the refrigerator for up to 8 weeks.

Cooking
Cut off the top in the same manner as for a pepper (see above), then scoop out the seeds and the stringy pulp. Using a heavy knife, cut the hard pumpkin flesh into chunks. Pumpkin can be baked, steamed or boiled to serve as a vegetable, in risotto and as a filling for ravioli.

Radishes

UK season: June–July

Radishes are used chiefly for salads and for crudités (see **Canapés**, page 172).

Choosing
The radishes should be firm and smooth. The leaves should not be wilting.

Place in a plastic bag and store in the refrigerator for up to 7 days.

Radishes are usually eaten raw. They can be *blanched* before eating if desired, although their colour fades.

Rocket

UK season: June–July

Rocket is a peppery salad leaf related to the dandelion. The rocket that is sold as wild rocket has spiky leaves and a very peppery flavour.

Choosing
Look for bright green leaves without any signs of wilting.

Storing
Wrap gently in kitchen paper, place in a plastic bag and store in the refrigerator for up to 2 days.

Using
Rocket is popular served as a salad dressed with a little olive oil and shavings of Parmesan.

Spinach

UK season: February–April

Baby spinach (pousse) can be served raw in a salad. It is sometimes served with a warm bacon dressing that partially wilts the leaves.

Choosing
Look for bright green leaves without any signs of wilting or yellowing. Choose spinach without a lot of stems.

Storing
Place in a plastic bag lined with kitchen paper and store in the refrigerator for up to 2 days.

Using
Wash the spinach thoroughly in several changes of water to remove any sandy soil. Cut out the large stems.

To cook spinach, sauté in lightly browned butter, using only the water that clings to the leaves after washing. Cooked spinach can be very wet and needs to be squeezed dry before serving or using in other dishes. Season with grated nutmeg.

Sautéed Spinach

SERVES 2

This can be served as an accompaniment or used as part of another dish.

225 g|8 oz spinach	salt and freshly ground black pepper
30 g|1 oz butter	freshly grated nutmeg

1 Wash the spinach and remove any stems.

2 Heat half the butter in a sauté pan over a medium heat until it starts to brown. Place the washed spinach in the pan and turn it over continuously using 2 large wooden spoons. The spinach is ready when it is wilted.

3 Place the spinach in a sieve to drain, then use your hands to squeeze it dry. Chop the spinach.

4 To reheat, melt the remaining butter in a sauté pan until it starts to brown lightly.

5 Stir in the spinach. Season with salt, pepper and nutmeg.

Sautéed Spinach: What has gone wrong when...

The spinach is bitter.
- The spinach is overcooked.

The spinach is watery.
- The spinach has not been squeezed sufficiently.

Spring Greens

UK season: March–April

Spring greens are a type of cabbage. They make a good accompaniment for roast pork and game. They are deep-fried and served as 'seaweed' in Chinese restaurants.

Choosing
As for *Spinach*, above.

Storing
As for *Spinach*, above.

Using
As for *Spinach*, above.

Squash

UK season: September–November

There are several members of the squash family (see below). They are characterized by thick skins and hard flesh.

As for *Pumpkin*, above.

As for *Pumpkin*, above.

Butternut: As for *Pumpkin*, above.

Gem: Cut in half and bake, boil or steam until tender.

Spaghetti Squash: Cut in half lengthways and remove the seeds. Dot with butter and cover with kitchen foil. Bake in the oven preheated to 200°C | 400°F | gas mark 6 until tender. Use a fork to scrape out the flesh into spaghetti-like strands.

Sugar-snap Peas

See *Mangetout*, above.

Swede

UK season: October–December

Swede is called turnip in Scotland. It is traditionally served with Haggis.

Choosing

Select medium-sized swedes without any soft spots.

Storing

As for *Celeriac*, above.

Cooking

Boil swede as for root vegetables (see *Methods of Cooking Vegetables*, above). It can be substituted in recipes for parsnip, turnip or celeriac (see *Turnips, Roasted Glazed Vegetables*, below) or cooked in the traditional manner by boiling then mashing with a fork and seasoning with butter, salt and pepper, for Bashed Neeps.

Sweetcorn

UK season: August

Choosing

Choose ears with moist, green husks and moist silk. Split the husks to check the size of the kernels. They should not be too large.

Baby sweetcorn is imported from Thailand. Avoid any with brown tips. It is most often used in stir-fries (see *Mangetout, Stir-fried Vegetables*, above).

Storing

The natural sugars in sweetcorn start to convert to starch as soon as it is picked, so it is best to cook it as soon as possible. If necessary, it can be placed in a plastic bag and stored in the refrigerator for 1 day.

Cooking

Remove the husks just before cooking. Place in a pan of boiling water with 1 tablespoon sugar added for every 4 ears. Do not salt the water as it tends to toughen the corn.

Sweet Potatoes

UK season: October–November

Sweet potatoes or yams are orange-fleshed with a deeper purplish skin. They have a sweet nutty flavour, rather similar to *Butternut squash* (see above) and can be substituted for potatoes in any potato recipe (see **Potatoes**, page 541).

Choosing

Look for firm, unblemished potatoes without any soft spots.

Storing

Place in a paper bag and store in a cool, dark, well-ventilated place for up to 2 weeks. Do not refrigerate.

Using

Bake or boil as for root vegetables.

Swiss Chard

UK season: October–March

Swiss chard resembles spinach but has either bright white or ruby-red flat stems. Baby red chard is now often seen as a salad leaf. It has a slightly more bitter flavour than spinach.

Choosing

Look for dark green glossy leaves not much bigger than 20 cm|8 in with firm white or red stalks.

Storing

Wrap in kitchen paper, then place in a plastic bag and store in the refrigerator for up to 2 days.

Cooking

Cook the leaves of older Swiss chard as for *Spinach*, above. The stems taste much like celery and can be thinly sliced and boiled.

Tomatoes

UK season: August–September

There are a wide variety of tomatoes imported year round, but they are often flavourless when out of season. Canned tomatoes are a good substitute for fresh when used for a sauce, but do not have as good a flavour as ripe tomatoes in season.

Choosing
Look for firm, deep-coloured tomatoes without any soft spots.

Storing
To ripen, keep in a single layer in a warm place for up to 1 week. Do not refrigerate tomatoes as this gives them a woolly texture.

Using
Tomatoes are widely used in cooking, for sauces (see **Sauces, Savoury**, page 607), for soups and to give flavour to a variety of meat and fish dishes. They are also eaten raw as a salad or as a garnish. Enhance their flavour by sprinkling with a little sugar.

Slicing: Cut across the width to prevent the seeds from falling out, using a thin serrated knife.

Peeling: Plunge the tomato in boiling water for 10 seconds, then place in cold water. Using a paring knife, nick the skins and then peel off. The skin should peel away easily. If it does not, return the tomatoes to the boiling water for a further 2 seconds. If the tomato is left in the water for too long, the surface under the skin will start to cook, giving it a furry texture.

Concassé: This is the term for a small dice of tomatoes. Peel as above, then cut into quarters from top to bottom. Scoop out the seeds, using a teaspoon. Use a cook's knife with the roll-slicing action (see **Knife Skills**, page 67) to cut the tomatoes into pea-sized dice.

Turnips

UK season: June–September

Choosing
Look for small turnips no larger than an egg, without any signs of wrinkling.

Storing
Place in a plastic bag and store in the refrigerator for up to 1 week.

Cooking
Boil as for root vegetables or steam small specimens. Baby turnips can be used in salads. Turnips can also be baked, as in the recipe below.

Roasted Glazed Vegetables

SERVES 4

225 g | 8 oz carrots	2 tablespoons vegetable oil
225 g | 8 oz turnips, celeriac or parsnips	2 tablespoons clear honey
225 g | 8 oz swede	30 g | 1 oz butter
225 g | 8 oz celery	1 tablespoon chopped fresh parsley

1 Preheat the oven to 200°C | 400°C | gas mark 6.

2 Top, tail and peel the carrots and turnips or celeriac and parsnips. Peel the swede. Cut into even-sized chunks about 3 cm | 1¼ in or turn into barrel shapes (see *Knife Skills*, page 75).

3 Destring the celery and cut into pieces the same size as the other vegetables.

4 Heat the oil in a roasting tin. Toss the vegetables in the oil, then roast for 45 minutes, turning occasionally.

5 Add the honey and butter to the tin and turn the vegetables in the mixture.

6 Return to the oven and roast for a further 10 minutes.

7 Toss with the parsley and serve.

Roasted Vegetables: What has gone wrong when...

The vegetables are shrivelled and hard.

- The vegetables are overcooked. The tin was too big or the oven was too hot.

The vegetables are pale and hard.

- The vegetables are undercooked. The tin was too small or the oven temperature was too low.
- The pieces of vegetable were too big.

Freezing Vegetables

Vegetables must be blanched prior to freezing to retard enzyme action that causes loss of colour, flavour and nutritional value. The recommended blanching times are given in the chart below.

Blanching Vegetables for Freezing

Use a large amount of water in a stockpot or a very large saucepan. A chip basket is useful for immersing the vegetables in the boiling water and removing them quickly. Process the vegetables in batches of 500 g | 1 lb.

1 Bring the water to the boil, then immerse the vegetables in the boiling water. Cover with a lid. Start timing when the water returns to the boil, then remove the lid.

2 When the time is up, plunge the vegetables into a bowl full of ice-cold water to stop the cooking.

3 Drain, then spread the vegetables on to trays to cool quickly and completely.

4 Freeze on the trays. This is called 'open-freezing' and means that the vegetables freeze separately, not in one solid lump. Vegetables frozen in this manner are easier to use as you can take just as much as you need from the freezer. In addition, they cook more quickly from frozen.

5 Store the frozen vegetables in freezer bags and label with the date. Strong-smelling vegetables such as onions and Brussels sprouts should be wrapped in 2 layers of plastic.

The following vegetables freeze successfully:

Vegetable	Preparation	Blanching time in minutes	Storage time in months
Asparagus	Do not tie in bunches	2–3	12
Artichoke (globe)	Remove stalks and outer tough leaves	5	12
Artichoke (Jerusalem)	Freeze once cooked into a purée	5	9
Beans, broad	Sort by size	$1\frac{1}{2}$	12
Beans, French	Trim ends	2–3	12
Beans, runner	Slice thickly	$1\frac{1}{2}$–2	6
Beetroot	Freeze completely cooked and skinned. Slice if large	–	6
Broccoli	Trim stalks	$2\frac{1}{2}$–4	12
Brussels sprouts	Choose small, firm sprouts. Remove outer leaves	3–4	12
Carrots	Choose small young ones with good colour. Scrape, Freeze whole	3	12
Cauliflower	Break heads into florets	3–4	6
Celery	Will be soft when thawed, but good for soups and stews	2	12
Corn on the cob	Remove husks and silks	4–6	12
Kale	Remove stalks	1	6
Leeks	Slice thinly; chop in chunks or leave whole	1–3	12
Mushrooms	Do not peel. Freeze unblanched for up to 1 month. For longer storage, cook in butter	$1\frac{1}{2}$	3
Onions	Store unblanched onions, sliced or chopped, for up to 3 months. Sliced or chopped onions can be blanched in water or oil. Button onions can be blanched whole	1–3	2
Mangetout and Fresh Peas	Choose young, very fresh peas	1	12
Potatoes	New	4	12
	Chips: blanch in oil		
	Boiled or mashed: freeze cooked and cold	–	3
Root vegetables	Cut into chunks; blanch, or cook completely	3	12
Spinach	Move about in water to separate leaves	1	12
Tomatoes	Make into a tomato sauce (see *Sauces, Savoury*)	–	12

Part three
Terms and Tables

Cookery Terms

Acidulate, to: To turn cooking liquor or a dish slightly acid, or piquant, by adding an acid such as lemon juice or vinegar.

Agar agar: A setting agent made from tasteless seaweed widely used in Asia. (See **Gelatine**, page 299.)

Al dente: Italian term, literally meaning 'firm to the tooth' which describes the degree to which pasta and some vegetables are cooked. (See **Pasta**, page 502.)

Antipasto: Italian term for cold hors d'oeuvres, often served with an aperitif before the pasta course.

Aromatic ingredients: Leaves, flowers, seeds, fruits, stems, roots and bulbs of fragrant plants (herbs such as parsley, thyme, chervil and tarragon) and vegetables (carrots, celery, onions, shallots and garlic), used essentially for their fragrance, to flavours boiled or braised dishes, vinegars, oils, stuffings, court bouillon, marinades, fumets and macerations.

Bake, to: To cook food in the dry heat of the oven at temperatures usually exceeding 150°C│300°F│gas mark 2.

Bake blind, to: To bake an empty pastry case. (See **Pastry**, page 509, and **Baking**, page 96.)

Baking powder: A mixture of sodium bicarbonate and acid, in the form of cream of tartar, used as a raising agent in baking. (See **Cakes**, page 139, and **Baking**, page 105.)

Bain-marie: A water bath, either hot or cold. A hot bain-marie is used to keep food such as sauces warm. A roasting tin half filled with hot water which is used to protect food, such as *Baked Custard* and terrines, from the fierce heat of the oven. The steamy atmosphere also keeps the food from drying out (See **Eggs**, *Baked Custards*, page 226.) A cold bain-marie consists of ice set in a bowl of water and is used to cool food quickly or keep food cold.

Ballotine: Boned stuffed meat, poultry or game birds, poached or braised and normally served hot. Sometimes used interchangeably with *Galantine*. (See **Poultry**, *Ballotines*, page 441.)

Barbecue, to: Term originally used to describe roasting over an open fire. Now describes cooking food on a grill over burning charcoal, hot coals or wood embers in the open air. (See **Meat**, page 350.)

Bard, to: To tie bacon or pork fat over a joint of lean meat, game or poultry before roasting, to prevent the meat from drying out. (See **Meat**, *Points to Remember When Roasting Meat*, page 343.)

Baste, to: To spoon over stock or fat during cooking to prevent drying out and to promote browning. (See **Meat**, *Points to Remember When Roasting Meat*, page 343.)

Batter: A farinaceous mixture of thick liquid consistency used to make drop scones (pancakes), crêpes, and to coat food before deep-frying. (See **Batters**, page 111, and *Deep-frying*, page 206.)

Bavarois: A creamy pudding made with eggs and cream set with gelatine. (See **Gelatine,** *Using Leaf Gelatine*, page 297.)

Baveuse: Term describing the half-cooked, wobbly consistency of a correctly cooked soufflé or omelette. (See **Soufflés**, *Hot Soufflés*, page 647.)

Beat, to: To work a substance or mixture energetically.

Beignets: Savoury or sweet fritters normally made from choux pastry deep-fried in oil.

Beurre manié: Butter and flour in equal quantities worked together to a soft paste and used as a liaison or thickening for liquids. (See **Sauces, Savoury**, page 583.)

Beurre noisette: Butter cooked over a medium heat until the milk solids turn nut-brown and delicately toasted in flavour. (See **Dairy Products**, page 205.)

Bind, to: To bring the ingredients in a mixture together using a binding ingredient such as egg, gelatine, aspic or white sauce. (See *Forcemeats*, page 271, *Terrines, Pâtés and Raised Pies*, *Binding Ingredients*, page 703.)

Biscuit: French term meaning twice-cooked, used to describe individual small, crisp, sweet or savoury pastry (See *Baking*, *Biscuits*, page 97.)

Bisque: Shellfish soup, smooth and thickened. (See *Soups*, page 659.)

Blanch, to: To boil briefly (see *Vegetables*, page 716), to part-cook or to soak in water to whiten (see *Meat*, *Offal*, page 452) or to remove excess salt (see *Meat*, *Pork, Ham*, page 410).

Blanquette: A stew made without first browning the meat. Usually used for lamb, chicken or veal (see *Meat*, *Veal, Braising and Stewing*, page 376). The sauce is often thickened with an egg and cream liaison (see *Sauces, Savoury*, *Thickening and Enriching Sauces with Egg Liaisons*, page 584).

Blend, to: To mix two or more substances together, either by hand using a spoon, or in a food processor or liquidizer.

Blood temperature: 37°C|98.6°F.

Bloom: Butcher's term to describe the bright red or rosy-pink colour of freshly cut raw meat (see *Meat, The Colour of Meat*, page 335) or the white markings on chocolate (see *Chocolate*, page 197).

Boil, to: To cook in boiling liquid. The point at which the surface of a heated liquid is covered with breaking bubbles. Water boils at 100°C|212°F at sea level.

Bone, to: To remove the bones from a joint of meat, poultry, fish or game, often in preparation for stuffing. (See *Lamb*, page 388.)

Bottling and canning: A method of preserving by hermetically sealing food in jars, bottles or cans and then heating it to temperatures above 100°C|212°F to destroy all micro-organisms and enzymes that may cause the contents to spoil.

Bouchées: French term for mouthful, used to describe small puff pastry cases used for canapés. (See *Canapés*, page 167.)

Bouillon: Strained broth or uncleared stock made from cooking vegetables and/or meat or fish in water.

Bouquet garni: A bundle of aromatics (see above). Parsley stalks, small bay leaf, fresh thyme, celery stalk, a blade of mace, tied together with string and used to flavour stews. Removed before serving. (See *Herbs*, page 306.)

Braise, to: To cook meat, fish or vegetables slowly, on a bed of vegetables in the case of meat or fish, with a small amount of liquid, such as water, stock, wine, beer or cider, in a pot with a close-fitting lid, either on the hob or in the oven. (See *Meat*, *Braising*, page 353.)

Brine: A salt solution used to preserve fish, meat or vegetables. (See *Preserving*, page 552.)

Brochette: A large, slightly flattened skewer on which pieces of meat, vegetables or fish are threaded for char-grilling or pan-frying.

Brown, to: To pan-fry meat, fish, poultry and vegetables in hot fat or oil until they reach a deep brown colour on all sides. (See *Meat, Browning*, page 343.)

Brunoise: Vegetables cut into very small regular dice. (See *Knife Skills*, *Cutting Batons, Dice and Julienne*, page 72.)

Cake: A raised, sweet baked mixture of flour, sugar or other sweeteners, fat and eggs with a moist, tender texture and small crumb. (See *Cakes*, page 136.)

Canapé: A small bread or biscuit base, sometimes fried and spread with savoury paste, or garnished with a wide variety of ingredients. Used for cocktail nibbles or as an accompaniment to meat dishes. Sometimes used to denote the base only. (See *Canapés*, page 167.)

Caramel: The stage at which melted and heated sugar crystals turn deep brown. (See *Caramel*, page 174.)

Caramelize, to: To turn sugar into caramel by gently heating it, or to brown vegetables, such as small onions, carrots or turnips, by lightly sautéing them in butter and a little sugar.

Caraque: Chocolate curls. (See **Chocolate**, *Using Tempered Chocolate*, page 195.)

Cartouche: Wetted greaseproof paper placed directly on top of food before covering with a lid, to retain a steamy atmosphere and reduce the risk of burning during slow cooking. A dry *cartouche* of greaseproof paper is used to line uncooked pastry cases before weighting it down with beans to bake blind (see above).

Casserole: A heavy dish made of metal, enamelware, ceramic or earthenware with a close-fitting lid. Also a term used for the food cooked and served in a casserole dish.

Caul: Thin membrane, laced with fat, surrounding the stomach of a pig. Also known as crépin. It is used to hold meat ingredients together and prevent them from drying out during cooking.

Char-grill, to: To grill food on a metal grid over intense heat provided by burning charcoal or hot coals. (See **Meat,** *Char-grilling*, page 348.)

Chateaubriand: Roast fillet steak from the thick end serving 2 people or more. (See **Meat**, *Beef, Frying and Grilling*, page 365.)

Chaudfroid: French term meaning hot-cold, used to describe cooked food served cold. Cooked meats and fish are decorated with a thin layer of white or brown sauce set with gelatine, then glazed with aspic. (See **Aspic**, *Chaudfroid*, page 93.)

Chiffonnade: Broad leaves such as lettuce, basil, chicory and cabbage, cut into strips of varying widths. (See **Knife Skills**, page 68.)

Chill, to: To cool food or drink rapidly to below 4°C|40°F, either in a refrigerator or by placing in an ice bath.

Chine, to: To cut through the ribs next to the backbone. Carving is almost impossible if the butcher has not chined the meat. (See **Meat**, *Lamb, Best End of Neck or Rack of Lamb*, page 390.)

Chop, to: To cut food into small pieces.

Chowder: A thick, creamy soup, based on milk, traditionally containing fish or shellfish and vegetables such as sweetcorn. (See **Soups**, page 665.)

Clabber, to: The process of curdling milk with rennet or a vegetarian coagulant in the early stages of cheese-making. (See **Cheese**, page 182.)

Clarified butter: Butter that is made clear by removing the milk solids, whey and salt so that the butter can be subjected to high heat without burning. (See **Dairy Products**, *Butter*, page 204.)

Clean, to: To remove the viscera and membranes from fish, poultry or game before cooking.

Clear, to: To make a cloudy liquid clear, using fine filters or protein. The process, called clarification, is used to purify stocks used for consommés and aspic, fruit syrups for jellies, and beverages such as wine, beer and cider. (See **Aspic**, *Clearing Stocks for Aspic*, page 90.)

Coagulation: When protein solidifies when subjected to heat or acid. (See **Eggs**, *Cooking Eggs*, page 216.)

Coating consistency: A term to describe the consistency of a liquid or sauce when it coats the back of a spoon lightly and evenly. If the sauce runs off the spoon or a line drawn through the sauce with a finger disappears, the sauce is too thin and requires thickening. (See **Sauces, Savoury**, page 580.)

Coddle, to: To cook gently in a sealed container placed in hot water. A method traditionally used to cook eggs.

Collops: Thick slices of meat taken from a tender cut, such as best end neck of lamb. (See **Lamb**, *Collops of Lamb*, page 393.)

Concassé: The skinned, seeded flesh of tomato, chopped into small dice. (See **Vegetables,** *Tomatoes*, page 746.)

Concasser: To chop roughly. (See **Knife Skills**, page 69.)

Consommé: Soup served hot or cold, made from the cleared stock of meat, poultry or fish. (See **Soups,** *Clear Soups*, page 662.)

Confit: Pork, goose or duck cooked and covered in its own fat and preserved in a pot. (See **Preserving**, page 553.)

Cookie: An American term meaning biscuit, derived from Dutch *koekje*. (See **Baking,** *Biscuits,* page 97.)

Coulis: A thick sauce made from puréed cooked or raw fruit (e.g. summer berries) or vegetables (e.g. tomatoes). (See **Sauces, Savoury**, page 608, and **Sauces, Sweet**, page 617.)

Court Bouillon: An aromatic, acidulated cooking liquor used for poaching fish. (See **Stocks**, page 693.)

Couverture: Plain dark chocolate with a relatively high proportion of cocoa butter, meaning blanket or covering. Used mainly for confectionery as it becomes shiny and brittle once tempered. (See **Chocolate,** *Types of Chocolate*, page 190.)

Cream, to: To beat ingredients together to incorporate air, such as butter and eggs when making a sponge cake. (See **Cakes,** *Creaming Method*, page 142.)

Cream yeast, to: To mix yeast with a little liquid (water or milk) and sometimes a pinch of sugar to break it down to a creamy consistency before it is added to dry ingredients. (See **Bread,** *Yeast*, page 118).

Crêpes: Thin French pancakes. (See **Batters**, page 112.)

Croquettes: Stiff purée or paste of mashed potatoes and sometimes poultry, fish or meat, bound with a fairly thick sauce, such as a *Béchamel*, formed into small balls or patties, coated in egg and breadcrumbs and deep-fried.

Croustade: Bread brushed with melted butter and baked in a patty tin until crisp. Used to contain hot savoury mixtures for a canapé, savoury or garnish.

Croûte: French for crust. Sometimes a pastry case, to accompany Fillet of Beef en Croûte, or fried bread for Scotch Woodcock or scrambled eggs on toast. Croûte also describes bread sliced and cut into squares or rounds, dipped in butter, baked and topped with savoury mixtures for hors d'oeuvres. (See **Soups,** *Soup Garnishes*, page 667.)

Croûtons: Small, even-sized cubes of fried bread used as a garnish for soups and salads. (See **Soups,** *Soup Garnishes*, page 667.)

Crush, to: To reduce a solid ingredient to very small pieces using a mortar and pestle, a food processor or the end of a rolling pin.

Crystallize, to: A preserving technique most frequently applied to fruit, flowers and nuts. The ingredient is gently heated then cooled in increasingly concentrated sugar syrup solutions until the syrup replaces the water in the fruit, preserving it for up to 6 months.

Curd: The coagulated semi-solid protein and fat constituents of separated milk. (See **Cheese**, page 182.)

Curdle: When the solid and liquid components of an emulsion separate (e.g. cake mixture or *Mayonnaise*). (See **Eggs**, page 200.)

Cure, to: To preserve food, such as fish or meat, by covering it, immersing it or exposing it to substances that inhibit the growth of bacteria, such as salt, vinegar, nitrates, alcohol, sugar and smoke. (See **Preserving**, page 549.)

Cut, to: To incorporate solid fat into dry ingredients until lumps of the desired size remain, using 2 knives or an electric mixer. (See **Pastry,** *Shortcrust Pastry*, page 510.)

Deep-fry, to: To cook food quickly by immersing it in hot oil. (See **Deep-frying**, page 206.)

Deglaze, to, or déglacer: To loosen and liquefy fat, sediment, and browned juices from the bottom of a pan by adding liquid, usually stock, water or wine to the hot pan and stirring with a wooden spoon while boiling. (See **Meat,** *Braising*, page 353.)

Déglaçage: The liquid left in the pan once the sediment has been loosened with water, wine or stock. The déglaçage is used to enrich the colour and flavour of soups, casseroles, braised dishes, gravies and sauces. (See **Meat,** *Braising*, page 353.)

Degorge, to: To extract the juices from meat, fish or vegetables by salting. Usually done to remove indigestible or strong-tasting juices. (See **Vegetables,** *Aubergines*, page 720.)

Degrease, to, or dégrasser: The removal of liquid fat from the surface of a cooling liquid, using a ladle or kitchen paper.

Dépouiller: To remove the scum from a reducing or boiling sauce or stock. A splash of cold stock or water is added to the boiling liquid to bring the scum and fat to the surface, which can then be skimmed more easily. (See **Stocks,** *Simmering and Skimming*, page 682.)

De-salting: Removing excess salt from salted and brined foods by blanching or soaking in water.

Détrempe: The dough base for layered pastry, consisting of flour and a little fat and water. (See **Pastry,** *Layered Pastries*, page 518.)

Devein, to: To remove veins and arteries from meat, offal and poultry. Also refers to the removal of the intestine from prawns. (See **Shellfish**, page 627.)

Devilled: Food combined with hot and spicy seasonings or served with a piquant sauce containing vinegar, mustard and cayenne.

Draw, to: To remove the intestines and vital organs from game so that it can be hung for a period of time to tenderize the meat and develop its flavour. (See **Game,** *Feathered Game*, page 458.)

Dredge, to: To coat food lightly and evenly with a powdered ingredient such as flour or icing sugar.

Dress, to: To decorate food with a single ingredient or a selection of ingredients.

Dripping: The melted fat and juices that run from a roasting joint of meat.

Dropping consistency: The consistency of a mixture that drops reluctantly from a spoon, neither pouring off nor obstinately adhering. (See **Pastry,** *Choux Pastry*, page 525.)

Drying: Preserving food by drying it in hot dry air. (See **Preserving**, page 549.)

Dumpling: Savoury dough made of flour and fat, often flavoured with herbs, spices or mustard, steamed on top of a stew. Served as a garnish for traditional British meat

stews. The term dumpling is also used for certain Chinese Dim Sum where egg or rice wrappers are filled with minced fillings and deep-fried or poached. (See, **Steaming,** *Dumplings*, page 679.)

Duxelles: Finely chopped raw mushrooms, onions or shallots, sautéed in butter and used as a stuffing, garnish or flavouring for a sauce.

Egg wash: Beaten raw egg, sometimes with salt added, used for glazing pastry or bread to give it a shine when baked. (See **Eggs,** *Uses in Cooking*, page 224.)

Emulsion: A suspension of a fatty liquid such as oil or melted butter and an aqueous liquid such as egg yolk, vinegar, water or lemon juice. The suspension will only be stable if an emulsifier such as egg yolk is added, as in the preparation of *Hollandaise Sauce* and *Mayonnaise* (see **Sauces, Savoury,** *Emulsified Sauces*, page 597). Unstable emulsions include French *Vinaigrette* (see **Salad Dressings**, page 572).

Enrich, to: To increase the fat and protein content of a mixture or sauce by adding cream, butter, eggs or egg and cream liaison to improve the consistency and flavour. (See **Sauces, Savoury,** *Finishing Sauces*, page 582.)

Entrecote: Sirloin steak. (See **Meat**, *Beef*, page 365.)

Entrée: Traditionally a dish served before the main course, but today usually refers to a main course.

Escalope: A thin slice of lean white meat, sometimes beaten out flat to make it thinner and larger. (See **Meat**, *Veal*, page 378.)

Farce: Stuffing or forcemeat. (See **Forcemeat**, page 271, and **Terrines, Pâtés and Raised Pies**, page 703.)

Fécule: Farinaceous thickening, usually arrowroot or cornflour. (See **Sauces, Savoury,** *Thickening Sauces with Fécules*, page 586.)

Fillet, to: To remove the bones from fish (see **Fish,** *Preparing Fish*, page 243.)

Filter, to: To strain through kitchen paper or muslin.

Fines herbes: A French term for a classic mixture of chopped aromatic herbs such as chervil, tarragon, chives and parsley, used to flavour sauces, cream cheeses, meat and egg preparations. (See **Herbs**, page 306.)

Finish, to: To complete the preparation of a dish by adjusting the seasoning, consistency or appearance.

Flamber (to flame): A French term, meaning to set spirits alight over food, to burn off most of the alcohol to enhance the flavour of the food and for dramatic effect.

Fleurons: Small crescents of baked *Puff Pastry*, generally used to garnish fish and poultry served in a sauce.

Flooding a plate: To coat the base of a plate or serving dish with a sauce of thin coating consistency, to enhance the appearance of food placed on top.

Flour, to: To sprinkle an item of food lightly or a work surface with flour.

Foie gras: The grossly enlarged and fattened liver of goose and duck, force-fed on corn. (See **Meat**, *Offal, Foie Gras*, page 446).

Fold, to: To stir a whisked or beaten mixture with a gentle lifting motion, to retain as much of the air in the mixture as possible. This method is applied when adding whisked egg whites to a cake (see **Cakes**, *Whisked Sponges*, page 147) or mousse mixture (see **Eggs**, *Folding in Egg Whites*, page 235).

Forcemeat: A seasoned mixture of raw or cooked ingredients, chopped or minced, used to stuff meats, fish and vegetables. Also forms the basis of pâtés, terrines and raised meat pies (see **Forcemeat**, page 271, and **Terrines, Pâtés and Raised Pies**, page 703).

Fraiser: To mix butter, eggs and flour together with a smearing motion when making French pastry. (See **Pastry**, *French Flan Pastry*, page 515).

Frappé: Iced, or set in a bed of crushed ice.

Freeze, to: To cool solid or liquid food quickly to −18°C|0°F or lower in order to preserve it or to make iced foods such as ice cream and sorbets.

Fricassé: A white stew made with cooked or raw poultry, meat or rabbit and *Velouté Sauce* (see **Sauces, Savoury**, page 591), sometimes thickened with cream and egg whites.

Fumet: A strong-flavoured liquid obtained by reducing a stock or other cooking liquor.

Galantine: Boned poultry, meat or fish that is stuffed, poached and served cold. Sometimes glazed with aspic. (See **Poultry,** *Galantines*, page 443.)

Galette: Food shaped into a flat, round cake. A galette ranges from cakes and filled *Puff Pastry* desserts to discs of layered thinly sliced potato, pan-fried in butter.

Game: A wild animal, bird or fish, killed for eating by hunting, shooting or fishing. (See **Meat**, *Game*, page 454.)

Game chips: Thinly sliced potato, fried in oil to garnish roast game birds. Potato crisps are often warmed in the oven as an alternative. (See **Meat**, *Game, Feathered Game*, page 462).

Ganache: A filling for cakes and chocolates made from plain chocolate and double cream. (See **Chocolate**, page 197.)

Garnish: An item of food or a mixture of ingredients added to a finished dish to enhance its appearance, flavour and texture.

Gastrique: Sugar dissolved in vinegar then caramelised, used to enhance the flavour of *Tomato Sauce* and to give a sweet and sour flavour and brown colour to sauces made with stock. (See **Sauces, Savoury**, *Tomato Sauce*, page 607.)

Gelatine: Available in powdered form or colourless leaves. It is used to set many savoury and sweet foods such as stock for aspic, fruit syrups for jelly, mousses and cold soufflés. (See **Gelatine**, page 294.)

Ghee: Clarified butter cooked until all the moisture is evaporated and the butter starts to brown, giving it a nutty flavour.

Glace de viande: Reduced, syrupy, strongly flavoured *Brown Stock*. Used as an essence to add body and colour to sauces. Can also be used as the base to a sauce. (See **Stocks**, *Glace de Viande*, page 684.)

Glaze, to: To create a glossy surface on food to enhance its appearance and to prevent discolouration caused by contact with the air. Cold savoury food, mainly charcuterie items, are brushed with aspic jelly and stock glazes; desserts such as fruit tarts are glazed with a fruit glaze of finely sieved apricot jam or redcurrant jelly.

Goujons: Strips of delicate fish, such as sole or plaice, or chicken, coated in egg and breadcrumbs, deep-fried and served with a piquant sauce. (See *Deep-frying*, page 208.)

Grain: A term to describe the direction in which muscles run through muscle or meat. (See *Meat*, *The Structure of Meat*, page 333).

Granita: An Italian water ice made from fruit, liqueur or coffee syrups containing a high proportion of water. (See *Sorbets*, *Granitas*, page 645.)

Grate, to: To reduce a solid food to coarse or fine threads (cheese, carrots, onion, etc.) or into fine fragments (the zest of citrus fruits) or powder (nutmeg) by repeatedly rubbing it over one of the various faces of a grater, perforated with small, sharp-edged holes of different size and shape.

Gratiner: To brown food under a grill after the surface of the dish has been sprinkled with breadcrumbs and butter or grated cheese. Dishes finished like this are sometimes called *gratinée* or *au gratin*.

Grill, to: To cook or brown food quickly under the intense heat of an electric element, gas flame or on a metal grid suspended above burning charcoal or hot coals.

Hang, to (*mortifier*): To hang meat and game on hooks in a cool, well-aerated place for a varying period of time, to tenderize and improve the flavour of the flesh. (See *Meat*, *Hanging Meat*, page 335.)

Hors d'oeuvre: Traditionally the first dish to be served at a meal to whet the appetite. The term has also come to mean a selection of hot and cold savoury foods served with an aperitif before sitting down to dinner.

Ice, to: To decorate the surface of cakes and biscuits with sugar-based toppings known as icing. (See *Cake Icings and Decoration*, page 155.)

Infuse, to: To steep or flavour a liquid with an aromatic ingredient by slowly heating to boiling point and then allowing to cool. The resulting flavoured liquid is called an infusion.

Joint, to: To cut meat, game and poultry into portions.

Julienne: Vegetables or citrus peel cut into thin matchsticks or very fine shreds, strictly 1–2 mm | $\frac{1}{25}$–$\frac{1}{12}$ in wide and 3 cm | $2\frac{1}{4}$ in long. (See *Knife Skills*, page 72.)

Junket: A set milk pudding. The milk is coagulated and solidified to curds by the addition of rennet.

Jus or jus de viande: God's gravy. Primarily the gravy of a roast made by diluting juices from the meat with wine, stock or water in the roasting pan. The resulting liquid is then reduced by boiling which also acts to absorb the browned sediment on the base of the pan strengthening both the flavour and colour of the gravy. (See *Sauces, Savoury*, *Gravy*, page 592.)

Jus lie: Thickened gravy. (See *Sauces, Savoury*, *Brown Sauces*, page 596.)

Kippers: Smoked herrings. (See *Fish*, *Smoked Fish*, page 263.)

Knead, to: To manipulate dough by pushing it across a work surface, flipping it over and pulling it back. (See *Bread*, *Yeast, The Stages of Bread-making*, page 122.)

Knock back, to: To punch down or knead out the carbon dioxide in risen dough so that it resumes its original bulk (See *Bread*, *Yeast, The Stages of Bread-making*, page 123.)

Knock up, to: To separate the layers of raw *Puff Pastry* with the blade of a knife around the cut edge of the pastry to facilitate rising while it is baked. (See *Pastry*, *Layered Pastries*, page 518.)

Lard, to: To thread strips of bacon fat through lean meat with a larding needle. As the meat cooks, the fat melts, moistening, tenderizing and adding flavour to the meat. (See *Meat*, *Veal, Veal Fricandeau*, page 317.)

Lardons: Small strips or cubes of pork fat or bacon, generally used as a garnish in casseroles and salads. (See *Meat*, *Pork, Lardons*, page 396.)

Leaven, to: To incorporate a leavening (raising) agent (e.g. yeast, baking powder, eggs) to a batter, cake mixture or dough to make it rise. (See *Eggs*, page 230, *Cakes*, page 139 and *Bread*, *Yeast*, page 118.)

Legume: Collective term for plant species that have seed pods that split along both sides when ripe. These include lentils, peas and beans. (See *Pulses*, page 559.)

Let down or thin, to: To add water or a water-based liquid, such as stock, to a sauce, soup or gravy to thin its consistency. (See *Sauces, Savoury*, *Thinning Sauces with Water or Stock*, page 587.)

Liaison: Ingredients that bind and thicken sauces, soups or other liquids. Classic examples are roux, beurre manié, egg yolk and cream liaisons, blood and fécules such as cornflour and arrowroot. (See *Sauces, Savoury*, page 584.)

Lighten, to: To incorporate air and lighten the texture of a mixture with whisked double cream or egg whites.

Loosen, to: To stir a spoonful of whisked egg white into a mixture to make it easier to incorporate the remaining egg white by folding. (See *Eggs*, *Eggs whites whisking*, page 233.)

Macédoine: A mixture of vegetables, usually including root vegetables such as turnip and carrot, cut into small dice. Used as a garnish for meat and poultry, or served cold in aspic or bound in *Mayonnaise* and used to stuff tomatoes. A term also used for fruit, as in fruit salad.

Macerate, to: To soak raw, dried or preserved foods, such as dried fruits, in liqueur, brandy or sugar syrups, sometimes infused with aromatic spices. As the food absorbs the liquid it improves in flavour and softens in texture.

Marbling: The fine streaks and flecks of fat, resembling the mineral patterns in marble, running through red meat, especially beef. (See *Meat*, *Beef, Fat*, page 344.)

Marinade: A liquid usually containing oil, aromatic vegetables, herbs and spices, and an acid such as wine, lemon juice or vinegar in which meat, game, fish or vegetables are steeped or for a varying length of time. (See *Meat*, page 340.)

Marinate, to: To soak fish, vegetables, meat and game before cooking in a flavoured, acidulated liquid, called a marinade. (See *Meat*, page 340, and *Fish*, page 248.)

Medallions: An item of food cut or formed into a flat, round or oval shape. Often used to describe a small, even, tender cut of meat. Fish, vegetables, poultry, foie gras and biscuits are also shaped into medallions of varying thickness.

Mezze: A selection of small Greek or Turkish cold or hot spiced dishes, served either as hors d'oeuvres or served one after the other as an entire meal.

Mille-feuille: French for a thousand layers. A term used to describe the characteristic appearance of a traditional French layered dessert made with *Puff Pastry*. (See *Pastry*, page 522.)

Mince, to: To reduce food to very small pieces, either with a knife or using a mincing machine.

Mirepoix: A bed of diced aromatic vegetables (carrots, onions and celery) placed in the bottom of heavy lidded ovenproof dish to enhance the flavour and add moisture to braised and pot-roasted meat and game. Often used to garnish the finished dish. (See *Meat, Braising*, page 353.)

Mirror, to: To glaze (adding shine and gloss) the base of a plate or serving dish with a thin layer of clarified aspic to enhance the appearance of the food arranged on top. (See *Aspic*, page 90.)

Mise en place: Literally, to put in place. Preparing and setting out ingredients and utensils in an organized manner prior to preparing and serving a meal.

Mix, to: The process of combining two or more ingredients.

Molasses: Also known as black treacle. (See *Sugar, Sweeteners and Sugar Syrups*, *Black Treacle*, page 697.)

Monter au beurre: French for to mount with butter. A small amount of butter is whisked or shaken into richly flavoured and coloured sauces, just before serving, to thicken and improve their consistency and add shine. (See *Sauces, Savoury*, *Thickening and Enriching Sauces with Butter*, page 584.)

Mousse: A French term meaning foam or froth, describing the light, airy consistency of savoury or sweet mousses obtained by the addition of whisked egg whites. (See *Mousses*, page 489.)

Mousseline: A delicate mixture of puréed fish, shellfish, veal, pork, and poultry and feathered game bound with cream and eggs. Used as a stuffing for fish and poultry or formed into *Quenelles* and poached or steamed. Served in a sauce, or as a garnish to other dishes. (See *Mousselines*, page 487.)

Napper: To coat, mask or cover a prepared food evenly.

Needleshreds: Fine, evenly cut shreds (or julienne) of citrus zest, generally used as a garnish. (See *Fruit*, *Oranges*, page 283.)

Noisette: French for hazelnut. Usually means nut-brown, as in Beurre Noisette, butter browned over heat to a nut colour. Also used to describe a small tender round cut of meat, usually lamb, from the rib or loin, surrounded by a thin band of fat to protect it during cooking.

Nouvelle cuisine: Style of cooking that promotes light and delicate dishes, often using unusual combinations of very fresh ingredients, arranged delicately on the plate.

Oeuf mollet: A hard-boiled egg just set in the centre. (See *Eggs*, *Timing Boiled Eggs*, page 216.)

Offal: The edible internal parts and some extremities of an animal, removed before the carcass is cut up, such as the kidneys, liver, brain, heart, intestines, feet, ears, sweetbreads and tongue. (See *Meat*, *Offal*, page 446.)

Oven spring: The last rising of the bread in the oven before the yeast dies often evidenced by a crack in baked bread where the crust has separated from the body of the loaf. (See *Bread, Yeast*: *What has gone wrong when . . .*, page 128.)

Oyster: A bivalve mollusc. Also used to describe a small tender piece of meat found on either side of the backbone of a chicken.

Panade or panada: Very thick mixture made from milk, butter and flour, used as a binding and thickening base for soufflés, forcemeats, stuffings and fish cakes. Also the name given to the *Choux Pastry* base before egg yolks are added.

Paner: To coat delicate ingredients, such as goujons of fish (see *Deep-frying*, *Coatings*, page 207), croquettes or small pieces of cheese in flour, egg and breadcrumbs, before deep-frying.

Pan-fry, to: To cook quickly small, thin tender pieces of meat and other foods in up to 5 mm | ¼ in oil or fat in the base of a wide, shallow pan over a medium to high heat. (See *Meat*, *Frying and Sautéing*, page 345.)

Papillote: Greaseproof paper cut into heart or circular shapes, on which a portion of meat, fish, fruit, vegetables and aromatic ingredients are placed. (See *Potatoes*, page 542.)

Parboil: To half boil or partially soften by boiling. Potatoes are parboiled before roasting.

Parfait: A French term meaning perfect used to describe the smooth texture of an iced dessert, made with fruit syrups or purées and softly whipped cream. (See *Ice Creams,* *Mousse-based Ice Cream*, page 314.)

Pass: To strain or push a substance through a sieve.

Pasteurization: The process of briefly heating a liquid, e.g. milk, to kill any micro-organisms that might be harmful to consume. (See *Cheese*, page 181.)

Pastry: A combination of flour, fat and usually liquid to make a dough which is shaped and baked. Pastry is used to hold, cover or support other ingredients. (See *Pastry*, page 507.)

Pâté: A savoury paste of liver, pork, game, etc. (See *Terrines, Pâtés and Raised Pies*, page 710.)

Pâtisserie: Sweet or savoury pastries and cakes. The name also applies to the shop where the pastries are made and sold. (See *Pâtisserie*, page 530.)

Paupiette: A thin slice of meat such as beef, pork or veal, spread with a layer of farce or forcemeat, rolled up, tied with string and pan-fried or braised. Also known as olives. Fillets of delicate fish such as sole may also be stuffed, rolled, tied and then poached in *Fish Stock*.

Pavé: French term, literally meaning slab or block, used to describe the shape of the food.

Pectin: A carbohydrate found in the pulp, skin, core, seeds and pips of fruit, responsible for setting jams and jellies when fruit is boiled with sugar. (See **Jams, Jellies, and Other Preserves,** *Pectin*, page 322.)

Peel, to: To remove thinly the skin of fruits and vegetables, using a knife or vegetable peeler. (See **Knife Skills**, page 73.)

Petits fours: Bite-sized items of pâtisserie, such as tartlets, little cakes and biscuits, or chocolates and candied fruit, served after a meal with coffee. (See **Pâtisserie**, page 530.)

Pickle: A condiment made of fruit or vegetables (or both) preserved in spiced vinegar. Usually served with cold meats, curries or cheese.

Pickle, to: To preserve foods in a solution of high acidity such as vinegar.

Pinbone, to: To remove the fine bones sometimes found in the flesh of round fish fillets (see **Fish**, page 246.)

Pinch: A very small quantity, amounting approximately 3–5 g | ⅛ teaspoon, of a dry powdered ingredient, such as salt, pepper or spice, taken between the thumb and forefinger and added directly to the food being prepared.

Pipe, to: To press a soft substance, such as meringue, icing or whipped cream through a piping bag fitted with a shaped metal or plastic nozzle to produce decorative details on a cake, or to form a food into an interesting shape for presentation purposes.

Piquant: Sharp, tangy, spicy in flavour.

Piquer: To insert flavourings into cuts made in meats or poultry. Also used to describe studding an onion with cloves to flavour casseroles.

Pith: The soft white layer under the outer skin of citrus fruit. When zesting or peeling the zest of citrus fruit, be careful to leave the pith behind as it has an unpleasant bitter taste.

Poach, to: To cook food gently by immersing it in liquid moving with the barest tremble.

Pot-roast, to: To bake meat with very little liquid in a pot with a tightly fitting lid, either in the oven or over a low heat. (See **Meat,** *Pot-roasting*, page 352.)

Poussin: Baby chicken. (See **Meat,** *Poultry, Types of Poultry*, page 415.)

Praline: Almonds cooked in boiling sugar, until the sugar caramelizes to a rich brown colour. The mixture is then cooled and crushed to a powder. Used for flavouring desserts and ice cream. (See **Caramel,** *Praline*, page 178.)

Preserves: A term mostly applied to fruit preserved with sugar in the form of jams and jellies. (See **Jams, Jellies and Other Preserves**, page 320.)

Preserving: Perishable foods prepared in such a way that they will keep longer than they would do if untreated. (See **Preserving**, page 549).

Press, to: Weighting food either to firm its texture (terrines) or to squeeze the juices out of meat or fish (Gravad Lax).

Prove, to: The last rising of a bread dough into its final shape before it is baked. (See **Bread,** *Stages of Bread-making*, page 116).

Purée: Fruit or vegetables, delicate meats and fish liquidized, sieved or finely mashed to a smooth consistency.

Quenelle, to: To shape soft, smooth foods with 2 spoons into egg-shaped portions. (See **Mousselines**, page 488.)

Ragoût: A stew.

Raising agent: An ingredient or substance that causes a mixture or dough to rise and increase in volume when cooked such as yeast and the chemical raising agents baking powder and sodium bicarbonate.

Réchauffée: A dish made with previously cooked food that is then reheated.

Reduce, to: To reduce the amount of a liquid by rapid boiling, to concentrate its flavour and colour and to thicken its consistency. (See **Sauces, Savoury**, *Thickening Sauces by the Reduction Method*, see page 582.)

Refresh, to: To pass boiled green vegetables under cold running water or to immerse them in iced water to prevent them from cooking further in their own steam and to set their colour.

Relax or rest, to: To set aside pastry or pasta dough in a cool place to allow the gluten, which will have tightened during rolling, to soften. Batters are also set aside to allow the starch cells to swell with liquid, giving a lighter result when cooked. (See **Pastry**, *Resting Pastry*, page 519.) Roast meat is also rested before it is carved. (See **Meat**, *Carving Meat*, page 344.)

Render, to: To melt solid fat, e.g. from beef or pork, slowly in the oven.

Rennet: An extract from the stomachs of unweaned calves or lambs, containing the enzyme rennin, which causes milk to coagulate. Rennet is used in the first stages of cheese-making before salt is added and for thickening junket (see above). (See **Cheese**, *The Cheese-making Process*, page 181.)

Repere: Flour mixed with water to form a paste used to seal the lid to the pan when cooking a dish slowly, e.g. Lamb Ragoût, to prevent the cooking liquid from evaporating.

Revenir: French term, literally meaning 'to return', used to describe passing meat or vegetables through hot fat to warm.

Ribbon, to the: The stage at which whisked egg yolks become sufficiently thick to leave a trail on their surface when dribbled from the whisk held above the bowl. (See **Eggs**, *Egg Foams*, page 232).

Roast, to: Cooking meat, poultry, game or fish at high temperatures using the radiant, dry heat of an oven (oven-roasting) or turning the food over a flame or grill (spit-roasting). (See **Meat**, *Roasting*, page 342.)

Rouille: Literally meaning 'rust' in French. A Provençal emulsion sauce flavoured and coloured to a rich orange with red chillies, saffron and garlic. Rouille is served with the Provençal fish soup known as Bouillabaisse. (See

Sauces, Savoury, *Mayonnaise: Daughter Sauces*, page 601.)

Roux: Equal amounts of butter and flour cooked together and used as a liaison to thicken sauces and soups. (See **Sauces, Savoury**, *Flour-based Sauces*, page 588.)

Rub in, to: To mix flour and fat together lightly with the fingertips until the mixture resembles breadcrumbs. (See **Pastry**, page 510.)

Sabayon: A light, foamy sauce or dessert made with eggs whisked over heat with sugar, sweet wine or liqueur. (See **Sauces, Sweet**, *Sabayon Sauce*, page 616.)

Salmis: A stew made with cooked game, or partially roasted game, such as woodcock, wild duck, pheasant.

Salt, to: To preserve meat and fish with salt, often combined with smoking and drying. (See **Preserving**, page 550.)

Sauté, to: To cook small pieces of food quickly by shaking and tossing in very little hot oil and/or butter until brown, using a wide, shallow pan called a sauté pan. (See **Meat**, *Frying and Sautéing Meat*, page 347.)

Scald, to: To immerse food briefly in boiling water to kill micro-organisms on its surface, to loosen the skins of fruit and vegetables for easier peeling and to make feathers and hairs easier to remove from the skin of birds and meat. To scald milk means to heat milk until just before the point of boiling, when some movement can be seen at the edges of the pan but there is no overall bubbling. Jam jars, muslin cloths and other kitchen items are also scalded by immersing in clean boiling water, generally to sterilize before use.

Score, to: To make shallow, long cuts, using a small knife, along the surface of fish, meat, vegetables and fruit to assist flavouring with marinades, to reduce cooking times and for decoration. Baked apples are scored around their middles to prevent them from bursting. The skins of chestnuts, tomatoes and peaches are scored before blanching to facilitate peeling.

Scum: Impurities such as coagulated blood, fragments of flesh and fat that collect on the surface of simmering stock, casseroles and sauces. The scum is removed, using a ladle or a large metal spoon to improve their appearance and flavour. (See **Stocks,** *Equipment for Making Stock,* page 684.)

Seal, to: A term often used in conjunction with 'seizing' meat (see below). It was originally thought that browning the surface of meat, poultry or game quickly before baking or roasting would seal in the juices. This theory has been rejected as the juices in cooking meat are squeezed out as the protein fibres shrink and set in the heat. Browning the meat does, however, enhance its flavour and appearance. (See **Meat,** *Browning,* page 346.)

Season, to: To use small quantities of salt, pepper, spices, sugar and other flavourings such as lemon, vinegar and oil to balance, enhance but not dominate the flavour of a dish or food. (See **Sauces, Savoury,** page 579.) Also describes the preparation of new cooking equipment such as iron griddles and frying pans to prevent subsequent rusting and sticking. (See **Kitchen Equipment,** *Cast-iron,* page 43.)

Seize, to: To brown the surface of meat, game, poultry or fish quickly in very hot fat before roasting, braising or stewing, to improve the colour and flavour of a dish. Also describes melted chocolate hardening into a solid unworkable lump when small quantities of liquid are added.

Separate eggs, to: To separate the yolks from the whites.

Setting point: The point at which a mixture containing gelatine starts to set and thicken. (See **Gelatine,** *The Setting Power of Gelatine,* page 295.) Also applies to the temperature (105°C|220°F) at which jams and jellies containing the natural setting agent pectin begin to set and thicken. (See **Jams, Jellies and Other Preserves,** page 325.)

Shape dough, to: To give a prepared dough its final shape before proving.

Shell, to: To remove the shells from shellfish or nuts or peas from their pods.

Sherbet: An American-style water ice containing milk.

Shred, to: To slice food into long, thin strips.

Sift, to: To pass one or more dry ingredients through a wire mesh sieve to remove lumps and combine and aerate ingredients. Drum sieves are used for sifting large quantities of ingredients.

Simmer, to: To cook food in liquid that is just below its boiling point (around 98°C|208°F) so that the liquid's surface trembles, with small bubbles breaking the surface.

Singe, to: The process of rotating poultry or game birds over a gas flame to burn off any feathers or down that remain after plucking.

Skim, to: To remove impurities from the surface of a simmering liquid with a ladle.

Skin, to: To remove the skin from fish, poultry, meat and game.

Slake, to: To mix thickening ingredients such as flour, arrowroot or cornflour to a thin paste with a small quantity of cold water, before adding to a sauce or soup, to prevent lumps from forming. (See **Sauces, Savoury,** *Thickening Sauces with Fécules,* page 586.)

Smoke, to: To preserve food by exposing it to smoke from burning wood or wood shavings in a sealed area either at cool or hot temperatures. (See **Preserving,** *Smoking,* page 549.)

Smoke point: The temperature at which the molecular structure of fat or oil begins to break down and smoke. (See **Deep-frying,** *Smoke Point of Oils,* page 207.)

Soft ball: The term used to describe sugar syrup reduced by boiling to a viscosity, that when dropped into cold water and squeezed gently between finger and thumb forms a soft ball. (See **Sugar, Sweeteners and Sugar Syrups,** *Stages of Sugar Syrup,* page 701.)

Sorbet: French term for water ice, made by freezing fruit, wine and liqueur syrups. (See **Sorbets,** page 643.)

Soufflé: French term, meaning puff, used to describe a light, sweet or savoury dish, either hot or cold, enriched with egg yolks, lightened with whisked egg whites and flavoured with vegetables, fish, cheese, fruit, chocolate or alcohol. (See **Soufflés,** page 647.)

Spatchcock: A small chicken or other bird, split open along the breastbone, flattened, secured with skewers and grilled or barbecued. (See **Poultry,** *Spatchcocking,* page 425.)

Spice: Seeds, roots, leaves and stems of plants with a powerful, sharp aroma, used to flavour food. (See **Spices**, page 669.)

Spice rub: A dry marinade of spices rubbed on to meat or fish to impart flavour and sometimes colour.

Sponge gelatine, to: To sprinkle powdered gelatine over cool water or liquid and leaving it to absorb the liquid until it becomes spongy in texture. (See **Gelatine**, *Using Powdered Gelatine*, page 295.)

Steam, to: To cook food by direct steaming in hot vapour in a perforated container over boiling liquid (usually water). Alternatively, food such as steamed puddings may be indirectly steamed by cooking it in a sealed container (usually a pudding basin) placed on a trivet, half submerged in a pan of boiling water. (See **Steaming**, page 673.)

Steep, to: To saturate fruit and cakes such as a savarin or baba with syrup or liqueur to flavour and moisten them.

Stew, to: To slowly cook meat, fish or vegetables immersed in liquid in a pot with a close-fitting lid, either on the hob or in the oven. (See **Meat**, *Stewing*, page 354.)

Stir-fry, to: To quickly fry food using the Chinese method, in a wok over a high heat, using very little oil and moving the food all the while.

Strain, to: To separate pieces of raw or cooked food from water, a marinade or cooking liquid, using a sieve, colander or strainer.

Suet: Saturated fat taken from around the kidneys of animals, usually cattle. Used for making steamed suet puddings, dumplings and suet pastry.

Supreme: Used to describe a choice portion of poultry from the breast and wing or a fine fillet of fish, such as sole or brill.

Sweat, to: To cook gently, usually in butter or oil, but sometimes in the food's own juices, to soften and to concentrate the food's flavour without frying or browning.

Syrupy: A term used to describe the consistency of a liquid or sauce when it is thickened to the viscosity of a thin sugar syrup and will evenly coat the back of a spoon. (See **Sauces, Savoury**, page 582.)

Tammy, to: To squeeze a sauce through a fine muslin cloth to remove impurities.

Temper, to: To heat, cool, then warm chocolate to precise temperatures so that it is shiny when set. (See **Chocolate**, *Tempering Chocolate*, page 193.)

Tenderize, to: To break down the tough muscle fibres in a joint or portion of meat to make it more tender to eat. (See **Meat**, *Factors Affecting the Tenderness of Meat*, page 338.)

Thicken, to: To add body and improve the consistency of a liquid such as soup, sauces and gravy by adding starch, using fécules, roux or beurre-manié; using egg yolk, cream or blood, reducing the liquid by boiling. (See **Sauces Savoury**, *Finishing Sauces*, page 587.)

To the thread: Term used to denote degree of viscosity achieved when reducing sugar syrup, i.e. the syrup will form threads if tested between a wet finger and thumb. (See **Sugar, Sweeteners and Sugar Syrups**, *Stages of Sugar Syrup*, page 701.)

Tomalley: The green-coloured liver of a lobster, often used to thicken lobster sauce.

Toss, to: To agitate food gently in order to mix ingredients or coat delicate food in a dressing or sauce.

Tournedos: A round slice of fillet steak, 2.5 cm|1 in thick. (See **Meat**, *Beef, Grilling Beef Steaks*, page 365.)

Truss, to: To tie or secure poultry, game birds and stuffed joints of meat with string or skewers to maintain their shape during cooking. (See **Meat**, *Poultry, Trussing*, page 418.)

Turn vegetables, to: To shape vegetables into uniform, barrel shapes using a turning knife. (See **Knife Skills**, *Using the Turning Knife*, page 75.)

Turn olives, to: To remove the olive stone (pit) with a spiral cutting movement.

Vol au vent: A large pastry case (15–20 cm|6–8 in in diameter) with lid, made from puff pastry with high raised sides and a deep hollow centre, filled after baking with chicken, seafood, sweetbreads or mushrooms, bound in a sauce and served hot. (See **Pastry**, *Puff Pastry*, page 522.) *Bouchée* (bite-sized) cases also available.

Well: A large bow-like hollow made in the centre of a mound of flour, either on a work surface or in a bowl, to hold liquid ingredients. A technique used in batter-making (See *Batters*, page 111).

Whey: The liquid residue of cheese-making after the solids and most of the fat have been separated to form cheese. The Italian cheese ricotta is made from whey enriched with cream and eaten fresh. (See *Cheese*, page 181.)

Whisk, to: Beating a substance (or substances) together vigorously to incorporate air, using a whisk or an electric mixer with whisking attachment.

Yeast: A single-celled micro-organism of the fungus family used to leaven bread and pastries. (See *Bread*, *Yeast*, page 118, and *Pâtisserie*, page 534.)

Classic Garnishes

Garnishes are often named after the chef who invented them (e.g. Carême), after historical figures e.g. (Rossini, Du Barry), after the region or town where an ingredient is found in profusion (e.g. Lyonnaise, Périgueux or Bordelaise) or after a selection of ingredients making up the garnish (e.g. bouquetière, jardinière).

À l'Alsacienne: Roast and braised pork, duck and goose dishes garnished with sauerkraut, smoked bacon, ham and sausage.

À l'Ancienne: Fricassée or white stew made with chicken, veal or lamb, garnished with sliced onion and button mushrooms.

À l'Andalouse: Large joints of red meat garnished with sautéed red peppers, aubergine, tomato, chorizo and rice.

Aurore: Eggs, vegetables and fish garnished with a Velouté or Béchamel Sauce (see *Sauces, Savoury*, page 589), flavoured and coloured to flame-red with tomato purée.

Bonne Femme: To cook in the simple way: e.g. sautéed chicken served with white wine gravy, lardons, button onions and croquette potatoes; fish served with white wine sauce, mushrooms and buttered potato purée.

À la Bordelaise: Eggs, fish, shellfish, offal and meat dishes flavoured with bone marrow, shallots and wine (white wine for white meat and fish dishes, red wine for red meat).

À la Boulangère: Lamb and fish dishes garnished with sliced potato and onion, braised in White Stock (see *Stocks*, page 683).

À la Bourguignonne: Dishes from Burgundy, such as Beef Bourguignonne, cooked in red wine and garnished with button mushrooms, button onions and lardons.

À la Bretonne: Mutton or lamb garnished with puréed or whole haricot beans. Also a purée of root vegetables served with gigot (leg) of lamb.

À la Catalane: Garnishes inspired by ingredients widely used in Spanish cooking such as fried aubergine, rice pilaf, pitted olives, braised artichoke hearts and tomato fried with garlic.

Chasseur: Sautéed chicken or veal served with a sauce of sautéed mushrooms, shallots, tomatoes and white wine.

Choron: Named after the chef who served grilled fish, tournedos steaks and poached eggs with Hollandaise Sauce (see *Sauces, Savoury*, page 602), flavoured with tomato purée.

Clamart: Named after the district of Hauts de Seine, famous for its pea crops. A garnish of artichoke hearts filled with buttered petits pois or a purée of peas.

Clermont: Dishes garnished with products characteristic of Auvergne, of which Clermont-Ferrand is the capital, such as chestnuts or cabbage. Cabbage is stuffed into paupiettes, and chestnuts are puréed and served in braised artichokes.

À la Créole: Savoury meat, poultry, fish and shellfish dishes inspired by West Indian cooking, garnished with buttered rice, tomatoes and sweet peppers. Desserts containing or garnished with rum, banana or pineapple.

Doria: Dishes garnished with cucumber fried in butter, named after the Genoese Doria family.

Du Barry: Dedicated to the Comtesse Du Barry and referring to the use of cauliflower. A joint of meat is garnished with florets of boiled cauliflower, masked in Mornay Sauce (see *Sauces, Savoury*, page 589) and browned under the grill.

À la Duchesse: Meat and fish dishes garnished with Duchess potatoes (puréed potatoes piped into decorative shapes and baked in the oven until golden-brown) or pâtisserie containing almonds.

À la Flamande: Garnishes using produce from Northern France, such as braised cabbage cooked with sausage, glazed carrots, baby onions and turnips, chiffonnade of chicory and purée of Brussels sprouts. Served with joints of beef and pork.

À la Florentine: Usually dishes containing leaf spinach or spinach purée.

À la Forestière: Portions of meat, poultry, eggs or vegetables garnished with wild mushrooms such as chanterelles, Morels and ceps, cooked in butter. Other accompanying garnishes may include fried bacon lardons and puréed potato.

Grand-mère: Very similar to *Bonne Femme* (see above), referring to home-cooked dishes where a recipe is not always used, such as a chicken casserole garnished with fried bacon lardons and mushrooms, sautéed potatoes and brown glazed onions.

À la Grecque: Refers to dishes of Greek origin such as vegetables marinated in olive oil and lemon, with tomatoes or other vegetables stuffed with rice, sultanas and herbs.

Gremolata: An Italian garnish of finely chopped parsley, finely grated lemon or orange zest and sometimes toasted and chopped nuts (pine nuts or almonds) sprinkled on to fish, poultry and veal dishes.

À la Hollandaise: Egg, boiled vegetable or poached fish dishes served with or coated in Hollandaise Sauce (see *Sauces, Savoury*, page 602).

À la Hongroise: Refers to dishes coloured and flavoured with paprika.

À l'Indienne: Dishes flavoured with curry powder and often served with rice.

Jardinière: A garnish of mixed vegetables such as carrots, turnips, French beans and peas, often served with roast meat and casseroled poultry.

Lyonnaise: Denotes the use of onions as a garnish, usually sliced and fried gently in butter.

À la Maltaise: Refers to dishes flavoured with orange. Maltaise Sauce is an Hollandaise Sauce flavoured and coloured with the juice and zest of blood orange and served with poached fish (see *Sauces, Savoury*, page 605).

À la Meunière: A method of cooking whereby fish is dusted in flour and fried in butter, then served with *Beurre Noisette* (see *Dairy Products*, *Butter*, page 205), lemon and chopped parsley.

À la Milanaise: Tomato sauce, with shredded ham, pickled tongue, mushrooms and truffles, served with macaroni and small cuts of meat.

Mornay: Foods such as fillets of sole, cauliflower and broccoli florets and soft-boiled eggs, coated in a Béchamel Sauce (see *Sauces, Savoury*, page 589), flavoured with a strong cheese, such as Gruyère, and browned under the grill.

À la Nantua: Dishes containing lobster or crayfish, either whole or puréed, in a sauce or in savoury butter.

À la Napolitaine: Food such as pasta, pizza and grilled meat dishes served with Pizzaiola Sauce, made with tomatoes, garlic, basil and olive oil.

À la Niçoise: Name given to many dishes from the region around Nice in southern France, garnished with olives, tomatoes, garlic, olive oil, fine green beans and anchovies or tuna.

À la Normande: Meat, fish and chicken dishes from Normandy garnished with mushrooms or apple slices and a creamy sauce flavoured with cider or Calvados.

Parisienne: Potatoes or other root vegetables scooped into small balls with a melon baller, and usually fried until golden-brown.

Parmentier: Denotes the use of potato as a base or garnish.

Paysanne: Meaning peasant. A term to describe braised meats or fish cooked with softened vegetables, such as carrot, turnip and potato, cut roughly into rounds. The term is also used for a mixture of root vegetables and cabbage, cut into dice and fried, to garnish soups and stews.

À la Périgourdine: Dishes made with small cuts of meat, game or poultry, served with a Périgueux Sauce, Madeira Sauce (see *Sauces, Savoury*, page 595) flavoured with finely diced truffles.

Persillade: Describes a garnish of finely chopped parsley, garlic and sometimes breadcrumbs, added to a dish just before it is served.

À la Portugaise: Small cuts of meat, poultry, fish, or vegetables garnished or flavoured with tomatoes or tomato purée.

À la Printanière: Meat, fish or egg dishes garnished with a mixture of spring vegetables glazed in butter.

À la Provençale: Dishes predominantly flavoured with tomatoes, black olives and garlic.

Rossini: Dishes named after the composer Rossini, such as steak tournedos, poached or scrambled eggs, omelette and poultry, garnished with thinly sliced foie gras, finely chopped truffles sautéed in butter, and a Demi-glace Sauce (see *Sauces, Savoury*, page 595).

À la Russe: Shellfish coated in aspic jelly and mayonnaise, accompanied with Russian salad, finely diced vegetables in mayonnaise. Also describes dishes garnished with caviar, gherkins, chopped egg and herrings.

Soubise: Roasted cuts of meat, particularly lamb, and egg dishes served with Soubise Sauce, made with a purée of gently cooked onions added to Béchamel Sauce (see *Sauces, Savoury*, page 589).

St Germain: Describes dishes garnished with peas and Pommes Parisienne (see above).

Vichy: A garnish of small carrots, glazed in butter.

Conversion Tables

METRIC	IMPERIAL	METRIC	IMPERIAL
7–8 g	$\frac{1}{4}$ oz	15 g	$\frac{1}{2}$ oz
20 g	$\frac{3}{4}$ oz	30 g	1 oz
55 g	2 oz	85 g	3 oz
110 g	4 oz ($\frac{1}{4}$ lb)	140 g	5 oz
170 g	6 oz	200 g	7 oz
225 g	8 oz	255 g	9 oz
285 g	10 oz	310 g	11 oz
340 g	12 oz ($\frac{3}{4}$ lb)	370 g	13 oz
400 g	14 oz	425 g	15 oz
450 g	16 oz (1 lb)	560 g	$1\frac{1}{4}$ lb
675 g	$1\frac{1}{2}$ lb	900 g	2 lb
1 kg	2 lb 4 oz	1.15 kg	2 lb 8 oz
1.35 kg	3 lb	1.8 kg	4 lb
2.3 kg	5 lb	2.7 kg	6 lb
3.2 kg	7 lb	3.6 kg	8 lb
4 kg	9 lb	4.5 kg	10 lb

Lengths

Imperial	Metric
$\frac{1}{2}$ in	1 cm
1 in	2.5 cm
2 in	5 cm
6 in	15 cm
8 in	20 cm
12 in	30 cm

Approximate American/European Conversions

	USA	METRIC	IMPERIAL
Flour	1 cup	140 g	5 oz
Caster and granulated sugar	1 cup	170 g	6 oz
Brown sugar	1 cup	170 g	6 oz
Butter/margarine/lard	1 cup/2 sticks	225 g	8 oz
Sultanas/raisins/currants	1 cup	140 g	5 oz
Ground almonds	1 cup	85 g	3 oz
Uncooked rice	1 cup	170 g	6 oz
Grated cheese	1 cup	110 g	4 oz
Chopped nuts	1 cup	100 g	$3\frac{1}{2}$ oz

1 American pint = 16 fl oz = 450 ml

1 tablespoon = 3 teaspoons = 15 ml

1 lb = 16 oz = 450 g

2 lb 4 oz = 1,000 g │ 1 kg

1 average bottle of wine 75 cl │ 750 ml

1 average bottle of spirits 70 cl │ 700 ml

1 lt = 1,000 ml = 100 cl = 10 dl = $1\frac{3}{4}$ imperial pints

Liquid measures

Imperial	ml	fl oz
1 teaspoon	5	
2 scant tablespoons	28	1
$\frac{1}{4}$ pint (1 gill)	150	5
$\frac{1}{3}$ pint	190	6.6
$\frac{1}{2}$ pint	290	10
$\frac{3}{4}$ pint	425	15
1 pint	570	20

Oven Temperatures

°C	°F	Gas mark	AMERICAN
70	150	¼	
80	175	¼	COOL
100	200	½	
110	225	½	
130	250	1	VERY SLOW
140	275	1	
150	300	2	SLOW
170	325	3	MODERATE
180	350	4	
190	375	5	MODERATELY HOT
200	400	6	FAIRLY HOT
220	425	7	HOT
230	450	8	VERY HOT
240	475	8	
250	500	9	
270	525	9	EXTREMELY HOT
290	550	9	

Wine Quantities

Imperial	ml	fl oz
Average wine bottle	750	25
1 glass wine	100	3
1 glass port or sherry	70	2
1 glass liqueur	45	1

Bibliography and Suggested Further Reading

General
Corriher, *Cookwise*, William Morrow and Company, Inc., New York, 1997

Cracknell and Kaufman, *Practical Professional Cookery, 3rd Edition*, Macmillan, London, 1992

Davidson, *The Oxford Companion to Food*, Oxford University Press, New York, 1999

Herbst, *The New Food Lover's Companion*, Barron's Educational Series, New York, 1995

Kamman, *The New Making of a Cook*, William Morrow and Co., New York, 1997

Kimball, *The Cook's Bible*, Little, Brown and Company, New York, 1997

Larousse Gastronomique, Hamlyn, London, 1988

Leith and Waldegrave, *Leiths Cookery Bible*, Bloomsbury, London, 2003

Leith's School of Food and Wine, *Chef's School*, Bloomsbury, London, 1998

McGee, *On Food and Cooking*, HarperCollins, London, 1991

Norman, *Masterclass, Expert Lessons in Kitchen Skills*, Hobhouse Ltd, 1982

Spry and Hume, *The Constance Spry Cookery Book*, J. M. Dent and Sons, 1961

Canapés
Treuille and Blashford-Snell, *Canapés*, Dorling-Kindersley, London 1999

Cheese
Masui and Yamada, *French Cheeses*, Dorling-Kindersley, London, 2000

Rance, *The Great British Cheese Book*, Macmillan, London, 1982

Chocolate
Bloom, 'All About Chocolate', *Fine Cooking*, Feb/Mar 1995

Magieri, *Chocolate*, HarperCollins, New York, 1998

Stanes, *Chocolate, the Definitive Guide*, Grub Street, London, 1999

With thanks to Gerard Ronay

Fish
Waldegrave and Jackson, *Leith's Fish Bible*, Bloomsbury, London, 1995

Whiteman, *The World Encyclopedia of Fish and Shellfish*, Anness Publishing, Canada, 2000

Forcemeat

Labensky and Hause, *On Cooking, Techniques from Expert Chefs*, Prentice-Hall, New Jersey, 1999

Food Safety

Basic Food and Hygiene Coursebook, Institution of Environmental Health Officers, 1992

Total Nutrition: The Only Guide You Will Ever Need, Mount Sinai School of Medicine, St Martin's Press, New York, 1995

Ice Cream and Sorbet

Liddell and Weir, *Ices, the Definitive Guide*, Grub Street, London, 1995

Nutrition

Total Nutrition: The Only Guide You Will Ever Need, Mount Sinai School of Medicine, St Martin's Press, 1995

Preserving

Schwartz, *Preserving*, Dorling Kindersley, London, 1996

Sauces

Roux, *Sauces, Sweet and Savoury, Classic and New*, Quadrille Publishing, London, 1996

Soups

Bareham, *A Celebration of Soup*, Penguin, London, 1994

Terrines and Pâtés

Labensky and Hause, *On Cooking, Techniques from Expert Chefs*, Prentice-Hall, New Jersey, 1999

Recipe List

General Index

Notes